GENEALOGICAL RESOURCES IN NEW YORK

Edited by Estelle M. Guzik

Published by the Jewish Genealogical Society, Inc.
P.O. Box 286398
New York, NY 10128

2003

∞ The paper used in this publication meets the minimum requirements of the
American National Standard for Information Sciences—Permanence of Paper
for Printed Library Materials, ANSI Z39.48-1984.

Library of Congress Control Number: 2003101418

ISBN 0-9621863-1-7

Printed in the United States of America

10 09 08 07 06 05 04 03 6 5 4 3 2 1

CONTENTS

APPENDICES

INDEXES

MAPS

INTRODUCTION

The Jewish Genealogical Society, Inc. (JGS) is proud to present this new *Genealogical Resources in New York*. Its origins date back to 1985, when the JGS hosted the Fifth National Summer Seminar on Jewish Genealogy and produced a loose-leaf binder for participants. Because of the attention it received from the larger genealogical community, it evolved into *Genealogical Resources in the New York Metropolitan Area* published in 1989. That book was selected as one of the outstanding reference books of the year by the New York Public Library.

This edition includes 12 new facilities in New York City and Albany and expands upon each of the original repositories in the five boroughs of New York City. It was our intent to produce an updated edition for the 19th Annual Conference on Jewish Genealogy. We missed that goal but hope our friends in the genealogical community will understand. Much has happened in New York City and in the genealogical world since then.

To create this book, we built upon the work of volunteers who contributed to the original volumes — and added much more. Archivists, librarians and government agency staff were consulted in updating the chapters covering their facilities. Since 1989, there has been an explosion of new books, indexes, computerized catalogs, and more. Computers have become a working tool of every organization. The Internet is now a part of our daily lives and a tremendous source of information for genealogists. So, you may ask, do we really need another book? Read the pages that follow and you will know the answer! Most reference books are consulted occasionally on an as-needed bases. This book is intended to be read. Readers will find buried treasures in each and every repository. We hope *Genealogical Resources* will give you the tools necessary to better explore what is available — both here in NYC and around the world.

GEOGRAPHIC AREAS COVERED:

Genealogical Resources in New York covers the five boroughs/counties that make up New York City as well as several New York State agencies located in Albany, NY. The majority of the facilities, as before, are located in Manhattan. Readers will find that a knowledge of the basic records maintained by public agencies in these New York City counties will help them locate records in other counties as well.

Historical differences in county/borough boundaries are noted in the text. But this time, we have added a superb article, "Before the Five Boroughs," written by Harry Macy, Jr. providing more detail and maps. The article was published originally by the New York Genealogical and Biographical Society and is reprinted here with their permission. See Appendix H.

Counties are subdivisions of the State of New York. Boroughs are subdivisions of New York City. Within New York City today, county and borough boundaries are identical but three have different county/borough names: New York/Manhattan, Kings/Brooklyn and Richmond/Staten Island. These differences are noted in the text. To reduce confusion, both names are used.

ORGANIZATION:

As before, the material is arranged geographically by borough. Borough or county offices are grouped with other public and private facilities in that borough, rather than with offices of similar function. For example, the Board of Elections has five borough offices — in Manhattan, Bronx, Brooklyn, Queens and Staten Island. Each office is found under the county/borough subheading. We have also added maps showing the location of most repositories. This should assist researchers in coordinating visits to facilities within a particular area.

There is one exception to this format: The Family History Centers (LDS). We have included the Family History Center in Manhattan and provided details on its indefinite loan holdings. In that chapter, we list the addresses of each of the Family History Centers in the New York metropolitan area. Hours vary for each facility, so be sure to call before going.

Collections housed at the Center for Jewish History — American Sephardi Federation, American Jewish Historical Society, Center Genealogy Institute, Hadassah Archives of the American Jewish Historical Society, Leo Baeck Institute, YIVO Institute for Jewish Research and Yeshiva University Museum — are grouped under Center for Jewish History. Some facilities included in the 1989 book have been merged with existing facilities and are no longer listed separately here. In 1992, the Bund Archives, formerly a separate repository, was transferred to YIVO and became a division of YIVO's Archives. Records of City Clerk's Offices that were in the outer boroughs — Bronx, Brooklyn, Queens and Staten Island — can now be obtained from the Manhattan office. The Brooklyn Center for Holocaust Studies has closed and its collections were transferred to the Museum of Jewish Heritage whose other collections are also included in this edition. Naturalization records of the U.S. District Court, Eastern District of New York and U.S. District Court, Southern District of New York were transferred to the National Archives-Northeast Region, as have most naturalization records of the U.S. District Court, New Jersey. Queens College, Historical Documents Collection closed and its holdings were divided among the Queens Borough Public Library, the NYC Municipal Archives and the NYS Archives.

New additions to this book include the American Sephardi Federation, American Jewish Historical Society, Center for Jewish History, Center Genealogy Institute, Ellis Island - American Family Immigration History Center, Ellis Island - National Park Service Archives and Library, John Jay College of Criminal Justice Library, Museum of Jewish Heritage, New York Public Library - Manuscript and Archives Division, and Science, Industry and Business Library, Old York Library, and New York State Department of State, Division of Corporations and Division of Licensing.

INFORMATION PROVIDED:

In addition to basic information about each facility — name, title of facility director, address (and mail address if different), phone number, cross streets, closest public transportation, travel directions, hours of operation, description of resources, finding aids, description of facility, fees/copies and restrictions on use — we have added wheelchair accessibility, fax number, e-mail address and website, where these exist. Genealogists looking back will find it hard to believe that these latter tools were rarely available or non-existent when the early editions of this book were published!

We are pleased to provide information on wheelchair accessibility for the first time. The universal wheelchair symbol [&] is displayed next to the facility's address if *both* an entrance *and* a bathroom in the building are wheelchair accessible. An asterisk (*) next to the wheelchair denotes some qualification. An explanation will be found under "Directions" on the same page. If an entrance to the building is accessible but we found no bathroom that appeared to be accessible, no symbol was "awarded" but a note on entrance accessibility was included under "Directions." More detail on accessibility will appear on our website in the next few months. Check www.jgsny.org for the latest information. We would like to hear directly from users on this issue.

Generally, the first subway (or train) listed under "Closest Public Transportation" is closest to the facility. Directions are given for transportation requiring the shortest walk from the subway/train station. We have added maps to each section so that readers can better coordinate research plans.

Under "Description of Resources," we have made a concerted effort to include the precise time span and geographic scope covered by each record group. Records relating to many ethnic/racial groups are included. In a given repository, unique collections of Jewish records as well as collections of other ethnic/racial groups are listed. NOTE: Many of the books cited in one library are available also in others. For this reason, we use standard library citations (including the YIVO-adopted standard for Yiddish books). This should ease locating books in NYC or out-of-town libraries not included here. Because of language limitations, diacritical marks for most foreign languages are not reproduced here.

A detailed description of available indexes is included under "Finding Aids." Where a record group or finding aid is also available at other facilities or on the Internet, this is generally noted. If a cross-referenced facility is covered in this book, its name is given in small CAPITAL LETTERS.

Under "Description of Facility," readers will learn the number of seats, staff, microfilm readers/printers, computers, photocopy machines, etc. and whether researchers have direct access to records and books. "Fees/Copies" describes the cost of using the facility and of copying materials.

Limitations on the use of records or advance order requirements are noted under "Restrictions on Use." Where telephone orders are taken, it is so noted.

In addition to Appendix H, described above, the following are included in the Appendix:

Appendix A provides a description of the various Soundex code systems in use by government and private agencies. This Appendix has been updated to correct an error recently discovered in the National Archives description of its Soundex code. See Tony Borroughs' article, "The Original Soundex Instructions," *NGS Quarterly,* Volume 89, No. 4, December 2001, pages 287–298 for more detail. Appendix B includes an updated and expanded list of Yizkor books memorializing communities destroyed in the Holocaust. This list has been revised by including the current country, adding cross-references to current town names, and using standard library citations for book titles.

Appendix C includes current sample forms to order birth, marriage and death records from New York City and New York State agencies covered in this book. Other appendices include a much expanded list of city directories in the New York Public Library (NYPL) collection as well as detailed lists of foreign telephone directories and U.S. and foreign newspapers in the NYPL collection. An updated and more complete list of cemeteries in the New York metropolitan area is included in Appendix G together with the Sprung cemetery map, published with permission of the Sprung Monument Corporation.

INDEXES:

There are three indexes — name, place and subject. The <u>name index</u> includes names of authors, names of people in collections that are cited in the text and names that appear in the title of a collection. Names of people in collections are cited only when they are few in number or when indicating the first or last name in an index. For all other collections, use the libraries' finding aids to locate information on family members.

The <u>place index</u> includes all localities — countries, cities, villages and neighborhoods that are mentioned under "Description of Resources." It includes the name of a locality when it is mentioned in the title of a book and, if relevant to the contents of a book, where the book is published. Generally, the latter are *not* included in the index. Place names are included as they appear in the text. Exceptions are noted in the index in parentheses. For example, references to Brooklyn as "Kings County" are indexed under "Brooklyn." The index entry is "Brooklyn (Kings County)" to denote this variation. Similarly, a collection such as *Italian Historical Documents* will be found in the place index under "Italy (Italian)." Appendices are not included in the place or name index.

The <u>subject index</u> covers subjects listed primarily under "Description of Resources." In rare cases (when citing a published resource not covered under "Description of Resources"), "Finding Aids" are also indexed. This index includes also the names of organizations and agencies cited in the book. Entries in CAPITAL LETTERS are repositories for which there are separate chapters in this book.

<u>Underlining</u> is used to denote either a primary source of the records or a more significant collection than found on other pages cited. Where two pages are connected by a hyphen, the subject continues to the second page. In all other cases, a hyphen is used as a space saver to connect three or more pages mentioning the subject.

IS THIS BOOK MEANT FOR JEWISH GENEALOGISTS ONLY?

No! Of the libraries, archives and public agencies covered in the book, only 25% are specifically Jewish in character. Sixty hold records or books on all groups (mostly non-Jewish). And, some of the remainder hold records of interest to non-Jewish researchers as well. For example, Yizkor books often contain photographs and maps of small towns and villages in eastern Europe which may be the only published sources of information on these localities.

IS THIS EVERYTHING?

Absolutely not. Be sure to check the catalogs and finding aids of these and other institutions for additional materials. We have tried to include as many of the significant collections as possible to give researchers a taste of what is available. Who would have imagined that they might find records of an ancestor who was employed as a theater matron? Who would have thought information would be available on push-cart owners? Or that Leo Baeck Institute, an organization that collects materials from German-speaking lands would have a collection of case files of displaced persons in *Italy*? This book is an invitation to explore each of these repositories for more. You will surely find something wonderful!

ACKNOWLEDGMENTS:

In preparing this book, we built upon the efforts of those volunteers who helped prepare the 1985 and 1989 editions and were assisted by key staff in each of the agencies described in this book. Contributors to this edition included:

Mark Adams	Gloria Freund	Esther Oriol
Gary Baxter	Ada Greenblatt	Mildred Redman
Debra Braverman	Lucille Gudis	Toby Sanchez
Linda Cantor	Claus Hirsch	Steven W. Siegel
Jeffrey Cymbler	Roger Joslyn	Paul Silverstone
Stewart Driller	Barbara Kahn	Maralyn Steeg
Karen Franklin	Hadassah Lipsius	June Walzer
Robert Friedman	B-Ann Moorehouse	Paula Zieselman

B-Ann Moorehouse was the creator of that wonderful vital records list available at the NYC Municipal Archives which was reproduced in the 1989 edition of this book and updated here. That list for the first time opened the world of NYC town records to genealogists everywhere.

Key staff in each of the agencies and repositories described in *Genealogical Resources in New York* helped tremendously in putting this material together. Directors and/or staff of every facility reviewed the material or provided detailed answers to my questions. Special thanks to those whose extraordinary efforts, dedication and willingness to put up with my endless questions and requests. They make researching a joy:

Bruce Abrams, Old Records Division, County Clerk's Office, New York County
Adina Anflik, American Jewish Historical Society
Aviva Astrinsky, YIVO Library
Gunnar Berg, YIVO Archives
Ruth Carr, NYPL, Irma & Paul Milstein Division of U.S. History, Local History and Genealogy
John Celardo, National Archives-Northeast Region
Kenneth Cobb, Municipal Archives
Renate Evers, Leo Baeck Institute
Richard Gelbke, National Archives-Northeast Region
Gabe Goldstein, Yeshiva University Museum
Leo Greenbaum, YIVO Archives
Alice Hudson, NYPL Map Division
Faith Jones, NYPL Dorot Jewish Division
Yeshayah Metal, YIVO Library
Bonni-Dara Michaels, Yeshiva University Museum
Fruma Mohrer, YIVO Archives
Mark Nusenbaum, Bronx County Clerk's Office
Joy Rich, New York Genealogical and Biographical Society
Leo Rivers, NYS Department of Health
Keven Rothermel, Queens County Clerk's Office
Diane Spielmann, Center for Jewish History
Gilsa Stewart, Schomburg Center for Research in Black Culture
Felix Torres, Staten Island County Clerk's Office
Joseph Van Nostrand, Old Records Division, County Clerk's Office, New York County
Oleg Vinogradov, YIVO Library
Marek Web, YIVO Archives

Many thanks also to Herbert Lazarus of YIVO who scoured the stacks pulling an endless number of books.

NYC and Albany maps were prepared by the Community Mapping Assistance Project (CMAP) of the New York Public Interest Research Group, Inc. (NYPIRG), under the direction of Steven Romalewski.

Any errors or omissions are wholly my responsibility. While working on the American Jewish Historical Society chapter, I came across the perfect preface by Cyrus Adler in the introduction to his work on Jewish soldiers who served in the Spanish-American War. He said,

> "To save persons who will be called upon to criticize this list the trouble or undue expenditure of time, I will point out some of the most glaring defects. It is inconsistent and inconvenient in arrangement; it contains names which should have been omitted, and omits names which should have been included; it frequently gives names incorrectly or with insufficient data or under wrong commands, and it even contains some repetitions. These faults are mentioned so that those who might otherwise be obliged to give their time in discovering them will use it in aiding me to correct them..." Cyrus Adler, American Jewish Yearbook, 1900–1901, p. 528.

Just change the word "list" to "book" and you have my message. I could not have said it better! I hear in Adler's note a call for future volunteers. Whether it is a book, a list, an index or a website — we can make it better with your help!

Finally, I want to thank my family — Marsha and Peter, Adrienne, Michael A., Rachel, Michael L., Michelle and Hal — for all their support and good advice and for giving us Caroline, Elizabeth, Daniel, Helena, Julia, Eva, Jesse and more. That's what this book is all about — creating a family tree!

Good luck in your search!

Estelle M. Guzik
Editor

February, 2003

MANHATTAN

(New York County)

Lower Manhattan Repositories

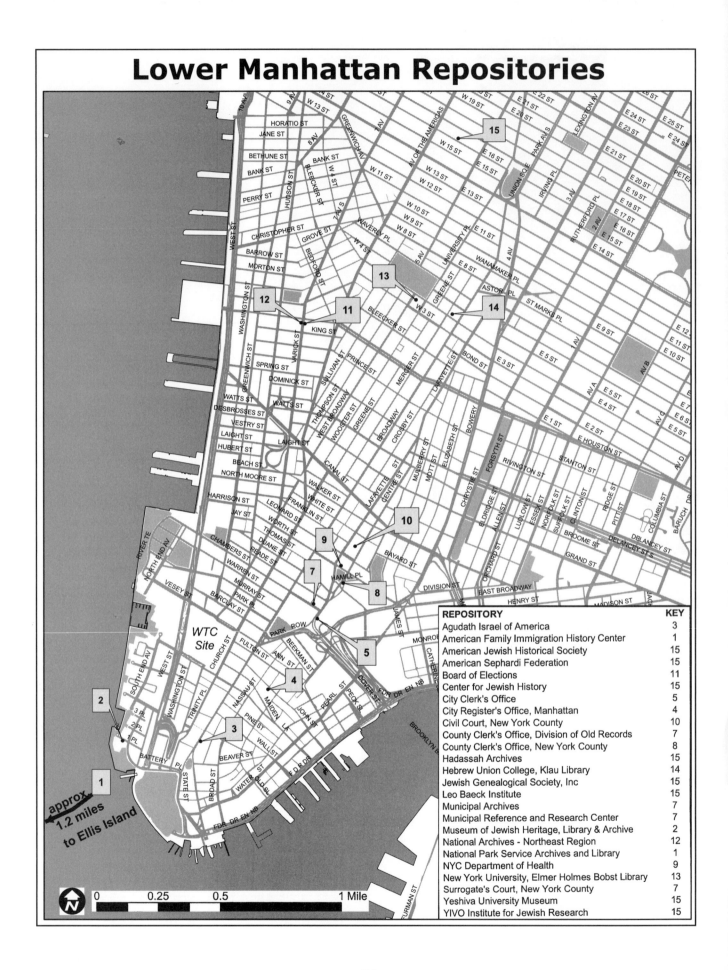

REPOSITORY	KEY
Agudath Israel of America	3
American Family Immigration History Center	1
American Jewish Historical Society	15
American Sephardi Federation	15
Board of Elections	11
Center for Jewish History	15
City Clerk's Office	5
City Register's Office, Manhattan	4
Civil Court, New York County	10
County Clerk's Office, Division of Old Records	7
County Clerk's Office, New York County	8
Hadassah Archives	15
Hebrew Union College, Klau Library	14
Jewish Genealogical Society, Inc	15
Leo Baeck Institute	15
Municipal Archives	7
Municipal Reference and Research Center	7
Museum of Jewish Heritage, Library & Archive	2
National Archives - Northeast Region	12
National Park Service Archives and Library	1
NYC Department of Health	9
New York University, Elmer Holmes Bobst Library	13
Surrogate's Court, New York County	7
Yeshiva University Museum	15
YIVO Institute for Jewish Research	15

Midtown Manhattan Repositories

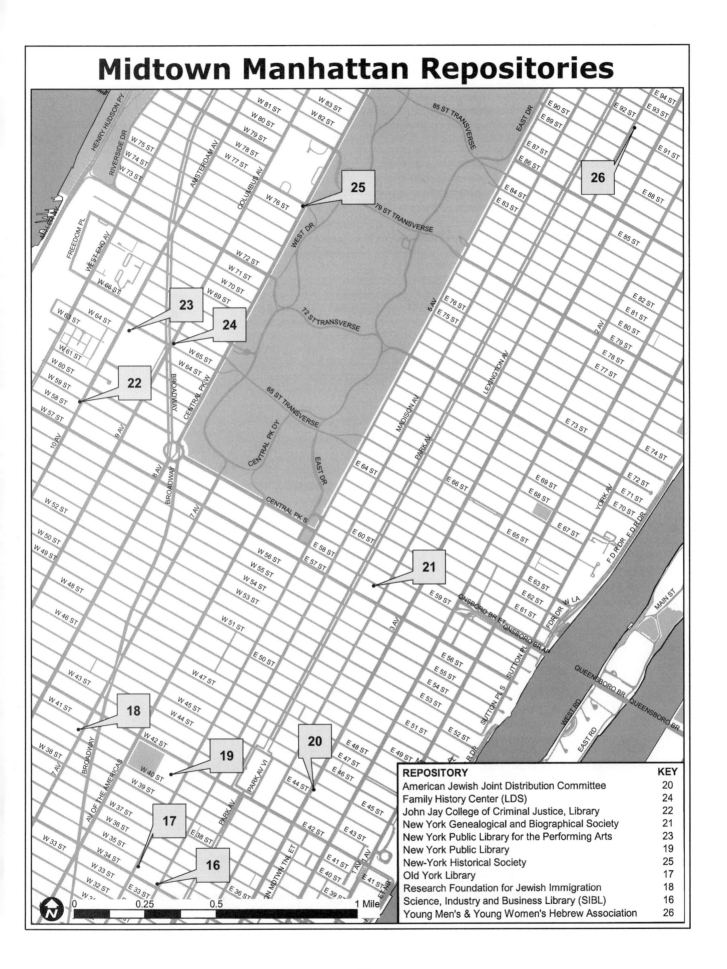

REPOSITORY	KEY
American Jewish Joint Distribution Committee	20
Family History Center (LDS)	24
John Jay College of Criminal Justice, Library	22
New York Genealogical and Biographical Society	21
New York Public Library for the Performing Arts	23
New York Public Library	19
New-York Historical Society	25
Old York Library	17
Research Foundation for Jewish Immigration	18
Science, Industry and Business Library (SIBL)	16
Young Men's & Young Women's Hebrew Association	26

Upper Manhattan Repositories

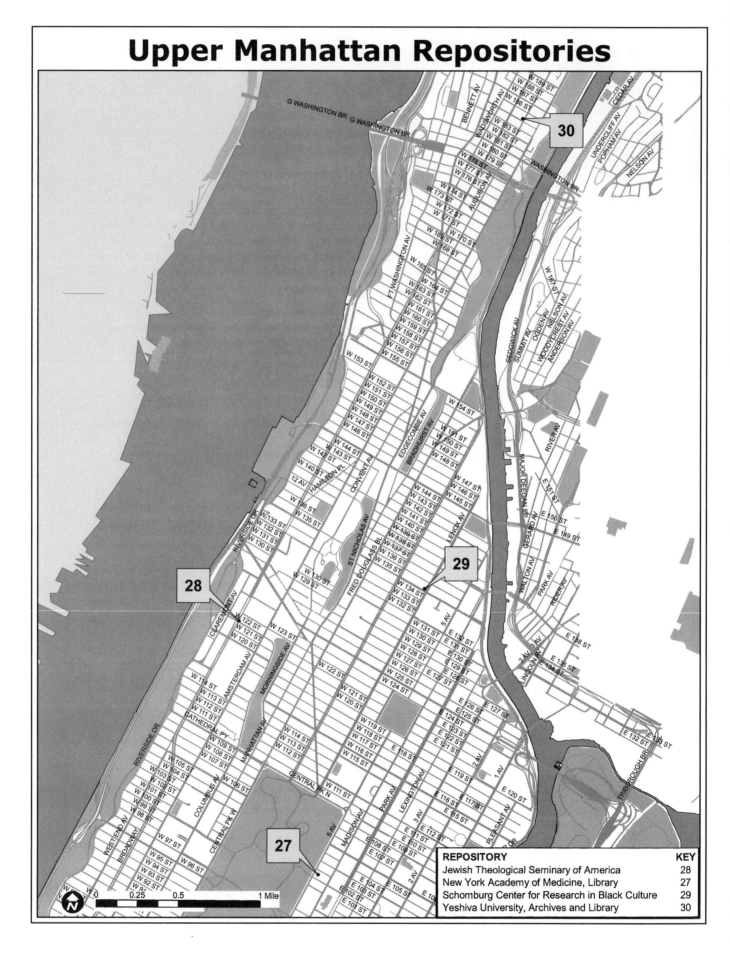

REPOSITORY	KEY
Jewish Theological Seminary of America	28
New York Academy of Medicine, Library	27
Schomburg Center for Research in Black Culture	29
Yeshiva University, Archives and Library	30

AGUDATH ISRAEL OF AMERICA
ORTHODOX JEWISH ARCHIVES

Facility Director:	Rabbi Moshe Kolodny, Archivist
Address:	42 Broadway, 14th Floor
	New York, NY 10004-1617

(Cross Street: between Exchange Place and Morris Street)

Phone:	(212) 797-8179
Fax:	(212) 269-2843
E-mail:	news@agudathisrael.org
Website:	none

Hours of Operation:

Monday to Thursday:	9:30 am to 5:00 pm
Friday:	9:30 am 12:00 noon

Closed Friday afternoon, Saturday, Sunday, Jewish and legal holidays. Note: Appointment suggested.

Closest Public Transportation:

Subway: 4 or 5 to Wall Street (Broadway)
J, M or Z to Broad Street (Exchange Place)
N or R to Rector Street (Trinity Place)
2 or 3 to Wall Street (William Street)

Bus: M1 or M6 (South) to Broadway and Morris Street
M1 or M6 (North) from Trinity Place and Morris Street

PATH train from New Jersey to World Trade Center suspended 9/11/01.

Directions:

Take the #4 or #5 train to the Wall Street station. Exit at the middle of the platform. Go up the stairs to "Broadway/Exchange Place." Walk <u>south</u> on Broadway to #42. The entrance to #42 is wheelchair accessible. The Archives is located on the 14th floor.

Description of Resources:

The Orthodox Jewish Archives collections cover Jewish immigration from the turn of the century to the present; the work of the Vaad Hatzala (Orthodox Jewish Rescue Committee) in providing relief and rescue to Jews trapped in Nazi Europe; Jewish educational activities; children's camps; employment and social welfare programs. The Archives houses an extensive collection of newspapers and periodicals documenting Jewish life in Eastern Europe pre-WWII.

Collections which may be of interest to genealogists include:

1. <u>Periodicals</u>: The Archives has a collection of current Orthodox journals and newspapers from the U.S.A., Israel and Great Britain, as well as newspapers from Europe pre-WWII. The collection includes:

Beth Jacob and *Agudath Israel,* Poland, 1930s (Hebrew/Yiddish)
Der Jud, Warsaw, 1919–1929 (includes lists of people by town who made contributions to alleviate economic distress in Ukraine)
Der Israelite, Frankfurt au Main, 1869–1939
Dos Yidishe Togblat, Warsaw, 1929–1939
Dos Yidishe Licht [The Light of Israel], NYC, 1923–1927
Dos Vort, Vilna, 1925–1937 (microfilm)
Ha Modia, Poltowa, Russia, 1910–1915 (photocopy)
Ha-Modia, Jerusalem, 1954–1991
Heijnt, Riga, Latvia, 1938–1939 (single copies)
Kol Yisrael, Jerusalem, 1923–1949 (weekly)
Machsike Hadas, Lemberg (Lviv), 1879–1913

2. <u>David Kranzler Collection</u>: Yearbooks and journals from students of orthodox yeshivot in the New York area, 1910 to present; and bills of divorcement from northeast U.S.A. rabbinical courts, 1910–1948.

3. <u>West Side Institutional Synagogue Collection</u> (Manhattan), 1935–1959: Lists of students and Jewish schools in Poland and Lithuania, 1937–1939.

4. <u>Nathan Baruch Collection</u>, 1947–1948: Data on displaced persons (DPs) and Jewish survivors after the Holocaust.

5. <u>Harry Fischel Papers</u>: Includes his autobiography.

6. <u>Joan Fredericks Collection</u>: Research material on the train of 1,200 inmates rescued from Theresienstadt Concentration Camp including interviews and correspondence with survivors.

7. <u>Harry Goodman Collection</u>, 1936–1960: Includes the *Jewish Weekly* (*Yiddishe Vochenzeitung*) and the *Jewish Post* published in London, England.

8. <u>Herman Landau Collection</u>: Two minute books of Orthodox youth groups in Fuerth, Germany, 1919–1936.

9. <u>Yeshiva Torah Vodaath, Community Service and Public Relations Collection</u> (Brooklyn), 1948–1980: Placement records and solicitation letters for the school throughout the U.S. and Canada.

10. <u>Rabbi Michael Munk Collection</u>: Biographical material on his father, Rabbi Ezra Munk of Berlin, and letters to the Rabbi from individuals. In addition, the collection includes documents on the Jews of Prague in the late 1700s.

11. <u>Otto Schiff Collection</u>: Includes 34 boxes containing immigration files of individuals assisted by the Refugee Immigration Division of Agudath Israel, 1946–1970s. The files include draft copies of Petitions for Naturalization and sometimes affidavits of support, visa applications, tax returns, marriage and birth certificates and personal correspondence.

12. <u>Jacob Oppenheim Papers</u>: Include the diary of Siegfrid Oppenheim covering his observations of the Holocaust beginning with Kristallnacht, November 10, 1938 and his stay in Buchenwald. [Translated into English by Michael Jacobovits, January 1998.]

13. <u>Moreinu Yaakov Rosenheim Collection</u>: Correspondence of the Orthodox Jewish rescue efforts for Jews trapped in the Holocaust includes letters on behalf of Jews in Czechoslovakia, Sweden, France, Germany, Romania, Italy, Poland and China (Tientsin). Includes a list of surviving children and their location (Box F/Switzerland Folder #9); case histories of child survivors: Rachkowsky, Cimbalista, Stopniczer, Gniwisch, Fogliemann, Zygmond (Box 5, Belgium); list of deportees in Bergen-Belsen, Germany who had Ecuadorian passports (1944), including birth dates and occasionally, birth place.

14. <u>Asher Hertzberg Collection</u>: Includes list of surviving Jews in Warsaw as of June 5, 1945 prepared by the Central Jewish Committee in Poland and submitted to the World Jewish Congress.

15. <u>Rabbi Nathan J. Goldstein Collection</u>: Includes *Sefer Anshe Shem*, a lexicon of prominent Rabbis throughout the world. Edited by Rabbi Samuel Z. Zarski, Moshe David Schiff. Tel Aviv, 1947; and *Sefer Hashana, First Year Book of the Hebrew Teachers College Students*. (First graduating class). Boston, 1925. Includes a list of the students (in Hebrew).

16. <u>Russian Immigrant Services and Education, Project Rise</u> (B-36 & B-37): Includes circumcision records of Russian Jews, 1980 & 1982. Arranged by Hospital and/or name of doctor. Records include name, address, birth date and place, parents names including mother's maiden name.

17 <u>Charles Richter Collection (C-16)</u>: Includes lists of people and their addresses in occupied Poland to whom parcels were sent in March 1941.

18. <u>Congregation Beth Hamidrash Hagadol, Roxbury, MA (a.k.a. Crawford Street Synagogue)</u>: Includes the 10th Anniversary Souvenir Book, 1914–1924, and the Men's Club Book, 1922–1923. Both include Who's Who biographical sketches and photographs of men and women in the Congregation. The Men's Club book includes also biographical sketches of the graduation class of the Yavneh Hebrew School of the Congregation.

19. <u>Michael G. Tress Collection (I-24)</u>: Includes lists of refugees in displaced person camps, 1946–1948.

20. <u>Photographs</u>: The Archives also has extensive photographic holdings of European and American religious personalities. In addition, it has c. 200 relief and refugee photos from World War II, DP camps and Israel.

Finding Aids:

The Archives has a 15-page booklet, *Checklist of Jewish Materials in Archives of Agudath Israel of America,* which describes 40 collections in its holdings. A copy of the *Checklist of Materials* can be obtained for a nominal fee ($2 for mailing to individuals) or free to institutions. See the Archivist for finding aids to collections acquired after the *Checklist* was published.

Description of Facility:

This is a small office which also serves as a research facility. Records can be obtained immediately. Space can be made available to serve up to 3 people at a time. There are two staff members to assist researchers. The Archives has one microfilm reader/printer.

Fees/Copies:

A photocopy machine is available at $.25 per page. Copies from microfilm cost $.30 per page.

Restrictions on Use:

The collections are subject to the privacy privileges of living individuals or family members and general copyright laws where applicable. All records of Agudath Israel created after 1960 require the consent of the Board of Directors before being used.

NOTE: The executive offices of the BOARD OF ELECTIONS are also located at 42 Broadway. Their computer room is located on the 6th floor.

AMERICAN GATHERING OF JEWISH HOLOCAUST SURVIVORS

Facility Director:	Benjamin Meed, President
Address:	122 West 30th Street, Suite 205 New York, NY 10001
	(Cross Streets: 6th and 7th Avenues)
Phone:	(212) 239-4230
Fax:	(212) 279-2926
E-mail:	mail@americangathering.org
Website:	none
Hours of Operation:	Mail requests only.

Description of Resources:

The Benjamin and Vladka Meed Registry of Jewish Holocaust Survivors was created in 1981 by the American Gathering of Jewish Holocaust Survivors in Jerusalem and developed further at its Washington Gathering in 1983. In April 1993, this computerized database was turned over to the U.S. Holocaust Museum in Washington, DC and is available there as well.

The database, now including over 180,000 survivors and their children, provides current name, address, places of residence before the War, places of internment or residence during the War, occupation, name before and during the War, maiden name, date and place of birth, spouse's name and information on spouse and other family members. Date of death has been added to the database where known. The database may indicate whether an oral history was recorded by the survivor and, if so, the year recorded and place in which the oral history can be found.

The original aim of the American Gathering was to document all survivors living in the U.S.A. and Canada in this historical archive. This goal has been broadened to include survivors living worldwide.

Finding Aids:

The published *Benjamin and Vladka Meed Registry of Jewish Holocaust Survivors* is a four-volume work with three indexes: survivors cross-indexed by previous and most current name (volumes 1 and 2); survivors indexed by place of birth and town of residence pre-war (volume 3); and survivors indexed by wartime location or locations (volume 4). The published *Registry* does not include current address, date of birth or other personal information about family members. Copies of the *Registry* are available in major libraries in NYC and around the world, including the CENTER FOR JEWISH HISTORY. [On open-shelf: D810.J4 N3 2000]

To obtain additional information by mail, the researcher must complete a Search Form which can be obtained from the American Gathering or from the U.S. Holocaust Memorial Museum website at www.ushmm.org. If the correct spelling of the name is unknown, a special soundex system can be utilized for the search. The American Gathering will forward letters to survivors. See "Restrictions on Use."

Fees/Copies:

Although there is no charge for a search, a contribution (tax-deductible) is appreciated. Send a self-addressed stamped envelope with your inquiry. NOTE: The *Benjamin and Vladka Meed Registry of Jewish Holocaust Survivors* can be purchased on CD-ROM for $175.

Restrictions on Use:

Because of confidentiality restrictions, survivor address and phone number are not released. However, in certain circumstances, arrangements can be made to forward a letter to the survivor.

NOTE: Researchers can access a computerized version of the published *Registry* when visiting the U.S. Holocaust Memorial Museum in Washington, DC. The *Registry* is located on the 2nd floor of the Museum and is open to the public from 10 am to 5 pm.

AMERICAN JEWISH JOINT DISTRIBUTION COMMITTEE ARCHIVES

Facility Director:	Sherry Hyman, Director, Archives and Records
Address:	711 Third Avenue, 10th Floor ♿ * New York, NY 10017-3898
	(Cross Streets: East 44th and 45th Streets)
Warehouse Address:	The Fortress 49-20 Fifth Street (entrance on 49th Avenue) Long Island City, Queens, NY
Phone:	(212) 687-6200
Fax:	(212) 370-5467 or (212) 682-7262
E-mail:	sherry@jdcny.org
Website:	www.jdc.org

Hours of Operation:

Monday to Thursday, 9:30 am to 4:00 pm; Friday, 9:30 am to 2:00 pm
By appointment only after research application has been approved.

Closed Saturday, Sunday, Jewish and legal holidays.

Closest Public Transportation:

Subway: 4, 5, 6 or 7 to Grand Central/42nd Street

Bus: M101 or M102 to Lexington Avenue and 44th/45th Street (southbound)
          M101 or M102 to 3rd Avenue and 44th/45th Street (northbound)

Directions:

Take the #4 or #5 (express) train to Grand Central/42nd Street station. Exit the train and walk east one block to Third Avenue. Walk north on Third Avenue to #711. *NOTE: Notify staff of accessibility needs.

Description of Resources:

The American Jewish Joint Distribution Committee (JDC) was established in 1914 by three American Jewish organizations — the American Jewish Relief Committee, the Orthodox Central Relief Committee and the People's Relief Committee — in response to the devastation of European Jewry. During WWI and postwar its functions included the distribution of food, clothing and medical supplies; the reconstruction of decimated areas and resettlement of refugees. The Holocaust era included efforts to rescue Jews from Nazi-occupied lands and negotiations with American and foreign governments. Post-WWII activities included the administration of displaced persons (DP) camps, relocation of refugees and migration to Israel.

Because of the extensive nature of this collection, only a sampling of the files are noted below. Researchers should consult the finding aids for additional subjects and place names mentioned. File numbers are in brackets.

1. Photographic Archives: Beginning with the portrait of the very first members of the JDC Executive Committee in 1918, circa 50,000 photographs are available that illustrate the JDC's work. The collection includes over 10,000 photographs from the DP period, including 200 from Bergen-Belsen Displaced Persons camp; and photographs of Jewish refugees in Shanghai and at Sousa in the Dominican Republic.

2. Records, 1914–1918: Files of particular interest to genealogists are organized under the following sub-headings:

Organizational Structure of JDC: Includes records of relief funds sent by the Transmission Bureau to individual families in Europe from relatives in America. Names and addresses are often included.

Subject Matter: Includes files on the following subjects: refugees in Russia (from Poland and Lithuania), refugees in Salonika (from Monastir, Serbia [now Bitola, Macedonia]); rabbis (refugees) in Alexandria and in Austria; prisoners of war by location, e.g. Austria and Germany (from Russia), Bulgaria (from Romania); American citizens deported from Palestine; relatives and friends, information service, 1915–1916 (arranged alphabetically); students in Switzerland (from Russia); and writers in Copenhagen and Switzerland (from Russia).

Geographical Areas: Includes files on the following places in Lithuania: Kovno, Lida, Pren (Prienai), Schaulen (Shavli or Siauliai), Skaudvile, Suwalki, Vilna and Wladyslawow.

3. Records, 1919–1921: This collection of 800 files includes documentary material on prevailing conditions in Eastern Europe such as pogroms (eye-witness accounts, diaries, memoirs and lists of victims); prisoners of war in Siberia (hand-written messages, photographs and minute books of POW camps). Materials are arranged under the following sample sub-headings:

JDC Administration, NY [1–60]: Executive staff [7–15]; personnel [28–43]; transmission of funds (includes lists of names of remitters). [55–60]

Overseas Administration [61–71]: Overseas personnel. [68]

Subject Matter [88–108]: Child care [88–89]; emigration and immigration [91]; pogroms and persecution [94]; POWs; refugees [99]; relatives and friends [100–100a]. These latter files include, by city, lists of persons in Europe seeking relatives in New York. The names and European addresses of the searchers are included.

Localities [109–290]: These files are grouped by country.

4. Records, 1921–1932, 1933–1944 and 1945–1964: Materials in the 1921–1932 collection are arranged in a similar manner to those above. The 1933–1944 collection includes 1,141 folders which span the Nazi and Holocaust eras. The majority of these files are arranged by country and region, although similar Subject Matter files as those described above are also included. The 1945–1964 files are listed by file name only.

The 1933–1944 collection includes Passenger Lists (under the heading, "Emigration/Sailings"), 1939–1944. During this period, the JDC's Transmigration Bureau assisted 12,700 Jewish refugees to emigrate to the U.S.A. via Spain and Portugal, and 1,300 via Siberia and Japan. Passenger lists for such vessels as the S.S. *Carvalho Araujo*, S.S. *Excalibur*, S.S. *Exeter* and S.S. *Exochorda* [369], S.S. *Guinea* [373], S.S. *Mouzinho* [375], S.S. *Nyassa* [377], S.S. *Serpa Pinto* [387], S.S. *Nea Hellis* [388], S.S. *Siboney* [389]; as well as lists of refugee children [233–239, 343–345, 589] are included. In addition, there are lists of refugees traveling from Europe to Buenos Aires [372]; Cuba [374, 376, 377]; Canada [454]; and arrivals in Istanbul, Turkey [1052]. Among these are lists from the S.S. *St. Louis* and documentation of efforts made to find a sanctuary for S.S. *St. Louis* refugees in 1939. [378–386; lists in 384]

The collection includes for Shanghai, a list of 1,578 refugees who registered for emigration to Canada [455]; list of Jewish refugees from Japan, 1941 [726]; list of 506 persons who were part of rabbinical groups (yeshiva students rabbis, and their families) in Shanghai, 1946/1947 [465, 487]; individual records ("hard core" refugees), 1950, 1955 [478–481]; passenger lists, S.S. *Gen. Gordon* arriving in San Francisco, 1949 [493]; passenger list of refugees on flights from Harbin and Tientsin to Israel, 1950/1951 [494, 496–498]; list of DPs who sailed on the S.S. *Anna Salen* to Naples, 1950 [496]; emigration lists from Shanghai to various countries, 1952–1964 [499]; and a list of 7,570 JDC files of Shanghai emigrants to the U.S.A., Canada, South America, Europe, Israel and Australia [500]. The actual files were impounded by the government in Shanghai at the end of the war and have never been recovered.

Organization files found in this collection can provide useful background information. Examples include, American Friends Service Committee [205–209]; German (European) - Jewish Children's Aid [233–239]; Emergency Committee in Aid of Displaced German Scholars [222–222n]; and U.S. Committee for the Care of European Children. [343–345]

See also CENTER FOR JEWISH HISTORY -YIVO INSTITUTE FOR JEWISH RESEARCH - ARCHIVES and LEO BAECK INSTITUTE for additional AJDC records.

Finding Aids:

In order to locate specific information of interest, the researcher should consult the finding aids at the Archives. There are five finding aids arranged in groups of years: 1914–1918, 1919–July 1921, August 1921–December 1932, 1933–1944, and 1945–1964. A sixth finding aid is a guide to the papers of Saly Mayer, JDC's representative in Switzerland, 1940–1949. The seventh finding aid lists the records of the Dominican Republic Settlement Association (DORSA), the governing body of a unique experiment in Jewish farming in the Dominican Republic, 1939–1977.

Each finding aid, except 1945–1964, provides details of the holdings by file number. Use this file number plus any other key information that is contained in the description to request the file. The 1919–1921 finding aid includes three appendices arranged alphabetically: Index of Localities; Reference List of Individuals; List of Landsmanshaftn.

There is a partial computerized index to the photograph collection.

Description of Facility:

All archival materials are now located at an off-site facility, the Fortress, in Long Island City, Queens. Prior to making an appointment, researchers are required to complete a 3-page Research Application and Statement of Compliance form. To receive an Application, send an e-mail, letter, fax or call JDC. Once the application is submitted and approved, an appointment can be made. Archives staff will advise whether the material will be made available for viewing at the Fortress or at the office in Manhattan. Researchers coming to the 3rd Avenue office must check in on the 10th floor. Staff escort visitors to the office or to the Fortress (by #7 subway to Vernon Boulevard/Jackson Avenue Station). Limited work space is available at both sites. There is one microfilm reader/printer at the 3rd Avenue office.

Fees/Copies:

Photocopy services are provided at a cost of $.25 per page. Copies of microfilm are $.20 per page. Any photocopy request exceeding one hour of labor will be billed an additional $12 per hour. Prices are subject to change.

Restrictions on Use:

Photo identification must be presented upon entering the 3rd Avenue building.

The use of some materials is restricted by date or content. Employment or personnel files may be restricted regardless of date. Researchers are provided a copy of the JDC Access and Restrictions Policy.

BOARD OF ELECTIONS
MANHATTAN BOROUGH OFFICE

Facility Director: Rosanna Kostamoulas-Rahmouni, Chief Clerk
Inez Ward, Document Record Unit

Address: 200 Varick Street, Room 1000   ♿
New York, NY 10014

(Cross Streets: West Houston and King Streets)

Phone: (212) 886-3800
(212) 807-8619 (Warehouse)

Fax: (212) 886-3820
(212) 225-5648 (Warehouse)

E-mail: none

Website: www.vote.nyc.ny.us

Hours of Operation:

Monday to Friday: 9:00 am to 5:00 pm. Document Record Unit closes at 4:45 pm.

Closed Saturday, Sunday and legal holidays.

Researchers should arrive no later than 4:00 pm. Persons wishing to view records at the warehouse, 448 West 16th Street, must call in advance for an appointment. A prior appointment is also recommended to view records at the Varick Street office during the weeks immediately before and after primary and general elections.

Closest Public Transportation:

To 200 Varick Street:
Subway: 1 or 9 to Houston Street.
C or E to Spring Street

PATH: To Christopher Street (from New Jersey)

Bus: M10 or M21 to West Houston and Varick Streets

To Warehouse, 448 West 16th Street, 4th floor
Subway: 1, 2, 3, 9, F or V to 14th Street

Bus: M11 or M14 to 9th Avenue and 15th Street

Directions:

To 200 Varick Street: Take the #1 or #9 train to the Houston Street station. The building is on the southeast corner of Houston and Varick Streets. Take the elevator to the 10th floor. Enter the reception area through the double doors next to the elevators (Room 1000).

Warehouse: Take the #1, #2, #3, #9 or F train to the 14th Street station. Walk or take the M14 bus west to 9th Avenue and 15th Street. The main entrance to 448 West 16th Street is closed. Enter through the Chelsea Markets at 75 9th Avenue (between 15th and 16th Streets). Go straight ahead passing the indoor "waterfall" and the overhead clock. Turn right about 50 paces after the clock. Go down the ramp next to the elevator with the traffic light. Take the elevator at the end of the ramp (on the right) to the 4th floor. Ring the bell to enter the Board of Election's Manhattan Warehouse.

Description of Resources:

The Manhattan office has voter registration records for voters residing in Manhattan from 1916–1920 (gaps) and 1923 to the present. See NEW YORK CITY DEPARTMENT OF RECORDS AND INFORMATION SERVICES, MUNICIPAL ARCHIVES for records, 1872–1922 (gaps).

Records before 1957 were maintained in ledgers (at the warehouse). Records, 1957–1995 are on microfilm (at Varick Street). Registrations still active in 1993 and new registrations filed 1993 or later have been digitized.

Registration information filed before 1995 may include date and court where naturalized, age or birth date, current and prior address, length of time at current address (and in State/County), AD/ED of the voter's address, date registered, and employer's name. If one is a citizen by marriage or through a parent, the name of that person and citizenship information may be recorded.

Records of new voters filed from 1995 to the present, include address, birth date, citizenship ("yes" or "no"), year last voted and prior address. Naturalization and birth place information were eliminated from the NYS registration form after the National Voter Registration Act went into effect (January 1, 1995).

Digitized registrations, 1993 to the present, are available in the Archival Voter Information Data (AVID) system. AVID combined and replaced the older Election Administration System (EASY Screens), a computerized database which was previously accessible to the public, and SCRIBE, digitized copies of voter applications ("buff" cards) previously accessible to staff only. EASY was implemented in Manhattan in 1986. SCRIBE was implemented in 1993. (SCRIBE = Signature Capture Reproduction & Imaging for the Board of Elections.) As a result, data on Manhattan voters active in 1986 or who registered 1986 or later are in the AVID system. Digitized copies of records of Manhattan voters still active in 1993 or who applied 1993 or later can also be seen in AVID. NOTE: AVID can access records from all five boroughs. Borough offices implemented these systems over a range of years, i.e. EASY (1985–1987), SCRIBE (1991–1993). Check BOARD OF ELECTIONS, BOROUGH OFFICES to determine the years covered by AVID for each borough.

At present, researchers have access only to the EASY system in Manhattan. However, the Board of Elections plans to addpublic-access computers for AVID in each borough in the near future. Such access is already available to researchers in the BOARD OF ELECTIONS, STATEN ISLAND BOROUGH OFFICE and QUEENS BOROUGH OFFICE.

Finding Aids:

The voter registration index includes Manhattan voters, 1986 to the present, accessible by researchers at the EASY Screens computers available in the Document Record Unit. Researchers can search by full name, surname only or by address. The latter can be helpful if names of spouse or adult children are unknown. The EASY Screens index includes name, current (last) address, birth date, AD/ED, date last voted and status code. Status codes which can be useful to genealogists are (A) Active; (1) moved, (2) inactive 4 years or more, (3) death; (4) felon; (5) not U.S. citizen; (7) incompetent; and (9) court order.

Digitized Manhattan records, 1993 to the present, can be accessed quickly by Document Record Unit staff using the AVID system.

Researchers can search the microfilms for earlier records. However, canceled records, pre-1980, are arranged by Assembly/Election District (AD/ED) and then alphabetized by surname. These records can be accessed only if the address and AD/ED are known. The 200 Varick Street office no longer has maps for these years. AD/ED maps, are available for some years at the Warehouse. See "Restrictions on Use." The NEW YORK PUBLIC LIBRARY, GENERAL REFERENCE DIVISION, has NYC AD/ED maps 1911 to the present (gaps), call number [**SEH+++(NYC Election Board Maps Showing the Assembly District of the City of New York)]. The NEW YORK PUBLIC LIBRARY MAP DIVISION has NYC AD/ED maps for 1914 and 1925. Maps through 1973 are also available at the NYC DEPARTMENT RECORDS AND INFORMATION SERVICES, MUNICIPAL REFERENCE AND RESEARCH CENTER on microfiche, 1872–1956, or paper, 1956–1973.

Canceled Records, 1980–1991 (microfilm), are in one alphabetical series. Canceled records (microfilm), 1992 to 1995 (microfilm), are arranged by year and then alphabetically. NOTE: Use AVID for 1993 or later cancellations.

Description of Facility:

This is a NYC government office. Computer printouts listing current Manhattan voters are located in the reception area in Room 1000. For access to the EASY Screens computer terminals or for viewing microfilms of Manhattan records, register at this office first. Researchers are then provided a name tag which serves as a pass to the Document Record Unit. Exit the reception area and turn left. There are 10 computer terminals for use by researchers in accessing the EASY Screens index and one dedicated computer on which the clerk can access digitized records in AVID. The office has two microfilm readers. The two staff people in this room are helpful and available to explain how to use the computers.

Records (in ledgers), 1916–1920 (gaps), 1923–1956, and AD/ED maps for a scattering of years (see "Restrictions on Use"), are located in the Board's Warehouse at 448 West 16th Street (between 9th and 10th Avenues).

Fees/Copies:

There is no charge for viewing (or hand copying) these records. Mail requests are accepted for a $3 fee (certified check or money order payable to the Board of Elections, City of New York). This covers a search for one name in one year at one address. Each additional name and/or year or address is $3. No refund is made if the record is not found. For an in-person search, the cost of a printout from the AVID system is $.25 per page for an uncertified copy or $3 certified.

Provide the full name at registration, address where residing at the time of registration, and date of birth or age. For pre-1957 records, use the address in a Presidential election year when the individual was more likely to have voted.

Restrictions on Use:

Active records are not available for examination ten business days before or after primary and general elections. During these periods, researchers should call before coming.

In Manhattan, digitized records can only be accessed by the Document Record Unit staff.

The Varick Street office no longer has the AD/ED maps. Pre-1980 research cannot be done without this information. Maps were transferred to the Warehouse but are scattered in different locations in no particular order at that facility. Some volumes are in open boxes near the back exit, and some were found on tables along the back wall. Maps appear to be available from 1918 to 1984 (with more than 10 year gaps for some periods).

NOTE: The Board of Elections' central office is also located in Manhattan at 42 Broadway. (This building is also the home of the AGUDATH ISRAEL OF AMERICA, ORTHODOX JEWISH ARCHIVES.) The Broadway office has 10 EASY Screens computer terminals that are open to the public, but it does not provide public access to AVID or microfilms of any of the borough offices. The computer room at this location can be entered through the Hearing Room on the 6th floor. It is the room opposite the reception desk. EASY Screens computers at this location can search all boroughs in one action.

CENTER FOR JEWISH HISTORY
LILLIAN GOLDMAN MAIN READING ROOM

Facility Director:	Rabbi Joshua E. Plaut, Director, Center for Jewish History
	Diane Spielmann, Public Services Coordinator
Address:	Center for Jewish History ♿
	15 West 16th Street
	New York, NY 10011
	(Cross Streets: Fifth and Sixth Avenues)
Phone:	(212) 294-8301
Fax:	(212) 294-8302
E-mail:	cjh@cjh.org
Website:	www.cjh.org

Hours of Operation:

Monday to Thursday: 9:30 am to 5:00 pm

Friday research available by prior appointment only, at the discretion of the appropriate partner organization.

Closed Saturday and all major Jewish and legal holidays. The Genealogy Institute may open on some Sundays and weekday evenings. Check the Center's website or call before coming.

Closest Public Transportation:

Subway: F, L, V to 14th Street/6th Avenue
4, 5, 6, L, N, Q, R, W to Union Square/14th Street
1, 2, 3, 9 to 14th Street/7th Avenue (or 1, 9 to 18th Street/7th Avenue).

Bus: M2, M3, M5 to 5th Avenue/17th Street (southbound)
M5, M6, M7 to Avenue of the Americas (6th Avenue/17th Street (northbound)
M6, M7 to Broadway/17th Street(southbound)
M14 to 5th Avenue/14th Street

Directions:

Take the F or V train to 14th Street and 6th Avenue (Avenue of the Americas). Exit the train at the <u>north</u> end to 16th Street and 6th Avenue. Walk less than one block <u>east</u> to the Center.

Description of Resources:

The Center for Jewish History, which opened its doors in 1999, is home to the AMERICAN JEWISH HISTORICAL SOCIETY, AMERICAN SEPHARDI FEDERATION, LEO BAECK INSTITUTE, YESHIVA UNIVERSITY MUSEUM and YIVO INSTITUTE FOR JEWISH RESEARCH. The combined holdings of the partners include approximately 100 million archival documents, a half million books, and thousands of photographs, artifacts, paintings and textiles. The Center is the largest repository documenting the Jewish experience outside of Israel. In 2000, the Center established a CENTER GENEALOGY INSTITUTE in association with the Lillian Goldman Main Reading Room, to provide assistance to patrons researching their family histories. Descriptions of holdings of the partner organizations and the Institute are included in the pages that follow.

NOTE: In 1992, the Bund Archives, formerly a separate repository, was transferred to YIVO and became a division of YIVO's Archives. See YIVO INSTITUTE FOR JEWISH RESEARCH - ARCHIVES for a description of Bund collections of interest to genealogists. HADASSAH ARCHIVES, now housed with the AMERICAN JEWISH HISTORICAL SOCIETY at the Center, is also included here.

The Reading Room Reference Collection consists of encyclopedias, directories, bibliographies, periodicals, dictionaries, indexes and other frequently used materials from the collections of the Center partners. Reference works representing diverse Jewish communities around the world include registers of Holocaust victims and survivors, biographical dictionaries, rabbinic resources, gazetteers, finding aids to other libraries and archives, and much more.

Finding Aids:

By the Spring 2003, the Center will have an integrated online catalog covering the collections of each library and archive located here. There are seven public computers with catalogs and Internet access outside the Reading Room. Existing card catalogs of YIVO INSTITUTE FOR JEWISH RESEARCH - LIBRARY, and the AMERICAN JEWISH HISTORICAL SOCIETY are also located in this area. Published and printed inventories of archival collections can be requested from each Reference Librarian at the reference desk upon entering the Reading Room. Researchers may also consult with Public Service librarians before entering the Reading Room to focus their research.

Description of Facility:

Researchers ready to access the vast collection of primary materials held by the Center partners can do so in the Lillian Goldman Main Reading Room on the third floor. Multi-lingual Reference Librarians from the Leo Baeck Institute, American Jewish Historical Society, YIVO Library and YIVO Archives, are represented at the Reference Desk (in that order). Librarians/Archivists from the American Sephardi Federation and Hadassah Archives can be called upon as needed. Appointments are recommended for these latter institutions. Researchers wishing to see materials from the Yeshiva University Museum (YUM) collection should write or e-mail YUM detailing requests. YUM catalogs available at the Center can be viewed without an appointment.

The Reading Room includes 32 study areas each equipped with outlets for use of laptop computers. Reference works from the partners' collections, are arranged by Library of Congress catalog number. The vast majority of the collections are in the stacks although some American Jewish Historical Society and YIVO Institute for Jewish Research materials are located off-site. See "Restrictions on Use" for each organization.

Researchers visiting the Center for the first time are asked to register at the reception desk in the outer area before entering the Reading Room. There are three work tables that can seat 16 researchers in this reception area. Computers accessible to the public are located to the left of the reception desk. The Shaul and Riteve Microfilm Room, the Center Genealogy Institute and its open-stack reference collection can be found here. The Microfilm Room has 6 microfilm readers, two of which are microfilm/microfiche readers. All can access one of the three printers located in this room.

The Center's bookstore, located on the main floor, carries newly published genealogy books. The 248-seat auditorium on the main floor features many programs of interest to genealogists, including those of the Jewish Genealogical Society, Inc.

Fees/Copies:

Photocopies for on-site researchers are made by staff at $.25 per page. See "Fees/Copies" for mail inquiry policies of individual partner agencies. Cost to reproduce photographs vary. Consult with the appropriate librarian. Checks or money orders must be in U.S. dollars drawn on a U.S.A. bank.

There is a charge of $3.75 per month (up to 3 months), to borrow films on interlibrary loan from the Family History Library in Salt Lake City for viewing at CJH. Only checks or money orders are accepted.

Restrictions on Use:

All coats must be checked in the main floor coat room. Briefcases and bags may be checked in the coat room or in lockers on the 3rd floor. Researchers obtain a visitor's pass at the ground floor reception desk. Photo identification must be left at the desk in exchange for the pass and is returned upon departure. First time researchers are asked to complete a registration card at the 3rd floor reception desk before entering the Lillian Goldman Main Reading Room.

Copyright laws of the United States (Title 17, US Code) govern the making of photocopies or other reproductions of material. No photocopying is permitted of rare, fragile or brittle materials. No more than one third of any publication or manuscript may be copied. Copying of some materials requires written permission of the donor or the author of the document. Staff will advise if this is the case. Center for Jewish History staff members are the final arbiters of what may be photocopied.

Only blank or lined paper, pencils and laptop computers (without the case) may be brought into the Reading Room. No personal books, large bags, pens, mobile telephones, cameras, scanners or strollers are permitted. A copy of the Center's policy is provided to each researcher upon entering the Reading Room and is also available online.

No materials can be borrowed.

CENTER FOR JEWISH HISTORY
AMERICAN JEWISH HISTORICAL SOCIETY

Facility Director: Michael Feldberg, PhD, Executive Director
Lyn Slome, Director of Library and Archives

Address: 15 West 16th Street ♿
New York, NY 10011

(Cross Streets: Fifth and Sixth Avenues)

Phone: (212) 294-6160
Fax: (212) 294-6161
E-mail: ajhs@ajhs.org
Website: www.ajhs.org

Hours of Operation:

Monday to Thursday: 9:30 am to 5:00 pm. Appointments are recommended.

Closed Friday, Saturday, Jewish and legal holidays

Closest Public Transportation, Directions, Description of Facility and Fees/Copies:

See CENTER FOR JEWISH HISTORY, LILLIAN GOLDMAN MAIN READING ROOM

Description of Resources:

Founded in 1892, the American Jewish Historical Society has an extensive collection of archival and published sources documenting Jewish contributions to religious, economic, cultural and political life in the Americas. Its holdings, from the 1590s to the present, include more than 40,000,000 documents and 50,000 books, many of them rare, including the first Hebrew books published in America. Also available here are thousands of historic paintings, posters and photographs including some of early Jewish settlers in the American Wild West. The collection includes the papers of individuals, as well as national and local Jewish organizations.

1. <u>Personal and Family Papers</u>: More than 700 collections of 18th, 19th and 20th century American Jewish political and communal leaders, such as Haym Salomon, financier of the American Revolution; Uriah P. Levy, the nation's first Jewish Commodore; Adolphus S. Solomons, co-founder with Clara Barton of the American Red Cross; and Emma Lazarus, poet laureate of America's immigrants. Of particular note are:

<u>Aaron Lopez Collection, 1731–1782</u> [P-11] includes shipping records, 1765–1794, pertaining to Lopez' import/export activities [Boxes 1–5]; and correspondence with individuals with whom Lopez traded. These are arranged by location (Boston, Dartmouth, East Greenwich, Kingston, Newport, Providence, Salem, Swansey, Warren, Worcester and some foreign ports) and by surname.

<u>Jacques Judah Lyons Collection</u> [P-15] contains his notes and original documents he collected related to the Jews of North and South America, in particular New York, Newport, Philadelphia and the West Indies. Lyons served as minister of the Spanish Portuguese Congregation of New York (Congregation Shearith Israel). He began collecting after the Civil War (1861) until his death in 1877. The Society's *Publication of the American Jewish Historical Society,* volumes 21 (1913) and 27 (1919), provide detailed name/subject finding aids to this collection. Volume 21, includes a reproduction of the earliest extant minute books of Congregation Shearith Israel; and volume 27 includes complete reprints of some of the most genealogically relevant materials, such as:

Registry of circumcisions in New York by Abraham I. Abrahams, 1756–1781; names of subscribers to Shearith Israel's religious school, 1793, including number of their children; names of boys and girls in the religious school, 1795; memorandum of marriages and births, 1804–1816; map of New Bowery and 21st Street cemeteries; lists of those interred in 19th Street and 21st Street cemeteries; names of some disinterred from Oliver Street and reburied in 21st Street, 1855; published article, 1775, on Jewish cemeteries in NYC including Bnai Jeshurun, Oliver Street, Portuguese cemeteries, with names/year of burials; tombstone inscriptions from the Beth Haim Cemetery, Newport, RI, 1885; names of women in the congregation by marital status, including husband's name, 1828–1839.

Excerpts from Lyons' notebook relating to the Gomez, Hays, Moses, Levy, Seixas, Simson, and Solomons families of New York; and Tuoro and Gould families of Newport. Records include Seixas family registers with family genealogies; excerpts from Gomez family bibles listing births, marriages and deaths, c. 1693–1852, and family tree; excerpts from diary of Aaron Levy, 1805–1834; records of births, marriages and deaths in Newport, RI copied from the family bible of Moses Seixas, 1744–1787; Simson family birth, marriage and death records transcribed from the records of Shearith Israel Congregation; history of Aaron Soria (DeSoria), 1762–1852, provided by his son in 1871.

Samuel Oppenheim Collection, c. 1650–1850 [P-255] includes Oppenheim's hand written research notes documenting a wide range of records on Colonial American Jewry and early Jewish settlers in other parts of the Americas. Oppenheim notes are from the Dutch West Indies Company records, newspapers, synagogue and court records. The collection includes files with information on over 1,100 individuals (alpha index by name) [Boxes 1–17]; and such varied information as a Jewish grantor/grantee alpha index from libers of conveyances (New York), 1790–1855 [Box 16/1–4]; Newark, NJ Town Records, 1720–1742 [Box 20/1]; New York directory of Jews, 1664–1734 [Box 20/9]; early history of the Jews of New York, 1664–1720 and 1721–1735 (unpublished) [Box 34]; Newport, RI Superior Court, 1720–1811, defendants/plaintiffs indexes [Box 20/4]; list of Jews in San Francisco, CA, 1849–1852 [Box 21]; Congregation Shearith Israel (New York), register of marriage certificates, 1758–1834. [Box 23]; notes on genealogies of Frank, Simson and Louzada families [Box 34]; Jewish owners of ships registered at the Port of Philadelphia, PA, 1730–1775; and at Newport [Box 35]; list of wills of Jews of Barbados up to 1800; and in Jamaica, 1731–1750 [Box 32], and much more.

Rabbi Tobias Geffen Papers [P-516]. Rabbi Geffen served in NYC, 1904–1907, Canton, OH, 1907–1910 and Atlanta, GA, 1910–1970. The collection covers the Atlanta period primarily. Includes autobiography and family correspondence [Boxes 1, 3–6]; c. 70 divorce cases [Boxes 16–18]; correspondence with congregants, soldiers and prisoners at the Atlanta Penitentiary [Box 19]; and Shearith Israel (Atlanta) religious school record cards, 1930–1932. These include pupil's name, address, parent's name, age or birth date. With the exception of the Shearith Israel records, most of the collection is in Yiddish. See "Restrictions on Use."

Rabbi Milton Steinberg Papers, 1920–1981 [P-369] Includes extensive correspondence with family and friends [Boxes 1–5]; congregants at Beth El Zedek synagogue, Indianapolis, IN, 1929–1949, and Park Avenue Synagogue, New York, NY, 1933–1949; correspondence with German refugees and American servicemen. [Boxes 16–17]

Rabbi Stephen S. Wise Papers [P-134] includes correspondence and individual case files. [Box 98]

Phillip Applebaum Collection, 1944–1993 [P-583] includes magazine articles about American Jews who attained prominence in various fields including sports, business and entertainment. Files are arranged by name.

Solis and Solis-Cohen Family Papers [P-642] includes correspondence, diaries and genealogies of the Cardozo, Etting, Menken, Nathan, Nones, Peixotto and Solis families. Ehrenreich Family Genealogy [P-96] includes Waterman, Krensky and Wise families; Louis Lipsey Papers [P-672] include genealogies of the Capin, Davidson/Borison, Lipshitz/Konheym, Mauerberger/Mayesberger and Wistenetzky families. Nones Family [P-334] includes DeLeon, Andrew, Moise and Menken families; Mielziner Family [P-342]; Phillips Family [P-192] includes Moss-Harris, Nathan, Samuel, Lopez-Moses, DeLeon-Hendricks. Other family genealogies include Jacobi-Schlossberg [P-705]; and Rose (Roos) Family [P-129]. See *Resources for Jewish Genealogy in the Greater Boston Area,* edited by Warren Blatt, page 46, for a list of additional genealogies available here.

2. Orphanage Records. This collection includes records from the mid-19th century to the early 1940s. A detailed description of these organization and records can be found in Nancy Arbeiter's excellent article, "New York Orphan Asylum Holdings at the American Jewish Historical Society," *Avotaynu,* Spring 1995, Vol XI, No. 1. See also a survey of child care institutions in the U.S.A. published by the U.S. Census in *Benevolent Institutions, 1910,* listing all such institutions by State/City and including year founded, address, population statistics and financial information. [I-42/Box 13]. See "Restrictions on Use."

Brooklyn Hebrew Orphan Asylum, 1878–1969 [I-230], founded in 1878, includes scrapbooks, 1912–1917 and 1927–1940; and 5 admission and discharge ledgers, 1879–1953, arranged chronologically by date of admission. Ledgers 1879–1913 and 1913–1914 include child's name, age, nativity (country), parent name and nativity, date of discharge, and name/address of person to whom discharged [Box 6]. These two indexes include cross references to pages in other indexes. Ledger, 1887–1910, includes the child's age, country of birth, as well as country in which both parents were born (but not parents' names). Ledger, 1889–1953, which covers children discharged 1911–1953, includes child's date of birth and nativity as well as date admitted and discharged [Box 7]. A typed discharge ledger, 1914–1938, includes name, dates admitted/discharged, age (through February 1930) or birth date (for later years) and person to whom discharged [Box 8]. A name index for Admissions and Discharge ledgers, 1879–1925, is being computerized.

Hebrew Orphan Asylum of the City of New York, 1855–1985 [I-42] includes applications for admission, 1864–1869, 1871–1879, 1887–1893, 1901–1924 [Box 28–33]. There are alpha indexes in each volume (except vols. 1871–1879). Applications include child's name, applicant's name and relationship, place of birth (many include city), parents' names, reason for admission and either age, year of birth or birth date. Applications, 1871 and later, include number of siblings and their ages; applications, 1915–1924, include names of other siblings, as well as mother's maiden name. Applications, 1906–1924, include date of arrival in the U.S.A. and New York City.

In addition to applications, there are vouchers submitted to the Commissioner of Charities, NYC, 1874, 1876, 1889–1894 [Box 13] which include alphabetical lists of children with dates admitted/discharged; and ledgers, 1884–1907, 1892–1901, 1936–1941 [Boxes 36, 41–42], which include child's name, where born, admission and discharge dates, and to whom discharged (often with relationship). The 1884–1907 and 1892–1901 ledgers also include applicant (and relationship to orphan) or name of parent or guardian.

Discharge ledgers are available from 1872–1875, 1899–1906, 1909–1940, 1939–1961, and are generally bound applications for discharge requested by the applicant (usually a relative), providing relationship and reason for discharge request. For some years, more detail information about the applicant or child are included. [Boxes 14–27, 36]. Admissions and Discharge ledger, 1862–1884, [Box 34], primarily a discharge ledger, lists children by sex and status at discharge, i.e. withdrawn, adopted, death, mercantile pursuits, trades, etc. These include name of child, dates entered and dates discharged. For those "adopted," the ledger includes by whom and address; for "trades," the ledger identifies which trade.

This collection also includes Friendly Home Admissions and Discharges, 1916–1941 [Box 37]; student ledger, 1902–1905 [Box 14]; conduct books, 1872–1875 (not indexed), and 1877–1884, 1891–1899 (indexed) [Boxes 34, 36, 41]; register of visitors to orphans, 1904–1905 [Box 47]; after-care department, 1912–1942 [Box 50]; and legacies and bequests, 1885–1898, 1902–1926. [Box 68]

Index of children, 1860–1900 [Box 73] is available online. Index, 1891–1918 [Box 38], is being computerized. These indexes include admission and discharge dates. See AJHS "Selected Finding Aides" online.

Hebrew Sheltering Guardian Society (HSGS), New York, 1879–1970 [I-43] founded in 1879, includes admission and discharge ledgers, 1907–1942. Discharge Ledgers, 1907–1910, provide child's name, age, parent/guardian name, address and occupation. [Boxes 11–12]

Admission and Discharge ledgers, 1908–1915, 1917–1932, have separate listings by month arranged by date of admissions and age of child [Boxes 12 & 20]. Unbound ledger-size pages, 1913–1919, arranged by the first letter of the child's surname, include age, birth date/place, parents' names and country of birth. Each of these ledgers include for Admissions "where transferred from," if relevant. Ledger, 1918–1942, includes child's name, birth date, age, to whom discharged and address, as well as parents' names (sometimes including mother's maiden name) and country of parent's birth. [Box 21]. The child's city/state numbers (I.D. number) and dates of admission/discharge are included in all these ledgers.

The collection includes a January 1898 voucher submitted to the Commissioner of Charities, NYC, alphabetically listing children under HSGS' care during that month with admission date and date of expiration [Box 15]; and Crows & Ravens: War Service Cavalcade, biographical sketches and reports on graduates and their sons serving in WWII, 1944 (includes some photographs).

Hebrew Infant Asylum of the City of New York, 1895–1934 [I-166], opened in 1895. Includes admission and discharge ledgers, 1895–1908 (indexed); children's records, 1896–1903 (not indexed); and admitting physicians' report ledgers, 1895–1908 (1903–1908 indexed).

Home for Hebrew Infants, 1922–1953 (New York) [I-232] includes admission and discharge ledgers, 1922–1943 [OS-1]. Arranged chronologically. See "Restrictions on Use."

Seligman Solomon Society, 1912–1922 [I-6], the alumni association of the Hebrew Orphan Asylum of NYC. Records include letters from soldiers, 1917–1918. [Box 4]. See also Hebrew Orphan Asylum of the City of New York [I-42/Boxes 79–81] which includes journals of this Society, 1889–1955 (gaps) and of the Academy Alumni Society, 1946–1954.

See also Hartman-Homecrest Collection (New York), 1921–1971 [I-223], founded in 1956.

3. Immigration Organizations:

Baron de Hirsch Fund Records, 1870–1991. [I-80] This collection is divided into seven subseries:

Administration/Organization of the Fund [Series 1/Boxes 1–63] includes applications for student aid from the Baron de Hirsch Student loan fund, c. 1892–1912 [Boxes 12–13]. These applications include birth place, marital status and education/employment history. Jewish Agricultural Society [Series 3/Boxes 67–85] includes student aid loan applications, c. 1940–1970); Delphi Agricultural School Scholarships, 1927–1933 [Box 80]; Farmingdale, Long Island, students, c. 1930–1935 [Box 81]; information on farming colonies in New York and New Jersey [Boxes 82–83]. For additional information on farming colonies, see Jewish Farming Colony. [Series 2/Boxes 64–66]

Woodbine Colony [Series 4/Boxes 86–124] includes correspondence with or about families wishing to move to Woodbine. [Box 87]; correspondence with c. 250 property holders (listed alphabetically in the finding aid) [Boxes 103–111]; and lists of Woodbine young men who enlisted or were drafted in WWI [Box 123]. Woodbine Agricultural School [Series 5/Boxes 125–139] includes admission applications, c. 1912–1915; list of 267 applicants to the School, c. 1914–1915, arranged by first letter of surname and State of residence; list of students admitted, 1914–1915, including length of residence in the U.S.A., education and previous occupation. [Box 131]; scholarship applications, 1918–1925, with name, occupation and nationality of parent [Boxes 136–137]; list of graduates, 1893–1918 (includes only first initial of first name); student followup reports, 1905–1920, including present occupation and year graduated; list of graduates serving in WWI. [Box 132]

Baron de Hirsch Trade School, [Series 6/Boxes 140–194] includes "statistics" on employees, 1917, providing position, birth date/country, age, date of employment, years served [Box 164]; employee case files, c. 1896–1935; applications for positions ranging from janitor to instructor, 1910–1933 [Boxes 183–184]; student rosters (graduates), 1893, arranged by occupation; student followup, 1927, including name, graduation class, education and employment history [Box 150]; pupil record books with name, address, nationality, parent/guardian name, occupation and means of support [Boxes 154–162]; and class pictures by class and department, 1925–1968.

Boston HIAS Records [I-96], include case files from the late 1920s to the 1970s arranged alphabetically by surname in two series: Boxes 1–179, cover the 1920s to early 1960s; and Boxes 181–210 include files to the 1970s; correspondence concerning arrivals, arranged alphabetically [Boxes 215–218]; 25,000 Arrival Cards, 1882–1929, for the ports of Boston, MA and Providence, RI, arranged alphabetically including name, age, marital status, port of entry, ship name and U.S. person responsible for the immigrant. [Boxes 215–218]

This collection also includes select passenger lists, 1905–1952, such as the S.S. *General Gordon* sailing from Shanghai to San Francisco, February 4, 1949 (602 names); and S.S. *General Meigs*, sailing from Shanghai to Israel via San Francisco and New York, February 15, 1949 (107 names). [Boxes 180, 211–214]. See "Restrictions on Use."

Industrial Removal Office Records (IRO), 1899–1922 [I-91], include ledgers with over 40,000 records of immigrants relocated mostly from New York City and some from Philadelphia to the interior of the U.S.; and correspondence from relocated immigrants [Boxes 6–17]. The collection is arranged chronologically. Ledgers include name, address, age, number of family members, occupation, nativity, and number of years in the U.S.A. Some correspondence in this collection has been reproduced and indexed by Robert A. Rockaway in, *Words of the Uprooted: Jewish Immigrants in Early 20th Century America*, Ithaca, 1988, also available here. [E184.J5W885 1998]. NOTE: A computerized index to IRO ledgers is in process. See AJHS "Selected Finding Aides" online.

Jewish Immigrant Information Bureau (Galveston, Texas), [I-90]. Galveston immigration plan records, 1901–1920, include ship passenger lists of immigrants who came through Galveston from Germany; internal correspondence of JIIB staff, and correspondence between JIIB and other organizations. There is a surname index online to this collection identifying passenger lists and correspondence in which the immigrant is mentioned; source and box/folder location are provided. See AJHS "Selected Finding Aides" online.

Organization of Jewish Colonies, 1931–1935 [I-47], predecessor of American Jewish Land Settlements in America. Records include questionnaires completed by interested individuals providing biographical information and preferred form of farm settlement. [Box 3]

4. Military Records:

American Jewish Committee, Office of War Records, 1918–1921 [I-9], include questionnaires completed by 6,300 Jewish servicemen after World War I. There were two versions of the questionnaire — a 4-page one for officers, wounded and next of kin of those killed in service; and a shorter, 2-page version for others. Some are arranged by branch of service (Army/Navy) and rank [Box 2]; others by originating city (Baltimore, MD, Canton, OH,

Cleveland, OH, New York, NY, Pittsburgh, PA, St. Paul, MN, Washington, DC) and rank [Boxes 3–4]; or status (wounded) and rank [Boxes 6–16]. Responses from civilian war workers [Box 17] and non-Jewish soldiers [Boxes 18–21] are included. There are three rosters of casualties and deaths of NYC servicemen which include address and next of kin. [Box 4]. Computerized indexes are available online for: questionnaires (c. 6,300); deceased soldiers (c. 3,000) and soldiers who received military honors (c. 1000). See AJHS "Selected Finding Aids" online.

Cyrus Adler Collection [P-16/Series III]. Includes correspondence and other materials collected by Adler to compile data on Jewish servicemen who served in the U.S. Armed Forces during the Spanish-American War. The list was published in the *American Jewish Yearbook, 1900–1901* (Jewish year, 5661), pages 529–622. Adler indicates the sources for information on officers of the Army/Navy were official registers; for non commissioned officers and enlisted men, Jewish newspapers and private information; and for volunteer troops organized by the States, published rosters, private information and the Jewish press.

National Jewish Welfare Board, Bureau of War Records, 1940–1969 [I-52]. Includes data cards on individuals from the New York metropolitan area who were in the service, 1941–1969, arranged alphabetically (Alpha Master Cards) [Boxes 313–419]; by geographic location (Geographic Master Cards) [Boxes 420–548]; and by New York City borough or suburb (Bronx, Brooklyn, Manhattan, Queens, Long Island, Long Beach and Greater New York Area) [Boxes 549–651]. These latter cards are further grouped by "ordinary servicemen" and "casualties and awards" for most geographic areas. Boxes 313–573 are on site.

See also, *American Jews in World War II: The Story of 550,000 Fighters for Freedom* [Lists Jewish soldiers who died in their country's service or who received awards/recognition of valor], compiled by Isidore Kaufman. 2 vols. Vol. 2 compiled by Bureau of War Records of the National Jewish Welfare Board. New York, 1947. [D810.J4 K3]

The Society has records also of the National Jewish Welfare Board, Army-Navy Division, [I-180] which include correspondence of JWB personnel and U.S. military chaplains concerning Jewish men serving in the Armed Forces. There is no detailed finding aid for this collection.

National Jewish Welfare Board, Military Chaplaincy Records, 1917–1984, [I-249]. Include detailed questionnaires completed by chaplains providing name, date/place of birth, date of entry into the U.S., date of citizenship, marital status and wife's name including maiden name, education, rabbinical positions held, military service record and a short history. Photographs are frequently included [Boxes 42–45]. Questionnaires are arranged alphabetically in two alpha series. This collection also includes correspondence from Jewish chaplains describing concentration camps and the condition of survivors.

Other collections, such as the Rabbi Bernard C. Ehrenreich Papers, 1871–1971 [P-26], Rabbi in Montgomery, AL and director of Camp Sheridan, AL include letters from soldiers, WWI, 1918–1919. [Box 3 & 4]. The Solis and Solis-Cohen Family of Philadelphia Papers [P-642, Series VII] includes a register of Jewish officers and men of New Jersey in the Revolutionary War. [Box 5/Folder 9]

5. Court Records: These collections are (microfilm) copies of select records of individuals and organizations with Jewish sounding names filed in NYC courts:

Mayor's Court (New York, NY), selected briefs, 1674–1860 [I-151]. Approximately 6,000 court documents including summons, complaints, affidavits and jury lists arranged chronologically. The collection is indexed by surname of litigant.

Selected Naturalization Certificates, 1816–1845 [I-152]. Includes c. 500 Declarations of Intention filed in the Court of Common Pleas and Superior Court (New York County), 1829–1845; and reports of aliens made to the clerk of the Court, 1816–1828. Alien reports include place of birth, age, nationality, place from which emigrated, occupation and place of intended settlement. Declaration records are arranged alphabetically by surname of declarant.

Selected Insolvent Debtors' Cases, c. 1787–1861 [I-153] includes approximately 2,000 cases, arranged alphabetically by surname of debtor. Some records contain an inventory of the debtor's assets.

Incorporation papers, 1848–1920 [I-154] filed in New York County (Manhattan) of approximately 10,000 Jewish organizations, including landsmanshaftn, fraternal organizations, political clubs, synagogues, social clubs and professional organizations indexed by the name of organization. See www.jgsny.org for index to Landsmanshaftn.

6. Jewish Organizations: Records of more than 300 Jewish communal organizations including national organizations, local fraternal societies, synagogues, landsmanshaftn and schools are located here and listed in the Society's Institutional collections. (Check also the Society's "vertical files," "miscellaneous" (MS) collections, and catalog of published volumes for additional material on organizations.) These include:

Council of Jewish Federations and Welfare Funds, Oral History Collection, 1985–1989 [I-59]. Includes 26 interviews with individuals who were actively involved in the development of the Jewish Federation movement. These include Avrunin, Becker, Bernstein, Citrin, Cohen, Epstein, Fisher, Fox, Goldsmith, Hexter, Hiller, Kravitz, Morris, Myers, Rice, Ritz, Rosenberg, Rosenwald, Rosichan, Schaenen, Silberman, Solender, Weinstein, Wolfe and Zucker. See also *The Oral History Collection,* Federation of Jewish Philanthropies. [F128.9.J5G65 and supp.]

National Jewish Community Relations Advisory Council (NJCRAC) [I-181], c. 1970–1976. Includes reports, articles and letters of appeal from Soviet Jews who wanted to emigrate or become "olim." These are arranged alphabetically by surname. The finding aid includes alpha groupings for each box [Boxes 49–53]. Printouts and lists of prisoners of conscience include father's name, year of birth, occupation, marital status and history of refusal by Soviet authorities. Some include date of arrest and trial date. [Boxes 55–59]

Bnai Brith. Records of several Bnai Brith Lodges, including from the New York area the Arnon Centennial Lodge #39 [I-30] and the Manhattan-Washington Lodge #19, 1871–1931 [I-31] which absorbed the Mt. Sinai Lodge #270 and Washington Irving Lodge #312. Membership records are included.

Workmen's Circle, 1903–1993 [I-304]. Subseries III, includes publications of 37 branches of which 17 were landsmanshaftn, 1912–1967 [Boxes 4–6] arranged by branch number. Subseries IV, includes school records such as journals and year books arranged by school location (mostly in New York City), 1926–1956 [Boxes 6–8]. See Workmen's Circle [MS-LAB.W1] (14 boxes); and the AJHS card catalog for additional publications of Workmen's Circle branches. See also CENTER FOR JEWISH HISTORY, YIVO INSTITUTE FOR JEWISH RESEARCH for additional Workmen's Circle collections. [RG 575 and Bund Archives, RG 1400]

7. Jewish Community Records including Vital Records:

Baltimore, MD. Henry Hochheimer Collection [P-74]. Includes records of 930 marriages, 1850–1912, performed by Hochheimer, chiefly in Baltimore. Includes index by groom's name.

Baltimore, MD and Washington, DC. M. Polack Papers [P-72], 1836–1862, Mohel book. 910 records of circumcisions performed in various eastern and southern locations (mainly Baltimore and Washington, DC).

Barbados. Barbados, 1679–1901, 1995 [I-139]. Includes an index of Jewish names/ages in the 1715 census of Barbados; and list of taxes charged to Jewish inhabitants of Barbados, 1679.

Boston, MA. Ber Boruchoff [P-157], 1906–1939, and Aaron Grovitz Papers [P-87], 1910–1936, include records of marriages in the greater Boston area. See "Restrictions on Use."

Curacao. Curacao Jewish Community Papers, 1683–1876 [I-112], include records of births, 1723–1891, and deaths, 1883–1912.

New York, Pennsylvania and Quebec, Canada. Jacob Raphael Cohen Papers [P-118] 1776–1843. Includes photocopy of a record book begun by Cohen with 500 records of circumcisions, marriages, and deaths in New York, Pennsylvania and Quebec, Canada.

Rochester, NY. Beth Joseph Center,[I-262]. Includes marriage records, 1945–1949.

Niederstettin, Germany. Abraham Selz Collection [P-385] includes a photocopy of mohel book, 1853–1881, for Niederstettin, Germany and surrounding area (450 records) in Hebrew, Yiddish and German.

8. Mexican Inquisition Collection, 1572–1914 [I-3]. Includes 23 "procesos" (transcripts of trials) of individuals accused of "judaizing," 1572–1768. Family names include: Almeida, Antonio, Campos, Caravajal, Diaz, Enriquez, Hernandez, Matos, Mendez, Morales, Nunez, Payba, Reyes, Rivera, Rodriquez, Silva, Sobremente, Texosso, Zarate.

9. Synagogues: In addition to New York County (Manhattan) Incorporation papers [I-154] described above, the Society has a collection of synagogue records, bulletins and books about synagogues in the U.S.A. and around the world:

American Synagogue Directory, 5717-1957, and *5221-1961.* Later publications of this directory, *American Jewish Organizations: Directory,* 1969 to 1987 (6th to 12th edition) also include other Jewish organizations such as homes and hospitals, schools, social service agencies, hotels, caterers and restaurants. [BM 205.A6]

Connecticut. *One Hundred Years of Jewish Congregations in Connecticut: An Architectural Survey, 5603–5703,* published by the Jewish Historical Society of Greater Hartford. Connecticut Jewish History, vol 2, #1, Fall 1991. [F 105.J5 C632]

Illinois. *Chicago Churches and Synagogues: An Architectural Pilgrimage,* by George Lane. Chicago, 1981. [NA 5235.C4 L3]

Kentucky. *The Synagogues of Kentucky: Architecture and History,* by Lee Shai Weissbach. Lexington, 1995. [NA 5230.K4 W45]

Maryland. *Synagogue Buildings in Baltimore during the 19th Century,* by S. E. Zalesch. 1984. [NH 4690.225]

New Jersey. *Southern New Jersey Synagogues: A Social History Highlighted by Stories of Jewish Life from the 1880's – 1980's,* by Allen Meyers. Sewell, NJ 1990. [BM 223.N3 M2]

New York. *The Changing Face of New York Synagogues, 1730–1974,* by William Aron. New York, [1975]. [BM225.N5 A4]

- *Guide to the Archives: Central Synagogue.* New York, 1994. This inventory covers records of Congregation Ahawath Chesed, 1849–1898, which merged with Congregation Shaar Hashomayim, 1898 to form Congregation Ahawath Chesed Shaar Hashomayim (later known as Central Synagogue); and records of the Bohemian American Israelite Congregation, 1929–1944, which merged with Central Synagogue. Includes description of marriage, bar/bat mitzvah and funeral records; and cemetery records (Cyprus Hills, Linden Hill and Salem Fields), 1859–1987. NOTE: The records are located at Central Synagogue. [CD 950.N432]
- *Jewish Calendar, Lodge and Society Directory: containing description and location of charitable, educational, religious and social institutions, synagogues, temples, homes, hospitals, asylums, dispensaries, sanitoriums, sick and benevolent associations, sisterhoods and ladies' societies etc,* by Alex Eli Jacobs. New York, 1905. Includes officers of many of these synagogues and organizations. [F 128.9.J5 J12]
- *Synagogues of NYC: A Pictorial Survey in 123 photographs,* by Oscar Israelowitz. New York, 1982. And, *Synagogues of NYC: History of a Jewish Community.* Brooklyn, 2002. [BM225.N49185 2000]
- *The Synagogues of New York's Lower East Side,* by Gerard R. Wolfe and Jo Renee Fine. New York, 1978. [BM225.N49 F56]

Pennsylvania. *Pittsburgh and the Synagogue Tradition,* by Walter Jacob. Pittsburgh, 1983. [BM 225.P57 J3]

Canada. *Treasures of a People: The Synagogues of Canada,* by Sheldon Levitt. Toronto, 1985. [NA 5240.L49]

Morocco. *Synagogues of Morocco: An Architectural and Preservation Survey,* by Joel Zack. New York, 1993.

Venezuela and Caribbean. *Synagogues in Venezuela and the Caribbean: Past and Present,* edited by Pynchas Brener, Marianne Kohn Beker, Caracas, [1999]. [BM 288.S95 1999]

Works Progress Administration (WPA), Historical Records Survey of synagogues and churches, published and unpublished materials, include:

U.S.A. *Directory of American Jewish Congregations,* unpublished manuscripts (June and September, 1939), of U.S.A. synagogues (includes NYS but not NYC); arranged by State and county and includes name and address of each synagogue, date founded, name of Rabbi, president, secretary and number of members. NOTE: The June draft is entitled, *Inventory of the Church Archives of NYC.* [BM 205.H3]

New York. *Brooklyn Synagogues,* 2 vols., typed draft (unpublished), includes for 430 synagogues in Brooklyn, name, address, date founded, date of incorporation, affiliation, number of members, history of location, Rabbi and records available, c. 1939–1941. [BM 205.H3]

- *Guide to Vital Statistics in the City of New York,* 1939–1942. Includes synagogues and churches that had, at the time of the survey, membership, birth, confirmation, marriage or death records. [CD 3408.N5 H52]

Colorado. *Inventory of Churches: Jewish Bodies.* 1941. [CD 3130.H48]

Michigan. *Inventory of Churches and Synagogues of Michigan: Jewish Bodies.* 1940. [CD 3300.H48 J44]

Mississippi. *Inventory of Churches and Synagogue Archives of Mississippi: Jewish Congregations and Organizations,* 1940. [CD 3320.H48 J11]

Additional WPA directories, 1939–1941, listing synagogues and churches (name/address) are available here for the District of Columbia, Florida, Northern California (Alameda County), Rhode Island, Tennessee, and Wyoming.

10. Cemeteries: Books and other publications about cemeteries, many with tombstone inscriptions, include:

U.S.A.

Albany, NY. *Old Beth Emmeth Cemetery: Listings and Inscriptions,* by V. C. Dolina. Albany, 1985. [F 129.A5 D5]

Gonzalez, TX. *Inscriptions from the Tombstones in the Old Jewish Cemetery of Gonzalez, TX,* by Mrs. Harry Gurinsky. 1932. [F 394.G5 G8]

Macon, GA. *The Burials of Congregation Beth Israel, Macon, GA in William Wolff Cemetery and in the Hebrew Burial Ground,* by Marian W. Kaufman. Macon, 1983. [F 294.M2 K18]

Philadelphia, PA. *Index of Names in Jewish Cemeteries, Ninth and Spruce Streets, Philadelphia,* by L. Emaleh. May, 1906. [F 158.9.J5 E5 Supplement]

Savannah, GA. *Savannah's Old Jewish Community Cemeteries,* by B. H. Levy. Macon, c. 1983. [F 294.S2 L47]

Schenectady, NY. *Listings and Inscriptions of Temple Gates of Heaven Cemetery as of September 1983,* by Virginia C. Dolina. [F 129.S4 D5]

Sumter, SC. *The Jewish Cemetery of Sumter, SC: A Transcription of the Names and Dates on the Tombstones, 1874–1942,* by Harold Moise. Sumter, 1942. [F 279.S8 M4]

Caribbean, Europe and South America

Bridgetown, Barbados. *The Monumental Inscriptions in the Churches and Churchyards of the Island of Barbados, British West Indies,* edited by Viere Landfred Oliver. London, 1915. [F 2041.O48]

Eisenstadt, Austria. *Die Grabshriften des Alten Juden Friedhofes in Eisenstadt,* by Bernhard Wachstein. Vienna, 1922. [DS 135.A9 W25]

Rio de Janeiro, Brazil. *Sepulturas de Israelitas: S. Francisco Xavier, Rio de Janeiro,* by Egon Wolf. Sao Paulo, 1976. [F 2646.W5]

St. Thomas, Virgin Islands. *299 Epitaphs from the Jewish Cemetery in St. Thomas, WI, 1837–1916,* by Julius Margolinsky. Copenhagen, 1957. [F 2105.M17]

Toledo, Spain. *Nuevo Hallazgo de una Inscripcion Sepulcral Hebraica en Toledo,* by Abraham Shalom Yahuda. Madrid, 1915. [DS 135.S7 Y3]

Vienna, Austria. *Die Inschriften des Alten Judenfriedhofes in Wien,* by Bernhard Wachstein, Vienna, 1912–1917. [DS 135.A9 W3]

11. Biographies: The collection includes such informative books as:

Biographical Dictionary of Early American Jews, Colonial Times through 1800, by Joseph R. Rosenbloom. Lexington, 1960. [E 184.I5 R63]

The Concise Dictionary of American Jewish Biography, 2 vols., edited by J. R. Marcus and J. M. Daniels. Cincinnati, 1994. Includes 24,000 biographical sketches of mostly deceased persons. [E 184 J5 C653 1994]

The Jewish Community Blue Book of Newark, Newark, c. 1925. Includes a history of the Jewish community and many Jewish organizations in Newark, NJ; membership lists of various synagogues and organizations; and who's who in Newark. [F 145.J458]

12. Photographs: In addition to the photographs described above, the Society has photographs from all over the United States of businesses, synagogues, cemeteries, institutions, families and individuals. Among these are:

Graduate School for Jewish Social Work (New York, NY), 1925–1950 [I-7]. Lower East Side Project includes 300 photographs documenting Jewish life, 1932–1934. [Series IV/Boxes 4, 5, 8]. This collection also includes student registers, 1925–1939 [Series 1/Box 2]; and original letters to *Der Tag,* 1932–1933. [Series III/Box 3/31–48]

Baron de Hirsch Fund Records [I-90]. 1,500 photographs include class photos from the trade school with names of students, as well as many photographs of farms and farmers, class activities, schools, synagogues, houses and factories.

Finding Aids:

A computerized index is being developed and many finding aids are already online. Researchers may also use the Society's card catalog which includes books, periodicals, as well as archival collections. For lists showing all archival collections, see the AJHS Librarian at the Reading Room desk. There are four separate lists: (1) Personal Papers, call numbers begin with "P-"; (2) Institutional Records, call numbers begin with "I-"; (3) Miscellaneous collections, call numbers "MS-", and (4) vertical files. For "Selected Finding Aids" to Personal and Institutional records online, see: www.cjh.org/academic/findingaids/AJHS/institutionlist.html.

In addition, the Society has more detailed inventories for many of the Institutional and Personal collections in notebooks behind the Reference Desk. The card catalog includes name indexes to correspondence in the Rabbi Tobias Geffen Papers, Rabbi Milton Steinberg Papers, and Rabbi Stephen S. Wise Papers. Other finding aids for specific collections are mentioned above in "Description of Resources."

Restrictions on Use:

Researchers are advised that permission to examine and review manuscript materials may be subject to restrictions placed on the material by donors and depositors or by AJHS.

Orphanage Records: Only records more than 75 years old are open to researchers.

Tobias Geffen Collection. Users must receive prior permission from the Geffen family to publish any material from this collection.

NOTE: In addition to the Center for Jewish History, AJHS has a New England facility at Hebrew College, Gann Library Building, 160 Herrick Road, Newton Centre, MA 02459 (telephone: 607-559-8880; fax: 617-559-8881; e-mail: reference@ajhs.org). Many AJHS holdings, including most of those involving the New England states and collections awaiting microfilming are accessible only in Newton. Advance appointments are recommended to assure that appropriate staff are available and to determine if relevant materials are accessible on site.

CENTER FOR JEWISH HISTORY
AMERICAN SEPHARDI FEDERATION

Facility Director:	Vivienne Roumani-Denn, Director of Library and Archives
	Randy Belinfonte, Librarian
Address:	15 West 16th Street ♿
	New York, NY 10011
	(Cross Streets: Fifth and Sixth Avenues)
Phone:	(212) 294-8350
Fax:	(212) 294-8348
E-mail:	vroumani@asf.cjh.org
Website:	www.asfonline.org

Hours of Operation, Closest Public Transportation, Directions, Description of Facility and Fees/Copies:

See CENTER FOR JEWISH HISTORY, LILLIAN GOLDMAN MAIN READING ROOM.

Description of Resources:

The American Sephardi Federation is an umbrella organization representing 25 Sephardic organizations in the U.S.A. It has undertaken an ambitious program to collect books, historical documents and artifacts concerning the history and culture of Jews from Sephardic communities, including Greece, Spain, Portugal, Turkey, North Africa and Middle Eastern countries. The Library's collection includes:

1. Vital Records:

    Burma, Rangoon (Yangon, Myanmar). *Musmeah Yeshua Synagogue, Birth Register, 1896–1979.* [CS 3010.Z9 R36 1979]. The register has been computerized and is available on ASF's website, www.asfonline.org.

    England, London. *Bevis Marks Records,* edited by Lionel D. Barnett. 3 vols. Vol. 1, early history of the Spanish and Portuguese Congregation of London...to 1800; vol. 2, abstracts of ketubot (marriage contracts), to 1837; vol. 3, abstracts of ketubot, 1837–1901. [BM 295.S7 L6 1940]

    Netherlands, Amsterdam. *Handleiding bij de index op de Ketuboth van de Portugees-Israelietische Gemeente te Amsterdam van 1650–1911* [Register of Sephardi Jewish marriages in Amsterdam, 1650–1911], compiled by Dave Verdooner and Harmen J. W. Snel. [Netherlands, 1990]. [DS135.N5A7 1990 Ref]

    • *Lijst der Aangegeven Lijken in Amsterdam: ingeschreven tussen 1806–1811* [List of Jewish inhabitants who died in Amsterdam, 1806–1811], by Dave Verdooner and Harmen Snel. [Netherlands, 1991] [DS 135.N5 A7 V37 1991]

    Netherlands, Den Haag. *Den Haag Portugees-Israelitische Hwelijeken: 1711–1714 en 1730–1778* [The Hague: Sephardic marriages, 1711–1714 and 1730–1778], compiled by the Nederlandse voor Joods Genealogie. [Netherlands, 1990]. Includes also circumcisions and births, 1755–1818 in 's Gravenhage. [DS 135.N5 H32 Ref]

    • *Huwelijken in Joods Den Haag,* 1681–1811 [Marriages of Jews in the Hague 1681–1811], with indexes, compiled by the Nederlandse voor Joods Genealogie. [Netherlands, 1990]. [DS 135.N5 H33 Ref]

    Tunisia: *Registres matrimoniaux de la communauté Juive Portugaise de Tunis aux XVIIIe–XIXe siècles* [Marriage registrations of the Portuguese Jewish community of Tunis from the 18th and 19th centuries], by Robert Attal and Joseph Avivi. Israel, 1989. [DS 135.T72 T863 1989]

    • *Pinkas ha-ketubot shel ha-kehilah ha-Portugalit be Tunis (603–614),* by Robert Attal and Joseph Avivi. Jerusalem, 2000. [DS 135.T72 T8632 2000]

2. Local Histories:

    Argentina, Australia and South Africa. *Jewish communities in Frontier Societies - Argentina, Australia and South Africa,* by Daniel Judah Elazar. New York, [1983]. [F 3021.J5 E4 1983]

    Algeria and France. *Les Juifs D'Algerie et la France (1830–1855),* by Simon Schwarzfochs. Jerusalem, 1981. [DS 135.A93 S33 1981]

    Brazil, Recife. *The Records of the Earliest Jewish Community in the New World,* by Arnold Wiznitzer. New York, 1954. [F 2659.J5 W59]

Bulgaria. *Bulgaria and her Jews: the History of a Dubious Symbiosis,* by Vicky Tamir. New York, 1979. [DS 135.B8 T351 1979]

Egypt. *Les Juifs en Egypte: depuis les origines jusqu'a ce jour,* by Maurice Fargeon. Cairo, 1938. [DS 135.E3 F22 1938]

Greece. *Les Juifs de Grèce de l'expulsion d'Espagne à nos Jours: Bibliographie,* by Robert Attal. Jerusalem, 1984. [DS 135.G7 A85 1984]

India. *The Jewish Communites of India: Identity in a Colonial Era,* by Joan C. Poland. New Brunswick, 1992. [DS 135.I6 R66 1992]
- *Turning Back the Pages: Chronicle of Calcutta Jewry,* by Esmond David Ezra. London, 1986. [DS 135.I62 C344 1986]

Morocco, Tangier. *A History of the Jews of Tangier in the 19th and 20th centuries*, by M. Mitchell Serels. New York, 1991. [DS 135.M85 T367 1991]

Netherlands, Amsterdam. *Memorias do estabelecimento e progesso dos judeos portuguezes e espanhoes nesta famosa citade de Amsterdam* [A Portuguese chronicle of the history of the Sephardim in Amsterdam up to 1772], by David Franco Mendes. Assen, 1975. [DS 135.N5 M46]

Netherlands Antilles. *History of the Jews of the Netherlands Antilles,* by Isaac and Suzanne Emmanuel. 2 vols. New York, 1970. Includes marriages grouped by family, 1600s–c.1965, pp 841–1007; and immigrants to Curacao aided by the Amsterdam Parnassim, 1658–1772, pp 774–780. [F 2049.E44 1970]

Rhodes. *The Jews of Rhodes: The History of a Sephardic Community,* by Rabbi Marc D. Angel. New York, 1978. [DS 135.G72 R482 1998]

Singapore. *The History of the Jews in Singapore, 1830–1945*, by Eze Nathan. Singapore, 1986. Appendix includes casualties and deaths that occurred during the Japanese occupation, March 1942–September 1945; list of internees; and list of burials in Thomson Road Cemetery, 1904–1911. [DS 135.S44 N38 1986]

Spain. *The Jews of Spain: A History of the Sephardic Experience*, by Jane Gerber. New York, 1992. [DS 135.S7 G47 1992]

Spain. *The Mezuzah in the Madonna's foot: oral histories exploring five hundred years in the paradoxical relationship of Spain and the Jews,* by Trudi Alexy. New York, [1993]. [DS 135.S8 A433]

Sudan. *Jacob's Children in the Land of the Mahdi: Jews of Sudan,* by Eli S. Malka. Syracuse, 1997. [DS 135.S85 M35 1997]

Turkey. *Jews of the Ottoman Empire and Turkish Republic,* by Stanford J. Shaw. New York, 1991. [DS 135.T8 S46 1991b]

3. <u>World Monuments Photo Archive</u>: Includes photographs of Moroccan and Syrian Jewish sites such as synagogues, cemeteries and Jewish quarters and ghettos.

4. <u>Newspapers</u>:

   North Africa. *ha-Itonut ha-Yehudit bi-Tsefon-Afrikah: reshimat ha-osafim ha-nimtsaim bi-Mekhon Ben-Tsevi: be-Vet-ha-sefarim ha-leumi veha universitai bi-Yerushlyim, ba-Arkhiyon ha-Tsiyoni uve-Osef Avraham Hatal bi-Yerushalaim,* by Robert Attal. [Jewish newspapers of North Africa: List of collections that are found in Mekhon Ben-Tsevi; in the Leumi library and at the University in Jerusalem, at the Zionist Archives and in the collection of Avaham Hetal in Jerusalem.] Jerusalem, 1980. [Z 6367.A88 1980]

5. <u>Cemeteries</u>:

   Barbados, Bridgetown. *Monumental Inscriptions in the Burial Ground of the Jewish Synagogue at Bridgetown, Barbados,* by Eustace M. Shilstone. New York, 1956. [F 2041.S56 1988 Ref ASF]

   Curacao. *Precious Stones of the Jews of Curacao: Curacaon Jewry 1656–1957,* by Isaac S. Emmanuel. New York, 1957. Includes tombstones and index. [F 2049.E42 1957]

   Greece, Saloniki. *Matsevot bet ha-almin shel Yehude Saloniki,* by Michael Molho. Tel Aviv, [1974]. [PN 6297.H4 M6 1974]

   Jamaica. *Monumental inscriptions of Jamaica.* London, 1966. [F1865 .W74 1966]
   - *The Jews of Jamaica: Tombstone inscriptions, 1663–1880,* by Richard D. Barnett and Philip Wright. Jerusalem, 1997. [F 1896.J48 B37 1997 Ref]

   Netherlands, Middelburg. *De Joodse Begraafplaatsen te Middelburg,* compiled by the Nederlands voor Joodse Genealogie, 1998. [PN 6297.H4 J6 1977]
   - Groningen. *Joodse Begraafplaatsen in Groningen en Oost-Friesland,* by K. Jongeling. Groningen, 1977. [PN 6297.H4 J6 1977]

- Ouderkerk. *Het Beth Haim van Ouderkerk: beelden van een Portugees-Joodse begraafplaats* [The Beth Haim of Ouderkerk aan de Amstel: images of a Portuguese Jewish cemetery in Holland], by L. Alvares Vega. Assen, 1975. [DS 135.N5 0937 1975]

New York. *Portraits Etched in Stone,* by David de Sola Pool. New York, 1952. [F 128.9.J5 P66 1952]

6. Holocaust:

Greece. *Jewish martyrs of Rhodes and Cos,* by Husky M. Franco. Zimbabwe, [1994]. [DS 135.G72 R484 1994]
- *In Memoriam: Hommage aux victimes juives des Nazis en Grèce,* edited by Michael Molho. Thessalonique, 1973. [D 810.J4 M58 1973]
- *Remember the Holocaust in Greece,* published by the Sephardic Jewish Center of Forest Hills, Inc. Atlantic Beach, NY, [1995]. [DS 135.G7 R46 1995]
- *Jewish Community of Salonika, 1943,* compiled by Aure Recanati. Jerusalem, 2000. Includes Nazi required forms documenting possessions of each family. [DS 135.G72 T495 J39 2000]

Italy. *Benevolence and betrayal: five Italian Jewish families under fascism,* by Alexander Stille. New York, [1991]. [DS 135.19 A17 1991]
- *The Italians and the Holocaust persecution, rescue and survival*, by Susan Zuccotti. New York, [1987]. [DS 135.I8 Z83 1987]

Netherlands. *Joods leven in de Friese hoofdstad, 1920–1945 voltooid verleden tijd,* by Salomon de Jong, [Leeuwarden], 1970. Includes list of Jews from Leeuwarden who died, 1940–1945. [DS 135.N5 L4 1970]
- *The Destruction of the Dutch Jews,* by Jacob Presser. Translated by Arnold Pomerans. New York, 1969. [DS 135.N4 P6732 1969]

7. Genealogies, Family Histories and Memoirs:

The library has a growing collection of published genealogies, family histories and memoirs including those of the families of Aciman, Arie, Batkin, Capadose, Charlap, DePinto, Ezra, Graziani-Levy, Hazan, Machlin, Modiano, Molho, Nasi, Picciotto, Sassoon, Shadur, Silva and Varons. In addition the collection includes:

Genealogia Hebraica Portugal e Gibraltar, secs. XVII a XX, [Jewish Genealogy of Portugal and Gibraltar] by J. M. Abecassis. 5 vols. Lisbon, 1990–1991. For family trees documented in each volume, see *Sephardic Genealogy Sources,* at www.orthohelp.com/geneal/namelists.htm#Abecas. [DS 135.P7 A37 1990 Ref]

Los Judios de Alepo en Mexico, [Jews from Alepo in Mexico] by David Marguen and Liz Hamus de Halabe. [Mexico, 1989]. Includes an appendix with family genealogies arranged by surname of the head of household. [F 1392 J4 J815 1989]

Noble families among the Sephardic Jews, by Isaac da Costa. London, 1936. [DS 135.S7 C6 1936]

8. Name Indexes:

The Complete Book of Muslim and Parsi Names, by M. Gandhi. New Delhi, 1994. [CS 2970.G36 1994 Ref]

9. Archives:

Central Sephardic Community of America Records, 1935-2000: includes lists of survivors of the Holocaust; list of Spanish Jews arrested by the Nazis in Greece, 1944; list of losses suffered by Greek Jews in 1944; honor roll of soldiers; and immigrant case files, 1944-1952. [Case file access restricted to 2010.]

International Committee of Jews from Arab lands, Restitution Files: class-action law suit by Sephardic refugees who were expelled from Arab countries. These include written testimony documenting losses in Arab countries. The Committee is seeking information on assets pertaining to synagogues, mikvaot, schools, cemeteries and Jewish quarters.

Membership Files: ASF is asking its members to submit genealogical information including ancestry.

Oral Histories of over 100 individuals from the Libyan, Syrian, Moroccan and Salonikan Jewish communities, 1998.

Finding Aids:

The Library has a computerized catalog accessible at the 7 terminals outside the Reading Room and available online. A search can be made by author, title, subject and keyword. This catalog will be integrated into the Center's unified catalog, once complete.

Restrictions on Use:

There is no librarian on duty in the Reading Room. A call must be made to the librarian's office to retrieve books. It is recommended that researchers make an appointment in advance to assure that staff are available.

CENTER FOR JEWISH HISTORY
CENTER GENEALOGY INSTITUTE

Facility Director: Dr. Rachel Fisher, Director

Address: Center for Jewish History   ♿
15 West 16th Street
New York, NY 10011
(Cross Streets: Fifth and Sixth Avenues)

Phone: (212) 294-8324
Fax: (917) 606-8222
E-mail: gi@cjh.org
Website: www.cjh.org

Hours of Operation, Closest Public Transportation, Directions, Description of Facility, Fees/Copies, and Restrictions on Use:

See CENTER FOR JEWISH HISTORY, LILLIAN GOLDMAN MAIN READING ROOM.

Description of Resources:

In 2000, the Center partners established a Genealogy Institute to help guide researchers in using the vast collection of materials at the Center. The Institute houses genealogy reference works including books, atlases, maps, newsletters and other materials supplementing those found in the collections of the Center's partners.

1. <u>Genealogy Newsletter</u>: The Institute has one of the most complete collections of newsletters published by Jewish genealogical societies and special interest groups around the world including:

Argentina, *Toldot,* 1996–	Illinois, Chicago, *Morasha,* 1989–
Australia, *The Kosher Koala,* 1993–	Israel, *Sharsheret Hadorot,* 1986–
Brazil, *Geracoes/Brasil,* 1995–	Latvia, *Latvia SIG,* 1996–
Canada, Toronto, *Shem Tov,* 1988–	Massachusetts, Boston, *Mass-pocha,* 1992–
California, Los Angeles, *Rootskey,* 1982–	Michigan, Detroit, *Generations,* 1988–
California, San Francisco, *ZichronNote,* 1985–	New York, New York, *Dorot,* 1979–
France, *Cercle de Généalogie Juive Revue,* 1985–	New York, Long Island, *Lineage,* 1988–
Germany SIG, *Stammbaum,* 1992–	Romania, *ROM-SIG News,* 1992–
Great Britain, *Shemot,* 1989–	Sephardic, *Etsi,* 1998–
Grodno SIG, *Jewish Grodno Gubernia,* 1998–	Switzerland, *Maajan-Die Quelle,* 1989–

2. <u>Genealogy Resource Books:</u> The Institute's open-stack collection includes:

Europe. *How to Document Victims and Locate Survivors of the Holocaust,* by Gary Mokotoff. Teaneck, 1995. See pages 79–83, for an inventory of some of the survivor and victim lists available at YIVO.

Austria and Germany. *A Guide to Jewish Genealogy in Germany and Austria,* edited by T. Skyte, *et. al.* London, 2001.

France. *Guide Pratique de Généalogie Juive,* by Basile Ginger. Paris, 2002.

France. *Sur les traces de vos ancétres à Paris: la recherche des origines,* published by Archives de Paris. Paris, 1997.

Germany. *Library Resources for German-Jewish Genealogy,* by Angelika Ellmann-Krueger and Edward D. Luft. Teaneck, 1998.

Great Britain. *Jewish Ancestry: A Beginner's Guide to Jewish Genealogy in Great Britain,* edited by Rosemary Wenzerul. [London], 2000.

Hungary. *Handy Guide to Hungarian Genealogical Research,* by Jared H. Suess. Logan, 1980.

Israel. *A Guide to Jewish Genealogical Research in Israel,* by Sallyann A. Sack, PhD and the Israel Genealogical Society. Revised edition. Teaneck, NJ, 1995.

Poland, Ukraine and Moldova. *Jewish Roots in Poland: Pages from The Past and Archival Inventories,* by Miriam Weiner. New York, 1997; and *...Ukraine and Moldova,* New York, 1999. Include comprehensive inventories of Jewish vital records and other genealogical holdings of local archives in Poland, Ukraine and Moldova.

NOTE: See also Miriam Weiner's website, www.rtrfoundation.org, for excerpts from these books, as well as previously unpublished material on <u>Belarus</u> and <u>Lithuania</u>

Slovakia. *A Guide to the Slovak Archives,* by Zuzana Kollarova and Jozef Hanus. Presov, 1999.

Ukraine. *Some Archival Sources for Ukrainian Jewish Genealogy,* by Aleksander Kronik and Sallyann Amdur Sack, Teaneck, [1997].

<u>United States</u>

Illinois. *Chicago and Cook County: A Guide to Research,* by Loretto Dennis Szucs. Salt Lake City, 1996.

Massachusetts. *Resources for Jewish Genealogy in the Boston Area,* by Warren Blatt. Boston, 1996.

New York and New Jersey. *Genealogical Resources in the New York Metropolitan Area,* edited by Estelle M. Guzik. New York, 1989. Includes select New Jersey and New York State counties.

Texas. *Dallas Jewish Genealogical Guide,* by David A. Chapin. Dallas, 1993.

United States. *Sourcebook for Jewish Genealogies and Family Histories,* by David S. Zubatsky and Irwin M. Berent. Teaneck, 1996.

United States. *First American Jewish Families; 600 Genealogies,* 1654–1977, by Rabbi Malcolm Stern. 3rd edition. Baltimore, 1991.

United States. *How to locate anyone who is or has been in the military: Armed Forces locator directory,* by Lt. Col. Richard S. Johnson. 4th edition. Houston, 1991.

3. <u>Gazetteers and Maps</u>: In addition to detailed maps of many European countries, the Institute assists researchers in locating their ancestral town using:

Magyar Helysegnev-Azonosito Szotar [Hungarian Geographical Dictionary], by Gyorgy Lelkes. Talma Konyvkiado, 1998. Includes cross-reference indexes to Croatian, Latin, Polish, German, Russian, Serbian, Slovak, Slovenian and Ukrainian names of towns formerly in "Greater" Hungary (1867–1920), as well as some border areas in Romania (Moldavia) and Bosnia-Herzegovina.

Shtetl Finder, by Chester G. Cohen. Bowie, 1989.

Where Once We Walked, by Gary Mokotoff and Sallyann Amdur Sack. Teaneck, 2002. Includes more than 23,500 towns in Central and Eastern Europe and provides latitude/longitude, distance from closest major city, Jewish population before the Holocaust, and citations to other reference books. A soundex index is provided to assist users when exact town name spelling is not known

4. <u>Name Indexes</u>:

A Dictionary of Jewish Surnames from the Russian Empire, by Alexander Beider. Teaneck, 1993.

A Dictionary of Jewish Surnames from the Kingdom of Poland, by Alexander Beider. Teaneck, 1996.

Jewish Family Names and Their Origins: An Etymological Dictionary, by Heinrich W. Guggenheimer and Eva H. Guggenheimer. [Hoboken], 1992.

5. <u>Jewish Vital and Other Records</u>: *Records in the Family History Library Catalog for Jewish Research,* compiled by the Genealogical Society of Utah includes volumes for the United States, Australia-Great Britain-New Zealand, Canada, Hungary, Germany (2 vols), Poland and International (2 vols). Films listed can be ordered through interlibrary loan from the Family History Library in Salt Lake City.

6. <u>Lectures on Tape</u>: The Institute has an extensive collection of lectures on audio tape from Jewish genealogy conferences held in NYC and around the world.

7. <u>Electronic Resources</u>: Researchers at the Institute have direct access to the Internet and CD-ROMs including:

Ancestry.com

Dachau Prisoner Information

Germans to America, 1875–1888

Jewish Records Indexing Project - Poland

Naturalization Records:
    Brooklyn (Kings County), 1907–1924
    Philadelphia, 1789–1880

Passenger and Immigration lists,
    Boston, 1821–1850
    New York, 1820–1850

Russians to America, 1850–1896

Sephardic House

U.S. Census, 1910, New York City

U.S. Census, Mortality Index, 1850–1880

Finding Aids:

Volunteers have created a series of fact sheets on genealogical resources at the Center and elsewhere to help guide patrons in their research. Staff and volunteers are available to answer questions about family history research and the genealogical holdings of the Center partners.

CENTER FOR JEWISH HISTORY
HADASSAH ARCHIVES AT THE AMERICAN JEWISH HISTORICAL SOCIETY

Facility Director: Susan Woodland, Archivist

Address: 15 West 16th Street ♿
New York, NY 10011-6301

(Cross Streets: 5th and 6th Avenues)

Phone: (917) 606-8259
Fax: (212) 294-6161
E-mail: swoodland@hadassah.org
Website: www.hadassah.org

Hours of Operation:

Monday to Thursday: 9:30 am to 1:00 pm, 2:00 pm to 4:30 pm, Monday to Thursday.

Closed Saturday, Sunday, Jewish and legal holidays. An appointment is recommended.

Closest Public Transportation, Directions, Description of Facility, and Fees/Copies:

See CENTER FOR JEWISH HISTORY, LILLIAN GOLDMAN MAIN READING ROOM.

Description of Resources:

The Hadassah Archives, housed with the American Jewish Historical Society at the Center for Jewish History, holds records documenting the history of Hadassah, a Jewish women's organization. Hadassah was formed in 1912 as a membership and fund raising organization to support medical and educational projects in Palestine and later, in Israel. The collection includes over 800 linear feet of records chronicling the work of Hadassah national presidents, board members and other leaders of Hadassah Medical Organization in Jerusalem. Items of interest to genealogists include:

1. Photographs: Mostly of national presidents, national board members and national leaders. The collection includes also photographs of Hadassah's projects: Hadassah Medical Organization, Youth Aliyah, Young Judaea and Hadassah vocational education programs, as well as Junior Hadassah and Hadassah conventions.

2. Hadassah Leaders [RG 7]. The Archives has the papers of many Hadassah leaders including Anna Tulin Elyachar, 1937–1985; Denise Tourover Ezekiel, 1936–1981; Miriam Granott, 1946–1979; Martha Grossman, 1919–1948; Tamar de Sola Pool, 1925–1979; Rose Halprin, 1930–1964; Jessie Zel Lurie, 1947–1980; Miriam Freund Rosenthal, 1879–1986; Alice L. Seligsberg, 1917–1942; Bernice Salpeter Tannenbaum, 1962–1985; Charlotte Jacobson, 1945, 1964–1991; Lola Kramarsky, 1962–1983; Ruth Popkin, 1978–1984; and Bertha Schoolman, 1941–1969. Several include family correspondence and biographical material. Examples are:

    Rose G. Jacobs Papers, 1910–1960 (microfilm). Autobiographical material [Reel 2], and correspondence concerning the Jacobs family, 1932–1933 and 1946 [Reel 3]. Drafts and notes for a history of Hadassah that Jacobs planned but never completed are included in the series on Zionist Personalities, 1910–1955, and Rose Jacob's *History of Hadassah*, 1921–1948. These include memoirs of her husband, Edward; biographical material on many Hadassah leaders; and memoriam essays for many others associated with Hadassah. [Reel 4]

    Henrietta Szold Papers, 1875–1965. Include Szold family correspondence, 1889–1942 [Boxes 1–3], documents relating to the life of her father, her own life and Szold genealogical materials, 1888–1964. [Box 7]

3. Hadassah Israel Education Service, 1940–1962 [RG 6]. Includes lists of Youth Reference Board Members, 1961–1969 [Box 3/6]; discussion of candidates for principal of the Alice Seligsberg High School, 1942 [Box 11/4]; correspondence, 1951–1967, and obituary of Dr. Elizer Ervin Arnstein, founder and director of the Hadassah Vocational Guidance Institute. [Box 14/2]

4. Hadassah Medical Organization (HMO) Papers, 1918–1984 [RG 2]. Biographical information and resumes [Boxes 103, 108]; Medical Advisory Council minutes, 1948–1959 [Box 77], Hebrew University Medical School Implementation Committee minutes, 1950–1963, and Dental School Implementation Committee minutes, 1958–1969, concerning medical staff positions and appointments [Reels 8 and 10]; correspondence on cases of disabled soldiers treated by the Occupational Therapy Department, 1948–1949 [Box 51/6]; material documenting Arab attacks on Jews in 1929, 1936–1938 [Box 55]; and the massacre of HMO workers by Arabs on Mt. Scopus

Road, 1947–1948 [Box 68 and 153/11]. Also found here are statements of Hadassah personnel (Karpas, Michaelson, Harris, Makin and Saltz) describing their involvement in the 6-day War [Box 120/10]; the kidnaping of Dr. Shlomo Samueloff and his 99 days of captivity as a hostage of the Syrians [Box 137/4]; and an unpublished manuscript by Olga Rubinow Lurie, *From Riverside Drive to Jaffa Road, 1920–1922,* including material on her father and many other Hadassah leaders [Box 144]. Researchers should check the finding aids for additional biographical material scattered throughout this collection.

5. Oral History, 1970s–1991 [RG 20]. Includes interviews with Hadassah presidents, National Board members, honorary members, 1970s–1980s; and interviews with HMO doctors, nurses and others conducted 1979–1991. Written transcripts sometimes accompany the cassettes.

6. Youth Aliyah Papers, 1933–1960 [RG 1]. Case files of former Youth Aliyah leaders and students (Leshkowitz, Gelbart, Haendler, Warschauer), 1941–1944; list of 768 Romanian Jewish passengers (names/ages) who died when the S.S. *Struma* sank in the Black Sea, 1942 [Box 4/16–19]; bulletins of Rescue Committee of the Jewish Agency for Palestine, which contains a report on the death of four Youth Aliyah graduates (Adato, Tenenbaum, Ottenheimer, Steinfeld), 11/27/45; and eyewitness accounts of the slaughter of Jews in Eastern Galicia, Pinsk, Polish White Russia, Transnistria, Salonika, Crete and various camps. Includes individual accounts of Igre, Mosenzik, Singer, Mannheimer, Mendelson, Ivnitzer, Wechselblatt, Lichtenstein [Box 11/57–59]. Memorial booklets (German/Hebrew) for Hans Beyth, Director of Youth Aliyah, slain by Arab snipers on 26 Dec 1947 [Box 12/17–18]. NOTE: This collection does not include case files or name lists of the c 20,000 young people rescued by Youth Aliyah during this period.

7. Young Judaea, 1911–1986 [RG 8]. Includes Masada and Trumpeldor club membership lists (undated) [Box 4]; Palmach club registration and membership information, c. 1940s, 1961. [Box 4]

8. Zionist Political History I, 1894–1985 and II, 1939–1985 [RG 4], documents Hadassah's role in Zionist history. Includes such items as the Gertrude Rosenblatt diaries, 1911–1914 [Box 2/17]; autobiographies of Shulamit Cantor and Helena Kagan, M.D. [Box 3/28–28A]; biographical sketch of Bertha Landsman, 1937, and Landsman family correspondence, 1921–1924 [Box 4/29–30]; World Zionist Congress-Hadassah delegate lists, 1946. [Box 24/182]

9. Annual Conventions Archives, 1914–1971 [RG 3]. These files include speeches made at conventions by various individuals for all years, correspondence related to the conventions, and delegates' lists for 1937–1955, 1958–1960, 1964–1967 and 1971–1975. The 1943 files also include a membership list. [Box 11/7]

Finding Aids:

In addition to *A Guide to the Hadassah Archives,* published in 1986, the Archives has published finding aids for seven collections and black loose-leaf binders with finding aids for the remaining collections. Each published finding aid, available in the Reading Room, includes an introduction, chronology or biographical sketch, scope and content note, series listing and descriptions, and box and folder lists. Some are still available and can be purchased at $5 per copy .

The Alice L. Seligsberg and Rose G. Jacobs Papers, 1918–1957.
The Papers of Denise Tourover Ezekiel, 1936–1981.
The Henrietta Szold Papers, 1875–1965.
The Hadassah Medical Organization Papers, 1918–1981; and The Hadassah Medical Organization Archives, 1947–1984: A Guide to the Microfilms.
The Archives of Youth Aliyah, 1933–1960.
Zionist Political History in the Hadassah Archives, 1894–1985. (2 vols.)

NOTE: It is anticipated that finding aids to the Hadassah Archive collection will be included in the Center for Jewish History online catalog.

Restrictions on Use:

Some materials are restricted by date and subject matter.

CENTER FOR JEWISH HISTORY
LEO BAECK INSTITUTE
LIBRARY - ARCHIVES

Facility Director:	Carol Kahn Strauss, Executive Director
	Dr. Frank Mecklenburg, Director of Research, Chief Archivist
	Renate Evers, Head Librarian
	Viola Voss, Archivist
Address:	Center for Jewish History ♿
	15 West 16th Street
	New York, NY 10011
	(Cross Streets: Fifth and Sixth Avenues)
Phone:	(212) 744-6400
Fax:	(212) 988-1305
E-mail:	lbaeck@lbi.cjh.org
Website:	www.lbi.org

Hours of Operation:

Monday to Thursday: 9:30 am to 4:30 pm (appointment recommended)

Closed Friday, Saturday, Sunday, Jewish and legal holidays.

Closest Public Transportation, Directions, and Description of Facility:

See CENTER FOR JEWISH HISTORY, LILLIAN GOLDMAN MAIN READING ROOM.

Description of Resources:

The Leo Baeck Institute (LBI) was founded in 1955 by the Council of Jews from Germany to document the history and culture of German-speaking Jewry. Its Archives and Library offer the most comprehensive collection of documents, manuscripts, photographs and books dealing with the life and history of Jews in German-speaking lands from earliest times to the present. Materials are mostly in German with some in English, Hebrew and Yiddish. The Archives and Library contain over 10,000 archival collections, a specialized library of 60,000 volumes, over 600 periodicals and newspapers, almost 1,300 memoirs, and an art collection of over 5,000 items.

Library:

The Library has an outstanding collection of German-Jewish communal histories, biographical dictionaries, and genealogical resources. Books and microfilm are available on interlibrary loan. In addition, the collection includes such general references as encyclopedias in English and German and German-English/English-German dictionaries. The following is only a sample of items of interest to genealogists. Call numbers are listed in brackets.

1. Biographical Dictionaries:

> Austria. *Oesterreichisches biographisches Lexikon, 1815–1950.* 11 vols. Graz-Koeln, 1957–2001 ("A" to "Schw" published so far). [Ref CT 913 O35]
>
> Austria, Czechoslovakia and Germany. Hagemann, Harald and Claus-Dieter Krohn, *Biographisches Handbuch der deutschsprachigen wirtschaftswissenschaftlichen Emigration nach 1933.* [Biographies of economists dismissed by universities in Germany after 1933 and in Austria and Czechoslovakia after 1938.] Munich, 1999. [Ref HB 76 B56 1999]
>
> Czech Republic. Bohemia. Sturm, Heribert, *Biographisches Lexikon zur Geschichte der Boehmischen Laender.* 3 vols. Munich, 1979–1999. ("A" to "Scho" published so far.) [Ref DB 202 B56]
>
> Central Europe. Strauss, Herbert A. and Werner Roeder, *International Biographical Dictionary of Central European Emigrés, 1933–1945.* 1980–83. Vols I & III (index) in German; Vol. II (pts. 1–2) in English. Munich, 1980. [Ref CT 1053 B56]
>
> Germany. Heuer, Renate, editor, with Andrea Boelke-Fabian, et al., *Lexikon deutsch-juedischer Autoren, Archiv Bibliographica Judaica.* [Lexicon of German-Jewish Authors.] Includes parents' names, spouse and children. 10 vols. Munich, 1992–2002 ("A" to "Hein" published so far). [Ref DS 135 G5 L49]

Germany, Austria, Switzerland and other German speaking lands. *Deutsches Biographisches Archiv* [German Biographical Archive], and index, edited by Willi Gorzny, et. al. 4 vols. Munich, 1986. Includes 1431 microfiche with entries taken from 264 biographical dictionaries, encyclopedias and almanacs published between 1700 and 1910. [Ref. Z 2230 D48]

Germany. *Dokumentation zur juedischen Kultur in Deutschland 1840–1940: die Zeitungsausschnittsammlung Steininger.* Includes biographical sources for information on Jewish artists, painters, actors, entertainers, composers. Archiv Bibliographia Judaica, Munich, [n.d.]. [X Mfiche 1]

Germany. *Wer ist's?* [Who's Who]. 1908, 1922, 1935. (Title changed to:) *Wer ist Wer,* 1951, 1958, 1965, 1967, 1974/5, 1983. Leipzig and Berlin. [Ref DD 85 W3]

Prussia. Lowenthal, Ernest G., *Juden in Preussen: Biographisches Verzeichnis.* [Jews in Prussia, a biographical dictionary.] Berlin, 1981. [Ref DS 135 G34 L68]

Worldwide. Stern, Desider, *Werke von Autoren juedischer Herkunft in deutscher Sprache: Sonderausgabe 3. Auflage1970 fuer Bnai Brith Loge Wien.* [Biographies of Jewish authors who wrote in the German language: Special edition, 1970]. Vienna, 1970. [Z 2231 S7 1970]

Worldwide. Wininger, Salomon, *Grosse juedische National-Biographie, mit mehr als 8000 Lebensbeschreibungen namhafter juedischer Maenner und Frauen aller Zeiten und Laender* [More than 8,000 biographies of well known Jewish men and women from all countries]. 7 vols. Cernauti, 1925–1936. [Ref DS 115 W5]

Worldwide. Landman, I., *The Universal Jewish Encyclopedia...,* 10 vols. New York, 1939–1944. [DS 102.8 U5]

2. Holocaust:

Germany. *Gedenkbuch: Opfer der Verfolgung der Juden, 1933–1945.* [Memorial book: Jewish victims of persecution, 1933–1945.] Koblenz, 1985. 2 vols. (This book lists over 128,000 Jews of West Germany who perished, with birth place, how they died and where; appendix gives data on each concentration camp.) [Ref DS 135 G33 G38]

Berlin. *Gedenkbuch Berlins der juedishen Opfer des Nationalsozialismus.* Berlin, 1995. [Ref DS 135 G4 B4 1995]

Frankfurt am Main. Diamant, Adolf, *Deportationsbuch der von Frankfurt am Main aus gewaltsam verschickten Juden in den Jahren 1941 bis 1944.* Frankfurt am Main, 1984. [Ref DS135.G4 F7 D5]

Hamburg. Sielemann, Juergen. *Hamburger juedische Opfer des Nationalsozialismus: Gedenkbuch.* Hamburg, 1995. [q DS 135 G4 H32 H34 1995]

Hannover. Schulze, Peter, *Namen und Schicksale der juedischen Opfer des Nationalsozialismus aus Hannover.* [Names and fate of Jews sacrificed by the Nazis in Hannover.] Hannover, 1995. [DS135 G4 H38 S381 1995]

Leipzig. Diamant, Adolf, *Deportationsbuch der in den Jahren 1942 bis 1945 von Leipzig ausgewalsam verschickten Juden.* [Frankfurt am Main], 1991. [q D 810 J4 D52]

Mannheim. Keller, Volker. *Deportation Mannheimer Juden nach Gurs.* Mannheim, 1990. [q DS135 G4 M36 M35]

Silesia. *Gross-Rosen, ein Konzentrationslager in Schlesien.* By Isabell Sprenger. Includes a chronological transport list, pages 316–359. Koeln, 1996. [D 805 G3 G7 1996]

See also "Deportation and Concentration Camp Lists" under "Archives" below.

3. Refugees

Shanghai, China. *Emigranten Adressbuch fuer Shanghai mit einem Anhang: Branchen-Register.* Original, Shanghai, 1939. Reprint Hong Kong, 1995 (English). 1995 edition lists also town of origin and occupation. [DS 135 C5 E4 1995]

United States. *Guide to the Archival materials of the German-speaking emigration to the United States after 1933,* by John M. Spalek, et at. 4 vols. Charlottesville, [1978–1997]. [Ref E 184 G3 S68]

United States. *Research Foundation for Jewish Immigration: Jewish Immigrants of the Nazi period in the USA.* 6 vols. New York, 1978–1992 [Ref E184 J5 J558]. Vols. 1, 3 and 5 are of particular interest to genealogists. Volume 1: *Archival Resources,* by Steven W. Siegel, 1979; volume 3, part 1: *Guide to the Oral History Collection of the Research Foundation for Jewish Immigration, New York,* by Joan Lessing, 1982; and volume 5: *The Individual and Collective Experience of German-Jewish Immigrants, 1933–1984, An Oral History Record,* by Dennis Rohrbaugh, 1986. See also Research Foundation for Jewish Immigrants Collection [AR 6290] described below.

4. Genealogical Resources:

Brandt, Edward R., et al. *Germanic genealogy: a guide to worldwide sources and migration patterns.* 2nd edition. St. Paul, [1997]. [q CS 611 G47 1997]

Brilling, Bernhard. *Familiennamen der Juden in* <u>*Westfalen*</u>. Bonn, 1958–59. [BM 729 N3 B7]

Czellitzer, Arthur. *Mein Stammbaum* [My Genealogy]. Berlin, 1934. [CS 14 C99 M4]

Dreifuss, Erwin Manuel. *Die Familiennamen der Juden, unter besonderer Beruecksichtigung der Verhaeltnisse in <u>Baden</u> zu Anfang des 19. Jahrhunderts. Ein Beitrag zur Geschichte der Emanzipation.* Frankfurt am Main, 1927. [DS 135 G4 B167 D74]

Heintze, Albert and Paul Cascorbi. *Die deutschen Familiennamen, geschichtlich, geographisch, sprachlich.* Halle an der Saale, 1925. [Ref CS 2541 H4 1925]

Jersch-Wenzel, Stefi, *et al. Quellen zur Geschichte der Juden in den Archiven der neuen Bundeslaender.* 6 vols. For each archive in the former DDR (East German), lists holdings related to Jews. Munich, 1996, 1999–2001. [Ref CD 1222 Q8]

Juedische Familien-Forschung [Journal of Jewish genealogy]. nos. 1–50. Berlin, 1924–1938. [P-B184]

Ellmann-Krueger, Angelika. *Auswahlbibliographie zur juedischen Familienforschung vom Anfang des 19. Jahrhunderts bis zur Gegenwart.* [Selected bibliography of Jewish family research from the beginning of the 19th century to the present.] Wiesbaden, 1992. [Z 6374 B5 E4]

Ribbe, Wolfgang and Eckart Henning. *Taschenbuch fuer Familiengeschichtsforschung.* [Address book of archives.] Neustadt and der Aisch, 1995. [Ref CS 11 T37 1995]

Riemer, Shirley. *The German Research Companion.* Sacramento, 1997. [Ref CS 11 R54 1997]

Finding aides for genealogists in the Reading Room include a blue loose-leaf binder labeled, *German Jewish Genealogy: Resource Book from LBI,* which includes excerpts from articles on German genealogy, addresses of archives, Internet resources, and names of resource people in the U.S.A. and Europe with expertise in specific areas.

5. Marriage Records

Alsace. Fraenckel, A.A., *Memoire Juive en Alsace: contrats de mariage au XVIIIeme siecle.* Strasbourg, 1997. [Ref DS 135 G32 F73 1997]; and, 2-vol. index by R. Leeson and D. N. Leeson. [Ref DS 135 G32 F73 1999]

Berlin. Jacobson, Jacob. *Juedische Trauungen in Berlin, 1723–1759.* [Jewish marriages in Berlin, 1723–1759]. Berlin, 1938. [DS 135 G4 B4 J318]

Berlin. Jacobson, Jacob. *Juedische Trauungen in Berlin, 1759–1813; mit Ergaenzungen fuer die Jahre von 1723 bis 1759.* [Jewish marriages in Berlin, 1759–1813; with and addendum for the years 1723 to 1759] Berlin, 1968. [DS 135 G4 B4 J32]

Moselle. Fleury, Jean, *Contrats de mariage juifs en Moselle avant 1792: recensement à usage généalogique de 2021 contrats de mariage notariés.* Paris, 1999. [Ref (q) DS 135 F82 F54 1999]

See also "Archives, Marriage Records" below.

6. Communal Histories:

Austria. Gold, Hugo. *Geschichte der Juden in Oesterreich; ein Gedenkbuch.* Tel Aviv, 1971. Includes biographical information on Austrian Jewish writers and Austrian Jews in the world, pages 143–176. [Ref DS 135 A9 G65]

Bavaria. Schwierz, Israel, *Steinere Zeugnisse juedischen Lebens in Bayern: eine Dokumentation.* Munich, 1992 [DS 135 G36 S395 1992]

Berlin. Jacobson, Jacob. *Die Judenbuergerbuecher der Stadt Berlin, 1809–1851; mit Ergaenzungen fuer die Jahre 1791–1809.* Berlin, 1962. [DS 135 G4 B4 J31]

Bohemia. Gold, Hugo. *Die Juden und Judengemeinden Boehmens in Vergangenheit und Gegenwart.* Bruenn-Prag, 1934. [q DS 135 C954 G63]

Bovenden. Busch, Ralf. *Die juedischen Einwohner Bovendens vom 17. bis 18. Jahrhundert.* Goettingen, 1971. [DS 135 G4 B648 B81]

Breslau. Brilling, Bernhard. *Geschichte der Juden in Breslau von 1454–1702.* Stuttgart, 1960. [DS 135 G4 B66 B711]

Chemnitz. Diamant, Adolf. *Chronik der Juden in Chemnitz, heute Karl-Marx-Stadt; Aufstieg und Untergang einer juedischen Gemeinde in Sachsen.* Frankfurt am Main, 1970. [DS 135 G4 C52 D5]

Dresden. Diamant, Adolf. *Chronik der Juden in Dresden; von den ersten Juden bis zur Bluete der Gemeinde und deren Ausrottung.* Mit einem Geleitwort von Robert M. W. Kempner. Darmstadt, 1973. [DS 135 G4 D74 D5]

Eschwege. Cohn, Joseph. *Das Eschweger Memorbuch; ein Beitrag zur Geschichte der juedischen Stadt- und Landgemeinden im Kreise Eschwege.* Hamburg, 1930. [DS 135 G4 E82 C6]

Essen. Samuel, Salomon. *Geschichte der Juden in Stadt und Stift Essen bis zur Saekularisation des Stifts, von 1291–1802; mit urkundlichen Beilagen und einer Stammtafel.* Essen-Ruhr, 1905. [DS 135 G4 E88 S24]

Frankfurt am Main. Arnsberg, Paul. *Die Geschichte der Frankfurter Juden seit der franzoesischen Revolution.* Darmstadt, 1983. [Ref DS 135 G4 F7 A71]

Frankfurt am Main. Dietz, Alexander, translated by Frances Martin. *The Jewish Community of Frankfurt: A Genealogical Study, 1349–1849*. Cronwall, 1988. (English) [Ref DS 135 G4 F7 D5412]. Original in German, *Stammbuch der Frankfurter Juden. Geschichtliche Mitteilungen ueber die Frankfurter juedischen Familien von 1349–1849, nebst einem Plane der Judengasse.* Frankfurt am Main, 1907. [DS 135 G4 F7 D54]

Frankfurt am Main. Dietz, Alexander. *Frankfurter Buergerbuch; geschichtliche Mittheilungen ueber 600 bekannte Frankfurter Familien aus der Zeit vor 1806.* Frankfurt am Main, 1897. [DD 901 F75 D54]

Freiburg. Lewin, Adolf. *Juden in Freiburg i. B.* Trier, 1890. [DS 135 G4 F74 L48]

Hannover. Gronemann, Selig. *Genealogische Studien ueber de alten juedischen Familien Hannovers.* Berlin, 1913. [CS 627 H3 G7]

Heilbronn. Franke, Hans. *Geschichte und Schicksal der Juden in Heilbronn; vom Mittelalter bis zur Zeit der nationalsozialistischen Verfolgungen (1050–1945).* Heilbronn, 1963. [DS 135 G4 H44 F73]

Hesse. Arnsberg, Paul. *Die juedischen Gemeinden in Hessen; Anfang, Untergang, Neubeginn.* Frankfurt am Main, 1971. [Ref DS 135 G4 H48 A75]

Leipzig. Freudenthal, Max, *Leipziger Messgaeste, 1675–1764.* Frankfurt am Main, 1928. Genealogical data on Jews who attended the Leipzig fairs, 1675–1764. [DS 135 G32 F74 L4]

Munich. Cohen, Arthur. *Die Muenchener Judenschaft 1750–1861; eine bevoelkerungs- und wirtschaftsgeschichtliche Studie.* Berlin, 1931. [DS 135 G4 M86 C64]

Oldenburg. Schieckel, Harald. *Die juedischen Wehrpflichtigen in Oldenburg von 1867–1918 und ihre Vorfahren.* Neustadt, 1971. [DS 135 G4 O5 S3]

Palatinate. *Dokumentation zur Geschichte der juedischen Bevoelkerung in Rheinland-Pfalz und im Saarland von 1800 bis 1945*, published by the Landesarchivverwaltung Rheinland-Pfalz. 9 vols. Volume 8 includes a personal name, place name and subject author index. Koblenz, 1972–1982. [DS 135 G4 P35 P3]

Posen. Heppner, Aron and Herzberg, Isaac, *Aus Vergangenheit und Gegenwart der Juden und der jued. Gemeinden in den Posener Laenden*, Koschmin, 1909. [Ref DS 135 G4 P69 H4]

Schwaben. Pfister, Doris, editor. *Dokumentation zur Geschichte und Kultur der Juden in Schwaben.* Augsburg, 1993. [q DS135 G37 D6 1993]

Tuebingen. Zapf, Lilli. *Die Tuebinger Juden; eine Dokumentation.* Tuebingen, 1974. [DS 135 G4 T84 Z3]

Vienna. Bato, Ludwig. *Die Juden im alten Wien.* Wien, 1928. [DS 135 A92 V5 B37]

Vienna. Gold, Hugo. *Geschichte der Juden in Wien: ein Gedenkbuch.* Tel Aviv, 1966. Includes biographical information on Vienna Jews in the world, pages 135–156. [Ref DS 135 A92 V5]

Worms. *Zum 900 jaehrigen Bestehen der Synagoge zu Worms. Eine Erinnerungsgabe des Vorstands der Israelitischen Religionsgemeinde Worms.* Berlin, 1934. [DS 135 G4 W6 Z8]

Wuerttemberg. Jeggle, Utz. *Judendoerfer in Wuerttemberg.* Tuebingen, 1969. [DS 135 G37 J4 J8]

7. Cemeteries:

Berlin. Nachama, Andreas, et al. *Juedische Grabstaetten und Friedhoefe in Berlin: eine Dokumentation.* [Berlin], 1992. [GT 3250 B4 J8]. See also Jacob Jacobson Collection. [AR 7002/MF 447]

Frankfurt am Main. Brocke, Michael. *Der alte juedische Friedhof zu Frankfurt am Main: unbekannte Denkmaeler und Inschriften.* Frankfurt am Main, 1996. [q GT 3250 F72 B76 1996]

Hannover. Wahl, Margret. *Der alte juedische Friedhof in Hannover.* Hannover, 1961. [DS 135 G4 H38 W3]

Hohenlimburg. Boening, Adalbert and Matthias. *Der juedische Friedhof in Hohenlimburg.* Hagen, 1986. [GT 3250 H64 B6]

Jebenhausen and Goeppingen. Bar-Giora Bamberger, Naftali. *Memor-Buch die juedischen Friedhoefe Jebenhausen und Goeppingen.* Goeppingen, 1990. [fGT 3250 J43 B3]

Lippstadt. Fennenkoetter, Hans Christopher. *Die juedischen Friedhoefe in Lippstadt.* Lippstadt, 1898. [GT 3250 L56 F4]

Mainz. Levi, Sali. *Beitraege zur Geschichte der aeltesten juedischen Grabsteine in Mainz; herausgegeben anlaesslich der Rueckfuehrung dieser Steine auf den alten "Judensand" Mainz.* [n.p.] 1926. [DS 135 G4 M35 L4]

Mannheim. Bernhard, Franz, et al. *Die Friedhoefe in Mannheim: Wegweiser zu den Grabstaetten bekannter Mannheimer Persoenlichkeiten.* Mannheim, 1992. [GT 3250 M35 F7]

Rexingen. Adler, Renate Karoline. *In Stein gehauen: Lebensspuren aus dem juedischen Friedhof in Rexingen; Dokumentation des Friedhofs und des Schicksals der 300 Jahre in Rexingen ansaessigen juedischen Gemeinde.* [Includes an alphabetical list of Jews buried in Rexingen]. Stuttgart, 1997.

Schwelm. Boening, Adalbert. *Hebraeische Inschriften auf dem juedischen Friedhof in Schwelm.* Schwelm, 1988. [GT 3250 S39 B6]

Soest. Brocke, Michael, et al. *Der juedische Friedhof in Soest: eine Dokumentation in Text und Bild.* [Includes list of members of the Jewish Community of Soest, 1700–1945.] Soest, 1993. [q GT 3250 S62 J8 1993]

Sulzberg. Kohout, Jiri. *Der juedische Friedhof in Sulzburg.* [Karlsruhe, 1990]. [q GT 3250 S85 K6]

Ulm. Brann, Marcus. *Juedische Grabsteine in Ulm.* Breslau, 1917. [DS 135 G4 U44 B72]

Waibstadt. Waibstadt Israelitischer Verbands-Friedhof. *Graeber-Verzeichnis.* Rappenau, 1914. [GT 3250 W28 W3]

Wesel. Brocke, Michael, et al. *Nur Graeber bleiben mir; juedische Friedhoefe in Wesel: Zeugnisse juedischen Lebens.* Koeln, 1988. [GT 3250 W48 B7]

Wuerttemberg. Wuerttemberg Israelitische Religionsgemeinschaft. *Juedische Gotteshaeuser und Friedhoefe in Wuerttemberg.* Stuttgart, 1932. [q BM 317 W84 J8]

See also cemetery lists, registers and death records in archival collections described below.

8. Military Records

Die juedischen Gefallenen des deutschen Heeres, der deutschen Marine und der deutschen Schutztruppen, 1914–1918; ein Gedenkbuch. Published by the Reichsbund Juedischer Frontsoldaten. Berlin, 1932. [D 609 G4 R4]; and 1933 [D 609 G4 R4 1933]

Der Schild, 1921–1938. Organ of the Reichsbund Juedischer Frontsoldaten. Includes photographs of former soldiers and biographical data in various issues. [y B345; P-B345]

Juedische Frontsoldaten aus Wuertemberg und Hohenzollern. Published by the Centralverein Deutscher Staatsbuerger Juedischen Glaubens, Wuerttembergischer Landesverband. Stuttgart, 1926. [D 639 J4 C47]

Kriegsbriefe gefallener deutscher Juden. Includes excerpts from letters written by fallen soldiers with date/place of birth and death. Published by the Reichsbund Juedischer Frontsoldaten. Berlin, 1935. [D 639 J4 R44] and, 1961. [D 639 J4 K74]

9. Newspapers: LBI's periodicals collection includes over 600 titles including:

Berlin. *Juedische Rundschau,* 1896–1938 [P-B225]
Breslau. *Juedische Zeitung,* 1900–1937 [P-B234]
Frankfurt am/M. *Neue juedische Presse,* Sept. 1907–Feb. 1922 [P-B76]
Hamburg, *Juedische Schulzeitung,* Oct. 1925–Nov. 1938 [P-B227]
Leipzig. *Allgemeines juedisches Familienblatt,* Nov. 1925–Dec. 1930
Munich, *Das Juedische Echo,* 1914–1933 [P-B181]
New York. *Aufbau,* 1934– [P-y B21]
Paris. *Pariser Tageblatt,* Dec. 1933–Feb. 1940 [P-B389]
Strassburg. *Das Juedische Blatt,* Sept. 1911–Jul. 1914 [P-B176]
Vienna. *Juedische Volksstimme,* 1900–1934 [P-B240]
Wiesbaden, Umgebung. *Juedische Wochenzeitung...,* 1928–1933 [P-B 473]
Zurich. *Juedische Presszentrale Zuerich...,* 1918–1939 [P-B222]

NOTE: See www.jewishgen.org/databases/Holocaust/Aufbau.htm for an index to lists of survivors and victims published in the *Aufbau*, September 1944 to September 1946.

Archives:

The Archives collection is so rich in source material that the following list is a sample of only some of the items of use to genealogists. See "Finding Aids" below to locate other materials. "MF" in the call number indicates the collection in now on microfilm:

1. Adoption of German Surnames

Several collections at the LBI Archives help document the change from patronymics to surnames in early 19th-century Germany. These include the literary estates of Berthold Rosenthal (b.1875–d.1957) and Jacob Jacobson (b.1888–d.1968). The Jacobson estate includes substantial remnants of the Gesamtarchiv der deutschen Juden (Archives of German Jewry) established in Berlin in 1905 as the central depository for the records of German-Jewish communities and organizations. Information in brackets identifies the particular item in the collection; JJC refers to the Jacob Jacobson Collection [AR 7002/MF 447]:

Baden - includes c.500 pages of detailed notes about the name changes and family names adopted by the Jews of Baden in 1809. Volumes are organized alphabetically by town name. The collection includes historical material about the history of Jews in Baden and the Palatinate as well as 70 family trees. [Berthold Rosenthal Collection, AR 637/MF 484]

Berlin files contain lists of Jewish families living legally in Berlin on 24 March 1813, lists of family names taken in 1812, and a list of Jews who had taken family names and Christian first names before 1812 (379 entries). [JJC I:51, I:58, and I:82]

Lippe-Detmold, 1810, list of family names. [JJC III:50]

Marienwerder district, West Prussia (Jacobson estate), 1845, lists of family names. [JJC III:88 and VIII:61]

Posen, alphabetical register of Jews naturalized, copied by Isidor Hirschberg, Bromberg, 1836 [JJC III:32]. See also *The Naturalized Jews of the Grand Duchy of Posen in 1834 and 1835: An Alphabetical list...,* compiled by Edward David Luft. Atlanta, 1987. [Ref DS 135 G4 P69 N3 1987]

Individual family histories tell stories such as the Strauss family [AR 4492] and the Heilner family. [AR 4471]

2. Circumcision and Birth Records

The following communities and years are represented by circumcision registers in the LBI Archives. Information in brackets identifies the particular item in the collections.

Aurich, 1758–1801. [JJC III:4]

Berlin, Circumcision registers and index, 1714–1840; and Mohelbuch, 1715–1805 with 2,786 entries [JJC I:1-4, I:19, I:55, I:75-76, and I:96]. Also alphabetical birth registers, 1778–1811, 1813–1840. [JJC I:7, I:42-43, I:50]

Filehne, Circumcision register, 1812–1850, of Rabbi A. Wreschner, containing 200 entries from Filehne and 32 entries from other places, and register, 1817–1864, of the Rabbinical Judge Aron Lazarus, containing 335 entries. [AR 2470]

Frankfurt am Main, Register, 1698–1836, kept by the ancestors of Moritz Abraham Stern, 63 pages. [AR 380/MF 324 (1)]

Fuerth, Registers, 1761–1806, of Benjamin Berlin and Mordechai Jafe. Handwritten copy in German. [JJC III:20]

Kurhessen, Mohelbuch, 1802–1841, 433 entries. [JCC III:42]

Munich, Mohelbuch, 1826–1874, of Rabbi Hirsch Aub, including entries for Prague, 1816, and Baiersdorf, 1819; registers, 1840–1878 and 1834–1885. [Elizabeth and Ernst Kitzinger Collection, AR 3086]

Munich, Circumcision register (Mohel book), 1913–1938, by Jewish community official Heinrich Glaser, 300 entries. [AR 143]

Prague, Worms, Pfalz, Mohelbuch, 1782–1823, 403 entries. [JJC III:65]

Randegg/Baden, Register, 1828–1881, of Baruch Bloch, copy with explanations by Dr. S. Moos-Moore, 1972; and list of births, marriages and deaths in 1810–1868. [AR 2483]

Schildberg/Posen, Register of Elkan Lewy, 1866–1906, 376 entries. [AR 3126/No. 1]

Schildberg, 1838–1866, and Bunzlau, 1867–1887. Photocopies of register of Abraham Unger. [JJC III:76]

Schleswig-Holstein, 1775–1817. [JJC III:77]

Vienna, birth registers, 1826–1938, and indexes, 1826–1929, from the Juedische Gemeinde Wien. [MF 548]

Wuerttemberg, 1880–1908. [AR 1471]

Among other community and family collections in the LBI Archives are numerous examples of individual birth certificates and announcements.

3. Marriage Records

The LBI Archives contain marriage registers of communities, contracts (ketubot), individual engagement and wedding announcements, as well as special newspapers issued for weddings. The following communities and years are represented by marriages registers in the LBI Archives:

Berlin, list of marriages (Trauungsliste), 1759–1813. [JJC I:12]

Berlin, register, 1813–1829, 1830–1837, 1837–1847, 1847–1851, photocopies made by the Reichsstelle fuer Sippenforschung. [JJC I:9-10, I:12, I:40-41, I:46-47, and I:63]

Breslau, 1789–1818. [JJC III:10]

Dresden, table of births, marriages, and deaths, 1786–1819/20. [JJC I:2 and I:55]

Nuernberg, 1872–1912, including four pages of marriages in Switzerland. [AR 1706/MF 328]

Vienna, marriage registers, 1857–1938, and indexes, 1857–1929, from the Juedische Gemeinde Wien. [MF 548]

4. Death Records

It is important to remember that rights of domicile were not always synonymous with burial privileges. Thus, no Jew could be buried in Breslau until 1671. Jews from Breslau were buried in Krotoschin, Zulz, and other outlying communities; the death certificates are therefore filed with these towns rather than with Breslau records. The following communities and years are represented by death records in the LBI Archives:

Ahlen. Includes a cemetery map and list of names/dates of deceased. [AR 10937]

Allersheim near Wuerzburg, list of deceased, 1779–1903, typed in German. [JJC III:1]

Altstrelitz, cemetery register, c. 1740–1923. [JJC III:2]

Arnswalde, miscellaneous tombstone inscriptions and documents, earliest c. 1780, mostly from 19th century. [JJC III:3]

Berlin, death registers, 1751–1813, 1818–1829, 1830–1837, 1841–1857, 1847–1855. [JJC I:5-6, I:34, I:44, VIII: 56c]

Berlin, inscriptions and dates of death, from gravestones at Schoenhauser Allee cemetery, Berlin, 19th century [JJC I:17]; inscriptions from grave monuments in the old Jewish cemetery, Grosse Hamburgerstrasse 26, by L. Landshuth, 2,767 entries, mainly in Hebrew, 13 volumes. [JJC I:20-32]; alphabetical register (by Hebrew first name) of all burials in the old Jewish cemetery of Berlin, 1671–1827 [JJC I:56]. List of tombstones, Weissensee cemetery; and burial list at Grosse Hamburgerstrasse. [AR 88/MF472]

Bretten/Baden, Memorbuch, 1725–1884. [AR 2799/MF 328]

Duesseldorf, Memorbuch, 1714. [JJC III:13]

Dyhernfurth, Chevra Kadisha records, 1782–1807. [JJC III:14]

Frankfurt am Main, death register, 1805–1808. [JJC III:17]

Gnesen, record book (Pinkas) of the Chevra Baalei Hamisakim Ubikur Cholim (burial society and society for visiting the sick), including list of deaths, 1841–1892. [JJC III:22]

Haigerloch, photographs of Jewish tombstones. [JJC VIII:57]

Hannover, Memorbuch. [JJC III:29]

Harburg, Memorbuch. [JJC III:30]

Koenigsberg (today Kaliningrad, Russia), requests for birth, marriage, and death certificates, 1847. [JJC III:39]

Koeslin, cemetery register [JJC III:41]

Krotoschin, Chevra Kadisha and death records, 1785. [JJC III:41a]

Potsdam, Jewish tombstone inscriptions, 1746–1836, typed list. [JJC I:54]

Vienna, death registers, 1826–1938, and indexes, 1874–1929, from the Juedische Gemeinde Wien. [MF 548]

Wandsbek, death register to 1884; and cemetery register, 1840–1883. [JJC II:29 and VIII:55c]

5. Other Collections with Regional Materials

The following collections at the LBI Archives contain material of particular interest to the genealogical researcher:

Alsace and Lorraine Jewish Communities Collection [AR 2863/MF 509] is divided into the following folios: Censuses [1–173]; Consistorial tax lists, 1816–1825 [226–592]; list of Notables of the Regional Lower Rhine Consistory, 1820–1840s, of the Metz Consistory, 1818–1850, and of the Nancy Consistory, 1818–1873 [797–809, 1560–1571, 1983–2013]; Rabbis and cantors in the Lower Rhine, 1853–1864 [935–941], in the

Upper Rhine regional Consistory, 1822–1848 [1244–1253], and election of cantors in Delme (Neurthe-et-Moselle), 1841–1860 [2265–2275], and Guebwiller, Upper Rhine, 1847–1866. [2362–2389]

American Jewish Joint Distribution Committee [AR 7196/MF 488], case files of individuals attempting to emigrate from Germany, 1933–1941 [Boxes 1–30]; and case files of displaced persons is Italy, 1945–1947. [Boxes 31–32]

Arthur Czellitzer Collection: includes personal and family papers as well as information on the genealogical society he created, the Gesellschaft fuer Juedische Familienforschung [discussed in *Toledot,* Summer 1977 and in *Search,* Winter 1987]. A full set of this organization's periodical, *Juedische Familien-Forschung,* 1924–1938, is available in the LBI Library (see above). [AR 302]

Austrian Heritage Collection: currently includes 2,400 questionnaires completed by survivors and 110 oral interviews. This is an ongoing project. Names are included in the online catalog. [AR 10378]

Berlin Jewish Address Book Collection, *Juedisches Adressbuch fuer Gross-Berlin.* 1929–1931. [AR 10980]. 1929/30 edition (photocopy) is in the Reading Room. [Ref DS 135 G4 B4 J83 1929-30]

Berthold Rosenthal [AR 637/MF 484] and Jacob Jacobson Collections [AR 7002/MF 447] referred to earlier are obviously rich in vital statistical and historical data for the genealogist. The Jacobson collection has been restored and microfilmed. It contains records from Berlin, Hamburg and other communities in northern and eastern Germany, mostly for the 18th and 19th centuries.

Bnai Brith Collection. Includes an album, *In Memoriam - Bnai Brith Leo Baeck Lodge #1531* (New York), with photographs and dates of birth/death of 192 members. [AR 4087]

Buttenhausen Jewish Community Collection. Includes tax book, 1940. [AR 2057/MF 306]

Ele Toledot, compiled by Shlomo Ettlinger during the first half of this century. The work is in three parts (no part "A"): Part "C" (22 volumes) lists the Jews of Frankfurt a/M chronologically by date of death, 1241–1824. Part "B" (9 volumes) list male (Maenner) Frankfurt Jews alphabetically by surname; and (2 volumes) list women (Frauen) by their first name. Part "D" (2 volumes) lists the remainder (Reste) and converts (Judentaufen), 1241–1811. Biographies usually mention parents and children. [AR 5241/MF 536]

Jews in Shanghai Collection: includes Project Shanghai Haven interviews by the Oral History Institute of Salt Lake City Utah; and a list of 1,443 "Central-European Jewish refugees who died in Shanghai." [AR 2509]

John H. Bergmann Collection: includes a vast amount of material about the community of Laupheim in Baden as well as other German communities including individual biographies, family histories, cemetery records, citizen lists, home ownership records and lists of rabbis [AR 4861]. See "Restrictions on Use."

John H. Richter Collection: includes many family trees, material about Jews in the film industry, name change documents, as well as research materials for his book, *From the Rhineland to Wisconsin,* and materials relating to German families who settled in Wisconsin. [AR 1683/MF 534]

Karl D. Darmstaedter Collection: unusually rich in materials about Jews from Mannheim and their fate in Nazi Germany. The documentation about Mannheim, Baden, and Worms includes photocopies and photographs of cemeteries in Prague and Neckarbischofsheim. [AR 15]

Leipzig Jewish Community Collection, 1874–1999: includes 9 microfilm reels containing the membership card files of the Jewish community of Leipzig as of 1935, with data on over 12,000 individuals; and a deportation list, 1940s. [AR 2167]

Max Markreich Collection: includes extensive typed manuscripts about the Jewish communities in Aurich, Bremen and Ostfriesland. Markreich was head of the Jewish community in Bremen and emigrated to the United States by way of Trinidad. His collection contains material as diverse as original documents on the Jewish community of Leer, 1748–1749; the Aurich mohelbuch; items on Jewish life in Trinidad, 1939–1940; and records of Congregation Shaare Zedek of Astoria (New York City), 1942. [AR 7048/MF 248]

Memoir Collection: includes almost 1,300 memoirs written over the past 200 years. Most are unpublished and written in German. [These are cataloged individually starting with the prefix "ME."]

Michael Berolzheimer Collection: includes over 50 family trees for the families Berolzheim, Berolzheimer, Besels, Brilin, Gosdorfer, Mannlein, Offenbacher, Rindskopf, Wertheimer, and Simon Wolf Oppenheim (Oppenheimer). The papers include copies of Jewish community registries from 18th and 19th century Bavaria;

copies of the <u>Fuerth</u> Testamentenbuch (register of wills, estates, and death dates of selected members of the community--translated by Rabbi Max Freudenthal), 1788–1818; a Schutzgeldliste (tax list for rights of residence of protected Jews) from Fuerth for 1716–1718; and other valuable genealogical notes. [AR 4136]

Research Foundation for Jewish Immigration Collection: includes approximately 25,000 files on individual refugees from Nazi Germany, including an alphabetical index and a category index. These 87 microfilm reels represent source material used for the *International Biographical Dictionary of Central European Emigrés 1933–1945* [AR 6290]. See also RESEARCH FOUNDATION FOR JEWISH IMMIGRATION.

Rudolf Jakob Simonis Collection: contains several hundred family trees, family histories, and related correspondence for <u>Berlin</u>, northern <u>Germany</u>, and <u>Sweden</u>. There is also a copiously illustrated Simonis family tree. [AR 7019/MF 551]

Vierfelder Family Collection: includes a six-generation history of the Vierfelder family from <u>Buchau</u>. The collection also includes 52 photographs of the Jewish community in Buchau and copious newspapers and historical clippings about Buchau. [AR 890/MF 408]

Westphalia Jewish Population 1933–1942. Collection of names of 8,112 Jews living in <u>Westphalia</u> between 1933–1942 with birth date, place of residence, date and destination of emigration, deportation or date of death. Compiled by Bernhard Brilling and Peter W. Lande. [AR 10911 (diskettes)]

6. <u>Deportation and Concentration Camp Lists</u>

Augsburg: deportation list, November 1941–February 1945, c. 400 names. [AR 990/MF 303]

Baden: 11 Gestapo lists of Jews still resident in Baden on 1 February 1941, including full Jews and those living in mixed marriages, 840 names from 12 or more towns; Jews who moved to the East, Easter 1942, 78 names; Jews who moved to the East, Summer 1942, 45 names; Jews who "emigrated" from Baden to Theresienstadt, 22 August 1942, 139 names, and addenda, 90 names; Jews deported from Baden-Baden, Freiburg, Heidelberg, Mannheim, etc. on 22 August 1942; Jews expelled from Baden on 1 March 1943. [AR 138; see also Adolf Loebel Collection, AR 4185]

Bielefeld: Lists of deportees and survivors. [Hans Kronheim Collection, AR 3156]

Bremen: List of Jews deported to Minsk, January 17, 1941, 426 names. [Max Markreich Collection: AR 7048/MF 248]

Gross Rosen Concentration Camp Collection includes a list of male camp inmates as of April 18, 1945. [AR 10975]

Koblenz: 4 Gestapo lists, 1942. Includes 867 Jews deported from Koblenz and the region, especially Bendorf-Sayn (printed by the Jewish community, c. 1947–1948). [AR 5473]

Konstanz: names, dates of birth, and last residence of the Jews of Konstanz, deported to Gurs (Vichy France) in 1940 (photocopies of Nazi documents). [AR 2166]

Nuremberg: List of Jews deported from Nuremberg, by name of individual and camp destination, 1941–1944. [AR 1706/MF 328]

Pfalz: 2 Gestapo lists, (early 1940s), 220 names; also a list for transports from Rheinpfalz, undated, 11 names. [AR 2039/MF 328]

Regensburg: deportees who arrived in Theresienstadt, 24 September 1942, 117 names. [AR 1425]

Wuerzburg: transport II/26 of Jews who arrived in Theresienstadt, 24 September 1942, 610 names. [AR 3788]

Several other lists of Jews deported to Gurs, Rivesaltes and Theresienstadt are located in the LBI Archives in the Bernhard Kolb [AR 360/MF 228] and Karl D. Darmstaedter [AR 15] collections; and lists of those interned in Theresienstadt, Lodz Auschwitz, Vittel and elsewhere, can be found in the Max Plaut collection [AR 7094]. See also, <u>Holocaust.</u> under "Library."

7. <u>Census</u>

German Minority Census of 1939 (dated 17 May 1938). This was a census of all "non-German" minorities living in German territory in 1939, including Sudetenland annexed from Czechoslovakia. [MF 466]

A useful finding aid to these 292 microfilms is, *The German Minority Census of 1939: An Introduction and Register,* compiled by Thomas K. Edlund. Teaneck, 1996. [st 742]

8. Photographs

LBI's collection holds over 30,000 photographs including portraits, cemeteries, and communities.

Finding Aids:

The Leo Baeck Institute now has one searchable database for the archives, library and periodicals. This computerized Master Catalog [MC-LBI] can be accessed online and from each of the 7 computers on the third floor outside the Reading Room (near the Genealogy Institute). A search can be made by keyword, author, title, subject and call number. Detailed descriptions of many archive collections are included. There is a separate catalog online for the Photograph Collection.

There are also two published catalogs of LBI archival materials, one in English and one in German, which are also available for sale. These are on open shelves in the Reading Room:

Leo Baeck Institute New York: Catalog of the Archival Collections, edited by Fred Grubel, et al. New York, 1990. English. This reference catalog divides the collections into 284 "major" and 3,825 "minor" collections and is arranged alphabetically by name of the collection. The book includes a detailed subject index; a summary of the content of the major collections and brief highlights of the remainder. [Ref Z 6373 G4 L4 1990]

Catalog of Archival Collections. No. 1, published by Leo Baeck Institute. New York, 1971 (German). This catalog is divided into three parts: German-speaking Jewish communities; newspapers, periodicals, yearbooks; memoirs. [Ref Z 6373 G4 L4]

In addition to the above, the Institute has a series of brown loose-leaf inventory binders located behind the reference desk. Collections are arranged alphabetically (no "major" or "minor" distinction). Each inventory includes a summary of the content as well as detailed descriptions of materials in each folder. For some collections, name lists can be found here that are not included in the online catalog. The online Master Catalog includes all of the material in the published catalog plus all collections added since publication. It includes much, but not all, of the information found in the brown binders. NOTE: The brown binders do not include all of the Institute's collections. The brown binder catalog was discontinued after the Master Catalog was in place. Check the Master Catalog under "Finding Aid" to determine if there is an inventory available for the collection (number of pages indicated).

All memoirs are cataloged with the prefix "ME." All archival collections have the prefix "AR" and all periodicals/ newspapers are cataloged with the prefix "P."

LBI has published a newsletter since 1960, the *LBI News* [y C134 LBI]. Details on new accessions are reported.

Fees/Copies:

For photocopying charges in the Reading Room, see CENTER FOR JEWISH HISTORY, CENTER GENEALOGY INSTITUTE.

Inquiries to LBI sent by fax, mail or e-mail should be sent on the Family Research Application Form available on LBI's web page, www.lbi.org. Inquiries should include mailing address as well as e-mail address. LBI staff suggest that researchers submit a copy of their family tree. There is a service fee for mail requests, payable in advance. Prices and instructions are available on the web page. There is a base charge for mail requests of $25 plus shipping up to $10, and photocopying at $.50 per page.

LBI members ($50 student membership; $100 general) receive invitations to lectures, *LBI News*, and discounts on publications. Higher-level contributors receive the annual *Yearbook,* containing articles and lectures, chiefly in English, and special invitations to luncheons and briefings.

Restrictions on Use:

Difficulties may be encountered in reading German-Gothic or Judaeo-German (German in Hebrew letters) particularly in the communal records. There is a sample page of German-Gothic to help readers decipher the alphabets at the Reference Desk.

Staff is helpful with finding materials and quick translation or interpretation of German-Gothic script or print. They cannot do research.

A few collections are restricted by donors. These are identified in the Master Index.

CENTER FOR JEWISH HISTORY
YESHIVA UNIVERSITY MUSEUM

Facility Director: Sylvia A. Herskowitz, Director

Address: Center for Jewish History   ♿
      15 West 16th Street
      New York, NY 10011

Phone: (212) 294-8330, ext. 8815 or 8813
Fax: (212) 294-8335
E-mail: info@yum.cjh.org
Website: www.yumuseum.org

Hours of Operation: Mail or e-mail requests only.

      NOTE: Yeshiva University Museum galleries are open:
      Tuesday, Wednesday and Sunday: 11 am to 5 pm
      Thursday: 11 am to 8 pm

Closest Public Transportation. Directions and **Description of Facility**:

See CENTER FOR JEWISH HISTORY, LILLIAN GOLDMAN MAIN READING ROOM.

Description of Resources:

Yeshiva University Museum (YUM), established in 1973, collects artifacts representing Jewish cultural, intellectual and artistic achievements around the world from the Bronze Age to the present. The diversity of this collection consisting of approximately 8,000 objects reflects YUM's interdisciplinary approach and includes fine art, archaeological artifacts, documents, photographs and objects of material culture. YUM also has a research library consisting of books, journals, monographs and sale catalogues on Jewish art, history and culture.

1. Photographs: The collection includes approximately 3,000 portraits of individuals and soldiers; family celebrations; family businesses; homes and towns, mostly dating before WWII.

2. Oral Histories: produced by junior high school students under the auspices of YUM. These oral histories were recorded and transcribed in 1987 as part of a National Endowment for Humanities grant tracking German Jews of Washington Heights. The 23 interviewees from 21 different villages, towns and cities in Germany recalled their lives in Europe in the 1920s–1940s and their American experience as residents of Washington Heights. *The German Jews of Washington Heights: An Oral History Project* includes abstracts of each interview.

3. Historical Documents: include ketubot, circumcision record books, business and family documents and diaries. The Museum has also c. 60 wimpel (torah binders with birth record information) from Germany and Washington Heights, New York.

4. Artist files: In addition to exhibition catalogs and monographs, YUM collects information on Jewish artists and these resources are available in vertical files and archival collections. For Israeli art and artists, check the Kathryn M. Yochelson Papers, 1948-2000.

Finding Aids:

For archival collections, check "Selected Finding Aids" online at www.cjh.org/academic/findingaids/yum/. YUM's artifacts collection inventory is fully cataloged on a computer accessible to staff. Staff can search by name of donor, subject (which could include the name of individuals in a photograph or location), artist, place of origin and bibliographic references. YUM's reference library is currently available online as part of YULIS, the Yeshiva University online catlog. NOTE: The catalog of YUM's artifacts collection will be incorporated into the Center for Jewish History online catalog.

YUM's published catalogues for individual exhibits provide a wealth of information on documents in its collection as well as those borrowed from other museums and private collectors. To find these in the CJH partners' holdings, enter "Yeshiva University Museum" under "Author." Call numbers below indicate the catalogue is in the collection of a YUM partner at the Center for Jewish History and may be viewed in the Reading Room. Check in particular:

Ashkenaz: The German Jewish Heritage includes such genealogical listings as mohel books (birth records), Kempen, 1784–1823, Lehman family papers, 1808 list of Judenshutzgelder (protection money) owed by 96 Jews of Homburg von der Hohe (Austria), Ettlinger family tree and family documents. [YIVO: /82092; LBI: DS 135.G3 A75]

The Changing Face of New York Synagogues, 1730–1974, by William Aron and Oscar Israelowitz. Includes photographs and a short history of 41 synagogues in the five boroughs of New York City. [AJHS: BM 225.N5 A4]

The German Jews of Washington Heights: An Oral History Project. [LBI: F 128.9 J5 Y4]

Mordecai Manuel Noah: The First American Jew [AJHS: E 335.Y27]

The Sephardic Journey, 1492–1992, [YIVO: /85005] includes a country-by-country listing of materials exhibited. Under each country, check the category "Life Cycles" which lists items of interest to genealogists. Each entry describes the document, place originated, year, collection from which it was borrowed and its city (or YUM and its catalog number). For example, item 101 in this catalogue reads:

"101. Ketubbah (Marriage contract)
Salonika, 1862. Ink and watercolor on paper, 19 1/4 x 13 3/8 in. Einhorn Collection, Tel Aviv.

Groom: Yeuda [sic] son of Mikhael
Bride: Miriam daughter of Mordekhai Krispin..."

Theodore Herzl: if you will it, it is not a dream. [LBI: DS 151 H4 T38 1997]

Tradition and Fantasy in Jewish Needlework includes biographical sketches of more than 60 Jewish artists whose works were exhibited. [YIVO: /85120]

Treasures of Dubrovnik. [YUM]

Copies/Fees:

See CENTER FOR JEWISH HISTORY, LILLIAN GOLDMAN MAIN READING ROOM. A complete list of YUM exhibition catalogues available for sale can be found on YUM's website.

NOTE: Admission to the Museum is $6 for adults; and $4 for seniors and students. Children under 5 and YUM members enter free. Individual membership begins at $36. Supporting members ($100) receive a 30% discount on Museum catalogues and free Sunday parking.

Restrictions on Use:

YUM's research library is primarily for staff use. Most publications are available in other libraries. However, information about the collection may be obtained by writing or e-mailing the Collection Curator. In select cases, researchers may consult materials from this collection by submitting a written request for specific information about a topic and explaining the research purpose. Allow two weeks for processing and answering inquiries.

CENTER FOR JEWISH HISTORY
YIVO INSTITUTE FOR JEWISH RESEARCH
ARCHIVES

Facility Director: Dr. Carl Rheins, Executive Director
         Fruma Mohrer, Chief Archivist

Address: Center for Jewish History   ♿
         15 West 16th Street
         New York, NY 10011

         (Cross Streets: Fifth and Sixth Avenues)

Phone: (212) 246-6080
Fax: (212) 292-1892
E-mail: yivomail@yivo.cjh.org
Website: www.yivoinstitute.org

Hours of Operation, Closest Public Transportation, Directions, Description of Facility and Fees/Copies:

See CENTER FOR JEWISH HISTORY, LILLIAN GOLDMAN MAIN READING ROOM.

Description of Resources:

YIVO, an acronym for Yidisher Visnshaftlekher Institut (Yiddish Scientific Institute), was founded in 1925 in Vilna, Poland (Vilnius, Lithuania today) and relocated its headquarters to New York in 1940, where an affiliate of YIVO was already in existence. YIVO Archives has an extensive and fascinating collection of materials relating to Eastern European Jewry. Its archival holdings include more than 22,000,000 documents, photographs, recordings, films, videotapes and artifacts in 1,700 collections of organizations and individuals. For the most part, the individuals are people who were famous and/or published authors in Eastern Europe.

Researchers, please be aware that many of these materials are in Yiddish, Hebrew, Polish and/or Russian. In addition, there are many items that are hand-written in Hebrew or Cyrillic script, some of which are illegible even to the YIVO staff. <u>Do not go to YIVO with unrealistic expectations</u>. The degree of success in utilizing YIVO's collections is directly related to a researcher's reading ability in the above languages. Although titles and descriptions of materials may be given in English, assume that most of the items are in a foreign language. Members of YIVO's staff are available to help find materials (and their assistance is invaluable), but they cannot provide translations.

A sample of the collections of importance to students of genealogy and family history follows. Record Group numbers are in brackets. For a description of additional collections cataloged, consult *Guide to the YIVO Archives*, compiled and edited by Fruma Mohrer and Marek Web:

1. <u>Landsmanshaftn (immigrant mutual aid societies)</u>:

 a. <u>The Landsmanshaftn Archive</u>: YIVO has gathered material on more than 1,000 landsmanshaftn, of which c. 500 are included in separate collections. The remainder are in file folders in the <u>Landsmanshaftn Collection</u> [RG 123]. According to *A Guide to YIVO's Landsmanshaftn Archive,* these collections may include:

  "minutes...; financial records, including membership dues books; records of special committees (relief, burial, loan fund, old age...); membership records (application lists, cards, censuses); burial records (golden books listing names, dates of death, records of interments, endowments, cemetery maps, burial permits); anniversary celebration and banquet programs, menus, journals, photographs; correspondence, meeting announcements, and bulletins; honorary certificates and citations; memorial (<u>yizkor</u>) books, publications manuscripts and materials..."

 b. <u>AJDC (American Jewish Joint Distribution Committee) Landsmanshaftn Department</u> [RG 335.7]. Many of these societies were formed in response to a particular disaster (such as a pogrom) and worked closely with the AJDC to provide disaster relief. The records are arranged by town in two series: 1937–1940 and post-1945.

 c. <u>Bund Collection - Landsmanshaftn [M-13] and Workmen's Circle Records [WC]</u>: YIVO's Bund Collection includes a small collection of landsmanshaft records [M-13] and extensive materials from various Workmen's Circle branches (by branch number) several of which were organized as landsmanshaftn. In addition, YIVO's <u>Records of the Workmen's Circle</u> [RG 575] includes more branch files as well as the Workmen's Circle Social

Services Department "dead files," 1937–1948. Records include membership cards with information on spouse and children, trade, income, rent, citizenship and date of death. Social Service Department files are arranged alphabetically. See "Restrictions on Use."

See also AMERICAN JEWISH HISTORICAL SOCIETY for additional landsmanshaftn records.

2. Holocaust:

a. French Holocaust Archives: Contains over 200,000 documents including the full records of the French Judenrat, Union Général Des Israélites de France (UGIF) [RG 210]. This collection (on microfilm) includes between 35,000 and 65,000 cards completed by members of the Jewish community in France, 1943–1944 providing name, address, date/place of birth, citizenship and occupation [Folder 22.3]; and a census of the Jews of France (Paris not included) submitted by UGIF local offices. Some localities included birth date/place, parents names, occupation, length of residence in France and address. Others included address, as well as personal and business assets [Folder 6.1/Reel 6]. Kehillat Haharedim of France (Association des Israélites Pratiquants) [RG 340], the underground Lubavitch children's rescue project records include admission forms for children to Boissy-St. Legers home [Folder 182] and child candidates for Kehillat Haharedim nurseries in France, 1945–1946 [Folder 205]. These forms included birth date/place and sometimes parents' names. For most, the word "déporté" appears instead. The collection also includes lists of deportees, survivors and a list of Jews in Dachau [Folder 241]. Rue Amelot [RG 343], another underground rescue agency records include lists of people in camps and refugees, 1943 [Folder 77]; and correspondence with internees in various camps arranged by camp. [Folders 42–80]

b. Records of Displaced Persons (DP) Camps and Centers [RG 294]: Some 300,000 pages including correspondence, minutes of meetings, leaflets and posters on Displaced Persons Camps have been placed on microfilm. The documents show how survivors of the war ran their daily affairs as they were relocated in dozens of DP camps in Germany, Austria and Italy. Lists of displaced persons and questionnaires completed in many of the camps are included. The collection includes material on those camps that were under the supervision of the American Army and agencies established by the United Nations.

c. Bund Collection - Holocaust: includes a number of original Auschwitz prisoner registration forms, c. 1943–1944 with biographical information on prisoners and their families, arranged by number [S2/87]; an Auschwitz register, "Block 8, Zu und Abgange Buch" listing prisoners by arrival date [MK 521]; list of 314 mostly Polish Jews who perished in the Holocaust and whose ashes are buried in the cemetery at Hannover-Bothfeld, Germany [S-1/75]; typed accounts (Polish) by children of their survival during the Holocaust. (Family names Akierman, Buchman, Bursztyn, Cieszynsk, Dembinsky, Halinki, Jakubowicz, Kucyk, Kutner, Mudrig, Pizyc, Sercanek, Sztockman, Wajnrajch and Was/Wons.) Some children are identified by first name only: Szymon, Wladka, Halinka, Hannah, Sabina, Bronka [S-2/4]. Includes also Jewish Labor Committee lists of Polish bundists in Shanghai (31 names) and Japan (41 names), 1941, most with birth date/place, occupation, parents' names [M-7/21]; published lists of Jewish survivors, 1945, in *La'karow v La'rahok, Reshimot Nitzalim, Register of Jewish Survivors: List of Jews Rescued in Different European Countries* (60,000 names) and *Re'Shimot Ha'Shredim Shel Yehude Polin* (arranged by town). [M-7/4 and 27]. See also Bund [JLC Box 8/25] for a booklet, *Jewish Children: Back to Life,* including summaries of some of the above child accounts in English.

d. Eyewitness Accounts of the Holocaust Period, 1939–1945 [RG 104], includes over 1,500 interviews in the language of the survivors, arranged in three series, (1) 1945–1948, primarily from informants in DP camps; (2) 1954, from YIVO-Yad Vashem Documentary Project; and (3) testimonies received by YIVO since the 1960s. Name indexes for each series (in Yiddish) are available in a card catalog. An inventory list arranged by locality is available for the first series only. See also, the Julian (Yehiel) Hirszhaut Collection [RG 720] and the Philip Friedman Collection [RG 1258]. These collections include several hundred additional eyewitness testimonies. The Hirszhaut Collection includes testimonies taken c. 1945 by Jewish historical commissions in Bialystok, Katowice, Krakow, Lublin, Lodz and Warsaw.

Other YIVO collections that include lists of survivors are Committee of Jewish Nazi Survivors' Organizations in USA [RG 1234]; Jakob Apenszlak Collection, 1939–1945 [RG 732] Polish refugees and survivors; and National Council of Bessarabian Jews, 1950–1972 [RG 1029], list of survivors from Bessarabia; HIAS and HICEM Main Office, New York, Europe [245.4.12] and Palestine [245.4.11] subseries; HIAS Transportation [245.4.20] which includes passenger lists as well as lists of survivors; HIAS Individual Cases and Lists of Immigrants [RG 245.4.21]; HICEM European Office, 1935–1953 [RG 245.5], France Series 4; and HICEM/HIAS Office in Lisbon [RG 245.6], Subseries II, Transportation Companies.

3. Immigration/Refugees:

   a.   HIAS (Hebrew Immigrant Aid Society) Collection [RG 245]: Includes records from the main office in New York as well as those of several agencies that merged or worked with HIAS over the years such as United Service for New Americans, HICEM offices in Europe (Lisbon, Paris and Prague) and the United HIAS office in Chile. HICEM was a joint agency of HIAS, the Paris/London-based ICA (Jewish Colonization Association) and the Berlin-based Emigdirect. The collection is divided into 10 series with several divided further into subseries. HIAS historical files, 1910–c.1970, containing inter-office memos and correspondence can be found here. An individual might be mentioned in a letter or memo in the correspondence files of the collection, but retrieving this information is extremely difficult and time-consuming as the material is not indexed by name. However, thousands of case files are scattered throughout the collection. Years vary for each subseries. Most are from 1945 to 1950. Some include only internal matters such as correspondence on transit payments; others have substantive genealogical information. The following include case files:

HIAS Ellis Island Bureau Records, 1905–1923 [RG 245.2]: Includes troublesome cases involving deportation, illness, or detention requiring the services of the HIAS Ellis Island Bureau. These records are arranged alphabetically by name of person being detained or about to be deported. These are the only pre-1937 case files that survived from HIAS' New York office. The inventory includes the location of groups of cases arranged by first few letters of the surname (e.g. "A to Br," "Li to NA") and indicates the reel/file numbers where they can be found. (24 microfilms). See also Records of Arrival [RG 245.4.41], AJDC War Orphans Bureau [RG 335.3] and Borenstein-Eisenberg Collection [RG 406] below, for additional pre-1937 immigrant records.

HIAS Foreign Relations Department, 1915–1973 [RG 245.3]: Includes correspondence requesting HIAS' assistance in locating individuals in behalf of relatives in the U.S.A. These letters were arranged by year and then alphabetically by the name of the individual who initiated the search. Most of the letters and signatures are in Yiddish. There is no name index. (23 microfilms)

HIAS AND HICEM Main Offices, New York, Individual Cases and Lists of Immigrants [RG 245.4.21]. Includes case folders, 1940–1942, for over 450 cases. Names are listed in the finding aid. Correspondence concerning more than one case may be together in one file. The microfilm includes a hand written page preceding each group of cases and listing the surnames included in that file. [Folders 73–84/microfilms MKM 15.60 and 15.61]

HICEM European Office, 1935–1953 [RG 245.5]. France Series III (1940–1945) and Series IV (1945–1953) subsections include individual cases processed. These are listed under "Refugee Dossiers" in the inventory. [Series III, Folders 3–65, 51 microfilms; Series IV, Folders 119–164, 10 microfilms]. Each folder is identified by the letters of the surname covered, i.e. Kla-Klee.

HICEM/HIAS Office in Lisbon [RG 245.6]. Subseries I includes Lisbon central refugee case files, arranged by the first 3 or 4 letters of the surname. [Folders 1–307, 22 microfilms]. Subseries II, Transportation Companies, includes biographical data sheets of refugees registered with HICEM (Lisbon) in 1945. [Folders 558–562]; and Departure Cards from HICEM's central card catalog for individual refugees leaving Marseille, Spain and Portugal, 1941–1944. [Folders 564/1 to 564/19; 13 microfilms]

United HIAS Service, Main Office, New York, 1954–1967 [RG 245.8]. This Office processed a substantial number of cases from 1940–1959. The actual number of cases in YIVO's collection is not known at this time. Cases are filed by year/case number and are stored in a warehouse off-site. An index to some of these files can be found in three series, all arranged by HIAS Soundex index: (1) NRS-USNA-UHS Case File Index Cards [RG 245.8.1], also known as the Holocaust Index, 1935–1953 (most are 1940s, post war). These index cards include cases handled by HIAS, National Refugee Service and United Service for New Americans. NOTE: Volunteers are working to computerized this index. (2) HIAS Records on Arrival, Master Index Cards, [RG 245.4.41], 1938–1972 (most date from 1945–1970). And, (3) Cross Reference Index, 1955–1982 (most from the 1960s and 1970s), that includes cross references to other persons mentioned on the Master Index Cards as well as Index Cards for later cases held by HIAS. See "Restrictions on Use."

NOTE: For a more detailed description of these indexes and other records still in HIAS' possession, see HIAS (HEBREW IMMIGRANT AID SOCIETY). See also Appendix A for an explanation of HIAS' Soundex index.

United HIAS Service Office in Chile, 1946–1970 [RG 245.9]. Includes individual case files arranged by agency, year and then alphabetically by the first three letters of the applicant's surname [Series 1/1–216]. Some are listed alphabetically by name in the finding aid [Series 1/217–429; Series 5/758–864]. Case files, 1957–1970, include immigrants arriving following the 1956 Hungarian uprising. The collection includes also family search case files, 1953–1971, arranged alphabetically in the finding aid by first letter of the surname of the person being sought [Series 3/568–582]; local address card files; and sponsor index cards arranged alphabetically. [Series 1/Boxes A-F; MKM 31.1]

HICEM Office in Prague, 1927–1939 [RG 245.10], a.k.a. Central Committee for German Speaking Refugees (Prague). Series III includes more than 1,800 refugee case files, 1936–1939. These cases are listed by name in the inventory list. Check both the primary list and the addendum.

Records of Arrival, 1909–1978 [RG 245.4.41]. This subseries includes Arrival Cards (71 reels), 1909–1978. The Arrival Cards include information on immigrants that were assisted by HIAS at ports of entry all over the U.S.A. They are arranged by year of arrival, port of entry, then alphabetically by surname. See HIAS (HEBREW IMMIGRANT AID SOCIETY) for a detailed description of these cards and for Arrival Cards, 1979–1985.

b. AJDC (American Jewish Joint Distribution Committee) Personal Service Department (formerly the Transmigration Bureau), 1946–1957 [RG 335.6], immigrant case files, 1946–1952. This collection includes 1,770 folders containing groups of case files, in four series. Three are arranged alphabetically and the fourth by country. See also AMERICAN JEWISH JOINT DISTRIBUTION COMMITTEE and LEO BAECK INSTITUTE for additional AJDC case files.

c. AJDC War Orphans Bureau [RG 335.3], includes 389 case files of Jewish orphans brought to NYC, 1919–1923, for whom foster families were found [Files 1–40]; and case files of children relocated to communities in Illinois, Massachusetts, New Jersey, Pennsylvania and other locations in the U.S.A. There are two indexes to New York City case files (by child's name and by foster parent's name). Both include name/address of foster parent, child's name, former city of residence in Europe and case number [File 207]. In addition, there are Disposition Reports from Warsaw [Files 41–44; with photographs] and Bucharest [Files 48/49] for children transported from these areas; and geographic lists (district/shtetl) of orphans providing child's name, age, former residence, whether parents alive, and if not, cause/year of death. Extensive lists are available for the districts of Lemberg (Lviv), Rowno, Brest-Litovsk, Bialystok. A third set of index cards included in this collection, arranged by child's surname, provides case number and a brief description of the child's family situation [File 206]. NOTE: "Orphans" include also children with one living parent. See "Restrictions on Use."

d. USNA (United Service for New Americans), 1946–1954 [RG 246.4]. Includes 8,000 case files. In 1954, USNA merged with HIAS to form the Untied HIAS Service. These case files are located off-site and are arranged by case number.

e. National Refugee Service, 1938–1946 [RG 248]: Includes lists, correspondence and some case files of refugee internees at various camps, prospective immigrants from various countries, and detentions and deportations from the U.S.A. Lists of refugee children include those inducted into the armed forces (c. 100 names) with date of arrival in the U.S.A., age at admission, present age, draft date, citizenship, and information on the whereabouts of parents [File 536]; list of immigrant children from England, 1939, includes date/ship of arrival in the U.S.A. and parents names [File 608]; lists of prospective immigrants include sponsors' names [File 610]. Individual forms with biographical information completed by some immigrants are arranged in folders by first letter of surname. [Files 602–606]

f. German Jewish Children's Aid, 1933–1953 (later known as European Jewish Children's Aid) [RG 249]: The GJCA was established in 1934 by a coalition of the New York Foundation, the Baron de Hirsch Fund, Bnai Brith, the Hofmeimer Foundation, the American Jewish Committee and the Women's Committee of the American Jewish Congress to receive and place refugee children. The collection includes individual case files of children in Europe waiting to emigrate, 1939–1951 [Series 3 & 8]; cases of children settled in the U.S.A., 1946–1951 [Series 4 & 10]; certificates of identity issued by the U.S. Consulate and the Quakers to children in Europe, 1941–1948 [Series 7]. Administrative files, arranged by country, include materials, such as: children's applications with photographs (Holland), 1940–1941 [Series 1/73]; list of German and Austrian children in the South of France, 1941 [Series 1/318]; and biographies of children in the U.S.A. with relatives in Europe, 1946. [Series 1/261]. Series 5 includes reports written by adult escorts of groups of children arriving in the U.S.A. These are arranged by date and name of arriving ship.

g. Jewish Labor Committee [RG 1400, Bund Collection/JLC]: Questionnaires completed in 1962 by Jews who emigrated to the U.S.A. after WWII include age, country of birth, marital status, year of arrival in the U.S.A., places of residence between 1939 and arrival, occupation, income, age of children, and citizenship status. [JLC /36]. Includes also eight case histories of children awaiting assistance (Spielman, Talkman, Gottlieb, Tannenbaum, Solnik, Sztern, Teper, Sztark); and JLC publication, *Jewish Children: Back to Life.* [JLC/25–26]

h. Borenstein-Eisenberg Collection on Early Jewish Migration [RG 406] has several passenger lists from the 1880s and early 1890s, including a list of 315 emigrants to New York, dated Koenigsberg, March 30, 1870 [1/9–14]; lists of Russian Jews who arrived in Algeria, Cairo, Constantinople, Marseilles, etc, c. 1882 [17/524–531]; passenger lists, testimonies from passengers, 1881–1882 [19/552–566]; lists of departed from Brody, 1881 [44/1691–1778]; lists of refugees leaving Hamburg, November 2 and 8, 1881 [48/1774–1797]; lists of emigrants traveling through National Steam Ship Company of Antwerp, 1881 [49/1798–1832]; lists of victims of the Zhitomer pogrom of April 23, 1905 [103/4970–4975]; and list of 46 immigrants who settled in Galveston with the help of the Jewish Emigration Association of Kiev, Jan/Feb 1911. [117/5436]

4. Biographical/Autobiographical Collections:

a   Biographies of Bundists and Labor Leaders [RG 1400]: The Bund collection includes over 600 biographies of Bundists around the world who are not included in *Doires Bundistes* (see YIVO LIBRARY); and questionnaires (in Yiddish) completed by Bundists c.1955 and 1968. The c.1955 questionnaire included birth date/place, occupation, education, parents' names, parents' occupations. Some have photographs. Folders are by arranged by first letter of surname. The latter questionnaire included year of arrival; former home town, occupation, whether a union, workmen's circle or landsmanshaft member; names of family members and their addresses. [MG-2/429A]. The Bund collection also includes biographical information on over 300 American [M-2] and 375 European [M-6, M-16, M-18] labor leaders; and many United Hebrew Trades and labor union activists [UHT/120A-145]. These are mostly fragile newspaper clippings.

b. Collection of Autobiographies [RG 102]: Includes 350 autobiographies (mostly in Yiddish) prepared by immigrants to America in response to a YIVO-sponsored contest in 1942. The contestants describe why they left Europe and what they accomplished in America. Family backgrounds are included.

c. Autobiographies of Jewish Youth in Poland, 1932–1939 [RG 4]. Includes over 380 written autobiographies (not interviews) each at least 25 pages, submitted to YIVO in Vilna as entries to three YIVO contests (1932, 1934, 1939). Covers recollections of years during WWI and the interwar period. The contestants included Jewish men and women between the ages of 16–22. Most were living in Poland or Lithuania. Some submissions include diaries. The finding aid includes a name index. The collection is arranged by number (not name) although each file includes a penciled slip of paper with the name of the contestant. (Yiddish, German).

d. Memoirs of American Jewish Soldiers, 1945–1946 [RG 110] Includes 52 essays submitted by contestants who wrote on the theme, "My Experiences and Observations as a Jew and Soldier in World War II."

e. Leksikon fun der Nayer Yidisher Literatur [RG 1150]. Includes correspondence, photographs and autobiographies submitted by Jewish writers from around the world to the Lexicon editors c. 1955. This collection includes also autobiographies and photographs which were not accepted for publication. See also YIVO's Bund Collection - Congress for Jewish Culture [Files 42A–47A] which includes additional autobiographies and photographs received by the Congress for this 8-volume reference work. (Yiddish). YIVO's Vilno Collection on Yiddish Writers [RG 3] includes similar material on writers active in Europe between 1900–1939. This latter collection includes c. 1,600 autobiographies, as well as photographs and correspondence (72 boxes) submitted by these writers to Zalman Reisin. Reisin was the editor of *Leksikon fun der Yidisher Literatur un Prese,* published in Warsaw, 1914.

f. Oral History Collection on the Labor Movement, 1964–1968 [RG 113]. Includes 43 transcripts of taped interviews with labor leaders and activists from the early years of the labor movement in the United States. (Yiddish, English). These include Belson, Berezer, Chait, Deutchman, Dubno, Farbman, Fenster, Feuer, Gutterman, Haskel, Held, Hendel, Halpern, Hershkovitz, Gershin, Gittelson, Glass, Goldman, Katzer, Krindler, Lilienblum, Lipsky, Margolin, Mendelowitz, Meyer, Nelson, Newman, Rabinowitz, Rubin, Rugoff, Shapiro, Shatin, Sher, Scherer, Schlesinger, Schveid, Schwartz, Shapiro, Shoenholtz, Walinsky, Weiss, Wisotzky, Wolff, Zimmerman, Zirlin.

5. Community Records including vital records can be found in the following collections:

a. Jewish Community Council of Minsk, 1825–1921 [RG 12]: This collection contains fragmentary registers of births, marriages, and deaths. The records are hand-written in Cyrillic.

b. Lithuanian Jewish Communities, 1844–1940 [RG 2]: These are mainly community records, 1921–1926, such as minutes of council meetings about tax collections or elections in those towns that were part of the independent Republic of Lithuania. Most of the material in the collection was generated by the Ministry of Jewish Affairs and is in Yiddish or Lithuanian. A total of 89 folders are listed in the finding aid as having vital records although some include only statistical summaries. A more detailed finding aid is being developed. The following communities are listed: Alanta, Alytus, Anyksciai, Ariogala, Baisogala, Balberiskis, Barstyciai, Birzai, Darsuniskis, Dotnuva, Dusetos, Eisiskes, Gargzdai, Garliava, Jonava, Joniskelis, Jurbarkas, Kaisiadorys, Kalvarija, Kaunas, Kedainiai, Kelme, Klikoliai, Krakes, Kraziai, Krekenava, Kretinga, Kuliai, Kupiskis, Kursenai, Kybartai, Laizuva, Lazdijai, Leipalingis, Liubavas, Marijampole, Mazeikiai, Nemunelio Radviliskis, Obeliai, Onuskis, Pagiriai, Pandelys, Panemunis, Panevezys, Pasvalys, Pasvitinys, Pikeliai, Pilviskiai, Plunge, Prienai, Pumpenai, Radviliskis, Raguva, Ramygala, Raseiniai, Rokiskis, Rudamina, Rumsiskes, Salociai, Saukenai, Seda, Seduva, Seirijai, Seredzius, Siaulenai, Siauliai, Siesikai, Siluva, Skapiskis, Skaudvile, Skiemonys, Skuodas, Sudargas, Surviliskis, Suvainiskis, Svedasai, Taujenai, Taurage, Telsiai, Troskunai, Ukmerge, Utena, Uzpaliai, Vabalninkas, Varena, Varniai, Vasiliski (in Belarus), Vaskai, Vegeriai, Veisiejai, Veivirzenai, Veliuona, Vieksniai, Vilkaviskis, Vilkija, Virbalis, Vyzuonos, Ylakiai, Zagare, Zapyskis, Zarasai, Zasliai, Zeimelis, Zidikai.

c. Jewish Community Council of Ostrowo, 1834–1919 [RG 13], Krotoschin. 1828–1919 [RG 14], and Briesen, 1871–1926 [RG 15]. The Ostrowo files include lists of eligible voters, lists of community members showing profession and citizenship status; copies of some birth records, 1847–1874 [File 38]; and records of Jewish weddings, 1836–1844 [File 123]. The Krotoschin collection includes a tax list, 1835 [File 1]; and fragmentary information on marriages [File 17] and deaths [File 24]. The Briesen files include many tax lists; burials, 1890–1893; lists of synagogue seat owners and applications for position of Rabbi and cantor.

d. Personenstandarchiv Koblenz [RG 242]: Jewish vital records were confiscated by this branch of the Nazi Reichssippenamt (Reich Racial Office) in the 1930s and 1940s and used to determine the pedigree of individuals. In 1950/51, Gregor Raskin, a YIVO representative in Germany, made photocopies. Examples include:

Ashenshausen (Thuringen): register of Jewish graves, 1710–1880 (145 graves).
Berlin, Germany: register of orphans cared for by the Orphans' committee of the Berlin Jewish Community. Lists birth dates, parents' names, guardians, schooling, date of acceptance and release. Index, 1861–1872.
Brandenburg (city): death records, 1758–1860; birth records, 1794–1825; marriages attestations, 1840–1844.
Coswig: death records, 1801–1875; births, 1803–1865.
Danzig: list of Jews made citizens and new family names, 1814 (605 names).
Erfurt (Prussian Saxony): Jewish marriage register, 1847–1869, birth register, 1847–1869, death register, 1863–1865, list of graves, 1818–1891 and cemetery register, 1878–1907.
Frankfurt an der Oder: cemetery register, 1677–1866; death register, 1814–1876.
Waldenburg (Silesia): list of burials, 1934–1938, marriages, 1934–1937, pidyon haben, 1937, divorces, 1938.

Other communities with materials in this collection include: Altmark, Aschersleben, Bergstadt, Berkach, Berlinchen, Bernburg, Bernstein, Bleicherod, Brieg, Crossen an der Oder, Dessau, Dreissigacker, Egelin, Eisleben, Ellrich, Festenberg, Flatow, Frauenburg, Freinwalde, Freystadt, Gardelegren, Garnsee, Groeningen, Gross(en) Muehlingen, Guttentag, Halle an der Saale, Harzgerode, Hundsfeld, Jastrow, Jawor (Jauer), Poland, Katowitz, Koethen, Krappitz, Krojanke, (Bad) Landeck, Lauenburg, Liebenwalde, Loewen, Luckenwalde, Magdeburg, Maerkisch Friedland, Mecklenburg-Schwerin, Muehlhausen, Nackel, Neumittelwalde, Neustadt, Neustettin (Pomerania); Nysa, Poland (Neisse), Oels, Offenbach, Ohlau, Oppeln, Potsdam, Reichenbach, Sagan, Satulung, Romania, Schloppe, Schweidnitz, Sprottau, Stargard, Tempelburg, Trebbin, West Prussia, Wolczyn, Poland (Konstadt), Wronke, Wschowa, Poland (Fraustadt), Zerbst.

e. Simon Dubnow Collections. 1632–1938 [RG 87]. This collections includes originals and copies of Jewish community registers (pinkasim) and other historical documents from Birzai, 1755–1796; Bobowno, 1829; Dubno, 1670–1671; Lublin, 18th century; Miedzyrzec, 1816; Mstislavl, 1760–1895; Novaya Ushitsa, 1839–1840; Pinczow, 1632–1740; Piotrowice, 1726–1809; Stary Bykhow, 1686–1869; Tykocin, 1769–1777; Zabludow, 1650–1783. Includes materials on pogroms in Kishinev (1903), Gomel (1903), Bialystok (1906).

f. Tcherikower Archive [RG 80]: Contains miscellaneous records on Jewish life in the Ukraine; includes lists of victims of Ukrainian pogroms, 1919–1921; and eyewitness accounts by locality. Thorough knowledge of Yiddish and Russian script is required to use this collection.

6 Labor Movement:

a. Bund Archives of the Jewish Labor Movement [RG 1404]: In 1992, this Archive were accessioned and became a branch of YIVO's Archives. The Jewish Labor Bund began as an underground political movement in Tsarist Russia in 1897. Two years later, the Bund Archives was established in Switzerland. It specialized in materials relating to the history of the Jewish labor and socialist movements, particularly in Eastern Europe and the Americas. For the genealogist whose relatives were active in the labor movement, this collection offers a wealth of biographical and historical material. The Archives' socialist and labor holdings (1,247 linear feet) date from the 1870s to 1992. The collection includes rare manuscripts, letters, minutes, newspaper clippings, books, pamphlets, photographs and personal documents. A large percentage of the collection is unique and not available elsewhere. In addition to materials on the Bund itself, the collection includes important materials on Russian Social-Democrats, the Socialist Revolutionary Party (SR), Poalei Zionists, Anarchists, Jewish Communists, Trade Unions and Polish Parties.

7. School Records:

   a. Records of Vaad Hayeshivot [RG 25]: This was an office in Vilna, Lithuania that arranged for financial support of 70 yeshivot and their students throughout Lithuania. It had contact with about 350 towns that sent students to the yeshivot. The correspondence, written in Yiddish script, is mainly from the 1920s and 1930s.

   b. Hebrew Technical Institute [RG 754]: Includes detailed alumni career records of the oldest vocational school for Jewish boys in New York City. The career of each individual student was recorded as he moved from position to position. Records include annual reports and catalogs (9 vols.); alumni career records, class years, 1886–1939 (13 vols.); class standing records, 1884–1939 (34 vols.); and roll books, mainly 1896–1939 (27 vols).

8. Photo Collections:

   YIVO's photograph collections document people and places around the world. See "Restrictions on Use." Major photograph collections include:

   a. Territorial Photographic Collection, 1860s –1970s [RG 120] Includes photographs of Jewish life in 65 countries around the world including street scenes, synagogues, members of organizations, community leaders, and much more. About one-half the collection is "Poland," defined as those areas that were politically part of Poland between 1919 and 1939. Russia and the United States are also well represented. The bulk of the Polish collection and parts of the Russian, Lithuanian, Estonian, and Latvian photographs are cataloged and available on videodisc. Those taken during the Holocaust are indexed in a computerized database. For other related photographs, see, Displaced Persons Camps and Centers: Photographs [RG 294.5], includes 70 DP Camps in Austria, Germany and Italy.

   b. Photographs of Personalities, 1880s–1970s [RG 121], includes writers, scholars, historians, scientists, philosophers, community and political leaders, rabbis, musicians and cantors; Photographs from the Vilna Archives, 1910s–1930s [RG 9], includes photographs of personalities, blood-libel trials, pogroms; Yiddish Theatre Photographs, 1910–1960s [RG 119] includes actors, directors and producers. Solomon Shmuelewitz-Small, 1920s–1930s [RG 214] and Benedict Stambler Collection [RG 1014] include photographs of cantors.

9. Collection on Genealogy and Family History: The Archives has an extensive collection of genealogies and family histories from all over the world deposited here by genealogists or other family descendants. A computerized catalog is being prepared and will be available online. The existing card catalog includes, where available, the town, country or time period covered by the collection.

10. Other Collections:

   a. National Desertion Bureau [RG 297]: This New York-based organization assisted Jewish families in which a parent had deserted, by attempting to locate the parent. The collection covers roughly 25,000 families from the 1920s to the 1950s. See "Restrictions on Use."

   b. Monika Krajewska Photo Collection [RG 1137]: Exhibit prints and contact sheets of photos, 1974–1986, taken in preparation for Monika Krajewska's book on Polish cemeteries, Czas Kamieni [A Tribe of Stones], Warsaw, 1982 (published also in English, 1993 and available in YIVO LIBRARY [/80867 and /85625]). The collection includes photos of tombstones in almost 100 cemeteries; an article about the Jewish cemetery in Sieniawa written in September 1982 (Polish); and information and photographs of some synagogues.

Finding Aids:

General Archival Collections: The 448-page Guide to the YIVO Archives, compiled by Fruma Mohrer and Marek Web includes summaries of each collection cataloged through RG 1300. The Guide is arranged alphabetically by collection name but includes a subject index. For collections cataloged since the publication of the Guide, check the RG Description Sheets. These are contained in black loose-leaf binders at the Reference Desk. The sheets are arranged by

RG number. They contain information about each collection and usually indicate whether it has been inventoried. For select collections, the Archives has more detailed Inventories also located at the Reference Desk. Work is underway to include these folder-by-folder descriptions of the collections in the online catalog. Several hundred of the more than 1,500 collections have such inventories. Additional inventories can be found in archival boxes at the Reference Desk. Finally, the Archives has name indexes to several collections on index cards.

NOTE: YIVO is always acquiring new collections. Check with the Archivist for uncataloged material.

1. The Landsmanshaftn Archive: YIVO has a published volume, *A Guide to YIVO's Landsmanshaftn Archive,* to assist in locating these records. The *Guide* is arranged alphabetically by place name for locality-based societies and alphabetically by society name for non-locality-based societies (mutual aid societies based on occupation, family circles and synagogue benevolent societies). For additional materials received prior to 1998, see the *Guide to the YIVO Archives.* NOTE: YIVO's list of cataloged landsmanshaftn can be found on the Internet at www.jgsny.org. The inventory folder for Landsmanshaftn Collection [RG 123], also includes pages for the Bund landsmanshaftn collection as well as lists of additional landsmanshaftn records received by YIVO but not yet cataloged. The inventory to AJDC Landsmanshaftn Department Records [RG 335.7] is arranged by locality in two series: 1937–1940 and post-1945.

2. Holocaust: A detailed inventory is available for Union Général Des Israélites de France [RG 200], providing descriptions of each folder and its location on microfilm by reel/frame number. Resident card files are arranged by first letter of the surname and census of Jews by town name. Detailed inventories are also available for Kehiles Haharedim of France [RG 340] and Rue Amelot [RG 343].

Displaced Persons Camps and Centers [RG 294] In order to find an individual, the researcher must know the name or location of the camp where the individual lived after the war. The collection is subdivided by country in which the DP camps were located: Austria [RG 294.4]; Germany [RG 294.2]; and Italy [RG 294.3]. The inventory reflects the administrative departments of the camp organizations. Materials in the finding aid can easily be found using the folder/reel/frame numbers.

Bund Collection - Holocaust [RG 1400/S] Check the S1/S2 folder in the Bund inventory box. The S1/S2 materials are Holocaust related. Additional materials on the Holocaust can be found throughout the Bund collection.

There are name indexes to the Eyewitness Accounts of the Holocaust Period [RG 104] in Card Catalog drawers YA 31–33 (Series 1–3). All are in Yiddish. The inventory for Series 1 is arranged also by locality. A separate name index is available for the Julian (Yehiel) Hirszhaut [RG 720] collection in drawer YA 34. The inventory for the Philip Friedman Collection [RG 1258] includes a list of people who gave testimony [File 831] and a list by locality and then surname. [Files 840–871]

3. Immigration/Refugees:

HIAS Collection: There are detailed inventories for most series in this collection. See descriptions above for specific collections with case files. See also HIAS (HEBREW IMMIGRANT AID SOCIETY), LOCATION AND ARRIVAL RECORDS DEPARTMENT. An explanation of the HIAS Case Name Indexing (Soundex) system is included in Appendix A. A series of computerized finding aids have been created and are being placed online; and *A Guide to the HIAS Archives at YIVO* will be available shortly.

AJDC War Orphans Bureau [RG 335.3]. There are two name indexes for this collection - one by name of orphan [File 206] and an alphabetical list of foster parents.

National Refugee Service Collection, 1938–1946 [RG 248]: The inventory for this collection includes folder and reel number but no frame numbers, making records on microfilm more difficult to find. Biographical questionnaires in Folders 602–606 are arranged by first letter of the surname. Bund Collection - Jewish labor Committee [RG 1400/JLC] inventory list can be found in the Bund box, "American" file. There is a detailed inventory list showing the contents of each folder for the Borenstein-Eisenberg Collection. [RG 406]

4. Biographies/Autobiographies:

Biographies of Bundists and labor leaders [RG 1400]: The relevant inventories for Bund related materials can be found in the "M" and "ME" folders of the Bund inventory box at the Reference Desk. The inventories for Bund biographies, ME-16, ME-17 and ME-40, include surname lists. These are arranged alphabetically by the Hebrew alphabet although the finding aid is written in Roman characters; surnames in folders for American and European biographies can be found in the "M" inventory list. Congress for Jewish Culture inventory can be found in the "American" organizations folder. Surnames in this finding aid are arranged as those in the "ME" inventory.

There is a card index arranged by surname for the Collection of Autobiographies [RG 102] located in file drawer YA 67 of the Card Catalog. There is no surname index to the Memoirs of American Jewish Soldiers [RG 110]. The surname index to Autobiographies of Jewish Youth in Poland [RG 4] is in Yiddish and can be found in the inventory of the Vilna Archives after the listing for folder 3887. See above for surnames in the Oral History Collection of the Labor Movement. [RG 113]

The inventory list for the Leksikon fun der Nayer Yidisher Literature [RG 1150] includes an alphabetical index; the inventory for the Vilna Collection on Yiddish Writers [RG 3] is arranged by surname of the writer.

5. Community Records:

Jewish Community Council of Minsk [RG 12]: For Minsk records, there is a written inventory (in Yiddish), arranged chronologically. Lithuanian Jewish Communities [RG 2] inventory is arranged alphabetically by name of town. Jewish Communities of Ostrowo [RG 13], Krotoschin [RG 14] and Briesen: [RG 15] and Personenstandarchive Koblenz [RG 242] inventories described the contents of each file.

Tcherikower Archive (RG 80): The inventory is handwritten in Yiddish and sometimes Russian script. Simon Dubrow Collection [RG 87] inventory can be found on pages 155–252 [Files 913–1043] of the Tcherikower Archive finding aid.

6. School Records:

Records of Vaad Hayeshivot [RG 25]: This inventory is arranged by town.

Hebrew Technical Institute: There is an inventory which specifies the nature of the files and reflects the organizational structure of the school. There is no name index.

7. Photograph Collections: Pre-World War II photographs on videodisc are indexed by town name and subject. These can be viewed on CJH computers (3rd floor) and online (http://yivo1000towns.cjh.org). For photographs taken during the Holocaust period and for those that were part of the Yiddish Theatre collection, there is a computerized keyword index. Photographs of Personalities are arranged alphabetically. Card indexes of personalities exist for several other photograph collections.

8. Collection on Genealogy and Family History: An index card file is available. A sample of the entries are listed above under "Description of Resources." A computerized index is planned.

9. Other:

National Desertion Bureau: YIVO has an alphabetical card index for these records.

Monika Krajewska Photo Collection: Not indexed. Cemetery location is noted on the back of each photograph.

Fees/Copies:

Photocopies are $.25 per page (researcher on premises); $.35 (mail orders) and $.35 from microfilm. Add an additional $10 service charge for shipping and handling in the U.S. and $13 to foreign countries. Extended research (limited availability) is $25 per hour plus $.35 per photocopy (maximum 50 copies in Archives/150 copies in Library). YIVO will make copies of photographs at $35 per photo (5"x 7" or 8"x 10"). There is an additional usage fee for commercial publication or reproduction of each original ranging from $30 to $125 per photo. Requests for permission to reproduce materials for publication should be made in writing to the Archives/Library. See YIVO Services Price List for more information. *Guide to the YIVO Archives*, compiled by Fruma Mohrer and Marek Web is available for sale ($100).

Restrictions on Use:

Photograph Collections: An advance appointment is necessary to view photograph collections other than those on videodisc. Contact the Photo Archivist at (212) 246-6080 to make an appointment.

National Desertion Bureau records are for scholars who use them for random statistical purposes. Access to these files for other purposes can only be obtained through the donor, the Jewish Board of Family and Children's Services.

HIAS Collection: Most case files are off site and cannot be accessed easily. Permission to view the HIAS case files must be obtained from the YIVO Archivist or from HIAS.

Monika Krajewska Photo Collection: Photos can be reproduced but credits have to be given by anyone who plans to use them as source material in his/her own research.

Other: There may be some restrictions on materials permitted to be photocopied. Check with the Archivist.

CENTER FOR JEWISH HISTORY
YIVO INSTITUTE FOR JEWISH RESEARCH
LIBRARY

Facility Director:	Aviva Astrinsky, Head Librarian
Address:	15 West 16th Street ♿ New York, NY 10011-6301
	(Cross Streets: Fifth and Sixth Avenues)
Phone:	(212) 246-6080
Fax:	(212) 292-1892
E-mail:	yivomail@yivo.cjh.org
Website:	www.yivoinstitute.org

Hours of Operation, Closest Public Transportation, Directions, Description of Facility, Fees/Copies and Restrictions on Use: See CENTER FOR JEWISH HISTORY, LILLIAN GOLDMAN MAIN READING ROOM.

Description of Resources:

YIVO Library houses over 350,000 books and periodicals. These include the Vilna Collection of 40,000 volumes and 25,000 rabbinical works, some dating from the early 16th century. For the genealogical researcher, the following materials are of particular interest (call numbers are in brackets):

1. <u>Memorial or Yizkor Books</u>: YIVO has one of the most extensive collections in the world of memorial books. Included are both the better-known yizkor books commemorating communities destroyed by the Nazis and the lesser-known books written after World War I about towns desecrated by pogroms. Call numbers for YIVO's yizkor books (post-WWII) are included in Appendix B. Most yizkor books are in Hebrew and/or Yiddish. Some contain small sections in English. About 80% of the books do not have indexes.

2. <u>Geographical material</u>: YIVO has many items that will help locate small towns, verify the spelling of their names, and give descriptions of the towns or the areas in which they are located. In addition to old maps and atlases from the period between the two World Wars, the Library has:

   100 evreiskikh mestechek Ukrainy: istoricheskii putevoditel, Podoliia [Historical Guide: 100 Shtetls of Ukraine, vol. 1 and 2, Jewish communities of Podoliya], edited by Viktor M. Lukin and Boris N. Khaimovich. Vol. 1 includes detailed essays on the communities of Medzhibozh, Zinkov, Proskurov, Satanov, Letichev and Derazhnya; and shorter entries on Gorodok, Kuzmin, Kupin, Mikhalpol, Nikolayev, Staraya Sinyava, Tarnoruda, Felshtin, Chornyi Ostrov, Sharovka and Yarmolintsky. Vol. 2 includes Bershad, Bratslav, Chernivtsy, Chechelnik, Myastkovka, Peschanka, Shargorod, Shipikov, Tomashpol, Trostyanets, Tulchin and Yampol and brief essays on 16 smaller communities. Jerusalem and St. Petersburg, 1997–2000. [/90828]

   The Encyclopedia of Jewish life before and during the Holocaust, edited by Shmuel Spector and Geoffrey Wigoder. 3 vols. New York, 2001. Translates into English and condenses information describing Jewish life of c. 6,500 communities included in *Pinkas ha-kehilot* (see below). [DS 135.E8 E45 2001]

   Entsiklopedyah shel galuyot: sifre zikaron le-artsot ha-golah ve'edoteha [Encyclopedia of the Jewish Diaspora]. Vol. 1, Warsaw (1952); vol. 2, Brest-Litovsk (1955); vol. 3, Tarnopol (1955); vol. 4, Lvov (1956); vol 5, Lublin (1957); vol. 6, Warsaw 2 (1959); vol. 7, Carpatho-Ruthenia (1959); vol. 8, Sokolka (1968); vol. 9, Grodno; vol. 10, Bulgaria (1967); vol. 11, Bessarabia (1971); vol. 12 Warsaw 3 (1973). Jerusalem, 1952–1973. Also Suchowola (1957), Bursztyn (1960) and Ozeryany (1959). [DS 135.E7 E55]

   Evreiskaia entsiklopediia [Jewish Encyclopedia], 16 vols. St. Petersburg, 1906–1913. (Russian). Contains entries about cities and many small towns in Russia. [DS 102.8.E7 1906]

   Pinkas ha-kehilot [Encyclopedia of Jewish communities]. 1969–. (Hebrew). Includes the following volumes: Romania (2 vols.), Germany (Bavaria), Germany (Wuerttemberg, Hohenzollern, Baden), Germany (Hesse, Hesse-Nassau, Frankfurt), Hungary, Poland (Lodz region), Poland (Eastern Galicia), Poland (Western Galicia), Poland (Warsaw), Poland (Volhynia and Polesie), Poland (Poznan, Pomerania, Gdansk), Poland (Lublin, Kielce), the Netherlands, Yugoslavia, Latvia and Estonia, Lithuania, Libya-Tunisia, Greece. [DS 135.E81...] (See Yizkor Book list, Appendix B).

   Placenames of Russia and the former Soviet Union: origin and meanings of the names for over 2,000 natural features, towns, regions and countries, by Adrian Room, Jefferson, NC, [1996]. [DK 15.R66 1996]

Slownik geograficzny Krolestwa Polskiego i innych krajow slowianskich [Polish Gazetteer]. Warsaw, 1880–1902 (Polish). Reprint 1975–1977. A 16-volume gazetteer that provides the name of the town, its population, the district it belongs to, and more. [DK 403.S5 1975]

Yahadut Lita [Lithuanian Jewry]. 4 vols., 1959–1984. (Hebrew). Volume 3 includes community descriptions and, in some cases, photographs. Includes also almost 600 biographical entries. [DS 135.L5 Y3]. **Indexed in *Latter Day Leaders...* See below.

3. Rabbinic Resources: These sources may be used both to trace rabbinic ancestors and to gather information about the religious heritage of the towns ancestors were from. In addition to biographies of individual rabbis and their descendants, the Library has:

Anshe ha-shem be-Artsot ha-berit [Encyclopedia containing biographical sketches of rabbis, scholars, writers and other eminent figures in American Jewry], by Benzion Eisenstadt. St. Louis, 1933. [/5781], [E 184.J5 E3]

Atlas eytz chayim, by Raphael Halperin. Vols. 1–2, 5–14. Bio-bibliographical encyclopedia of rabbis. [Israel], 1978–1987. [BM 750.H3]

Conservative Judaism in America: A Biographical Dictionary and Sourcebook, edited by Pamela S. Nadell. New York, 1988. [BM 750.N33 1988]

Dorot ha-aharonim [Recent Generations], by Benzion Eisenstadt. 3 vols. New York, [1913–1915]. Biographies arranged by first name. [14/17818], [DS 125.3.A2 E5]; and [1936/37–1940/41], [DS 115.E36 1936]. **Indexed in *Latter Day Leaders...* See below.

Dor rabanav ve-sofrav [Generations of Rabbis and Authors], by Benzion Eisenstadt. Warsaw, [1895–1903]. [14/17818], [DS 125.3.A2 E4]

Eleh ezkerah: osef toldot kedoshe 700–735 [These will I remember: biographies of leaders of religious Jewry in Europe who perished in the years 1939–1945], edited by Dr. Isaac Lewin. 7 vols. (Hebrew). Arranged by first name of rabbi in each volume. New York, 1956–. [DS 125.F8 E645 1956], [4/48359]. **Indexed in *Latter Day Leaders...* See below.

Entsiklopedyah le-toldot gedole Yisrael [Encyclopedia of great men in Israel], edited by Mordecai Margulies. Tel Aviv, 1946–1950 (Hebrew). Includes rabbinic personalities from the 9th to the end of the 18th century. [DS 115.E5 1946]

ha-Hasidut, by Yitshak Alfasi. Tel Aviv, [1974]. (Hebrew). Contains information on Hasidic rabbis from the Ba'al Shem Tov to the present and has an index of towns and an index of rabbis (by first names). [BM 198.A5]

Hakhme Yisrael ba-Amerikah [Israel's Scholars in America], by Benzion Eisenstadt. Includes American rabbis, authors and artists with photographs. [14/17818] [E 184.J5 E33]. **Indexed in *Latter Day Leaders...* See below.

Latter Day Leaders, Sages and Scholars born between late 18th and early 20th century, compiled by Emanuel Rosenstein and Neil Rosenstein. (English) Includes over 5,500 entries from all over the world arranged by groups of countries. Indexes ten rabbinic dictionaries (**) by surname, first name and town and includes volume and page number of these reference works. Elizabeth, 1983. [BM 750.L3 1983]

Le-toldot Yisrael ba-Amerikah, by Benzion Eisenstadt. New York, 1917. [/202613]

Meore Galitsyah: *entsiklopedyah le-hokhame Galitsyah* [Encyclopedia of Galician Rabbis and Scholars], by Rabbi Meir Wunder. 5 vols. Jerusalem, 1978–1997. (Hebrew). Includes biographical sketches of rabbis and sometimes their family trees. Arranged by surname in Hebrew. [BM 750.W8]

Otsar ha-rabanim [Rabbis' Encyclopedia: Rabbinate Era from 970 to 1970], by Nathan Zebi Friedmann. [Bnei Brak, 1975]. (Hebrew). Includes for c. 20,000 rabbis, year of birth or death, father's name, sons and sons-in-law, other biographical information and a list of the rabbi's works. Arranged alphabetically by first name. [BM 750.F7]

Reform Judaism in America: A Biographical Dictionary and Sourcebook, edited by Kerry M. Olitzky, Lance J. Sussman and Rabbi Malcolm H. Stern. Westport, CT, 1993. [BM 750.R39 1993]

Sefer Ohole-shem by Shemuel N. Gotlib. Pinsk, 1912. (Hebrew). Biographical sketches of 1,500 rabbis in Eastern Europe, Asia, Africa, Australia and the United States in 1912. Frequently includes ancestry. Arranged by locality. Indexed by first name. [BM 750.G6]

Sefer melitse esh: ...kolel toldot tahalukhot ve-kurot haye gedole Yisrael, by Abraham Stern. 3 vols. New York, [1962]. (Hebrew). Detailed biographical sketches arranged by yahrzeit date. There is a Hebrew name index to these c. 2,000 entries arranged by first name. [BM 750.S7]

Shevet mi-Yehudah: nerot-neshamah li-yeme zikaron ule-et-sefod li-shelume-emune-Yisrael mi-dor-dor, by Yisrael Erlikh. Lists of rabbis arranged by yahrzeit date and year. Includes also kinnui (nickname), father's name, locality where served and book authored; surname index and an extensive bibliography of rabbinical sources. Tel Aviv, 1997. [BM 750.E744 1997]

Toldot Anshe Shem, Part I, by Oscar Rand. Includes biographical sketches and photographs of European rabbis who came to the U.S.A. Surname index in English and Hebrew. New York, 1950. [BM 750.R3]

4.. <u>Holocaust and Related Resources</u>: YIVO's library contains an important collection of materials relating to the Holocaust in addition to the yizkor books noted above. These include:

Accession List of the Bulletin, "To Those Near and Far," compiled by Jewish Agency in Palestine, Search Bureau for Missing Relatives. Includes an inventory of lists, date of printing and number of survivors listed. Jerusalem, 1945. [3/22777]

Blackbook of Localities whose Jewish population was exterminated by the Nazis. [Jerusalem], 1965. Published by Yad Vashem. (English). Lists communities in the Soviet Union and Europe and Jewish population of each town. Sections on Poland and Germany are arranged by province. [D 810.J4 Y2 1965]

The Documents of the Lodz Ghetto: An Inventory of the Nachman Zonabend Collection [RG 241], compiled by Marek Web. New York, 1988. [D 810.J4 D6]

Encyclopedia of the Holocaust, chief editor Israel Gutman. 4 vols. (English). London, 1990. These volumes were also published in Hebrew [5 vols. and index volume] and German. [D 810.J4 E6 1990]

Guide to Unpublished Materials of the Holocaust Period. 1970–. (YIVO has vols. 1–5). A series of books that list, by town, original documents in the Yad Vashem archives. An entry might include documents relating to deportations, war criminals, refugees, orphanages, etc. Researchers can write to Yad Vashem to determine the cost of copying documents. [D 810.J4 G8]

How to Document Victims and Locate Survivors of the Holocaust, by Gary Mokotoff. Teaneck, 1995. See pages 79–83, for an inventory of some of the survivor and victim lists available at YIVO. [D 810.J4 M65 1995]

Yad Vashem Central Archives: Collection of Testimonies Memoirs and Diaries [Record Group 033], Part 1, compiled by Bronia Klibansky. Jerusalem, 1990. [D 810.J4 Y27 1990]

<u>Lists of Victims:</u>

Death Books from Auschwitz: Remnants, edited by Jerzy Debski, State Museum of Auschwitz-Birkenau. 3 vols. Munich, 1995. [/90347]

Kuudiatud 1941: General Index of Deportees from Estonia, compiled by Vello Salo. Brampton, ON, Canada, 1993. [/86007]

Lerer yizker bukh [Teachers' Memorial Book], by Hayyim S. Kazdan. New York, 1954. Includes biographies of Yiddish teachers in Poland who were lost in the Holocaust. [LC 746.P6 K34]. NOTE: YIVO Archives has photographs published in this book.

Lodz-Names: List of the Ghetto Inhabitants, 1940–1944. 5 vols. Published by Yad Vashem and the Organization of Former Residents of Lodz in Israel. Jerusalem, 1994. [/89156] [DS 135.P62]

Liste Officielle des Décédés des Camps de Concentration, published by the Ministere des Anciens Combattants et Victimes de Guerre. 6 vols. Paris, [1945-1949]. Includes Mauthausen, Neuengamme, Auschwitz, Bergen-Belsen, Flossenburg, Dachau and others. [3/22775]

Memorial dates (Yorzait) of the martyred Jews in Dachau, compiled by Joel Zak, Josef Lindenberger and Jacob Silberstien. Vol. 11, Jews Born in Poland. New York, 1947–. [/99325]

Mémorial de la Déportation des Juifs de Belgique [Memorial of the Deportation of the Jews of Belgium], edited by Serge Klarsfeld and Maxime Steinberg. New York, 1982. [9/81068]

Le Mémorial des Enfants Juifs Déportés de France [Memorial of the Deported Children of France], edited by Serge Klarsfeld. [Paris], 1994. (French); and New York, 1996 (English). Includes photographs of many of the children. [/87687-French; /89327-English]

Le Mémorial de la Déportation des Juifs de France. Paris, 1978. (French), compiled by Serge Klarsfeld. English ed.: *Memorial to the Jews Deported from France, 1942–1944.* New York, 1983. Lists transports of Jews to concentration camps, including both those that originated in France and those that passed through France. Information relating to about 90 transports is given. The names of victims are listed alphabetically for each transport and, when known, the birth date and place of birth are included. Also given are the number of people who survived each transport and its destination. [9/76780-French; /79227-English]

In Memoriam: Le-zekher [Netherlands]. A list of 103,000 names of Jewish and Dutch people who did not survive WWII. Den Haag, 1995. [Netherlands, 1995]

Nevek a hajdu megyebol kiuzott zsidok nevie [Names of the Deported Jews of Hajdu County, Hungary], published by the Beate and Searge Klarsfeld Foundation. New York, 1992. [Hajdu-Bihar Megye (Hungary) 1992]

Nevek munkaszazadok vesztesege: a keleti magyar hadmuveleti teruleteken [Names of Jewish Victims of Hungarian Labor Battalions], edited by Dr. Gavriel Bar Shaked. New York, 1992. [Hungary, 1992]

Terezinska Pametni Kniha: Zidovske Obeti Nacistickych Deportaci z Cech a Moravy, 1941–1945 [Jewish Victims of Nazi Deportations from Bohemia and Moravia, 1941–1945], edited by Miroslav Karny. 2 vols. Prague,

1995. Arranged by transport. Includes 81,397 deportees who perished, were liberated or whose fate was unknown; listing name, birth date and when/where deported. [D 805.5.T54 T47 1995] [/94622]. See also *Terezin Memorial Book: A Guide to the Czech Original* (in English). [DS 805.5.T54 T472 1996]

De toten fon Dachau: Deutsche und Osterreicher, compiled by Dr. Paul Husarek. Includes lists of Polish Jews who were transferred from Dachau to other camps. Munich, [1948]. [3/45499]

Lists of Polish Jews who Perished in Dachau, Germany. [Germany, 1945]. Includes name, birth date/place and date of death. [3/45499]

Vilniaus getas: kaliniu sarasai [Vilnius ghetto: lists of prisoners], chief editor Evsey Tseitlin. 2 vols. Vilnius, 1996–1998. [/98659-/98660, /89610]

Lists of Survivors

The Library has one of the most extensive collections of survivors lists by location in 1945–1946. These include survivors of concentration camps, specific groups of survivors and lists by location at the end of the War, such as:

Benjamin and Vladka Meed registry of Jewish Holocaust survivors, compiled by the United States Holocaust Memorial Museum in cooperation with the American Gathering of Jewish Holocaust Survivors. 4 vols. Washington, DC, 2000 [D 810.J4 N3 2000]. See AMERICAN GATHERING OF JEWISH HOLOCAUST SURVIVORS.

International Refugee Organization: Professional Medical Register, compiled by Health Division, Headquarters. Geneva, [1949]. Includes name, age, nationality, marital status, languages, religion, medical education and degrees of surviving medical professionals. [/88243]

List of Persons Liberated at Terezin and List of Children at Terezin, compiled by the Czechoslovak Jewish Committee. Includes 15,000 names. New York, 1945. [3/22777E], [3/22772]

Reshimah: Talmide Yeshivot Hakme Lublin [Register of Yeshiva Students of Lublin], compiled by B. Sh. Shneurson. Jerusalem, 1965. (Hebrew). [/88245]

She'erit Ha-peletah [Lists of Survivors], compiled by the Central the Central Committee of Liberated Jews in Bavaria. Includes lists of survivors by concentration camp including, Dachau, Bergen-Belsen, Buchenwald, Camp Felding, Flossenberg, Hasag-Altenburg, Hamburg, Hannover, Hillersleben, Kamer, Linz, Regensburg, Turkheim, and others. 7 vols. Dachau, etc. 1945. [3/22768 I-V], [3/22769], [3/22769A]

Lists of person liberated (1945/1946):

Budapest [3/22766 I-IV]	Poland [3/2276A], [3/45499]
Belgium [3/22777B]	Riga [3/227C]
Czechoslovakia [3/22777F]	Slovakia [3/22767]
Czestochowa, Poland [3/22768A]	Sweden, [/22774], [/8846]
Fuerth, Germany [/88247]	Thessalonike [3/22777D]
Hamburg, Germany [3/22777K]	Warsaw [3/22767A], [3/2277G]
Italy [3/22773 I- III]	Yugoslavia [3/22771]
Lithuania [3/22770]	Various locations [/88244 I-II],
Lublin, Poland [3/22777H], [/88248]	[3/22766A(I)], [3/22777]
Netherlands [3/22777A]	

5. Biographies: The Library has an extensive collection of individual biographies, personal narratives, *Who's Who* in Jewish communities around the world and biographical dictionaries such as:

Africa
South African Jewry (1976–1977), by Leon Feldberg. Johannesburg, [1976 or 1977]. [DS 135.A26 S6 1976]

Europe
Bibliographie des Juifs en France, by B. Blumenkranz. [Toulouse, 1974]. Includes 320 biographies. [Z 6373.F785]

Doires Bundistes [Bundist biographies], edited by Jacob Sholem Hertz. 3 vols. New York, 1956–1968. (Yiddish). Index by surname. [/47591]

The Encyclopedia of Russian Jewry: Biographies A–I, edited by Herman Branover, Zeev Wagner, Sir Isaiah Berlin. Northvale, NJ, [1998]. [DS 135.R9 R6713 1998]

Oyf ale teg fun a gants yor, by J. Gutkowicz. Warsaw, 1966. Includes biographies of Jewish writers, artists, actors and intellectuals in Polish history. Entries arranged by date of birth. [CT 205.G8]

Polski slownik biograficzny [Polish Biographical Dictionary], published by the Polska Akademya Umiejaelnosci and Polska Akademia Nauk. 39 vols. Warsaw, 1935–1999. Includes prominent Polish men and women including those who were Jewish, from the beginning of Poland's history to the present. [DS 413.P6 1935]

Slownik biograficzny dzialaczy polskiego ruchu robotniczego [Biographical dictionary of activists in the Polish Labor Movement], edited by Feliks Tych. 3 vols., A–K. Warsaw, 1978. Includes many Jewish labor activists. [HD 8538.A1 S5 1978]

Zsidó lexikon, edited by Peter Ujvari. Reprint of biographies of Hungarian Jews originally published in 1929. [S.1], 1987. [DS 102.8..Z6 1987]

Israel

Entsiklopedyah le-halutse ha-yishuv u-bonav, [Encyclopedia of the pioneers and builders of the Yishuv], edited by David Tidhar. 19 vols. Includes photographs and biographies of settlers in Israel from 1700. Tel Aviv, 1947–1971. [DS 125.3.A2 T5 1947]

Oral History Division, Catalog No. 3, Hebrew University of Jerusalem, The Institute of Contemporary Jewry. Jerusalem, 1970. [Z 6621.H4 H4]

Who's Who in Israel, 1952, 1955, 1956, 1958 and 1969/70. [DS 125.3.A2 W53]

North America

Arbeter ring boyer un tuer [Workmen's Circle Builders and Pioneers], edited by E. Jeshurin and Y. Sh. Herts. New York, 1962. Appendix includes a 4-page list of prominent Workmen's Circle members and some non-members buried in Workmen's Circle cemeteries, including date of death and name of cemetery. A second appendix lists important people, the positions they held over the years on various WC national committees from 1900–1962, with dates served and title. [HD 7126.W7]

A Biographical Dictionary of Canadian Jewry, 1909–1914: from the Canadian Jewish Times, by Lawrence F. Tapper. Teaneck, [1992]. [F 1035.J5 F76 1992]

Bibliography of American and Canadian Jewish Memoirs and Autobiographies in Yiddish, Hebrew and English, compiled by Eziekiel Lifschutz. New York, 1970. [E 36.L5 1970]

Who's Who in American Jewry, 1926, 1928, 1938/39 and 1980. Includes biographies of American and Canadian Jews. [E 184.J5 W6]

Worldwide

Famous Musicians of Jewish Origin, by Gdal Saleski. New York, 1949. Includes almost 400 composers, conductors, violinists, cellists, pianist, singers and others. [ML 385.S2 1949]

Great Jews in Music, by Daryl Lyman. New York, 1986. Includes over 450 biographical sketches. [ML 385.L95 1986]

Leksikon fun der nayer Yidisher literatur [Biographical dictionary of modern Yiddish literature], edited by S. Niger and Y. Shatski. New York, Congress for Jewish Culture, 1956–1981. 8 vols. (Yiddish). Incudes c. 7,000 entries arranged alphabetically by the author's Yiddish surname. [PJ 5121.L4]. See YIVO INSTITUTE FOR JEWISH RESEARCH- ARCHIVES, for original materials submitted and photographs not used in publication. [RG1150 and Bund Collection]

Leksikon fun Yidishn teater [Lexicon of the Yiddish Theater], compiled and edited by Zalman Zylbercweig. 6 vols. New York, Warsaw and Mexico, 1931–1969. [PN 3035.Z9 1931]

Leksikon ha-sifrut ha-ivrit [Encyclopedia of Modern Hebrew Literature], by Getzel Kressel. 2 vols. (Hebrew). Merhavyah, 1965–1967. [PJ 5006.K7 1965]

Shures Poyle-Tsi'en: portretn [Poalei-Zion Portraits], collected and edited by Shlomo Schweizer. Includes over 400 biographies of Poalei Zion leaders. (Yiddish). Tel Aviv, 1981. [DS 150.L4 S39]

Who's Who in Labor, edited by Marion Dikerman and Ruth Taylor. New York, 1946. Includes many Jewish labor activists. [uncataloged]

Who's Who in World Jewry, 1955, 1965, 1972, 1978, 1981 and 1987. [DS 125.3.A2 W5]

6. ## Name Indexes

A Dictionary of Jewish Names and their History, by B. C. Kaganoff. New York, 1977. [CS 3010.K28 1977]

Dictionary of Ashkenazic Given Names: Their Origin, Structure, Pronunciation, and Migrations, by Alexander Beider. Bergenfield, NJ, 2001. [CS 3010.B18 2001]

Jewish and Hebrew Onomastics, A Bibliography, by Robert Singerman. New York, 1977. [CS 3010 .S5 1977]

Jewish Family Names and their Origins: an etymological dictionary, by Heinrich W. Guggenheimer and Eva H. Guggenheimer. Hoboken, NJ, 1992. [CS 3010.G84 1992]

Jewish Surnames in Prague (15th–18th Century), by Alexander Beider. Teaneck, [1995]. [/87158], [CS 3010.B44 1994]

Les noms des Israelites en France: histoire et dictionnaire, by Paul Levy. Paris, 1960. [/63089]

Sefer ha-prenumerantn [Hebrew subscription lists], by Berl Kagan. New York, 1975 [Z291 K3]. Prenumeranten or "priornumbers" refers to lists of people in 8,767 communities in Europe and South Africa who ordered copies of rabbinic works before publication. Kagan's book includes a place index to these subscription lists. The books covered were published in the last 200 years with the majority in the 1850–1910 period. (Yiddish/Hebrew). [Z291.K3 1975]

7. Resource Books: Guides to YIVO's Archive as well as those of other institutions around the world can be found here. These include:

Archives and Manuscript Repositories in the USSR: Estonia, Latvia, Lithuania, and Belorussia, by Patricia Kennedy Grimsted. Princeton, 1981. [CD 1735.B34 G74 1981]

Archives and Manuscript Repositories in the USSR: Ukraine and Moldavia, Book 1: General Bibliography and Institutional Directory, by Patricia Kennedy Grimsted. Princeton, 1988. [CD 1735.U4 G75 1988]

Archiwa panstwowe w Polsce: przewodnik po zasobach, edited by Andrzeja Biernata and Anny Laszuk. Warsaw, Poland, 1998. [CD 1740.A825 1998]

Catalogue of Memoirs, William E. Wiener Oral History Library of the American Jewish Committee. 3 vols. New York, 1978–1993. 165 East 56 Street, New York, NY 10022 (212) 751-4000. [E 194.J5 W5 1978]

Dokumenty po istorrii i kulture evreev v arkhivakh Moskvy [Jewish Documentary Sources in Moscow Archives], edited by M. S. Kupovetskii, E. V. Starostin and M. Web. Moscow, 1997. [DS135.R9 D624 1997], [/94907]

Guide to the Holdings of the American Jewish Archives, by James W. Clasper and M. Carolyn Dellenbach. Cincinnati, 1979. [E 184.J5 H4]

A Guide to the Archival Holdings at the Jewish Public Library of Montreal, compiled by Florence Cymbalista Silverstone and Rose Switzman Rosaminer. Montreal, 1991. [Z 6621.J39 1991]

A Guide to Manuscript on Microfilm Collections of the Research Library of the Balch Institute for Ethnic Studies, compiled by Monique Bourque and R. Joseph Anderson. Philadelphia, [1992]. [Z 6621.B3 1992]

Guide to Polish Libraries and Archives, by Richard Casimir Lewanski. Boulder, 1974. [Z 817.A1 L48 1974]

Guide to the Sources for the History of the Jews in Poland in the Central Archives: Ginzei Am Olam, Central Archives of the Jewish People, edited by A. Teller. Jerusalem, 1988. [Z 6621.C4 C8 1988]

Guide to the YIVO Archives, edited by Marek Web and Fruma Mohrer. New York, [1998]. [Z 6375.Y59 1997]

Inventory of the American Jewish Committee, 1906–1980, by Seymour J. Pomerenze. Ann Arbor, 1981; and *Index...* by Jessica L. Milstead and Beverly A. Pajer. New York, 1994. Indexes AJC records located at the AJC's Jacob Blaustein Library in New York City (c. 1906-1930s) and AJC's Records Center (later records). Includes records transferred from the Records Center to YIVO (1930-1970s) now part of RG 347. [Reference Desk]

Jewish Documentary Sources in Russia, Ukraine and Belarus: A Preliminary List, edited by Dorit Sallis and Marek Web. New York, 1996. Includes information on 1,300 collections of Jewish provenance in the Russian, Ukrainian and Belarussian archives including addresses, collection number and dates covered. [DS 135.R9 S4 1996]

Jewish Roots in Poland: Pages from the Past and Archival Inventories, by Miriam Weiner. New York, 1997. Includes detailed inventories of Jewish vital record and other genealogical holdings of local archives in Poland. [CS 877.J4 W45 1998]

Jewish Roots in Ukraine and Moldova: Pages from the Past and Archival Inventories, by Miriam Weiner. New York, 1999. [Ref Desk: DS 135.U4 W45 1999]

Magyar zsido leveltari repertorium [Directory of Archival Holdings Relating to the History of Jews in Hungary: Hungarian Archives], edited by Gyorgy Haraszti. 2 vols. Budapest, 1993. [Z 6620.H9 H3 1993]

Printed Books on Jewish Cemeteries in the Jewish National & University Library in Jerusalem, by Mathilda A. Tagger. Jerusalem, 1997. [DS 115.T3 1997]

The Russian Consular Records Index and Catalog, compiled by Sallyann Amdur Sack and Suzan F. Wynne. New York, 1987. [CS 856.J4 S23 1987]

Some Archival Sources for Ukranian-Jewish Genealogy, by Aleksander Kronik, et al. Teaneck, 1997. [CS 861.S6 1997]

8. Jewish Organizations: The Library has many publications listing Jewish organizations in New York City and other localities. These include:

American Jewish Yearbook, 1899–. [DS 101.A5]. Of interest to genealogists:
    Lists of every Jewish organization in the US: 1900/01, 1907/08, 1919/20.
    Biographical sketches of rabbis and cantors: 1903/04; 1904/05.
    Biographical sketches of communal workers: 1905/06.
    Necrologies - every volume.
    Individual biographies of prominent Jews

Bridges to an American City: A Guide to Chicago's Landsmanshaftn, 1870 to 1990, by Sidney Sorkin. New York, [1993]. [/85988]

Di Yidishe landsmanshaftn fun New York [Jewish Landsmanshaftn of New York], edited by Isaac Rontch. Federal Writers Project, New York, 1938. (Yiddish). Includes an index to 1,841 societies functioning in 1938. Family circles arranged by Yiddish family name. [HS 2229.M4]

Jewish Communal Register of New York City, 1917–1918, edited and published by the Kehilah of New York. New York, [1919]. Second edition. Includes the history and function of almost 3,700 organization in the City during that period. [HV 3192.N5 1919]

Jewish Hometown Associations and Family Circles in New York: The WPA Yiddish Writer's Group Study, edited by Hannah Kliger. Indiana, [1992]. [/84702]

9. Synagogues:

Bohemia and Moravia. *Jewish Sights of Bohemia and Moravia,* by Jiri Fiedler. Prague, 1991. Guide book includes photographs of synagogues and cemeteries. [/85858]

England, London. *The Synagogues of London* by Paul Lindsay. London, 1993. Appendix 2 includes maps showing location. Appendix 3 includes an address directory of synagogues in Greater London arranged by affiliation. [/87487]

Europe. *Synagogues of Europe: Architecture, History, Meaning,* by Carol Herselle Krinsky. New York, [1985]. [NA 5450.K75 1985]

Romania. *Sinagogi din Romania* [Synagogues of Romania], by A. Streja and L. Schwarz. Bucharest, 1997. [/92892]

Poland. *Wooden Synagogues,* by Maria and Kazimierz Piechotka. Warsaw, 1959. [12/51537]

Poland. *Zachowane synagogi i domy modlitwy w Polsce: katalog* [Preserved Synagogues and Houses of Prayer in Poland], by Eleonora Bergman and Jan Jagielski. Warsaw, 1996. [DS 135.P6 B35 1996]

United States. *Synagogues of the United States: a photographic and architectural survey*, by Oscar Israelowitz. New York [1992]. [/84350]

10. Military:

Belarus. *Pamiats: Aktsiabrski raion...* [Memorial: Aktsiabrski District (Belarus)] [/98931]. Each volume includes biographical information about Jewish and non-Jewish residents of the district who died fighting in WWII, as well as those who perished in the repressions which occurred in the 1930s. Other volumes in this *Pamiats* [Memorial] series cover the districts (raion) of *Babruiski* [/99185, /98874]; *Barysau, Barysauski* [/105162]; *Bialynitski* [/99439]; *Chacherski* [/99442]; *Cherykauski* [/99237]; *Dobrushski* [/99444]; *Dziatlauski* [/105163]; *Elski* [/105781]; *Hluski* [/105779]; *Homelski* [/98871, /98872]; *Horatski* [/98950]; *Kalinkavitski* [/99440]; *Kastsiukovitski* [/106686]; *Kirauski* [/98951]; *Klichauski* [/98877]; *Klimavitski* [/98873]; *Kruhlianski* [/99187]; *Loeuski* [/99481]; *Mahiliou* [/98952]; *Mahiliouski* [/99186]; *Mazyr, Mazyrski* [/98930]; *Mstsislauski* [/99441]; *Naraulianski* [/99224]; *Petrykauski* [/98932]; *Rahachouski* [/98876]; *Rechytski* [/98884, /98885]; *Shklouski* [/98875]; *Slauharadski* [/99443]; *Svetlahorsk, Svetlahorski* [/105328]; *Vetkauski* [/98869, /98870]; *Zhlobini, Zhlobinski* [/105780]; *Zhytkavitski* [/98883] and more. 38 vols. Minsk, 1988–1998. (Cyrillic).

Germany. *Die Hamburger Juden in Kriege, 1914–1918,* by Dr. Urias. Hamburg, 1933. Includes lists of Jewish soldiers from Hamburg, Altona, Bremen, Bremerhaven, Cuxhaven, Kiel, Lubeck, Wandsbek, Germany. [/11727]

Great Britain. *British Jewry book of honour* [World War I], edited by Michael Adler. London, 1922. [/59136]

Lithuania. *Fighting back: Lithuanian Jewry's armed resistance to the Nazis, 1941–1945,* by Dov Levin; translated by Moshe Kohn and Dina Cohen. New York, 1985. Appendix includes a list of over 200 people whose testimonies were used in researching the book; and identifies the archive in Israel where the complete record can be found (pages 287–290). [/79669]

Poland. *Jewish Military Casualties in the Polish Armies in World War II,* by Benjamin Meirtchak. 2 vols. Tel Aviv, 1994–1996. Volume 1, Jewish soldiers and officers of the Polish People's Army killed and missing in action, 1943–1945, includes 1,596 soldiers, birth year/place, father's name, place/date of death, military rank and regiment. Volume 2, Jewish military casualties in September 1939 Campaign and casualties in the Polish armed forces in exile includes an additional 1,647 names. [/86325]

- *Jews-officers in the Polish armed forces, 1939-1945,* by Benjamin Meirtchak. Tel Aviv, 2001. Includes 4,879 Jewish officers in the Polish army and in the armed forces in exile with birth date, sometimes birth place, rank, assignment, and if killed-in-action, date and place of death. [/107209]

Ukraine. *Knyha Pamiati Ukrainy* [Memorial Book Ukraine], edited by Ivan Oleksandrovych Herasymov. 54 vols., including the following oblasts: *Chernigovskaia* [/105165], *Ivan-Frankivska* [/105167], *Khmelnytska* [/98878]; *Lvivska* [105169], *Rivnenska* [/105170], *Sumska* [105168], *Ternopilska* [/105171], *Volynska* [/98879],

Zakarpatska [/98880]; *Zhytomyrska* [/105166] and City of Kiev (Kyiv) [/105172]. [Ukraine], 1993–2000. Includes Jews and non-Jews from these provinces who died or were missing in action during WWII. (Cyrillic). Biographical data such as father's name, year of birth, date of death or date missing in action, occupation and religion are provided. Each volume contains c. 15,000 names. A c. 250-volume series is planned.

Soviet Union. *Kniga pamiati voinov-evreev pavshikh v boiakh s natsizmom, 1941–1945* [Memorial book of Jewish soldiers enlisted in the army of the Soviet Union, who were killed in action in the war against the Nazis, 1941–1945], edited by M. F. Marianovskii, et al. Includes biographical sketches of over 70,000 Jewish soldiers providing father's name, date/place of birth, date/place of death, military address, rank, place of burial, source of information (record number) and archive. 6 vols. Moscow, 1994–1995. [Cyrillic]. [/87763a], [106782]

Soviet Union. *Under Fire: the stories of Jewish heroes of the Soviet Union*, compiled by Gershon Shapiro. Jerusalem, 1988. Includes 150 biographies of Jews awarded as "Heroes of the Soviet Union."

Worldwide. *140 Jewish marshals, generals & admirals*, by E. Rubin. London, [1952]. Includes biographies of Jewish officers from Australia, Austria, Belgium, China, France, Germany, India, Israel, Italy, Poland, Turkey, South Africa, Great Britain and the U.S.A. [/41832]

Worldwide. *Schalom libertad!: Juden im spanischen Burgerkrieg*, by Arno Lustiger. Frankfurt am Main, [1989]. Includes biographies of Jewish soldiers from many countries, including U.S.A., Poland, Germany, Israel, and France, who fought in the Spanish Civil War, 1936–1939. [/84404]

11. Newspapers and Periodicals:

The Library has embarked upon a program to systematically acquire microfilms of all Jewish newspapers ever published in Eastern Europe, as well as those published in the East European diaspora (North America, South America and South Africa). Its collection includes:

Der Fraind (St. Petersburg), 1903–1913 [Y-1]
Der Moment (Warsaw), 1912–1938 [Y-5]
De Yidisher Shtime, (Kovno), 1919–1940 [Y-29]
Jewish Chronicle (London), 1933–1947 [80-Y-1168]
Jewish Daily Forward (NYC), 1897–1997
Jewish Displaced Persons Periodicals:
    Jidisze Cajtung, 1946–1948 [Reels 1 & 2]
    Idisze Bilder, 1947–1948 [Reel 3]
    Ilustrirter Ort Magazin, 1948 [Reel 4]
    Admonter Hajnt, 1946–1948 [Reel 11]

Het Joodsche Weekblad (Amsterdam), 1941–1943 [62-35-133]
Morgn Frayhayt (NYC), 1923–1986 [Y96-1544]
Nasz Przeglad (Warsaw), 1923–1939 [Y-96-1543]
Nowy Dziennik (Krakow), 1918–1924 [Y-96-1548]
South African Jewish Chronicle, 1902–1959
Tageblatt (New York), 1888–1928 [Y-41]
Transylvania Yiddisher Zeitung, 1894–1936 [Y-26]
Tzeit (Vila), 1932–1939 [Y-3]
Unzer Freund (Vilna), 1932–1939 [Y-2]

NOTE: See *A Guide to the Microfilms edition of Jewish Displaced Persons Periodicals from the Collections of the YIVO Institute*, edited by Zachary Baker. New York, 1990. Includes a complete list of c. 150 titles of newspapers, journals, flyers and one-time only publications in this collection. [D 809.G4 J4 1990]

Finding Aids:

YIVO is in the process of computerizing its catalog. To date, all Roman character books and books acquired 1992 or later are included. Until the new system is fully operational, users must search the card indexes located at the entrance to the Reading Room for books not in the computerized catalog.

The Library's holdings were originally cataloged according to the language in which the material was written. As a result, there are separate catalogs for materials in the Latin alphabet, the Cyrillic alphabet, the Hebrew language, the Yiddish language and for a special collection of rabbinical books (mostly in Hebrew). The catalogs are arranged by author and title though titles are not always indexed. This problem should be resolved once the computerized catalog is available.

In addition, the Library has one numerically classified subject catalog which includes, in one sequence, works found in the four separate author-title catalogs. The Library has an innovative finding aid to the English (and Yiddish) catalogs which refers English-speaking researchers to the subject catalog: Green index cards have been added to both the English and Yiddish catalogs, directing readers to relevant classifications in the subject catalog.

The only materials not in the subject catalog are the holdings that were part of the original collection of rabbinica rescued from Vilna during WWII. To locate books in this collection, consult the librarian.

NOTE: YIVO reference materials in the reading room are arranged by the Library of Congress classifications and have been assigned a Library of Congress call number.

CITY CLERK'S OFFICE
MARRIAGE LICENSE BUREAU

Facility Director:	Victor Robles, City Clerk
Address:	Municipal Building 1 Centre Street, Room 252 New York, NY 10007
	(Cross Streets: Brooklyn Bridge and Chambers Street. Chambers Street runs through the center of the building.)
Mail Address:	Add "Attention: Marriage Record Unit" to lower left corner of the envelope.
Phone:	(212) 669-8898
Fax:	(212) 669-3300
E-mail:	none
Website:	none

Hours of Operation:

Monday to Friday: 8:30 am to 4:00 pm (to order records)

Closed Saturday, Sunday and legal holidays.

Closest Public Transportation:

Subway: 4, 5 or 6 to Brooklyn Bridge
J, M or Z to Chambers Street/Lafayette Street
N or R to City Hall
A or C to Chambers Street/Church Street (north end)
2 or 3 to Park Place

Bus: M1 or M6 to Broadway and Chambers Street
M15 or M22 to Centre and Chambers Streets

Directions:

Take the #4 or #5 (express) or #6 (local) train to the Brooklyn Bridge station. Go up the staircase at the center of the platform. Turn at the top of the stairs and go straight ahead to the exit. Go up the wide staircase. You will emerge on the street level of the Municipal Building. Turn right, around the staircase, to the entrance to the building. The office is on the 2nd floor. Be sure to enter at the south end of the building, i.e. near the subway entrance. The 2nd floor of the north end does not connect. NOTE: The south side entrance is wheelchair accessible.

Description of Resources:

City Clerk's Office marriage records, 1930 to the present and City Clerk's marriage indexes, 1908 to the present for all boroughs (microfilm), are available in the Manhattan office. The City Clerk's record consists of the application (affidavit) filed by the couple before the wedding and the marriage license filed after the wedding by the officiating person (e.g. rabbi) certifying that the wedding actually occurred and showing the date, place and witnesses. As a result, copies of applications for marriages that never took place are among the affidavits filed here.

NOTE: Two independent sets of records existed for the years 1908–1937 when both the Department of Health and the City Clerk's Office maintained marriage records. The Health Department records (known as "certificates"), 1866–1937, and earlier City Clerk's Office records (affidavits/licenses), 1908–1929 can be viewed at the NEW YORK CITY DEPARTMENT OF RECORDS AND INFORMATION SERVICES, MUNICIPAL ARCHIVES. Of note, City Clerk's marriage records often include more detailed information than Health Department records.

See also NEW YORK PUBLIC LIBRARY, MILSTEIN DIVISION OF UNITED STATES. HISTORY, LOCAL HISTORY AND GENEALOGY, NEW YORK GENEALOGICAL AND BIOGRAPHICAL SOCIETY LIBRARY, and the FAMILY HISTORY CENTER - MANHATTAN for Health Department marriages. Only the MUNICIPAL ARCHIVES has copies of City Clerk marriage records and indexes, 1908-1929. Microfilm copies of City Clerk indexes, 1930-1951, will be available for viewing at the MUNICIPAL ARCHIVES shortly.

Finding Aids:

For the years, 1908–1971, the City Clerk's Office has microfilm copies of its original alphabetical ledger indexes for brides and grooms. These handwritten ledgers were arranged by borough in which the affidavit was filed, then by the first 2 letters of the surname, and then chronologically by date of application (not date of marriage). Separate ledgers existed within each borough for groups of months in each year, i.e. Jan–Feb, Mar–Apr, etc. When the ledgers were microfilmed, all pages for a particular borough, alpha page, and year (January to December), were filmed consecutively. Nevertheless, searching for a name can be time consuming. If the marriage occurred before 1938 and the groom's name is known, check the published Health Department marriage indexes to learn the date and borough in which the marriage took place. This may help narrow the search. (Affidavits could be filed up to 60 days prior to the marriage.) A complete set of NYC Health Department published marriage indexes, 1898–1937, are available here.

NOTE: City Clerk's marriages records, 1908 to May 1943, were required to be filed in the borough in which the bride resided (not necessarily the borough in which the marriage took place). For out-of-city brides, the record was filed in the borough where the license was obtained. After May 1943, all marriage certifications were filed in the borough in which the couple obtained their license. There was no requirement that the couple obtain their license in the borough in which the marriage took place or in which the bride or groom resided. The license could be obtained in any county in New York State.

The Office has a computerized index including both brides and grooms from 1950 to the present. From, 1972–1983, these are also maintained in bound volumes by borough; and from 1984 to the present, in printouts. The bound computerized index and printouts show both bride's and groom's names, the date they filed their application and, after 1973, the bride birth date. See "Restrictions on Use."

Description of Facility:

The Office is located on the 2nd floor of the Municipal Building. Researchers may obtain records by submitting a request form by mail or in-person to the clerk in Room 252; or by requesting special permission to conduct the research themselves and paying an additional fee. See "Restrictions on Use." Only a limited number of authorized genealogists can be accommodated for direct research. The Office makes one microfilm reader available for two-hour appointments (12:00 to 2:00 pm). A prior appointment for on-site research is necessary.

Researchers who know the date of marriage may submit a request form in-person in Room 252. The clerk behind the counter will do the search (one-year, one-Borough if pre-1950) which can take an hour or more. If the date is unknown, a same-day search will not be conducted. Responses to such requests will be mailed. NOTE: Researchers can do the search themselves using indexes available at the MUNICIPAL ARCHIVES.

Fees/Copies:

Applications for copies of records are available in Room 252. (See also Appendix C-1.) Submit the completed application for processing. You will be called when the search for your record is completed. Only then will you be asked to pay the fee.

A fee of $15 is charged for records which can be searched by computer (1950 or later). For earlier records, 1930–1949, the fee is $15 for the first year (fee includes one certified copy at $10; and one-Borough search at $5); $1 for the second year searched and $.50 for each additional year. For on-site research of two hours, the fee is $5. All payments must be made by certified check, postal or international money order, payable to "The City Clerk of New York." Personal checks and cash are not accepted.

Restrictions on Use:

Records less than 50 years old are provided only to the couple or their authorized representative. Genealogists should indicate their relationship to the couple or a statement providing dates of death. Authorization from one of the parties or their next-of-kin may be necessary to obtain later records.

Researchers wishing to conduct their own research must present a letter of authorization from an attorney or recognized genealogical society; and have an appointment. Bring the letter of authorization and a $5 money order to the counter outside the Executive Office, Room 265. (Turn left when exiting the elevator and continue down the hallway to reach this counter.) An advance appointment is necessary.

CITY REGISTER'S OFFICE
MANHATTAN

Facility Director:	John Lariviere, City Register
	Gladys Leonard, Deputy City Register
Address:	City of New York, Manhattan Business Center ♿
	66 John Street, 13th Floor
	New York, NY 10038
	(Cross Streets: Nassau and Dutch Street)
Phone:	(212) 361-7550 (City Register's Office)
	(212) 361-7660 (Real Property Assessment Bureau)
Fax:	(212) 361-7699
E-mail:	see website
Website:	www.nyc.gov/html/dof/

Hours of Operation:

Monday to Friday: 9:00 am to 4:00 pm

Closed Saturday, Sunday and legal holidays.

Closest Public Transportation:

Subway: 2, 3, 4, 5, J, M or Z to Fulton Street
            A or C to Broadway/Nassau Streets

Bus: M1 or M6 to Broadway and Fulton Street

Directions:

Take any of the above subway lines to Fulton Street or Broadway/Nassau Streets. The building, "City of New York, Manhattan Business Center," 66 John Street, is one block south of Fulton Street and two blocks east of Broadway (passing Nassau Street). If exiting at Fulton and Broadway, walk east on Fulton to Dutch Street. Turn south and walk to the end of the block. The building on the south side of John Street is #66. Take the elevator to the 13th Floor. Turn left when exiting the elevator for the City Register's Office; or turn right for the Real Property Assessment Bureau.

Description of Resources:

New York County (Manhattan) deeds, mortgages and filed maps, from 1654 to the present are available here. The Office also has miscellaneous real estate items. These may include wills, transfer of dowager rights, etc.

The records for sections of the Bronx that were annexed to New York County at the end of the 19th century are located in the City Register's Office in the Bronx. However, the Manhattan grantor/grantee and mortgagor/mortgagee indexes, 1874–1891, include western Bronx properties.

All records in this office are on microfilm reels or in microfilm jackets (except Torrens properties, described below), arranged chronologically by date recorded. NOTE: Microfilm jackets arranged by block/lot for Manhattan were discarded in June, 2001 when the Office moved to its new location. The City Register's Office is digitizing deed and mortgage records, 1966 to the present. Property record indexes and digitized document images for Manhattan, 1966 to the present, and indexes, 1982 to the present for the Bronx, Brooklyn and Queens, may be online by January 2003.

Finding Aids:

Records in this office may be searched either by name of property owner or by property location. From 1982 to the present, a computer search can be made four ways: by borough and surname; borough, block and lot number; borough, reel and page number; or borough and address. For instruction on how to conduct a computer search, see *City Register Public Access Quick Reference Guide*, (one page) available at the Microfilm Counter. NOTE: At least one computer in each borough office can access information for all NYC boroughs except Staten Island. At present, copies of actual documents can be found only in the borough office where the property is located. (This may change if records are digitized.)

To identify all records for a particular person or corporate body, there are indexes for grantor, grantee, mortgagor and mortgagee, for various time periods from the 17th century to the present. Alphabetical indexes are available for the years 1675–1981 (microfilm); and 1982 to the present (microfiche or computer). Grantor/ Grantee indexes, 1949–1982, are also available in libers under the third and fourth counters (counting from the wall to the right of the entrance). For deeds recorded up to 1856, there is also a published set of volumes, *Index of Conveyances* (separate grantor and grantee books), located under the third counter. Grantor/grantee indexes (microfilm, microfiche and libers) are not easy to use since names are indexed only by the first two letters of the surname, in chronological sequence. NOTE: Grantor (seller), grantee (buyer) and mortgagor (borrower) indexes include names of property owners. Mortgagee indexes include primarily lending institutions.

Indexes 1982 to the present have been computerized and a search can be made by borough and surname. To conduct a search by name, clear the screen ["Clear" button], type "F378" (for a Real Property search) or "F377" (for a Personal Property search) and press the "enter" key. After the new screen appears, enter the "Party Name" (surname, comma, first name or surname alone followed by a comma) on the appropriate line, and press "PF17" (at the top of the keyboard). The computer provides a list of property owners in the borough by that name or surname and address. NOTE: "Real Property" includes single family homes, apartment buildings, condominium apartments and commercial property. To see more detail, including block and lot number, enter the list number desired at the bottom of the screen ("Next Function"), tab to the "Data" field and press "PF19" at the top of the keyboard. The screen will display all instruments filed, and for each it will list reel and page number, type of filing, date of filing, parcel ID (block and lot number) and party type (grantor/grantee, mortgagor/mortgagee).

The computerized index also includes a separate database for personal property, a.k.a. Uniform Commercial Codes (UCC) filings from October 1988. "Personal property" includes liens on cooperative apartments, equipment for stores, etc. Clear the screen and type "F377" to begin a personal property search.

To trace the ownership of a particular piece of property, the street address or location must be converted into a block and lot number. Every parcel of land has a unique block and lot number. There are several ways to obtain these numbers:

1. If the building still exists, use the computers in the City Register's Office, 13th floor, to obtain the block/lot numbers. To search by address, type the word "Find." Fill in the borough code, house number and street address as indicated on the screen to obtain the block and lot number. If no deed or mortgage was filed after 1981, a "no records" message will appear at the bottom of the screen. Should this occur, use one of the following alternatives to find block/lot numbers.

2. The Office has a copy of the *Real Estate Directory of Manhattan* published by First American Real Estate Solutions. Locating block and lot numbers is very easy if this volume is used. It is arranged by address and shows block and lot numbers, as well as other information such as name, address and telephone number of the current owner of each parcel. Both the NEW YORK PUBLIC LIBRARY, SCIENCE, INDUSTRY AND BUSINESS LIBRARY and the BROOKLYN BUSINESS LIBRARY, Reference Desk, have copies of this Manhattan directory; or,

3. The Office has an atlas of block and lot numbers on a standing carousel of sectional maps. The maps show block and lot numbers for each parcel, along with other recent information about each property; or,

4. If the building no longer exists or if the street name and/or numbering has changed, consult the Real Property Assessment Bureau, Information Desk, also located on the 13th floor. That office can look up information on any property in Manhattan and provide the block/lot or advise of physical changes to the buildings, streets and/or numbering sequences. If they are not busy, current block and lot number may be provided by telephone. Call (212) 361-7660.

5. Block and lot may also be obtained by accessing the NYC Department of Finance website. Go to "Real Estate Tax"; and then click on the "Property Tax Bills" button. Scroll down to "Search by Address" and enter the borough, street (house) number, and street name. Press "search."

   NOTE: An alternative page on NYC's Department of Finance website which provides block/lot information, is "Property Address Search" at http://webapps.nyc.gov:8084/CICS/fin1/find001I.

6. For the years 1891–1917, records were recorded by (land) section number, as well as block and lot numbers. There is a chart pasted on a microfilm reader at the front of the Microfilm Counter listing block and lot numbers in each (land) section. Use this chart to obtain section number.

Once section, block and lot number (1891–1917) or block and lot numbers (for all other years) are known, consult the several different indexes described below to obtain the liber and page numbers (or reel and page numbers if recorded after 1968) for deeds, mortgages and other instruments on file for a particular parcel:

1. Indexes by block (on microfilm) are on open shelves near the windows at the far left of the room. The original index volumes (paper copy) are available against the wall or under the counters to the right of the entrance. For the 1654–1965 series, within groups of years there are separate libers (or reels) for each type of instrument (deed or mortgage). The libers (or reels) are arranged by block number and date recorded. The series for deeds, 1654–1917, has block maps and historical information on farm ownership displayed at the start of each block's pages. These *Block Index of Re-Indexed Conveyances*, 1654–1917, are typed and located under the 2nd and 3rd counters.

   Comprehensive liber indexes (Block/Lot Tickler Indexes), which include all types of instruments in one index, are available from 1966 to January 1982. These libers (or reels) are arranged in groups of years, by block number and date recorded.

   For records 1982 or later, including Torrens properties (described below), researchers should use one of the 14 computer terminals located here. Clear the screen, type "F379" and press enter for a document search of the property. Type in the block and lot number, and "R" for a Real Property search or "P" for a Personal Property search in the appropriate fields. (Use the "Tab" key to move around the screen.) Press "Enter" to see on screen a list of all recordings during this period including type of record (deed, mortgage, etc), reel and page numbers (for viewing the actual record) and date of the filing; or press "PF16" to print a report with this information.

   NOTE: Plans are underway to computerize indexes in the Manhattan, Bronx, Brooklyn and Queens from 1966 to the present over the next years and these indexes will be accessible from all offices (except Staten Island). Digitized deed and mortgage records for Manhattan from 1966 to the present and indexes from 1982 for Bronx, Brooklyn and Queens may be online by January 2003. The office anticipates online access to 1966 records and indexes for all boroughs (except Staten Island) by 2004. Check http://nyc.gov/html/dof/html/acris.html for the new Automated City Register Information System (ACRIS).

2. There is another useful index for deeds and mortgages created originally by the Works Progress Administration (WPA) and located along the walls to the left of the entrance and on the Microfilm Counter wall. These WPA indexes (faded green-covered books) are arranged by block and lot and list all deeds and mortgages recorded for a particular lot, from the late 19th century to about 1966. At the start of each block (most blocks take up more than one volume), there are maps of the block, with street numbers as well as lot numbers marked. Different instruments are on color-coded pages. These WPA indexes are not considered "official" records although the City Register's Office did continue to maintain them after the WPA project was completed.

3. Researchers should be aware that some properties were not filed by block and lot number. These were recorded under the Torrens Land Title Registration System. They include large tracts of land which, for example, may have been owned by the same family through several generations. Transfers were made by Memorial Certificates rather than by deed. Fewer than 15 Torrens properties still exist in Manhattan. The Block index may indicate "Torrens" or "Land Title Registration" instead of liber/page numbers. As new instruments are filed for these properties, they are being converted to the block/lot system. Records for all will be entered into the computer and will be identifiable by the fact that they have dates of action prior to 1946, the earliest date that will be entered for all other properties.

Deeds and Mortgage Records: To examine an instrument recorded for a particular property, researchers may use the microfilms (self service) or microfiche (at Microfilm Counter). Use the liber and page numbers obtained from the index (either the name index or block and lot indexes) to locate the film for pre-1968 records and reel and page number for records, 1968 and later. Where film is not available on self-service shelves, request a microfiche copy at the Counter.

Maps: In addition to the sectional maps described above, the Office also has on film all maps filed with the City Register's Office. These are on open shelves.

Sanborn, Manhattan Land Book of the City of New York, TRW-REDI Property Data maps, available at the Real Property Assessment Bureau, may also be useful in identifying information about a particular property.

Description of Facility:

The City Register's Office is a large, busy government office occupying most of the 13th floor at 66 John Street. The Real Property Assessment Bureau is located also on this floor.

All index libers are on open shelves under the counters and along the walls in the Public Research Section. The block and lot atlas is on a standing carousel to the right of the entrance (after passing the cashiers). Four long counters provide stand-up reading space for referencing the volumes. All records are immediately available. The Office has 36 microfiche and 23 microfilm readers of which 9 are microfilm reader/printers. Many are unusable. Where possible, work with the computers or ledger indexes. There are two photocopy machines and 14 computer terminals supported by printers. One computer, labeled "All Boros" on top, can access information from all boroughs. Microfilms are on self-service open shelves. Staff will answer short questions but they cannot conduct searches for the public.

Fees/Copies:

There is no cost for computer printouts of the index. Paper copies of microform records can be made at $.25 per page. Purchase a copycard from the cashier at the entrance to the Public Research Section. If you provide the clerks with block and lot, liber (or reel) and page numbers, certified copies of records can be made by the Office. Certified copies take 5-10 days. There is a fee of $4 per page.

This office will accept cash, certified checks or money orders. No personal checks are accepted.

Restrictions on Use:

Researchers may take up to 5 microfilm reels at a time for viewing.

Grantor/Grantee indexes (microfilm) are not on the self-service shelves. Request these films at the Microfilm Counter. These are not frequently used by title searchers and staff are unfamiliar with them. Be persistent. NOTE: Box covers which identify the content information were missing from some films.

Copies of records can be made only from microfilm or microfiche. Photocopy machines in this office are for Uniform Commercial Code records.

No mail requests for searches can be honored. Researchers may conduct their own searches or use Title searchers for official purposes. Contact the New York State Land Title Association, 2 Rector Street, Room 901, New York, NY 10006, (212) 964-3701 for the names of qualified Title searchers. This organization of underwriting companies, abstracters and title insurance agents will provide a listing of all of its members who operate within a particular County. These firms are not inexpensive. Contact them for their fee schedule prior to requesting a search.

The City Register's Office will supply certified copies of real property instruments by mail only when sufficient document location data is supplied (document type, date, liber/reel and page numbers) and a check for the proper amount ($4 per page) is enclosed.

No pens may be used when working with the index libers.

Computers are very old and not user-friendly.

CIVIL COURT OF THE CITY OF NEW YORK
MANHATTAN (NEW YORK COUNTY)

Facility Director: Mary Lee Andronaco, Clerk of the County

Address: 111 Centre Street (also known as 75 Lafayette Street), Room 118   ♿
New York, NY 10013

(Cross Streets: Franklin, White and Lafayette Streets)

Phone: (212) 374-7915 (General Clerk's Office)
Fax: none
E-mail: none
Website: see www.courts.state.ny.us

Hours of Operation:

Monday to Friday: 9:00 am to 5:00 pm

Closed Saturday, Sunday and legal holidays.

Closest Public Transportation:

Subway: 4, 5 or 6 to Brooklyn Bridge (or 6 to Canal Street)
           J, M or Z to Chambers Street
           N or R to City Hall
           A or C to Chambers Street (north end)

Bus: M1 or M6 to Broadway and Worth Street (south)
        M1 to Centre and Worth Streets (north)
        M6 to Church and Worth Streets (north)
        M22 to Worth and Lafayette Streets (west)

Directions:

Take the #4 or #5 (express) or #6 (local) train to the Brooklyn Bridge station. Go down the staircase at the <u>north</u> end of the platform. Turn right at the bottom of the stairway, then left and follow the signs to "BMT & Pearl Street." Go up the stairs at the end of the long corridor, exit through the gate and go up the next flight of stairs ahead to the far right. Walk north three blocks on Centre Street to the New York City Civil Court building at 111 Centre (or walk north on Lafayette Street to #75). Or, take #6 (local) train to Canal Street and walk 2 blocks south on Lafayette Street to the building. Room 118, General Clerk's Office, is located on the first floor (north side) of the building.

Description of Resources:

The Court has change of name records from May 1887 to the present. Records 1887–1962, were those filed in the City Court. After 1962, this became the Civil Court of the City of New York.

For the period May 1887 to June 13, 1906, the case records explaining why the name change was requested and the Court's decision on the case are in bound volumes in groups of years. From June 14, 1906 to 1936, the bound volumes include only the Court's decision. The June 14, 1906 to December 31, 1931 case files, including the explanation of why the name change was requested, appear to have been lost or were destroyed. From 1932 to the present, separate file folders are available on each case.

Finding Aids:

This office has both ledger (1887–January 2001) and computerized (1994 to present) indexes. The ledger indexes are either at the front of each record book (through 1936) or in separate ledger volumes (1937 to January 2001) and are arranged alphabetically by the first letter of the surname.

The ledger indexes include both the old and new names but are alphabetized only under the old name pre-1938 and from 1958 to the present. From 1938 to 1957, both the old and new surnames are alphabetized by the first letter of the surname.

The Civil Court's computerized index (1994 to the present) includes name changes. These can be recognized by the letters "NCN" in the case number. New names are denoted by "NN" in the Defendant/Plaintiff column and old names by "ON." Older records may be included in this database if a certified copy of the file was requested after 1994.

Description of Facility:

Ledger indexes, 1887 to January 2001, are located behind the counter in the General Clerk's Office, Room 118 (first floor). There are three computers with Civil Court case indexes (1994 to present) in this Office.

Name change record files covering the years 1932–1952 are in Room 118. These and earlier records stored elsewhere in the building, must be requested from the clerk behind the counter in Room 118.

NOTE: The Civil Court does not have its own website. However, information about various NYS courts can be found on the *New York State Unified Court System* website (www.courts.state.ny.us).

Fees/Copies:

There is one photocopy machine available in Room 118. Copies are $.10 per page. The clerk can provide a certified copy at $5 per document.

Restrictions on Use:

None.

COUNTY CLERK'S OFFICE - STATE SUPREME COURT
NEW YORK COUNTY (MANHATTAN)

Facility Director: Norman Goodman, County Clerk
                               Joseph Antonelli, Chief Clerk

Address: 60 Centre Street, Room 103B ♿
               New York, NY 10007

               (Cross Streets: Worth Street and Foley Square)

Phone: (212) 374-4704, 8344
Fax: none
E-mail: none
Website: www.courts.state.ny.us/supctmanh/county_clerk_operations.htm

Hours of Operation:

Monday to Friday: 9:00 am to 5:00 pm
                            9:00 am to 3:00 pm (Record Room)

Closed Saturday, Sunday and legal holidays.

Closest Public Transportation and Directions:

See CIVIL COURT OF THE CITY OF NEW YORK, MANHATTAN (NEW YORK COUNTY). The State Supreme Court building is to the left of the U.S. Court House. Go up the main stairs to the rotunda and take an elevator down one flight to the basement level. NOTE: Wheelchair accessible entrance at ground level on Pearl Street (south side of building).

Description of Resources:

This Office has filed records and court cases for New York County (Manhattan). The following are available in the State Supreme Court building. For earlier Court records, see COUNTY CLERK'S OFFICE - STATE SUPREME COURT - NEW YORK COUNTY (MANHATTAN), DIVISION OF OLD RECORDS.

1. Business Names include:

    Certificates of Incorporation, 1947 to the present (includes incorporation records for synagogues and landsmanshaftn societies)
    Limited Partnerships, 1925 to June, 1991 (microfilm)
    Trade Names "Doing business as...," 1925–1989 (microfilm), 1990 to the present (originals)

    See NYS DEPARTMENT OF STATE, DIVISION OF CORPORATIONS for limited partnerships, July 1, 1991 to present.

2. Military Discharge Records are filed on a voluntary basis by veterans from the first World War to the present. See "Restrictions on Use."

3. Name Changes filed in Supreme Court, New York County, 1935 to the present.

4. Court Cases filed in Supreme Court, New York County, 1941 to the present. Includes all cases filed in New York County during this period, except those being held for microfilming at the COUNTY CLERK'S OFFICE - STATE SUPREME COURT, NEW YORK COUNTY (MANHATTAN), DIVISION OF OLD RECORDS. See "Restrictions on Use."

5. Matrimonial Records - divorces, separations and annulments brought in New York County, 1941 to the present. Includes all records filed in New York County during this period, except those being held for microfilming at the COUNTY CLERK'S OFFICE - STATE SUPREME COURT, NEW YORK COUNTY (MANHATTAN), DIVISION OF OLD RECORDS. See "Restrictions on Use."

6. Incompetency Records and Conservatorships involving persons who could not handle their own affairs or persons committed. The records are available from 1941 to 1980 and 1996 to the present. (See COUNTY CLERK'S OFFICE - STATE SUPREME COURT, NEW YORK COUNTY (MANHATTAN), DIVISION OF OLD RECORDS for pre-1941 and 1981–1995 records.

7. Surrenders of Children filed from 1927 to the present. See "Restrictions on Use."

Finding Aids:

1. A computer index (printout) is available for <u>Business Names</u> registered in New York County. This index is arranged alphabetically by company name and covers Trade Names "Doing business as.." and General Partnerships from 1812 to 1996, Limited Partnerships to 1991, and Certificates of Incorporation to 1995. NOTE: Bound computer printouts for Business Names are mislabeled "1800–1996."

    In addition, the office has a computerized index for <u>Trade Names "Doing business as"</u> and General Partnerships from 1996 to the present; and <u>Incorporations</u>, 1995 to the present.

    NOTE: See NYS DEPARTMENT OF STATE, DIVISION OF CORPORATIONS AND DIVISION OF LICENSING for an online statewide index to corporations and limited partnerships active on or after December 5, 1977.

2. <u>Matrimonials</u>, <u>Incompetency Records</u> and all other <u>Court Cases</u> involving individuals, 1971 to the present have been computerized and can be accessed by name of plaintiff or defendant at any of the computer terminals in Room 103B and 141B. From 1941 to 1971, there are alphabetical card indexes arranged by groups of years, i.e 1948–1961, 1962–1970. See "Restrictions on Use."

    Of the five NYC counties, only New York County has a "Commercial" Division (opened in 1995) to handle complicated commercial cases. (Other NYS counties with this Division are Albany, Erie, Monroe, Nassau, Suffolk and Westchester.) New York County has digitized and posted online commercial case decisions, c. 2000 to the present. <u>Commercial decisions</u> can be searched by case number or "content" (try surname) and can be viewed at "New York State Supreme Court, Commercial Division, Decision Search":

    http://decisions.courts.state.ny.us/nyscomdiv/search/AdvComDivquery.asp

    NOTE: A separate index to all pending New York County (Manhattan) Supreme Court <u>Civil Cases</u> requiring judicial intervention ("RJI" cases) is available on the NYS Unified Court System CaseTrac website: http://e.courts.state.ny.us. Online searches can be made by surname of plaintiff, defendant, firm/attorney, or index (case) number. Digitized decisions are added at the conclusion of the case and are already accessible for New York (Manhattan), Kings (Brooklyn), and Queens counties. After a two week period, closed cases are removed from CaseTrac but decisions remain online. To search online decisions by surname, click on "Full Text Search of Decisions Now Available" at:

    http://portal.courts.state.ny.us/pls/portal30/CMS_dev.DYN_NDASEARCH.show.

    A separate index for <u>Criminal Cases</u> includes pending criminal cases from Criminal and Supreme Courts of 21 counties. All five boroughs of NYC and suburban counties (Nassau, Putnam, Rockland, Suffolk, Westchester) are included. The <u>Criminal Case</u> index online can be searched by case number only.

3. <u>Military Discharge Records</u> are indexed in an alphabetical card file. See "Restrictions on Use."

4. <u>Name Change Records</u>: Liber indexes for <u>Name Change</u> records are available from 1923 to the present. Liber indexes pre-1947 include name changes of corporations as well as individuals. Indexes from 1947 to the present include only individual. For 1923–1946, the index is arranged by the first letter of the old and new surnames. For 1947 to the present, these are arranged alphabetically by the first letter of the old surname only.

    There are also index cards for Name Change records, 1941–1971. However, these are not open to the public. The clerk behind the counter in Room 103B can search this index.

    If the name change occurred before 1935, researchers should use the index cards (alphabetical) available in the COUNTY CLERK'S OFFICE -STATE SUPREME COURT - NEW YORK COUNTY (MANHATTAN), DIVISION OF OLD RECORDS.

Description of Facility:

These offices are located on the basement level of the New York State Supreme Court Building. Researchers are not permitted behind the counters. There is no seating available in most rooms. The exception is the Business Section (Room 117B) where there is seating for 16 researchers at two long tables and the Record Room (Room 103B) which can seat 46 researchers. There are 1-2 staff persons in each room who take record requests.

Records and indexes can be found in the following rooms:

1. <u>Business Names</u>: The computer printout, 1812–1996, (mislabeled 1800–1996) and records are in Room 117B. Two computer terminals for later records are in Room 109B.

2. <u>Military Discharge Records</u>: Indexes and records are located in Room 109B (to the far right) behind the counter.

3. Name Changes: Liber indexes pre-1947 are in Room 141B on the shelves to the far left (before the entrance to Room 103B). Records, 1935–1946, are in Room 117B (Prefix "M"). Later name change records are available in Record Room 103B.

4. Matrimonials, Incompetencies and other Court Cases: There are 4 computer terminals which include the index 1971 to the present in Room 103B opposite the clerks' desk. In addition, there are 3 computer terminals in Room 141B. Card indexes to case files 1948 to 1971, are to the right when you enter Room 103B. There is also a card file for 1941 to 1948, accessible to the clerks only.

5. Surrenders of Children: Records of surrenders are maintained in a vault in Room 109B. See "Restrictions on Use."

Fees/Copies:

Business records and Name Change records may be examined by researchers. Copies may be made at $.25 per page. Copy machines are available at the entrance to each room in addition to the 7 machines in Room 103B. There are also 2 microfiche reader/printers in Room 103B. Copies are $.25. A change machine for $1 or $5 is available in Room 103B.

Most case files are open and may be copied. See "Restrictions on Use" for limitations. For older records on microfiche or microfilm, a copy will be provided to the researcher.

Restrictions on Use:

Business Records on microfilm must be ordered from the clerk. Microfilm is not accessible to the public. The record will be copied by the clerk and the copy will be available to the researcher the next day.

Matrimonial cases are closed except to the involved parties or their attorneys. Indexes are open.

Court Cases and Matrimonial Cases are being microfilmed in groups of years. During this period, the records are held by the COUNTY CLERK'S OFFICE - STATE SUPREME COURT, NEW YORK COUNTY (MANHATTAN), DIVISION OF OLD RECORDS. Check the index at the County Clerk's Office here before going to the 31 Chambers Street.

Case files from 1941–1954 are off-site and must be ordered in Room 103B. Turnaround is 2-3 days. Case files 1955–1979 have been microfilmed (see note re microfilmed records above). Files 1980–1995 will be microfilmed over the next few years and are being held in the COUNTY CLERK'S OFFICE - STATE SUPREME COURT, NEW YORK COUNTY (MANHATTAN), DIVISION OF OLD RECORDS during this period. Files 1996 to the present are available in hard copy.

Access to Military Discharge Records is restricted to the concerned individual or his/her immediate family.

Surrenders of Children (indexes and records) are closed except by court order.

COUNTY CLERK'S OFFICE - STATE SUPREME COURT NEW YORK COUNTY (MANHATTAN)
DIVISION OF OLD RECORDS

Facility Director:	Joseph Van Nostrand, Archivist/Senior Management Analyst Bruce Abrams, Archivist/Principal Court Analyst
Address:	31 Chambers Street, Room 703 New York, NY (Cross Streets: Centre and Elk Streets)
Mail Address:	New York County Clerk's Office 60 Centre Street, Room 161 New York, NY 10007
Phone:	(212) 374-4376, 4781
Fax:	none
E-mail:	none
Website:	www.courts.state.ny.us/supctmanh/county_clerk_records.htm

Hours of Operation:

Tuesday, Thursday: 9:00 am to 1:00 pm, 2:00 pm to 5:00 pm*
Monday, Wednesday, Friday: By appointment only*. Closed Saturday, Sunday and legal holidays.

*NOTE: Hours may change to 9:00 am to 3:00 pm daily. Call before coming.

Closest Public Transportation:

Subway: 4, 5 or 6 to Brooklyn Bridge
J, M or Z to Chambers Street
N or R to City Hall
A or C to Chambers Street (north end)

Bus: M1, M6 to Broadway and Reade/Chambers Streets (south); and Church and Reade/Chambers Streets (north)
B51 or M22 to Centre Street and Reade/Chambers Streets

Directions:

Take the #4 or #5 (express) or #6 (local) train to the Brooklyn Bridge station. Exit to "City Hall/Park Row/Chambers Street." The exit is at the South end of the platform. Go up the stairs, turn right and exit the gate. After the gate, go up the stairs to the right. You will emerge at the corner of City Hall Park on Chambers and Centre Streets. 31 Chambers Street is the Surrogate's Court building located across Chambers Street. Take the elevator to the 7th floor. NOTE: There is a service entrance (steep incline) at the back of the building (Reade Street) which provides access to wheelchair users.

Description of Resources:

This Division of the County Clerk's Office is the custodian of old records of the State Supreme Court in New York County and its predecessor courts, as well as other materials which fall within the jurisdiction of the County Clerk. For more recent business, matrimonial, military and court records, see COUNTY CLERK'S OFFICE - STATE SUPREME COURT, NEW YORK COUNTY (MANHATTAN). The following records are located at this office:

1. Census Records

   U.S. Census, New York County (Manhattan), 1860 (Ward 18/Divisions 1-6 only) and 1870. The New York County (Manhattan) enumeration of the 1870 Census was done twice. The first enumeration is available here.
   NY State Census, New York County (Manhattan), 1855 (originals), 1905 (includes the Bronx), 1915, 1925 (on microfilm). See"Restrictions on Use."

   NOTE: NEW YORK PUBLIC LIBRARY, MILSTEIN DIVISION OF U.S. HISTORY, LOCAL HISTORY AND GENEALOGY and NEW YORK GENEALOGICAL AND BIOGRAPHICAL SOCIETY have the 1855, 1905, 1915 and 1925 Censuses on microfilm for New York County; as well as the 1860 and 1870 U.S. Census; the NEW YORK STATE DEPARTMENT OF EDUCATION, NEW YORK STATE LIBRARY has the 1855, 1915 and 1925 Census (microfilm).

2. Name Changes

   Individuals whose names were legally changed, 1847–1934

3. Naturalizations

   Petitions for Naturalization filed in NY County:
   State Supreme Court, 1868, 1896–1906 (microfilm)*; 1907–1924 (originals & microfilm)
   Court of Common Pleas, 1792–1895 (microfilm)*
   NY County, Superior Court, 1828–1895 (microfilm)*
   *NOTE: Originals of these records are off-site and cannot be accessed. Dexigraph copies of these New York County court Petitions, 1792–1906, are available for viewing at the NATIONAL ARCHIVES, NORTHEAST REGION.

   Declarations of Intention filed in New York County:
   State Supreme Court, 1896–1906 (originals), 1907–1924 (originals & microfilm)
   Court of Common Pleas, 1802–1895
   NY County, Superior Court, 1828–1895
   NOTE: Naturalization Petitions and Declarations records, 1907–1924, have been microfilmed by the Mormon Family History Library and are available if ordered at any FAMILY HISTORY CENTER around the world.

   Microfilm index, 1792–1906 to Petitions for Naturalization in New York County (non-federal) courts. These index cards contain much of the key information available on the Petitions for this period. NOTE: This index is *not* the same as the WPA index available at the NATIONAL ARCHIVES, NORTHEAST REGION, NEW YORK PUBLIC LIBRARY, MILSTEIN DIVISION OF U.S. HISTORY, LOCAL HISTORY AND GENEALOGY and at FAMILY HISTORY CENTERS (LDS) around the world. In addition to the New York County Courts, the WPA index includes records in courts in all five NYC counties.

4. City Directories

   Manhattan/Bronx* City Directories (paper copies) for 1850–1868, 1870–1901, 1909, 1911–1913, 1916–1918, 1920–1922/23, and 1933/34. The Division also has damaged Directories for 1905/6 and 1908–1910. Use may be restricted because of condition. *NOTE: Parts of the Bronx are included from 1875 to 1895 and all of the Bronx from 1896 to 1933/34.

   The Directories alphabetically list head of household by surname (male adults primarily; women usually are included only if widowed), occupation, home address and/or business address. Entries for businesses (except for 1931) are also included. The Directories make excellent finding aids for the 1890 Police Census, the NYS Census and the U.S. Census.

5. Business Names

   Certificates of Incorporation, 1804–1946 (includes incorporation of synagogues and landsmanshaftn). See "Restrictions on Use."
   Limited Partnerships, 1822–1912
   Registered Business Names (a.k.a. Trade Names "Doing business as..."), 1900–1924. See "Restrictions on Use."

6. Maps

   Enumeration and Assembly Districts for 1855 and 1870, New York County (Manhattan)
   Maps/Condemned Areas (contained in condemnation case files, as well as individual maps), 1797 to the present
   Maps of Manhattan, 1893–1894

7. Matrimonial Records

   Divorce, separation and annulment cases brought in New York County, 1784–1940, in the following Courts:

   Court of Chancery and Supreme Court, 1784–1940
   Court of Common Pleas, 1847–1895
   Superior Court, 1847–1895

   Later records are available at the Old Records Division on a temporary basis (see COUNTY CLERK'S OFFICE - STATE SUPREME COURT, NEW YORK COUNTY (MANHATTAN). See "Restrictions on Use."

8. Marriage Records

   Marriages performed by the Mayors of New York, 1830–1850 (2 volumes)

9. Military Records

   1917 Militia Enrollment List, State of New York, Adjutant General's Office: New York County (includes name, address, age, birth date, occupation and prior military service of men ages 18 to 45 liable for service)

10. Other Court Records

   Attorneys admitted to practice in NY, 1754–1895. (For records filed after 1895, contact the First Appellate Division of NY Supreme Court, Admissions Committee, 60 Madison Avenue, New York, NY or call 212-779-1779.)

   Court of Chancery, 1754–1847 (85% of these records are after 1820). See also NEW YORK STATE DEPARTMENT OF EDUCATION, NEW YORK STATE ARCHIVES.

   Mayor's Court (after 1821, became Court of Common Pleas), 1674–1895

   Supreme Court of Judicature, Parchments, 1685–1848. (Most of the records date from 1780–1800.)

   Supreme Court, Pleadings, 1754–1910

   Superior Court Cases, 1828–1895

   Supreme Court Common Law Judgments, 1799–1940. (After 1910, case folders include all papers filed in the case in addition to the final judgment.) Later records are available at the Old Records Division on a temporary basis (see COUNTY CLERK'S OFFICE - STATE SUPREME COURT, NEW YORK COUNTY (MANHATTAN).

   Supreme Court Equity Cases, 1847–1910. (After 1910, equity cases were filed together with Supreme Court Common Law Judgments.)

11. Incompetency Records and Conservatorships involving persons who could not handle their own affairs or persons committed, pre-1941 and, 1981–1995. See COUNTY CLERK'S OFFICE - STATE SUPREME COURT, NEW YORK COUNTY (MANHATTAN) for records 1941 to 1980 and 1996 to present.

12. Adoptions

   Adoptions arranged through New York County SURROGATE'S COURT, 1874–1934. (These are duplicate orders filed with the County Clerk. The actual case files are on file in the SURROGATE'S COURT.) See "Restrictions on Use."

Finding Aids:

Census Records. Use 1855/1860 and 1870 Ward maps to narrow the search for Census Records in these years. There are no street addresses in the 1855, 1860 or 1870 Censuses. The Office does have an address index to the 1905, 1915 and 1925 NYS Censuses. NOTE: In 1860, Ward 18 covered East 14th to East 27th Street from 6th Avenue to Broadway.

Naturalization Records. There are three Naturalization indexes for 1907–1924: (1) a card index arranged alphabetically by surname, 1907–1924; (2) liber indexes, grouped by years and indexed by the first letter of the last name; and (3), a digitized index created from the card index (available also online.through *Ancestry.com* or *Ancestry.plus*).

There are liber indexes for Declarations of Intention, 1907–1924 arranged by groups of years and the first two letters of the surname. Pre-1907 Declarations have an index in each of the 393 volumes. See "Restrictions on Use."

For the New York County courts, pre-1907, there is a microfilm index which covers the Petition records of all three courts. A more comprehensive index including all NYC, NYS and Federal Courts that processed Naturalization cases is available at the NATIONAL ARCHIVES, NORTHEAST REGION. and the NEW YORK PUBLIC LIBRARY, IRMA & PAUL MILSTEIN DIVISION OF U.S. HISTORY, LOCAL HISTORY AND GENEALOGY.

Court Records are indexed by computer, alphabetical card indexes, and libers: These include:

i. Computerized indexes, "Supreme Court Civil Branch In-House Databases," searchable by name of plaintiff or defendant, and arranged in three databases:

   Historical Records I: includes Court of Common Pleas, 1786–1895; and Superior Court cases, 1828–1895.

   Historical Records II: includes Supreme Court Equity Judgements, 1847–1910; and Pleadings, 1754–1910.

   Matrimonial Records: includes Matrimonials, 1784–1910. NOTE: In addition to this index, there are two other indexes that should be searched for Matrimonial records: Historical Records I, which includes matrimonial cases of the Court of Common Pleas, 1847–1895 and Superior Court, 1847–1895; and Supreme Court, 1911–1940 (card index).

   To conduct a new search, click on "go" and then "back." A blank search screen will appear.

ii. Alphabetical card indexes are available for each of the following record groups:
   | Court of Chancery | 1765–1848 |
   | Mayor's Court/Court of Common Pleas | 1786–1895 (included in Historical Records I) |

Supreme Court of Judicature, Parchments	1685–1848
Supreme Court, Pleadings	1754–1910 (included in Historical Records II)
Superior Court Cases	1828–1895 (included in Historical Records I)
Supreme Court Common Law Judgments	1799–1910
Supreme Court Cases	1911–1940

iii. The following records are indexed in a combined alphabetical card index, the Miscellaneous Records Index:

| Name Changes | 1847–1934 |
| Marriage Records | 1830–1850 |

iv. Liber Indexes, arranged by year or groups of years and then alphabetically or by the first letters of the surname, are available for:

Attorneys Admitted (three volumes)	1754–1895
Limited Partnerships	1822–1922
Supreme Court Equity Judgements	1847–1910 (included in Historical Records II)
Matrimonials (divorces and annulments)	1784–1910 (included in computerized Matrimonial Records)

NOTE: Typed Matrimonial indexes, 1784–1910 (6 volumes), are arranged by first letter of the surname, and first letter of the given name.

Business Records: A computer index (printout) is available for Business Names registered in New York County. This index is arranged alphabetically by company name and covers all records from 1812 to 1986. See COUNTY CLERK'S OFFICE - STATE SUPREME COURT, NEW YORK COUNTY (MANHATTAN), Room 117B for printouts through 1996, and Room 109B for the computer terminals which access the index to later business records.

Military Records: 1917 Militia Enrollment List is arranged by first letter of the surname. Searches can be time consuming where there is more than one ledger to browse.

Description of Facility:

The Old Records Division occupies the 7th and 8th floors of 31 Chambers Street. The Reading Room (Room 703) is on the 7th floor to the right of the elevator lobby. Seating is available for 8 researchers at two sloped tables. Three staff members can provide assistance. There is one microfilm reader, one reader/printer and one computer on which the public can accessed the computerized databases.

Census volumes, 1855, 1860 and 1870, Naturalization Petitions, 1907–1924, City Directories, and all indexes described above are on open shelves or in cabinets on the 7th floor. Declarations of Intention are located on the 8th floor. Microfilms are located on the 7th floor and accessed through the Reading Room.

Fees/Copies:

Copies of Naturalization records must be made from the microfilm. A photocopy machine is available at $.25 per page and a microfilm reader/printer at $.50 per page. Bring change. Mail requests for Naturalization records are $10 per copy and Census searches are $10 per name, per address and year. State-mandated fees for photocopies of other records are as follows: Court records, $8 per document; Business Records, $10 per document. Payment by certified check or money order, payable to the New York County Clerk, must accompany the order. Allow 2-3 weeks for a return reply.

Restrictions on Use:

Declarations of Intention pre-1907 are not very accessible. Each of the 393 volumes is indexed separately. Further, separate volumes exist for each year or for parts of a year, by country of origin and also by court. Only three major country groupings were used: Germany, Great Britain/Ireland and Italy. Declarations by immigrants of such countries as Poland, Russia or Austria are usually located in the volumes for Germany. Researchers must know approximately in what year and court the Declaration was filed. Direct access to these volumes is currently limited since they are located on the 8th floor which is off-limits to the public. However, the public can search the microfilm copies.

Business Records (Certificates of Incorporation, 1921–1946, and Registered Business Names (1900–1924); Matrimonial Records, 1911–1940; and Name Change Records are now stored off-site. These records can be retrieved in 1-2 weeks.

Matrimonial cases are only available if more than 100 years old. Indexes are open.

Adoption indexes and records are sealed and cannot be viewed except by court order. Some materials are accessed by the staff only and can be used only under staff supervision, e.g. fragile parchments or books.

Visitors to 31 Chambers Street must present photo identification to the guards at the building entrance.

ELLIS ISLAND IMMIGRATION MUSEUM
AMERICAN FAMILY IMMIGRATION HISTORY CENTER

Facility Director: Jan DeDeka, General Manager, History Center

Address: Ellis Island, NY   ♿

Mail Address: The Statue of Liberty-Ellis Island Foundation, Inc.
292 Madison Avenue, 14th Floor
New York, NY 10017

Phone: (212) 561-4500
(212) 269-5755 (Ferry schedule)

Fax: (212) 779-1990

E-mail: historycenter@ellisisland.org

Website: www.ellisisland.org

Hours of Operation:

Daily, 9:30 am to 5:00 pm, except Christmas Day, December 25.

NOTE: Advance reservations to use the American Family Immigration History Center can be made online at www.ellisisland.org. Prior appointment recommended. Reservations are grouped into three periods — 9:45 am, 11:45 pm and 1:45 pm. The exact time of reservation is provided upon arrival at the History Center check-in counter at Ellis Island. No reservation is needed to visit the Museum or the American Immigrant Wall of Honor.

Closest Public Transportation:

Subway: 4 or 5 to Bowling Green Station
N or R to Whitehall Street
1 or 9 to South Ferry

Bus: M1, M6 or M15 to Broadway/South Ferry

Ferry: Circle Line Ferry departs from Battery Park every 45 minutes, 9:00 am to 3:30 pm; last departure from Ellis Island, 5:15 pm. (Longer hours and 30-minute departures during summer months.)

NOTE: From New Jersey, take the Central Avenue bus to Liberty State Park. Ferry ticket office at Park.

Directions:

Take the #4 or #5 train to Bowling Green Station. Exit the train and cross through Battery Park to reach the Circle Line ferry ticket office at Castle Clinton (circular building). Take the next Statue of Liberty/Ellis Island Ferry to Ellis Island. (Ellis Island is the second stop.) Turn left immediately upon entering the Museum and walk straight ahead through the door marked "Learning Center, American Family Immigration History Center." Check in at the desk for assignment of a work station. NOTE: Ferry travel time from Battery Park is 40 minutes. Allow extra time for long lines in summer months.

Description of Resources:

The American Immigration History Center and the American Immigrant Wall of Honor were developed and funded by The Statue of Liberty-Ellis Island Foundation, Inc. The Center opened in April 2001. Researchers can access:

1. Passenger Arrivals, Port of New York, 1892–1924. An interactive database of 22 million passenger records including 17 million immigrants and 5 million other passengers and crewmen who arrived at the port of New York, 1892–1924. The database was compiled by 12,000 volunteers of the Mormon church and is also accessible online (www.ellisisland.org).

   Each passenger record includes immigrant's given name and surname, ethnicity, last residence (town/country), date of arrival, age at arrival, gender, marital status, name of ship, port of departure and page/line. The manifest can be viewed to determine family members traveling with the immigrant, and place of birth (1906 or later).

2. Family Scrapbooks: Members of The Statue of Liberty-Ellis Island Foundation may create Family History Scrapbooks using the equipment available in one of the 10 work studios at the Center. Visitors can scan family

documents brought from home — birth certificates, marriage licenses, family photos and even small three-dimensional objects such as military medals or jewelry; take a family photo using a special digital camera; create brief digital audio messages; add stories or songs; write a family history; and include a copy of the ship manifest and photograph in the scrapbook which can be saved either on special archival paper, CD-ROM or online for public access (with password protection). NOTE: Scrapbooks can also be created online.

3. <u>The American Immigrant Wall of Honor</u>. In an outdoor area, visitors will find a monument with over 600,000 names of ancestors who emigrated to the U.S.A., and were memorialized by having their names inscribed here. Additions can be made by donation to the Foundation. Panel location of names on the Wall can be obtained at computer workstations on the first floor of the Museum. See also www.wallofhonor.com.

Finding Aids:

<u>Passenger Lists</u>: After using the swipe-card to activate the computer, researchers will see a short (10 minute) video and easy to follow instructions. The search screens at the History Center differ from those online and are easier to use. After entering the name, researchers are immediately given a choice of limiting the search by gender, year, and ethnicity. The results, shown on screen, are divided into three categories: the name exactly as entered, close matches and alternate spellings. Just click on a name to see the "passenger record," a one-page extract of eleven fields that appear on the manifest. Click on "Manifest" to see the actual record.

NOTE: Researchers using computers at home may find additional web pages created by Dr. Stephen P. Morse helpful in locating passenger records. To search the Ellis Island database in one step or customize your search, use http://home.pacbell.net/spmorse or www.jewishgen.org/databses/EIDB. This website includes four search tools. One allows researchers to search the Ellis Island database in one step and permits a customized search by year, ethnicity, and more. A second, created by Morse and Michael Tobias, allows researchers to narrow the search further to those who were identified as "Hebrew." Researchers using that site can search also by town and Daitch-Mokotoff soundex. The third, created by Morse, Tobias and Eric Steinmetz, is a "short form" for searching the Ellis Island database for any passenger by town of origin and/or by Soundex. And, the fourth assists researchers in finding scanned images of missing manifests that are in the database. This latter tool was created by Morse with contributions from Tobias, Alex Calzareth and Yves Goulnik.

Description of Facility:

The History Center is housed in the Ellis Island Immigration Museum's West Wing. There are 31 computers for passenger list searches and 10 private work stations for work on family scrapbooks. Reservations for use of a computer may be made at least 24-hours in advance (by completing a reservation form online). Go to the check-in desk at the History Center to receive a swipe-card which will activate your computer. Computer stations can seat 3 to 7 people.

Each of the 10 private work studios available to create a Family History Scrapbook are equipped with a computer, color scanner, digital camera and audio equipment.

Fees/Copies:

Circle Line Ferry from Battery Park is $10 round trip; $8 for seniors; $4 for children ages 3-17. There is no entrance fee to the Museum. A $5 per session fee is charged to use a History Center Search Station. Each search session lasts 35 minutes of which 25 minutes is available for the actual search. Scrapbook sessions are approximately 55 minutes. If desired, go to the check-in desk to determine if additional sessions are available. An additional $5 is charged per session. Reservations can be made online up to 90 days in advance.

Members of the Statue of Liberty-Ellis Island Foundation (contribution of $45 or more) can use one of the work studios to create a Family History Scrapbook. Donors receive a 10% discount at shops on Ellis Island, Liberty Island, including the Food Court and the Foundations' online gift shop; and a $.50 discount on Audio Tours of Ellis Island. Additions to the Wall of Honor can be made by donation of $100 or $200 per name (depending on format). Discover card users may receive a 5% discount. NOTE: Discounts cannot be combined.

Photocopies of passenger manifests are $25 per page on 11" x 17" archival paper. A copy of the passenger ship is $12.50. NOTE: Copies of passenger manifests can also be made at NATIONAL ARCHIVES - NORTHEAST REGION.

Restrictions on Use:

All passengers are screened prior to boarding the Circle Line ferry. Early arrival is recommended to allow extra time for security screening. No packages, backpacks, coolers, parcels, tools or weapons of any kind are permitted.

ELLIS ISLAND IMMIGRATION MUSEUM
NATIONAL PARK SERVICE ARCHIVES AND LIBRARY

Facility Director: George Tselos, PhD, Archivist
Janet Levine, PhD, Oral Historian

Address: Ellis Island, NY ♿

Mail Address: Statue of Liberty National Monument
U.S. Department of Interior, National Park Service
Attention: Library
Liberty Island
New York, NY 10004

Phone: (212) 363-3206, Ext. 158 (Library)
(212) 363-3206, Ext. 157 (Oral History Program)
(212) 363-3206, Ext. 137 (Genealogy Workshops)
(212) 269-5755 (Ferry schedule)
Fax: (212) 363-6302
E-mail: STLI_Library@nps.gov (Library)
Janet_Levine@nps.gov (Oral History Program)
Website: www.nps.gov/elis/index.htm

Hours of Operation:

Monday to Friday: 9:30 am to 4:30 pm. Appointment recommended.

Closed Saturday, Sunday and all legal holidays. NOTE: The Museum is open daily, 9:30 am to 5:00 pm, except Christmas day, December 25.

Closest Public Transportation and Directions:

See ELLIS ISLAND IMMIGRATION MUSEUM, AMERICAN FAMILY IMMIGRATION HISTORY CENTER. Take the elevator to the Archives and Library on the 3rd floor, west wing.

Description of Resources:

Library has a collection of books, unpublished manuscripts, photographs and archival materials related to Ellis and Liberty Islands in particular, and immigration in general, some of which are of interest to genealogists. These include:

> *The Famine Immigrants: Lists of Irish Immigrants Arriving at the Port of New York, 1846–1851,* edited by Ira A. Glazier. 7 vols. Baltimore, 1983. [E184.I6 F25 1983]
> *German Immigrants: Lists of Passengers Bound from Bremen to New York,* compiled by Gary J. Zimmerman and Marion Wolfert, 1985–. [Lists only passengers with specific places of origin] vol. 1, 1847–1854, vol. 2, 1855–1862, vol. 3, 1863–1867. [E184.G3 Z56 1985]
> *Who's Who Among Hispanic Americans, 1994–1995.* Detroit, [1995]. [E184.H5X]

Archives include historic photographs, maps and building plans related to Liberty and Ellis Islands, and files abandoned on-site when the facility was closed in 1954. While these were mostly administrative files, a small number are deportation case files and passenger lists. Case files listed in the finding aid by name include: Bolard, Cordts, Doucette, Heaghney, Newman, Quagliotti, Rosenberg, Summerton, Weir and Werblow. See "Restrictions on Use." [Boxes 9, 12, 13, 46]. Passenger lists include the S.S. *Nordan* (1905, 1908, 1944); and S.S. *Rydan* (1908). [Box 14]

Ellis Island Oral History Program: This ongoing project, begun in 1973 and dedicated to preserving the first-hand recollections of immigrants coming to the United States during the years Ellis Island was in operation, already includes circa 2,000 taped and/or transcribed interviews. Most, but not all, are immigrants who passed through Ellis Island. Interviews were conducted also with people interned as enemy aliens, those deported from Ellis Island, as well as former Ellis Island employees and people who served in the coast guard at Ellis Island and the Statue of Liberty.

NOTE: Some 136 transcribed interviews (but not audio tapes) conducted for the book, *American Mosaic: the immigrant experience in the words of those who lived it,* by Joan Morrison and Charlotte Fox Zabusky (Pittsburgh, 1980) are available here.

Finding Aids:

The Library has a binder that includes a description of its archival collection by box and file number.

Oral History Program: The computerized index at each listening station includes over 1,000 of the taped interviews. These interviews can be accessed by surname, country, year of entry, year of birth, or name of ship. Researchers can enter the first letter of the surname to locate possible alternate spellings (results not in alpha order).

For a complete listing including donated interviews and transcribed interviews, see the typed listings available in a binder in the office of the Oral Historian and arranged by name and by country. The name index, arranged alphabetically, includes birth date, country of origin, year of entry into the U.S.A., age at entry, name of ship, date of interview, running time, name of interviewer, and interview number. Additional information such as relationship to other interviewees and description of content is sometimes included. The index is also arranged by country, cross referenced by name and interview number. Transcribed *American Mosaic* interviewees are listed separately.

Description of Facility:

The Library and Oral History listening stations are located on the 3rd floor, west wing. Both the reading room and the listening room are large sky-lit chambers. The reading room can accommodate 32 researchers at four tables. The Oral History listening room has 20 listening stations and monitors and can accommodate 50 people (2-4 at each station).

The National Park Service and the NATIONAL ARCHIVES - NORTHEAST REGION conduct genealogy workshops for visitors at Ellis Island who wish to learn how to research their family immigration history. Workshops are held monthly, from April to October, on the third Thursday of the month at 1:00 pm and 2:30 pm and are free to all Ellis Island visitors. Call (212) 363-3200 for schedule.

Fees/Copies:

The Circle Line Ferry from Battery Park costs $10 round trip; $8 for seniors; $4 for children ages 3-17. There is no entrance fee to the Museum or Library.

Copies of Oral History Project tapes can be ordered at $15. Photocopies cost $.30 per page. Copies are free if total cost is under $5 (16 pages or less).

Restrictions on Use:

All passengers are screened prior to boarding the Circle Line ferry. Early arrival is recommended to allow extra time for security screening. No packages, backpacks, coolers, parcels, tools or weapons of any kind are permitted. These should be left at home.

Researchers wishing to use the Research Library must make a request 72 hours in advance and register at the Library upon arrival. Pens may not be used in the Library. Materials may only be used on-site in the presence of a Library staff member.

FAMILY HISTORY CENTER (LDS)
MANHATTAN

Facility Director:	Lynda Gunther, Co-Director
	Paul Gunther, Co-Director
Address:	125 Columbus Avenue, 2nd floor ♿
	New York, NY 10023
	(Cross Streets: 65th Street and Broadway)
Phone:	(212) 873-1690
Fax:	(212) 496-2436
E-mail:	NewYork.familyhistorycenter@verizon.net
Website:	www.familysearch.org

Hours of Operation:

Tuesday to Friday	1:00 pm to 7:00 pm
Saturday:	11:00 am to 5:00 pm

Closed Sunday, Monday and legal holidays. Check hours before visiting. Family History Centers are staffed by volunteers. See "Restrictions on Use."

NOTE: THE FAMILY HISTORY CENTER CLOSED FOR RENOVATION ON DECEMBER 1, 2002 AND WILL REMAIN CLOSED FOR AT LEAST SIX-MONTHS. During this period researchers may order and view films at other Family History Centers in the New York/New Jersey metropolitan area (see addresses below); at the CENTER FOR JEWISH HISTORY (CJH), 15 West 16th Street, NYC; or at the NEW YORK GENEALOGICAL AND BIOGRAPHICAL SOCIETY, 122 East 58th Street, NYC.

Closest Public Transportation:

Subway : 1 or 9 to 66th Street/Lincoln Center
A, B, C or D to 59th Street/Columbus Circle

Bus: M5, M7 or M104 to Broadway and 65th Street
M10 to Central Park West and 65th Street
M66 to Broadway and 66th/65th Street (crosstown)

Directions:

Take the #1 or #9 train to 66th Street/Lincoln Center station. Cross Columbus Avenue/Broadway and walk one short block south to 125 Columbus Avenue on the corner of 65th Street. Sign in at the desk in the lobby. Take the stairs or elevator to the Library on the 2nd floor.

Description of Resources:

The Family History Center in Manhattan is one of many branches of the Mormon Family History Library in Salt Lake City. The Library has the most extensive collection in the world — currently 2.2 million rolls of microfilm and 742,000 microfiche — including materials and records of interest to Jewish genealogists. These materials are available for loan to Family History Centers for a small fee. The Manhattan Center currently has the following records on indefinite-loan:

- 1938 German census of Jews (299 rolls), including Sudetenland and Czechoslovakia
- 19th-century vital records for Jewish communities in Eastern and Central Europe, including Budapest, Krakow, Kielce, Lodz, Lomza, Radomsko, Tarnow, Vienna (Wien), and Warsaw.
- Hamburg passenger lists, direct lists 1851–1934; index of direct lists 1851–1935; card index of direct lists 1856–71; index of indirect lists 1880–91(Some early years missing from indexes)
- *Slownik geograficzny Królestwa Polskiego i innych Krajow slowianskich* [Geographical dictionary of the Kingdom of Poland and other Slavic countries], 15 vols., 1880–1902
- *Allgemeines geographisch statistisches Lexikon aller österreichischen Staaten.* General gazetteer of the Austrian Empire, including areas later located in Austria, Czechoslovakia, Hungary, Italy, Poland, Romania, Ukraine and Yugoslavia. 1845–1853.

- *Gemeindelexikon der im Reichsrate vertretenen Königreiche und Länder* [Gazetteer of the Crownlands and territories represented in the imperial council], 14 vols., 1903–1908. Includes Galicia.
- *Meyers Orts- und Verkehrs-Lexikon des Deutschen Reichs* [Gazetteer and directory of the German Empire], 1912
- *Spis miejscowosci Polskiej Rzeczypospolitej ludowej* [Spis Gazetteer of Poland], 1968
- Gazetteer-Hungary, 1877, 19 fiche
- Cook County, IL birth index, 1871–1916
- Cook County, IL death index, 1871–1916
- Street Index 1881 and 1891 to the Census of England and Wales
- 1881 Census of England by county, surname index, birthplace index, census index
- 1850 U.S. Census of New York State
- Ireland - civil registration indexes to births, 1864–1946; marriages, 1845–1921, 1933–1942 and deaths, 1864–1926, 1930–1944.
- Florida combined marriage index, 1927–1969
- Florida combined death index, 1877–1969
- New York City, vital records, Manhattan deaths, 1798–1865
- New York City Health Department, indexes to vital records (marriage indexes are for grooms only unless otherwise noted). Manhattan indexes (*) include the western Bronx from 1874 and eastern Bronx from 1895.

Births (all borough)	1898–1965	Deaths (Brooklyn)	1895–1897
Births (Manhattan and Brooklyn)	1881–1897*	Marriages (all boroughs)	1898–1937
		Marriages (Manhattan)	1888–1897*
Deaths (all boroughs)	1898–1965	Marriages (Brooklyn)	1894–1897
Deaths (Manhattan)	1888–1897*	Marriages (Bronx)	1898–1937 (Brides)

NOTE: Many other NYC records have been microfilmed by the Mormon Family History Library and are accessible to researchers around the world.

Electronic Resources: In addition to the Library's catalog, researchers can access the following on the Library's website:

1. *Ancestral File*, consisting of names and other vital information (birth, marriage, death dates) organized into family groups and pedigrees. The name/address of the researcher who contributed the file is included.

2. *International Genealogical Index (IGI)*, an index of over 600 million names of deceased persons, including vital information such as birth or marriage dates and places. Many names in the index come from vital records from the early 1500s to 1885. Others have been submitted by LDS members.

3. *Pedigree Resource File*, contains names, family relationships and birth, marriage and death information. The information in each file appears as originally submitted and is not merged with information submitted by others.

4. 1880 United States Census, 1881 Census of the British Isles, and 1881 Canadian Census. These three databases, with 55 million names, include all persons listed in these censuses and can be searched together or individually. Included are year of birth, country of birth, age, occupation, marital status, race, name of head of household, relation to head of household, and, for the U.S. census, country of father's and mother's birthplace. Information provided for those listed in the Canadian Census includes ethnic origin and religion. For Census of the British Isles, information includes disability.

Finding Aids:

The complete catalog of the Library's worldwide collection is available on the Internet (see above). A search can be made by place, title, author, film/fiche number, keyword and subject. The catalog is also available on CD-ROM. The Manhattan FHC has a loose-leaf notebook listing all microfilms/microfiche on indefinite loan. These are arranged by country/locality as well as film number. A copy of this listing is available online at www.jgsny.org.

NOTE: Films can be ordered also on inter-library loan at the CENTER FOR JEWISH HISTORY - GENEALOGY INSTITUTE. (CGI). A listing of films of particular interest to Jewish genealogists is available at the CGI in 10 brown leather bound binders and on CD-ROM, *Jewish Records in the Family History Library Catalog as of 1 February 2001.*

Description of Facility:

An up-to-date list of Family History Centers around the world, including hours open, can be found on the Family History Library's website (see above). Those in the New York/New Jersey metropolitan area include:

<u>New York</u>

Bronx, NY (Bronx)	211 East Kingsbridge Road. (718) 561-7824
Brooklyn, NY (Kings)	1212 Glenwood Road. (718) 434-8245
Lynbrook, NY (Nassau)	10 Peninsula Blvd. (516) 599-8079
Middletown, NY (Orange)	790 Silverlake Scotchtown Road. (845) 692-0364.
Newburgh, NY (Orange)	Mt. Airy Road, New Windsor. (845) 564-6785
Plainview, NY (Nassau)	160 Washington Avenue. (516) 433-0122
Poughkeepsie, NY (Dutchess)	204 Spakenkill Road. (845) 462-2470
Queens, NY (Queens)	86-16 60th Road, Elmhurst. (718) 478-5337
Scarsdale, NY (Westchester)	60 Wayside Lane. (914) 564-6785
Staten Island, NY (Richmond)	913 Rockland Avenue. (718) 698-0668
Terryville, NY (Suffolk)	372 Terryville Road, Port Jefferson Station. (631) 642-2096
Yorktown, NY (Westchester)	801 Kitchawan Road, Route 134. (914) 941-9150

<u>New Jersey</u>:

Caldwell, NJ (Essex)	209 Mountain Ave, North Caldwell. (973) 226-8975
East Brunswick, NJ (Middlesex)	303 Dunhams Corner Road. (732) 254-1480
Emerson, NJ (Bergen)	840 Soldier Hill Road. (201) 262-7357
Irvington, NJ (Essex)	1064 Clinton Avenue.
Mahwah, NJ (Bergen)	30 Youngs Road. (201) 327-1940
Short Hills, NJ (Essex)	140 White Oak Ridge Road. (973) 379-7315
Union City, NJ (Hudson)	2500 New York Avenue. (201) 866-8118

NOTE: Addresses are not mailing addresses. Because of limited staff, Family History Centers cannot respond to mail inquiries.

The Manhattan Center has 14 microfilm, 5 microfiche readers, 3 reader/printers, 9 computers with a shared printer and 5 computers with Internet access. The standard complement of microfiche and CD-ROMs (including the Social Security death index) is available, as well as a library of books and periodicals.

Fees and Copies:

Films can be order from the Family History Library as follows:

- Films already on indefinite loan: No cost
- 30 days $3.75
- renewal for 60 days   3.25
- second renewal (indefinite loan) 3.25

Microfiche can be ordered at $.15 per fiche. These remain on indefinite loan.

There are three photocopy machines available at $.25 per copy. Printouts from the catalog may be made to paper at $.10 per copy or to disk at $.50 per disk. Copies from microfilm/microfiche printers are $.25 per copy.

Restrictions on Use:

All microfilms and microfiche must be used in the local Family History Center. The typical wait is 2-3 weeks from the date ordered.

No books can be borrowed by mail from the Library in Salt Lake City.

Call before visiting a Family History Center. Hours are subject to change.

HEBREW UNION COLLEGE - JEWISH INSTITUTE OF RELIGION
THE KLAU LIBRARY

Facility Director:	Dr. Philip E. Miller, Librarian
Address:	One West Fourth Street ♿
	New York, NY 10012-1186
	(Cross Streets: Broadway and Mercer Street)
Phone:	(212) 824-2258
Fax:	none
E-mail:	See online Information Search Service, "Ask Libbie" at:
	http://library.cn.huc.edu//vtlseng/english/requests/iss.html
Website:	www.huc.edu

Hours of Operation:

Monday to Thursday:	9:00 am to 5:00 pm
Friday:	9:00 am to 3:00 pm

Closed Saturday, Sunday, Jewish and legal holidays.

Closest Public Transportation:

Subway: N or R to 8th Street
           6 to Astor Place
           A, C, E, F, V or S to West 4th Street/Washington Square

Bus: M1 (South Ferry), M5 or M6 to Waverly Place and Broadway (southbound)
           M1, M2 or M3 to 8th Street and Broadway (southbound)
           M1 to Lafayette and East 4th Street (northbound)
           M5 or M6 to Avenue of the Americas and West 4th Street (northbound)

Directions:

Take the N or R train to the 8th Street station. Exit the station and walk south on Broadway to West 4th Street. Turn west on West 4th Street to the entrance.

Description of Resources:

The Klau Library is a major Judaica library in NYC with over 140,000 volumes. Of special note are the microfilms of portions of the holdings of the American Jewish Archives in Cincinnati. The following is a bibliographical sampling of available works useful for genealogical research. Call numbers are in brackets:

1.   Cemetery Records:

    Algiers. Bloch, Isaac. *Algiers Cemeteries.* Paris, 1888. [HS/210]
    Barbados. Shilstone, E. M. *Jewish Monumental Inscriptions in Barbados.* New York, 1956. [HS/1260]
    Czech Republic. Prague. Lion, Jindrich. *Der alte Prager Judenfriedhof* [The old Jewish cemetery of Prague]. Prague, 1960. [HS/191]
    Czech Republic. Prague. Lieben, Koppelman. *Grabensteininschriften des Prager israelitischen alten Friedhofs* [Gravestone inscriptions of the Old Prague Israelite cemetery]. Contains the most complete record of epitaphs - in German gothic type. Prague, 1856. [HS/190]
    Denmark. Copenhagen. Margolinsky, Julius. *Jodiske Dodsfald 1693–1976* [Jewish cemetery]. Copenhagen, 1978. [HS/1206]
    Germany. Frankfurt am Main. Hulsen, Julius. *Der alte Judenfriedhof in Frankfurt a.M.* [The old Jewish cemetery in Frankfurt am Main]. Frankfurt, 1932. [HI/472.3]
    Germany. Rheinpfalz. Friedmann, Hugo. *Merischonim loachronim: Verstorbenlisten der juedischen Gemeinden der Mittelmosel von Wintrich bis Enkirch* [From first to last: Death lists of the Jewish communities of the central Mosel valley, from Wintrich to Enkirch]. (typescript) Berncastel-Cues, 1929. [HS/407]
    Greece. Salonika. Molho, Michael. *Matsevot Bet ha-alamin shel Yehude Saloniki* [Tombstones of the Jewish cemetery of Salonika]. Salonika, 1975. [HS/889.2]

Hungary. Budapest. Scheiber, Alexander. *Newly found Jewish tombstones at Buda.* Budapest, 1953. [HS/415]

Israel. Jerusalem. Cohen, Shear Yashub. *Har ha-zetim* [Mt. of Olives]. Jerusalem, 1969. [LB]

Spain. Cantera Burgos, Francisco and Jose Maria Millas y Vallicrosa. *Las Inscripciones Hebraicas de Espana* [Hebrew inscriptions of Spain]. Madrid, 1956. [HS/756]

Ukraine and Moldova. Goberman, David N. *Evreiskie nadgrobiia na Ukraine i v Moldove* [Jewish Tombstones in Ukraine and Moldova], Moscow, [1993]. [N7415.5 S5 1991 vol.4]

United States. Galveston, TX. Dreyfus, A. Stanley. *Hebrew Cemetery No. 1 of Galveston, TX.* (mimeographed) [ALU]

2. Vital Records and Lists

England. London. *Bevis Marks Records,* edited by Lionel D. Barnett. 4 vols. Vol. 1, early history of the Spanish and Portuguese Congregation of London...to 1800; vol. 2, abstracts of ketubot (marriage contracts), to 1837; vol. 3, abstracts of ketubot, 1837–1901; vol. 4, circumcisions, 1715–1775. London, 1940, 1973. [HS/337], [f BM295.S7 L6 1940]

Italy. DiGrassi, Liliana. *Ketubbot Italiane: antichi contratti nuziali ebraici miniati* [Italian ketubbot: illuminated Jewish marriage contracts]. Milan, 1984. [NK 1672 K4 1984]

Portugal. Coimbra. Bivar Guerra, Luiz de. *Inventario dos Processos da Inquisicao de Coimbra (1541–1820)* [Catalog of the trials of the Inquisition of Coimbra, Portugal, 1541–1820]. Names are indexed in vol. 2. Paris, 1972. [HS/772]

Other. Sabar, Shalom. *Ketubah: Jewish Marriage Contracts of the Hebrew Union College Skirball Museum and Klau Library.* Philadelphia, 1990. [ND 2935 H4 1990]

3. Communal Histories and Yizkor Books (Pre- and Post-World War II)

Yizkor books at this library are included in the *Bibliography of Eastern European Memorial (Yizkor) Books* (see Appendix B). The following books are not included in this bibliography:

Bavaria. Weinberg, M. *Die Memorbuecher der juedischen Gemeinden in Bayern* [Memorial books of the Jewish communities in Bavaria]. Frankfurt, 1937–1938. [HS/323]

Bavaria. Salfeld, Sigmund. *Das Martyrologium des Nuernberger Memorbuch* [Martyrology of Jews in Bavarian towns]. Berlin, 1898. [HS/350]

Brest-Litovsk. *Brzesc nad Bugiem (Brisk) Ir Tehilah* [Brisk, City of Prayer]. Warsaw, 1886. (Hebrew) [HI/912]

Busk. *Toldot Yehudim* [History of the Jews]. Tel Aviv, 1962. [HI/926.3]

Krakow. Friedberg, B. *Luhot zikaron* [Tablets of Memory]. Frankfurt am Main, 1904. [HI/929.1]

Lithuania. *Da'at kedoshim* [Wisdom of the holy], by Israel T. Eisenstadt. Includes the descendents of two martyrs, Yizrael Zak and Tuviah Bachrach killed in a 1659 pogrom. Families mentioned include: Altshuler, Ashkenazy, Auerbach, Babad, Bachrach, Berlin, Berliner, Broida, Eizenstadt, Eskeles, Ettinger, Frenkel, Friedland, Gunzburg, Grayever, Halberstadt, Heilprin, Horowitz, Hochgelerenter, Jaffe, Katzenellenbogen, Landau, Lipshutz, Luria, Margolis, Meizel, Meizels, Mintz, Mirkes, Morwitz/Morvits, Neumark, Parness, Polak, Rabbinovitch, Rapaport, Rokeach, Volozhiner, Zak and Zusman. St. Petersburg, 1897/98. [HI/921]

Lithuania. Dubnow, Simon. *Pinkas ha-medinah Lita* [Ledger of the province of Lithuania]. Berlin, 1925 (photocopy). [HI/917]

Lodz. *Ha-Yehudim be-Lodz* [The Jews in Lodz]. Warsaw, 1893. [HI/926.1]

Lodz. Yasni, A. Wolf. *Die geshikhte fun Yidn in Lodz* [The history of the Jews in Lodz]. Israel, 1960. [HI/922.3]

Lublin. Balaban, Majer. *Die Judenstadt von Lublin* [The ghetto of Lublin]. Berlin, 1919. [HI/907] and Hebrew edition [HI/907.2]

Lviv. *Zydzi Lwowscy* [Jews of Lwow]. Lwow, 1909. (Polish) [HI/903.2]

Lviv. *Anshe shem* [Men of renown]. Krakow, 1895. (Hebrew) [HI/904]

Lviv. *Die Lemberger Juden pogrom Nov. 1918–Jan. 1919.* [HI/910]

Minsk. Eisenstadt, Benzion. *Ravnei Minsk* [Chief Rabbis of Minsk]. Vilna, 1898. [HI/921.1]

Ostraha/Ostrov. *Mazkeret li-gedole Ostraha* [Memorandum of the Leaders of Ostraha]. 1907. [HI/906]

Pinsk. Aharoni, Avraham. *Maftehot shemot ha-ishim veha-yishuvim shel sifre Pinsk* [Indexes of the names of the men and settlements of the records of Pinsk]. Haifa, 1982. [DS135.R93 P5433 1982]

Russia. *Juden pogrome in Russland* [Jewish pogroms in Russia - giving the story of each community]. 2 vols. Koeln/Leipzig, 1910. [HP/100]

Ukraine. Revyuk, E. *Polish atrocities in the Ukraine.* 1931. [HP/73]

Vilna. Fein, Rabbi Samuel Joseph. *Kiryah Ne'emanah* [Faithful City]. Vilna, 1915. [HI/926]

Vilna. Haivrit b'Vilna. *Toldot ha-kehilah* [History of the Community]. Vilna, 1935. [HI/923.2]

Zolkiew. *Sefer Zolkiew* [The book of Zolkiew]. 1843. [HI/905]

4. Gazetteers

Cohen, Chester G. *Shtetl Finder.* Los Angeles, 1980. [REF DS135.R9 C58]
Szajkowski, Z. *Analytical Franco-Jewish Gazetteer, 1939–45.* New York, 1966. [HP/166]

5. Biographical Dictionaries

Who's Who in American Jewry. 1926, 1928, 1938–39, 1980. [E184 J5 W6]
Who's Who in World Jewry. 1955, 1965, 1972, 1978, 1980. [DS 125.3 A2 W5]
Whittemore, Henry. *Progressive, Patriotic, and Philanthropic Hebrews of the New World* [Biographies of leaders of the NYC community with a history of their philanthropic institutions]. New York, 1907. [Kiev HL collection]
Tapper, Lawrence F. *A Biographical Dictionary of Canadian Jewry, 1909–1914: From the Canadian Jewish Times.* Teaneck, [1992]. [fF1035.J5 F76 1992]

6. Periodicals

Allgemeine Zeitung des Judenthums [General Newspaper of Jewry], Germany, 1837–1921
The American Hebrew, New York, 1879–1884, 1890–1900, 1926–1941
American Jewish Historical Society: *Publications,* 1892–1947, *American Jewish Historical Quarterly,* 1947–1977, *American Jewish History,* 1977–
American Jewish Archives, 1948–1996
American Jewish Year Book, 1899–
Canadian Jewish Year Book, 1939–1941
Chicago Jewish Forum, 1942–1969
The Israelite (edited by Isaac Mayer Wise, now *The American Israelite*), Cincinnati, 1854–1913
Jewish Times, New York, 1869–1872.
The Occident (edited by Isaac Leeser), Philadelphia, 1843–1868
The Reform Advocate (edited by Emil G. Hirsch), Chicago, 1891–1922.
Western States Jewish Historical Quarterly, 1968–.

7. American Jewish Archives (AJA) Microfilms

Portions of the holdings of the AJA in Cincinnati are on microfilm in the library. These include some congregational records, family histories and other data. The following are the records of genealogical interest. Film numbers are in brackets:

Amsterdam. Portuguese Congregation ketubot, 1690–1893. [833–840]
Barbados. Ledger books and burial records, 1696–1887. [822]
Efroymson-Feibleman-Kahn genealogy. [2764]
Hamburg, Germany. Sephardim, 1672–1682. [751]
Jamaica, West Indies. Wills, 1692–1798. [140]
Lisbon, Portugal. Inquisition records: New Christians, America to Lisbon. [606–650, 736–745, 842–847]; Mexico. [720–722]; Brazil to Lisbon. [783–794]
Mexico. Inquisition records, 1597–1718. [856–859]
St. Thomas, VI. Vital records, 1786–1956. [125]
Surinam. Portuguese Congregation records, 1754–1920. [67-67o]
Portugal. Portuguese Community records. [176-198]
Portugal. Records of the Portuguese Jews. [527-527t]
United States. American Jewish Joint Distribution Committee, papers, 1918–1980. [2798]
- Atlanta, GA. Hebrew Benevolent Congregation (The Temple), vital records, etc., 1890–1950. [552]
- Charleston, SC. Congregation Beth Elohim, minutes, 1838–1850. [84]
- Cincinnati, OH. Judah Touro Cemetery, 1856–1970. [2160-61]
- Cincinnati, OH. United Hebrew Cemetery, records, 1850–1951. [48]
- Cincinnati, OH. United Hebrew Cemetery, burials, 1850–1930, 1951–1959. [439-439a]
- Erie, PA. Congregation Anshe Chesed, minutes, etc. 1875–1936; cemetery records, 1865–1920. [3066-3069]
- Nashville, TN. Vine Street Temple, marriages and deaths, 1881–1928. [592]
- New Orleans, LA. Touro Synagogue and Hebrew Rest Cemetery, 1846–1955. [221-222]
- New York, NY. Congregation B'nai Jeshurun, records (marriages, 1825–1930; deaths, 1853–1928). [493-493h]

- New York, NY. Congregation Shearith Israel (Spanish & Portuguese), records, 1706–1949. [1-1g]
- New York, NY. *New York Herald Tribune,* Index, 1875–1906. [3-3b]
- Philadelphia, PA. Association for the Protection of Jewish Immigrants, 1884–1921. [137-137d]
- Philadelphia, PA. Reform Congregation Kneseth Israel, minutes, 1847–1880. [90]
- Piqua, OH. Anshe Emeth Congregation records, 1874–1956. [560]
- St. Louis, MO. Mt. Sinai Cemetery, 1859–1972. [861]

8. Electronic Resource:

Bar-Ilan Responsa Project
Encyclopedia Britannica
Encyclopedia Judaica
Index to Jewish Periodicals

Finding Aids:

The Library's computerized catalog is accessible online (Online-VTLS Gateway) at: http://library.cn.huc.edu/

Holdings of the (New York) Klau Library acquired since 1972 (Roman-alphabet items) and 1989 (Hebrew/Yiddish items) are included in this catalog. In addition, the catalog includes the holdings of HUC libraries in Cincinnati, Los Angeles and Jerusalem. For earlier acquisitions, check the Library's three card catalogs (adjacent to the library entrance):

1. The original (Kiev) catalog, created by former librarian Edward Kiev, includes author, subject, and title. Call numbers consist of letters, usually followed by numbers (e.g. HS/88). Note that Hebrew books are cataloged separately in drawers following A–Z.

2. The newer catalog is subdivided into author-title and subject catalogs using the Library of Congress system.

3. A catalog of post-1964 acquisitions in the Cincinnati campus Klau Library.

In addition, the Library has the following large-sized, bound catalogs, located in the first bookcase beyond the desk:

4. *Catalog of the Klau Library of Hebrew Union College-Jewish Institute of Religion.* 32 vols. Cincinnati, 1964. Each volume is arranged alphabetically by subject, author and title. For example, under the heading "Poland," there are 45 pages of listings of individual cities and towns and other subjects.

5. *Manuscript Catalog of the American Jewish Archives.* 4 vols. Cincinnati, 1971; supplement, 1 vol. 1975. A short description of each collection is included in the *Guide to the Holdings of the American Jewish Archives,* by J. W. Clasper and M. C. Dellenbach, Cincinnati, 1979.

6. *Catalog of the Jewish Collection, New York Public Library.* 14 vols., 1960; supplement 7 vols., 1975.

For photographs in the Library's Cincinnati collection, see *An Index to the Picture Collection of the American Jewish Archives,* by Jacob R. Marcus, Cincinnati, 1971, which includes a surname index.

Description of Facility:

This is primarily a research library in a spacious area on the second floor of the building, accessible only by elevator. There are individual carrels (working tables) with comfortable chairs and one microfilm reader. Two staff members are usually on duty to obtain materials and provide assistance.

Encyclopedias, many histories, bound periodicals and the finding aids described above are on open stacks in the reading room. Most of the works mentioned above are in the stacks and are available only on request at the desk at the hours specified. See "Restrictions on Use."

Fees/Copies:

A photocopy machine is available for use with a VendaCard at $.10 per copy.

Restrictions on Use:

All visitors must secure an admission badge from the receptionist in the lobby, and must sign in at the library counter facing the elevator. Material is brought from the stacks only 3 times per day — 11:00 am, 2:00 pm and 4:00 pm. It is best to notify the Library in advance of the works you wish to consult. Return all books and materials to the cart at the desk. Five microfilm reels at a time may be requested. Only HUC-based personnel are permitted to borrow books.

HIAS (HEBREW IMMIGRANT AID SOCIETY)
LOCATION AND ARRIVAL RECORDS DEPARTMENT

Facility Director: Leonard Glickman, President and Chief Executive Officer
                            Valery Bazarov, HIAS Location and Family History Specialist

Mail Address: 333 Seventh Avenue, 17th Floor
                            New York, NY 10001

Phone: (212) 613-1409
Fax: (212) 967-4356
E-mail: location@hias.org
Website: www.hias.org

Hours of Operation:

Monday to Friday: 9:00 am to 5:00 pm.
Closed Saturday, Sunday, Jewish and legal holidays.

Closest Public Transportation, Directions, Description of Facility:

Not applicable. Inquiries may be made by mail, e-mail, fax or telephone. Search request forms ("Location Service Request" and "Arrival Card Request") are available online.

Description of Resources:

HIAS, founded in 1881, is the oldest international migration and refugee resettlement agency in the U.S.A. and is an important resource for immigrant family information.

1. Case Files: Case files 1979–1988 (microfilm) and original records, 1991 to the present, are at HIAS' Office. Case files, 1960–1990, are in HIAS' warehouse. See "Restrictions on Use."

   See YIVO INSTITUTE FOR JEWISH RESEARCH - ARCHIVES for pre-1960 HIAS case files and other HIAS records. YIVO also has case files of agencies affiliated with HIAS such as the Joint Distribution Committee, German-Jewish Children's Aid, National Refugee Service, United Service for New Americans. See also AMERICAN JEWISH HISTORICAL SOCIETY for HIAS Boston office case files, late 1920s–1970s and arrival cards, 1882–1929.

2. Photo Archives: HIAS has a collection of photographs including some of refugee ships bringing displaced persons to the United States after WWII.

3. HIAS Location Service:

   The HIAS Location Service was established to help emigres and others around the world re-establish contact with relatives and friends. It is now possible to access Location Service information and initiate search requests online.

   a. In addition to using HIAS own case files, the Location Service works closely with a network of affiliated agencies around the United States, Jewish organizations worldwide, other international agencies, libraries, and national archives.

   b. HIAS maintains an online forum for persons who do not provide enough information for an individual search. Notices submitted on a HIAS Location Service Search Request form (available online) may be translated into Russian and placed on the HIAS Location Service web page. This online forum is updated monthly.

   c. For those engaged in genealogical research, HIAS Location Department assists in finding archival records or other related information from the countries of the former Soviet Union.

Finding Aids:

HIAS uses the following indexes to locate records:

1. Arrival Index Cards, 1909–1985 (81 reels), include information on immigrants that were assisted by HIAS. For the earlier years, these include immigrants at ports of entry all over the U.S.A. The cards, arranged by year of arrival, port of entry, then alphabetically by surname, summarize information about each member of the family traveling together and include: date of arrival, conveyance (name of ship/plane), port, family name, first names of each family member, birth dates and country of birth, sex, marital status, country of last residence, occupation, sponsor and

sponsors' address. Case file numbers appear on these cards beginning in 1955. Ports of entry <u>pre-1940</u> included New York, Boston, Baltimore, Galveston, Philadelphia, Providence, San Francisco and Seattle. <u>For1940–1964,</u> they included also Bradley Airfield (Hartford County, CT), Charleston, Gulfport, Laredo (TX), Miami, Mobile, New Orleans, Newport, Niagara Falls, Norfolk, Oswego, Portland, Rouses Point, Savannah, and Wilmington (DE). <u>Arrival Cards, 1965–1967</u> include only "eastern U.S. ports" and are arranged by year and surname. <u>Arrival Cards, 1968–,</u> include arrivals at the port of New York only. There are three additional series included here — "Canadian arrivals (various cities)" for 1921–1923, 1927, 1939–1952, 1954; "Portland," 1914, 1915, 1921 and "S.S. *St. Louis*" passengers, 1939. NOTE: The quality of these films vary. Some cards are illegible.

2. <u>Master Card Index-Central Files Cases</u>, c. 1938–1979 (5 reels). This index, arranged by HIAS' Case Name Indexing System (Soundex), identifies all members of the traveling party. (See Appendix A for a description of HIAS' Soundex.) Index cards include case number, name of immigrant, wife's name including maiden name, names of other "case unit members" (i.e. children), birth dates, country of birth, marital status, relationship to first person listed and arrival date. The back side of the card includes "interested U.S. persons," their address (or borough), case number if serviced by HIAS and their relationship to the immigrant. Listed at the bottom under "Cross Reference Cases - Changes- Additional Data" are names of later arrivals and their case numbers where the immigrant here is listed. Index, 1970–1979 (original cards), include alternate spellings of the surname, and if wife previously married, the surname from her first marriage.

3. <u>Cross Reference Index-Central Files Cases</u>, c. 1955–c. 1982 (most from the 1960s and 1970s) are arranged by HIAS' Soundex (46 reels). A separate card is included for all adults (except head of the immigrant household) for cases opened in the 1960s. For cases opened 1970–1979, there is a card for each adult (<u>including</u> head of household). The cards for head of household appear to be duplicates of the Master Card Index, 1970–1979. Separate cards are included for (1) immigrant wife (by her maiden name), (2) alternate names for the immigrant husband ("man") and (3) names of relatives and friends provided by the immigrants. If any of this latter group were HIAS clients, their case numbers are included.

Researchers should check both the Master Cards <u>and</u> the Cross Reference Index to find an adult included in a 1960s case but need only check the Cross Reference Index for 1970s cases.

4. <u>Computerized Index</u>. From 1980 to the present, HIAS has a computerized case index accessible to HIAS staff.

5. <u>Holocaust Arrivals, c. 1935–c. 1953</u> (most from 1940s, post-war) also known as the <u>NRS-USNA-UHS Case File Index Cards</u> (10 reels). These 4" x 6" cards are arranged by HIAS Soundex for immigrant head of household's surname. The cards include case number, name of immigrant, wife including maiden name, children, birth dates and countries of birth, dates of arrival, U.S. address (or addresses), address abroad, affiant(s) and address of affiant, date case was opened/closed. The back side of the card includes "cross references," usually name(s), addresses of relatives showing the relationship to immigrant and that person's case number if also assisted by HIAS. NOTE: "NRS" is the National Refugee Service; "USNA" is the United Service for New Americans. "UHS" or United HIAS Service was the name used by HIAS when it merged in December, 1953 with these two agencies.

6 <u>Joint Distribution Committee (JDC) index cards</u>, c. 1946–1949 (5 reels). This index is arranged alphabetically by surname. The form for this card includes surname and first names of members of the family. Space is provided for birth date and place, present address (in Europe), dates case opened and closed, persons interested and relationship. These fields are mostly blank. Names, address and date case opened are generally filled in. There are no case numbers on these cards.

Fees/Copies:

There is a fee of $25 for either posting inquiries online, for conducting a basic search or for a copy of an arrival record. There may be an additional fee if an advanced search is requested, depending on labor and expenses incurred.

Restrictions on Use:

Searches cannot be conducted by researchers at HIAS' office. However, researchers can view microfilm of the <u>Arrival Index Cards</u>, 1909–1979, <u>Master Index Cards</u>, c. 1938–c. 1972 (mostly 1960s), <u>Cross Reference Index</u> [MKM 28], <u>NRS-USNA-UHS Case File Index Cards</u> (Holocaust Cards) and <u>JDC Index</u> at the YIVO INSTITUTE FOR JEWISH RESEARCH, ARCHIVES; and Arrival Cards, 1882–1929, ports of Boston, MA and Providence, RI at the AMERICAN JEWISH HISTORICAL SOCIETY. Copies of individual case files at HIAS, 1960 to the present, can be made only for the individual or a relative.

JEWISH THEOLOGICAL SEMINARY OF AMERICA
LIBRARY

Facility Director:	Dr. Mayer E. Rabinowitz, Librarian
	Naomi Steinberger, Executive Librarian
Address:	3080 Broadway ♿
	New York, NY 10027-4649
	(Cross Streets: West 122nd and 123rd Streets)
Phone:	(212) 678-8081 (Library Reference Desk)
	(212) 678-8077 (Special Collections)
	(212) 678-8082 (Circulation Desk)
Fax:	(212) 678-8998; (212) 678-8891
E-mail:	library@jtsa.edu
Website:	www.jtsa.edu/library

Hours of Operation:

Library:	Winter/Summer Semesters	Academic Recess
Monday to Thursday:	8:00 am to 10:00 pm	8:00 am to 5:00 pm
Friday:	8:00 am to 5:00 pm*	8:00 am to 5:00 pm*
Sunday:	9:30 am to 10:00 pm	Closed
	*or earlier, i.e. Seminary closing time	

Special Collections:		
Monday to Thursday:	12:00 noon to 4:00 pm	12:00 noon to 4:00 pm
Friday:	10:00 am to 2:00 pm	10:00 am to 2:00 pm

Audio-Visual Center and Reference Desk:		
Monday to Thursday:	9:00 am to 7:00 pm	9:00 am to 5:00 pm
Friday:	9:00 am to closing	9:00 am to closing
Sunday:	11:00 am to 7:00 pm	closed

NOTE: Fall, spring and summer semesters generally run from September to the end of July. Academic Recess hours generally apply to the month of August and any days between semesters. The entire facility is closed Saturday, Jewish and legal holidays.

Closest Public Transportation:

Subway: 1 or 9 to 116th Street and Broadway

Bus: M4 or M104 to 122nd Street and Broadway
M5 to 122nd Street and Riverside

Directions:

Take the #1 or #9 train to the 116th Street station. Exit at the center of the platform. Walk 6 blocks north on Broadway to 122nd Street. The entrance to the building is on the northeast corner. Enter the courtyard, turn right, walk down the right side of the quadrangle. Enter the building and go up to the 2nd floor to reach the Library.

Description of Resources:

The Library of the Jewish Theological Seminary, founded in 1893, houses 375,000 books, 11,000 manuscripts, 25,000 rare books, 13,000 reels of microfilm (primarily of Hebrew manuscripts), 750 current periodical subscriptions, 1,000 video records and other materials covering all aspects of Jewish life. The Library serves as a research center for JTS faculty and students while also satisfying the information needs of the Jewish community.

General Collections:

1. The Library has a large collection of Yizkor books (See Appendix B) and rabbinic biographies. Its holdings include hundreds of histories of local Jewish communities throughout the world. See CENTER FOR JEWISH HISTORY - YIVO INSTITUTE FOR JEWISH RESEARCH for many titles available here also.

2. <u>Periodical Collection</u> includes local Jewish newspapers from communities in Europe, America, North Africa and the Near East some dating from the 19th century. These include such diverse titles as:

Ami d'Israél, Strasbourg, April, 1841 (microfilm), 1851–1858, 1862
The Canadian Jewish Chronicle, 1914/15–1930, 1941–1948
Davar Aher, Calcutta, 1918
Emanu-el, San Francisco, 1903–1930
Esra, Vienna, 1919–1920
The Jewish Chronicle, London, 1841–1842, 1844–1899, 1900–1939 (gaps), 1956–1988; index, 1841–1880 (on microfilm, except 1900–1939)
Jewish Daily Bulletin, New York, 1924–1935
Jewish Times, Baltimore, 1869–1951
Juedische Rundschau, Berlin, 1902–1906, 1924–1938 (microfilm), 1933, 1936

3. <u>Jewish Archival Survey Publications,</u> part of Project Judaica, a cooperative effort by JTS, YIVO and the Russian State University for the Humanities in Moscow to comprehensively survey Jewish archival collections in the former Soviet Union. Publications to date include:

Dokumenty po istorrii i kulture evreev v arkhivakh Moskvy [Jewish Documentary Sources in Moscow Archives], finding aid (in Russian) with descriptions of over 400 collections in 21 Moscow archives. [CD1711.J482]
Jewish Documentary Sources in Russia, Ukraine and Belarus: A Preliminary List, edited by Dorit Sallis and Marek Web, New York, 1996. Includes information about, and finding aids for, 1,300 collections of Jewish interest in these three countries. [CD1711.J48]

4. <u>Jewish Cemeteries</u>:

Austria. Eisenstadt, Mattersdorf (Mattersburg), Deutschkreutz, Kobersdorf, Lackenbach, Frauenkirchen and Kittsee. Goldstein, Moshe. *Maamar sheva kehilot* [Command of seven communities]. Tel Aviv, [1954 or 1955]. [DS135.A92 B9 G63 1955]
Austria. Graz. Herzog, David. *Die juedischen Friedhofe in Graz.* Graz, 1937. [DS135.A92 H45 1937]
Czech Republic. Prague. Jerabek, Luboes. *Der alte Prager Judenfriedhof* [The old Jewish cemetery of Prague]. Prague, 1903. [DS135.C96 P8 J4 1903]
Czech Republic. Prague. Muneles, Otto. *Ketovot mi-bet ha'almin ha'Yehudi ha'Atik be Prag* [Epitaphs from the Ancient Jewish Cemetery of Prague]. Jerusalem, 1988. [DS135.C96 P8 M36 1988]
Germany. Wuerttemberg. *Juedische Gotteshaeuser und Friedhoefe in Wuerttemberg* [Jewish synagogues and cemeteries in Wuerttemberg]. Stuttgart, 1932. [BM318.W7518 1932]
Greece. Salonika. Emmanuel, Isaac S. *Gedole Saloniki le-dorotam* [Leaders of Salonika in their generations]. 500 inscriptions, 1500–1660. Tel Aviv, 1936. [DS135.G72 S2 1936]
Hungary. Scheiber, Sandor. *Jewish Inscriptions in Hungary from the 3rd century to 1686.* Leiden, 1983. [CN745.S32 1983]
Israel. Jerusalem. Benvenisti, Meron. *Ir ha-menuhot: bate ha' almin shel Yerushalayim* [Jerusalem's City of the Dead]. Jerusalem, [1990]. [DS109.B384 1990]
Lithuania. Vilna. Klausner, Israel. *Korot bet ha-almin ha-yashan be-Vilnah* [History of the old cemetery in Vilna]. Jerusalem, 1972. [DS135.R93 V5 K56 1972]
Netherlands. Amsterdam. de Castro, David Henriques. *Keur van grafstenen op de Portugees-Israelietische begraafplaats te Oudekerk aan de Amstel* [Selected gravestones from the Dutch Portuguese Jewish Cemetery at Ouderkerk aan de Amstel with descriptions and biographical notes]. Reprint of the Dutch/German 1883 edition, preceded by an English translation and descriptions of six additional gravestones]. Ouderkerk aan den Amstel, 1999. [PJ5034.8.N48 C372 1999]. The library also has the original.
United States. Charleston, SC. Elzas, Barnett A. *The Old Jewish Cemeteries at Charleston, S.C.: a transcript of the inscriptions on their tombstones, 1762–1903.* Charleston, 1903. [F279.C4 E5]

5. <u>Resources of other Libraries</u> (<u>Louis Ginzberg Microfilm Collection</u>): The Library has microfilm copies of rare Judaic and Hebraic manuscripts and books located in other libraries around the world, such as the British Museum, the Cambridge University Library, Bodleian Library (Oxford), Kaufman Collection of the Hungarian Academy of Science, Parma Library (Italy), Austrian National Library, Biblioteca Escorial (Madrid), Firkovich Collection (St. Petersburg), Bibliotheque Nationale and Alliance Israelite (Paris) and the Gunzburg Collection (Moscow).

<u>Special Collections</u> include (1) the Archives, which consist primarily of collections of personal and family papers of rabbis, scholars, writers and other individuals from Europe and America associated with the Conservative movement and records of communities; (2) rare books, many dating from the 15th and 16th centuries; and (3) the Joseph and Miriam

Ratner Center for the Study of Conservative Judaism which collects and preserves historical records of the Conservative movement. Special Collections include Hebrew manuscripts such as fragments from the Cairo Geniza and manuscripts of medicine, math, astronomy, astrology, Jewish philosophy, poetry and drama. Of particular interest are:

1. Family Genealogies: The collection includes genealogical charts of European and American families including the Rothschilds, the Caro Rabbinic dynasty, the Oppenheimer family (Frankfurt), the Phillips family (London and America) and the Yehya family (Spain).

2. Ketubot (Jewish marriage contracts): The Library houses one of the most extensive collections of ketubot in the world. The collection includes over 750 ketubot dating from an 11th century Geniza document and including ketubot from 15th century Spain, Italy, the Ottoman Empire, Iran, Kurdistan, India, England, Germany, 16th century Greece and 20th century Israel and United States. These have been photographed.

3. Community records include documents from around the world such as:

   Algeria. Consistoire records, 1847–1905 [RG 8]
   Detroit, Michigan, marriage and divorce [RG 30-1] includes religious divorces and some marriage documents (not indexed)
   France. Consistoire records, 1808–1905; Jewish communities records, 1648–1946 [RG 36]; Marseilles Consistoire records [RG 78]. See also Temple Israélite (Paris, France), minute books, 1851–1875.
   Historical Documents, 15th–20th centuries (Jewish communal records — German, French and Italian communities) [RG 52]
   Italian Historical Documents [RG 57]
   Morocco. Jewish community records, 20th century (Fez mostly, but also Meknes, Rabat, Safe, Sale, Sefrou and Tangier) [RG 87]

4. Community Record Books: Over 400 communal record books (Pinkasim) from Jewish communities in Europe, North America, Africa and Asia, which date from the 16th to the 20th centuries. These include Pinkasim of the Chevra Kadisha (burial societies) and lists of burials, tombstone inscriptions, yahrzeits or departed from (call numbers are in brackets):

[MS 3873]	Alsace-Lorraine, France, 1799–1815	[MS 4028]	Krotoszyn, Poland, 1777–1840
[MS 9286]	Louisville, KY, 1892	[MS 3872]	Lissa, Poland, 1833–1854
[MS 8499]	Madi, Hungary, 1793–1890	[MS 3960]	Lugo, Italy, 1680–1825
[MS 3874]	Bohemia, Czechoslovakia, 1775–1869	[MS 3947]	Pesaro, Italy, 1693–1810
[MS 4018]	Greishaber, Germany, 1733–1825	[MS 9676]	Sefad, Israel, 1856–1895
[MS 4014]	Heidingsfeld, Germany, 18th & 19th century	[MS 8510]	Sulzberg, Austria, 1825
		[MS 4031]	Schwersenz, Poland, 1773–1809
[MS 9370]	Ihringen, Germany, 1791–1823	[MS 8513]	Trimbach, Switzerland, 19th & 20th century
[MS 3797]	Ivancice, CZ, 19th century		
[MS 3932]	Jungholtz, France, 1787–1892	[MS 10287]	Tukkum, Latvia, c. 1834–1872

5. Mohel books (records of circumcisions) of mainly European communities, 17th to 19th centuries. These manuscripts contain the names of the mohel, child, parents and date of circumcision. A sample of those available in the Rare Book Room include:

[MS 3707]	Alsace, France, 1794–1862	[MS 3706A]	Germany, 1823–1870
[MS 10318]	Amsterdam, Netherlands, 1650–1696	[MS 3835]	Hammerstein, Germany, 1780–1801
[MS 3613]	Bohemia, Czechoslovakia, 1760–1826	[MS 10354]	Hungary, 1789–1868
[MS 3861]	Bohemia, Czechoslovakia, 1835–1866	[MS 3882]	Italy, 1666–1734
[MS 3610]	Carpentras, France, 1743–1772	[MS 3560]	Italy, 1810–1869
[MS 9584]	Central Europe, 1791–1810	[MS 3592]	Philadelphia, San Francisco and other U.S. cities
[MS 9644]	Csanad, Hungary, 1834–1855		
[MS 10343]	Damascus, Syria, 1840	[MS 3880]	Venice, Italy, 1718–1728
[MS 3698]	Frauenberg, E. Prussia, 1819–1874	[MS 9369]	Vienna, Austria, 1859–1883
[MS 3700]	Germany, 1834–1870	[MS 8999]	Zsambek, Hungary, 19th century

The Rare Book Collection has many other Pinkasim such as: London, Beit Din, 1834–1855 [MS 3584]; Venice, Pinkas of payments 1575–1734 [MS 8593]; Koszeg (Guns), Hungary, weddings, 1851–1885 [MS 9738]; Leghorn, Italy, divorces, 1706 [MS 9367]. NOTE: A list of pinkasim, arranged alphabetically by source location, is available in the May 1992 issue of *ZichronNote*, the newsletter of the San Francisco Bay Area JGS. This list was derived from the five-volume *Guide to the Hebrew Manuscript Collection of the Library of the Jewish Theological Seminary of America* (1991). Check also the JTS Aleph catalog under "Pinkasim."

6. <u>Synagogue Records</u> of those affiliated with the Conservative movement including:

<u>Baith Israel Anshei Emes - Kane Street Shul</u> (Brooklyn): A list of marriages, 1913–1917 (included in the financial records of the synagogue); seat books, 1908–1949 (gaps), 1975–1981; membership receipts, 1922–1923; membership lists and contributions, 1930; scrapbook, 1955–1956; souvenir journals, 1916–1986 (gaps); and centennial banquet book, 1956. Includes the Baith Israel sunday school register of pupils, 1889–1890; and Talmud Torah Anshei Emes tuition book, 1922–1924; records of plots in Beth El, Washington and Mt. Carmel cemeteries, c. 1919, and cemetery board records, 1919–1930.

<u>Brooklyn Jewish Center</u>, 1921–1983: Includes the *Brooklyn Jewish Center Bulletin*, 1922–1986 (gaps) [Box 32]; the *Brooklyn Center Review*, 1933–1885 (gaps) [Box 7]; and Hebrew school register lists including father's name, 1939–1940. [Box 13]

<u>Chisuk Emuna Bnai Russia Congregation</u> (Harrisburg, PA): Includes cemetery lot records, 1937–1968; cemetery correspondence, sale of lots, perpetual care and legal papers, 1879, 1884, 1904, 1931, 1949–1974; blueprint of plots, 1945; fiscal records of membership accounts, 1926–1949; holiday honors, 1935–1949; and congregational minutes, 1893–1897 and 1929–1970 (gaps).

<u>Congregation B'nai Jeshurun</u> (New York City): Marriage certificates, 1826–1973; wedding book, 1897–1902; registers of deaths, including name, age, date, 1853–1928; cemetery burial permits, 1914–1934; perpetual care lists (index at 1972, 1975 and 1978); cemetery account ledgers, 1882–1926; minutes of the Joint Cemetery Committee (B'nai Jeshurun and Shaaray Tefila), 1857–1901; a "Book of Life" which includes yahrzeit dates of benefactors of B'nai Jeshurun, 1862–1965; eight files on estates and burial plots of congregants; correspondence concerning condolences, 1953–1954, and congratulatory correspondence, 1950–1952.

The collection includes Rabbi Israel Goldstein's index cards, 1926–1982 for rites performed, including Bar Mitzvahs, 1926–1972, with father's or mother's name and occupation; weddings, 1950s–1982, listing birth dates, date of marriage, marriage license number, parents and witnesses names; eulogies, 1920s–1960s, with name of cemetery, date of funeral and sometimes obituary; and yahrzeits, 1862–1980, arranged by month, including English and Hebrew names, date of death, and name address of relative.

Also available is the Religious School register, 1855–1919 (listing name, address, parent's name, and attendance of students), and 1946–1947 (listing names and addresses of students); a Bar Mitzvah Information Book (including name, parent's name and address), 1945–1953; and a copy of *The Clarion,* the B'nai Jeshurun Religious School year book, 1952.

There are members' dues ledgers, 1904–1923; lists of congregation members (names and addresses), 1928–1931, 1935–1946, 1949–1951 and 1957; seat deeds, 1886–1958; contribution acknowledgments, 1947–1954; minute books of the congregation, 1825–1966 (gaps); correspondence of its rabbis, cantors and officers; and rabbis' letters and applications for a pulpit position, 1917.

<u>Flatbush Jewish Center</u> (Brooklyn, NY) 1925–1988, newsletters. See also, <u>Bialik School of the Flatbush Jewish Center Records, 1955–1989</u>: Includes yearbooks of graduation classes, 1955–1988; directory of alumni, 1976, with achievements and interests; and lists of parents, 1972–1973, 1979–1987.

<u>Shaare Zedek</u> (New York): Includes copies of ketubot (marriage contracts), 1841–1929 (4 volumes, no index); religious school records, 1891–1903, 1915–1921. School journals, 1891–1902, include father's name and child's age. The collection includes bound ledgers of Bayside Cemetery which Congregation Shaare Zedek owns. Day books are available for burials, 1887–1928; and cemetery plot book, 1907–1925, listing individuals and organizations owning plots during this period. See "Restrictions on Use."

<u>Temple Beth Zion - Beth Israel</u> (Philadelphia, PA): Includes 8 volumes on the congregation's history; typed "History of 100 years of Temple Beth Israel, 1840–1940" (23 pp.); centennial celebration book, 1940; and five notebooks of names on memorial tablets. Includes records of donations, 1840–1895; a book of Board Managers, 1901–1960; account books, 1842–1900, showing seats, pew rents, offerings and/or membership; cemetery account book, 1934–1948; account book for receipts and disbursements, 1949–1963; minute books, 1873–1907 (annual general meetings) and 1926–1940 (Board of Managers meetings). See also <u>American Jewish History Center</u> below.

<u>Temple Shomrei Emunah</u> (Montclair, NJ): Includes minute books of general meetings, 1905–1955 (gaps); Sisterhood meetings, 1940–1948; Board of Trustees meetings, 1951–1969; congregational correspondence, 1929–1940; newsletter, 1936–1969; and fifth anniversary bulletin, 1955.

American Jewish History Center [RG 10]: This Archives collection includes:

Anshe Chesed Synagogue/Euclid Avenue Temple (Cleveland, OH) minute books, 1907–1921; excerpts from minute books of the following Milwaukee synagogues: Congregation B'ne Jeshurun (Milwaukee), 1875–1927; Congregation Emanu-El (Milwaukee), 1880–1927; Chevra Bikur Cholim (Milwaukee), 1883–1927; and information on Jewish servicemen from Milwaukee during WWII [Box 10-10]. Records of Congregation Beth Israel (Philadelphia, PA) include notebooks listing memorial tablets with names/addresses of known descendants (1940–1943), minute books, 1840–1849, 1907–1959] and minutes of the Daughters of Beth Israel, 1893–1897, 1915–1919 and 1947–1962. [Box 10-27]

7. Personal Papers of scholars and rabbis, many of whom were associated with the Conservative movement or with the Seminary, including those of Cyrus Adler, Solomon Schechter, Israel Rosenberg, Moritz Steinschneider, Zadoc Kahn, the Adler family of London, Albert Bettelheim, Louis Levitsky and others. Papers of Conservative rabbis of the 19th and 20th centuries, part of the Ratner collection, have biographical material, sermons and correspondence. These include Ben Zion Bokser, Abraham Hurvitz, Ario Hyams, Nathan Kollin, Israel H. Levinthal, and Louis Levitsky. A few, like the Rabbi Isaac Klein collection include wedding sermons, Buffalo and Springfield, and ketubot (in which Rabbi Klein was involved); Jewish divorces given or held by him; and eulogies.

8. Jewish Theological Seminary Collections: Include the Cantors Institute/Seminary College of Jewish Music Collection, 1940s–1970s [RG 19] containing award, prize and scholarship files, 1952–1957 [Box 1/57-74]; placement reports, 1968, 1971, 1972 and 1974 [Box 4/61]; and commencements, 1954–1975.

Jewish Theological Seminar, Teachers' Institute, Alumni Association Records, c. 1930s–c. 1990 [RG 12c], including class lists, photographs and surveys of alumni gathered for publication in the Association's bulletin. The questionnaires were completed by members of the classes of 1912–1971 in 1968–1969 [Box 5/6–43, 53], and the classes of 1912–1979 in 1977. These questionnaires, arranged by class, include information about the alumnus' career, family, education, communal affiliations, achievements and in some cases letters, resumes, and biographical sketches. Also available is an Alumni Directory, 1959 [Box 5/45]; and class lists, 1912–1971, created in 1984, showing address/telephone or "deceased" [Box 1/45]. A related collection is JTS Rabbinical School, Alumni Files, 1894–1965 [RG 15/Series A] which includes a file of correspondence with each alumni. The finding aid includes names of every individual ordained by the Seminary during this period. See "Restrictions on Use."

Oral Histories Collection includes interviews with individuals important to the history of JTS and the Conservative movement such as: Joseph Abrahams, Gerson Cohen, Hadassah Finkelstein Davis, Moshe Davis, Sylvia Ettenberg, Jessica Feingold, Louis Finkelstein, Carmel Bentwich Forsyte, Theodore Friedman, Joel Geffen, Simon Greenberg, Abraham Millgram, Naomi Flax Tepfer, Mordecai Waxman and Joseph Zeitlin.

9. Prints, Photographs and Postcard Collections. The Ratner collection includes approximately 6,000 photographs of individuals, Jewish communities, synagogues and cemeteries associated with the Conservative movement. In addition, the Archives has an estimated 5,000 photographs (60 boxes) and other items from the 17th to 20th centuries not yet sorted. The Postcard collection includes 3,200 from the early 20th century to the present. The Library also has the Yad Vashem: Archives of Destruction (microfiche), which include over 15,000 photographs taken in Europe during and immediately after the Holocaust.

Finding Aids:

All Latin character books can be found in the computerized catalog, ALEPH. Hebrew books cataloged since 1990 can be found in ALEPH as well. Eventually, all books will be included. There are computer stations located on the 2nd and 3rd floors of the Library. The catalog can be searched by author, title, subject, keyword, place of publication, year of publication, publisher and call number. ALEPH can be searched in either English or Hebrew. It is also available online, through the Library's website. If a Hebrew book citation is not in ALEPH, check the Library's card catalog located on the 2nd floor.

The card catalog is divided into five sections: General Catalog, Old Catalog, Subject Catalog, Hebrew Title Catalog and Periodical Title Index. No new records have been entered into the Card Catalog since it was "closed" on June 15, 1990. The Hebrew Title Catalog is arranged by title only. Not all editions of a work are listed. Check the General Catalog to locate all editions owned by the Library.

Yizkor books (memorial books) can be found by utilizing the call number in Appendix B. Since JTS uses Library of Congress call numbers and its holdings are on open shelves (2nd and 3rd floors), one can find most of these books as well as books related to pre-WWII pogroms in the series beginning DS135 (3rd floor, south of elevator). For example,

DS135.R93 includes books on communities in Russia; DS135.P62 in Poland; DS135.H92 in Hungary; DS135.C96 in Czechoslovakia and Czech Republic; and DS135.S55 in Slovakia.

Genealogy books are arranged under the CS series, and rabbinic biographies primarily under BM750 (collective biographies) and BM755 (individual biographies). These are all on open shelves on the 3rd floor.

All materials from the Audio-Visual collection (except microfilms) and the Special Collections are now included in the ALEPH catalog. These items have been assigned Special Call Numbers (SCN), and may be retrieved through a regular ALEPH search. SCN codes are "KET" for ketubah, "MS" for manuscripts, "RB" for rare book, and "REEL" for microfilm reel number. To determine whether the Library has a pinkas for a community, check the ALEPH catalog by name of community or by looking under "Pinkasim." To locate a ketubah, search using the subject "Ketubah." Most of the Ratner Collection finding aids can also be accessed on the web (not included in ALEPH).

Check two red binders for records in the Ratner Collection (mostly synagogues and personal papers); and a black binder for other Archival collections. These describe both cataloged and uncataloged collections. For the French records, see *An Inventory to the French Jewish Communities Records Group (1648–1946)* by Roger S. Kohn.

There is a computerized index to the Ratner <u>Photograph Collection</u> and a printed index by locality of the <u>Yad Vashem: Archives of the Destruction</u>.

Description of Facility:

The Library's reference collection, JTS dissertations, bound periodicals and Stack Books PJ–Z, are located on the 2nd floor. Stack Books A–PI are on the 3rd floor. All post-1840 materials in the Library (except special collections) are on open shelves. The Library can seat 300.

Special Collections including archival material, rare books and records of the Ratner Center can be accessed in the Special Reading Room (formerly known as the Rare Book and Manuscript Center) on the 5th floor. Finding aides for these collections are on open shelves in this Room. Materials can be obtained through hourly paging.

The Audio-Visual Center, located on the 2nd floor, houses all materials on microfilm and microfiche including the Library's extensive collection of periodicals and copies of rare manuscripts from libraries around the world. The index to the <u>Yad Vashem: Archives of the Destruction</u> is in the Audio-Visual Center. There are 3 microfilm and 2 microfiche readers, 2 reader/printers and 2 VCRs. Permission to use the Audio-Visual Room may be obtained from the Reference Librarian on the second floor.

Fees/Copies:

There are 6 photocopy machines available on the 2nd floor at $.10 per page. Special collection mail requests are charged $.25 per page plus postage and a $5 handling charge.

Restrictions on Use:

Researchers may obtain a day pass to use the Library upon presentation of a valid photo ID to the Librarian at the Circulation desk. Users of Special Collections are required to store all briefcases and other personal materials behind the control desk. No pens may be used here.

Use of fragile materials such as the <u>Shaare Zedek's</u> Bayside Cemetery day books may be restricted by the staff.

Some <u>Jewish Theological Seminary Records</u> dating from 1973 to the present are closed. Check with the Archivist.

Members of Friends of the JTS library (annual membership fee $300) may borrow books up to four weeks. The general public may not borrow books.

JOHN JAY COLLEGE OF CRIMINAL JUSTICE, CITY UNIVERSITY OF NEW YORK
LLOYD GEORGE SEALY LIBRARY

Facility Director: Professor Larry E. Sullivan, Chief Librarian

Address: 899 Tenth Avenue ♿
New York, NY 10019

(Cross Streets: West 58th and 59th Streets)

Phone: (212) 237-8246 (Reference Desk)
(212) 237-8225 (Library Hours/Travel)
(212) 541-0965 (Appointment/Special Collections)
Fax: (212) 237-8221
E-mail: libinfo@jjay.cuny.edu
Website: www.lib.jjay.cuny.edu

Hours of Operation:

	Semester	June and July
Monday to Thursday:	9:00 am to 10:00 pm	Monday, Tuesday & Thursday: 10:00 am to 8:00 pm
Friday:	9:00 am to 5:00 pm	Wednesday: 10:00 am to 10:00 pm
Saturday and Sunday:	12:00 noon to 5:00 pm	Friday: 11:00 am to 5:00 pm (part of June only)
		Saturday and Sunday: closed

For holiday, summer and intersession schedules, call ahead. The schedule may be different from the above.

Closest Public Transportation:

Subway: A, B, C, D, 1 or 9 train to 59th Street/Columbus Circle
R or N train to 57th Street/7th Avenue

Bus: M11 north to 58th/10th Avenue (south on 9th Avenue)
M31 or M57 to 10th Avenue/57th Street

Directions:

Take the A, B, C, D, #1 or #9 train to 59th Street and Columbus Circle/8th Avenue. Walk or take the M57 or M31 bus west on 57th Street to 10th Avenue (Amsterdam Avenue). The Library entrance is on 10th Avenue between 58th and 59th Streets. NOTE: Wheelchair users may take the elevator to reach the Library.

Description of Resources:

The Library's holdings include 300,000 books and 2,770 serial subscriptions. Its collection includes materials related primarily to criminal justice, law, social sciences, public administration and related fields. Of interest to genealogists in the Library and Special Collections are:

1. <u>Biographies and Autobiographies</u> of prisoners, ex-convicts, attorneys, judges and others involved with the criminal justice system. In addition, to *Martindale-Hubbell Law Directory* [KF190.M3], the Library has the *National Association of Criminal Defense Lawyers: Member Handbook,* 1997 to present. Includes name, address, telephone, fax and e-mail address. Biographies and photographs are included for life members, leadership and staff. [KF190.N3 and KF195.L7 N4]

2. <u>New York City Police Department blotters for the Borough of Manhattan,</u> 1916–1935. The blotters record daily arrests and other occurrences in each precinct. They are arranged by precinct and chronologically by date. Details included vary by precinct. Not all precincts are represented for each year. See "Restrictions on Use."

3. <u>Trial Transcripts of the County of New York, 1883–1927.</u> The Library has (on microfilm) c. 2,700 verbatim trial transcripts from criminal courts of New York County. The records are predominately those of the Court of General Sessions of the Peace (371 of 425 reels), 1886–1927. Other courts included are the New York State Supreme Court (Manhattan), 1896–1922, Court of Oyer and Terminer, 1886–1895, District Police Courts 1887–1894, City Magistrate's Court, Sheriff's Court and Coroner's Office, 1883–1907, 1926; and Court of General Sessions, New York Supreme Court (Grand Jury), 1883–1920. [Special Collections]

For more information on this collection, see *Trial Transcripts of the County of New York, 1883–1927: A Historical Introduction with an Index to the Microfilm Collection,* by Eli Faber and Eileen Rowland. New York, 1989 [Ref Desk KF220.F33 1989]. This small book provides a history of the collection and the courts involved. Volume 3, Supplementary Index, is arranged by name of defendant, names of judges and attorneys, case number and charge; and cross references volumes 1 and 2 to provide case name, charge and reel number on which the transcript can be found.

4. Richard Louis Dugdale Papers. Includes his "Jukes" family studies relating family history to crime and poverty. This collection consists of large worksheets containing raw data on over 800 individuals compiled by Dugdale for his study published c. 1877. Worksheets include name, age, year died, occupation, crimes, vices, legitimacy of self and children, pauperism, cross reference to parents (if on worksheets) and more. [Special Collections X106]

5. English Criminal Biographies, 1651–1722, includes 58 criminal biographies and autobiographies gathered by Robert R. Singleton for his dissertation. [Special Collections PR3409.P6 S55 1916a]

6. Prelect Program Student Profiles, 1970–1973. The Prelect program provided college courses at John Jay one day each week for law enforcement personnel such as probationary patrolmen, recruits, field training officers, correction aids and investigators. An estimated 3,800 officers and agents from the NYC Police Department, NYC Housing Authority and NYC Transit Authority participated in the program. Includes birth date/place, education and employment history. [Special Collections]. See "Restrictions on Use."

7. Oral History Collection. Includes interviews conducted by Professor Gerald Markowitz on video with 35 faculty and friends of John Jay College for its 25th Anniversary in 1988. Persons interviewed included Adams, Best, Bohigian, Bowker, Bracey, Buiar, Cammett, Clancy, Collins, Colville, Cook, Edelstein, Hegeman, Lindsay, Loewenthal, Loughery, Lynch, MacNamara, Malone, Moran, Murphy, Pfeffer, Pinckert, Preston, Price, Riddle, Rothlein, Sherman, Smith, Tabor, Umansky, Wagner, Walker, Wilson and Yarmus. [Special Collections]

8. Law Enforcement News Interviews (audio tapes and transcripts) with five police officers from France, Great Britain and Ireland (Durin, Byford, Hallett, Powis and Sheehan). See also, *European Policing: The Law Enforcement News Interviews,* by Michael Balton, New York, c. 1978 [HV8194.A2 E9] which includes 10 interviews including these five. [Special Collections]

9. Lewis E. Lawes Papers. Includes personal papers, prisoner related correspondence, 1919–1942; photographs, correspondence with the Lawes family; scrapbooks, such as the "Black Sheep," Sing-Sing football team scrapbook; and letters of Lewis E. Lawes, warden of Sing Sing prison from 1920–1941. [Special Collections X101]

10. Tuskagee Institute News Clipping File, 1899–1966, includes articles from 300-500 newspapers, magazines and other publications arranged in three series (microfilm). Series 2, arranged by subject, includes lynchings, 1899–1966 [Reels 221–236]; necrology, 1912–1966 [Reels 237–240]; theatrical individuals and troupes, 1912–1939, [Reel 241]; soldiers, 1918–1920 [Reel 244], and more. Series 3, includes ten editions of *Negro Yearbook,* published between 1912–1952 [Reels 250–252]. [Special Collections E185.5.T77]

11. Court Cases: In addition to trial transcripts, the Library has the following published materials:

    American State Trials: A collection of the important and interesting criminal trials which have taken place in the U.S. from the beginning of our government. 17 vols. Wilmington, DE, 1972 [Reference Law KF220.L38 1972] Includes trials from 1657 to 1920 including trials of a runaway slave, a train robber and Massachusetts witch trials. Cases include court-martial, impeachment and ecclesiastical tribunals. There is a surname index to these cases including defendants, plaintiffs, victims, witnesses, judges and lawyers, compiled by Elysabeth Kleinhans. [Ref Law KF220.L382]

    Complete Oral Arguments of the Supreme Court of the United States. Frederick, MD. (microfiche). Transcripts of all oral arguments presented, 1969 to present. Case name indexes are available, 1969–1986/87 (published); and index cards, 1987– (microfiche). [KF101.9.C65]

    Sixty Famous Cases: 29 English cases — 31 American cases, from 1778 to the present, trials selected and accounts narrated, by Marshall Van Winkle. Long Branch, NJ, 1956. 10 vols. Index in volume 1. [KF223.V2]

    The Annals of Murder: a bibliography of books and pamphlets on American murders from colonial times to 1900, by Thomas M. McDade. Oklahoma, 1961. [KF221.M8 M3]

Finding Aids:

The Library's collections are included in CUNY+ online catalog ("location" = John Jay). The website also includes a general description of the Library's Special Collections; and "*Specialties of the House,*" by Katherine B. Killoran, describing some of the more unusual resources of the Library. A large black notebook maintained at the Reference Desk,

Guide to the Manuscripts Collections and Archives of John Jay Collection of Criminal Justice, includes collection descriptions and finding aids to assist in locating manuscript materials.

A finding aid to the <u>Tuskagee Institute News Clipping File</u> can be found on reel #1 of that collection.

Description of Facility:

The Library is located on the basement level and first floor of this renovated building. Catalog computer terminals and Reference Desk are on the first floor. There are two librarians at the Reference Desk to assist researchers. Special Collections are in a locked room on the first floor. An appointment is necessary to use these collections. Photocopy machines are on both levels. To reach the Library's first floor, researchers must take an escalator down to the lower level and then walk up a staircase at the back. Wheelchair users may take the elevator.

Fees/Copies:

Self service photocopies and copies from microfilm reader/printers cost $.10 per page.

Restrictions on Use:

Researchers who are not John Jay students or faculty may use this facility only if the materials sought are not available elsewhere in New York's public libraries. A referral to the City University of New York is necessary in the form of a METRO card provided by a local library which cites the unique title of the reference source needed. Without this METRO referral or valid CUNY ID, researchers will not be given access to this Library. Check with a branch New York, Brooklyn or Queens public library for this referral. For access to Special Collections, an appointment is necessary. Call (212) 541-0965 for more information.

<u>NYC Police Blotters</u> have no name index or precinct index. Researchers need to know the precinct number and date of arrest in order to find anything about a detainee.

<u>Prelect Program Student Profiles</u> are not indexed and are closed to the public because of privacy concerns.

MUSEUM OF JEWISH HERITAGE - A LIVING MEMORIAL TO THE HOLOCAUST
LIBRARY & ARCHIVE

Facility Director:	Dr. David G. Marwell, Director
	Dr. Julia Bock, Librarian
	Bonnie Gurewitsch, Archivist

Address: 18 First Place, East Wing ♿
Battery Park City
New York, NY 10004-1484

(Cross Street: Battery Place)

NOTE: The Library/Archives are temporarily located at 1 Battery Park Plaza (entrance at 24 Whitehall Street), 25th floor, New York, NY 10004-1484, and will remain there until construction of the East Wing of the Museum is completed. Expected opening of the new wing is Fall, 2003.

Phone:	(212) 968-1800
Fax:	(212) 968-1368
E-mail:	collections@mjhnyc.org
Website:	www.mjhnyc.org/home.htm

NOTE: Effective January 1, 2003, JewishGen (www.jewishgen.org), became a division of the Museum.

Hours of Operation:

Monday to Friday: By appointment only
Closed Saturday, Sunday, Jewish and legal holidays.

Closest Public Transportation:

Subway: 4 or 5 to Bowling Green
1, 9, N or R to Rector Street
J, M or Z to Broad Street
2 or 3 to Wall Street

Bus: M9 to Little West Street and Battery Place
M20, M22 to West Thames Street and South End Ave
M 1, M6 to Broadway and Morris Street or Battery Place

Directions:

Take the #4 or #5 train to Bowling Green station. Exit the station and walk <u>west</u> on Battery Place. Cross West Street and Little West Street and continue <u>north</u> along Battery Place until reaching the Museum. The Library is in the new East Wing (opening date planned for Fall, 2003).

To reach the Library/Archives at its temporary location, exit the Bowling Green station, cross State Street and walk along Battery Park (a.k.a. State Street) to Bridge Street (the building is on this corner). Turn left on Bridge Street to the building entrance at 24 Whitehall Street. Take the elevator to the 25th floor.

Description of Resources:

The primary purpose of the Library and Archive, founded in 1986, is to support the internal needs of the Museum. Materials from the former Center for Holocaust Studies, Documentation and Research in Brooklyn are now available here. The Library has over 8,000 books, periodicals, journals and pamphlets. There are over 2,700 collections in the Archive. The following are of particular interest:

1.   <u>Yizkor Books</u>: The library has over 200 yizkor books and its collection is constantly growing.

2.   <u>Jacob Kestenbaum Papers</u> (1938–1956) [RG 865]: Kestenbaum, an immigrant from Tarnow, Poland and resident of the Flatbush community in Brooklyn, was approached by many Landsmen (people from his hometown) and family members for aid during and after World War II. The collection includes correspondence, affidavits and other documents concerning Kestenbaum's efforts to assist over 700 Jewish refugees in Europe emigrate to the U.S.A.

3. Personal Histories and Personal Documents: The Museum has over 2,800 audio tapes and written histories of Holocaust survivors, American soldiers and liberators received from the former Center for Holocaust Studies in Brooklyn. Personal documents including letters, memoirs, diaries, Kennkarten (identification cards), passports, ration cards, affidavits, photos and other artifacts covering the 1933–1946 period, are sometimes included. Audio tapes from this collection have been preserved and transferred to CD-ROM. In addition, the Museum has over 1,000 videotaped interviews with Holocaust survivors, rescuers, former Allied Service people and other eyewitnesses.

   NOTE: It is anticipated that the Museum will be one of five repositories linked to Steven Spielberg's Survivors of the Shoah Visual History Foundation with access to some or all of its 50,000 videotaped interviews. The other four repositories are the Fortunoff Video Archive for Holocaust Testimonies, Yale University, New Haven; Simon Wiesenthal Center, Los Angeles; US Holocaust Memorial Museum, Washington DC; and Yad Vashem, Jerusalem, Israel.

4. Fred Neumann Collection [RG 852]. Neumann, a U.S. Military Intelligence officer during World War II, was responsible for interrogation of German prisoners of war. Reports of these interviews and U.S. military government denazification efforts in Germany are included in this collection.

5. Oskar Schreyer Collection, 1941–1942, includes 290 letters mailed to refugees in Barcelona, Spain or Lisbon, Portugal, which were never delivered or claimed. The mail came from 29 different countries including the U.S.A. (71), France (49), Germany (47), Luxembourg (16), England (16) and were in the custody of Albert Nussbaum, who was chairman of the Transmigration Office of the Joint Distribution Committee in Lisbon. Oskar Schreyer, on behalf of the Nussbaum estate, transferred the collection to the Center for Holocaust Studies.

6. Family Trees. The collection includes family trees of the Bienenfeld (Warsaw, Poland), Razumny (Riga, Latvia), Ziman-Bernstein (Kovno/Slobadka) and Lindenfeld families.

7. Vital Records and other artifacts: The Museum has a scattering of artifacts that may be genealogical in nature. These include such items as a circumcision record book from Livorno, Italy, 1883–1890; a birth register from Lomza, 1826–1912 [58.94]; birth register for Bratislava, 1898–1901 [1940.90]; a register from the Jewish Congregation of Bratislava listing births and marriages (dates unknown). [1943.90]

8. Photographs and films: The Museum's collection includes photographs and documents for Bardejov (Bartfeld) collected for use in a memorial book for that community; and home film footage of shtetl life in Kolbuszowa, Rymanow, Rzeszow, Suchostaw and Zborow in eastern Poland, taken on trips there in 1929.

Finding Aids:

The Library has a computerized catalog. Search under "Yizkor" for a complete listing of the Yizkor Book collection. These are further indexed by locality name, author and title.

The Archive has finding aids for the larger collections. Jacob Kestenbaum Papers are indexed by name of refugee assisted. Index cards include name and box number in which the file is located. The Archives has a card index arranged by surname for Personal Histories and Personal Documents. These are also indexed by town, shtetl, ghetto or concentration camp. The Archive is planning an online index to this collection that will allow surname and subject searches including place name. The Oskar Schreyer Collection includes a hand written 31-page list including name of writer, person to whom the letter or postcard was addressed and a summary of the contents of the letter.

A published description of some of the collections of the former Center for Holocaust Studies is available in *Guide to Historical Resources in Kings County (Brooklyn) New York Repositories,* vol. I, [1987], published by New York Historical Resources Center.

Description of Facility:

The new East Wing of the Museum is currently under construction. Researchers who have appointments will be announced by the reception desk in the lobby. Space can be made available for 1-2 researchers.

Fees/Copies:

Photocopy fees to be determined (on-site research only). No mail research can be conducted. Archives/Library staff service the research needs of the Museum itself.

Restrictions on Use:

Picture Identification must be presented upon entering the building.

NATIONAL ARCHIVES AND RECORDS ADMINISTRATION
NORTHEAST REGION (NEW YORK CITY)

Facility Director: Dr. Robert C. Morris, Director

Address: 201 Varick Street, 12th floor   ♿
New York, NY 10014-4811

(Cross Streets: Corner of West Houston Street)

Phone: (212) 337-1301
Fax: (212) 337-1306
E-mail: newyork.archives@nara.gov
Website: www.nara.gov

Hours of Operation:

Monday, Wednesday
     and Friday: 8:00 am to 4:30 pm
Tuesday and Thursday: 8:00 am to 8:00 pm (microfilm research only after 4:30 pm)
First and Third Saturday
     each month: 8:30 am to 4:00 pm (microfilm research only)
Closed remaining Saturdays, Sunday and federal holidays.

Closest Public Transportation:

Subway: 1 or 9 to Houston Street
            E to Spring Street

PATH: To Christopher Street (from New Jersey)

Bus: M20 to West Houston and Varick/7th Avenue (South) or West Houston and Hudson Street (North)
        M5, M6 or M21 to West Houston & 6th Avenue (Avenue of the Americas)

Directions:

Take the #1 or #9 train to the Houston Street station. The building is on the southwest corner of W. Houston and Varick Streets. Enter on Houston through the second doorway west of Varick Street. After passing security, take the elevator to the 12th floor. Turn left and follow the signs to the National Archives. On Saturdays use the Varick St. entrance.

Description of Resources:

Although the National Archives was not established until 1934, its major holdings date back to 1638. The National Archives, Northeast Region (New York City), is one of 13 regional repositories for historically valuable records of the federal government. The holdings of this branch of the National Archives are chiefly of regional interest but also include microfilm copies of many of the most important records in the National Archives, Washington, DC. The following describes the records of the National Archives, Northeast Region (New York City):

1. <u>U.S. Census Records</u> (microfilm): All existing population schedules for the U.S.A. are available here. These include 1790, 1800, 1810, 1820, 1830, 1840, 1850, 1860, 1870, 1880, 1890 (fragments), 1900, 1910, 1920 and 1930. NOTE: The 1890 Census was destroyed for most states by water damage resulting from a fire. The only surviving fragments in the New York metropolitan area are Jersey City, New Jersey; Eastchester, New York (in Westchester County); and Brookhaven Township, New York (in Suffolk County).

    Special schedules available include:
    Mortality schedules, 1850, 1860, 1870 and 1880
    See also <u>Military Records</u> below, for veterans' schedules, 1890

2. <u>Immigrant and Passenger Arrivals</u> (microfilm) include passenger lists of vessels arriving at:

    <u>Port of New York</u>:
    New York harbor, 1820–1957 [M237; T715]. Post-World War II passenger lists include Holocaust survivors and non-Jewish displaced persons who came to the U.S. The American relief agency that assisted these individuals is identified in the record.

Indexes to Port of New York lists, 1820–1846 [M261], and 1897–1902 [T519] are arranged alphabetically by surname. Indexes, 1902–1943 [T621] and 1944–1948 [T1417] are arranged by NARA's Soundex system. The 1944–1948 index includes addition and correction cards for arrivals <u>prior to 1944</u>, some going as far back as 1902. See also www.ellisislandrecords.org for index and records, 1892–1924.

Book indexes to Port of New York lists, 1906–1942, grouped by shipping line, and arranged chronologically by date of arrival. [T612]

Registers of vessels arriving at the Port of New York, 1789–1919. These registers were arranged, for the most part, alphabetically by name of vessel and then chronologically. [M1066]

<u>Upstate New York</u>:

Buffalo, Lewiston, Niagara Falls and Rochester, NY, 1902–1954. Manifest cards arranged by Soundex. Includes over 1.0 million arrivals. [M1480]

Upstate New York arrivals, alphabetical card manifest, July 1929–April 1956. Includes over 22,000 arrivals at Alexandra Bay, Cape Vincent, Champlain, Clayton, Ft. Covington, Mooers, Rouses Point, Thousand Island Bridge and Trout River, NY. [M1481]

Upstate New York arrivals, Soundex card manifests, July 1929–April 1956. Includes almost 19,000 arrivals at Hogansburg, Malone, Morristown, Nyando, Ogdensburg, Rooseveltown and Waddington, NY. [M1482]

<u>Canadian Border Crossings</u>:

Canadian border entries through small ports in Vermont, 1895–1924, index (alphabetical), 1895–1924 [M1462]

Canadian Pacific and Atlantic port manifests of passenger arrivals into St. Albans, VT District, 1895–1954 [M1464]; and indexes (Soundex), 1895–1924 [M1461] and 1924–1952 [M1463]. NOTE: Indexes are not complete after 1917. See www.nara.gov/publications/prologue/stalbans.html.

Canadian Pacific port manifests of passenger arrivals in the St. Albans, VT District, 1929–1949. [M1465]

<u>Alabama, Florida, Georgia and South Carolina</u>, index to passenger lists arriving at ports in these States, 1890–1925. [T517]

Tampa, Florida, passenger lists, November 2, 1898–December 31, 1945 (gap December 1902–September 1904; May 1915–November 1915). [M1844]

<u>Atlantic and Gulf Coasts and ports on the Great Lakes</u> manifests, 1820–1873 [M575] and index (alphabetical), 1820–1874 [M334]. Includes passenger arrivals for various years at 65 small ports including Bridgeport, CT (1870), Bridgeton, NJ (1828), Cape May, NJ (1828), Hartford, CT (1832), Little Egg Harbor, NJ (1831), Newark, NJ (1836), New Haven, CT (1820–1847), New London, CT (1820–1873), Oswegatchie, NY (1820–1823), Perth Amboy, NJ (1820–1832), Rochester, NY (1866); Sag Harbor, NY (1829–1834) and Saybrook, CT (1820). Among other ports included are Galveston, TX (1846–1871), Georgetown, DC (1820–1821); Providence, RI (1850–1867); Richmond, VA (1820–1844), Savannah, GA (1820–1868), and Wilmington, DE (1820–1849). See reel #1 for a complete list of ports and years covered.

<u>Maine</u> (all arranged alphabetically):

Calais, Maine. Manifest cards of alien arrivals, c. 1906–1952. Includes some arrivals, 1877–1905. [M2042]

Jackman, Maine. Manifest cards of alien arrivals, c. 1909–1953. Includes also some cards, 1899–1908. [M2046]

Ft. Fairfield, Maine. Manifest cards of aliens, c. 1909–1953 and citizen arrivals, c. 1927–1952. Includes also some arrivals at Easton, ME, Houlton, ME, Boston, MA and Buffalo, NY; and some alien departure records [M2064]. These arrivals are also indexed in St. Albans, VT index. [M1461]

Van Buren, Maine. Manifest cards of alien arrivals, c. 1906–1952. [M2065]

Vanceboro, Maine. Manifest cards of alien arrivals, c. 1906–1952. Includes some arrivals 1888–1905 and a few arrivals at Halifax, Nova Scotia and St. John, New Brunswick, Canada. [M2042]

<u>Boston, Massachusetts</u> manifests, 1820–1891 [M277]; index (alphabetical), 1848–1891 [M265], 1902–1920 [T521, T617]; and book indexes (by date of arrival), 1899–1940. [T790]

<u>Philadelphia, PA</u> manifests, 1883–1945 [T840]; index (Soundex), 1883–1948 [T526]; and book index (arranged by date of arrival), 1906–1928. [T791]

<u>Galveston, Texas</u> manifests, 1896–1951 [M1359]; index (alphabetical), 1896–1951. [M1357, M1358]

<u>Published and CD-ROM indexes</u> at the Archives include:

Germans to America: Lists of Passengers Arriving at U.S. Ports, 1840–1845, and 1850–1897, 69 vols., edited by Ira A. Glazier and P. William Filby, 1988–. See also, *Germans to America, 1850–1888.* [CD-ROM 28 and 29]

The Famine Immigrants: Lists of Irish Immigrants Arriving at the Port of New York, 1846–1851, edited by Ira A. Glazier. 7 vols. Baltimore, 1983.

*Irish Passenger Lists 1847–1871: Lists of Passengers Sailing from Londonderry to America on Ships of the J. &.
J. Cooke Line and the McCorkell Line*, compiled under the direction of Brian Mitchel, Baltimore, 1988. See
also, *Irish to America, Passenger Immigration Lists, 1846–1888* [CD-ROM 47] and *Irish Immigrants to North
America, 1803–1871*. [CD-ROM 30]

Italians to America: *Lists of Passengers Arriving at U.S. Ports, 1880–1899*, edited by Ira A. Glazier and P. William
Fillby, 1992–. See also *Italians to America, 1880–1893*. [CD-ROM 31]

Migration from the Russian Empire: Lists of Passengers Arriving at the Port of New York, 1875–1891, edited by
Ira A. Glazier. 6 vols., 1995–. See also *Russians to America, 1850–1896.* [CD-ROM 53]

For additional published indexes, see NYPL IRMA AND PAUL MILSTEIN DIVISION OF UNITED STATES HISTORY, LOCAL
HISTORY AND GENEALOGY.

3. <u>Hamburg Passenger Lists, Direct Index, 1855–1899</u>: Index to departure lists of individuals from central and eastern
Europe who left through the port of Hamburg, Germany and sailed directly to their destinations without stopping
at other European ports, April 1855–March 1899. The index provides date of departure and name of ship. Since
there is no comprehensive index to arrival lists for the port of New York for these years, this index can be used to
assist researchers in searching New York arrival lists. NOTE: A partial index is available at www.hamburg.de.

4. <u>Military Service Records</u> include Veterans Administration, War Department, Adjutant General's Office and other
records as follows:

Civil War Union Veterans and Widows of Union Veterans, enumeration schedules, 1890 [M123]. Indexes include
1890 Veteran's Census Index New York (microfiche); and *Veterans' Schedules: U.S. Selected States*, for 31
states including New Jersey. [CD-ROM 45]

Civil War, index to compiled service records of volunteer Union Soldiers who served in organizations from the
States of New Jersey [M550] and New York. [M551]

Revolutionary War rolls, 1775–1783 [M246]. An index to these records is available on *Ancestry.com/Ancestry.plus.*

Revolutionary War, compiled service records of soldiers who served in the American Army [M881] and index
[M860 or T515]; and compiled service records of American Naval personnel and members of the Departments
of Quartermaster General and the Commissary General of Military Stores [M880] and index. [M879 or M860]

Revolutionary War pension and bounty-land-warrant applications files (in alpha order), 1800–1900. [M804]

War of 1812, index to compiled service records of volunteer soldiers. [M602]

War of 1812, records relating to prisoners-of-war (primarily American soldiers and some British). [M2019]

Patriots' War, 1838, alphabetical index to compiled service records of volunteer soldiers who served from the State
of New York. [M631]

World War I Draft Registration cards, New York State, New Jersey and Puerto Rico. Registration cards are
arranged by state, county/city, local Draft Board, and then alphabetically by surname of the individual
registrant. New York City alone had 189 Boards. [M1509]

World War II Draft Registration cards, 4th Registration, men born between April 28, 1877 and February 16, 1897,
New York City, New Jersey and Puerto Rico. New York City and New Jersey registration cards are arranged
by county and then alphabetically. Puerto Rico cards are filed in one alpha series.

The Archives also has *History of Ships and Navies* [CD-ROM 40] which includes photographs of many passenger
and military vessels; *The Civil War CD-ROM* which includes the following volumes: *The War of the Rebellion:
A Compilation of Official Records of the Union and Confederate Armies,* Dyer's *Compendium of the War of
Rebellion, Fox's Regimental Losses in the American Civil War,* National Archives, *Guide Index to the Official
Records of the Union and Confederate Armies, 1861–1865.* [CD-ROM 43]; and *Civil War, Massachusetts Soldiers,
Sailors and Marines, 1861–1865.* [CD-ROM 33]

5. <u>Naturalization Records</u> are available for the following Courts in Federal Region 2 (New York, New Jersey and
Puerto Rico). Naturalization records include Declarations of Intention (sometimes referred to as "first" papers),
Petition for Naturalization and name changes. Very few Declarations of Intention were filed after 1951 since they
were no longer required. Since 1952, immigrants could file a Petition for Naturalization directly, after living in the
U.S. for 5 years. Declarations were filed only if the immigrant elected to do so, e.g. documentation needed for
employment. For naturalizations filed after 1991, check with the Immigration and Naturalization Service. With
the exception of name changes and the administration of oaths, Federal and local courts were no longer involved
in the naturalization process after 1991.

 i. <u>"Old Law" Naturalization Records for New York City</u>: Photocopies (dexigraphs) of Naturalization Records
filed in Federal, State and local courts in New York City, 1792–1906. Any naturalization completed prior to
October 1906 in <u>any</u> NYC court should be found in this group of records. These courts include:

Federal Courts:

U.S. Circuit Court, Southern District, New York, 1846–1876
U.S. District Court, Southern District, New York, 1824–1906
U.S. District Court, Eastern District, New York, 1865–1906

State and Local Courts:

Court of Common Pleas for the City and County of NY, 1792–1895
Marine Court of the City of New York, 1806–1849
Superior Court of the City of New York, 1828–1895
Supreme Court, 1st Judicial District, formerly Supreme Court, City and County of NY, 1868, 1896–1906
City Court of Brooklyn, 1836–1894
County Court, Kings County, 1856–1906
County Court, Queens County, 1799–1906
Surrogate's Court, Queens County, 1888–1898
County Court, Richmond County, 1869–1906

ii. U.S. District Court for the Eastern District of New York (covers Kings, Queens, Richmond, Nassau and Suffolk Counties)

Petitions for Naturalization, 1865–1991
Declarations of Intention, 1865–1979
Military Petitions, 1918–1920 (WWI), 1942–1946 (WWII), 1950–1956 (Korea)
Name changes 1991–present, arranged by date of naturalization (no index).

iii. U.S. District Court for the Southern District of New York (covers Manhattan, Bronx, Westchester, Putnam, Rockland, Orange, Dutchess and Sullivan Counties. However, most records are for residents of Manhattan and the Bronx. Residents of other jurisdictions, e.g. Brooklyn, may also have been naturalized in this Court.)

Petitions for Naturalization, 1824–1991
Declarations of Intention, 1842–1959, 1967–1991. NOTE: Declarations 1960–1966 are missing and presumed to have been destroyed.
Military Petitions, World War I (1919), World War II and Korea
Repatriation Petitions, 1937–1970
Name Changes, 1991–1996 (arranged by date of naturalization)

iv. U.S. Circuit Court, Southern District of New York (same jurisdiction as U.S. District Court)

Petitions for Naturalization, 1846–1876 and 1906–1911
Declarations of Intention, 1845–1911

v. U.S. District Court, Western District of New York (covers Erie, Monroe and surrounding counties. These counties include the cities of Buffalo and Rochester.)

Petitions, 1903–1966
Declarations of Intention, 1906–1963
Military Petitions (Fort Porter and Fort Niagara), 1918–1920

vi. U.S. District Court, Northern District of New York (covers Albany, Broom, Syracuse, Utica and surrounding counties.)

Petitions, 1821–1855, 1906

vii. U.S. District Court, District of New Jersey

Camden Office - Petitions, 1932–1981; Declarations of Intention, 1933–1968. NOTE: The index to Petitions includes, 1982–1991 which are not available here. NOTE: For copies of 1982–1991 petitions filed in Camden, contact the U.S. District Court, Mitchell H. Cohen Courthouse, 1 J. F. Gerry Plaza, P.O. Box 2797, Camden, NJ 08101.
Newark Office - Petitions, 1914–1982; Declarations of Intention, 1914–1982
    Military Petitions, WWII overseas, 1942–1945; Korean War overseas, 1955–1956
    Picatinny Arsenal and Port Newark, 1918

NOTE: The Newark Office opened in 1911 and began Naturalizations in 1913. For petitions, 1982–1991, filed in Newark, contact the U.S. District Court of New Jersey, Martin Luther King Courthouse, Room 4015, 50 Walnut Street, Newark, NJ 07101.

Trenton Office - Petitions and Declarations, 1838–1906; Petitions, 1931–1988; Declarations, 1930–1983 Military Petitions, Camp Dix, WWI, 1918–1919; and WWII, 1942–1946

viii. U.S. District Court for Puerto Rico

Petitions, 1898–1972
Declarations of Intention, 1917–1963

ix. Other Naturalization Records

Essex County, NY, index and Petitions, 1799–1879
Clinton County, NY, index and Petitions, 1851–1906
Nassau County, NY, index to Petitions, 1899–1986
Suffolk County, NY, index to Petitions, 1853–1990

Military Naturalization index (includes WWI petitions filed at Aviation Field #2, Camp Mills, Camp Dix; Camp Upton, Fort Slocum; and WWII and Korean War petitions filed in U.S. District Courts, Eastern and Southern Districts of New York).

Nassau and Suffolk County indexes to Petitions and Military Naturalization index can be searched online at www.italiangen.org/databases.stm. Kings County (Brooklyn) index to Petitions and Declarations, 1907–1924, can be searched on the Jewish Genealogical Society, Inc. website at www.jgsny.org. Links to other online NYS naturalization indexes including Rockland and Westchester counties are also available on this website.

6. Chinese Re-entry Permits [RG 85]: Case files, 1880s–1944, of some 30,000 Chinese immigrants who applied for re-entry permits under the Chinese Exclusion Acts of 1882 and 1902 are located here. The case files include correspondence, reports, transcripts of interrogations and testimony, as well as the original identification forms issued by the Immigration and Naturalization Service. A computerized index, *Chinese Case Files*, can be accessed on the Archives computers and online through *Ancestry.com* (by *Ancestry.com* members) or *Ancestry.plus* (at libraries with this enhanced version of *Ancestry.com*).

7. Other Court Records [RG 21]: Court cases filed, 1685–1968, in the U.S. District Courts in New York State, New Jersey and Puerto Rico; the Court of Appeals-Second Circuit (cases appealed from New York State, Connecticut and Vermont); and all Circuit Courts in New York State and New Jersey. Dates vary for each court. (NOTE: The functions of the Circuit Courts were absorbed by the U.S. District Courts in 1911.) The cases filed in these courts include legal proceedings in bankruptcy, and criminal, admiralty and civil actions. Records for Circuit Court, Southern District of New York, 1791, include also a list of attorneys. For a more detailed description of records of District Courts, see *Guide to Records in the National Archives-Northeast Region,* compiled by John Celardo and Nancy Malan, 1996. A virtual *Guide* is available online.

8. Income Tax Records: Post-Civil War income tax records relating to business and corporate taxes for the following district offices are available: Albany, 1910–1917; Buffalo, 1862–1917; Lower Manhattan (Second Collection District), 1910–1917; Lower Manhattan (Third District), 1913–1917; Newark, 1917; Syracuse, 1883–1917. In addition, the Archives has Assessment Lists for New York State, 1867–1873, and New Jersey, 1868–1873.

9. Internal Revenue Service (IRS) Employees [RG-58]: Registers of individuals employed by the IRS in Brooklyn, 1885–1919, and Buffalo, NY, 1875–1919. These include employee name, position title, compensation, date of appointment, date and reason for termination of service, place and year of birth and information concerning the employee's prior civil and military service.

10. Russian Consular Records for the New York Consulate, 1844–1929 [M1486]: Includes correspondence about army registrations, 1917; passports applications, 1917–1926; nationality certificates, 1917–1919; extradition files, 1908–1912; missing persons, 1919–1925; deceased persons and estates, 1903–1915; Russian seamen, 1917–1919; and visa applications, 1916–1920.

11. Concentration Camp Records: These records include at least partial lists of inmates, including:

Buchenwald inmate questionnaires, death records, and transport list; Dachau registers and lists of persons liberated; Natzweiler questionnaires; Mauthausen inmate personnel cards, death records, victims list; lists of Belgium Jews in Mauthausen and survivors; and Bergen-Belsen death certificates, 1945. In addition, there are Gestapo transport lists, Berlin, and names of Jews whose German nationality was annulled.

12. Public Health Service Records, 1831–1970 [RG-90], include Seamen's Fund and Retreat and its successor, the Marine Hospital, Staten Island, NY, patient case histories, 1831–1882 [vols. 35–55]; registers of patients, 1831–1870 [vols. 22–34]; register of deaths, 1831–1874 [vol. 56]; and autopsy reports [vol. 57]. This collection includes also medical examination records of crew members and passengers from the New York Quarantine Station on Staten Island.

13. Department of Navy, Bureau of Medicine and Surgery Records, 1831–1922 [RG-52], include a register, 1831–1894, for U.S. Naval Hospital, Brooklyn, listing officers buried in the naval hospital cemetery and a separate list for officers who died at the hospital but were not buried there. The register provides name, age, rank date/place of death, whether died in the hospital, at home or on a ship, cause of death, place of burial, and sometimes, by whom buried. A burial plot register lists men buried in the Brooklyn Navy Yard cemetery and provides name, rank and death register line number.

    This collection also includes a register of Navy, Marine Corp and Army personnel whose remains were returned from Europe after WWI (November 1919–March 1922) by request of family, and reburied at a national or private cemetery. The register includes name, rank, branch of service, sometimes cause of death, name/address of next of kin, date body was shipped and date arrived, name of ship, and remarks (which usually provide some information on place of burial). Surname index included.

14. Veterans Administration Records, 1876–1934 [RG-15/M1749], include records of the New York State Soldiers' and Sailors' Home, Bath, New York. The home was transferred from the State to the Federal government and became a branch of the National Home for Disabled Volunteer Soldiers. Records include registers of veterans' admissions. (15 reels)

15. City Directories: City Directories are available for over 500 cities in the United States (more than 1,000 rolls of microfilm) covering the 1920s and 1930s. These will be of assistance to researchers in using the 1930 Census. In addition, the following city directories are available for New York City:

    NYC (generally Manhattan and parts of the Bronx): 1869–1873, 1878–1882, 1888–1924, 1931, 1933/34
    Brooklyn: 1897–1910, 1912/13, 1933/34
    Queens: 1898, 1909/10, 1912

    For a list of additional City Directories available at NARA, see www.nara.gov/genealogy/citydirs.html.

16. Vital Record Indexes:

    New York State Births, 1881–1927
    New York State Marriages and Deaths, 1881–1952

    NOTE: It is anticipated that New York State birth indexes more than 75 years old, and death and marriage index more than 50 years old will be provided to the Archives annually. Copies of the actual records must be obtained from the NEW YORK STATE DEPARTMENT OF HEALTH, or the local registrar of vital statistics (for communities outside New York City) or the NEW YORK CITY DEPARTMENT OF RECORDS AND INFORMATION SERVICES, MUNICIPAL ARCHIVES for events that occurred prior to 1898 in municipalities now part of New York City. A complete list of local registrar addresses is available in a loose-leaf binder.

    See also CD-ROMs in the Archives collection which include indexes to marriage records in select Illinois, Indiana, Kentucky, Ohio and Tennessee counties [CD-ROM 41]; and the Social Security Death Index (1995 edition). [CD-ROM 13 and 14]

17. New York State Archives:

    The NEW YORK ARCHIVES has deposited a large collection of its microfilmed records formerly available only in Albany, at the National Archives-Northeast Region. See NEW YORK STATE DEPARTMENT OF EDUCATION, NEW YORK STATE ARCHIVES for a partial list.

18. Index to Freedman's Bank Records, 1865–1874. [CD-ROM 48]. See NYPL, SCHOMBURG CENTER FOR RESEARCH IN BLACK CULTURE for the registers of the Freedman's Savings and Trust Company, [M816] indexed here.

Finding Aids:

1. Census: Surname indexes (microfilm) to the 1880, 1900, 1910 and 1920 Censuses are arranged by state and then according to the National Archives Soundex system. (See Appendix A for a description of this system.) The 1880 Soundex index (microfilm) covers only households with children 10 and under. However, the LDS Family History

Library website (www.familysearch.org) has an online index to all persons in the 1880 Census (also on CD-ROM, see below). The index to 1890 Census fragments is arranged alphabetically.

The 1910 index (microfilm) is available for only 21 states (not Connecticut, New Jersey, and New York). However, the Archives has the Heritage Quest CD-ROM indexes for Connecticut and New York (Upstate and New York City). See also, *A Research Guide for the New York 1910 Federal Census*, compiled and edited by Ann Hunt, Pittsfield, PA, 1999, available here. This index of New York State (not including NYC) arranged by counties and towns shows enumeration districts, wards and precincts and where to locate them on the 1910 census microfilms. The Archives also has on microfiche, *Cross Index to Selected City Streets and Enumeration Districts, 1910 Census* [M1283] for 39 cities including New York City (Manhattan, Bronx, Brooklyn, Staten Island — but not Queens) and Elizabeth, Newark and Paterson, NJ. A similar index on microfilm exists for 1930 and includes Queens County. [M1931]

A Soundex index is available for all or part of 12 southern states for the 1930 Census [M2049-M2060]. None exists for New York, New Jersey or Connecticut. However, the Archives has acquired City Directories from all over the U.S.A. covering the 1920s and 1930s to assist researchers in locating records. In addition, Enumeration District (ED) descriptions for 1880–1950, including 1930 [T1224]; and laminated 1930 ED maps for NYC are available here. NOTE: To locate ED's in large cities not included in the Soundex index or the 1930 Street Index [M1931], or to learn that an index already exists for a particular city and its NARA reel number, see the online website created by Dr. Stephen P. Morse, Joel D. Weintraub and David R. Kehs, *Obtaining EDs for the 1930 Census in One Step (Large Cities)* at: www.stevemorse.org. See also *Ancestry.com* or *Ancestry.plus* for an all-person index to the 1930 Census for New York State, New Jersey, Connecticut and more.

The Archives is acquiring CD-ROM or computerized indexes as they become available. See the CD-ROM binder for a complete list. In addition to the 1910 indexes for New York and Connecticut described above, the Archives has indexes for all states, 1880; and 21 states including New York, New Jersey and Connecticut, 1870. Published indexes for most states, 1790–1870, are also available here.

2. Immigrant and Passenger Arrivals: Available indexes are included in "Description of Resources" above. In addition, the Archives has the following publications to assist in locating passenger arrivals:

Catalog of Ship Arrival Manifests, New York, 1899–1924, compiled by Marion Smith, Historian, Immigration and Naturalization Service. Lists ships by date of arrival in each roll of the passenger arrivals [T715 microfilm series].

Index to Ships Arriving at the Port of New York, compiled by staff and volunteers of NARA-Pittsfield, MA for the years 1907, 1909–1916. Includes an alphabetical list by name of ship, date of arrival, microfilm roll and volume number; and a list arranged by volume number (more or less date of arrival).

Morton Allan Directory of European Passenger Steamship Arrivals for the Years 1890–1930 at the Port of New York, and for the Years 1904–1926 at the Ports of Philadelphia, Boston and Baltimore. Baltimore, 1980. See also *Cimorelli Immigration Manifests, 1890–1930,* online at www.cimorelli.com.

3. Military Records: Most military record indexes available in this NARA branch are included under "Description of Resources" above. The *General Index to Compiled Military Service Records of Revolutionary Soldiers* [M860, previously known as, and identical to T515], includes also the names of Naval Personnel that are included in M879. NOTE: NARA-Northeast Region has copies of all three indexes — M860/T515 and M879.

World War I Draft Registration Cards. To assist in identifying the correct draft board in NYC, the Archives has maps of draft registration districts for Manhattan, Brooklyn, the Bronx and Queens. An alphabetical index to NYC Draft Boards 150 (partial), 151 and 152, created by Carole Glick Feinberg, is available online at the Jewish Genealogical Society's website, www.jgsny.org.

4. Naturalization Records: The Archives has a binder for Naturalizations showing the records, cabinet location and indexes available on microfilm for each record group. The following includes indexes on microfilm as well as other formats:

I. "Old Law" Naturalization Records for New York City (1792–1906)
Federal, State and local records are combined in one Soundex index (microfilm).

ii. U.S. District Court for the Eastern District of New York
Petitions, 1865–1906, may be accessed via the Soundex index listed above ("Old Law").
Petitions, 1865–1987, are indexed alphabetically by name and in groups of years in a card index. WWI military petitions are included in this index. There is no alphabetical index to petitions, 1988–1991. The Archives

has typed lists in loose-leaf binders arranged by date and certificate number covering this four-year period. The index to <u>Military petitions</u>, WWII and Korea, is included in the computerized Military Naturalization Index. See above 5(ix). A separate card index is also available.

Declarations of Intention, 1865–1916, are indexed alphabetically by surname in each individual volume. The Archives has ledger indexes covering the period 1909–1949. These are organized by year and then first letter of the surname. There is no alphabetical index to Declarations of Intention filed in 1950 or later.

iii. <u>U.S. District Court for the Southern District of New York</u>

Petitions, 1824–1906, may be accessed via the Soundex index listed above ("Old Law").

Petitions, 1824–August, 1989, are indexed alphabetically by name and groups of years in a card index. Repatriation and WWI petitions are included in this index. A computerized index, 1926–1949, is being developed by the Genealogy Federation of Long Island volunteers using *certificate* stubs. This work-in-progress is available at the National Archives - Northeast Region and on the Italian Genealogy Group website (www.italiangen.org/southern_district_records_intro.stm). NOTE: *Certificate* stubs do not include denied or canceled petitions. Check the card index if a record is not found in the computerized index. A separate computerized index is available at NARA for 1989–1991 petitions (also created by a volunteer).

Petitions, 1990–1991, are in a computer printout arranged by date and then alphabetically by surname for each day.

Declarations of Intention, 1842–October 30, 1915, are indexed alphabetically by surname in each of the 89 volumes covering this period. There is a ledger index, 1915–1916, covering the remainder of 1915 and 1916, arranged alphabetically by name. A computerized index is being prepared by volunteers for Declarations, working back from 1916. Declarations, 1917–1950 are indexed alphabetically by name in a card index.

Military Petitions for WWII and Korea are included in the Military Naturalization Index. See 5 (ix) above. A separate card index arranged alphabetically by surname is also available.

iv. <u>U.S. Circuit Court for the Southern District of New York</u>

Petitions, 1846–1876, may be accessed via the Soundex index listed above ("Old Law"). An alphabetical card index is also available for these records.

Petitions, 1906–1911, are indexed alphabetically by name in a card index.

Declarations of Intention, 1845–1906 are indexed by name in each volume. There is a ledger index for Declarations as well as Petitions, 1906–1911.

v. <u>U.S. District Court for the Western District of New York</u>

Petitions, 1903–1966 and Declarations, 1906–1963, are indexed alphabetically together by name in a card index. Military Petitions (Fort Porter and Fort Niagara), 1918–1920, are included in this index.

vi. <u>U.S. District Court for the Northern District of New York</u>

Hand written extracts of Petitions, 1821–1855 and 1906, created by a volunteer, are arranged alphabetically by name.

vii. <u>U.S. District Court for New Jersey</u>

Camden office - There are separate card indexes, Certificates of Naturalization, Petitions, 1932–1991, and Declarations, 1933–1968. Each are arranged alphabetically by name.

Newark office - There are two overlapping microfiche indexes, c. 1914–1984, covering Petitions and one for Declarations of Intention. One Petition index labeled "Index to Naturalizations" includes microfiche copies of the Naturalization stubs which include address, age or birth date of the immigrant. The second, labeled "Old and New Index" includes index cards with name and petition number as well as a scattering of stubs. Researchers should check both if an immigrant is not found in one. Both are arranged alphabetically by name. Picatinny Arsenal and Port Newark petitions, 1918, are not indexed.

Trenton office - There is a card index, 1838–1906, to Petitions and Declarations arranged alphabetically by name; and to Petitions, 1930–1988. A ledger index also exists for the 1838–1906 period and includes naturalizations filed in the Court of Common Pleas. The Archives has no index to Declarations, 1930–1983.

Camp Dix is included in the Military Naturalization Index. See 5 (ix) above. A separate index to petitions arranged alphabetically is available in a loose-leaf binder.

viii. <u>U.S. District Court for Puerto Rico</u>
The Archives has a one-volume index to Petitions, 1917–1929, arranged alphabetically by first letter of the surname.

ix. <u>Other Naturalizations</u>
Archives staff have created computerized indexes to <u>Clinton County, NY</u> Petitions, 1851–1906; and <u>Essex County, NY</u> Petitions, 1799–1879.

5. <u>Concentration Camp Records</u>: The finding aid, in a loose-leaf binder, is arranged by concentration camp and provides the reel number for each group of records. There is no surname index included in the finding aid. Some records are arranged alphabetically and reel numbers for alpha groups are provided.

6. <u>Chinese Re-entry Permits</u>: Case files are arranged numerically by case number. The Archives has created a computerized alphabetical name index.

7. <u>Other Court Records</u>: The Archives also has draft inventories of the records of each court. Case files can be located by court and case number. Minute, docket or order books may have name indexes but are not available for all courts. Check with the appropriate court for available indexes.

8. <u>Income Tax Records</u> of individual businesses are not easily accessed. These records are arranged by year, District or Collection Office, and type of tax. Further, the only index to this collection is a list arranged by year and box number.

9. <u>Internal Revenue Service Employees</u>: These records are not indexed. However, there are only three thin volumes of records which can be scanned quickly by the researcher.

10. <u>Russian Consular Records</u>: There is a loose-leaf binder, "Microfilm Publication Descriptive Pamphlets" that includes an inventory with reel and box numbers for these records. A name index, arranged by the Daitch-Mokotoff Soundex system, is included in *The Russian Consular Records Index and Catalog*, available at the Reference Desk. An explanation of the Daitch-Mokotoff Soundex System is available in the book. Record numbers beginning with "N" (listed in column "D") are those from the consulate in New York City and are available here.

11. <u>New York State Archives</u>: The Archives has a loose-leaf binder, *Guide to Microforms Deposited at the National Archives - New York Region*, kept behind the desk that includes a complete listing of the State microfilms available here.

12. <u>Public Health Service</u>, <u>Department of Navy</u>, <u>Bureau of Medicine and Surgery</u>, and <u>Veterans Administration Records</u>: The Archives has draft finding aids for these collections. Registers are arranged chronologically unless otherwise indicated.

For additional records and finding aids available at the National Archives, see NARA's website and *Guide to Genealogical Research in the National Archives of the United States*. Third edition, Washington, DC, 2000.

Description of Facility:

Two staff persons are available to assist researchers at the Reference Desk. Seating is available for 12 researchers at 6 tables. There are 48 microfilm readers, 2 microfiche readers and 2 microfilm/microfiche reader/printers. The Archives has three computers with access to computerized databases and CD-ROMs, 2 computers with public access to the Internet and one computer for use in converting surnames to NARA's Soundex code. Microfilm reels are in self-service file cabinets.

Fees/Copies:

The cost of copying a page from microfilm is $.30 and from paper records, $.15 when researchers make their own copy. When a staff member makes a copy, the charge is $.50 for paper copies and $1.90 from microfilm. Copies can be obtained immediately. Mail, fax or e-mail requests for Petitions of Naturalization are charged a minimum of $10.00. This can include more than one record. Personal checks, money order and credit cards are accepted. (All inquiries other than naturalization must be directed to Washington, DC.)

Restrictions on Use:

Researchers must provide building security with photo identification to enter the building. All briefcases/handbags and coats must be left in lockers in the entrance area. There is no charge for the lockers.

A snack bar is located across the hall from the National Archives. Researchers may bring food into this area. Food and drink are not permitted in the research room.

NEW YORK ACADEMY OF MEDICINE
LIBRARY

Facility Director: Maxine Rockoff, Librarian
                          Miriam Mandelbaum, Curator, Rare Books and Manuscripts
                          Lea Myohanen, Coordinator of Public Services

Address: 2 East 103rd Street, 3rd floor
                          New York, NY

                          (Cross Streets: Corner of Fifth Avenue)

Mail Address: 1216 Fifth Avenue
                          New York, NY 10029-5293

Phone: (212) 822-7300 (Reference desk)
                          (212) 822-7313 (Rare Book Room)
Fax: (212) 423-0266
E-mail: info@nyam.org
Website: www.nyam.org

Hours of Operation:

Reading Room
   Monday to Friday: 9:00 am to 5:00 pm
Malloch Rare Book Room
   Tuesday to Friday: 10:00 am to 4:00 pm, by appointment only.

NOTE: Stack retrieval and photocopying services cease at 4:30 pm.

Closed Saturday, Sunday and most legal holidays. The schedule for summer months may vary. Call in advance.

Closest Public Transportation:

Bus: M1, M2, M3 or M4 bus to Madison Avenue and 103rd Street (northbound) and Fifth Avenue and 102nd Street
         (southbound)

Directions:

From midtown, take the M1, M2, M3 or M4 bus north on Madison Avenue to 102/103rd Street. Walk west on 103rd towards Fifth Avenue. The entrance is on 103rd Street. NOTE: The entrance is wheelchair accessible.

Description of Resources:

The Library, founded in 1847, is one of the largest medical libraries in the U.S.A. Its collection includes more than one million volumes, 275,000 illustrations and portraits, and 1,600 current periodicals and journals.

The following are of particular interest to genealogists (call numbers are listed in brackets):

1.   National Medical Directories

   American Board of Medical Specialties [AMBS] Compendium of Certified Medical Specialists, 1986/7–1990/91
      [W 22.1 A1523], and *AMBS Directory of Board Certified Medical Specialists,* 1992/93–. [W 22.1 O32]

   American Medical Directory. 1906–1989, later known as the *Directory of Physicians in the United States, 1992–.*
      Published by the American Medical Association for the U.S. and Canada. The Directory is arranged
      alphabetically by state, locality and name. There is a cumulative index arranged alphabetically by surname.
      Entries include education, year of license, primary and secondary specialties, type of practice, awards and local
      address. [2AA (1906–1985); 2AA1.A512 (1986–1989); W 22.AA1 D5985 (1992–)]

   *Directory of Deceased American Physicians 1804–1929: A genealogical guide to over 149,000 medical
      practitioners providing brief biographical sketches drawn from the American Medical Association's Deceased
      Physicians Masterfile,* edited by Arthur W. Hafner. 2 vols. Chicago, 1993. [WZ 22 AA1 D598 1993]

   Directory of Medical Specialists. 1939– 1989/90. This Directory lists physicians alphabetically by specialty, state,
      locality and name. There is a Master Index arranged alphabetically by surname and including locality, state

and specialty. The Directory includes biographical information about the physician such as date and place of birth, education, career history, military record, awards, society memberships, office address and telephone number. [W 22 DA2 D5984]

Medical Obituaries: American Physicians' Biographical Notices in Selected Medical Journals Before 1907, by Lisabeth M. Holloway. New York, 1981. [ZWZ 112 H745m 1981]

Directories are available also for individual states including New York, New Jersey and Connecticut; and specific groups such as psychologists, nurses, dentists, pharmacists and other scientists. Examples include:

American College of Healthcare Executives: Biographical Dictionary of the Membership. 2000–. [WX 22.1 A512d]

Biographical Dictionary of Psychology, by Leonard Zusne. Includes a short biography of c. 1200 deceased Psychologists and individuals from other fields who made a contribution to psychology from antiquity to the present. Westport, 1984. [3.]

Blacks in Science and Medicine, by Vivian O. Sammons. New York, [1990]. [WZ 112 S189b 1990]

Directory, American College of Hospital Administrators: A Biographical Directory of the Membership. 1938–1984 (gaps). [2AA]

R. L. Polk & Co's Dental Register of the United States and Canada, 1898–1899. [2AA]

Who's Who in Dentistry. 1916, 1925. Biographical sketches of prominent dentists in the U.S. and Canada. [s.3]

Who's Who in the Nursing World, 1928. [2.H.A.]

Who's Who in American Nursing, edited by Jeffrey Franz. Washington, DC, [1984]. [3.]

2. <u>International Biographical Directories</u>

Australia. *Medical Directory of Australia.* 1962–. [W 22 KA8 M489]

Austria, West Germany, Switzerland. *Who's Who in Medicine,* edited by Karl Strute and Theodor Doelken. 2 vols. Worerthsee, [Germany], 1978, 1981. [3.]

Canada. *Canadian Medical Directory.* 1987–. [W 22 DC2 C212]

Czech Republic. *Biographisches Lexikon der Deutschen Medizinischen Fakultät in Prag 1883-1945,* by Ludmila Hlaváčková and Petr Svobodný. Prague, 1998. [WZ 140 GC75 H677B 1998]

France. *Guide Rosenwald: L'Annuaire du Medicin,* 1929–. [W 22 GF7 G946]

Germany. *Zahnarzte 1933–1945: Berufsverbot, Emigration, Verfolgung,* by Michael Kohn. Berlin, 1994. [WU 11GG4 K79z 1994]

Great Britain. *The Medical Register,* 1874–1959 (gaps) [W 22 FA1 M489]; and *The Medical Directory,* 1886-1998. [W22 FA1 M4]

Ireland. *Register of Scientific Research Personnel,* by Diarmuid Murphy and Donal Ó Brolcháin. Dublin, 1971. [Q 145 M97 1971]

Israel. *Directory of medical research in Israel: institutions and scientists,* by Donald S. Berns, Oded Abamsky and Michael Silbermann. Jerusalem, 1996. [W 22 J19 B531d 1996]

New Zealand. *New Zealand Medical Register, 1985–1988.* [W 22 KN4 N532]

Poland. *The Martyrdom of Jewish Physicians in Poland,* edited by Louis Falstein. Includes biographies pp. 303–498. New York, 1963. [S.3]

Switzerland. *Schweizerisches Medizinisches Jahrbuch Annuaire Medical Suisse.* 1929–. [W 22 GS9 S413]

U.S.S.R. *Akademiya Meditsinskiyh Nauk Soyuza Sovetskikh Sotssialisticheskikh Republik.* 1947. (Reference data concerning the active members of the Academy of Medical Science of the U.S.S.R.) [Q11054]

Worldwide. *Biographisches Lexikon der hervorragenden Aerzte aller Zeiten und Voelker,* edited by August Hirsch, et al. Vienna, 1884-1888. 5 vols. Includes physicians who achieved prominence by 1880. [ZWZ 129 B5821]

3. <u>Biography (Obituary) File</u>: This is a unique index created by the Academy Library c. 1920 and continued until c.1978. Obituaries and biographies of physicians are either pasted directly on an index card or the source, date, volume/page of the obituary/biography are noted on the card. The earliest date noted for a source is 1877, but there may be earlier ones. The Library stopped entering data c. 1978.

4. <u>Portraits Catalog</u>: Like the Biography (Obituary) File, this catalog is a unique tool created by the Academy Library. It is an index to photographs of physicians in books and periodicals acquired by the Library up to 1975. If a written biography is also available, the source, date, volume and page number are noted on the card. This catalog is arranged alphabetically by surname in 5 volumes to 1960, and in three supplementary volumes — 1959–1965, 1966–1970 and 1971–1975. The *Portraits Catalog* and supplements have been published by G. K. Hall and may be available in other libraries.

5. *Index Medicus* and its predecessor was published annually by the National Library of Medicine and is available in this Library from 1879 to 1975 in print form. This was an index to more than 2,700 biomedical journals. Two sets of volumes existed for each year — an Author Index and a Subject Index. Not all the journals covered by the index are available in this Library. The Library also has online access to *PubMed,* including *Medline,* an index to journals published from c. 1966 to the present; and *OldMedline,* 1958–1965. *Medline* contains over 11.0 million bibliographic citations and author abstracts from more than 4,300 biomedical journals published in the U.S. and 70 other countries.

6. <u>Historical Collection</u> includes 49,000 volumes on the history of medicine, science and other health related disciplines. 32,000 of these volumes date from 1700 BC to 1800 AD. Among these books are such unusual biographical titles as:

Cosenza, Mario Emilio. *Biographical and Bibliographical Dictionary of the Italian Humanists and of the World of Classical Scholarship in Italy, 1300–1800.* 2nd edition, 6 vols. Includes photo reproductions of Professor Cosenza's hand written cards providing brief biographies of Italian scholars and those who studied in Italy. Boston, 1962–1967. [RBS3]

Friedenwald, Harry. *Jewish Luminaries in Medical History and a Catalogue of works bearing on the subject of the Jews and Medicine from the private library of Harry Friedenwald.* Baltimore, 1946. [RB2]

Goldschmidt-Lehmann, Ruth P. *A bibliography of Anglo-Jewish medical biography.* Jerusalem, 1988. Includes a list of over 300 Jewish medical practitioners and cites articles, often obituaries, that have been published about them. Provides an excellent list of biographical sources. [Z 6659.5 G623b 1988]

Hellstedt, Leone M. *Women Physicians of the World: Autobiographies of Medical Pioneers.* Includes 91 autobiographies of women physicians from 27 countries. Washington, [1978]. [RB 3]

Hes, Hindle S. *Jewish Physicians in the Netherlands, 1600–1940.* Assen, 1980. [RB 3]

Jocher, Christian Gottlieb. *Allgemeines Gelehrten-Lexikon.* 4 vols. Leipzig, 1750–71; and supplements published in Leipzig and Bremen, 1784–1787; 1810, 1813–1819 and 1897 (7 vols.). Includes biographical sketches of scholars of many nationalities and including many physicians. [RB3]

Levy, Mary L. *Some Jewish Physicians at the English Court (1102–1921).* Marlow, 1961. [RB 145096]

Margalith, David. *Physicians: Forerunners of Modern Israel.* Tel-Aviv, 1973. [RB3]

7. <u>Electronic Resources</u>: The Library's online resources, *Important Figures in Health Sciences — their lives and works,* and *Databases,* includes links to websites providing biographies of doctors, nurses, nobel prize winners and more. Included is a link to *Canadian Health Obituaries* (www.health.library.mcgill.ca/osler/cfstand/chobit.htm).

Finding Aids:

In addition to the catalogs described above, the Library has an online catalog including all periodicals, all books published after 1950 and most books published since 1801. Researchers visiting the Academy Library may obtain books from the stacks that are in the computerized catalog by clicking on the "Request" key at the top of the screen displaying a book title. A window will open requesting seat number and name. Click on "Submit above information." A verification screen will be displayed. Click on "Request Selected Item." Books are delivered directly to your assigned seat. NOTE: An appointment must be made to see books in the Malloch Rare Book Room.

To find pre-1950 books, check also the Library's card catalog, arranged by author and title. The Library has two subject catalogs. The *Subject Catalog of the Library* is a set of blue volumes which include photo duplicates of the Library's subject card file on all materials acquired prior to 1969. Items acquired after 1968 are in the subject card catalog in the catalog room.

The catalogs do not contain any citations to individual journal articles. See *Index Medicus* or *PubMed* for such citations. Searches can be made by personal name, corporate/conference name, title, subject or key word.

To obtain books from the stacks that are in the card catalog (but not online), a call slip must be submitted to the circulation desk. No more than 5 call slips may be submitted at one time or a total of 10 in one day.

Description of Facility:

The Library is on the third floor of the New York Academy of Medicine building. This is an institutional building, erected in the 1920s, with meeting rooms, high ceilings, flowing spaces and a club atmosphere. The Library Lobby is a large gallery which houses the card catalog, six computers, the circulation desk and some biographical dictionaries. The Biography (Obituary) card file is located behind the reference desk in the Lobby.

The Library has one very spacious room, the Main Reading Room (Woerishoffer Hall), and a smaller one, the Current Periodicals Room. The Main Reading Room has seating for about 100 researchers. The Current Periodicals Room seats 36. The *Index Medicus* volumes (1879–1975) and early copies of the *American Medical Directory* and *Directory of Physicians in the United States* can be found in the Current Periodicals Room. The *Subject Catalog of the Library,* and the *Portraits Catalog* are located in the Main Reading Room on a table near the center of the room.

The Malloch Rare Book Room is located on the Mezzanine floor, one floor above the Library. It can be accessed by taking the elevator to the Mezzanine floor or going up the spiral staircase (with staff permission) from the area at the far end of the Library Lobby.

Fees/Copies:

Photocopies are made by the staff at $.25 per page. Place the order at the circulation desk. Copies of photographs or slides can be made from photographs in the Library's collection at a cost of $50 (black and white).

The Library will respond to mail requests for research. If the research takes 15 minutes or less, there is no charge. If more time is needed, the inquirer will be informed that a $80 per hour research fee is charged. Requests are usually responded to within 2 weeks but may take longer.

Restrictions on Use:

The Library is open to the public. However, it is necessary to make an appointment to use the Rare Book collection. Call numbers beginning with [RB] would be located here.

Only Fellows of the Library and Library Subscribers (usually firms heavily into medical research) have borrowing privileges. However, the Library does participate in the inter-library loan program and non-reference materials can be borrowed in this manner. Requests may be submitted through an individual's local public library.

No orders for photocopies are taken after 4:30 pm.

When entering the New York Academy of Medicine building there is a checkroom to the left. Coats and bags must be checked. Only the minimum of notebooks, paper and writing implements may be brought into the Library.

NEW YORK CITY DEPARTMENT OF HEALTH AND MENTAL HYGIENE
OFFICE OF VITAL RECORDS

Facility Director: Rosalyn Williams, Director of Vital Records

Address: 125 Worth Street, CN-4, Room 133
New York, NY 10013-4090

(Cross Street: Centre and Lafayette Streets)

Phone: (212) 788-4500
(212) 788-4505 (recorded information)
(888) 849-1835 (credit card orders for Birth records, if calling from NYC)
(800) 908-9146 (credit card orders for Birth records, if calling from outside NYC)

Fax: (212) 962-6105 (credit card orders for Birth records)

E-mail: none

Website: www.nyc.gov/html/doh/

Hours of Operation:

Monday to Friday: 9:00 am to 4:30 pm

Closed Saturday, Sunday and legal holidays.

Closest Public Transportation and Directions:

See CIVIL COURT OF THE CITY OF NEW YORK, MANHATTAN (NEW YORK COUNTY). The Health Department building is straight ahead when you emerge from the subway. Enter on the Worth Street side. Turn right at the information booth. The office (Room 133) is the last room on the right on the ground floor. NOTE: Use the Lafayette Street entrance (west side of building) for wheelchair accessibility.

Description of Resources:

This office maintains for all five New York City boroughs, birth records, 1910 to the present, and death records, 1949 to the present. See "Restrictions on Use."

For older records see NEW YORK CITY DEPARTMENT OF RECORDS AND INFORMATION SERVICES, MUNICIPAL ARCHIVES.

Finding Aids:

This office has book indexes for each year of record. Indexes, 1910 to 1937, are arranged by year, borough and then alphabetically by surname. For the period after 1937 (except 1944–1945), annual citywide indexes are arranged alphabetically by surname. Citywide indexes for 1944 and 1945 are arranged by NYC Health Department's Soundex system (see Appendix A) applied to the child's surname and then by the Soundex of the mother's maiden name.

Indexes are printed volumes to 1986 for births and to 1983 for deaths. For later years, the indexes to births and deaths are computer printouts. This office also has geographic (address and hospital) indexes for births from 1910 to 1987. Alphabetical indexes can be viewed by the public for a daily or annual fee. See "Fees/Copies" and "Restrictions on Use."

NOTE: Birth and death indexes through 1982 (alphabetical) can be viewed at no charge at the NEW YORK PUBLIC LIBRARY, IRMA AND PAUL MILSTEIN DIVISION OF UNITED STATES HISTORY, LOCAL HISTORY AND GENEALOGY. They can also be viewed on microfilm (to 1965) at the NEW YORK GENEALOGICAL AND BIOGRAPHICAL SOCIETY and at Mormon FAMILY HISTORY CENTERS around the world.

Description of Facility:

This is a busy government office. Applications for copies of birth and death records and return envelopes are available near the entrance to the room, on the rear left wall. The least busy hours are 9:00 am-10:00 am and 3:00 pm to 4:30 pm. Applications are also available online and can be copied from the Department's web site. Applications for viewing birth/death indexes are available from the receptionist in the Director's office (door to the left of the tellers' windows). There are seven tellers at windows in Room 133. Each of these tellers also accepts applications and payment for viewing birth and death indexes. Researchers should be prepared to show a valid, signed photo identification. See "Restrictions on Use."

Fees/Copies:

To obtain a copy of a birth or death record, complete the appropriate application (see Appendix C-2 and C-3) and fill out a self-addressed envelope (no stamp needed). Submit these with your payment to a teller in Room 133 or send your request by mail. For birth records, orders may be placed also by telephone, fax or via the Internet. See "Restrictions on Use." Certified copies of the original records are available at $15 per copy. Searches include any two consecutive years. Additional years are $3 per year/per name.

Payments may be made by cash, personal check, money order or credit card for requests submitted in-person. Do not send cash when requesting by mail. There is an additional handling charge of $5.50 per order for credit card orders. For those requiring 2-3 day delivery, add an additional $11. All checks should be made out to "New York City Department of Health & Mental Hygiene" and must have your name and address imprinted on the check. If payment from a foreign country, send an international money order or check drawn on a U.S. bank. Mail requests should include a stamped self-addressed envelope.

At least two pieces of information about a deceased person (other than information found in the indexes) should be included in the application for a death record. Items such as parents' names, occupation of the deceased or spouse's name qualify. Be sure to indicate your relationship to the deceased person on the application.

For birth records (other than your own) and death records, a copy will not be provided immediately even if you come in-person. Allow up to 4 weeks for a return reply by mail.

Birth records from 1920 to the present are available in shortened computer form. These short form certifications of birth do not include parents' ages, place of birth, occupation or number of children previously born to the mother. The short form certifications also cost $15. You must specifically ask for the long form if you wish this additional information for post-1920 records. Birth records 1910 to 1919 are not available in computer form.

There is a fee of $15 per day for viewing the New York City Health Department birth and death indexes. Bring two pieces of valid, signed photo identification.

Restrictions on Use:

No records (except your own short form birth record) can be obtained immediately. Birth records pre-1936 and death records pre-1989 are stored off site.

Birth records are only available to the individual of record and/or a direct descendant. If the individual is deceased, a copy of the death certificate must accompany the request. If the person of record is living, the request must be accompanied by an original notarized letter of authorization from that individual, naming the person who may request a copy of the record. A valid, signed photo identification or two proofs of identity (letter from a utility or an entitlement letter from a government agency) must accompany mail requests for birth records.

Orders for birth certificates using the online "VitalChek" (www.vitalchek.com) may only be used for the applicant's own certificate or for his/her child, provided the applicant's name is on the child's certificate.

Geographic (address and hospital) birth indexes may not be viewed by the public.

NEW YORK CITY DEPARTMENT OF RECORDS AND INFORMATION SERVICES
MUNICIPAL ARCHIVES

Facility Director:	Kenneth R. Cobb, Director
Address:	31 Chambers Street, Room 103 New York, NY 10007
	(Cross Streets: Centre and Elk Streets)
Phone:	(212) 788-8580
Fax:	(212) 385-0984
E-mail:	Archives@doris.nyc.gov
Website:	www.nyc.gov/html/doris/html/collections.html

Hours of Operation:

Monday to Thursday: 9:00 am to 4:30 pm
Friday: 9:00 am to 1:00 pm
Closed Saturday, Sunday and legal holidays.

Closest Public Transportation and Directions:

See COUNTY CLERK'S OFFICE - STATE SUPREME COURT, NEW YORK COUNTY (MANHATTAN), DIVISION OF OLD RECORDS. The Municipal Archives is on the first floor of the Surrogate's Court building. NOTE: There is a service entrance (steep incline) at the back of the building (Reade Street) which provides access to wheelchair users.

Description of Resources:

The Municipal Archives, a division of the NYC Department of Records and Information Services (DORIS), has circa 100,000 cubic feet of historic records documenting New York City, its people and government. These include vital records, building records, films, photographs, papers donated by NYC elected officials, and NYC agency records. The following records are of particular interest to genealogists:

1. New York City Vital Records: Vital records are indexed and arranged according to the locality/borough in which they were originally filed. New York City, before 1898, consisted of Manhattan and parts of the Bronx. Manhattan records include the western area of the Bronx (Kingsbridge, West Farms and Morrisania), 1874–1897, and the eastern area of the Bronx, 1895–1897. These areas were annexed by New York City in 1874 and 1895 respectively. (The Bronx became a separate borough in 1898.) For vital records in these areas and years, a search of Manhattan records, as noted by *, should be made. See Appendix H, "Before the Five Boroughs," by Harry Macy, Jr., for a more detailed history and maps.

   A. Births and Deaths: Include birth records, 1898–1909, and death records, 1898–1948, for all five NYC boroughs; and records pre-1898 for localities that became part of NYC in 1898.

   B. Marriages: Includes marriage records, pre-1938 and indexes pre-1952. At least two independent sets of marriage records were maintained for each borough of NYC for the period 1908–1937. These include records filed with the NYC Health Department and those filed in the City Clerk's Offices. The Municipal Archives has all marriage records (and extant indexes) filed with the Health Department and has accessioned City Clerk's marriage records for the years, 1908–1929 and indexes for the years, 1908-1951. NOTE: A third set of marriage records are available for Queens County for the 1908–1920 period (gaps) and 1938. See COUNTY CLERK'S OFFICE, QUEENS.

   NOTE: Birth, marriage and death records (certificates) for Queens and Richmond Counties, 1881–1897, the eastern portion of the Bronx (then part of Westchester County), 1881–1895, and Kings County towns prior to annexation to the City of Brooklyn in the 1880s and 1890s, are available also from the NEW YORK STATE DEPARTMENT OF HEALTH in Albany. The Municipal Archives has liber records (registers) only for these communities and years. For Manhattan/Bronx* births, marriages and deaths, 1866–1887, and Brooklyn births and marriages, 1866–1879, and deaths, 1862–1879, the Archives has both liber records and certificates.

   For NYC birth records, 1910 to present, and death records, 1949 to present, see NYC DEPARTMENT OF HEALTH AND MENTAL HYGIENE, OFFICE OF VITAL RECORDS. For City Clerk's marriage records, 1930 to date and indexes 1952 to date, see CITY CLERK'S OFFICE - MANHATTAN. See Town Records (below) for additional pre-1898 Brooklyn records.

A list of existing liber records and certificates (on microfilm) for each locality/borough follows. Unless otherwise noted, records are <u>liber records</u>.

MANHATTAN (NEW YORK COUNTY)*

Births:	Manhattan	Jun 1, 1847–Dec 31, 1848
	Manhattan/Bronx*	Jul 1, 1853–Dec 31, 1887
	Manhattan/Bronx*	Jan l, 1866–Dec 31, 1897 (certificates)
	Manhattan	1898–1909 (certificates)

Deaths:	Manhattan	Jul 26, 1795–Oct 25, 1795
	Manhattan	Jan 1, 1802–Jul 31, 1804
	Manhattan	May 1, 1808–Jul 31, 1808
	Manhattan/Bronx*	Jan 1, 1812–Dec 31, 1887
	Manhattan/Bronx*	Jan 1, 1866–Dec 31, 1897 (certificates)
	Manhattan	Jan 1, 1898–Dec 31, 1948 (certificates)

Marriages:	Manhattan	May 12, 1829-May 17, 1846 (scattered)
		Jun 1, 1847–Dec 31, 1848
	Manhattan/Bronx*	Jul 1, 1853–Dec 31, 1887
	Manhattan/Bronx* - Health Dept. Records	Jan 1, 1866–Dec 31, 1937 (certificates)
	Manhattan/Bronx* - City Clerk's Records	1908–1913 (licenses/affidavits)
	Manhattan - City Clerk's Records	1914–1929 (licenses/affidavits)
	Manhattan - City Clerk Record of Certificates or Contracts of Marriage*	1902–1908
	Mayor's Office, Registry of Marriages*	1875–1897
	Delayed and Imperfect Marriages*	1873–1916
	Mayor's Office/City Court, Registry of Marriages by Judge Ehrlich*	1886–1895

BRONX

Births:	Morrisania (Town)	1872–1874
	S. Mt. Vernon & Wakefield (Village)	Aug 6, 1890–May 20, 1895
	Westchester (Town)	Jan 15, 1847–Dec 8, 1849, Feb 14, 1881–May 10, 1895
	Bronx (Borough)	1898–1909

Deaths:	Bronx (Borough)	Jan 1, 1898–Dec 31, 1948 (certificates)
	S. Mt. Vernon & Wakefield (Village)	Nov 11, 1878-Oct 27, 1881 (10 records), Aug 27, 1890–Jun 4, 1895
	Westchester (Town)	Jan 3, 1847–Dec 27, 1849, Dec 8, 1887–Apr 24, 1895

Marriages:	Bronx (Borough) - Health Dept. Records	Jan 1, 1898–Dec 31, 1937 (certificates)
	Bronx - City Clerk Records	1914–1929 (licences/affidavits)
	Bronx - County Clerk, Marriage License Religious Certificates	1914–1929 (certificates)
	S. Mt. Vernon (Village)	Nov 23, 1890–May 22, 1895
	Westchester (Town)	Dec 18, 1847–Dec 19, 1849, 1871–1873, 1876, 1881, Feb 1, 1882–Apr 24, 1894

BROOKLYN (KINGS COUNTY)

Births:	Brooklyn (City)	Jan 1, 1866–Dec 31, 1879
	Brooklyn (City/Borough)	Apr 3, 1866–Dec 31, 1909 (certificates)
	Flatbush (Town)	Jan 5, 1847–Dec 1, 1851, Dec 15, 1880–Apr 28, 1894
	Flatlands (Town)	Sep 4, 1880–Dec 30, 1895
	Gravesend (Town)	Nov 8, 1880–May 6, 1894
	New Lots (Town)	Mar 3, 1881–Jul 31, 1886
	New Utrecht (Town)	Nov 22, 1880–Jun 26, 1894

Deaths:	Brooklyn (City)	Jan 1, 1848–Dec 31, 1853, Jan 1, 1857–Dec 31, 1879
	Brooklyn (City/Borough)	Jan 1, 1862–Dec 31, 1948 (certificates)
	Flatbush (Town)	Feb 10, 1847–Nov 19, 1851, Dec 5, 1880–May 6, 1894
	Flatlands (Town)	Sep 5, 1880–Dec 31, 1895
	Gravesend (Town)	Aug 14, 1880–May 3, 1894
	New Lots (Town)	Jun 9, 1881–Jul 31, 1886
	New Utrecht (Town)	Dec 27, 1880–Jun 29, 1894

Marriages:	Brooklyn (City/Borough) - Health Dept. Records	Jan 1, 1866–Dec 31, 1937 (certificates)
	Brooklyn (Borough) - City Clerk License Records	1908–1929 (licenses/affidavits)
	Flatbush (Town)	Jan 11, 1847–Jul 16, 1851, Oct 1880–Apr 1894
	Flatlands (Town)	Dec 1880–Dec 1895
	New Utrecht (Town)	Dec 1880–Jun 1894
	New Lots (Town)	May 1881–Jul 1886
	Gravesend (Town)	Feb 1881–May 1894
	Delayed Registration	1875–1934
	Special Marriages	1898–1937
	Metropolitan Board of Health	
	Register of Marriages	1866–1879

QUEENS

Births:	College Point (Village)	Nov 1, 1889–Jan 16, 1898
	Far Rockaway (Village)	Dec 3, 1889–Dec 11, 1897
	Flushing (Town)	Jan 2, 1847–Dec 27, 1849,
		Jan 1, 1881–Oct 12, 1897
	Flushing (Village)	Oct 14, 1889–Dec 29, 1897
	Jamaica (Town)	Jan 23, 1847–Dec 30, 1848,
		Jul 9, 1881–Dec 16, 1897
	Jamaica (Village)	Jul 23, 1889–Jan 12, 1898
	Long Island City	May 2, 1871–Dec 31, 1897
	Newtown (Town)	Jan 31, 1847–Dec 22, 1849,
		Jun 23, 1881–Jan 2, 1898
	Richmond Hill (Village)	Dec 14, 1895–Dec 7, 1897
	Rockaway (Village)	Jun 29, 1897–Jan 14, 1898
	Whitestone (Village)	Sep 1, 1889–Dec 28, 1897
	Queens (Borough)	1898–1909

Deaths:	Queens (Borough)	Jan 1, 1898–Dec 31, 1948 (certificates)
	College Point (Village)	Nov 12, 1889–Jan 18, 1898
	Far Rockaway (Village)	Dec 12, 1889–Dec 21, 1897
	Flushing (Town)	Jan 4, 1847–Dec 31, 1849,
		Jan 1, 1881–Jan 6, 1898
	Flushing (Village)	Oct 17, 1889–Jan 13, 1898
	Jamaica (Town)	Jan 14, 1847–Dec 30, 1848,
		Jul 3, 1881–Jan 15, 1898
	Jamaica (Village)	Jan 17, 1881–Jan 16, 1898
	Long Island City	May 26, 1871–Dec 31, 1897
	Newtown (Town)	Jan 31, 1847–Jan 8, 1849,
		Jul 1, 1881–Jan 8, 1898
	Richmond Hill (Village)	Sep 8, 1895–Dec 28, 1897
	Rockaway Beach (Village)	Jul 20, 1897–Jan 3, 1898
	Whitestone (Village)	Oct 22, 1889–Dec 8, 1897

Marriages:	Queens (Borough) - Health Dept. Records	Jan 1, 1898–Dec 31, 1937 (certificates)
	Queens (Borough) - City Clerk License Records	1908–1929 (licenses/affidavits)
	Flushing (Town)	Jan 10, 1847–Dec 30, 1849
	Jamaica (Town)	Jan 1, 1847–Feb 9, 1848
	Long Island City	May 7, 1871–Jul 28, 1890,
		1881–1897
	Newtown (Town)	1881–1898
	College Point, Far Rockaway, Flushing,	
	Jamaica, Richmond Hill, Rockaway,	
	Whitestone	1881–1898

STATEN ISLAND (RICHMOND COUNTY)

Births:	Castleton (Town)	Jan 3, 1882–Dec 30, 1897
	Edgewater (Village)	Aug 25, 1885–Dec 22, 1897
	Middletown (Town)	May 3, 1882–Nov 23, 1897
	Northfield (Town)	Jan 25, 1882–Dec 11, 1897
	Port Richmond (Village)	Feb 10, 1888–Dec 24, 1897
	Southfield (Town)	Jul 9, 1882–Dec 29, 1897
	Tottenville (Village)	Jun 27, 1890–Dec 30, 1897
	Westfield (Town)	Apr 17, 1882–Dec 23, 1897
	Mixed Towns	Jan 4, 1847–Apr 28, 1852
	Staten Island (Borough)	1898–1909

Deaths:	Staten Island (Borough)	Jan 1, 1898–Dec 31, 1948 (certificates)
	Castleton (Town)/	
	New Brighton (Village)	Jan 2, 1881–Dec 30, 1897
	Edgewater	Sep 5, 1885–Dec 29, 1897
	Middletown (Town)	May 15, 1882–Dec 27, 1897
	Northfield (Town)	Jun 9, 1872–Feb 17, 1873,
		Nov 8, 1881–Dec 30, 1897
	Port Richmond (Village)	Feb 16, 1888–Dec 30, 1897
	Southfield (Town)	Jul 28, 1882–Dec 29, 1897
	Tottenville (Village)	Aug 19, 1890–Dec 31, 1897
	Westfield (Town)	Apr 26, 1882–Dec 29, 1897
	Mixed Towns	Jan 9, 1847–1850, 1852
Marriages:	Staten Island (Borough) - Health Dept. Records	Jan 1, 1898–Dec 31, 1937 (certificates)
	Staten Island (Borough) - City Clerk License Records	1908–1929 (licenses/affidavits)
	Castleton (Town)	Jan 5, 1848–Oct 31, 1849,
		Feb 21, 1882–Dec 30, 1897
	Edgewater (Village)	Jul 2, 1883–Dec 30, 1897
	Middletown (Town)	Apr 11, 1882–Nov 3, 1897
	Northfield (Town)	Jan 6, 1847–Dec 30, 1849,
		Feb 14, 1882–Aug 29, 1896
	Port Richmond (Village)	Feb 8, 1888–Dec 19, 1897
	Southfield (Town)	Feb 28, 1848–Dec 30, 1852,
		Oct 5, 1882–Sep 29, 1897
	Tottenville (Village)	Apr 21, 1864–Mar 19, 1865,
		Jul 29, 1890–Sep 27, 1897
	Westfield (Town)	Jan 2, 1882–Dec 31, 1897

MISCELLANEOUS

Deaths:	Bodies in Transit through Manhattan	1859–1894
	Daily Return of Deaths by Cholera	1866
	Still Births	1866–1887
	Tenement House, 2nd District	1875
	US Soldiers in Cuba & Puerto Rico	1898–May 1, 1900 (certificates)

2. 1890 New York City "Police" Census: This population census of Manhattan and the western Bronx is arranged by Assembly/Election District. It lists, by street address, the name of each resident, including children, their sex and age. NOTE: The NEW YORK PUBLIC LIBRARY, U.S. HISTORY, LOCAL HISTORY AND GENEALOGY DIVISION and the NEW YORK GENEALOGICAL AND BIOGRAPHICAL SOCIETY also have microfilm copies of this Census.

3. New York State Census: Kings County (Brooklyn), 1855, 1865, 1875, 1892, 1905, 1915, 1925; Richmond County (Staten Island), 1855, 1865, 1870 (Federal), 1875, 1880 (Federal-Short Form), 1892, 1915, 1925.

NOTE: The Archives has the 1880 "Short Form" Federal census for Richmond County (Staten Island). This lesser known 92-page document is a summary copy of the 1880 Federal census, and was required by the Census Act of 1879. It includes, name, age, sex and color of each member of the household. See, "The 'Short Form' 1880 and 1890 Federal Censuses" by Roger Joslyn, published in *The American Genealogist* in October 1994. The 1870 Federal census available here appears to be an incomplete copy (missing Castleton Town). A more complete version of the 1870 Federal census is available at the NATIONAL ARCHIVES - NORTHEAST REGION and at the NEW YORK PUBLIC LIBRARY, U.S. HISTORY, LOCAL HISTORY AND GENEALOGY DIVISION. Copies of the NYS Census, Kings and Richmond counties, are also available at the NYPL GENEALOGY DIVISION, and at the NEW YORK GENEALOGICAL AND BIOGRAPHICAL SOCIETY and NYS DEPARTMENT OF EDUCATION, NEW YORK STATE LIBRARY.

4. Jury Census Records: New York County (Manhattan), 1816 (except wards 4, 6, 7, 9), 1819 (except wards 1, 3) and 1821 (except wards 3, 8, 10). For 1816 and 1819, the census included the name of the head of household, his street and house number, occupation, age, reasons for exemption from jury service, total number of persons in the household, total number of jurors in the household and numbers of persons by race/sex, and whether a slave.

The 1821 Jury Census includes name of head of household, address, number of males over 21 in the household by various categories of assets and military service.

5. Almshouse Records, 1758–1953, include admission, discharge, census and housekeeping records for municipal institutions (Almshouse, Workhouse, City Home and hospitals) located on Blackwell's (Welfare) Island.

6. Court Records, 1684–1949. The Archives holdings pertain primarily to criminal court records:

New York County Court of General Sessions, Minutes of the Sessions, 1684–1920; indictment records, 1790–1893 Police Court/Magistrate's Court docket books, 1799–1930; papers filed in dismissed cases, 1807–1856

Court of Special Sessions, calendar of prisoners, 1829–1839

New York County Surrogate's Court, estate inventories, 1780s–1830s; insolvent assignments (bankruptcy), 1800–1830

Kings County Criminal Court indictment records, 1894–1965 (with gaps)

Kings County Special Sessions, bastardy proceedings, 1926–1936

Richmond County Special Sessions, bastardy proceedings, 1899–1939

Civil Court records (includes Kings County), "Papers in Suits" (papers related to civil actions)

7. <u>District Attorney Records</u>: Indictments, case files, docket books and other records relating to criminal investigations and prosecutions for New York County, 1790–1966; Kings County (Brooklyn), 1940–1945, Richmond County (Staten Island), 1913–1977.

8. <u>Photographs</u>: The Department of Taxes collection includes black and white photographs of every building in New York City, 1939–1941. These photographs were taken for assessment purposes and include each private home, apartment house and commercial property in the City. Vacant land was not photographed. The quality of these photos varies.

Other photographs are available depicting streets, highways, sewers, bridges and other public structures from the Manhattan Borough President's Office collection, 1915–1949, Brooklyn Borough President's Office, 1918–1956, Queens Borough President's Office, 1889–1950, and Department of Bridges/Plant and Structures, 1901–1938 (glass plate negatives). Photographs from the Department of Docks and Ferries, 1901–1970, depict waterfront scenes and airport facilities; and the Brooklyn Law Department collection, 1935–1945, includes buildings condemned for the construction of the Brooklyn/Queens Expressway. See also WPA Collection below.

9. <u>Works Progress Administration, Federal Writers' Project</u>, NYC Unit, 1936–1943. Rough drafts, notes, research materials, original manuscripts and photographs assembled for the *New York City Guide* and other publications. The collection includes a partial survey of NYC synagogue records as part of the Historical Records Survey, as well as material on the Jews of New York, Italians of New York and others. An index to the WPA synagogue records, created by Ada Greenblatt, appears on the Jewish Genealogical Society's website, www.jgsny.org.

10. <u>Voter Registrations</u>: Includes 50,000 volumes from the BOARD OF ELECTIONS:

New York County: records of naturalized voters, 1872–1878, and registers of voters, 1872–1922 (gaps). See "Restrictions on Use." Some volumes, 1916–1920, are at the warehouse of the BOARD OF ELECTIONS, MANHATTAN BOROUGH OFFICE.

Queens County: registers of voters, 1898–1948.

Richmond County (Staten Island): registers of voters, 1898–1957; and Town of Castleton, 1897. The Archives also has a Register of War Voters, 1944–1946, arranged by surname of voter and residence at the time of induction.

Voter registration information varies over time but generally includes name of registrant, country or state of birth, race, age, street address, length of residence in state, county, Assembly and Election District. Most important for the genealogist is the information showing native or naturalized voter, date of naturalization and court where naturalization occurred. The records may also indicate city and state where last registered, whether registrant owned his/her residence, marital status, whether a citizen by marriage, occupation, business location and party affiliation.

11. <u>Coroner's Office Records</u>: Include records of inquests and personal effects, day books, coronor's jurers and records of deaths. The records span the years 1823–1918, but are not available for all boroughs in each year. Office of the Chief Medical Examiner investigation of death case files, 1918–1939, are available for all boroughs. See "Restrictions on Use."

12. <u>Richmond County (Staten Island) County Clerk's Office Records</u>: The following records have been deposited with the Archives:

Appointment of City Officials, 1880–1900 and 1921–1929

Business records including Certificates of Incorporation, 1848–1897

Condemnation records, 1930–1943

Certificates of Notary Public, 1870–1929

Coroner's records including inquests, 1851–1897

Court records spanning the years 1706–1947. These include records of defunct courts on Staten Island, such as Sessions and General Sessions, Justice, Oyer and Terminer and County Court, as well as records of the Supreme Court, Richmond County. The records include Special Proceedings, 1840–1929, in which Name Change cases and Incompetency cases were filed, as well as Judgments, 1816–1934, Indictments, 1706–1931 and Actions, 1929–1947.

District Attorney Records, 1880–1977

Jury Lists, 1820–1890

Matrimonial records including Divorce Judgments, 1861–1933

Military records on service exemptions, 1917. Includes c. 60 letters from men of draft age requesting exemptions; a 52-page address list of members of the Fire Department, by unit; and address list of the Artillery Service Detachment of the Veteran Corps of Artillery, State of New York, August 6, 1917. [SI-437]

Orders of Filiation (child support), 1859–1897

Passport Applications, 1940–1953

Volunteer Firemen rolls and certificates of membership, 1900–1930

13. Town Records, 1591–1898, include records of cities, towns and villages in areas of Kings, the Bronx (formerly Westchester), Queens and Richmond (Staten Island) Counties prior to consolidation with New York City. These include Kings County (Brooklyn) town records transferred from St. Francis College, James A. Kelly Institute for Local Historical Studies in 1988. ["AN"=Accession number; "MF"= Microfilm number.] A sample follows:

Castleton Town (Richmond County), mortgages, 1849–1879; school district minutes.

City of Brooklyn Common Council minutes, 1846–1897 [AN 88-43, 44, 47]; Brooklyn Town meeting book, 1785–1823. [AN 88-119]

Bushwick Town records [AN 88-83], deeds and births of slaves, 1660–1825. [MF 116]

Flatbush Town records [AN 88-98], 1819–1851 [MF 2], 1888–1892 {MF 8}; Supervisors annual reports, 1886–1893 [MF 3]; School District 3 tax lists, 1877–1881 [MF 3]; Board of Health minutes, 1874–1876 [MF 4]; military records [MF 4]; military exemptions, 1862–1864 [MF 23]; chattel mortgages, 1883–1890 [MF 4]; State Census, 1845 (EDs 1 and 2) [MF 4]; school census district 3, 1893 [MF 4] ; assessment rolls, 1854–1894 [MF 9-MF 16]; Court of Common Pleas minutes, 1800–1833 [MF 8]; births and slave manumissions, 1799–1819 [MF 2]; slave holders, 1799–1826 [MF 8]; slave manumissions, 1805–1820 [MF 17]; removal of bodies, Health Department, 1891–1893. [MF 17]

Flatlands Town [AN 88-99] minutes, 1783–1895; police blotter, 1893–1896 [MF 76]; Board of Health minutes, 1880–1895 [MF 75]; road records, 1661–1868 [MF 75-MF 76]; military records, record of troops, 1861–1865 [MF 141]; assessment rolls, 1849–1884 [MF 77-MF 78]; personal mortgages, 1886–1892 [MF 78-MF 80]; chattel mortgages, 1847–1895 [MF 75]; school district records, 1844–1895 [MF 140]; slave records, 1799–1838. [MF 88]

Flushing Town (Queens), Town Clerk records, 1868–1885; school district records, 1860–1896; Town Board records, 1790–1893; tax records, 1891–1895; Trustees records, 1863–1885.

Gravesend Town records [AN 88-97], minutes of meetings, deeds and leases, 1646–1872 [MF 61-MF 62]; school district #1 records, 1857–1894 [MF 63]; persons liable for military service and records of troops, 1862–1865 [MF 63]; assessment rolls, 1859–1893 [MF 74]; Board of Health minutes, 1880–1894 [MF 68-MF 69]; school accounts, births of slaves, 1799–1819 [MF 63], 1830–1843. [MF 145]

Jamaica Town (Queens), Town records, 1660–1897; census of pupils, 1896–1897; overseer of the poor, record of applicants, 1879–1897; tax records, 1891–1895.

Morrisania Town (Westchester County, now part of the Bronx), voter registration rolls, 1863–1867; assessment rolls, 1858–1869 (gaps).

New Lots Town [AN 88-100] assessment rolls, 1857–1885. [MF 28-MF 40]

New Utrecht Town records [AN 88-96], historic deeds, 1659–1831 [MF 37]; school papers, 1827–1894; Town Meeting minutes, oaths, 1793–1894 [MF 37]; records of troops, persons liable for military duty, 1851, 1861–1865 [MF 39]; assessment rolls, 1822, 1830–1894 [MF 38, MF 43-MF 60]; chattel mortgages, 1850–1894 [MF 39]; Health Board, slave births, 1800–1822. [MF 38]

Newtown Town (Queens), Town Board minutes, 1692–1897 (gaps); records of schools, 1888–1897; military records, 1865; criminal dockets, 1659–1688, 1895–1897; tax records, 1883 and 1891–1895.

Westchester Town (Westchester County, now part of the Bronx), Town Board minutes, 1788–1879; births of slaves, 1800–1823; manumission of slaves, 1787–1816; military rolls, 1851–1852, 1854, 1862; 1665–1879 (gaps).

Williamsburg Town [AC 88-59] Clerk's Book, 1842–1855 [MF 161]; Town records, 1832–1837 [MF 154]; tax rolls, 1847–1853 [MF 157-MF 159]; City of Williamsburg Common Council minutes, 1852–1854. [MF 162/3]

Kings County, Board of Supervisors' minutes, 1714–1893 [AN 88-53]; lists of trial and grand jurors, 1897–1898 [AN 88-81]; court and road records, 1668–1825 [AN 88-101]; County Clerk applications for citizenship, c. 1900 [AN 88-102]; transcribed wills (3 vols.), 1658–1891 [AN 88-107]; religious incorporations, 1785–1875 [AN 88-111A]; deeds, 1679–1909 [AN 88-112]; mortgages, 1757–1811, and chattel mortgages, 1873–1895 [AN 88-112B]; horseshoer's register, 1896–1904 [AN 88-116]; oaths of office, 1838–1846 [AN 88-117]; Dutch slave records, 1760–1784, and manumission of slaves, early 1800s. [AN 88-118]

Kings County Surrogate's Court [AN 88-66]. Probated will proceedings, 1830–1866, 1881, 1889; Final Accountings, 1838–1869; Estates, 1815–1867; Administrations, 1844–1865; Guardian accounts, 1851–1862; Sales of Estates, 1790–1859.

Maps and charts, c. 1700s–1888 [AN 88-73, 88-108]: property lines, topographical and profile street maps, atlases and locality plats relating to Kings County, Brooklyn Town, the Towns of Gravesend, Flatbush, New Utrecht, Bushwick and the City of Williamsburg. Most are hand-drawn.

Vital records [AN 88-82], including births, marriages and deaths (folder) for Bushwick, 1857, Flatbush, 1847–1848, 1851, Flatlands, 1847, Flatlands Almshouse, 1847 (indexed); deaths, Lunatic Asylum and Kings County Almshouse, 1848; marriages performed by mayors of Brooklyn, 1837–1887 (and index); index to marriages, 1591–1831 (scattered years), includes Elsworth family tree (pp. 130–135); index to marriages, Kings County, June 1, 1864–May 31, 1865.

The Archives also has records from communities outside NYC such as:
Hempstead, North Hempstead and Oyster Bay tax records, 1891–1895 [AN 92-51]
Yonkers, Westchester County, Assessed Valuation of Real Estate, 1843–1844, 1853 [AN 94-54]

NOTE: Brooklyn Town became a City in 1834. In 1855, it absorbed the Town of Bushwick and the City of Williamsburg. In 1886, it annexed the Town of New Lots. The Towns of Gravesend, Flatbush and New Utrecht were annexed in 1894. The last Town, Flatlands, joined the City in 1896. In 1898, the City of Brooklyn became one of the five boroughs of New York City. See Appendix H, for a more detailed history.

14. Annual Record of Assessed Valuation of Real Estate: These are ledger books compiled yearly which list owner or occupant, description and value of real estate, including buildings. The pre-1898 books are arranged by ward. After 1897, the books are arranged by block and lot numbers. The Archives has:

Manhattan	1789–1792, 1794–1795, 1799, 1802, 1806–1978/79
Bronx	1897–1961/62
Brooklyn	1862–1974/75
Queens	1899–1987/88
Staten Island	1899–1978/79

15. Department of Personnel, Bureau of Examinations records include eligible lists Brooklyn City, 1883–1898, and New York City, 1895–1971; promotion lists, 1908–1929, 1932–1938 and 1945–1954; registers of applications, 1925–1936 and 1938–1945.

16. City Directories

New York (Manhattan/Bronx): 1869–1913, 1915–1918, 1920, 1922, 1924, 1931, 1933/34.
Brooklyn: 1796, 1802/3, 1811/12, 1822–1826, 1829–1910, 1912/13, 1933/34.

17. Potter's Field (Hart Island) records of burials, 1881–1985 (gaps). Arranged by trench number and date of burial. Includes name, age, date and place of death, cause of death, date of burial. For a history of Hart Island, see www.correctionhistory.org/html/chronicl/nycdoc/html/hart.html

18. Naturalization Records from select courts including:

Richmond County Clerk's Office (Staten Island) naturalization records such as affidavits, 1820–1906; certificates, 1902–1921; petitions, 1920–1926; posted petitions, 1920–1930; military petitions, 1918–1921; Department of Labor reports, 1918–1938; and hearings, 1936–1945.
Manhattan (New York County), Marine Court naturalization records, 1827–1845. (missing volumes 1 & 3).

NOTE: The Archives also has copies of two books, *Naturalizations in the Marine Court, New York City 1827–1935* and *Naturalizations in the Marine Court, New York City 1834–1840,* by Kenneth Scott, which include complete abstracts of naturalizations included in volumes 5–19 of the Marine Court.

19. Occupational Permits: The Archives has such unusual collections as :

Theatre Matrons Permits, 1940, NYC Department of Health, include 1,700 original applications, physical exam reports, personal histories, photographs and renewal applications [90-119]. See "Restrictions on Use."

Physicians and Surgeons Affidavits, 1908–1924, Kings County only. Includes name, address place and date of birth, license number and date issued. Sometimes also includes date of graduation and medical school from which graduated. [88-115]

Pistol Permits, 1932–1933, includes photographs of applicants. [68-005]

20. Department of Probation Case Records for Brooklyn, 1910–1950; Manhattan, 1945–1950. [93-21 and 93-22]

21. Religious Incorporation Records, New York County, 1784–1900 (microfilm) from the City Register's Office. Among the first to incorporate in New York was Congregation Shearith Israel on 11 June 1784. See also "Town Records" above for Religious Incorporations in Kings County (Brooklyn), 1785-1875.

Finding Aids:

Most of the collections in the Municipal Archives have some type of finding aid. These include:

1. New York City Vital Records: Indexes (microfilm) are arranged by locality or borough, year and surname. Researchers examining pre-1898 indexes should be aware that several indexes may exist for a particular year. Check with the staff to be sure that you have seen all the liber and published indexes for localities in a particular borough. For vital records in the Bronx, a search of Manhattan records, as noted by *, should be made.

Births/Deaths - The Archives has card, liber and published indexes (on microfilm) to birth/death certificates as follows:

		Card Indexes	Liber Indexes	Published Indexes
Births:	Manhattan/Bronx*	1866–1897	-	1881–1909 (Soundex)
	Brooklyn (City)	1866–1897	1880–1885, 1888–1894	1881–1909 (Soundex)
	Queens/Staten Island	-	-	1898–1909 (Soundex)
Deaths:	Manhattan/Bronx*	1868–1890	-	August 1888–1948
	Brooklyn (City/Borough)	1862–1897	1880, 1886–1894	1895–1948
	Bronx/Queens/Staten Island	-	-	1898–1948

The Archives also has the following indexes to liber records. NOTE: There are indexes for some years for which there are no records.

		Card Indexes	Liber Indexes	Published Indexes
Births:	Manhattan/Bronx*	1830–1865	1873–July 1888	-
Deaths:	Manhattan/Bronx*	-	1873–July 1888	-
	Brooklyn (City)	1848–1866	1848–1871	-

All card indexes and published death indexes are arranged alphabetically by name. Card indexes for births include parents' names. The Manhattan/Bronx card index to 1830–1856 births can be found on reel #1, labeled "1857 A..." Few records were recorded for these years. Published birth indexes, 1881–1909, are Soundex indexes. See Appendix A for a description of the Health Department's Soundex system. Liber indexes for Manhattan are arranged by the first letter of the surname and for Brooklyn by the first three letters of the surname.

NOTE: There are no indexes to Manhattan liber records for births, 1866–1872, or pre-1873 liber records for marriages and deaths. Manhattan liber records pre-1873 (births, deaths and marriages) are maintained by month/day/year of the registration of the event (not the event itself) and grouped by the first letter of the surname.

There are no indexes to Brooklyn liber records for births and marriages, 1866–1879, and deaths, 1872–1879. However, Brooklyn liber records for deaths, 1872–1879, are arranged alphabetically by the first letter of the surname.

In addition to these card, liber and published indexes for Manhattan/Bronx and Brooklyn, the Archives has liber or card indexes to some town/village liber records; a geographic index to birth certificates by street address for Manhattan (including western Bronx), 1880–1914, Bronx, 1898–1910, Brooklyn, 1898–1910, Queens, 1898–1917, Staten Island, 1898–1909; and a hospital index to birth certificates for Manhattan, 1880–1909, Bronx, 1942–1944.

NOTE: See also *Ancestry.com* (fee-based) or *Ancestry.plus* (at libraries) for an online index to NYC births records, 1891–1902; and index to NYC death records, 1892-1895 (based on published indexes for that period). Additional years may be added.

Marriage Indexes - The Archives has the following finding aids (on microfilm) for <u>Health Department</u> marriage certificates:

| | Card Indexes | | Liber Indexes | Published Indexes |
	Brides	Grooms	Brides/Grooms	Grooms
Manhattan*	1866–1937	1866–1910	-	1888–1937
Bronx	1898–1937	-	-	1898–1937
Brooklyn	1866–1910, 1930–1937	1866–1907	1880–1893	1894–1937
Queens	1905–1938	-	-	1898–1937
Staten Island	1898–1937	1898–1932	-	1898–1937

The <u>Health Department</u> published marriage indexes (all boroughs) are arranged alphabetically by name of the groom only. Card indexes are arranged in two alphabetical series by names of the bride and groom. Brooklyn liber indexes are arranged by the first three letters of the surname of both brides and grooms in one alphabetical series.

In addition to the indexes to marriage certificates, there are also liber indexes to <u>liber records</u> for Manhattan/Bronx, 1873–1888, arranged by the first letter of the groom's surname.

The Archives also has liber indexes to town/village marriage records pre-1898; the Health Department index to Delayed and Imperfect Marriages, 1874–1916, for Manhattan (including parts of the Bronx); an index to Special Marriages, Brooklyn, 1908–1934; and a book by Joel R. Simon, *1866 Brooklyn Marriage Index* that indexes marriages by bride and groom, April to December 1866 and has an appendix that lists marriages recorded in the *Brooklyn Daily Eagle* from January to April, 1866.

See also NEW YORK PUBLIC LIBRARY, U.S. HISTORY, LOCAL HISTORY AND GENEALOGY DIVISION, the NEW YORK GENEALOGICAL AND BIOGRAPHICAL SOCIETY LIBRARY, the NEW-YORK HISTORICAL SOCIETY and FAMILY HISTORY CENTER (MANHATTAN), for copies of some published and microfilmed NYC Health Department vital records and indexes.

The Archives has liber indexes (on microfilm) to <u>City Clerk</u> marriage license records, 1908–1951. These are arranged by borough, groups of months, and the first two letters of the surname. Licenses were filed by date of application (affidavit), not date of marriage.

2. <u>1890 NYC Police Census</u>: To locate an address in the 1890 census, researchers need both the "book number" (a.k.a. "volume number") and Assembly District/Election District (AD/ED). Use *Aid to Finding Addresses in the 1890 New York City Police Census,* compiled by Howard M. Jensen, to learn the book number. Check the Archives beige binder, *New York City "Police Census" 1890* to convert book number to AD/ED. Microfilm reels are arranged by volume (book) number, but AD/ED appears first on the film.

   NOTE: An index to 26 of the existing 894 volumes of this Census can be accessed online through *Ancestry.com* or *Ancestry.plus.*

3. <u>New York State Census</u>: Richmond County (Staten Island) census is arranged by Town. For the Kings County (Brooklyn) census, 1892, the Archives has Joseph Silinonte's *Street Index to the 1892 New York City Census.* Use Assembly District/Election District maps for 1905 and 1915. Ward maps are available for earlier years.

4. <u>Almshouse Records</u>: The Archives has a bound volume describing the holdings in this collection. For some institutions, records are arranged by date of admission or date of discharge. Others are arranged by date of death.

5. <u>Court Records</u>: Most records are arranged chronologically. There is an alphabetical printout available for General Sessions indictments, 1879–1893. Each volume of the Minutes of the Court of General Sessions is self-indexed by name of defendant. The New York County District Attorney Record of Cases, 1895–1966, is an alphabetical list of defendants that can be used to locate court records. Estate inventories are arranged alphabetically and there is a 2-volume name index to insolvent assignments.

6. <u>District Attorney Records</u>: Pre-1879 records are arranged chronologically (no alphabetical index). There is an alphabetical printout for later years. Closed cases, 1896–1965, are indexed by year of indictment and defendant's surname. There are also 12 inventory volumes arranged by date on top of the microfilm cabinet near the office entitled, *District Attorney Indictments, Court of General Sessions, Inventory*, 1879–1893, for New York County.

7. <u>Photographs</u>: To locate a building in the Tax Photograph collection, researchers need to determine the block and lot number of the building. This can be done in two ways:

(a) by using *Phil's Nicer Block & Lot* program which converts an address to block/lot number. NOTE: See also CITY REGISTER'S OFFICE, MANHATTAN for an online program that does a similar conversion.

(b) by locating the building in the land atlases. For Manhattan, use *Manhattan Land Book, 1934*; for Brooklyn, *Desk Atlas of the Borough of Brooklyn 1929*. For the Bronx, various Bromley Land Atlases in hard copy are available. For Queens and Staten Island, use the Sanborn maps available on microfilm. Once the block and lot numbers are known, these must be converted into a "File" number which is the key number to identifying the correct microfilm where the photograph will be found. For Manhattan, these block/lot lists showing corresponding "File" numbers have been printed out and are in black loose-leaf binders. The lists are on microfilm for each of the other boroughs.

There is a geographic card index to photographs from the Manhattan Borough President's Office. Most other collections have captions listed.

8. <u>Works Progress Administration, Federal Writers' Project (and Historical Records Survey)</u>: The box list identifies material on Jews and synagogues. The material is arranged by title of the publication and then alphabetically by folder (or subject) title. See www.jgsny.org for an index to synagogues included here.

9. <u>Voter Registrations</u>: The records are arranged by year, Assembly/Election District (AD/ED) and then alphabetized by surname or first letter of the surname. To locate records, the researcher must provide the Archives staff with the year and AD/ED. (Try to use a year in which there was a Presidential election.)

To determine the AD/ED, an address is required. Check the AD/ED maps in the DEPARTMENT OF RECORDS AND INFORMATION SERVICES, MUNICIPAL REFERENCE AND RESEARCH CENTER or at the BOARD OF ELECTIONS office in the appropriate borough. These maps are <u>not</u> available at the Archives. To verify that the person sought actually registered, consult the *List of Enrolled Voters* for that year and AD/ED. These lists are available at the MUNICIPAL REFERENCE AND RESEARCH CENTER and at the NYPL - SCIENCE, INDUSTRY AND BUSINESS LIBRARY (SIBL).

10. <u>Coroner's Office Records</u>: There is a surname index to New York County records, 1853-1917. For earlier records, 1823-1849, see Kenneth Scott's abstracts in *Coroners' Reports New York City, 1823-1842,* and *1843-1849* available at the NEW YORK GENEALOGICAL AND BIOGRAPHICAL SOCIETY. To locate unindexed records, be aware that inquests were generally held shortly after the date of death. See "Restrictions on Use" for Chief Medical Examiner records.

11. <u>Richmond County Clerk's Office Records</u>: The Archives has an inventory listing the subject, years and location/box number for each set of records. It does not have name indexes to these records. The indexes, where they exist, are in the COUNTY CLERK'S OFFICE - STATE SUPREME COURT, RICHMOND COUNTY (STATEN ISLAND).

The indexes at the COUNTY CLERK'S OFFICE include those for: Court Cases, 1930–1947 (includes Matrimonial records, 1930–1933, in the <u>Index to Rule Books</u>); Certificates of Incorporation, 1891–1897; and Special Proceedings (includes Name Change and Incompetency records), 1913–1929. These indexes cover only a small portion of the Richmond County material in the Archives' collection.

12 <u>Town Records</u>: The Archives has a bound volume, <u>Index to Old Records</u>, which includes some of these records and is arranged alphabetically by Town/Village and subject. Entries include the type of record, years covered and file number. In addition, the Archives has accession lists which provide some more detail on the remaining collection.

13. <u>Annual Record of Assessed Valuation of Real Estate</u>: The Archives has an atlas which can be used to convert addresses to block and lot numbers.

14. <u>Department of Personnel, Bureau of Examinations</u>: Records in this collection are not indexed.

15. <u>Potter's Field</u>: There is no index to these records. If a death certificate lists "City Cemetery" as the place of burial, check Potter's Field (Hart Island) records.

16 <u>Naturalization Records</u>: The <u>Index to Rule Book</u> in the RICHMOND COUNTY CLERK'S OFFICE includes Naturalization petitions. There is an alphabetical card index to naturalization records of the Marine Court, New York County.

17. <u>Occupational Permits</u>: There is a finding aid organized by permit number for <u>Theatre Matron Permits</u>. See "Restrictions on Use." There are no finding aids for Physician and Surgeon's Affidavits or Pistol Permits.

18. <u>Probation Case Records:</u> There is no finding aid to these records. Researchers need to know the date of sentencing. These records do not include individuals who were sentenced to prison.

19. <u>Religious Incorporations</u>: There is an alphabetical index at the beginning of each of the microfilmed volumes.

Description of Facility:

The Reference Room can seat 15-20 researchers at tables. There are 20 microfilm readers available. Two of these are reader/printers.

This is primarily a self-service facility. See the yellow binder, *Microfilm Cabinet Inventory* for location of microfilmed records. There is one staff member on duty behind the counter to assist researchers. New York City Vital Records (Health Department birth, marriage and death indexes and records), Census Records (1890 Police, Jury Census and Kings County) and City Directories on microfilm are in self-service cabinets at the front of the Reading Room [cabinets 1-5 and carousel]. Geographic birth indexes, Vital Record ledger indexes (pre-1898), City Clerk's marriage indexes and Coroner's Records are behind the counter and must be requested from the staff. City Clerk's marriage records (microfilm) are in open cabinets located along the Chambers Street window wall [cabinets 11-12].

Published birth indexes (microfilm) include some birth records with an "S" suffix, denoting "Special" births. These are births registered many years after the event occurred and are not included in the microfilms described above. Request these from the staff behind the counter.

Assessed Valuation of Real Estate (1789–1900), are in the wood cabinet on the Centre Street window wall [cabinet 8].

WPA Historical Records Survey [cabinet 12], are on the Chambers Street window wall (left of the photocopy machine).

District Attorney Records, Richmond County Census Records [cabinet 15] and some Court Records [cabinets 14 and 15] are in the cabinets along the Chamber Street wall.

Town Records (Kings County) [cabinet 7] and Tax Department photographs (microfilm) [cabinets 6 and 7], are to the left of the fireplace. The Sanborn maps used to determine block/lot numbers are in shelves along the Centre Street wall. *Phil's Nicer Block & Lot* index can be found on a computer in the Municipal Archives office. Ask staff for permission to use this computer. The loose-leaf notebook used to convert Manhattan block/lot numbers to "File" numbers is on the table near cabinets 7 & 8.

Fees/Copies:

There is no charge for use of this facility except when using the New York City Vital Records or Office of the Chief Medical Examiner Investigation Case Files (see below). Researchers can make copies of microfilm material (except New York City Vital Records) on the reader/printers at $.25 per page. A photocopy machine at $.15 per page is available. Copies 11" x 17" can be made at $.25 per page.

The Archives charges a $5 fee for use of the New York City Vital Records (microfilms of birth, marriage and death records) for a day or any part thereof. Researchers may hand copy records at no additional cost. Photocopies of vital records are made by staff only. The fee is $5 for a copy of a birth, marriage or death certificate (add $5 for a one year/one borough search if the certificate number is not provided). $2 is charged for each additional year searched and $2 for each additional borough searched. A certified copy of the certificate or transcript of the record is supplied, if found. Complete the Municipal Archives' Application for a Copy of a Birth Record, Death Record or Marriage Record (see Appendix C-4, C-5 and C-6 or print a copy from the Archives website (see above).

Prints (8" x 10") of photographs can be made for $25 a photo. (For larger prints, 11"x 14", the cost is $35; and for 16"x 20", $50). Add $2 for postage and handling of every 3 prints ordered ($2 minimum mail charge). If block and lot number is not included, add $5 search fee. See the Archives website for a copy of the Photograph Order Form. NOTE: Researchers can make a photocopy of a Tax Photograph for $.50 at the microfilm reader/printer in the doorway to the office.

Due to the fragile condition of the material within the investigation case files of the Office of Chief Medical Examiner, applicants will be supplied with photocopies (not originals) of all documents. There is a $1 per page fee for copies. Most case files contain fewer than 20 documents. Applicants should write "Not to Exceed $20" on their check memo line when requesting by mail.

Send mail requests with a check or money order payable to the NYC Department of Records and a stamped, self-addressed envelope. Allow 3-4 weeks for completion of orders.

Restrictions on Use:

City Clerk's Marriage Records: The Archives will search and make copies of Health Department marriage records but will not conduct searches of the City Clerk's records, 1908–1929, unless a search has been made of the Health Department series and a specific date (day/month/year) is provided. Records for this period can be copied if researchers provide the City Clerk license number (see fees above). For later City Clerk's records (1930 -1951), researchers may check the indexes at the Municipal Archives to learn the license number but must visit or write to the CITY CLERK'S OFFICE, MANHATTAN to obtain a copy.

No mail searches can be done for Census Records or City Directories.

Voter Registrations, Richmond County Clerk's Office, Department of Personnel, Occupational Permits, Probation Case Records, Naturalization records and many Court Records, and Town Records (except Kings County) are not on site and must be requested in advance. Materials are retrieved from other storage locations. Researchers wishing to see these records should be sure to order them at least one week in advance. It can take from one to seven days to retrieve records depending on staff availability.

Coroner's Records - Access can be granted to Office of the Chief Medical Examiner case files more than 60 years old for legitimate research, historical, genealogical or law enforcement objectives. Researchers are not permitted access to original materials. See "Fees/Copies." Researchers must indicate the purpose for which the record will be used and provide a copy of the Health Department death certificate. Written permission from the Municipal Archives Director is required before any material in a case file may be quoted directly or reproduced in any manner.

Richmond County Clerk's Office records cannot be accessed easily. The actual indexes are not available here. See COUNTY CLERK'S OFFICE - STATE SUPREME COURT, RICHMOND COUNTY (STATEN ISLAND).

Some Manhattan Voter Registration records were severely water damaged. Check with the Archives staff for the inventory of available records.

Other

Visitors to 31 Chambers Street must present photo identification to the guards at the building entrance.

Because of the limited number of microfilm readers, researchers are advised to arrive early.

There is a 30-minute limit on use of the microfilm reader/printer dedicated to making copies of Tax Photographs when others are waiting.

Only materials needed for research are permitted at the reading tables. All other personal belongings must be left at the coat rack near the door. (This prohibition does not apply to users of microfilm machines.)

Smoking, eating and drinking are not permitted. All notes must be taken with pencil, typewriter or recorder. No pens or ink allowed when using original records.

Physical condition of the materials may limit reproduction and photocopies. Reproductions are for the researcher's personal use only. Written permission must be obtained from the Director of the Municipal Archives if the copied material is to be used for publication. There may be a publication use fee. Certain collections, such as the Theatre Matron Permits are fragile and require special permission for usage. Call before coming.

The Municipal Archives appreciates receiving copies of any research results.

NEW YORK CITY DEPARTMENT OF RECORDS AND INFORMATION SERVICES MUNICIPAL REFERENCE AND RESEARCH CENTER

Facility Director:	Paul Perkus, Director
	Christine Bruzzese, Supervising Librarian (Public Services)
Address:	31 Chambers Street, Room 112
	New York, NY 10007
	(Cross Streets: Centre and Elk Streets)
Phone:	(212) 788-8590
Fax:	(212) 788-8589
E-mail:	Library@doris.nyc.gov
Website:	www.nyc.gov/html/doris/html/dorisref.html

Hours of Operation:

Monday to Friday: 10:00 am to 4:00 pm

Closed Saturday, Sunday and legal holidays.

Closest Public Transportation and Directions:

See COUNTY CLERK'S OFFICE - STATE SUPREME COURT, NEW YORK COUNTY (MANHATTAN), DIVISION OF OLD RECORDS. The Municipal Reference and Research Center is on the first floor of the Surrogate's Court building. NOTE: There is a service entrance (steep incline) at the back of the building (Reade Street) which provides access to wheelchair users.

Description of Resources:

The Municipal Reference and Research Center established in 1913 as the Municipal Reference Library, is a depository for all official reports and studies issued by New York City government agencies. In addition to approximately 250,000 reports, books and other publications, the Center has an extensive collection of clippings and pamphlets on New York City matters. These include:

1. Biographical Binders: These contain mounted clippings, from local New York City newspapers and other sources, about people in or having an impact upon New York City government and political life. The biographical clippings are mounted in binders and date from the early 1950s to the present.

2. Vertical Files: Newspaper clippings that deal with individuals or groups of people in the City's government are located in vertical files under "Officials and Employees" or in specific subject or Department files. In addition, the "NYC Politics" file contains information on selected campaigns, primaries and elections from 1917 to the present. A person who campaigned for office but was not elected may show up here.

3. New York City Neighborhood Files: These include newspaper clippings, pamphlets and other material on neighborhoods within New York City (all boroughs).

4. Street Name Historical File: This card file contains references to street names and street name changes within the five boroughs of New York City. This index is updated annually to reflect name changes approved by the Mayor and City Council. In some years, park and playground names were included also. Each card shows the name, location, date of name change, and, when available, background information on the name and history of the site. A high percentage of the name changes honor a person, usually a deceased person.

5. Map Collection: The Center has a microfiche collection of maps showing the boundaries of old Assembly Districts (AD) and Election Districts (ED) for Manhattan (1872–1956), the Bronx (1914–1954), Brooklyn (1914–1954) and Queens (1917–1954). Each AD is on a separate fiche. As a result, these maps may be difficult to use unless the researcher has a good idea of the location of the area being sought. Also, the Election Districts are color-coded and not easy to decipher because of poor color contrast.

    The Center has a complete set of AD/ED maps (paper copy), 1956–1973, and a scattering of earlier and later maps. Consult with the Research Librarian on other maps in the collection.

6. Civil Service Lists ("Civil Lists"): These are lists of New York City employees, including employees of the Board of Education, from 1883 to the present. Lists from 1952/1953 to 1969 are on microfilm and those from 1969 to the present are on microfiche. While the Center has paper copies of pre-1952/1953 lists, these are off-site. The NEW

YORK CITY DEPARTMENT OF RECORDS AND INFORMATION SERVICES, MUNICIPAL ARCHIVES (across the hall) has microfilm copies.

Pre-1969 lists include the Department in which employed, job title, surname, first name, date entered into service and salary.

1969 and 1970 include surname, first letter only of first name, home address, employee number, Department number, job title number and salary. (The Center has a complete set of job descriptions corresponding to these numbers.)

1971 to 1983 include the same data as above, except Social Security number and pension number replaced employee number. See "Restrictions on Use."

1984 to 1990, and 1993 to the present do not include the employee's home address, pension number or Social Security number. These lists include Department number, surname, first letter of the first name, job title number and salary. The 1991–1992 lists include this same information except that Social Security number was added. See "Restrictions on Use."

See also, *The Seventh Report of the Secretary of the Board of Retirement being the report for the 20th and 21st year of the New York City Teachers' Retirement Fund, 1915.* Includes for 2,018 teachers who retired between 1895 and 1915: name, address, date of appointment, date of retirement, salary, annuity, years of experience and date of birth. Includes also a list oa annuitents who died since the 6th annual report was issued and date of death, where known. New York, 1915. [Ed9.71 R31] NOTE: There is an alpha index on pages 35-46 and on *Ancestry.com/Ancestry.plus.*

7. Biographical Publications: The Center has a small but varied collection including:

    Architects in Practice, NYC, 1840–1900. Committee for the Preservation of Architectural Records. [82 F84 aipny]

    Spengler, Otto. *Das Deutsches Element der Stadt New York.* 1913. [920 Sp3]

    Old Merchants of New York. 1863, 1870, and 1968. [920.B27 omo]

    Register of the Associate Alumni of the College of the City of New York: Alumni Register 1853-1924, published by the City University of New York, City College. Includes for over 13,000 alumni: degree, year graduated, occupation, employment history, address, date of death, if known; and war service of alumni, 1860-1924. New York, [1925]. [Ed9.95 C68a]

    Who's Who in New York. 1904, 1909, 1911, 1914, 1918, 1924, 1929, 1938, 1947 and 1952. [920 W62N]

8. New York City Histories: The collection includes books written about New York City, its neighborhoods, government and people.

9. Proceedings: The Center has a complete set of minutes of the Common Council, 1675–1831; proceedings of the Board of Aldermen, 1831–1937; and proceedings of the City Council, 1938 to the present. In addition, the collection includes proceedings of the Board of Estimate, 1871–1980; a complete set of the *City Record,* 1871 to the present; and annual reports, journals or minutes of such agencies as the Civil Service Commission, 1908–1954, Board of Education, City Planning Commission, and Department of Public Charities (mid-nineteenth century).

    Information on individuals, scattered in these proceedings, may be included in resolutions in memoriam to a former or current member of the Board, Council, Commission or Department, announcements of appointments, etc. Of particular interest to genealogists are Civil Service Commission proceedings and Board of Estimate actions on the New York City Employees Retirement System.

    Civil Service Commission proceedings include actions related to individuals who were NYC employees. Information in these items varies but generally includes name, position title and salary.

    Board of Estimate proceedings list applications received from individuals for retirement benefits, disability benefits or the continuance of death benefits under the New York City Employee Retirement System. These lists are included in Board of Estimate proceedings, 1936–1969, and show employee name, job title, agency where last employed, current address (which may be the place to which the employee retired), years of service, date of membership (i.e. date of employment), date of retirement, details of the pension and Social Security number. Data on retirees appear in Board of Estimate proceedings prior to 1936 but are not organized in a manner that allows for convenient reference. See "Finding Aids."

10. *List of Enrolled Voters* and *Registry of Voters:* The *List of Enrolled Voters* (known as *Enrollments,* 1899–1912) were published annually in the *City Record* or as a separate publication of the BOARD OF ELECTIONS. They include

name, address, political party in which registered, Assembly District and Election District. Since 1957, the lists include also the voter's number and the names of voters who did not appear on the previous year's list.

Registry of Voters was also published in the *City Record*. Similar data is included (name, address, Assembly District, Election District) but the lists are organized differently. See "Finding Aids."

List of Enrolled Voters is available for 1899–1912 *(Enrollments)*, 1939–1974/1975. *Registry of Voters* is available for 1883–1887, 1896, 1901–1902, 1904–1969. NOTE: There are gaps in these sets.

The NEW YORK PUBLIC LIBRARY, SCIENCE, INDUSTRY AND BUSINESS LIBRARY has more complete sets of *List of Enrolled Voters* and *Registry of Voters,* 1881–1903, which are on-site and immediately accessible.

Finding Aids:

1. Biographical Binders: These binders are arranged alphabetically by the name of the individual.

2. Files: The Vertical Files are arranged alphabetically. An article about an individual would be either under "Officials and Employees" or the Department in which the individual worked. The "Officials and Employees" files are broken out alphabetically, i.e. A–M, N–P, Q–Z. A complete listing of subject headings in the vertical files can be found in a blue binder (front section) on the librarian's desk in the City/State room.

   An index to the Neighborhood Files is in the back of the blue binder. The neighborhoods are arranged by borough and then alphabetically by name. Each neighborhood has been assigned a number. The file can be located once the number is known.

3. Street Name Historical File: These index cards are filed alphabetically and are cross-indexed by the current and old names of the street.

4. Map Collection: The Assembly District maps on microfiche are arranged by borough, year and Assembly District. The Assembly District maps (paper copy) are arranged by year and borough in drawers. The lowest drawer has the oldest maps (1956 and 1957).

5. Civil Service Lists ("Civil Lists"): The annual lists from 1969 to the present are on microfiche arranged alphabetically by surname. The pre-1969 lists are more difficult to use. They are arranged by Department, sub-divisions of the Department, job title and finally surname. Sub-divisions of the Board of Education include offices within the Board's headquarters as well as each individual school. To determine on which microfilm reel a particular Department can be found, use the annual master lists printed in the *City Record*. These lists are located near the microfilm cabinets.

6. Biographical Publications and New York City Histories can be found in the catalog in the main room under "N.Y.C. Biographies" and "N.Y.C. History." Most of these volumes can be found on open shelves under classification numbers that begin with 920 or 974.

7. Proceedings: Indexes to proceedings are generally available and are located in each volume or the last volume of the year. Board of Estimate proceedings indexes, 1955–1980, are in separate volumes. The NYC Employee Retirement System (NYCERS) applications index, 1937–1969, is an addenda at the back of the annual Board of Estimate index. A similar list exists for 1936, but it is included within the regular Board of Estimate index under "Estimate and Apportionment, New York City Employee Retirement System." In earlier years, there was no separate listing for actions related to the NYCERS.

8. *List of Enrolled Voters* and *Registry of Voters:* Lists, 1965–1975, are in bound books on open shelves in the City/State room. Earlier volumes are not on-site.

   Prior to 1957, lists are organized by year, borough, Assembly District, Election District and the first letter of the surname. Lists, 1957–1960, are arranged in a similar manner except that voters who registered in the district for the first time are listed separately, in italics, after the printed listing of regular voters for each letter of the alphabet. Names are completely alphabetized beginning in 1957.

   Lists after 1960 are organized by year, borough, Assembly District, Election District, surname and first name. New voters are not separated out but are noted by an asterisk.

   Registry of Voters are organized by year, borough and Assembly District, Election District, street name, building number, name of voter. Names are not alphabetized. These volumes are not on-site.

   The reference librarian can consult an inventory of *Registry of Voters* and pre-1966 *List of Enrolled Voters* located at the desk in the main reading room to determine if the volume for a particular year is available.

Description of Facility:

The Center is located on the ground floor of the Surrogate's Court building opposite the main entrance. It consists of two public rooms, the main room and the City/State room. The Biographical Binders, vertical and neighborhood files, *List of Enrolled Voters,* proceedings, most biographical publications and New York City histories are located in the City/State room.

The Civil Service lists on microfiche are located at the desk at the entrance to the main room. These must be requested from the staff person on duty. As security, a photo-identification card must be deposited with the person on duty while using these materials. The lists on microfilm are located in the microfilm cabinet near the desk.

The Assembly District maps (microfiche) and Street Name Index are located in the Technical Services room which is not open to researchers. These must be requested from the librarian. No identification is needed. The Assembly District maps (paper copy) are located in the map cabinet in the main room near the entrance to the Technical Services Room.

There is one microfilm reader, one microform reader/printer and two photocopy machines. The library can accommodate 40 researchers. There is one reference librarian available to assist the public.

Fees/Copies:

Photocopies are $.15 per page. These machines can make change. Copies from microfilm or microfiche can be made at $.20 per page (exact change required).

Restrictions on Use:

Visitors to 31 Chambers Street must present photo identification to the guards at the building entrance.

Paper copies of Civil Service Lists (pre-1956), *List of Enrolled Voters* (pre-1966) and *Registry of Voters* (all) are not on-site and must be ordered in advance. One week notice is required to obtained these lists. The Center will accept requests by telephone. The NYC Law Department has determined that Social Security numbers are not public records. Therefore, Civil Service Lists 1971–1983 and 1991–1992 are no longer available to researchers.

The Municipal Reference and Research Center collections are primarily for reference use within the Center. Limited categories of materials are allowed to be circulated for short periods of time to city government employees only.

NEW YORK GENEALOGICAL AND BIOGRAPHICAL SOCIETY LIBRARY

Facility Director: Joy Rich, Director of the Library

Address: 122 East 58th Street
New York, NY 10022-1939

(Cross Streets: Park and Lexington Avenues)

Phone: (212) 755-8532
Fax: (212) 754-4218
E-mail: library@nygbs.org
Website: www.nygbs.org

Hours of Operation:

Tuesday to Saturday: 9:30 am to 5:00 pm

Closed Sunday, Monday, legal holidays and Saturdays preceding Monday holidays.

Closest Public Transportation:

Subway: 4, 5 or 6 to 59th Street
N, R or W to Lexington Avenue

Bus: M101 or M102 to East 59th Street/Lexington Ave (southbound); and 59th Street/3rd Ave (northbound)
M1, M2, M3 or M4 to Madison Avenue and East 58th Street (northbound)
M28 to Lexington Avenue and East 57th (crosstown)
Q32 (to Queens) or M103 (crosstown) to Lexington Avenue and East 59th Street

Directions:

Take the #4, #5 (express) or #6 (local) train to the 59th Street station. Exit to East 59th Street and Lexington Avenue. The exit is at the <u>south</u> end of the station. Walk one block <u>south</u> on Lexington Avenue to East 58th Street and turn <u>west</u> to the building. The Library is reached by elevator to the fourth floor. NOTE: The entrance can be made wheelchair accessible by placement of a wooden ramp over the stairs. Call in advance.

Description of Resources:

The Society's genealogical research library was established in 1869 with a focus on families in the State of New York from the colonial era to the present. The collection includes over 75,000 volumes, 30,000 manuscripts, 1,300 periodicals, 22,000 microfilms and microfiche, and 200 CD-ROMs on genealogy, local history and biography. The bulk of the collection is pre-20th century America with large segments devoted to New York State and the Northeast.

In 2003, the NYG&B became an authorized branch library of the Family History Library in Salt Lake City with access to its vast collection of materials. See FAMILY HISTORY CENTER (LDS), MANHATTAN for more information on records available on inter-library loan.

The following materials are in the NYG&B collection. Call numbers are given in brackets.

1. <u>New York City Vital Records</u> (microfilm; see "Restrictions on Use"). The NYG&B is expanding its collection of vital <u>records</u> and <u>indexes</u>. See the Library's website for a complete inventory of records available. The following list includes indexes only:

   <u>Birth Indexes:</u>
Manhattan/Bronx*	1830–1965
Brooklyn	1866–1965
	1847–1851, 1881–1894 (Flatbush town)
Queens	1871–1897 (years vary for each town/village)
	1898–1965
Staten Island	1898–1965

   The Library has alphabetical <u>and</u> soundex indexes to Manhattan/Bronx* births for the period 1888-1897.

Marriage Indexes:

Manhattan/Bronx*	1866–1937 (bride and groom indexes)
Brooklyn	1894–1937 (groom index)
Queens	1881–1898 (groom index; years vary for each town/village)
	1898–1937 (groom index)
	1905–1937 (bride index)
Staten Island	1882–1937 (bride and groom indexes)

Death Indexes:

Manhattan/Bronx*	1868–1965
Brooklyn	1848–1965
	1847–1849, 1880–1894 (years vary for each town/village)
Queens	1898–1965
	1847–1849, 1871–1897 (years vary for each town/village)
Staten Island	1898–1965

* NYC Health Department records and indexes for Manhattan include the western Bronx from 1874 and the eastern Bronx from 1895 until the Bronx became a separate borough in 1898.

See also MUNICIPAL ARCHIVES and NEW YORK PUBLIC LIBRARY, IRMA AND PAUL MILSTEIN DIVISION OF UNITED STATES HISTORY, LOCAL HISTORY AND GENEALOGY for additional indexes and records.

2. Census:

Census book indexes, 1790–1850 or 1860, are available for most states. In addition, the Society has on microfilm the following (see "Restrictions on Use"):

State Census: The Library's collection includes microfilmed New York State census records and indexes, 1825–1925, including from the New York metropolitan area:

New York County, 1855, 1905, 1915, 1925
New York City (Manhattan and western Bronx), 1890 "police" census.
Bronx County, 1915, 1925. NOTE: Bronx was included in the 1905 census for New York County.
Kings County (Brooklyn), 1855, 1865, 1875, 1892, 1905, 1915, 1925
Queens County, 1892, 1915, 1925
Richmond County (Staten Island), 1855, 1865, 1875, 1915, 1925
Nassau County, 1915, 1925. NOTE: Nassau was included in the 1892 Queens census.
Rockland County, 1855, 1865, 1875, 1892, 1905, 1915, 1925
Suffolk County, 1865, 1915, 1925
Westchester County, 1905, 1915, 1925

Federal Census:
New York State, 1790–1920; and 1880, 1900 and 1920 Soundex indexes. Indexes for 1870 (all NYS), and 1910 (NYC, Nassau and Suffolk Counties; and Upstate New York) are also available on CD-ROM.
New York State, 1890 (special schedule for soldiers, sailors, marines, and widows of veterans); and index.
New York State, special schedules (agricultural, industrial, mortality, social), 1850–1880
Connecticut, 1810, 1850 and 1910 index (CD-ROM).
New Jersey, 1850–1880; and 1880 Soundex index.

3. Probate Records:

Most probate records and their indexes are on microfilm, including wills, administration bonds, letters of administration, guardian bonds, and guardianships for New York City and many other counties throughout the state, extending from the mid 1700s to the early 1900s. Abstracts and indexes include:

Bronx:
The Library has a copy of the computerized index to Bronx County probate records available at BRONX SURROGATE'S COURT, 1914–1986. NOTE: This index is not yet accessible.

Brooklyn:
Abstracts of Wills of Kings County, recorded at Brooklyn, 1787–1843 (typescript), by DeWitt Van Buren. [K10]
Index of Wills probated in Kings County 1850–1890, by Gertrude A. Barber, 1949. [K12]
Index to the Wills, Administrations and Guardianships of Kings County, New York, 1650–1850, compiled and edited by Milton Halsey Thomas and C. Shepard, 1926. [K611]

<u>Manhattan</u>:

Abstracts of Wills for New York County, New York from 1801–1856, 20 vols., compiled by Ray C. Sawyer and Gertrude A. Barber.

Abstracts of Wills probated in the Common Pleas Court (also known as Mayor's Court), 1819–1892, Supreme Court of Judicature, 1821–1829, Supreme Court of Judicature, 1847–1856, Supreme Court of Judicature, 1856–1870, compiled by Ray C. Sawyer.

Index to Letters of Administration filed in New York County from 1743–1875, compiled by Gertrude A. Barber.

Index of Wills for New York County (New York City) from 1662–1850, compiled by Ray C. Sawyer.

Index of Wills for New York County, New York, from 1851–1875 inclusive, compiled by Ray C. Sawyer.

<u>Queens</u>:

Abstracts of Wills for Queens County, NY, by Ray C. Sawyer, 4 vols. in 2 (typescript, 1936–1937), v.1: 1797–1813; v.2: 1813–1828; v.3: 1828–1843; v.4: 1843–1850; McCormack, L.J. v.5: 1848–1856. [Q5]

<u>Staten Island</u>:

Richmond County, NY Index of Wills, 1787–1863; Index of Letters of Administration and Guardianship, 1787–1866 (typescript). [R12]

<u>New York State</u>:

Genealogical Data from New York Administration Bonds, 1753–1799 [Court of Appeals, Albany], by K. Scott. New York, 1969; and — *from further New York Administration Bonds, 1791–1795 and 1795–1798.* 1971.

See NEW YORK PUBLIC LIBRARY, MILSTEIN DIVISION OF UNITED STATES HISTORY, LOCAL HISTORY AND GENEALOGY, STATEN ISLAND HISTORICAL SOCIETY, and NEW YORK STATE LIBRARY, for additional abstracts of probate records.

4. <u>Marriage Announcements, Obituaries and Name Changes</u>:

The Library has an extensive collection of abstracts of marriage announcements and death notices published in 18th and 19th century newspapers (on open shelves) as well as other name indexes. The following are those for NYC:

Index of Marriages and Deaths in the New York Weekly Museum, 1788–1817, compiled by American Antiquarian Society. 1952.

Index to Marriage and Death Notices in the New-Yorker Stats-Zeitung, 1836–1870, by Frank A. Biebel. New York, 2000.

Index to Marriages and Deaths in the New York Herald, 1835–1855, compiled by James P. Maher. Baltimore, 1987; vol. 2, 1856–1863; vol. 3, 1864–1870. Alexandria, VA, 1991–2000.

Index to Staten Island Marriages and Deaths in the New York Herald, 1864–1867, by Holly Tooker. 2000.

Marriage and Death Notices from the New York Weekly Museum, 1789–1796, compiled by Consuelo Furman and Robert Furman, M.D. New York, 1950.

Marriages and Deaths from the New Yorker (Double Quarto Edition), 1836–1841, by Kenneth Scott. Washington, D.C, 1980.

Marriage Records from "The Herald" and "Morning Herald," Volumes 2 and 3, Published in New York City, 1836 and 1838, compiled by DeWitt Van Buren.

Nation-Wide Marriage Notices as Gleaned from the New York Weekly Tribune, compiled by Judith Rush. [Winter Park, FL], 1978. Includes some birth notices and divorce cases.

Newspaper Death Notices, New York, New Jersey, Connecticut (newspaper clippings). Vol.1, 1870–1890, indexed; vol. 2, 1872–1910, indexed.

New York City Marriages, 1810–1814, as reported in the Commercial Advertiser, compiled by Marie Kiersted Pidgeon. New York, 1933.

New York Evening Post Deaths Abstracts, 1801–1890, compiled by Gertrude A. Barber. 55 vols. 1933–1947.

New York Evening Post, New York City Marriages, 1811–1890, compiled and edited by Gertrude A. Barber. 23 vols. 1933–1947.

The New-York Magazine Marriages and Deaths: 1790–1797, edited by Kenneth Scott and Kristin Lunde Gibbons. New Orleans, 1975.

New York Marriage Bonds, 1753–1783, compiled by Dr. Kenneth Scott. New York, 1972.

New York Marriages Previous to 1784: A reprint of the original edition of 1860 with additions and corrections. Includes also *Supplementary List of Marriage Licenses; New York Marriage Licenses,* by Robert H. Kelby, and *New York Marriage Licenses, 1639–1706, with Index,* by Kenneth Scott. Baltimore, 1968.

New York Times Obituary Index, 1858–1978.

Petitions for Name Changes in New York City, 1848–1899, by Kenneth Scott. New York, 1984. Includes abstracts of 890 petitions for changes of name during this period.

The Library has abstracts for many other localities including such gems as, *Jewish Marriage Notices from the Newspaper Press of Charleston, SC, 1775–1906,* compiled by Barnett A. Elzas, New York, 1917.

5. Coroner's Records:

Coroner's Inquisitions, 1823–1898, New York County. (microfilm)
Coroners' Reports New York City, 1823–1842, abstracted by Kenneth Scott. New York, 1989. Includes c. 5,000 identified cases. (More than 1,000 not identified were omitted.) An index of c. 2,200 non-decedents (relatives or acquaintances) is included.
Coroners' Reports New York City, 1843–1849, abstracted by Kenneth Scott. New York, 1991. Includes c. 4,700 identified cases. An index of nearly 10,000 non-decedents (relatives or acquaintances) is included.

6. Naturalizations:

Denizations, Naturalizations, and Oaths of Allegiance in Colonial New York, by Kenneth Scott and Kenn Stryker-Rodda. Baltimore, 1975.
Early New York Naturalizations: Abstracts of Naturalization Records from Federal, State and Local Courts, 1792–1840, by Kenneth Scott. Baltimore, 1981. Includes 14,000-15,000 naturalizations.
Naturalizations in the Marine Court, New York City, 1827–1835, abstracted by Kenneth Scott. New York, 1990.
Naturalizations in the Marine Court, New York City, 1834–1840, abstracted by Kenneth Scott. New York, 1991.
Naturalizations in the Marine Court, New York City, 1838–1840, indexed by B. Abrams. New York City, 2000.
New York [County] Supreme Court naturalization petition index, 1907–1924. [CD-ROM]

7. City Directories (microfilm):
NYC Directories (Manhattan and parts of the Bronx), 1786–1934 (some gaps)
Brooklyn Directories, 1796–1934 (gaps)
The Society also has print copies of Buffalo City Directories, 1832–1869 (gaps), and several other U.S. cities.

8. Material on Other Localities:

The Society has a comprehensive collection for New York, New Jersey, Pennsylvania and the New England states, including genealogies, published cemetery inscriptions, vital records and town and county histories. Some of the latter material is on microfilm. See "Restrictions on Use."

9. Genealogical Publications and Indexes:

The extensive collection of reference works includes how-to books and pamphlets, lineage books, and 1,600 genealogical periodicals and indexes, including:

American Genealogical-Biographical Index, edited by F. Rider. [CS 44 A57]. The library owns approximately 75% of the books indexed. Also available on *Ancestry.com* and *Ancestry.plus.*
The American Genealogist and indexes. [CS 42 A51]. Worden, J.D. Subject Index to vols. 1–20. 1986. Name index to vols. 9–41 on CD-ROM. Also indexed in PERSI and GPAI.
Biography and Genealogy Master Index [to biographical dictionaries and encyclopedias, Who's Who, etc] on CD-ROM. [CT 214 U5 B57]
DAR Patriot Index. 3 vols. [E202.5A129 and E202.5A13]; and *Index to the rolls of honor (ancestors index) in the Lineage books of the National Society Daughters of the American Revolution.* 4 vols. [E202.5A15]
Genealogical Periodical Annual Index (GPAI). Vol. 1 to present (1962 to present). [CS42.11 G4]
Historical-Biographical Dictionaries Master Index. [CT 215 U5 H15]
National Genealogical Society Quarterly and indexes [CS 42 N4]. Also available on CD-ROM, vols. 1–85.
New York Genealogical and Biographical Society Record. Indexes: Worden's name index, 1870–1998 [CD-ROM]; and published indexes, Barber, G.A., *Surnames,* vols. 1–20, 21–40; *Subject,* vols. 39–76, 71–94. Worden, Jean D. *Master index,* 1870–1982; Macy, H. *Articles in The Record, 1983–1995, Indexed by Principal Surname or Location.* [CS 42 N49]
Periodical Source Index (PERSI). Vol. 1–17 (covering periodicals published, 1847–1985) and 1986–1997 annual supplements. [CS 42.11 A4]. Also available on CD-ROM.
Revised Master index to New York State DAR Genealogical Records Volumes. Collection at NYPL. [N.Y. G129.6 A15]
Surname Index to 65 Volumes of Colonial and Revolutionary Pedigrees, by G.R. Crowther. 1964. [CS 42 N43]

10. Land and Property Records:

Microfilm holdings include grantor/grantee indexes, mortgage indexes, and deed indexes for New York City and counties throughout the state from late 17th to 20th century (majority are through late 19th century).

11. Cemeteries:

   Cemeteries of the United States: a guide to contact information for U.S. cemeteries and their records. Detroit, [1994].
   Fairchild Cemetery Manual: a reliable guide to the cemeteries of Greater New York and vicinity, Brooklyn, [1910].
   Graveyard Shift: a family historian's guide to New York City cemeteries, by C. Innskeep. Orem, UT, [2000].
   New York State Cemeteries Name/Location Inventory, 1995–1997. 3 vols. Bowie, MD, 1999.

12. Manuscript Collection:

   Many of the holdings are one-of-a-kind. They include most towns and counties in New York and consist of genealogies, charts, transcriptions of gravestone inscriptions, town records, church records, vital records from family bibles, research notes by professional genealogists and family historians, and maps for census research. See "Restrictions on Use."

13. Electronic Resources:

   Ancestry.plus. See NEW YORK PUBLIC LIBRARY, IRMA AND PAUL MILSTEIN DIVISION OF UNITED STATES HISTORY, LOCAL HISTORY AND GENEALOGY for a sample of available resources on this website.
   Heritage Quest Online (a.k.a. *Genealogy & Local History Online*), includes more than 25,000 digitized genealogical books and serials; and full-text images of the U.S. Census, 1790-1930.
   ProQuest Historical Newspapers, New York Times, 1851–1999. NOTE: NYG&B members have access to this database and *Heritage Quest Online* at no cost from home via the NYG&B website.

Finding Aids:

In addition to the above indexes, the Society has a card catalog for books and periodicals alphabetically integrating author, title and subject and a computerized catalog. The card catalog for the Manuscript Collection and microform collections is subdivided by surnames, New York towns, New York counties, other states, other countries.

The library has many one-of-a-kind finding aids for the New York State censuses, including maps for finding election/enumeration districts, assembly districts, and wards. Finding aids are also available for federal censuses, land and property records, and Emigrant Savings Bank records. Staff members have prepared bibliographies of the library's holdings for different ethnic and religious groups including Jewish, Eastern European, and German.

Description of Facility:

The library occupies the 4th and 5th floors of the building. The Technology Center, located on the 3rd floor, houses 8 microfilm readers, a microfiche reader and three microfilm/fiche-reader/printers. Maps and CD-ROMs and all NYC vital record indexes are also located here. These are available for use by members only. Seating in the non-member area on the 4th floor can accommodate 10 people. At least one librarian is always available.

The collection is physically divided. Reference books that non-members can access are on open shelves in an area at the entrance to the library. They include a complete set of the *New York Genealogical and Biographical Record,* a collection of genealogical how-to books, general interest genealogy periodicals, and indexes to genealogy books and periodicals. The bulk of the collection is located beyond the railing in the larger members reading room, two balconies, and two other rooms. All books and periodicals are accessible to non-members by call slip.

Fees/Copies:

Suggested daily donation of $10 is requested of non-members. The donation can be applied toward membership by later presenting the receipt for it. Annual membership is $60 for individuals and $90 for joint membership (two famly members living at the same address). Membership includes full access to the library's collection including online electronic resources, a subscription to the quarterly journal, *The New York Genealogical and Biographical Record* and to the *NYG&B Newsletter,* and discounts on publications, lectures and other programs.

Photocopies cost $.35 per page. For non-members, photocopying is done by the staff. Up to 10 pages per book will be made if the material is not fragile. Members may make their own copies (up to 5 pages from a manuscript but never an entire manuscript). Researchers can order Family History Library microfilm for viewing at the NYG&B at $4 per reel for the first 30 days. Renewal is permitted for two additional 45-day periods at $4 per period.

Restrictions on Use:

Only NYG&B members can use manuscripts, microforms and electronic media. Staff will bring books to the non-member area and will check the manuscript catalog, but only members can use the manuscripts. Non-members can no longer view book indexes to NYC vital records since these are now housed in the Technology Center on the 3rd floor.

NEW-YORK HISTORICAL SOCIETY
LIBRARY

Facility Director: Margaret Heilbrun, Vice President for Library Services and Head Librarian

Address: 2 West 77th Street   ♿
New York, NY 10024

(Cross Streets: Central Park West and Columbus Avenue)

Phone: Reading Room: (212) 873-3400, ext. 225, 226; Manuscripts Department: ext. 265
Prints, Photographs and Architecture Collections: ext. 227, 228

Fax: (212) 875-1591
E-mail: reference@nyhistory.org (Reference Desk)
mssdept@nyhistory.org (Manuscripts)
printroom@nyhistory.org (Prints, Photographs and Architecture)
Website: www.nyhistory.org

Hours of Operation:

Tuesday to Saturday: 10:00 am to 5:00 pm

Closed Sunday, Monday and legal holidays; and closed Saturday during the summer (Memorial Day to Labor Day).
Prints, Photographs and Architecture Collections open to researchers <u>by appointment only</u> (11:00 am to 5:00 pm).
Museum open Tuesday - Sunday, 10:00 am to 5:00 pm.

Closest Public Transportation:

Subway: B or C to 81st Street
1 or 9 to 79th Street

Bus: M10 to West 76th/77th Street and Central Park West
M79 (79th Street Crosstown) to West 81 Street and Central Park West

Directions:

Take the B or C train to the 81st Street station. Exit at the <u>south</u> end of the station to Central Park West and 79th Street.
Walk <u>south</u> on Central Park West crossing West 77th Street. The building is on the corner.

Description of Resources:

The New-York Historical Society houses one of the oldest research libraries in the U.S.A. The Society was founded in
1804 and the nucleus of a library was formed in 1809. By 1813, when its first catalog was printed, the Society housed
4,265 books, 130 newspapers, and more. The Library's collection today encompasses more than 350,000 printed books
and pamphlets, 2 million manuscripts including diaries, letters, business records and patents, close to 10,000 newspapers,
over 30,000 maps and atlases, and more than 500,000 photographs, prints, architectural records and scrapbooks covering
four centuries of New York history. Materials of interest to genealogists include:

1. New York City Vital Records Indexes

   Birth, death and marriage indexes, 1889–1905. See "Restrictions on Use."

   NOTE: Pre-1898 these indexes include only New York County (Manhattan and the Bronx). Brooklyn, Queens and
   Staten Island were not included in these indexes until 1898. See NEW YORK CITY DEPARTMENT OF RECORDS AND
   INFORMATION SERVICES, MUNICIPAL ARCHIVES for actual records.

2. City Directories

   New York (Manhattan/Bronx), 1786–1925, 1933/34
   Brooklyn, 1822–1902, 1904, 1906–1907, 1909, 1912–1913, 1933/34
   Queens, 1890, 1891/92, 1893/94, 1902, 1904, 1906–1910, 1912, 1921–1923
   Staten Island, 1888, 1892/93, 1933/34

   The collection includes *Phillips' Elite Directory,* 1874–1903 [F128.22.A4], and *Dau's New York Blue Book,*
   1907–1937 [F128.22.A6], arranged by address.

3. Newspapers

The Society has an outstanding collection of New York City newspapers from the first NYC paper, the *New-York Gazette,* to present publications. It has the fourth largest collection in the country of original issues of newspapers published in the U.S.A. before 1820. The newspaper collection is in original format and on microfilm and microcards. Of note also, the Society has typed lists of announcements of deaths, and marriages, 1801–1890, from the *New York Evening Post.*

The collection includes a card index from the offices of *The Sun* (1913–1920) and its successors, the *Sun and New York Herald* (1920) and *New York Herald* (1920–1924). In addition, volume indexes are available for:

> *Brooklyn Daily Eagle,* 1891–1900 (see "Restrictions on Use")
> *New York Evening Post,* 1873–1921 (gaps)
> *New York Times,* 1851 to present
> *New York Tribune,* 1875–1906
> *New York World,* 1885–1890, 1892

4. Probate Records

Abstracts of Wills on file in the Surrogate's Office, City of New York, 1665–1800, 17 vols. plus index, published by the New-York Historical Society. Abstracts of New York County wills, 1665–1856, are available as well as indexes to wills and letters of administration until 1875.

5. Map Collection

The Society has some 30,000 maps and atlases (mostly American, some foreign) including large-scale insurance atlases of Manhattan, beginning with 1853.

6. Family Histories/Genealogies

The collection includes some 15,000 genealogies and family histories as well as 120,000 works on local history. Among the collections are papers of the Hendricks Family, 1790–1938, an early American-Jewish Sephardic family; and Jews in South Carolina, 1783 to 1897, listing burials in Jewish cemeteries. Many of the collections are in manuscript form. Some include naturalization records and passport applications. See the card catalog.

7. Military

The Society has one of the largest military and naval history collections in the U.S.A. It incorporates the libraries of the Military Order of the Loyal Legion (Commandery of the State of New York), the Naval History Society, the Lathrop C. Harper Spanish-American War Collection, the Eugene H. Pool Collection of Captain James Lawrence and the complete library of the Seventh Regiment, New York National Guard, c. 1813–1949, including Civil War regimental histories, officers accounts, rosters, company minute books, scrapbooks, photographs, court-martial records and muster rolls.

8. Photo Collection

The Department of Prints, Photographs and Architecture Collections of the Library houses more than 75 photograph collections, 1850s to the present. These include:

Irving Browning Collection (c. 1920–1939), 1,885 photographic prints of streets and buildings, including skyscrapers under construction and photographs of Lower East Side peddlers.
Liberman Collection includes photographs of every house of worship in Manhattan (4 volumes). Photographs were taken from 1966–1973 (starting at the Bowery and ending at the northern tip of Manhattan).
Photograph File includes 135 images by Alexander Alland of Black Jews in Harlem and Russian Gypsies on the Lower East Side (1940s).

Check also the Geographic Files arranged by street name, for photocopies of photographs in the collections that can be identified by street name and building number.

9. Advertising Ephemera Collection

The Bella C. Landauer Collection includes such diverse items as advertising cards (popular in the late 19th and early 20th centuries) and many manufacturers' catalogs, including those of Jewish manufacturers. An appointment must be made in advance to use this collection.

10. <u>Slavery and Black History</u>

The collection includes records of slave births, NYC, 1800–1818; Castleton Town Book (Staten Island), 1800–1827, listing children born to slaves after July 1, 1799; records of the New York Manumission Society, including a register of manumission of slaves, 1816–1818 and indenture and manumission of slaves, 1809–1829. Also available are account books of slave dealers, logbooks of slave ships, letters of abolitionists, slave diaries, genealogies, papers related to the "Colored Troops" of the Civil War and minutes of the Colored Orphan Asylum.

Finding Aids:

The Library has a card and electronic catalog (see below). Many special collections are cataloged separately, so be sure to ask a reference librarian for assistance. There is a genealogical catalog arranged by family name and separate catalogs for newspapers, manuscripts, maps, broadsides, sheet music and hotel men. Special collections such as the Seventh Regiment are cataloged separately. See also *A Guide to Newspaper Research at the New-York Historical Society Library;* and *A Guide to Military History Research in the Printed Collections at the New-York Historical Society Library* (free). The librarians are very helpful in locating uncataloged items.

NOTE: The New-York Historical Society electronic catalog is also accessible via the Internet as part of the BobCatPlus catalog of New York University (www.bobcat.nyu.edu). This catalog combines the resources of several libraries including NEW YORK UNIVERSITY, ELMER HOLMES BOBST LIBRARY. Computers in the New-York Historical Society Library access N-YHS materials only.

There are two separate card catalogs for Manuscripts (pre-1984 and 1984 to present) with entries under place names and personal names. There is also *A Guide to the Manuscript Collections of the New York Historical Society,* 1972, by Arthur J. Breton (2 vols).

A Guide to Print, Photograph, Architecture and Ephemera Collections at the New-York Historical Society by Helena Zinkham (1998), provides summary information on 75 collections. The Department of Prints, Photographs and Architecture Collections also houses the negatives index.

Description of Facility:

The Library reading room is located on the second floor and has a seating capacity of 52. There are three or more staff persons available to assist researchers. Materials can be obtained in 5-15 minutes; some reference books are on open shelves There are 2 computers with access to the Library's electronic catalog; 4 microfilm reader/printers, 2 microfiche and 1 microcard reader. The Department of Prints, Photographs and Architecture Collections is located on the 2nd floor. Eight to nine people can be seated at 3 tables in this room (by appointment only).

Fees/Copies:

Photocopy service costs $.35 to $.50 per page. Copies, exclusive of microfilm copies, are made by Library staff only. There is a limit of 20 pages per person per day. It can take from 5 to 35 minutes to obtain a copy in person. There are additional shipping and handling charges for mail orders. Some materials may not be photocopied because of the fragility but may be photographed by the Department of Rights and Reproductions. Requests for all services must be made before 4:30 pm.

Fees vary depending on size and format. Copies of photographs begin at $25 (black and white) or $50 (color). All requests for photographs must be in writing and a permission agreement detailing usage requirements must be signed. Pre-payment is required. Allow 3-4 weeks for processing orders. For more information, call the Department of Rights and Reproductions at ext. 282.

Membership fees start at $25 for students and seniors, $40 for an individual and $65 for dual membership.

Restrictions on Use:

Vital record indexes for New York City, City Directories and the *Brooklyn Daily Eagle* newspaper are originals and the Society prefers that the microfilm copies at the NEW YORK PUBLIC LIBRARY or the BROOKLYN PUBLIC LIBRARY be used by researchers.

Coats, bags, packages, briefcases, books, food and drink must be checked. They are not allowed in the Library. Adults only may use the facility. Use of pencil is mandatory. Hand-held copiers and cameras may not be used.

Researchers wishing to use rare books, newspapers, manuscript or the broadside collection are required to submit identification and are restricted to one item at a time.

NEW YORK PUBLIC LIBRARY - HUMANITIES AND SOCIAL SCIENCES LIBRARY
GENERAL RESEARCH DIVISION AND MICROFORMS ROOM

Facility Director: Elizabeth Diefendorf, Frederick Phineas and Sandra Priest Rose Chief Librarian, General Research Division

Alice Dowd, Assistant Chief Librarian for Microforms

Address: Fifth Avenue at 42nd Street, Rooms 100 and 315 ♿
New York, NY 10018-2788

(Cross Streets: 40th and 42nd Streets; 5th and 6th Avenues)

Phone: (212) 930-0830 (Library hours or to locate a book)
(212) 340-0849 (Mid-Manhattan telephone reference service)
(212) 930-0810 (Copy Services)
(212) 642-0139 (Microforms Room)

Fax: (212) 930-0572
E-mail: grdref@nypl.org
Website: www.nypl.org/research/chss/grd/index.html
catnyp.nypl.org (catalog)

Hours of Operation:

Deborah, Jonathan F. P., Samuel Priest and Adam Raphael Rose Main Reading Room, Blass Public Catalog Room, Microforms Room, DeWitt Wallace Periodical Room and Copy Services:

Thursday to Saturday   10:00 am to 6:00 pm
Tuesday and Wednesday 11:00 am to 7:30 pm

Closed Sunday, Monday and legal holidays

NOTE: Not all Divisions of NYPL are open these hours. Check the individual Division listings which follow. Research Libraries schedule is subject to change. Call before coming.

Closest Public Transportation:

Subway: B, D, F or V to 42nd Street/6th Avenue
7 to 5th Avenue/42nd Street
4, 5 or 6 to 42nd Street/Grand Central Station
1, 2, 3, 9, N, Q, R, S, W to 42nd Street/7th Avenue

Bus: M1, M2, M3, M4, M5 or Q32 to 42nd St/5th Ave (southbound); or 42nd St/Madison Ave (northbound)
M5, M6 or M7 to Avenue of the Americas (6th Avenue) and 42nd Street
M42 (crosstown) or M104 to 5th Avenue and 42nd Street

Directions:

Take the B, D, F or V train to the 42nd Street station. Exit at 42nd Street and 6th Avenue (Avenue of the Americas). Walk <u>east</u> on 42nd Street. Or, take the #7 to the 5th Avenue/42nd Street station. Exit at 42nd Street and 5th Avenue. Walk about 100 feet <u>west</u>. Enter the Library through the 42nd Street entrance (between 5th and 6th Avenues).

Description of Resources:

The New York Public Library was created in 1895 and moved into its current location on 42nd Street in 1911. Today, the Library consists of the HUMANITIES AND SOCIAL SCIENCES LIBRARY, the NYPL FOR THE PERFORMING ARTS, the SCHOMBURG CENTER FOR RESEARCH IN BLACK CULTURE, and the SCIENCE, INDUSTRY AND BUSINESS LIBRARY, as well as the branch libraries. The HUMANITIES AND SOCIAL SCIENCES LIBRARY, housed at 42nd Street and 5th Avenue, includes six major divisions including the GENERAL RESEARCH DIVISION, DOROT JEWISH DIVISION, MAP DIVISION, SLAVIC AND BALTIC DIVISION, MILSTEIN DIVISION OF UNITED STATES HISTORY, LOCAL HISTORY AND GENEALOGY and the Oriental Division. In addition, there are several special collections including the MIRIAM AND IRA WALLACH DIVISION OF ARTS, PRINTS AND PHOTOGRAPHS and the MANUSCRIPTS AND ARCHIVES DIVISION. The GENERAL RESEARCH DIVISION, with over 3.5 million volumes is responsible for more than one-half the total book holdings of the Research Libraries in the arts and humanities. It administers the Bill Blass Public Catalog Room, the Rose Main Reading Room, the DeWitt Wallace Periodical Room, the Microforms Room and Copy Services.

The Rose Main Reading Room houses over 25,000 books on open shelves including biographies, indexes, encyclopedias, dictionaries and other reference books covering a wide range of subjects. Items of interest to genealogists include:

1. Biographies: The collection is rich in collective and individual biographies, as well as biographical dictionaries. These include:

   Allgemeine Deutsche Biographie. Berlin, 1967–1971. 56 vols. (Reprint of 1875–1912 edition.) [SE Wall, Bookcase 20, *RR-AGK 71-74]

   Archivio Biografico Italiano [Italian biographical archive]. Includes entries from 321 biographical sources published between 1646 and 1934 covering more than 150,000 individuals [*XM-21964]; and index. [JFF 99-3346]

   Archivo Biográfico de España, Portugal e Iberoamérica. Munich, [1986-1996]. Includes biographical entries from works published between 1602 and 1995. [*XL-813, *XM-19,313, *XM-19,314]; and index. [*XL-813+]

   Australasian Biographical Archive. Munich, 1990. Entries from 181 reference works published from 1866 to 1983 include 100,000 people from Australia and New Zealand [*XM-19,308]; and supplement, 1995. [*XM-21,897]

   Biography and Genealogy Master Index, 1980–. [SE Wall, Bookcase 2, *R-AA 81-1683]. Available also through the Library's Selected Electronic Resources; and accessible online from home by NYPL card holders.

   Biography Index, 1946–. [SE Front Wall, Bookcase 10, *R-*D 86-2706]

   British Biographical Archive. Includes 168,000 biographical sketches from 324 English-language reference works published between 1601 and 1926 [*XM-16,823]; and index. [*R-AB 98-10070]

   Contemporary Authors, 1964–. [SE Wall, Bookcase 6–8,*R-AB 78-5024]

   Current Biography, 1940–. [SE Wall, Bookcase.3, *R-AA 98-1105]

   Dictionaire de Biographie Française, 1933–. [SE Wall, Bookcase 19, *R-AGI]

   Dictionary of National Biography (Great Britain), 1967. (Reprint of 1885–1901 with supplements covering 1901–1990.) [SE Wall, Bookcase 18, *R-AGH 73-1514]

   Dictionary of Scientific Biography, 1970–1980; and supplement, 1990. 18 vols. [SE Wall, Bookcase 12,.*R-AB]

   Dictionary of Literary Biography, 1978–1986. 71 vols. [SE Wall, Bookcase 11, *R-AB 79-1061]

   Neue Deutsche Biographie (Germany), 1953–. [SE Wall, Bookcase 20, *RR-AGK]

   The New York Times Index, September 1851–. [SE Front Wall, Front Bookcases 4 to 7, *R-*A]

   Scandinavian Biographical Archive, edited by Laureen Baillie. Munich, 1994. Includes 150,000 people who lived in Norway, Denmark, Sweden, Finland and Iceland. [*XM-19,320; index *R-AGQ 95-13042]

   Who's Who, an Annual Biographical Dictionary (Great Britain), 1849–. [Most current at Information Desk in Public Catalog Room; some on Southeast Wall, Bookcase 4, *RR- AA]

   Who's Who in France, 1953–. [SE Wall, Bookcase 19, *RR-AGI] and older volumes. [JFM 86-475]

   Who's Who in Italy, 1957/58, 1980, 1987–. [SE Wall, Bookcase 17, *R-AGF 89-2025]

2. Published Research Guides: The Division's collection includes the following of interest to genealogists:

   Library of Congress National Union Catalog of Manuscript Collections, 1959–1993 [North Hall, Northeast Corner, Bookcase 144–145, *R-GBI]. Describes 72,300 collections, including family collections and those of Jewish organizations, in 1,406 repositories. See also *Index to Personal Names in the National Union Catalog of Manuscript Collections, 1959–1984* (includes c. 200,000 name entries) and *Index to Subjects and Corporate Names in the National Union Catalog of Manuscripts, 1959–1984* [both indexes in Bookcase 144–145]; and *Genealogies Cataloged by the Library of Congress Since 1986,* Washington, DC, 1991 [AP 92-17295] located in NYPL - DIVISION OF UNITED STATES HISTORY, LOCAL HISTORY AND GENEALOGY. See also *ArchivesUSA* online.

   Guide to the Research Collections of the New York Public Library, compiled by Sam P. Williams. Chicago, 1975. [At Information Desk in the Bill Blass Catalog Room]

   Directory of Archives and Manuscript Repositories in the United States. Phoenix, AZ, 1988. [*R-*GBI 88-2158]

3. City Directories - U.S.A. (Microforms Room 100): A very extensive collection of U.S.A. city directories, from 1752–1960 is available in self-service cabinets. The Division has a standing order to purchase every city directory that is made available on microfilm. See Appendix D. Many paper editions of New York State, New Jersey and Connecticut city directories formerly at the Annex have been filmed and are available here.

4. City Directories - New York City (Microforms Room 100). The following NYC directories are in self-service cabinets:

   NYC (generally Manhattan and parts of the Bronx), 1786–1933/34
   Brooklyn, 1796, 1802/3, 1812/13, 1822–1826, 1829–1910, 1912/13, 1933/34

Queens, 1902, 1904, 1906–1912, 1933/34
Richmond (Staten Island), 1933/34

For additional NYC city directories (Queens and Staten Island), see NYC city directories available in Room 119 of the NYPL, IRMA AND PAUL MILSTEIN DIVISION OF UNITED STATES HISTORY, LOCAL HISTORY AND GENEALOGY.

5. New York and Suburban Area Telephone Directories (Microforms Room 100)

	White Pages	Yellow Pages	Address Directories
Manhattan*	1878 to current	1929–	1929–1980, 1986, 1993
Manhattan (includes Bronx)	1924–1928	1928	
Bronx	1929–	1929–	1929–1980, 1986
Brooklyn, Queens & SI	1924–1928/29	-	
Brooklyn	1929–	1929–	1929–1980, 1986
Queens	1933–	1929–	1929–1980, 1986
Staten Island	1927–	1921–1924, 1928–	1929–1980, 1982,1986
Rockaway (Queens)	1928–1976	same	see Queens
Rockaway (Queens) and 5 towns	1977	same	see Queens
Suffolk, Nassau, Queens	1910–1947	-	see Queens only
Nassau	1913–	1929–	-
Rockland	1910–	1927/1928–	-
Suffolk	1928–	1929–	-
Westchester	1915–	1956–	1956–1980, 1986

Pre-1924, Manhattan telephone directories include other New York City boroughs, Nassau/Suffolk, Westchester and some New Jersey communities. See description on Reel #1 of the Manhattan telephone directory.

See also NEW YORK PUBLIC LIBRARY - SCIENCE, INDUSTRY AND BUSINESS LIBRARY for *Cole's* directories (address directories). NOTE: Staten Island Business Telephone Directories/Yellow pages, 1921–1924, and 1928/29 are in Room 119 (with City Directories).

6. US Telephone Directories: The Library has a large collection of telephone directories in various formats. Subscriptions to paper copies were canceled in 1998. Telephone directories after 1998 are either on Phonefiche or microfilm. The Microforms Room has a complete set of Phonefiche telephone directories for cities in the U.S.A. and Puerto Rico — primarily those over 15,000 in population. Phonefiche copies start in 1976 but not all cities were included from the start. Phonefiche (white and yellow pages) for the last 2 years are at NEW YORK PUBLIC LIBRARY - SCIENCE, INDUSTRY AND BUSINESS LIBRARY.

The Microforms Room 100 has pre-1976 telephone directories for U.S.A. cities in addition to those in the NYC area. These include (in stacks):

Baltimore, 1914–1945
Boston, 1909–1917, 1919–1945
Buffalo, 1910–1919
Chicago, 1909–1920
Cleveland, 1919–1920
Los Angeles, 1909–1920, 1925

New Orleans, 1912–1950
Philadelphia, 1913–1919
Pittsburgh, 1912–1950
St. Louis, 1912–1950
San Francisco, 1910–1950
Washington DC, 1907–1950.

Other pre-1976 U.S.A. telephone directories are in paper copy and are off site. The Information Desk in the Bill Blass Public Catalog Room has an 86-page bound book, *Domestic Telephone Directories at the Annex,* that lists all the U.S.A. telephone directories in the Library's collection.

7. Foreign City Directories: The Division has a collection of Canadian City Directories, 1843–1949, (paper copies/off-site) and some European City Directories. The Canadian collection includes (with gaps):

Halifax, 1871–1935
Montreal, 1843/44–1949

Ottawa, 1882–1934.
Toronto, 1883–1937

For London and Berlin, the Division has (in the stacks):

London Directories from the Guildhall Library, 1677–1900. [*ZAN-G68]
Post Office London Directory, 1799–1967. [CO (London Post Office Directory)]
Kelley's Post Office London Business Directory, 1968–1984. [CO (London Post Office Directory)]
Berliner Adressbuch, 1896, 1905, 1913, 1923, 1925, 1927, 1932, 1936, 1939. [*ZAN-13187]

8. <u>Foreign Telephone Directories</u>: Phonefiche are available for Australia, Canada, Great Britain, Italy, Scotland, and Switzerland. Access is also available to telephone directories via the Internet. Paper copies pre-1998 previously at the Annex are either in the stacks, off-site or in the Microforms Room. Check first in the Microforms Room to see if the directory is available there. See Appendix E for a list of select Foreign Telephone Directories in the Library's collection.

9. <u>Social Club Directories</u>: An assortment of social club directories (mostly non-Jewish) from around the U.S.A. previously at the Annex have been microfilmed. For New York City and State, these include:

Andiron Club of New York City: Directory, 1927, 1929, 1931, 1934, 1937, 1940. [*ZAN-10018 no. 1]
Club Men of New York, 1893–1903. [*ZAN-11133]
Club Members of New York, 1913/14, 1915/16–1921/22, 1924–1932/33, 1937, 1940. Includes men and women of
    prominence in social, professional and business life. [*ZAN-9641]
Directory of the Phi Delta Theta Club of New York, 1922, 1932. [*ZAN-10721 no. 5]
Kiwanis Club of New York City, 1920. [*ZAN-9836 no. 1]
Parents League of New York City: Membership list, 1935. [*ZAN-11213 no. 2]
Piping Rock Club (Locust Valley, NY), 1919–1924, 1926–1927, 1929, 1932, 1937–1939. [ZAN 9656]
Saturn Club (Buffalo, NY), 1894, 1899. [*ZAN-10836 no.1]
University Club of Buffalo: Constitution rules and list of members, 1895, 1898, 1915. [*ZAN-10471 no. 1]

10. <u>Occupational Directories</u>: The Division has an assortment of U.S.A. and some international occupational directories (microfilm, in stacks) including:

Adams County (PA) Teachers' Institute, 1875. [*ZAN-10626 no. 4]
American Agriculturist Farm Directory and Reference Book of Oneida County, NY, 1917 [*ZAN-G563 no. 2]; and
    ... Otsego and Herkimer Counties, New York, 1917. [*ZAN-G563 no. 3]
American Association to Promote the Teaching of Speech to the Deaf, List of Officers and Members, 1890–1891.
    [*ZAN-12820 no. 3]
Directory of Federal and State Dairy Food, Drug, and Feedings Stuffs Officials, 1916–1917.
    [*ZAN-11403 no. 4]
Directory of Louisiana Sugar Planters, 1907, 1920. [*ZAN-11934 no. 4]
*Directory of Organizations and Individuals Professionally Engaged in Governmental Research and Related
    Activities*, 1940–1941. [*ZAN-11038]
Directory of Probation and Parole Officers in the United States and Canada, 1928, 1931, 1934, 1937, 1941, 1947.
    [*ZAN-10323]
International Association of Chiefs of Police, 1916/17, 1929, 1931 [*ZAN-10588 no. 1]
International Police and Detective Directory, 1926–1927. [*ZAN-10528]
International Who's Who Among Hotel Men, 1924/25, 1927/28. [*ZAN-11692]
Ithaca (NY) [List of city departments and officials], 1925–1926, 1928–1934. [*ZAN-12895 no. 1]
Official Directory: Central, Regional and State Administrative Offices, Works Projects Administration, 1940–1941.
    [*ZAN-10066 no. 2]
Official List of Insurance Brokers (Boston, MA), 1906. [*ZAN-9596 no. 6]
Mitgliederliste des Vereins Deutscher Lehrerinnen in Amerika [Woman's Association of German Teachers in
    America], 1902, 1904, 1906, 1909. [*ZAN-11479 no. 4]
National Science Teachers Association, 1952–1953. [*ZAN-11702 no. 1]
Who's Who Among the Blind in the Business and Professional World, c. 1951. [*ZAN-12304 no. 4]
Yearbook and List of Active Members of the National Education Association, 1903/04–1905/06, 1907/08–1917/18.
    [*ZAN-10739]

11. <u>Catalog of Copyright Entries, 1891–1982</u> (Microforms Room): Library of Congress, Copyright Office publications listing books, dramatic compositions, maps, charts, periodicals, musical compositions, engravings, cuts, prints, chromos, lithographs, photographs and fine arts registered in the Copyright Office of the Library of Congress. Includes names of claimants. For Copyright Office records since January 1978, check the Library of Congress web site at www.loc.gov/copyright.

12. <u>New York City Newspapers</u>: There are over 450 NYC newspapers listed among the Library's holdings in a binder located at the Microforms Room Information Desk (Room 100). These include (with gaps):

Brooklyn Citizen, 1887–1947
Brooklyn Daily Eagle, 1848–1938
Brooklyn Daily Times, 1859–1937

Brooklyn Daily Union, 1863–1876
Brooklyn Daily Union Argus, 1876–1883
Brooklyn Eagle, 1932–1963
Brooklyn Standard Union, 1911–1932
Brooklyn Union, 1883–1887
Bronx Home News (Bronx-Harlem-Washington Heights), 1911–1948
Daily Mirror (New York Mirror), 1924–1972
New York Daily News, 1855–1872, 1902–1905 [stacks], 1919– [self service]
New York Evening Post, 1744–1821
New York Herald, 1802–1817, [stacks], 1835–1924 [self service]
New York Herald Tribune, 1924–1966
New York Post, 1801– (microfilm index, 1873–1923)
New York Telegram, 1867–1931
New York Times, 1851– Published index, 1851– ; also, *New York Times Biographical Edition/Service,* 1970–1999;
   and *Personal Name Index to the "New York Times Index." 1851–1974* and supplement, *1975–1999.*
New York Tribune, 1842–1924 (microfilm index, 1875–1899) [self service]
New York Star, 1879–1899
New York Sun, 1833–1950
New York World, 1860–1931
New York World Telegram, 1931–1950
New York World Telegram and Sun, 1950–1966
Richmond County Gazette, 1859–1903
Village Voice, 1955– [self service]
Weekly Worker (Socialist Weekly), 1901–1908

This collection also includes many ethnic newspapers in NYC including those of the Chinese, Danish, French, Greek, Hispanic, Hungarian, Irish, Italian, Scot and Swedish communities in New York City. For Jewish community newspapers, see the NYPL DOROT JEWISH DIVISION.

13. *The New York Sun Morgue*

The Division has the morgue clipping files for the *New York Sun* (off-site) from the late 1890s to the end of the 1940s. Very few of the extant files predate 1926. Files are arranged by name and subject. See "Restrictions on Use."

14. U.S.A. Newspapers (Microforms Room): The Library has a collection of newspapers from around the U.S.A. See Appendix F for a select list. The Division will eventually include in its microfilm collection all obtainable issues of more than 2,000 early American newspapers published before 1820 and some later. A checklist of titles and dates received, *Early American Newspapers,* may be consulted at the Public Catalog Room Information Desk and at the Microforms Information Desk [*ZAN-7473]. For pre-Civil War newspapers not included on these lists or classmarks beginning with *KSC, check with the librarian in the RARE BOOK DIVISION. For a comprehensive list of later papers, see the 4-volume, *U.S. Newspapers in the New York Public Library - Index* [Microforms Div. 94-4575] at the Microforms Information Desk. U.S.A. newspapers with indexes available in the Library include [classmark provided if not on open shelf in Room 100]:

Albany Times Union, 1968–. Index, 1982–1987 [JFM 99-340]
Albuquerque Journal, 1969–. Index, 1999– [*XL-812]
Atlanta Journal/Constitution, 1945– (gaps). Published index, 1971–1979, 1982–
The Boston Globe, 1972–. Published index, 1983–
Chicago Tribune, Jan 1947– [self service]. Published index, 1972–
Denver Post, 1969– (gaps). Published index, 1992–
Detroit News, 1945–. Published index, 1976–
Houston Chronicle, 1995–. Published index, 1995–
Houston Post, 1969–1995. Published index, 1976–1994
Los Angeles Times, 1954– [self service]. Published index, 1972–
Minneapolis Star and Tribune, 1967–. Index, 1984–1985 [JFM 99-354]
New Orleans Times-Picayune, 1837–. Published index, 1972–
St. Louis Post-Dispatch, 1939–. Published index, 1980–
San Francisco Chronicle, 1865–. Published index, 1976–

USA Today, 1982– [self service]. Published index, 1982–
Washington Post, 1914– [self service]. Published index, 1972–

In addition to the above, researchers can access some newspaper indexes on the Internet via any "Selected Electronic Resources" computer.

15. Foreign Newspapers

See Appendix F for a select list of the Division's collection of foreign newspapers. Indexes are available for:

The (London) Times, 1785– [*ZY(Times, London)], Index, 1785–1790; *Palmer's Index to the (London) Times*, 1790–1905; *The Official Index to the (London) Times*, 1906–; *The (London) Times Obituaries*, 1991–1993. *The (Manchester) Guardian*, 1959– [*ZY (Guardian(Manchester, England)]. Index, 1986–

See also *Historical Newspapers Online* available among the Library's Selected Electronic Resources. For current periodicals, visit the DeWitt Wallace Periodical Room (Room 108) across from the Microforms Room (first floor).

Finding Aids:

The NYPL public catalog includes a computerized system, Catalog of the New York Public Library (CATNYP) and a retrospective 800-volume book catalog, *Dictionary Catalog of the Research Libraries of the New York Public Library, 1911–1972*, also known as the "Black Book Catalog" or the *Dictionary Catalog*. Most books found in the pre-1972 *Dictionary Catalog*, can now be accessed on the CATNYP computer terminals located in the Public Catalog Room (Room 315) and elsewhere around the building. CATNYP is now accessible also on the Internet. For materials published before 1972 and not found in CATNYP, i.e. serial publications such as newspapers which ended pre-1972 and some manuscript materials, consult the *Dictionary Catalog*. Some materials such as articles cataloged in the *Dictionary Catalog* may never be added to CATNYP. Books with Hebrew/Yiddish titles appear in CATNYP using the Hebrew alphabet and also have transliterated titles.

NOTE: The Library continues to work on conversion of the *Dictionary Catalog* so that eventually all books and serials will be recorded in CATNYP. Sets of the *Catalog* are available for consultation in the Bill Blass Public Catalog Room, the South Hall of the Main Reading Room (Room 315) and at other locations throughout the building. A list of libraries around the world that have copies of the 800-volume *Dictionary Catalog* can be found on the Library's web site.

Books and periodicals can be searched under author, subject, title, keyword or classmark number in the online catalog. Classmarks (call numbers) are found at the top of each entry display. If the classmark begins with "*R", the book is on an open shelf in either the South or North Halls. Classmarks beginning with "*Z" are on microfilm and "*XM*" are on microfiche and can be accessed through the MICROFORMS ROOM.

Once the classmark is identified, fill out a blue-and-white call slip for each book or periodical being requested. Most Library materials are in closed book stacks and may be retrieved only by Library personnel. Materials may be housed in other Divisions or at one of the other Research Library buildings. Researchers may wish to consult with a librarian at the Information Desk in the Public Catalog Room in order to determine the location of an item before handing in a call slip. A copy of the call slip with an assigned number will be returned to you by the clerk.

The Subject Guide to Reference Material on Open Shelves, in a loose-leaf binder at the Public Catalog Room Information Desk, outlines the types of materials on the open shelves of the Main Reading Room and provides the classmark and location by wall section.

For additional City Directories not listed in Appendix D, check the CATNYP catalog. U.S.A. City Directories are cataloged under classmark *ZAN-G... The Information Desk in the Bill Blass Public Catalog Room has an index card file for Canadian City Directories.

The Microforms Room (Room 100) has published indexes to several newspapers on open shelf at far end of the room. There are also 24 computers in the South Hall (Room 315) and one in the Microforms Room to access newspaper and periodical indexes on the Internet and on CD-ROM (Selected Electronic Resources). Click on "Newspapers and Periodicals" to access such websites as *Historical Newspapers Online* and *Ethnic NewsWatch*. See IRMA AND PAUL MILSTEIN DIVISION OF UNITED STATES HISTORY, LOCAL HISTORY AND GENEALOGY for a brief description of these websites.

While many U.S.A. Newspapers are cataloged in CATNYP, only some Foreign Newspapers appear in this computerized catalog. Check with the Information Desk in the Bill Blass Catalog Room for additional foreign newspapers in the Library's collection. See also Appendix F for a selected list.

Each volume of the Catalog of Copyright Entries includes a surname index of copyright claimants including the first initial of the first and middle names. Microfilms (1891–1977) are in Cabinet #52 of the Microforms Room. For

1979–1982, the volumes are on microfiche. The Library also has most of the published volumes in the South Hall of the Rose Main Reading Room.

Description of Facility:

The Bill Blass Public Catalog Room (Room 315), a spacious room on the third floor, houses 34 on-line computer terminals (supported by printers) with access to CATNYP. The 800-volume book catalog, which reproduces the pre-1972 card catalog, line the shelves around the room. Reference librarians at the Information Desk can assist researchers in locating materials throughout the Research Libraries. There are 6 long tables at which the bound catalogs can be consulted. Some seats (stools) are available. Books and other materials are requested at the desk to the left of the Information Desk. Pneumatic tubes carry the call slips to the stack floors. Pick up the books requested at the Main Reading Room Delivery Desk in the South Hall (for even numbers) or North Hall (for odd numbers) when the number appears on the Indicator Board above the Delivery Desk.

In addition to the reference works on open shelves in this room, there are 88 miles of shelves (not accessible to the public) located beneath the room where staff members with the aid of a computer-controlled dumbwaiter system provide requested items within 20 to 30 minutes. Retrieving material from the stacks under Bryant Park can take up to 90 minutes.

The Rose Main Reading Room, a vast space two city-blocks long with 636 reader seats, is entered through the Public Catalog Room. The room is divided into a North Hall and a South Hall. Thirty of the forty-two tables are wired so that readers may use laptop computers to gain access to the Internet. References from these sources may be printed or, in many cases, downloaded. Twelve tables, six at each of the far ends of the North and South Halls, are not equipped for computers and are exclusively for reading.

Forty-eight computer workstations are located in the South Hall, 20 are devoted to electronic databases ("Selected Electronic Resources") which include some on the Internet, 23 provide full Internet access, including e-mail access, and 4 provide access both to the Selected Electronic Resources and the Internet (but no e-mail access). One of these four is set aside for 15-minute "Express Search" usage. See "Restrictions on Use." Both the South and North Halls have reference desks where librarians provide assistance with computerized reference and traditional resources. See the MILSTEIN DIVISION OF UNITED STATES HISTORY, LOCAL HISTORY AND GENEALOGY for a description of the genealogical resources available through "Selected Electronic Resources" computers. NOTE: Researchers who have NYPL branch library cards have remote access to some of these same resources through their home computers using the bar code number on the card. Access via the NYPL Branch Libraries' electronic resources menu on the NYPL website.

The South Hall Reading Room includes an enclosed Multimedia Center with 4 audio-visual and multimedia workstations for reviewing audio and video materials or items that are digitally formatted [classmarks *WG, *B and *U]. This enclosure has a supervised reading area for use of materials in delicate condition or that have been borrowed through Inter-Library loan.

Biographies and biographical dictionaries are located in the South Hall of the Main Reading Room along the southeast wall. (This is the wall to the left, when you enter the South Hall). Biographical dictionaries [classmark *R-AA and *R-AB] are in wall bookcases 1–16 and individual biographies [classmark *R-AN] are in wall bookcases 32–37. Indexes to periodicals, such as *The New York Times Index* and the *Personal Name Index to the "New York Times Index"* are also in the South Hall [classmark *R-*D] in the southeast front wall, bookcases 7–31. Bibliographies are in the North Hall [classmark *R-*G]. Encyclopedias [classmark *R-*A] can be found in the South Hall along the southeast front wall and Dictionaries [classmark *R-R] in the northeast front wall.

Seven self-service photocopy machines are available in the North Hall behind the Information Desk. Approval by library staff is necessary before using these machines. Staff-assisted quick copy, required for fragile materials, is available at the Copy Services window also located in the North Hall. (See below).

The building is wheelchair accessible from the 42nd Street entrance. A wheelchair accessible restroom for women is on the ground floor and for men on the third floor.

The Microforms Room (Room 100) is located on the south end of the first floor. Most City Directories, some Newspapers and the Catalog of Copyright Entries are in self-service cabinets near the entrance to the room. There are 2 computer terminals available to access CATNYP and one Selected Electronic Resources computer. This Division has 3 microfiche readers, 16 microfilm readers and 25 microfilm/microfiche reader/printers. Researchers must sign up at the desk for use of the reader/printers. (30 minute time limit.) The 2 tables in Room 100 can seat 10 people.

NOTE: Beginning in 2003, researchers wishing to access materials in the New York Public Library's Research Libraries — HUMANITIES AND SOCIAL SCIENCE S LIBRARY, NYPL FOR THE PERFORMING ARTS, SCHOMBURG CENTER FOR RESEARCH

IN BLACK CULTURE, and SCIENCE, INDUSTRY AND BUSINESS LIBRARY — will need a personalized ACCESS Card to request materials from the stack collections. Eventually, ACCESS card holders will also be able to submit electronic call slips, make advance reservations for materials or computers, and gain remote access to electronic resources at the Research Libraries. Library users can register for an ACCESS card online or in person. Patrons then submit the forms at the registration desks within each Research Library. The user's photograph, name, barcode, ID number and signature will appear on the ACCESS card, which will be issued on the spot.

Fees/Copies:

Copico debit cards can be purchased for self-service photocopying and can be used throughout the Library. Copico cards may be purchased for $1, which includes a $.70 credit for printing and photocopying. These cards may be reused by adding value to them. There is a $.20 per page fee for printing from all public workstations, with the exception of the CATNYP work stations in the <u>Bill Blass Public Catalog Room</u> and self-service photocopy workstations in the <u>North Hall</u>. Printouts from CATNYP are free in the Bill Blass Public Catalog Room. Self-service photocopies cost only $.15 per page if the Copico debit card is used in the <u>North Hall</u> and $.20 per page using cash. Copies from microfilm reader/printers are $.25 per page. NOTE: Printouts from CATNYP work stations in the Microforms Room cost $.20.

Paper copies made by staff at the Copy Services Desk cost $.25 for an 8.5" by 11" page and $.50 for 11" x 17". More than one item can be included on a page. A copy of a map 36" x any length costs $5. Scanned photocopies 8.5" X 11" are $.40 and 11"x 17" are $.65. There are additional charges for fax (per page), express or foreign mail.

Prices for photographs start at $15 for an 8" x 10" black and white print and $21 for a color print. For a black and white photographic negative 4" x 5" add $15 and for color add $25. Color prints (8" x 10") from 35mm slides are $36. Microfilm copies cost $.20 per frame (minimum charge $25) and microfiche (from NYPL master only) $12 per fiche. A complete price list is available. There are additional charges for special handling of difficult work, for Express and foreign mail and for processing and mailing microfilm orders.

Payment can be made several ways: (1) by check drawn on a U.S. bank or a U.S. branch of a foreign bank; (2) by U.S. postal or bank money order; (3) by international money order drawn on a bank with a branch in the U.S.; or (4) by VISA, MasterCard and American Express credit cards. Prepayment in full is required.

NOTE: Many of the Library's electronic resource workstations allow researchers to save results to computer disks for later viewing. Bring your own supply of formatted computer disks.

In order to make copies of materials located in other Divisions (outside the Rose Main Reading Room), inform the librarian of that Division, get a pink pass to carry the material out of the room, and take it to the Copy Services Desk. The Division's librarian will note on the pass whether the material must be returned immediately or whether it may be left at the book return window in the North Hall.

NYPL *Express* provides research services such as biographical profiles, obituaries, maps, patents, newspaper clippings, and company profiles, for a fee. Research fees for a "standard" search (within 2 weeks) cost $75 per hour (billed in 15-minute increments). Photocopy fees, toll calls and postage are extra. Document fees begin at $15 ("Standard," 3-4 business days) and include the first 10 pages. Additional pages are $.25 per page. Fees for "Next Day," "Rush," or "Express" service are higher. See the Library's website (www.nypl.org/express) for more information. NYPL *Express* can be contacted by mail, phone (212) 592-7201; fax, (212) 592-7215 or e-mail, express@nypl.org.

Restrictions on Use:

There is a check room at the 5th Avenue entrance for all personal books, bags and coats. Bags and packages must be opened for inspection by the guard when leaving the Rose Main Reading Room and when leaving the building.

To use Selected Electronic Resources, Internet-access computers and multimedia workstations in the South Hall Reading Room, researchers must sign-in (and show identification) at the South Hall Information Desk. Reservations are limited to 30 minutes and can be made for up to 2 nonconsecutive hours per day. No sign-up is required for use of Internet Express workstations (up to 15 minutes of use). If there are many users in the Microforms Room, time is limited to 30 minutes on the microfilm/microfiche reader/printers.

No more than 3 items can be requested at a time in the Bill Blass Catalog Room. No materials can be borrowed.

Only materials in good condition may be photocopied using the self-service photocopy machines.

Some materials such as paper copies of <u>Canadian City Directories</u>, <u>U.S.A. Telephone Directories</u>, <u>Foreign Telephone Directories</u> and the <u>*New York Sun* morgue</u> are off-site and must be ordered in advance. The *New York Sun* morgue is in very poor condition and librarians may deny access to some parts of the collection.

NEW YORK PUBLIC LIBRARY
DOROT JEWISH DIVISION

Facility Director: Michael Terry, Dorot Chief Librarian

Address: Fifth Avenue at 42nd Street, Room 84 ♿
New York, NY 10018-2788

(Cross Streets: 40th and 42nd Streets; 5th and 6th Avenues)

Phone: (212) 930-0601
Fax: (212) 642-0141
E-mail: freidus@nypl.org
Website: www.nypl.org/reseach/chss/jws/jewish.html

Hours of Operation:

Thursday to Saturday   10:00 am to 6:00 pm
Tuesday and Wednesday   11:00 am to 7:30 pm

Closed Sunday and legal holidays.

Closest Public Transportation, Directions and Fees/Copies:

See NEW YORK PUBLIC LIBRARY - HUMANITIES AND SOCIAL SCIENCES LIBRARY, GENERAL RESEARCH DIVISION.

Description of Resources:

The Jewish Division has one of the great collections of Judaica in the world. It was established in 1897, just two years after the formation of the Library. Today, the Division contains some 300,000 books, microfilms, manuscripts, newspapers and periodicals from all over the world. The collection includes forty 15th-century works and over 1,500 16th-century works.

Items of interest to genealogists include (NYPL classmark indicated in brackets):

1. Census

    Jews in Alsace, 1784: *Dénombrement Générale des Juifs.* [*PXP+ 80-4713]

2. Rabbinic Responsa

    These books of answers provided by rabbis to questions on halakhic matters usually make some reference to the rabbi's lineage on the first page or may have an introduction that was added posthumously providing some biographical information.

3. Newspapers

    The Library has an extensive collection of newspapers and periodicals printed in Europe and America in the last two centuries. The complete list of newspapers available in the Dorot Jewish Division by place, language, and decade is online. Examples include:

    Afrikaner Idishe Tsaytung (Johannesburg, South Africa, Yiddish), 1942–1971 [*ZAN-*P49]
    Aufbau (New York, German and, in recent years, also English), 1934– [*ZAN-*P66]
    Australian Jewish News, 1935– [*ZAN-*P50]
    The Day (New York, Yiddish), 1914–1957 [*ZY-*P2]
    The Jewish Post (Winnipeg, Canada), 1941–1980 [*ZAN-*P229]
    Freie Arbeiter Stimme [Free Voice of Labor], (New York, Yiddish) 1890–1892, 1899–1952, 1963–1977 [*ZAN-*P183]
    Havaner Lebn (Cuba, Yiddish), 1932–1958 [*ZAN-*P175]
    Idishe Tsaytung: El Diario Israelita (Buenos Aires, Argentina, Yiddish), 1923–1973 [*ZY-*P11]
    Jewish Standard (Toronto, Canada), 1930–1977 [*ZAN-P578]
    Jewish Chronicle (London, England), 1841– [*ZAN-*P55]
    Jewish Daily Forward (New York, Yiddish), 1897 to present (complete collection). [*ZAN-*P142]
    Jewish Echo (Scotland, English), 1946–1955 [*ZAN-*P132]; 1956– [*PBE+]
    Juedische Presse (Berlin, German), 1872–1923 [*ZAN-P735]
    Wiener Morgenzeitung (Vienna, Austria, German), 1921–1926 [*ZAN-*P401]

4. Marriage Records

20 Italian Ketubot from the 17th and 18th centuries.

Verdooner, Dave and Harmen Snal. *Trouwen in Mokum: Jewish marriages in Amsterdam, 1598–1811.* 2 vols. Index of 15,238 intended Jewish marriages in Amsterdam. (Dutch and English).'s-Gravenhage, [1991]. [*PWO 92-4393]

5. Holocaust Resources

One of the largest collections of yizkor books in New York City (see Appendix B and Electronic Resources). See also,

Yad Vashem Archives of the Destruction: A Photographic Record of the Holocaust. [microfiche; *XMH-2067]

6. Community History

Books on Jewish communities around the world.

7. Gravestone Inscriptions

United States. De Sola Pool, David. *Portraits Etched in Stone: Early Jewish Settlers 1682–1831.* New York, 1951. [*PXY (Pool, D. De Sola)]

Austria. Wachstein, Bernhard. *Die inschriften des alten Judenfriedhofes in Wien...* 2 vols. Vol. 1, 1540–1670; vol. 2, 1696–1783. Vienna, 1912–1917. [*PXT+ (Wachstein, B...)]

Austria. Reises, Johannes. *Jungeren juedischen Friedhofes in Eisenstadt* [Cemetery in Eisenstadt, Austria]. Eisenstadt, 1995. [*PXT (Eisenstadt) 95-2697]

Czech Republic. Hock, Simon. *Mishpahat k.k. Prag.* Pressburg, 1892. [*ZP-822 no. 3]

Germany. Levy, Prof. Dr. M.A. *Juedische Grabsteine aus Aden.* [Leipzig, 1867]. [*ZP-*PBM p.v. 483, no. 7)] [*PWN 76-1288]

Germany. Hammer, Klaus. *Historische Friedhofe & Grabmaler in Berlin.* Includes photos of historic cemeteries and tombstones. Berlin, [1994]. [JFE 95-12730]

Germany. Melcher, Peter. *Weissensee: ein Friedhof als Spiegelbild judischer Geschichte in Berlin.* Berlin [1986]. [DS135 G4 B4677 1986]

Germany. Kober, Adolf. *Jewish Monuments of the Middle Ages in Germany* [110 tombstone inscriptions from Speyer, Cologne, Nuremberg and Worms, 1085–c.1428]. New York, 1944–1945. [*PXS (Kober, A....)]

Greece. Molho, Michael. *Matsevot bet ha-almin shel Yehude Salonik* [Tombstones in Thessalonike]. Tel Aviv, 1974. [*PWN 78-5700]

Israel. Klein, Samuel. *Juedisch-Palastinisches Corpus Inscriptionum* [Tombstones in Palestine]. Reprint of 1920 editon. Hildesheim, 1971. [*PWN 72-1014]

Netherlands. Mulder, Samuel Israel. *Iets over de begraafplaatsen der Nederlandsch-Israëlitische gemeente to Amsterdam.* Amsterdam, 1851. [*XMH-167]

Netherlands. Vega, L. Alvares. *Het Beth Haim van Ouderkerk: beelden van een Portugees-Joodse begraafplaats* [Beth Haim of Ouderkerk aan de Amstel: images of a Portuguese Jewish cemetery in Holland]. Assen, 1975. [*PWN 76-1228]

Poland. Jagielski, Jan. *Przewodnik po Cmentarzu zydoskim w Warszawie przy ul. Okopowej 49/51* [Guide to the Warsaw Jewish cemetery, 49/51 Okopowej Street]. 2 vols. Warsaw, 1995. [*PXV (Warsaw) 01-4001]

Poland. Yaari-Wald, Benjamin. *Bet ha'almin ha-Yehudi be-Tomashov-Mazovyetski* [Jewish Cemetery Tomaszow Mazowieki]. [Israel], 1996. [*PXV (Tomaszow Mazowieki) 98-64)]

Slovakia. Weiss, Izak. *Sefer Avne bet ha-yotser:...matsevat avne kodesh ve-toldot hakhme Yisrael...de-ir Presburg* [Tombstones in Bratislava]. Jerusalem, [1970]. [*PWN 75-759]

Sweden. Judiska Litteratursamfundet. *Gamla judiska gravplatser i Stockholm.* Tombstone inscriptions copied and translated by Moses Fried. Stockholm, 1927. [*PBV (Judiska)(Gamlas...)]

8. Biographies and Genealogies

An extensive collection of biographical texts and genealogies such as:

Azulai, Hayyim Joseph D. *Shem ha-gedolim ha-shalem* [An encyclopedia of 1300 rabbis in the 18th century]. 3 vols. Reprint of 1905 edition. Brooklyn, 1958. [*PWR (Azulai, H...)]

Bader, Gershom. *Medinah ve-hakhamehah* [Biographies of leading Jews in Galicia]. New York, [1934]. [*PWR (Bader, G...)]

Balaban, Meir. *Di yidn-shtot Lublin* [The Jews of Lublin]. Buenos Aires, 1947. [*ZP-1097 no. 5]

Bresler, Wolf and Samuel Glasserman Leksikon fun Idishe gezelshaftlekhe tuer in Argentine. Buenos Aires, 1941–, vol 1. (Spanish and Yiddish). Includes Hebrew name, parents names, year and place of birth, year of immigration. [*PXX 88-1225]

Chones, Shimon. *Toldot ha-poskim: leksikon li-geone u-gedole Yisrael...* [Rabbinic authorities and their works]. Warsaw, 1929. [*PWR (Chones, S.M...)]

Cohen, Israel. *Vilna.* Philadelphia, 1943. [*PXV (Cohen, I. Vilna)]

Dembitzer, Chaim. *Sefer Kelilat yofi.* Includes Rabbis of Poland, Lithuania and Ukraine (Lviv). Krakow, [1888]. [*PWR 90-5487]

Eisenstadt, Benzion. *Dor rabanav ve-sofrav* [Generations of Rabbis and Authors]. Warsaw, [1895–1905]. [*ZP-674]

Eisenstadt, Benzion. *Hakhme Yisrael be-Amerikah* [Israel's Scholars in America]. New York, 1903. [*PWR]

Federbusch, Simon. *Hokhmat Yisrael be-ma'arav Eropah* [Science of Judaism in Western Europe]. 3 vols. Jerusalem, [1958–1965]. [*PWR (Federbusch, S...)]

Freedman, Chaim. *Eliyahu's branches: the descendents of the Vilna Gaon.* Teaneck, 1997. [*PWO (Elijah...)]

Frumkin, Arieh L. *Sefer Toldot hakhme Yerushalayim: mi-shenat 5250 la-yetsirah ad 5630 la-yetsirah.* 2 vols. Jerusalem, [1927–1930]. Originally published in Vilna, 1874. [*PWR (Frumkin, A....)]

Ghirondi, Mordechai and Ch. Nepi. *Toldot gedole Yisrael u-geone Italyah* [History of the Scholars of Israel and the Sages of Italy] and *Zekher tsadikim le-verakhah.* Trieste, 1853. [*PWR (Ghirondi, M...)]

Halachmi, David. *Hakhme Yisrael: entsiklopedyah li-gedole Yisrael ba-dorot ha-aharonim.* [Biographies from the 13th to 20th century]. Tel Aviv, [1957]. [*PWR (Ha-Lahmi, D...)]

Halperin, Raphael. *Toledot am Yisrael mi-beriat ha-olam ve-ad yameinu: Atlas ets hayim* [Encyclopedia of rabbis and Jewish scholars]. 14 vols. Tel Aviv, 1978–. [*PWO-90-2183]

Horodetzky, Samuel. *Keren Shlomo* [Solomon Luria]. Drohobycz, 1896. [*PWZ]

Kohen, Yosef Yitshak. *Hakhme Transilvanyah* [Sages of Transylvania]. Jerusalem, [1988/1989]. [*PXM+ 6301]

Lifschitz, Aryeh L. *Avot atarah le-banim.* Includes Katzenellenbogen, Wahl, Lifschutz and related families. Warsaw, [1927]. [*PWZ (Wohl)(Lifshitz, A.J.L...)]

Rosenstein, Neil. *Rabbi Elijah (1720–1797), the Gaon of Vilna and his cousinhood.* Elizabeth, NJ, 1997. [*PWO+ Elijah...)]

Schwartz, Zigmund. *Shem ha-gedolim li-gedole Hungaryah.* Encyclopedia of c. 1,700 Hungarian rabbis and authors. Brooklyn, [1958]. [*PWR (Schwartz, S. Shem...]

Sherman, Moshe D. *Orthodox Judaism in America: A Biographical Dictionary and Sourcebook.* Westport, CT, 1996. [*PWR 96-2714]

Stern, Abraham. *Sefer melitse esh.* Includes c. 2000 medieval and modern rabbis and scholars. Jerusalem, [1974]. [*PWR 77-3833]

Unger, Menashe. *Admorim she-nispu ba-Shoah* [Biographies of rabbis who perished in the Holocaust]. Jerusalem, 1969. (Hebrew) [*PWR]. Also in Yiddish as *Seyfer Kdoyshim.* New York, 1967. [*PWR (Unger, M...)]

Walden, Aaron. *Sefer Shem ha-gedolim he-hadash* [An encyclopedia of rabbis in the 19th centuries]. Warsaw, 1864. [*PWR (Walden, A. Shem...]

Wininger, Salomon. *Grosse juedische national-biographie* [An international biographical dictionary of Jews from the Middle Ages to the 20th century]. Czernowitz, [1925–1936]. [*PWR (Wininger, S...)]

For a list of Rabbinic biographical dictionaries, many of which are in the collection of the Jewish Division, see *Toledot,* Vol. 4, No. 3, pp. 3–15, "Jewish Genealogical Materials in the Library of Congress" by Ellen Murphy; or David Einsiedler, "Rabbinic Genealogy Sources: A Bibliography by Type," printed for Jewish Genealogical Society Seminars, Israel and Los Angeles. See also CENTER FOR JEWISH HISTORY, YIVO INSTITUTE FOR JEWISH RESEARCH.

9. Name Indexes

Deich, Genrikh Markovich. *A List of Religious Personnel in Jewish Houses of Worship in Russian Provinces (1853–1855).* S.l., 1992. [*PXW 93-1103]

Gorr, Shmuel, joint venture with Gary Mokotoff. *Name Changes in the Palestine Gazette, 1921–1948.* Lists c. 27,000 Jews whose name changes were published in the *Palestine Gazette.* 1990. [*XMH-3031]

Guggenheimer, Heinrich W. and Eva H. Guggenheimer. *Jewish Family Names and Their Origins: An Etymological Dictionary.* Hoboken, 1992. [*P-Desk 92-4399]

Hebrew Free Loan Society of New York. List of Members and Patrons of the Hebrew Gemilath Chassodim Association. New York, 1903. [*ZP-1408]

Kaganoff, Benzion. *A Dictionary of Jewish Names and their History.* New York, 1977. [*P-*PWP 79-67]

Singerman, Robert. *Jewish and Hebrew Onomastics: A Bibliography.* New York, 1977. [*PCL 77-3586]

Snel, Harmen and Jits von Straten, *Joodse voornamen in Amsterdem: een inventarisatie van Asjkenazische en bijbehorende burgerlijke voornamen tussen 1669 en 1850* [Jewish first names in Amsterdam: an inventory of Ashkenazie and matching civil first names between 1669 and 1850]. Meppel, [1996]. [*PXR 98-1659]

Zubatsky, David S. and Irwin M. Berent. *Source Book for Jewish Genealogies and Family Histories.* Teaneck, 1996. [*PWO 96-3268]

See also, *DOROT: The Journal of the Jewish Genealogical Society*, Winter 1997-98, p. 10–11 for additional titles with name lists in the Dorot Jewish Division.

10. <u>Military</u>

Ben Hirsh, J. *Jewish General Officers: A Biographical Dictionary.* Includes biographies of 120 officers from English speaking countries and Israel. [Melbourne, 1967.] [*PWR (Hirsh, J.B.)]

Henry, Morris. *We Will Remember Them: A Record of the Jews who died in the Armed Forces of the Crown, 1939–1945.* London, 1989. [*PXQ 90-211]

Kaufman, Isidore. *American Jews in World War II: The Story of 550,000 Fighters for Freedom.* Lists Jewish soldiers who died in their country's service or who received awards/recognition of valor. 2 vols. New York, 1947. [*PXY]

Reichsbund Juedischer Frontsoldaten, *Die juedischen Gefallenen des deutschen Heeres, der deutschen Marine und der deutschen Schutztruppen, 1914–1918* (microfilm). [Berlin], 1932–1933. [*ZP 875 no. 5 and no. 6]

• *Unsere gefallenen Kameraden: Gedenkbuch fuer die im Weltkrieg gefallenen Muenchener Juden.* Includes photograph and full-page biography of each fallen soldier. Munich, 1929. [*ZP-875 no. 4]

Vervoort, Andre. *Les Juifs et la guerre.* Paris, 1915–1917. [*ZP-845 no. 4-5]

Young, Mel. *Where They Lie: the story of the Jewish soldiers of the North and South whose deaths — killed, mortally wounded, or died of disease or other causes — occurred during the Civil War, 1861–1865: someone should say Kaddish.* Lanham, MD, [1991]. [*PXY 91-2090]

11. <u>American Jewish Committee Oral History Library</u>:

Tapes and transcripts of 1,841 oral histories documenting the American-Jewish experience in the 20th century. The interviews are divided into two broad categories: general biography, consisting of the memoirs of prominent American Jews in a variety of fields, and special collections arranged by theme. While much of the material centers on New York, the regional collection contains interviews with Jewish residents of communities throughout the U.S.A. Special interview projects were conducted with Soviet emigres and Holocaust survivors. The collection is described and indexed in a 4-volume, *Catalogue of Memoirs of the William E. Wiener Oral History Library,* New York, 1978–1993. [*PAL 79-4400]. A name index is available on CATNYP arranged by first name and then surname.

12. <u>Guides to Archives/Libraries</u>:

Banchik, Nadezhda and Vasilii Shchedrin, et al. *Dokumentalnye istochniki po istorii evreev v arkhivakh SNG: putevoditel.* [Documentary sources on the history of Jews in archives of the commonwealth of Independent States (former Soviet republics).] Moscow, 1994–. [*PXW 97-561, Ch. 1]

Budziarek, Marek. *Judaica lodzkie: w zbiorach muzealnych i zasobach archiwalnych: praca zbiorowa.* [Judaica from Lodz: in museum collections and archives.] Lodz, 1994. [*PXV (Lodz) 96-824]

Eliashevich, D. A. *Dokumentalnye materialy po istorii evreev v arkhivakh SNG i stran Baltii: predvaritelnyi spisok arkhivnykh fondov* [Documentary sources on Jewish history in the archives of the federation of independent states and countries of the Baltic: A preliminary list of archival collections]. St. Petersburg, 1994. [*PAL 98-334]

Kazmierczyk, Adam. *Materialy zrodlowe do dziejow Zydow w ksiegach grodzkich dawnego wojewodztwa krakowskiego z lat 1674–1696.* [Source materials for the history of Jews in town books of Krakow voivodship from 1674–1696. Krakow, 1995–. [*PXV (Cracow) 95-3368 T.1]

Pilarczyk, Krzysztof. *Judaika polskie z XVI–XVIII wieku: materialy do bibliografii* [Polish Judaica from the 17th–18th centuries: materials and bibliography]. Krakow, 1995–. [*PAO 96-1570 Cz. 1]

Weiner, Miriam, *Jewish Roots in Poland: Pages from The Past and Archival Inventories.* New York, 1997. Includes detailed inventories of Jewish vital record and other genealogical holdings of local archives in Poland. [*P-Desk 98-1902]. NOTE: See also Miriam Weiner's website, www.rtrfoundation.org.

Weiner, Miriam, *Jewish Roots in Ukraine and Moldova: Pages from the Past and Archival Inventories.* New York, 1999. [*P-Desk 99-10116]

13. <u>Electronic Resources and CD-ROM:</u>

Bar-Ilan's Judaic Library, includes full text of halachic responsa.

Bibliography of the Hebrew Book, 1473–1960

Ethnic NewsWatch. For a list of Jewish newspaper titles available here, see the Jewish Division's website.

Forward, 2000- (name and subject index online)

Index to Jewish Periodicals: 1988–1999. This is an author/title index to 138 English language journals, including *Avotaynu.* A search can be made by part of the title (subject) as well.

Jerusalem Post, 1988–1994

Jerusalem Report, 1990–1995

Jewish Week, 1993- (name and subject index online)

Yizkor (Holocaust Memorial) Books in the Dorot Jewish Division's collection. NOTE: The Library plans to digitize the entire collection and put these books online.

Finding Aids:

See NEW YORK PUBLIC LIBRARY - HUMANITIES AND SOCIAL SCIENCES LIBRARY, GENERAL RESEARCH DIVISION for a detailed description of CATNYP (computer catalog) and book catalogs. For material of Jewish interest in any language and publications in Hebrew characters, cataloged before 1972, the bound volumes, *The NYPL: Jewish Collection Catalog* should be consulted. Books with Hebrew/Yiddish titles are *not* included in the book catalogs, 1981–1985 (black books).

All holdings, including Hebrew/Yiddish books cataloged since 1972 are included in CATNYP. There are four CATNYP terminals in this Division. Consult the librarian for Hebrew/Yiddish books not found in these catalogs. Librarians have access to a computer terminal which updates these catalogs, and to a Hebrew/Yiddish "in-process" file.

To find information about a particular community, see "Jews in ..." in the published catalog, or "Jews, (country), (city)" in the CATNYP catalog. To find books on gravestone inscriptions, see "Epitaphs" or "Epitaphs Jews" in each catalog.

All classmarks (call numbers) starting with [*P] are located in the Jewish Division. Classmark groupings of interest to genealogists include: Epitaphs [*PWN], Genealogy [*PWO], Biographical Material [*PWP], Collective Biographies [*PWR] and Individual Biographies [*PWZ]. Information about Jewish Communities are grouped in classmarks by country: Orient [*PXL], Israel [*PXLB], Italy [*PXN], Spain/Portugal [*PXO], France [*PXP], Great Britain [*PXQ], Germany [*PXS], Austria-Hungary [*PXT], Poland [*PXV], Russia [*PXW], America [*PXX] and U.S. and Canada [*PXY]. These call numbers are not unique and must always be used together with the title and author of the book.

Check the Catalog table beside the computer catalogs for loose-leaf binders listing all Jewish newspapers on microfilm and current newspapers in the Division's collection. For earlier newspapers only available in paper copy, check the bound catalogs.

Description of Facility:

The Jewish Division is located in Room 84 on the ground floor to the right of the entrance on 42nd Street (between 5th and 6th Avenues). The room can seat 40 researchers. Outlets are available for computer plug-in. Seven microfilm readers and one reader/printer are available. There are 1-2 librarians available to provide assistance and one paging assistant. Indicate your seat number on the call slip and the page will bring materials directly to your table.

Reference books (encyclopedias, biographical dictionaries, etc.) are on open shelves around the room. All other books are in closed stacks but can be obtained immediately. See "Restrictions on Use."

Restrictions on Use:

Researchers are requested to sign the registration book at the desk and to leave all bags in the cloakroom on the first floor. Laptop computers may be brought in but laptop carrying cases must be left in the cloakroom.

No more than five items can be requested at a time. No materials can be borrowed.

Picture identification is required to use some materials such as rare books and CD-ROMs. NOTE: See NEW YORK PUBLIC LIBRARY - HUMANITIES AND SOCIAL SCIENCES LIBRARY, GENERAL RESEARCH DIVISION, "Description of Facility" for photo ACCESS card to be required of <u>all</u> patrons.

NEW YORK PUBLIC LIBRARY
IRMA AND PAUL MILSTEIN DIVISION OF UNITED STATES HISTORY, LOCAL HISTORY AND GENEALOGY

Facility Director: Ruth Carr, Chief

Address: Fifth Avenue at 42nd Street, Rooms 119 and 121   &
New York, NY 10018-2788

(Cross Streets: 40th and 42nd Streets; 5th and 6th Avenues)

Phone: (212) 930-0828
Fax: none
E-mail: histref@nypl.org (complete online E-mail Reference Service form)
Website: www.nypl.org/research/chss/lhg/genea.html

Hours of Operation:

Thursday to Saturday   10:00 am to 6:00 pm
Tuesday & Wednesday   11:00 am to 7:30 pm

Closed Sunday, Monday and legal holidays.

Closest Public Transportation, Directions and Fees/Copies:

See NEW YORK PUBLIC LIBRARY - HUMANITIES AND SOCIAL SCIENCES LIBRARY, GENERAL RESEARCH DIVISION.

Description of Resources:

The Genealogy Division has an extensive collection of genealogical periodicals, newsletters, family histories, published genealogies, and county, town and village vital records and histories. Just a sample appear below. (NOTE: Book classmarks are included if *not* on open shelf). Microform (film or fiche) located in the Division microforms reading room (Room 119) or in the stacks (accessible through Room 119) are included here. See also NEW YORK PUBLIC LIBRARY, GENERAL RESEARCH DIVISION AND MICROFORMS ROOM (Room 100) for additional microform materials:

1. U.S. Census (self-service microfilm in Room 119)

   Connecticut: 1790–1880, 1910
   New York State, 1790–1880, 1900, 1910, 1920, 1930
   New Jersey, 1830–1880, 1910
   Puerto Rico: 1910, 1920, 1930

   Mortality schedules, 1850–1880, for New York and New Jersey
   Veterans and Widows of Union Veterans of the Civil War, 1890, all states (indexes for most).

   In addition to the above, the Division has a scattering of U.S. Census for various years and localities in 33 other states and District of Columbia. See NATIONAL ARCHIVES-NORTHEAST REGION for the complete collection of U.S. Census (every state), 1790 to 1930. See also NEW YORK PUBLIC LIBRARY - SCHOMBURG CENTER for U.S. Census of other states. SCHOMBERG has an almost complete collection of the U.S. Census through 1900 as well as the fragmentary 1890 and some states for 1910 and 1920.

2. New York State Census (self-service microfilm in Room 119)

   Bronx County: 1915, 1925
   Kings County (Brooklyn): 1855, 1865, 1875, 1892, 1905, 1915, 1925
   New York County (Manhattan: 1855 and 1905 (includes the Bronx), 1915, 1925. There is a card index for street
       addresses, 1905, 1915, 1925
   Queens County: 1915, 1925
   Richmond County (Staten Island): 1855, 1865, 1875, 1915, 1925
   Nassau County: 1915, 1925
   Suffolk County: 1855, 1915, 1925
   Westchester County: 1905, 1915, 1925

   1855 Census is also available here for 42 counties (including those noted above).

3. <u>New York City Police Census</u> (self-service microfilm in Room 119)

   1890 - Manhattan and western Bronx

4. <u>New Jersey State Census</u> (self-service in Room 119)

   The following years are available here:

   1855 (13 counties), 1865 (14 counties), 1875 (Sussex County only), 1885, 1895, 1905, 1915 (all 21 counties)

5. <u>Canadian Census</u> (microfilm)

   1871 [*ZI-353]

6. <u>City Directories</u> - New York City (microfilm/microfiche):

   NYC (generally Manhattan and parts of the Bronx), 1786–1933/34
   Brooklyn, 1822–1826, 1829–1910, 1912/13, 1933/34
   Queens, 1898, 1902, 1904, 1906–1912, 1933/34
   Richmond (Staten Island), 1882/83, 1884, 1888–1893/4, 1895/6, 1897/98, 1898–1900, 1903, 1906, 1933/4

   NOTE: There are two reverse NYC (Manhattan) City Directories arranged by street addresses included in the above City Directories: 1812 (Reel 6) and 1851 (Reel 14).

   The Division has an extensive collection of pre-1870 U.S. City Directories in paper copy. Many have already been microfilmed and are available in self-service cabinets in the MICROFORMS ROOM (Room 100). Check Appendix D. See the MICROFORMS ROOM also for earlier Brooklyn City Directories (1796, 1802/3, 1812/13), a duplicate set of some of the above and some foreign City Directories. See the GENERAL RESEARCH DIVISION for paper copies of Canadian City Directories.

7. <u>New York City Vital Records</u>

   <u>Records</u> (self service microfilm in Room 119):

   Deaths (Manhattan only), 1798–1865

   <u>Indexes</u>: The Division has the NYC Health Department indexes spanning the following years in either bound indexes, microfilm or microfiche:

Births	August 1888 to 1982
Deaths - All Boroughs	August 1888-1967, 1969-1982
Manhattan	1868–1890
Brooklyn	1848–1898
Staten Island	1847–1897
Marriages (grooms)	August 1888 to 1937
Marriages (brides):	
Manhattan	1869–1937
Queen	1905–1937
Bronx	1898–1937
Staten Island	1898–1937

   Brooklyn, Queens and Staten Island (Richmond) are not included until 1898 in birth and marriage indexes. Beginning in 1937 all boroughs of NYC are merged in one alphabetical listing. Prior to that year, separate listings (or volumes) were made for each borough.

   Birth indexes, 1898–1909 (microfiche), are arranged according to the NYC Health Department Soundex system. Birth indexes on microfilm are arranged alphabetically. The Soundex system was used again from 1943 to 1945 in both microfiche and paper copies of the birth indexes. See Appendix A for an explanation of this system.

   Marriage indexes for grooms are microfilms of the published NYC Health Department indexes. Marriages indexes for brides are microfilms of the Health Department's unpublished cards indexes.

   See also NEW YORK GENEALOGICAL AND BIOGRAPHICAL SOCIETY and NEW YORK CITY DEPARTMENT OF RECORDS AND INFORMATION SERVICES, MUNICIPAL ARCHIVES. The MUNICIPAL ARCHIVES has microfilm copies of Health Department vital records and indexes for births to 1909, deaths to 1948 and marriages to 1937; and CITY CLERK'S OFFICE marriage records, 1908-1929, and indexes, 1908-1951. For birth and death indexes 1983 to the present, see the NEW YORK CITY DEPARTMENT OF HEALTH AND MENTAL HYGIENE. For marriage indexes 1952 to the present, see the CITY CLERK'S OFFICE.

8. Vital Records Indexes - Other States (microfiche)

California:
   Deaths, 1940–1994 [*XMG-1850]
   Marriages (Bride Index), 1960–1986 [*XMG-1851]
   Marriages (Groom Index), 1960–1986 [*XMG-1852]

Florida:
   Deaths, 1877–1999 [*XLG-41+]
   Marriages, 1928–1999 [*XLG-42+]
   Divorce, 1927–1999 [*XLG-43+]

See also *RootsWeb* website for death indexes: California, 1940–1997; Kentucky, 1911–2000; Maine, 1960–1997 and Texas, 1964–1998. Web address for California ("ca") is: http://userdb.rootsweb.com/ca/death/search.cgi.

9. Marriage Announcements

Index to Marriages and Deaths in the New York Herald, 1835–1855, by James P. Maher. 1987.
In Remembrance: Abstracts of Marriage & Death Notices: Brooklyn Daily Eagle Newspaper, compiled by Maggie
   Coletta, 1999–. Vol. 1, 1881; vol. 2, 1882.
Marriages Taken from the Brooklyn Eagle (Index), October 27, 1841 to December 31, 1880, comp. by G. A. Barber.
New York Evening Post New York City Marriages (Index), November 16, 1801 to December 31, 1883 (Division has
   vols 1–23), compiled and edited by Gertrude A. Barber.
New York Marriage Bonds 1753–1783, by Dr. Kenneth Scott. 1972. [APRN 78-3023]
*Names of persons for whom Marriage Licenses were issued by the secretary of the province of New York previous
   to 1784,* reprint. Baltimore, MD, 1968.
10,000 Vital Records of Central New York, 1813–1850, by Fred Q. Bowman. 1986. [APR NYS 86-2821]
10,000 Vital Records of Eastern New York, 1777–1834, by Fred Q. Bowman. 1987. [APR NYS 87-1513]
10,000 Vital Records of Western New York, 1809–1850, by Fred Q. Bowman. 1986. [APR NYS85-1641]

NOTE: The three Bowman books index marriage and death announcements in 34 newspapers of 23 upstate New York communities (not NYC). Western New York is defined as all counties west of Geneva; Central New York includes counties between Geneva and Utica; and Eastern New York includes the remainder of the upstate area.

10. Obituaries

New York Evening Post, New York City, Deaths (Index), November 6, 1801 to December 31, 1890, by Gertrude A.
   Barber. 54 vols. 1933–1947.
Deaths Taken from the Brooklyn Eagle (Index), October 27, 1841 to December 31, 1880, by Gertrude A. Barber.
   27 vols. 1936–1966.
The New York Times Obituaries Index: 1858–1978. 2 vols. (See also, *Personal Name Index to the New York Times
   Index* for obituaries not found in this 2-volume set.)
Boston Evening Transcript. *The Index to Obituaries,* 1875–1899, 1900–1930 [APK+]
New York Tribune. *Obituaries 1875–1897* (At the Information Desk)
Deaths Reported by the Long Islander, 1878–1890, by D. Roberts, 1998. [APR (Long Island, NY (99-7243)]

See also, *Obituaries: A Guide to Sources*, by Betty M. Jarboe, Boston, 1989 for additional titles which may be in the Division's collection.

11. Cemeteries

The Division has an extensive collection of books about cemeteries in New York and elsewhere including:

Cemeteries of the U.S: A Guide to Contact Information for U.S. Cemeteries and their Records. Detroit, 1994.
   [*P-USLHG APA 94-606]
Fairchild Cemetery Manual: A Reliable Guide to the Cemeteries of Greater New York and Vicinity, by Fairchild
   Sons. Brooklyn, 1910. [*ZI-266]
The Graveyard Shift: A Family Historian's Guide to New York City Cemeteries, by Carolee Inskeep. Orem, Utah,
   2000. [*R-USLHG APA 00-4676]
United States Cemetery Address Book. Vallejo, CA, 1994/95. Includes all States, more than 25,000 cemeteries,
   addresses and locations. [*R-USLHG APA 94-1154]
*Where They're Buried: A Directory Containing More than 20,000 names of Notable Persons Buried in American
   Cemeteries...,* by Thomas E. Spencer. Baltimore, [1998]. [APK 99-9297]

Hillsborough County, Florida Cemeteries, 1840–1985, produced by the Florida Genealogical Society. 8 vols. Tampa, FL, [1986]. [APR (Hillsborough Co, FL) 86-3056]. Includes also Jewish cemeteries serving Tampa.

Jewish Cemeteries of Hartford, Connecticut: The Cohen/Goldfarb Collection by Edward A. Cohen and Lewis Goldfarb. Bowie, MD, 1995. [APR (Hartford, Conn) 96-5548]

Jewish Cemeteries of the Delmarva Peninsula: A Burial Index for Delaware & Maryland's Eastern Shore, by Julian H. Preisler. Westminister, MD, 1995. [APR (Middle Atlantic States) 96-5562]

12. Wills and Administrations - Abstracts and Indexes

Manhattan:

New-York Historical Society. *Abstracts of Wills on file in the Surrogate's Office, City of New York, 1665–1800.* 17 vols. and index. See NEW YORK GENEALOGICAL AND BIOGRAPHICAL SOCIETY for these volumes on CD-ROM.

Sawyer, Ray C. and Gertrude A. Barber. *Abstracts of Wills for New York County, 1801–1856.* 20 vols.

Sawyer, Ray C. *Index of Wills for NY County, New York, from 1851–1875 inclusive.* NY. 1950–51. 3 vols. [APRN]

Barber, Gertrude. *Index of the Letters of Administration filed in NY County from 1743–1875.* NY, 1950–51. [APRN]

Hershkowitz, Leo. *Wills of Early New York Jews, 1704–1799.* 1967 [APRN (Hershkowitz...)]

Brooklyn:

Thomas, Milton H. and C. Shepard. *Index to the Wills, Administrations, Guardianships of Kings County, NY, 1650–1850.* Washington, DC, 1926. [APR (Kings County)]

Barber, G.A. *Index of Wills probated in Kings County, NY Jan.1, 1850–Dec.31, 1890.* 3 vols. (typescript, 1949) [APR (Kings County)]

Queens:

Surrogate's Court Records in the Office of the County Clerk, Jamaica, Long Island, NY - 1680–1781. Wills and administrations, guardians, and inventories. Brooklyn, 1918. [APR (Queens County)]

Queens County, NY Surrogate Records at Jamaica, NY, 1787–1835. Brooklyn, 1905–1918. [APR (Queens County)]

Staten Island:

Hix, Charlotte M. *Staten Island Wills and Letters of Administration: Richmond County, New York, 1670–1800, as found in the Surrogate's Court, New York County, New York and abstracted by the New York Historical Society, 1892–1908, and Staten Island references found in the New Jersey colonial documents.* Bowie, MD, 1993. [APR (Richmond Col., NY.) 93-12553]

See NEW YORK GENEALOGICAL AND BIOGRAPHICAL SOCIETY for additional Brooklyn, Queens and Staten Island abstracts not in the New York Public Library collection.

13. Naturalization Records (self-service microfilm in Room 119)

Index (Soundex) to naturalization petitions filed in federal, state and local courts in New York City, 1792–1906. NOTE: Also known as the "WPA Index."

Index (alphabetical) to petitions for naturalization filed in the U.S. District Court for the Eastern District of New York, 1865-1957. [NOTE: Eastern District covered Brooklyn, Queens, Nassau, Suffolk Counties.]

Queens County naturalization petitions, 1794–1906; index to petitions, 1794-1941; and Queens County declarations of intention, 1906–1926 (index included in each volume).

Bronx County, index to naturalization petitions, 1914-1932; and index to declarations, 1914-1952.

See also, *Guide to Naturalization Records of the United States*, by Christina K. Schaefer, Baltimore, MD, 1997. NOTE: Records of the U.S. District Court, Eastern District of New York can be found at the NATIONAL ARCHIVES - NORTHEAST REGION. For Queens County naturalization records, see COUNTY CLERK'S OFFICE, QUEENS; and Bronx County naturalization records, see COUNTY CLERK'S OFFICE, BRONX

14. Passport Applications (self-service microfilm in Room 119). NOTE: Both NYPL callmarks (*ZI) and NATIONAL ARCHIVES film numbers (starting with "M" or "T") are included below for the convenience of researchers.

Registers and indexes for Passport Applications, 1810–1817, 1830–1831, 1834–1906. [*ZI-676; M1371] include:
Index to Emergency Passport applications (issued abroad), 1874–1906 [rolls 10 and 11]
Index to Special Passport Applications, 1829–1894 [roll 12]
Index to passport applications issued by the New York Passport Office, August 1861–February 1862, and other registers of miscellaneous special passports, 1835–1869. [roll 13]

Index to Passport Applications, 1850–1852, 1860–1880, 1881, 1906–1923 [*ZI-795; M-1848]. Includes also,
   Index to Passport Extensions, 1917–1920 [rolls 53–57]
   Index to Passport Extensions Issued Abroad, 1906–1918 [rolls 57–59]
   Index to Consular Registrations, 1907–1921 [rolls 59–61]
   Index to registration certificates — widows, divorced women and minors, 1907–1917. [roll 61]

15. Passenger Records and Indexes (self-service microfilm in Room 119)

Port of New York:
Passenger lists of vessels arriving at New York harbor from 1820 to 1910. These lists are arranged in order of arrival. [*ZI-131; M237, T715 (to roll #1615)]
Indexes: 1820–1846 [*ZI-80; M261]; June 16, 1897 to June 30, 1902 [*ZI-333; T519]; and July 1902 to December 1943 [*ZI-333A; T621]. See published indexes (below) for the 1846 to June 15, 1897 period.
Holland-America Line passenger lists and indexes, 1900–1940. [fiche, *XMG-1755]

Canadian Border Crossing: Soundex index to Canadian border entries through St. Albans, VT District, January, 1895–June 30, 1924. [*ZI-637; M1461]

Port of Baltimore, MD: Passenger lists, September 20, 1820 – March 30, 1837 [*ZI-781; M255, roll #1 only]

Port of Boston, MA: Passenger list index, 1902–1906 [*ZI-781; T521], 1906–1920 [*ZI-782; T617]

Miscellaneous Ports on the Atlantic and Gulf Coasts and the Great Lakes: Passenger lists, 1820–1873 for vessels arriving at 63 ports on the Atlantic and Gulf Coasts, and two ports on the Great Lakes. [*ZI-322; M575] See NATIONAL ARCHIVES AND RECORDS ADMINISTRATION, NORTHEAST REGION for a list of the ports included.

Published indexes (in Room 121) include: (Classmark provided if *not* on open shelf):

Czech Immigration Passenger Lists, by Leo Baca. 9 vols. Halletsville, TX, 1983–. Includes select lists of arrivals at the ports of Galveston (1848–1861, 1865–1871, 1880–1886, 1896–1914), New Orleans (1848-1899), New York (1847–1896) and Baltimore (1834–1899).
Dutch Immigrants in United States Ship Passenger Manifest, 1820–1880: An alphabetical listing by household heads and independent persons, compiled by Robert P. Swierenga. 2 vols. Wilmington, DE, 1983.
The Famine Immigrants: Lists of Irish Immigrants Arriving at the Port of New York, 1846–1851, edited by Ira A. Glazier. 7 vols. Baltimore, MD, 1983.
German Immigrants: Lists of Passengers Bound from Bremen to New York, compiled by Gary J. Zimmerman and Marion Wolfert. Baltimore, 1985–. Lists only passengers with specific places of origin. 4 vols. Vol. 1, 1847–1854, vol. 2, 1855–1862, vol. 3, 1863–1867 and vol. 4, 1868–1871.
Germans to America: Lists of Passengers Arriving at U.S. Ports, 1840–1845, and 1850–1897, edited by Ira A. Glazier and P. William Filby. Wilmington, DE, 1988–2002. Passenger lists were derived from original ship manifests and published in their entirety in chronological order of arrival date at U.S. east coast ports. The determining factor for inclusion of a list was the presence of 80% or more passengers with German surnames.
Greek Passenger Lists, 1885–1910, by Mary Voultsos. 3 vols. Worcester, MA, 1992.
Hamburg Passengers From the Kingdom of Poland and the Russian Empire: Indirect Passage to New York: 1855–June 1873, by Geraldine Moser and Marlene Silverman. Washington, DC, 1996.
Migration from the Russian Empire: Lists of Passengers Arriving at the Port of New York, 1875–1891, edited by Ira A. Glazier. 6 vols. Baltimore, 1995–.
Norwegian Immigrants to the United States: A Biographical Directory, 1825–1850, by Gerhard B. Naeseth. Madison, WI, 1993. Vols. 1 & 2 (1825–1846).
Passenger Arrivals at the Port of Baltimore, 1820–1834, edited by M. H. Tepper; transcribed by E. P. Bentley.
Passenger Arrivals at the Port of Charleston, 1820–1829, by Brent H. Holcomb. Baltimore, MD, 1994.
Passenger Arrivals at the Port of New York, compiled by Elizabeth P. Bentley. Baltimore, MD, 1999. Vol. 1, 1820–1829; vol. 2, 1830–1832.
Passenger Arrivals at the Port of Philadelphia,1800–1819, edited by Michael H. Tepper, transcribed by Elizabeth P. Bentley. Baltimore, MD, 1986.
The Wuerttemberg Emigration Index, by Trudy Schenk, et al. Salt Lake City, 1986. Covers emigration from the late 18th century to 1900, to North America and elsewhere. (Available also on *Ancestry.com* and *.plus.*)

16. Ships:

The Division has the following lists of vessels to assist the researcher in locating passenger records and learning more about the ships on which their ancestors arrived:

American Passenger Arrival Records: A Guide to the Records of Immigrants Arriving at American Ports by Sail and Steam, by Michael Tepper. Baltimore, 1993. Reprinted 1999. [*R-USLHG APK 00-11906]

Morton Allan Directory of European Passenger Steamship Arrivals, for the years 1890–1930 for the Port of New York, and 1904–1926 for the Ports of New York, Philadelphia, Boston and Baltimore. Baltimore, 1980. [Desk - USLHG, 80-974] (Second copy on open shelf in Room 119)

Passenger Ships Arriving in New York Harbor, vol. 1 (1820–1850), edited by B. W. Steuart. Bountiful, UT, 1991.

Register of Vessels Arriving at the Port of New York from Foreign Ports, 1789–1919. [*ZI-391, Room 119.]

Ships of our Ancestors, by Michael J. Anuta. Baltimore, MD 1983. Reprinted 1993. Photographs of nearly 900 steamships.

In addition to the above, the Division has a card index listing every ship and referencing articles in periodicals that describe the ship.

17. Military and Veterans (self-service microfilm in Room 119)

Revolutionary War pension and bounty-land-warranty application files, 1800–1900 [*ZI-132]; and published index.

American Loyalist Claims index and records in the Exchequer and Audit Department of the British Public Records Office. Series 1, 1776-1831; series 2,1780-1835. [*ZAN-H221]

1812 War, index to pension application files.

Mexican War, index to pension files, 1887–1926.

Civil War Veterans - index to the compiled service records of the volunteer Union soldiers who served in organizations from New York State, Connecticut, Maine, Massachusetts, New Hampshire, New Jersey, Rhode Island, Vermont.

General index to pension files, 1861–1934. Most records relate to Civil War (Union) veterans.

Index to compiled service records of volunteer soldiers who served during War of 1812, Indian Wars, Mexican War, Spanish-American War, and Philippine Insurrection.

Index to pension application files of remarried widows based on service in the Civil War and later wars and in the regular army after the Civil War.

Headstones provided for deceased Union Civil War veterans, c. 1879–c. 1903.

The Division has many books that provide the history of military regiments and/or lists of servicemen:

A Compendium of the War of the Rebellion, by Frederick H. Dyer. 3 vols. New York, 1959.

Histories, Personal Narratives, United States Army: A Checklist, by Charles E. Dornbusch. Cornwallville, NY, 1967. Includes nearly 3,000 entries representing WW I and II and the Korean War.

Military Bibliography of the Civil War, compiled by Charles Emil Dornbusch. 4 vols. Includes over 8,241 regimental histories. New York, NY, 1961–1987.

Official Records of the Union and Confederate Navies in the War of the Rebellion. 30 vols. Harrisburg, PA, 1987. (Reprint).

The Roster of Union Soldiers, 1861–1865, by Janet B. Hewett. Wilmington, NC, 1998.

The Roster of Confederate Soldiers, 1861–1865, by Janet B. Hewett. Wilmington, NC, 1996.

The Union Bookshelf: A Selected Civil War Bibliography, by Michael Mullins and Rowena Reed. Wendell, NC, 1982. [IK 85-1733]

United States Colored Troops, 1861–1865, by Janet B. Hewett. Wilmington, NC, 1999.

United States Army Unit Histories: A Reference Bibliography, by James T. Controvich. Manhattan, KS, 1983. [JFF 84-925] Includes over 6,000 entries. Relates to WW I, WWII, Korean and Vietnam Wars.

18. Name Indexes

American Genealogical-Biographical Index [name index to many genealogies, mostly non-Jewish]. (On open shelf). NOTE: Also available on *Ancestry.com* and *Ancestry.plus.* See Selected Electronic Resources (below).

Daughters of the American Revolution, New York Master Index - Genealogical Records [at Information Desk].

Dau's NY Blue Book. 1907–1935 (gaps). Lists name, address and household members of "prominent" New Yorkers (includes many Jewish families). [microfilm, *ZAN-4605]

Directory of Family Associations, by Elizabeth Petty Bently. Baltimore, MD, 1991. Includes information on circa 6,000 family associations. [APA 93-1581]

Index to Personal Names in Cole's History of Rockland County by Rev. David Cole, compiled by the Historians Roundtable of Rockland County; editor, Kathe Chipman. New City, 1986. [APR (Rockland Co, NY) 87-404]

The Soundex Daitch-Mokotoff Reference Guide, edited by Bradley W. Stewart. 2 vols. Bountiful, UT, 1994. Includes codes for over 500,000 surnames. [On open shelf in Room 119.]

19. <u>Genealogy Guides</u>

The Division has an extensive collection of "how to" books. Among those available here are:

Bailey, Rosalie Fellows. *Guide to Genealogical and Biographical Sources for NYC (Manhattan) 1783–1898.* New York, 1954 [APRN (Bailey...)]. Reprinted with new introduction by Harry Macy, Jr., 1998. [APB 99-9189]
Beard, Timothy F. and Denise Demong. *How to Find Your Family Roots.* New York, 1977. [APB 78-817]
Byers, Paula K. *Asian American Genealogical Sourcebook.* Detroit, 1995. [*R-USLHG APB 95-11592]
Chorzempa, Rosemary A. *Polish Roots: Korzenie Polskie.* Baltimore, MD, 1993. [*R-USLHG APB 93-9637]
Cole, Trafford R. *Italian Genealogical Records.* Salt Lake City, [1995]. [*R-USLHG APB 95-11311]
Crandall, Ralph J. *Shaking Your Family Tree: A Basic Guide to Tracing Your Family's Genealogy.* Dublin, NH, 1986. [*R-USLHG APB 86-2353]
Everton, George B. *The Handy Book for Genealogists,* Logan, UT, 1999. [located at Information Desk]
Gnacinski, Jan and Len. *Polish and Proud: Your Polish Ancestry.* Wisconsin, 1979. [APB 80-1324]
Grenham, John. *Tracing Your Irish Ancestors: the complete guide.* Dublin, [1999]. [Desk-USLHG 99-11545]
Hoff, Henry B. "Research in New York Downstate," *Tree Talks,* March 1982. [APR New York]
Kronman, Barbara. *Guide to NYC Public Records.* New York, 1992 (4th edition). [Desk-USLHG 95-15202]
Kurzweil, Arthur. *From Generation to Generation.* New York, 1980. [APB 80-3575]
Neagles, James and Lila Lee Neagles. *Locating Your Immigrant Ancestors: A Guide to Naturalization Records.* Logan, UT, 1986. [*R-USLHG APB 88-1184]
Rottenberg, Dan. *Finding Our Fathers.* New York, 1977. [APB 77-1002]
Ryan, J. G. *Irish Records: Sources for Family and Local History.* [Salt Lake City, 1997.] [Desk-USLHG 98-1547]
Ryskamp, George R. *Finding Your Hispanic Roots.* Baltimore, [1997]. Covers Spain, Portugal and Latin America. [Desk -*R-USLHG APB 97-2750]
Smith, Clifford N. and Anna P.C. Smith. *Encyclopedia of German-American Genealogical Research.* New York, 1976. [ATA 80-950]
Szucs, Loretto Dennis and Sandra Hargreaves Luebking, eds. *The Source: A Guidebook of American Genealogy,* Revised Edition. Salt Lake City, 1997. [Desk - USLHG 97-5998]
Wellauer, Maralyn. *Tracing Your Polish Roots.* [Milwaukee, 1978]. [APB 80-800]
Wellauer, Maralyn. *Tracing Your German Roots.* Milwaukee, 1991. [APB 92-3970]

20. <u>Gazetteers</u>: For genealogists researching localities in New York State, this Division has:

Gazetteer of the State of New York, by John H. French. Baltimore, MD, 1995. Reprint of original published with indexes, Syracuse, NY, 1860. [located at Information Desk]

See NYPL MAP DIVISION and NYPL SCIENCE, INDUSTRY AND BUSINESS LIBRARY for other gazetteers of interest.

21. <u>Photo Collections - NYC</u>

Photographic Views of New York City 1870's to 1970's [self-service microfiche in Room 121]. The collection had its origins in the 1920s and includes over 54,000 photos of streets and buildings in NYC. Each photo is accompanied by a description (street, cross street, date, direction of photo and name of building, if known). This collection is available both in Room 119 and 121. See also QUEENS BOROUGH PUBLIC LIBRARY.
Lloyd Acker Collection (self service microfiche in Room 119). Includes 45,000 views of NYC buildings from 1935 to 1975 by Lloyd Acker, a commercial photographer who photographed specific buildings and indexed them by address. Not all photos are dated.
Eugene Armbruster Collection of Long Island photographs, 1890s–1930s. Indexed by village, surname and subject.
William Williams Collection of Ellis Island views.
Lewis Hine Collection of immigration photographs, 1890–1930s.
New York City Scrapbooks. Illustrations and views from various old NYC newspapers and periodicals.

22. <u>Electronic Resources</u>: The Division has access to the following databases:

<u>CD-ROM</u> (in Room 121)

Griffith's Valuation of Ireland, 1848–1864, a database which includes more than a million names of individuals who owned property in Ireland during this period.
Official Records of the Union and Confederate Armies, includes information from 128 published books.
PERSI (Periodical Source Index), 1999. Index of articles from c. 5,000 genealogical and historical periodicals written in English or French (Canadian entries) since 1800. Created by the Allen County Public Library in Ft. Wayne, IN. Also included in *Ancestry.com* and *Ancestry.plus*.

<u>Selected Electronic Resources</u> (in Room 121, as well as the South Hall of the Main Reading Room, and many other locations throughout the Library):

Ancestry.plus, an enhanced version of *Ancestry.com,* with its extensive collection of databases, including:

AIS Census Index includes in one index census schedules, 1790–1870 for most states, and later years for some states, as well as some special censuses (Mortality, Veterans, Slaves). Includes for New Jersey, 1800 (Cumberland County only), 1830–1870; New York State, 1790–1870; Connecticut, 1790, 1810–1860; and 1890 veterans' schedules for New York, New Jersey and Connecticut.

American Genealogical-Biographical Index. (Also available in hard copy. See above.)

Gale's *Passenger & Immigration Lists Index,* lists over 2.8 million passengers arriving in the U.S. and Canada.

Social Security Death Index.

U.S. Federal Census Images, 1790–1930 (in progress).

World War I Draft Registrations, includes all registrants from Alaska, Delaware, Florida, Idaho, Mississippi and Nevada and some from other states such as New York (ongoing project). Index provides date of birth, birth place, city or county and state of residence.

Archives U.S.A. provides detailed indexing to manuscript collections from c. 5,500 U.S. repositories, integrating three major sources: *Directory of Archives and Manuscript Repositories in the United States, National Union Catalog of Manuscript Collections,* and *National Inventory of Documentary Sources in the United States.* (All three are also available in hard copy in the NEW YORK PUBLIC LIBRARY - HUMANITIES AND SOCIAL SCIENCES LIBRARY, GENERAL RESEARCH DIVISION.)

Biographical and Genealogical Master Index. (Also available in hard copy in the GENERAL RESEARCH DIVISION.)

Biography Resource Center.

Heritage Quest Online with access to more than 25,000 full-text family/local histories; and the U.S. Census, 1790-1930.

Literary Resource Center, includes *Contemporary Authors.*

Ethnic NewsWatch, provides full-text access to c. 200 ethnic and minority newspapers, 1990–.

Historical Newspapers Online which includes *Palmer's Index to the (London) Times 1790–1905, The Official Index to the Times, 1906–1980, Palmer's Full Text Online, 1785–1870* and the *New York Times index,* 1851-1923.

New York Times Historical Backfile, includes full-text and full-image articles, 1851–1999.

RLG (Research Libraries Group) Archival Resources includes close to 700,000 collections of manuscripts, oral histories and more, located in repositories around the world such as NYPL, NYS Library, Library of Congress, Jacob Rader Marcus Center of the American Jewish Archives, Harvard, Columbia, Cornell, Brandeis, and Princeton Universities, National Archives of Australia and South Africa, and many more.

NOTE: Every computer in the Library which has Selected Electronic Resources can access the above. Some, such as *Biography Resource Center,* are accessible at home via the Internet to NYPL Branch library card holders. There are many other online resources of interest to genealogists. See *Cyndi's List: A Comprehensive List of 70,000 Genealogy Sites on the Internet,* by Cyndi Howells, 2001. [On open shelf in Room 121]

23. <u>Other</u>: The Division has unusual material such as:

Registry of Voters, 1884, 1889–1890, 1898–1899, 1904–1954 [*ZAN-G430]. Bound volumes are available for 1955 to 1969 at the NYPL - SCIENCE, INDUSTRY AND BUSINESS LIBRARY, Within each Assembly District and Election District, voters are listed by address. NOTE: The Division has some voter registration lists from other localities in the U.S.A. and foreign countries. Check the catalog under subject, "Voting Registers."

New York Tax Book, New York: List of Persons, Copartnerships, and Corporations Who Were Taxed on $17,500 and Upward in the City of New York in the Year 1850, compiled by W. A. Darling, 1851. [IRH (Darling...)]

The Income Record: A List Giving the Taxable Income for the Year 1863, of Every Resident of NY, 1851.

Emigrant Savings Bank Records, 1850–1883 (microfilm in Room 119). This collection consists of records of the bank's c. 70,000 depositors and borrowers. Test Books often contain detailed personal and genealogical information about individuals such as occupation, birthplace, names of family members, date of arrival in the U.S.A., name of the ship on which the depositor arrived, port of embarkation and port of entry into the U.S.A. See the NEW YORK PUBLIC LIBRARY, MANUSCRIPTS AND ARCHIVES DIVISION for the complete archives. See also, Monica Bennett's index to these records (in progress) at www.genexchange.org/esb/.

Finding Aids:

1. <u>Catalogs</u>: For all genealogy books (regardless of when acquired) and other materials acquired after 1972, consult the CATNYP computer terminals in Room 121. All pre-1972 genealogy books have been added to the online catalog as part of the on-going conversion project. For a description of the Research Libraries' catalogs, see NYPL - HUMANITIES AND SOCIAL SCIENCES LIBRARY, GENERAL RESEARCH DIVISION. *Dictionary Catalog of the Local History*

and Genealogy Division (Green volumes), located in Room 121, includes the collection before 1972. Holdings are listed by author and subject, rarely by title. The librarians in the Genealogy Division are the best "finding aids." They are familiar with the materials most frequently requested and often have this material at the desk.

NOTE: Most materials with classmarks (call numbers) beginning with [A] or [I] can be obtained in Room 121. The Genealogy Division may be reclassifying in the future in order to place more materials on open shelves.

2. US Census Indexes: The Division holds published Census indexes, 1790–1870, for most states, and 1910, for some states. For the New York metropolitan area, available published indexes include: New York State and Connecticut, 1790–1870, and 1910; New Jersey, 1830–1870. The 1910 New York State published indexes (Heritage Quest) include New York City, Nassau and Suffolk Counties, 14 vols. (in one alpha index); and Upstate New York State, 11 vols. [*R-USLHG APR (New York) 02-1875, and 02-1365]. For 1890, there are published indexes to the Union Veterans and Widows census for New York and New Jersey. NOTE: See also CENTER FOR JEWISH HISTORY and NEW YORK GENEALOGICAL AND BIOGRAPHICAL SOCIETY for 1910 Census indexes on CD-ROM.

For 1800, the Division has *United States 1800 Census Index,* edited by Raeone C. Steuart, Bountiful, UT, 2000 [*R-USLHG 00-5231]. This index includes the following jurisdictions in one alphabetical series: Connecticut, Delaware, District of Columbia, Maine, Maryland, Massachusetts, New Hampshire, New York, North Carolina, Pennsylvania, Rhode Island, South Carolina and Vermont.

Room 119 has the Soundex index (on microfilm) for New York, New Jersey, and Connecticut, 1880; New York State, 1900 and 1920; and Puerto Rico, 1920. See Appendix A for an explanation of the National Archives Soundex system. There are also 1880 Street Guides for Manhattan and Brooklyn in Room 121.

In addition to the Heritage Quest published 1910 indexes, the library has *A Research Guide for the New York 1910 Federal Census,* compiled and edited by Ann Hunt, 1999. This index for New York State (not including New York County, Brooklyn or Queens) is arranged by County and Town, showing the Enumeration Districts/Wards/ Precincts and where to locate them on the 1910 Census. For New York City (except Queens), 1910, a paper copy of the street index to the Enumeration Districts (ED), *Guide to the Enumeration Districts, 1910 Census* is available on open shelves in Room 119. With this index (by borough/street/house number) the researcher can identify the ED in which the house was located. The Genealogy Division has a National Archives publication which converts these EDs into reel numbers. The Division also has (on microfilm) a copy of the 1910 *List of Enrolled Voters* for Queens. This list is arranged by Assembly/Election District and first letter of the surname.

See also, the *AIS Census Index*, 1790–1870, 1890 Veterans Schedules and index to 1930 U.S. Census (includes NY, NJ, CT and more) available on *Ancestry.plus* at the Selected Electronic Resource terminals in Room 121.

The Division has a collection of maps (on first table in Room 121) including: Census District maps for Manhattan, 1855, 1860, 1870 and Brooklyn, 1860, 1870 and 1880; Ward maps for Manhattan, 1797, 1803, 1808, 1817, 1824, 1828, 1831, 1840 and 1850 and Brooklyn, 1850. For 1900, there are Census Enumeration District maps for Manhattan and Queens; and for 1920, for all boroughs. See also,

> *Poles and Russians in the 1870 Census of New York City: full alphabetical index for the second enumeration (with a partial index for the first enumeration),* by Marlene Silverman, PhD. Washington, DC, 1993.
> *The New York Foundling Hospital: An Index to the Federal, State and Local Census Records (1870–1925),* by Carolee R. Inskeep. Baltimore, MD, 1995.
> *The Children's Aid Society of New York: An Index to the Federal, State, and Local Census Records of its Lodging Houses, 1855–1925,* by Carolee R. Inskeep. Baltimore, MD, 1996.

3. NYC Police Census: To locate an address in the 1890 census, researchers need both the "book number" (a.k.a. "volume number") and Assembly District/Election District (AD/ED). Use City Directories for addresses and *Aid to Finding Addresses in the 1890 New York City Police Census,* compiled by Howard M. Jensen, to learn the book number. Then use the blue binder in Room 119 (or black binder in Room 121), *1890 NYC Police Census ED Maps* to find the AD/ED number. See also *Ancestry.plus* or *Ancestry.com* website for a partial index to this census.

4. New York State Census: For 1905, 1915 and 1925, Manhattan (includes the Bronx in 1905), there is a microfilmed card index to addresses [*ZI-539]. See the black binder (on open shelf) in Room 119 for Manhattan/Bronx to assist in locating these reels. For Richmond County (Staten Island) 1925 census, see Theodore Nelson's *New York 1925 State Census Index,* a surname index (138,100 entries). Search by town in earlier Richmond County census records. For Kings County (Brooklyn) census, the Division has street finding aids for 1855, 1865, 1875, 1892 and 1905.

5. New Jersey Census: There are no name or street indexes to the New Jersey census. The census is arranged by City/Town. Room 119 has a black binder, "Guide to New Jersey State Census for 1885, 1895 and 1915."

6. <u>Canadian Census, 1871</u>: There is no index to this census. Use the *Catalog of Census Returns on Microfilm, 1666–1901* to locate the province and town sought (at Information Desk in Room 121).

7. <u>City Directories</u>: There is a card index to pre-1870 paper copies of City Directories in the Division's collection. Researchers should check the MICROFORMS DIVISION first since many have already been microfilmed.

8. <u>Vital Records Indexes</u>: Because of the aging condition of the indexes, the following are on microfilm or microfiche and can be found in Room 119:

Births	1888–1915, 1921 (microfilm)
	1898–1900, 1906–1907, 1910–1946, 1949–1959, 1962, 1965, 1968–1975 (microfiche)
Deaths	1888–1956 (microfilm)
Marriages	1888–1937 (microfilm)

Indexes in bound volumes are available in Room 121:

Births	1888–1889, 1913, 1916–1919, 1922–1927, 1929–1944, 1946–1963, 1965–1982
Deaths	1957–1982

9. <u>Photographs</u>: The index for <u>*Photographic Views of New York City*</u> is in three bound volumes. Volume 1, *Street Index,* has entries by street name and includes the cross street, date of photo, direction of photo and fiche and row/photograph numbers. Volume 2, *Building Index,* has similar entries by building name. Volume 3, *Subject Index,* has general entries such as "Synagogues." It does not identify the name or street, just the fiche and row/photograph numbers.

There are two sets of these materials. One is located in the Genealogy Division's Microfilm Room 119 and a second in Room 121. The fiche, in 3 long boxes near the microfiche reader in Room 121 (behind the counter in Room 119), are arranged alphabetically by street name. Index volumes are at the desk.

The card index (microfilm) for the <u>Lloyd Acker Collection</u> is in a self service cabinet in Room 119. It is a geographic index, arranged numerically for numbered streets and alphabetically for named streets.

10. <u>Emigrant Savings Bank Records</u>. The index to Test Books can be found on microfilm Reels 1 (1850–1866) and 2 (1867–1877). While there is an index on Reel 3 (1878–1880), the Library never received Test Books to which this index refers. MANUSCRIPTS AND ARCHIVES DIVISION has a finding aid with more information about this collection.

Description of Facility:

The MILSTEIN DIVISION OF UNITED STATES, LOCAL HISTORY AND GENEALOGY, also known as the Genealogy Division, is housed in Rooms 121 and 119 at the north end (42nd Street) of the first floor. Room 121 has a seating capacity of 51. Two librarians are usually on duty to help researchers. With the opening of this newly renovated facility, many more publications are accessible on open shelves. Published <u>Census indexes</u>, <u>passenger lists</u>, <u>vital records indexes</u> (NYC Health Department <u>Death indexes</u>, 1957–1982) and major genealogical periodicals are on open shelves which run the full length of Room 121. Published Health Department <u>Birth indexes</u> are available in Room 121 but must be requested at the Division's Information Desk. There are currently three CATNYP terminals, five computer terminals (dedicated for use in searching networked <u>Selected Electronic Resources</u>), one stand-alone CD-ROM reader and one microfiche reader in Room 121. Card indexes for paper copies of <u>City Directories</u> and <u>Ships</u> are under the stairs in Room 121.

The Division's microforms area in Room 119 has 9 microfilm readers, 2 microfiche readers and 2 microform reader/printers. NOTE: If there are no machines available in Room 119, researchers may request a pass to use films in Room 100. These films must be returned to Room 119. Most microfilms of interest to genealogists are in self-service cabinets around the perimeter of the room. Microfiche holdings must be requested from the staff at the desk. 1-2 staff persons are available to assist researchers in this room. All microforms with call numbers "ZAN-G," "*ZI," "*XLG" or "*XMG" are either located in Room 119 or can be ordered in Room 121. All other microform materials are in Room 100.

For materials not on open shelf, call slips must be completed (up to 4 at one time). However, call numbers are not always required. Consult the librarian on items of interest. When requesting material in Room 121, indicate "table" and "seat number" on the call slip, since staff will bring the books directly to that seat.

Restrictions on Use:

Researchers must sign the register before requesting materials in the Genealogy Division (Room 119 and 121). See NEW YORK PUBLIC LIBRARY, GENERAL RESEARCH DIVISION, "Description of Facility" for photo ACCESS card to be required of <u>all</u> patrons. Only 4 bound volumes or 6 reels of microfilm (from the stacks) may be requested at a time. No books or microfilms may be taken out of the room without a pass. Books must be returned to the designated return area in Room 121 when no longer needed. Microfilms are returned to the designated area in Room 119. Do <u>not</u> refile films.

NEW YORK PUBLIC LIBRARY
MANUSCRIPTS AND ARCHIVES DIVISION

Facility Director: William Stingone, Curator

Address: Fifth Avenue at 42nd Street, Room 328   ♿
New York, NY 10018-2788

(Cross Streets: 40th and 42nd Streets; 5th and 6th Avenues)

Phone: (212) 930-0801
Fax: (212) 302-4815
E-mail: mssref@nypl.org
Website: www.nypl.org/research/chss/spe/rbk/mss.html

Hours of Operation:

Tuesday & Wednesday: 11:00 am to 6:00 pm
Thursday to Saturday: 10:00 am to 6:00 pm

Closed Sunday, Monday and legal holidays.

Closest Public Transportation and Directions:

See NEW YORK PUBLIC LIBRARY - HUMANITIES AND SOCIAL SCIENCES LIBRARY, GENERAL RESEARCH DIVISION.

Description of Resources:

The Manuscripts and Archives Division holds approximately 29,000 linear feet of archival material in over 3,300 collections, dating from the third millennium BCE to the present. Manuscript collections contain original materials regardless of format, including not only paper documents but also photographs, sound recordings, films, videotapes, artifacts and electronic records. Of special interest:

1. <u>American Committee for the Guidance of Professional Personnel</u>, 1938–1945. Records include applications and sometimes photographs of refugee law personnel seeking retraining assistance. Case files includes curricula vitae, interview memoranda and correspondence. The curricula vitae form includes parents' names and father's place of birth and occupation.

2. <u>Diaries Collection</u>, 1755–1921, includes original and transcripts of diaries which the Division has received over the years. These range from the 1849 diary of James S. Tollen giving an account of his adventures as he crossed the plains to California during the days of the gold rush, to the journal kept by Isaac Watts Platt, Clergyman, 1847–1858 in West Farms, NY, which includes a complete record of baptisms, marriages and burials in his community.

3. <u>Emergency Committee in Aid of Displaced Foreign Scholars Records,</u> 1933–1945. Includes biographical information and correspondence with and about refugee scholars receiving (and not receiving) grants or fellowships. The files include curricula vitae, interview memoranda, evaluations, correspondence and sometimes photos and a description of what happened to the applicant in Europe. There were circa 6,000 applicants of whom 335 received assistance. Not all the "non-grantee" files are applicants. Most, but not all the applicants, were Jewish. The collection also includes two boxes of biographical statements, mostly curricular vitae of other refugees. These files are labeled "American Friends Service Committee, Biographical Data on Scholars." There are also lists of refugee scholars with birth dates, marital status, institutional affiliation and country of placement. The collection includes personnel records of prospective employees of the Committee.

4. <u>Emigrant Savings Bank Records</u>, 1850–1883, 59 volumes, some of which include personal and family information (mostly Irish). See NYPL - IRMA AND PAUL MILSTEIN DIVISION OF UNITED STATES HISTORY, LOCAL HISTORY AND GENEALOGY which has a microfilm copy of this portion of the collection. In addition, Society Accounts (Reel 23), 1922–1927, include some landsmanshaftn and other Jewish organization records. Nine volumes of minutes of the Irish Emigrant Society, 1841–1933 are included (Reels 42–49).

5. <u>Ernst Papanek papers</u>, 1928–1976, relate mostly to this Austrian-born child psychologist's work with refugee children during and after World War II. Includes records pertaining to patients or residents of the Brooklyn Training School and Wiltwyck School for Boys (Esopus, NY). See "Restrictions on Use."

6. Jewish Foundation for Education of Women Records, 1880–1988. Includes information about students who attended the Hebrew Technical School for Girls, and case files of women who received scholarships from the Foundation.

   Case files, 1937–1955, include applications for tuition loan or grants with personal and family history of the applicant and her parents including applicant's age, birth place, occupation and financial status. Some files include photographs. The collection also includes registers of scholarship recipients. See "Restrictions on Use."

7. New York Typographical Union #6 Records include new member rosters, 1908–1919 (in alphabetical order) and 1907–1963 (chronologically). The file also includes lists of deceased members, 1912–1951 (chronologically) and roll books with member signatures, 1859–1966.

8. Rockefeller Institute for Medical Research correspondence, 1933–1940, consists of correspondence of Phebus Aaron Levene of the Institute with displaced foreign physicians and chemists who sought to emigrate to the U.S.A. from Europe and especially Germany. Some files include curricula vitae.

9. Sol Bloom (New York City Congressman) papers, 1898–1949, include case files of Jewish refugees and displaced persons in Europe and elsewhere who sought permission to emigrate to the U.S.A. before, during and after World War II. Some files include first hand accounts of suffering experienced during the Holocaust. Later files, 1945–1949, include constituent requests for aid in obtaining civil service employment and in gaining entry to the U.S. Military Academy at West Point or the U.S. Naval Academy at Annapolis. A draft of the *Autobiography of Sol Bloom,* 1949, is part of the collection.

10. Personal and Family Papers make up a large part of this Division's 3,300 collections. Among these are the Straus papers which include a family tree and history of the descendants of Lazarus Straus (1809–1898); and the personal papers of Dorothy Schiff, John Jacob Robbins, Eleanora Mendelssohn, Fredericka Dembitz Brandeis, Stanley Isaacs, Elias Lieberman, Philip Loeb, Samuel Rosenberg and Amy Schwartz Oppenheim. Although some individual collections do not include personal files, the finding aid almost always includes a detailed biographical sketch.

   The James Riker Papers, 1660–1989 [W94a-231] include transcripts and extracts from original public records in NYC, Albany and other locations, such as the 1771 census of Newtown. Some, but not all of these materials were used by Riker, a historian and genealogist, in his books, *History of Harlem,* 1881 (revised and reprinted 1904 and 2001) [IRGN 01-9976], and *Annals of Newtown* [IRM (Newtown) 85-1163], containing some of the first published New York genealogies. For more detail on this collection, see "James Riker's Publications and Papers," by Harry Macy Jr., published in *The NYG&B Newsletter,* Spring-Summer 2002, p.37. NOTE: Riker's books are available in the NYPL, U.S. HISTORY, LOCAL HISTORY AND GENEALOGY DIVISION and at the OLD YORK LIBRARY.

Finding Aids:

The Manuscript and Archives Division has a card catalog that includes all materials acquired through 1985. It is alphabetically arranged by name, subject, geographic location and type of document (diaries, maps, etc). Descriptions of collections acquired after 1985 and all but a few of the large manuscript collections regardless of acquisition date, are in CATNYP. See NYPL GENERAL RESEARCH DIVISION AND MICROFORMS ROOM for a description of CATNYP. A list of major manuscript collections is on the Division's website. Detailed inventory lists for some can be accessed online.

The two-volume *Dictionary Catalog of the Manuscript Division* reproduces the card catalog of manuscript collections as of 1966. More detailed inventories for most collections are available in the Room 328. Most include a descriptive summary, biographical notes, administrative information, organizational history, scope and content and a container or box list. For some, the container/box list includes an index of correspondents or case files. (Be sure to indicate the box number in requesting material.) The Division has Survey Files, arranged by name, which serve as cross reference files to locate information across different collections. These surveys are not comprehensive and were not updated regularly but are a good place to start.

Researchers may place orders by phone, fax or mail in advance of their visits. E-mail requests can be sent but should not be used for orders for the same or following day. Call before coming if you wish to see a collection the same day. Some collections are stored off site and require 48-hour notice.

Emergency Committee in Aid of Displaced Foreign Scholars Records, 1933–1945. An alphabetical list of scholars receiving assistance (Grantees & Fellows) and those applicants or other corespondents who did not receive assistance (Non-Grantees), is included in the finding aid.

Emigrant Savings Bank Records. The index to the Test Books can be found on microfilm Reels 1 (1850–1866) and 2 (1867–1877) of this collection. While there is an index on Reel 3 (1878–1880), the Library never received the Test Books to which this index refers. The Division has a finding aid with more information about this collection. See also the IRMA AND PAUL MILSTEIN DIVISION OF UNITED STATES HISTORY, LOCAL HISTORY AND GENEALOGY which has Reels 1–20 of this collection in Room 119.

Jewish Foundation for Education of Women Records, 1880–1988. There is an online finding aid for this collecton at www.nypl.org/research/chss/spe/rbk/faids/jewishfound.html. Case files, 1937–1955, are arranged alphabetically by year and name of applicant. (Boxes 5–7, 19–21). Names are not included in the finding aid.

New York Typographical Union #6 Records. Lists of new members are in Box 8 (chronological) and Box 9 (alphabetical). Box 9 also includes the chronological lists of deceased members.

John Riker Papers. There is an online finding aid at: http://digilib.nypl.org/dynaweb/ead/human/mssjasriker/

Description of Facility:

Room 328, the Brooke Russell Astor Reading Room, is at the far end of the North Hall. It has 24 individual desks at which researchers can work. Three self-service file cabinets to the right of the Information Desk hold the finding aids describing the Division's collections. The Division has one Selected Electronic Resources and one CATNYP workstation. In addition, it has one microfilm reader, one video viewer and one audio cassette player. The *Dictionary Catalogs* are under the two tables adjacent to the computer workstation. The room is shared with the Rare Book Division and that Division's bibliographic reference books line the walls of the room.

Fees and Copies:

The Division has one photocopy machine. All photocopying is done by divisional staff (not at Copy Services). The charge is $.30 per page for an 8 ½" by 11" page or $.50 for an 11" x 17" page. Add an additional $2 for mailing.

See NEW YORK PUBLIC LIBRARY - HUMANITIES AND SOCIAL SCIENCES LIBRARY, GENERAL RESEARCH DIVISION for cost of making photographs. See the librarian for permission to make copies. See "Restrictions on Use."

Restrictions on Use:

A card of admission is required to use the Manuscripts and Archives Division. Apply for this card in the Office of Special Collections, Room 316 (opposite the Bill Blass Public Catalog Room). Each applicant must show traceable identification and supply the name and address of an individual who can verify the information on the application. Cards of admission must be obtained in person and are not transferable. They are granted for a period of up to six months. The entrance to Room 328 is locked. Researchers must hold their admission card to the window in order to be admitted. NOTE: See also NEW YORK PUBLIC LIBRARY - HUMANITIES AND SOCIAL SCIENCES LIBRARY, GENERAL RESEARCH DIVISION, "Description of Facility" for photo ACCESS card to be required of all patrons.

Readers are required to store all belongings not needed for research in the Library's coat check room on the first floor. This includes all coats, shopping bags, handbags, computer cases and newspapers. Valuables may be brought to the room in a clear plastic bag provided by the checkroom.

Manuscript and archival materials are delivered only four times a day. Call slips must be submitted at least 45 minutes in advance, i.e. by 11:15 am, 2:15 pm, 4:15 pm and 5:45 pm, for delivery at noon, 3:00 pm, 5:00 pm or the next morning.

The Division will not photocopy bound materials or fragile items and reserves the right to prohibit the photocopying of other materials. Microfilming or scanning of bound or fragile items may be possible.

Researchers are instructed not to remove materials to be copied from boxes or folders. A "Photocopy Request Flag" is provided, which must be inserted in the folder directly in front of the materials to be copied.

Ernst Papanek Papers pertaining to patients or residents of the Brooklyn Training School and Wiltwyck School are closed for 100 years from date of file (2048–2072).

Jewish Foundation for Education of Women Records. Users are required to sign a waiver attesting that they will not divulge the names/address or other identifying features of scholarship applicants and recipients.

NEW YORK PUBLIC LIBRARY
MAP DIVISION

Facility Director: Alice C. Hudson, Chief

Address: Fifth Avenue at 42nd Street, Room 117 &
New York, NY 10018-2788

(Cross Streets: 40th and 42nd Streets; 5th and 6th Avenues)

Phone: (212) 930-0587
Fax: (212) 930-0027
E-mail: mapref@nypl.org
Website: www.nypl.org/research/chss/map/map.html

Hours of Operation:

Tuesday: 1:00 am to 7:30 pm
Wednesday to Saturday: 1:00 am to 6:00 pm

Closed Sunday, Monday and legal holidays.

Closest Public Transportation and Directions:

See NEW YORK PUBLIC LIBRARY - HUMANITIES AND SOCIAL SCIENCES LIBRARY, GENERAL RESEARCH DIVISION.

Description of Resources:

The Map Division has the most extensive collection in New York City of gazetteers, maps, including pre-19th century maps and world atlases, produced in both the United States and Europe, dating from the 1800s through the present. The collection includes 405,000 maps and 18,000 atlases and books.

A. Gazetteers

> *U.S. Board on Geographic Names Gazetteer.* Despite the post-WWII dates, these gazetteers are particularly useful for locating very small towns in Poland and the former Soviet Union that are thought not to exist since the war. The complete set of 224 volumes provide latitude and longitude for every place name and also indicate place name changes in such countries as:

Austria, 1962	Italy, 1956
Bulgaria, 1959	Poland, 1955
Czechoslovakia, 1955	Romania, 1960
East Germany, 1959	Syria, 1983
France, 1964	USSR, 1970
Hungary, 1961	West Germany, 1960

> NOTE: U.S. Board of Geographic Names database is also available on the U. S. Department of Defense, National Imagery and Mapping Agency website at http://164.214.2.59/gns/html/index.htm.

> *Austria-Hungary 1913 Index,* a detailed place name index, based on *Stieler's Hand Atlas.* The accompanying map is also available. (See Map section below).

> *Bartholomew Gazetteer of the British Isles.* This place name index which describes each location is available for 1887, 1893, 1943, 1955 and 1970.

> *Columbia Lippincott Gazetteer of the World,* 1880, 1898, 1906, 1952, 1960 and *Columbia Gazetteer of the World,* 3 vols., 1998 [98-7372]

> Defense Mapping Agency/Army Map Service - *Index to Names on AMS 1:250,000 Map of Eastern Europe* (Series N50l). Provides latitude and longitude. (See <u>Maps</u> below.)

> *Genealogical Gazetteer of Galicia,* by Brian J. Lenius. Anola, 1999.

> *Lietuvos Zemelapis: Map of Lithuania,* compiled by Juozas Andrius. United States, 1956. (Map kept separately). This small book includes place names in Lithuania as of 1939, i.e. before the annexation of Klaipeda territory

by Nazi Germany and the Soviet invasion of June 1940. It includes also the Polish occupied (1920–1939) Vilnius region.

Nazwy Geograficzne Rzeczypospolitej Polskiej (Geographical Names of the Republic of Poland). Warsaw, 1991. Lists place names (from 1987), longitude and latitude and voivodship for 25,000 communities. [95-14686]

Postal Place Names in Poland by George K. Kay. Edinburgh, 1992. Provides a comprehensive listing of postal place names which are, or were, used in official lists of territories forming part of the Polish state over 150 years. For each place name, the years in which the places were listed in official sources are given, as well as name changes (and year) and voivodship. The book is arranged alphabetically by the (1988) place name or last-used Polish place name. [95-1858]

Rand McNally Commercial Atlas. This has the most detailed place name index for the U.S. It lists all communities, even those with zero population. It is published annually, and the Map Division has back editions since the 1880s. While not all editions are available, there is at least one per decade, usually for the year of (or following) the census, in order to provide accurate population data.

Ritters Geographisch-Statistisches Lexikon, 1874 (1983 reprint), 1905, 1906 and 1910 (in German). This is an excellent source for pre-war Central Europe place names, especially place names no longer in use. An English key to abbreviations in the text, created by the Map Division, is available at the Information Desk.

Shtetl Finder Gazetteer by Chester G. Cohen. Bowie, MD, 1980 [*R-85-1081]. Includes cities, towns and villages in the Russian Pale of Settlement as it existed in 1900; the Russian provinces of Samogita, Livonia and Kurland which were later combined with other Russian territory to form Lithuania and Latvia; and territory in the 19th century empire of Austria-Hungary. Place names are arranged alphabetically according to their Jewish pronunciation. Map names from the *National Geographic Atlas* and some other atlases are also given. The 1989 reprint can be found in the NYPL, DOROT JEWISH DIVISION and at the CENTER FOR JEWISH HISTORY.

The Times Atlas of the World. The latest edition of this classic British atlas, 1999, with its valuable A-to-Z gazetteer (with latitudes and longitudes) is available along with some back editions starting in 1895 (gaps).

Where Once We Walked: A Guide to the Jewish Communities Destroyed in the Holocaust, by Gary Mokotoff and Sallyann Amdur Sack. Teaneck, NJ, 2002. Documents more than 23,500 towns in Central and Eastern Europe where Jews lived before the Holocaust. Provides latitude and longitude, pre-Holocaust Jewish population and citations in other books that reference the town. The book includes alternate names for each town and a soundex index to assist users when the exact spelling of the town name is unknown.

In addition to the gazetteers in the Map Division, the SLAVIC AND BALTIC DIVISION (Room 217) has the 15-volume *Slownik Geograficzny* (geographical dictionary) which provides detailed late 19th-century information on most East European communities (in Polish).

B. Maps (U.S.A. and Foreign)

1. Greater New York Area: The Division has road maps, national atlases, NYC geographical and property maps from the 1600s to date, including:

Property Maps. These block maps delineating each property were produced by the Sanborn Fire Insurance, Sanborn Land Books, Robinson, E. Belcher Hyde, Bromley and Perris. The maps are available from 1850 for Manhattan, from 1855 for Brooklyn, 1870s for the Bronx and Staten Island, and 1891 for Queens.

Sanborn property maps (on microfilm) from the 1880s are available also for cities in Connecticut (to 1989), New Jersey (to 1991) and New York, other than NYC (to 1990).

The Division also has the most current *New York Boroughs* (microfiche) tax maps and property ownership information produced by First American Real Estate Solutions (formerly Real Estate Data, Inc., a.k.a. REDI) for the outer boroughs (Brooklyn, the Bronx, Queens and Staten Island), arranged by block/lot, address and owner's name [*XLK-4]. For Manhattan, the Division has the *Sanborn Manhattan Land Book of the City of New York* indexed by block and lot number for 1975/76 and from 1983 to the present. Ownership information is included. [*R-Map Div 83-2577]

See the NYPL - SCIENCE, INDUSTRY AND BUSINESS LIBRARY for copies of *New York Boroughs* (except current year) from 1987 [*XLF-426]; and additional NYC real property resources.

<u>Topographic maps</u> of NYC are available in the U.S. Geological Survey quadrangles, Borough Topographical Surveys, 1969 Plan for NYC contour maps, 1954 borough contour maps and the Bien Atlas sheets of 1891. Some are also available on interactive CD-ROM, such as TOPO! which covers the New York City metropolitan area including Long Island, the Catskills and the Poconos.

2. <u>United States and Canada</u> road maps and national atlases. The Map Division maintains an extensive historical file of maps of all 50 states going back to the 1700s as well as an extensive Canadian collection.

3. <u>Europe</u>. A wide variety of maps are available for Europe including:

<u>Military Surveys of Europe</u>: Detailed surveys from the mid-19th century to the present include:

1:250,000 AMS (Army Map Service) for Eastern Europe (N501 Series) and Western Europe (M501 Series)
1:200,000 set for Central Europe and much of the former U.S.S.R. (in Russian). Siberia is incomplete.
1:100,000 AMS series for Poland and Germany (nearly complete set)
1:75,000 AMS series for Austria-Hungary (includes 250 sheets)

Generally complete map sets for the Soviet Union on scales greater than 1:250,000

<u>Country Map Files</u>: The Division has extensive files of general maps for individual countries during different time frames. These are particularly good for reviewing a country's borders and assessing the geopolitics during particular historic eras.

<u>*Stieler's Hand Atlas*</u>: Several editions of this world atlas are available. It has good coverage of Europe, particularly in the 19th century. There is a detailed place name index. German spellings are used throughout.

<u>Austria-Hungary 1913 Map</u>: A large, very detailed map of this region has been reproduced from *Stieler's* and is available in this Division. A place name index in book form is also available. (See Austria-Hungary 1913 Index above.)

<u>Historical Atlas of East Central Europe</u> by Paul R. Magocsi. Toronto, [1993]. Includes maps showing the distribution of various ethnic groups including the Jewish population in East Central Europe c. 1900. Charts show the Jewish population in these European countries and several large cities. [94-10202]

C. <u>Computer Mapping Workstations</u>: The Division has two computer mapping workstations which includes the following CD-ROMs, among others:

British Library Map Catalog
Tripmaster '97
25 Rare Maps
Metro New York City: The Aerial Street Atlas of Greater New York
Civil War Records Atlas
Delorme Street Atlas USA

Finding Aids:

Materials received and cataloged since 1972 and most books acquired before 1972 are now in the Library's CATNYP catalog. The Map Division's 10-volume book catalog, *Dictionary Catalog of the Map Division,* is also used in locating materials cataloged prior to 1972. Flat sheet maps acquired prior to 1972 are not in CATNYP.

See NEW YORK PUBLIC LIBRARY - HUMANITIES AND SOCIAL SCIENCES LIBRARY, GENERAL RESEARCH DIVISION for a description of the CATNYP catalog.

The Map Division has a directory that lists many other map collections in the United States, such as the extensive holdings at Yale University and the University of California at Berkeley.

Description of Facility:

The Map Division is located on the first floor of the Library in Room 117. The room can seat 25 people at tables, and has one counter which serves as a work area for oversized maps. There is one staff member on duty at the reference desk. One microfilm and one microfiche reader are available. The catalogs are to the left of the entrance. There are 2 computer workstations.

Staff will conduct short place name searches in response to telephone requests. Typically, time permitting, they will look at two or three sources located at the reference desk to provide a latitude and longitude or a nearby city, as well as any alternative spellings. Patrons must come in to conduct actual research.

Fees/Copies:

Copies of maps can be made by the Map Division staff. Maps up to 36" wide (no limit on length) can be copied for $5.00 (in-person requests only). All copying is done at the discretion of the staff, depending on the map's condition and age. No fragile or antique maps can be copied. The staff will cooperate in finding alternative materials or ways of reproduction where appropriate. For example, researchers with staff permission may photograph (preferably with a 35mm camera on a sunny day using no flash) or make a tracing (only with a Mylar sheet, supplied by the staff, to protect the map and only in pencil). Or, the Division may recommend reproducing the map using the Library's Copy Services to make a photograph or slide. See NEW YORK PUBLIC LIBRARY - HUMANITIES AND SOCIAL SCIENCES LIBRARY, GENERAL RESEARCH DIVISION AND MICROFORMS ROOM for fees.

Restrictions on Use:

Researchers must sign in at the register and complete a call slip for each item requested. NOTE: See NEW YORK PUBLIC LIBRARY - HUMANITIES AND SOCIAL SCIENCES LIBRARY, GENERAL RESEARCH DIVISION, "Description of Facility" for photo ACCESS card to be required of all patrons.

Materials can be obtained quickly unless a lot of material is ordered. Five items can be requested at a time.

Researchers may be required to use a particular item for a limited time, if it is in high demand.

See "Fees/Copies" for limitations on copying.

NEW YORK PUBLIC LIBRARY
MIRIAM AND IRA D. WALLACH DIVISION OF ART, PRINTS AND PHOTOGRAPHS

Facility Director: Robert Rainwater, Chief Librarian, Arts, Prints and Photographs and
        Curator, Spencer Collection
Paula Baxter, Curator, Art and Architecture
Dr. Roberta Waddell, Curator, Prints

Address: Fifth Avenue at 42nd Street, Rooms 300 and 308   ♿
New York, NY 10018-2788

(Cross Streets: 40th and 42nd Streets; 5th and 6th Avenues)

Phone: (212) 930-0835 (Art and Architecture)
(212) 930-0817 (Prints)
(212) 930-0837 (Photographs)
Fax: (212) 930-0530

E-mail: artref@nypl.org (Art and Architecture)
prnref@nypl.org (Prints)
phgref@nypl.org (Photographs)
Website: www.nypl.org/research/chss/spe/art/artarc/artarch.html

Hours of Operation:

	Art and Architecture	Prints and Photography
Thursday to Saturday	10:00 am to 6:00 pm	1:00 pm to 6:00 pm
Tuesday and Wednesday:	11:00 am to 7:30 pm	1:00 pm to 6:00 pm

Closed Sunday, Monday and legal holidays.

Closest Public Transportation, Directions and Fees/Copies:

See NEW YORK PUBLIC LIBRARY - HUMANITIES AND SOCIAL SCIENCES LIBRARY, GENERAL RESEARCH DIVISION.

Description of Resources:

The Division's collections provide extensive biographical information on artists and artisans as well as samples of their work. There are pictorial and historical holdings covering places, both local and foreign, in the form of prints, photographs and original art. Pictures of eminent people are also available. Several specialties such as upholstering, goldsmithing and jewelry making are covered. Some aspects of life, such as costumes and religious attire, are covered from a historical and multinational perspective. The Division's holdings include:

A. <u>Art and Architecture Collection</u> (Room 300) contains a reference collection of 265,000 volumes including periodicals, scrapbooks and clippings on subjects such as the fine arts, antiques, architecture, design, furniture and interior decoration. It covers all peoples and periods.

    1.   <u>Art</u> - Several sources of information are available on artists:

        <u>The Artist Files</u> (on microfiche), includes over 90,000 files on individual artists arranged alphabetically by the artist's name, provides biographical information and includes newspaper and magazine clippings, press releases, catalogs, manuscripts, original photographs and reproductions. It covers both American and foreign artists, architects, collectors, crafts people and art historians. This file was developed during the Works Progress Administration and ends in 1972. There is a five-volume typewritten index to this collection.

        The Division's <u>Inside File</u> (drawers 1–95) is a cross-index by artist to books and periodicals in the Division's collection that have reproductions of a particular artist work or biographical information. The Inside File was created during the 1930s as a WPA project. For later information, researchers should consult *The Art Index* [MAC], a published index to 420 international art periodicals from 1929 to the present, or the *RILA* volumes (*Répertoire International de la Littérature de l'Art*), an international index to art literature.

        The Division also has a collection of <u>scrapbooks</u> now on microfilm that cover various subjects. Information on a particular artist or architect may be found in these microfilmed books. The <u>Inside File</u> (two drawers, "scrapbooks") indexes the contents of these scrapbooks by name of artist as well as subject.

Other reference publications include:

Allgemeines Lexikon der bildenden Künstler der Antike bis zur Gegenwart, edited by Ulrich Thieme and Felix Becker, 37 vols. Munich, 1992. [MAN 93-9188]
Allgemeines Lexikon der bildenden Künstler des 20. Jahrhunderts, by Hans Vollmer. 6 vols. Munich, 1992. [MAN 93-9189]
Artist Biographies Master Index, edited by Barbara McNeil. Detroit, [1986]. [MAO 87-274]
Dictionnaire Critique et Documentaire des Peintres, Sculpteurs, Dessinateurs et Graveurs de tous les Temps et de Tous les Pays, by Emmanuel Bénézit, 10 vols. Paris, 1976 [*R-ART 90-2371]; 1999 [MAO 00-7289]
Index to Artistic Biography, by Patricia Pate Havlice. 2 vols. Metuchen, 1973. [MAO 88-8106]
Mallett's Index of Artists: international-biographical, by Daniel T. Mallett. New York, 1948. [MAO (Mallett...]

NOTE: Not all periodicals or books listed in these indexes are in the Division's collections. See also "Electronic Resources" below.

2. Architecture - The Inside File (drawers 1–25) contains sources on European and American buildings in the Library's holdings, such as pictures of clubs, hotels, public buildings, prominent family houses/mansions, department stores, synagogues and churches. Architect biographies and portraits are also indexed here. Encyclopedias, dictionaries and periodical indexes available in this Collection include:

Architects in Practice, New York City, 1840–1900, by Dennis Steadman Francis, lists architects and their addresses. New York, 1979. [MQWO 80-2888]
Architects in Practice New York City 1900–1940, by James Ward. Union, NJ, [1989]. [MQWO+ 90-8210]
The Avery Index to Architectural Periodicals, covers over 1,000 architectural periodicals from 1934 to the present. [MQB+ 73-2854]. Useful to locate articles on architects and architectural structures. Available in hard copy, CD-ROM, and online (see below). See also *Avery Obituary Index to Architects,* 2nd Edition. Boston, 1980. [MQY+ 82-1920]
Biographical Dictionary of American Architects (Deceased), by Henry Withey, includes articles on over 2,000 architects and provides their dates of birth and death. Detroit, 1956. [MQY]
Contemporary Architects, by Muriel Emanuel. 3rd Edition. New York, [1994]. [MQY+ 95-9467]
The Macmillan Encyclopedia of Architects, editor-in-chief Adolf K. Placzek. 4 vols. New York, 1982. Covers architects internationally through the ages. Includes and index by building name. [MQY 84-1787]

3. Electronic Resources - Computers in Room 300 offer access to selected electronic resources. These include stand alone databases, CD-ROMs, and online databases. Among these are:

Art Index & Art Index Retrospective, 1929 to present. (See above for print copy)
ArtBibliographies Modern: Abstracts of the Current Literature of Modern Art, Photography and Design, 1974-.
AskArt, a database of more than 26,000 American artists, painters, sculptors and illustrators, listing books (and page number) with information about the artist.
The Avery Index to Architectural Periodicals, 1934 to present, with more than 455,000 records, updated daily. (See above for print copy.)
BHA: Bibliography of the History of Art, 1973 to present. Includes *Répertoire d'Art et d'Archeologie, (RAA)*, 1973–1989, and *RILA: Répertoire International de la Littérature de L'Art,* 1975–1989.
Design and Applied Arts Index, 1973 to present, includes more than 450 journals dealing with design and craft. (See MAC+ 90-2802 for print copy.)
Index to Nineteenth-Century American Art Periodicals, 1840–1907.

See also the Division's *Electronic Research Guide,* compiled by V. Rutigliano, Art & Architecture Collection.

B. Prints and Photography Collection (Room 308) has books and other pictorial resources. The Prints Collection has reference materials useful for studying the history of print making and individual print makers, as well as original prints. It covers the areas of engraving, woodcuts and lithography and includes some 180,000 prints and 15,000 books and pamphlets. The Photography Collection has over 200,000 photographs and 70,000 book entries in the catalog, and includes single photographs by subject and biographical material on photographers.

1. The Portraits File contains clippings, photographs and engravings of eminent, although not necessarily famous, people through 1900. The file is arranged by sitter. These could be prominent business people, professionals, leaders of organizations, unions, etc. NOTE: The Division's card index to separately cataloged portraits is located to the right of the librarian's desk. An index to portraits in selected books which are not shelved in the Print Division, "Portraits (Not in Room 308)," is located in the back room.

2. I. N. Phelps Stokes Collection of American Historical Prints covers historical events, cities, landscapes, maps and plans of American cities, 1497–1891. The collection includes 800 views and maps of New York City. A book catalog of this collection is arranged by year and indexed by artist, engraver and subject (views).

3. Eno Collection of New York City Views is similar to the Stokes Collection but covers only New York City. This Collection includes 477 New York views from the 17th through the19th century. A book catalog is available arranged by borough and year and indexed by artist and subject.

4. The Artist Files in the Print Room (The Print Makers File) (engravers, etchers, etc.) includes all sorts of ephemera, reproductions of works, exhibition notices, clippings, reviews and obituaries. It is arranged in envelopes by the name of the print maker.

   There is a card index which includes all reference material on print makers in published volumes and periodicals located in the Print Collection. This index is arranged alphabetically by name of print maker.

5. Book Illustrator's Index is a card index arranged alphabetically by name of book illustrator. It includes illustrated books shelved elsewhere in the Research Libraries.

6. Bookplate Index is a card index arranged alphabetically by the name of owners of bookplates included in books throughout the Research Libraries.

7. Photographer's File is a vertical file including clippings which may have biographical information about photographers as well as the subjects photographed. A card index to these files is arranged alphabetically by name of photographer.

8. The Photography Catalog of all materials in the Division is a card index arranged by name of photographer and the subject photographed.

Finding Aids:

See NEW YORK PUBLIC LIBRARY - HUMANITIES AND SOCIAL SCIENCES LIBRARY, GENERAL RESEARCH DIVISION for a description of the computerized catalog (CATNYP). Through retrospective conversion, pre-1972 Art, Prints and Photograph book records are now available on CATNYP. However, the Division's book catalogs may be more complete for this period. Original prints are not part of these catalogs, and photographs are only partially covered. Card files supplement the main catalog. Many of the special collections have their own catalogs

Staff members will help direct researchers to the appropriate catalog. The staff will also conduct short searches in response to telephone requests. Time permitting, they will look at two or three sources located at the reference desk to verify that information on an artist is available. Patrons must come in to conduct actual research.

Description of Facility:

Located on the third floor of the Library, the Art and Architecture Collection is in Room 300 (at the south end of the Rose Main Reading Room 315) and Prints and Photography Collections are in Room 308. The Art and Architecture room can seat more than 60 people while the Prints and Photography room can seat 20. There are eight computers with access to CATNYP and Electronic Resources; and three microfiche readers in Room 300. The "Inside File" is located behind the reference desk and under the staircases. Ask the Reference Librarian for access.

Restrictions on Use:

For research in the Prints and Photography Collections, a Card of Admission is required. Room 308 is always locked and only those with a card are admitted. Apply in person to the Office of Special Collections in Room 316. Proper identification and purpose of research must be stated. Normally, the card is issued immediately. A genealogical request, such as the need for information on a specific artist, or a print of a specific location, is considered sufficient. NOTE: See also NEW YORK PUBLIC LIBRARY - HUMANITIES AND SOCIAL SCIENCES LIBRARY, GENERAL RESEARCH DIVISION, "Description of Facility" for photo ACCESS card to be required of all patrons.

Researchers must sign in at the reference desk. Materials can be obtained quickly unless many items are ordered. Some photographic materials require 24-hour notice. Depending on the category of material, five items may be requested at one time (fewer if very busy). Researchers may be allowed to use a particular item for a limited time if it is in high demand. None of the materials in this Division can be sent to the Main Reading Room for use when the Division is closed. All copying is done at the discretion of the staff depending on the material's condition and age. No original, fragile or rare materials, such as prints or photographs, can ever be photocopied. The staff will assist in finding alternative materials or ways of reproduction. For example, staff permission may be granted to take a photograph (preferably with a 35mm camera using existing lights but no flash or special lights).

169

NEW YORK PUBLIC LIBRARY
SLAVIC AND BALTIC DIVISION

Facility Director: Edward Kasinec, Chief

Address: Fifth Avenue at 42nd Street, Room 217 ♿
         New York, NY 10018-2788

         (Cross Streets: 40th and 42nd Streets; 5th and 6th Avenues)

Phone Number: (212) 930-0713, 0714
Fax: (212) 930-0693
E-mail: Slavicref@nypl.org
Website: www.nypl.org/research/chss/slv/slav.balt.html

Hours of Operation:

Thursday to Saturday 10:00 am to 5:45 pm
Tuesday and Wednesday 11:00 am to 7:15 pm

Closed Sunday, Monday and all legal holidays.

Closest Public Transportation, Directions and Fees/Copies:

See NEW YORK PUBLIC LIBRARY - HUMANITIES AND SOCIAL SCIENCES LIBRARY, GENERAL RESEARCH DIVISION AND MICROFORMS ROOM.

Description of Resources:

The Slavic and Baltic Division (formerly the Slavonic Division) has over 460,000 books, 1,200 current serials, and 21,600 microfilm titles in 12 Slavic and 3 Baltic languages. The two largest components of the collection are in the Eastern Slavic vernacular languages (i.e. Belarusian, Russian, Ukrainian) and Western Slavic languages (e.g. Czech, Slovak, Polish) which constitute 44% and 14% of the collection respectively. Other holdings are in Bulgarian, Carpatho-Rusyn, Croatian, Latvian, Lithuanian, Macedonian, Serbian, Slovenian, and Sorbian. Judaica in the Slavic languages are usually found in the JEWISH DIVISION. For an overview and history of this Division, see *Slavic and Baltic Library Resources in The New York Public Library: A First History and Practical Guide,* by Robert H. Davis, Jr. New York 1994. [*R-Slav. Div 95-5116]. The following are some of the resources of interest to genealogists in this Division:

1. <u>Guides to Archives/Libraries</u>

  Archiwum Panstwowe w Polsce. [National Archives in <u>Poland</u>.] Warsaw, 1998. [R-Slav. Div. 99-5733]
  Boriak, Hennadii.V. *Natsionalna arkhivna spadshchyna Ukrainy ta derzhavnyi reiestr "Arkheohrafichna Ukrainika": arkhivni dokumentalni resursy ta naukovo-informatsiini systemy.* [The national archival heritage of <u>Ukraine</u> and the national register "Arkheohrafichna Ukrainika": archival documentary resources and scientific informational systems.] Kiev, 1995. [Desk-Slav.Div. 97-1309]
  Deich, Genrikh Markovich. *Putevoditel: arkhivnye dokumenty po istorii Evreev v Rossii v XIX-nachale XX vv.* [A research guide to materials on the history of Russian Jewry (19th and early 20th centuries) in selected archives of the former <u>Soviet Union</u>. Moscow, [1994]. [Desk-Slav. Div. 97-1275]
  Dokumenty Natsionalnogo arkhivnogo fonda Respubliki Belarus v Natsionalnoi biblioteke i muzeiakh sistemy Ministerstva Kultury i pechati Respubliki Belarus: spravochnik. [Documents of the National Archival Collection of the Republic of <u>Belarus</u> in the National Library and Museums of the system of the Ministry of Culture and presses of the Republic of Belarus: A handbook.] Minsk, 1995. [*R-Slav. Div. 96-7944]
  Eskenazi, Zhak. *Judaica Bulgarica: evreite po bulgarskite zemi: anotirana bibliografiia.* [Judaica <u>Bulgaria</u>: Jews from Bulgaria: annotated bibliography.] Sofia, 1999. [Desk-Slav. Div. 00-6510]
  Feldman, D. *Obzor dokumentalnykh istochnikov po istorii evreev v fondakh RGADA.* [A Review of documentary sources on the history of the Jews in the collections of the <u>Russian</u> State Archives of Ancient Acts.] Moscow, 1994. [*QGS 97-706]
  Grant, Steven and John H. Brown. *The <u>Russian</u> Empire and Soviet Union: A Guide to Manuscripts and Archival Material in the United States.* Boston, 1981. [*R-Slav.Div. 83-43]
  Grimsted, Patricia. *Archives and Manuscript Repositories in the <u>USSR, Estonia, Latvia, Lithuania</u> and <u>Belorussia</u>.* Princeton, [1981]. [*R-Slav.Div 82-1212]

- *Archives and Manuscript Repositories in the USSR: Ukraine and Moldavia.* Princeton, [1988–]. [*R-Slav.Div. 89-21057 Bk 1.]
- *Archives and Manuscript Repositories in the USSR: Moscow and Leningrad..* Princeton, 1971. [*R-Slav.Div. 82-829]; and supplement. Zug, Switzerland, [1976]. [*R-Slav.Div .82-830]
- *Archives of Russia: A Directory and Bibliographic Guide to Holdings in Moscow and St. Petersburg.* Armonk, NY, [2000]. [*R-Slav. Div. 01-427]

Grossman, Iu, et al. *Spravochnik nauchnogo rabotnika* [Handbook for Scholars]. Lvov, 1979. Lists the archives of the USSR with addresses. (Russian) [*R-Slav.Div. 84-2615]

Karlowich, Robert A. *A Guide to Scholarly Resources on the Russian Empire and the Soviet Union in the New York Metropolitan Area.* Armonk, NY, [1990]. [*R-Slav.Div. 90-4326]

Kracow Archiwum Aktów Dawnych Miasta Krakowa [Catalog of the Krakow Archive]. Kracow, 1907–1915. [*QR (Crakow...]

Kupovetskii, M. S., E. V. Starostin and Marek Web, *Dokumenty po istorii i kulture evreev v arkhivakh Moskvy: putevoditel'.* [Documents concerning Jewish history and culture in the archives of Moscow: A guidebook.] Moscow, 1997. [*R-Slav. Div 98-5225]

Lewanski, Richard C. *Guide to Polish Libraries and Archives.* Boulder, CO, [1974]. [Desk-Slav.Div. 83-1169]

Magocsi, Paul R. *Ucrainica at the University of Toronto Library: A Catalogue of Holdings.* 2 vols. Toronto, [1985]. A guide to Ukrainian material at the University of Toronto Library. [Desk-Slav.Div. 86-1866]

Marcinkowski, Stanislaw. *Archiwum Panstwowe w Kielcach i jego oddzialy w Jedrzejowie, Pinczowie i Starachowicach: przewodnik po zasobie archiwalnym: opracowanie zbiorowe.* [National archives in Kielce and its branches in Jedrejow, Pinczow and Starachowice: guide to archival materials: collective works.] Warsaw, 1993. [Desk-Slav Div 95-562]

Mehr, Kahile B. and Daniel M. Schlyter. *Sources for Genealogical Research in the Soviet Union.* 1983. [n.c.]

Moskva. Address book of Russian Institutions. Moscow, 1962. (Russian) [*QFP]

Obzor, dokumentalnykh istochnikov po istorii evreev v fondakh RGVIA. [A survey of documentary sources for the history of the Jews in the collections of the Russian State military-historical archive.] Moscow, 1994. [*OGS 97-705]

Odessa: Tsentral'na Naukova Biblioteka [Odessa Public Library Catalog]. Odessa, 1927–1929. (Cyrillic). [*QGAA]

Scott, Robert. *A Guide to East European Scholarly Resources in the New York Metropolitan Area.* New York, 1997. [Desk-Slav. Div. 97-1602]

Sturm, Rudolf. *Czechoslovakia, A Bibliographic Guide.* Washington, DC, 1967. [*QV 72-2125]

2. Gazetteers and related works

Atlas, U.S.S.R., 1969. Includes maps from 1:1,500,000. [*R-Slav.Div.]

Goroda Rossiiskoi imperii: na 1.01.1914 so svedeniiami o nikh na 1.01.1987: spravochnik. [Cities of the Russian Empire: from January 1914 to January 1987: A reference book.] St. Petersburg, 1996. [*R-Slav. Div. 96-8127]

Horecky, Paul L. *East Central and Southeast Europe.* 1976. A guide to basic publications about each country. [Desk-Slav.Div. 78-139]

Akademie der Wissenschaften und der Literatur. *Russisches Geographisches Namenbuch.* 10 vols., 1962–1978. A German-language gazetteer of the Russian Empire. Place names are in Cyrillic script. [*R-Slav.Div. (Russisches...)]

Room, Adrian. *Placenames of Russia and the Former Soviet Union: Origins and Meanings of the Names for Over 2000 Natural Features, Towns, Regions and Countries.* Jefferson, N.C., 1996. [*R-Slav. Div. 96-2247]

Semionov-Tyan-Shanski, Petr Petrovich. *Geografichesko-statisticheskii slovar Rossiiskoi Imperii* [Geographic Dictionary]. 5 vols. St. Petersburg, 1863–1885. (Russian) [QCF 96-2436]

Slownik Geograficzny. 1900. A 16-volume geographical dictionary which provides detailed late 19th-century information on most East European communities. (Polish) [*R-Slav.Div. 78-445]

Swiatkowski, H. *Taryffa domow miasta Warszawy i Pragi: z planem ogolnym i 128 szczegolowych planikow ulic i domow.* [Tariffs of houses, cities of Warsaw and Praga: including general maps and 128 detailed maps of streets and houses.] (Originally published in Warsaw, 1852). Warsaw, 1979. [Slav. Reserve 99-6219]

3. Biographical Dictionaries

The Division has an extensive collection of Who's Who and other biographical dictionaries from the Slavic and Baltic areas. These include:

Belarus. *Kto est kto v Respublike Belarus* [Who is who in the Republic of Belarus], edited by Anatolii I. Valakhanovich, et al. Minsk, 1999. [*R-Slav. Div. 00-3653]

Bulgaria. *Koi Koi e v Bulgariia 1998* [Who's Who in Bulgaria, 1998], by Nikola Kitsevski and Raicho Radulov. Sofia, 1998. [*R-Slav.Div. 01-2361]

Czech Republic. *Cesky biograficky slovnik XX. stoleti,* compiled by Josef Tomes. 3 vols. Prague, 1999. Provides information on 12,000 Czech and Slovak personalities who had a significant impact in various areas during the last century — from politics, national economy, to literature, science, arts and sport. Includes also emigres and deceased individuals with dates of birth and death. [*R-Slav.Div. 00-11677]

* *Kdo je kdo v Ceské republice na prelomu 20. stoleti: 5000 biografickych hesel nejvyznamnejsich osobnosti,* [Who's Who in the Czech Republic in the 20th century: 5000 biographies of the most important people], edited by Michael Trestik. Prague, 1998 [*R-Slav.Div. 99-4973]; 1991/92, 1994/95. [92-918]

Estonia, Latvia, Lithuania. *Baltisches biographisches Archiv* [Baltic Biographical Archive], edited by Axel Frey. Munich, [1995]. Entries taken from 218 biographical works published between 1650 and 1993. Includes more than 80,000 individuals. [*XLS-294]

Latvia. *Es vinu pazistu: latviesu biografiska vardnica* [I know him: Latvian Biographical dictionary], edited by Zanis Unams. Reprint of 1939 edition. Grand Haven, MI, 1975. [*R-Slav.Div. 78-3687]

* *Who is Who in Latvia, 1996: Biographical dictionary.* Riga, 1996. [*R-Slav.Div. 98-6266]

Lithuania. *Kas yra kas Lietuvoje* [Who is Who in Lithuania]. Vilnius, [1993–1997]. [*R-Slav.94-1162]

Poland. *Polski Indeks Biograficzny* [Polish Biographical Index], by Gabriele Baumgartner. 4 vols. Munich, 1998. Introduction in English. These entries were taken from 333 biographical reference works published between the 17th and 20th centuries [*R-Slav.Div. 98-8762]. NOTE: This is an index to biographies in the *Polish Biographical Archives* (719 microfiche covering 88,500 entries), not yet in the Divisions collection.

* *Tomasza Swieckiego Historyczne pamiatki i znamienitych rodzin i osob dawnej Polski* [Tomasz Swieck's Historic recollections of outstanding families and personalities of Poland's past.], by Juljan Bartoszewicz. 2 vols. Reprint of original published in Warsaw, 1858/1859. [*QR 86-1336]

* *Slownik biograficzny czlonków tajnych towarzystw gimnazjalnych w Wielkim Ksiestwie Poznanskim 1850-1918* [Biographical dictionary of members of secret grammar school societies in the Grand Duchy of Poznan 1850-1918], by Marian Paluszkiewicz and Jerzy Szews. Poznan, 2000. [*QR 01-2774]

Russia and the Soviet Union. *The biographical dictionary of the former Soviet Union: prominent people in all fields from 1917 to the present,* by Jeanne Vronskaya and Vladimir Chuguev. London, [1992]. Includes 6,500 entries. [*R-Slav.Div. 93-2617]

* *Khudozhniki russkogo zarubezhia, 1917–1939: biograficheskii slovar* [Russian Artists in foreign countries, 1917–1939: biographical dictionary], by O. L. Leikind. St. Peterburg, 1999. [*R-Slav. Div. 00-2976]

* *Russischer biographischer index* [Russian biographical index], edited by Axel Frey. 4 vols. Munich, 2002. Includes over 80,000 individuals from 162 works published between 1827 and 1995. [*R-Slav. Div. 02-6666]

* *Russkoe zarubezhe--Zolotaia kniga emigratsii: pervaia tret XX veka: entsiklopedicheskii biograficheskii slovar* [Russians Abroad: Gold Book of Emigration the first third of the 20th century: Biographical Encyclopedia], edited by V.V. Shelokhaeva. Moscow, 1997. [*R-Slav. Div. 97-9179]

* *The Soviet political elite: brief biographies, indices and tables on 989 members and candidate members of the CPSU Central Committee from 1912–1969, together with an overall analysis,* by Borys Lewytzkyj. [Palo Alto, CA, 1970]. [*R-Slav. Div. 77-1422]

* *Who was Who in the USSR: a biographic directory containing 5,015 biographies of prominent Soviet historical personalities,* edited by Heinrich E. Schulz, Paul K. Urban and Andrew I. Lebed. Metuchen, NJ, 1972. [*R-Slav. Div. 75-858]

Ukraine. *Khto ie khto v Ukraini: Polityky, pidpryiemtsi, viiskovi, naukovtsi, diiachi kultury, sportsmeny,* [*Who's Who in the Ukraine: politicians, businessmen, military men, scientists, cultural leaders and sportsmen*], by Hryhorii Andrushchak, et al. Kiev, 1997. (Cyrillic) [*R-Slav. Div. 97-9271]

* *Knyha Pamiati Ukrainy* [Memorial Book Ukraine], edited by Ivan Oleksandrovych Herasymov. 200 vols., including the following oblasts: *Cherkaska, Chernigovskaia, Donetskaia, Dnipropetrovska, Kharkivska, Khersonskaia, Khmelnytska, Kirovogradskaia, Kyivska (Kiev), Luganskaia, Lvivska (Lviv), Nikolaevskaia, Poltavska, Rivnenska, Sumska, Ternopilska, Volynska, Zakarpatska, Zaporizka.* (Ukraine), 1995–. Includes Jews and non-Jews from these provinces who died or were missing in action during WW2. (Cyrillic). [*R-Slav. Div. 96-7973]. See also YIVO INSTITUTE FOR JEWISH RESEARCH, LIBRARY.

4. Newspapers:

The Division has an extensive collection of newspapers and periodicals. See the following:

Chaban, Lev. *Current Slavic, Baltic and East European Periodical and Newspaper Titles Available in the Slavic and Baltic Division, the Periodicals Division and the Branch Libraries of the New York Public Library.* New York, 2002. Arranged by language of periodical. [Desk-Slav Div - Draft]

Horbal, Bogdan, Robert Davis, Jr and George D. Estafy. *Russian Periodicals, Newspapers and Almanacs, 1703–1939 at The New York Public Library.* 2 vols. New York, 1999. [*R-Slav.Div. 75-106 No. 94]

Karlowich, Robert. *Russian-Language Periodical Press in New York City from 1889–1914.* New York, 1981. (English) [Desk-Slav. Div. 85-392]

5. Census

Horn, Maurycy. *Regesty dokumentow i ekscerpty z Metryki Koronnej do historii Zydow w Polsce, 1697–1795.* [Registers of documents and excerpts from "Metryka Koronna [Crown Census]" concerning the Jews in Poland, 1697–1795.] 2 vols. Wroclaw, 1984–. [*QR 85-1117 v. 1, 2]

Tsentralnyi Statisticheskii Komitet. *Obshchii svod, 1–2.* 2 vols., 1897. This is a statistical summary of the 1897 census of the Russian Empire by region/city. (Russian-French) [*QB (Russia)]. Of particular interest are the tables which provide by Oblast/City, the following:

Table IV - religion of the population;
Table XI - number of cemeteries by religion; and,
Table XII - number of synagogues and churches.

6. Cemetery Lists (mostly non-Jewish)

Biernatowie, Andrzej and Barbara. *Cmentarz Powazkowski w Warszawie* [Powazkowski cemetery in Warsaw]. Includes tombstone inscriptions and cemetery plot maps. Vol. 3. Warsaw, 1980. [*QR 98-659]

Nicholas, Grand Duke of Russia. *Moskovskii Nekropol* [Tombstone Lists Moscow Area]. Pre-Russian Revolution. 1907–1908. [*QE]

Nicieja, Stanisław Sławomir. *Cmentarz Łyczakowski we Lwowie w latach 1786–1986* [Lyczakowski cemetery in Lviv, 1786–1986]. Wroclaw, 1988. Includes a name index. [*QO 89-26711]

Puget, Wanda. *Zabytkowe cmentarze i mogily województwa lomzynskiego* [Historical cemeteries and tombs in the Lomza voivodship]. Warsaw, 1991. List of cemeteries by locality includes some Jewish cemeteries. [*QR 97-2001]

7. Name Indexes

Sack, Sallyann and Suzan F. Wynne. *The Russian Consular Records Index and Catalog.* New York, 1987. [*R-Slav. Div. 87-4636]

Unbegaun, Boris O. *Russian Surnames.* Oxford, 1972. [*R-Slav. Div. 85-4708]

8. Encyclopedias

Brockhaus, F.A. and I.A. Efron, eds. *Novyi Entsiklopedicheskii Slovar* [New Encyclopedia - lists cities and shtetlach, and, in some cases, the Jewish population as of the 1897 census]. 1904. (Russian) [*QAC]

Evreiskaia entsiklopediia: svod znanii o evreistve i ego kulture v proshlom i nastoiashchem [Russian Jewish Encyclopedia], edited by Simon Dubnow, Juda Loeb Katzenelson, David Baron Gunzburg, and Albert Harkavy. 16 vols. Reprint of 1906–1913 edition. Moscow, 1991. [*QAC 97-3316]

Rossiiskaia evreiskaia entsiklopediia [Encyclopedia of Russian Jewry], edited by G. G. Branover. Moscow, 1994. Library has volumes 1–4. [*QAC (Subject) 00-6550]. NOTE: See NEW YORK PUBLIC LIBRARY, DOROT JEWISH DIVISION which has volume 1 in English. [*PBZ 99-930]

9. City and Telephone Directories

A sample of available Directories which list names of individuals are those for [classmarks *QCA or *QCA+]:

Ekaterinoslav, 1912	Russia, 1899, 1903, 1911/12
Gomel, 1908	St. Petersburg/Leningrad, 1895, 1899, 1902,
Kiev, 1911–1912	1939
Lviv, 1897, 1916	Saratov, 1911
Moscow, 1875–1895, 1908–1911, 1915–1917,	Siberia, 1908, 1924
1927–1931, 1936	Southwestern Region (Kiev, Podolsk and Volinsk
Odessa Gubernia, 1926, 1927	Gubernia), 1913
Omsk, 1911	

In addition, the Division has business and organization directories for various regions. [Slav. Reserve 96-7788] NOTE: The Lviv directory cited above is also a business directory. Most businesses were known by the proprietor's name. These include:

Austro-Hungarian empire, 1877: 49,000 trade, business, and stock companies in 6,237 locations.

Galicia, 1897: business and professional directory by town and type of business.

Galicia, 1901: industry.

Galicia, 1933: industry and commerce.

Poland (only Russian-Poland), 1906: factory industries.

Poland, 1922: industry, commerce and finance.

Poland (including Gdansk), 1926–1927, 1929: trade, industry, handicraft and agriculture.

Poland (telephone directory), 1930. Includes both business and residential listings by town.

For a more detailed description of these business directories, see "Polish Business, Street and Telephone Directories...NYPL," by Jeffrey Cymbler published in *DOROT, The Journal of the Jewish Genealogical Society, Inc.,* Volume 18, Numbers 2–3, Winter 1996–Spring 1997. See also NEW YORK PUBLIC LIBRARY - HUMANITIES AND SOCIAL SCIENCES LIBRARY, GENERAL RESEARCH DIVISION AND MICROFORMS ROOM for additional city and telephone directories in the NYPL's collection.

10. Photographs and Avant-Garde Books:

The Division's collection includes more than 40 albums containing photographs from the 1880s–1930s including geographic areas (cities, towns), religious subjects (churches, monasteries); and political subjects (tsars, revolution) and an extensive postcard collection. See also,

Russian and Ukrainian Avant-Garde and Constructivist Books and Serials at the New York Public Library: A First Census & Listing of Artists Represented, by Robert H. Davis, Jr. and Margaret Sandler. New York, 1998. Includes an index of graphic artists who designed covers or illustrated books.

Written in Light: Original Slavic, Baltic, East European and Eurasian Photographs in the NYPL, ca 1850–1935, compiled by HeGwone Yoo. (In preparation)

11. Dictionaries (On open shelf)

This Division has dictionaries of Slavic and Baltic languages (Russian, Polish, Ukrainian, Bulgarian, Czech, Lithuanian and Latvian) to English and other languages.

Finding Aids:

The 44-volume *Dictionary Catalog of the Slavonic Collection, Second Edition* includes the 1898–1972 holdings of the Division. Materials acquired and cataloged by the Division after 1972 and all Roman-script Slavic and Baltic titles acquired pre-1972 are included in the Library's online public access catalog, CATNYP. See NEW YORK PUBLIC LIBRARY, HUMANITIES AND SOCIAL SCIENCES LIBRARY, GENERAL RESEARCH DIVISION AND MICROFORMS ROOM for a description of CATNYP. Some but not all Cyrillic materials have been entered into CATNYP. Users must utilize the *Dictionary* catalogs to find most materials written in Cyrillic. In addition, there are 59 "supplemental" printed volumes, to the 44-volume core catalog. These are cataloged in CATNYP, and are available with the *Dictionary Catalog* in the corridor outside Room 217. Classmarks beginning with [*Q] can be found in the Slavic and Baltic Division.

The Division also has the *Bibliographic Guide to Slavic, Baltic, and Eurasian Studies* (formerly known as *Bibliographic Guide to Soviet and East European Studies*), 1979–. These annual publications include books and other materials cataloged by the Research Libraries of the NYPL and the Library of Congress.

Description of Facility:

The Slavic and Baltic Division is located on the second floor in Room 217. Four computers/printers with access to CATNYP are in the hallway immediately outside Room 217. The room can seat 24 persons. A Reference Librarian is available to assist researchers in finding materials. There are 2 microfilm and one microfiche readers in the room. The Division's extensive Reference Collection (23,500 volumes), line the walls of the Reading Room. Books with classmarks (call numbers) beginning with [*R] can be found on these open shelves. All catalogs are in the corridor outside Room 217.

Restrictions on Use:

No more than 5 books can be requested at one time.

Rare books (generally pre-1850) are provided to researchers at a designated table in the Slavic and Baltic Division. Researchers must show some identification when requesting these materials.

NOTE: See NEW YORK PUBLIC LIBRARY - HUMANITIES AND SOCIAL SCIENCES LIBRARY, GENERAL RESEARCH DIVISION, "Description of Facility" for photo ACCESS card to be required of all patrons.

NEW YORK PUBLIC LIBRARY FOR THE PERFORMING ARTS
DOROTHY AND LEWIS B. CULLMAN CENTER

Facility Director: Jacqueline Z. Davis, Executive Director
Donald McCormick, Curator, Rodgers and Hammerstein Archives of Recorded Sound
Madeleine Nichols, Curator, Jerome Robbins Dance Division
Robert Taylor, Curator, Billy Rose Theatre Collection
Charles Eubanks, Acting Chief, Music Division

Address: 40 Lincoln Center Plaza (111 Amsterdam Avenue), 3rd Floor ♿
New York, NY 10023-7498

(Cross Street: Corner of 65th Street)

Phones: (212) 870-1663 (Recorded Sound)   (212) 870-1639 (Theatre Collection)
(212) 870-1657 (Dance Division)   (212) 870-1650 (Music Division)

Fax: (212) 870-1720 (Recorded Sound)   (212) 870-1868 (Theatre Collection)
(212) 870-1869 (Dance Division)   (212) 870-1794 (Music Division)

E-mail: performingarts@nypl.org
rha@nypl.org (Recorded Sound)
dance@nypl.org (Dance Division)
theatrediv@nypl.org (Theatre Collection)
musicdiv@nypl.org (Music Division)

Website: www.nypl.org/research/lpa/lpa.html

Hours of Operation:

Tuesday, Wednesday,
  Friday, Saturday: 12:00 noon to 6:00 pm
Thursday: 12:00 noon to 8:00 pm

Closed Sunday, Monday and legal holidays.

Closest Public Transportation:

Subway: 1 or 9 to 66th Street/Lincoln Center

Bus: M5, M7 (north) or M104 to Broadway and 65/66th Streets
M11 (north) or M66 to 65th Street and Amsterdam Avenue
M7 or M11 (south) to Columbus Avenue and 66th Street

Directions:

Take the #1 or #9 (local) train to the 66th Street station. Exit the station to Lincoln Center Plaza. The Library is at the northwest corner of the Plaza (next to the Vivian Beaumont Theatre). A second entrance to the Library is on Amsterdam Avenue at 65th Street. NOTE: Use the Plaza entrance for wheelchair accessiblity.

Description of Resources:

The Library's performing arts collections began with acquisitions that formed the Music Division in 1888; the Theatre Collection in 1931; and the Dance Division in 1944. The Rodgers and Hammerstein Archives of Recorded Sound, originally part of the Music Division, became a separate research unit in 1965 when all these collections were united into one facility at Lincoln Center. Today, the NEW YORK PUBLIC LIBRARY FOR THE PERFORMING ARTS houses 9 million items including books, historic recordings, videotapes, manuscripts, correspondence, sheet music, press clippings, programs, posters and photographs. Materials in the research collections of specific interest to genealogists include:

1.   Rodgers and Hammerstein Archives of Recorded Sound: This repository houses approximately 500,000 recordings and videotapes of all types of music, including early operatic performances recorded on wax cylinders, poetry, popular music and historic broadcasts of famous personalities and statesmen.

    The Benedict Stambler Memorial Archives of Recorded Jewish Music is of particular interest to Jewish genealogists. The 78-rpm recordings in this collection date back to 1910 and the LPs (long playing records) to 1950.

The LPs have a performer index. The collection includes also the "Vistas of Israel" radio program; and the Ruth Rubin Collection of Yiddish Folk songs and Folklore, 1947–1966.

The Archives houses clipping files which include articles about the sound recording industry by country, artist and subject; and taped interviews with actors, directors, producers, singers and composers.

2. <u>Jerome Robbins Dance Division</u>: This Division is the largest and most comprehensive archive in the world devoted to the documentation of dance. It contains 29,000 reels of film and videotape of live dance performances, as well as 3,400 hours of taped interviews with well-known choreographers. The collection includes more than one million manuscript items, 26,500 files of newspaper clippings, 330,000 photographs, 1,900 original costume and set designs and 34,500 books as well as periodicals, diaries, notebooks and letters, covering all forms of dance — ballet, modern, social, ethnic and folk.

Of particular note are the <u>Collected Papers of Fred Berk</u>, who worked on a Bibliography of Jewish Dance during his lifetime. Videotapes and oral histories document the work of artists including Anna Sokolow, Jane Dudley, Pearl Lang, Edith Segal, Felix Fibich and Ze'eva Cohen. The complete professional papers of Jerome Robbins; and the manuscript, *Trattato dell'arte del ballo,* written by an Italian-Jewish dancing master, Guglielmo Ebreo da Pesaro, circa 1460, can be found here.

3. <u>Billy Rose Theatre Collection</u>: Every aspect of the entertainment world, including drama, film, radio, television, circus, vaudeville and magic is covered in this collection. The Yiddish theatre dating back to the 1920s is also documented.

The collection includes clipping files from newspapers and periodicals organized under 25,000 headings with files on individual performers, designers, dramatists and directors. Obituaries of theatre personalities are included. There are thousands of photographs, playbills, prints, posters, programs and scripts in the collection.

The Theatre Collection houses the <u>Robinson Locke Collection</u> of Dramatic Scrapbooks, 1870–1920, some 900 bound volumes and over 2,300 portfolios which include loose clippings and photographs; the <u>Hiram Stead Collection</u> on the British Theatre, 1672 to 1932, which contains letters, autographs and portraits in 600 portfolios; the <u>Henin Collection</u> which covers the Parisian stage from the 17th to 19th centuries; the <u>Chamberlain and Lyman Brown Collection</u>, which includes scrapbooks of stage and film personalities, 1910–1961; and the <u>Radio Writers Guild</u> which contains membership correspondence and records. The <u>Theatre on Film and Tape (TOFT) Archive</u> includes film and videotape of live Broadway, Off-Broadway, and regional theatre productions documented since 1970; theatre-related television programs; and dialogues between distinguished theatre personalities about their careers and techniques. See "Restrictions on Use." Stage photographs can be found in the White Studio Collection, 1910–1936 and in the Vandamm Studio Collection, 1920–1960.

Among those individuals whose papers are located here are Harold Clurman (1935–1978), including his daily diaries and a scrapbook given to him by the Habimah Theatre in Tel Aviv honoring his work there in 1949; Lillian Gish (1909–1992); Gypsy Rose Lee, (c. 1910–1970); Zero and Kate Mostel (1915–1956); Paul Muni (1920–1967); Harold Prince (1907–1986); Mary Pickford and Buddy Rogers Group (1943–1976).

4. <u>Music Division</u>: The world of music is documented in this Division through composers' scores, an extensive clipping collection, programs, photographs, original scene designs, manuscripts and books.

The Division has Biographical Index Cards to 1989 which include biographical data, paste-on clippings or references to sources with biographical information on a particular musician or composer; and thousands of composers' autographs from the 18th through the 20th centuries in various collections. Other holdings of interest include:

<u>Arthur M. Abell Papers</u> include letters from such individuals as Max Bruch, Serge and Olga Koussevitzky, Isidore Philipp and Richard Strauss; and a large collection of photographs.
<u>Letter File</u> includes several thousand letters of musicians and composers from the 18th to the 20th centuries.
<u>Mel and Shifra Gold Yiddish Music Project</u> has 85,000 folios of out-of-print Yiddish and Hebrew sheet music.
<u>Mendelssohn Family letters</u>, 1821–1847 includes 740 letters written by Felix Mendelssohn and his sister Fanny to their parents and each other.
<u>Otto Hess Collection</u> includes 4,000 photographs of jazz musicians in concert or at leisure.

Among the books in the Division of particular interest to Jewish genealogists are:

Federation of Jewish Philanthropies. *In the Jewish Tradition: A Directory of Performing Artists.* Includes photographs and biographies. Hazel Weinberger and Robin Mayers, eds. New York, [1985]. [JNC 87-4]
Nulman, Macy. *The Concise Encyclopedia of Jewish Music.* New York, [1975]. [JME 75-181]. (on open shelf)

Finding Aids:

The online CATNYP catalog now includes all materials in the Dance Division, almost the entire collection of books and periodicals of the Recorded Sound and the Music Divisions, and books acquired by the Billy Rose Theatre Collection. A full set of the NYPL *Dictionary Catalogs* can be found in the open-stack reference area adjacent to the Research Collections Reading Room. See NYPL GENERAL RESEARCH DIVISION for a description of these catalogs.

Each Division also has typed finding aides of archival collections, many of which are accessible online (see Digital Library Collection, http://digital.nypl.org/findingaids.html). Some, like that for the Stambler Archives, list holdings by name of performer. Additional finding aids include:

1. <u>Rodgers and Hammerstein Archives of Recorded Sound</u>: The Archives has a card catalog arranged by name of composer/artist, subject and title of work, for most acquisitions through 1979. The Reference Desk librarian also has access to ATLAS, a database covering LPs, audio tapes, CDs and videotapes cataloged after 1979; and AREV, an internal database covering unpublished sound and video recordings of the Rodgers and Hammerstein Archives. A separate card index exists for recordings that are included in the WNEW collection (78-rpm and 45-rpm recordings played on WNEW radio). This index has a "Performers" section.

    For old recordings (mostly 78-rpm), check the *Rigler-Deutsch Record Index* on microfiche. These microfiche are arranged by title, performer, composer and label. (This index also includes the record holdings of Syracuse, Yale and Stanford Universities and the Library of Congress.)

    The Archives has the *Schwann* catalog (U.S. recordings), 1949–2001, and *Gramophone* (English classical recordings), 1923 to the present. Not all records listed here are in the Archives collection.

2. <u>Jerome Robbins Dance Division</u>: In addition to CATNYP and typed finding aids, there are brief descriptions of major dance collections and a list of oral history project participants with year interviewed, on the web. The Dance Division holdings can be searched in CATNYP or seperately (updated daily), and are also on *Dance on Disk,* a CD-ROM which is updated annually; and published in annual supplements to the *Dictionary Catalog*. Each of these catalogs and the separate *Index to Dance Periodicals* (1990–), also serve as an index to more than 35 international dance journals. All special collections and clipping files have been integrated into these catalogs which are arranged by author, title and subject. Names of performers and choreographers are included here. *Dance on Camera, 2002: Videotapes Available for Viewing in the Dance Division*, can be consulted at the Dance Division Reference Desk.

3. <u>Billy Rose Theatre Collection</u>: There is an integrated card catalog (white label drawers) for non-book materials (programs, clippings, photographs, scrapbooks, etc.) acquired through 1993 which includes names of performers, subjects and titles of productions. The Reference Desk librarian has access to AREV, a database covering the Theatre Collection's non-book materials, 1993 to the present. Researchers can also consult Part III of the *Dictionary of the Theatre and Drama Collections* published by G.K. Hall and Company, for non-book items cataloged pre-1974. Check CATNYP first for Theatre Collection books, scripts and periodicals. If not found, check the card catalog (blue label drawers) for books, scripts and periodicals cataloged pre-1972.

    A binder at the Reference Desk of the Theatre Collection lists all films in the TOFT archive through November 1, 1996. Films are arranged by title of production. Names of performers and titles of later productions are listed in CATNYP. Advance appointments are recommended for viewing films. Only four viewing stations are held open for walk-ins. Call (212) 870-1641.

4. <u>Music Division</u>: Biographical Index Cards and the Letter File card index are arranged alphabetically by name. The Division has a subject card index but no name index for its extensive clipping files. These files, however, are arranged alphabetically by surname. Submit a call slip requesting a file on a particular person or all files with a particular surname. Other useful, although not current indexes include the Poets File, Jewish Music File, Black Music File, Musician's File (1800–1950) and Scrapbook File.

Description of Facility:

Researchers must go to the newly renovated Research Collections Reading Room on the third floor opposite the elevators to access collections in the four Divisions described above. There are reference librarians representing each of the four Divisions on duty at Reference Desks. The Reading Room, which extends across the width of the building, seats c. 150 researchers at eight study tables that are equipped with data jacks for use of laptop computers. The Reading Room houses 35 computers with access to CATNYP. Twenty-four of these can also access performing arts databases, electronic databases of the NEW YORK PUBLIC LIBRARY - HUMANITIES AND SOCIAL SCIENCES LIBRARY and other websites available free to researchers. Circulating materials can be found on the first and second floors of the Center. There are

66 computers on these floors with access to CATNYP. Of these, 22 can access electronic resources. An additional 15 computers with internet access are available near the Plaza entrance.

The Reading Room houses card catalogs of the Music Division and Billy Rose Theatre Collection. The Music Division's Black Music File and Jewish Music File are not in the public area of the Library but can be brought to researchers. The card catalog of the Rodgers and Hammerstein Archive of Recorded Sound is in the Reference Room adjacent to the Reading Room, which also houses open-stack reference materials and published *Dictionary Catalogs*. Typed finding aids in black binders for Recorded Sound and Music Division collections are on open shelves in the Reference Room. Dance Division and Billy Rose Theatre Collection finding aids are at their respective Reference Desks.

There are 20 monitors for viewing Dance Division materials; and 12 listening stations to hear Recorded Sound holdings. The Lucille Lortel Room, adjacent to the Reading Room, houses the Theatre Division's Theatre on Film and Tape Archive (TOFT) and 24 screening stations on which these films can be viewed.

There are 8 microfilm/microfiche reader/printers. Five of these are in the Reading Room and 3 are in the Copy Services center located to the far right of the entrance to the Reading Room.

The Katharine Cornell-Guthrie McClintic Room, to the far left of the Reading Room, is reserved for use of rare materials or materials in fragile condition.

Fees/Copies:

Copy Services provides quick copies and photographic reproductions of research materials, as permitted by Division librarians. If self-service copying is permitted, a purple form will be provided to the researcher by the Reference Desk librarian. For fragile, rare or oversized materials, a white form is provided. For photocopy, photographic service or research fees, see NEW YORK PUBLIC LIBRARY, HUMANITIES AND SOCIAL SCIENCES LIBRARY, GENERAL RESEARCH DIVISION. Copy Services on the 3rd floor has 3 self-service photocopiers.

Copies of LPs, 78-rpm recordings and other conventional formats cost $40 per hour of recording ($20 minimum). Cylinders, wire recordings and other non-standard formats are $50 per hour (one hour minimum). All digital recording (including compact discs) cost $60 per hour (minimum $30). This does not include the tape costs (from $3 to $25) or pitching to score ($100 per hour). Add $2.50 for shipping and handling charges in the U.S.A. Payment should be by check or money order, payable to the "NYPL/Rodgers and Hammerstein Archives." The Curator must approve all requests. See "Restrictions on Use."

Restrictions on Use:

Researchers wishing to enter the Research Collections Reading Room must check coats and briefcases on the first or third floors. None of the materials in the special collections described above may be borrowed. A maximum of 15 items may be requested for viewing at one time. NOTE: See NEW YORK PUBLIC LIBRARY - HUMANITIES AND SOCIAL SCIENCES LIBRARY, GENERAL RESEARCH DIVISION, "Description of Facility" for photo ACCESS card to be required of all patrons.

Photocopying of rare and fragile material is not permitted. Such items may sometimes be reproduced by other reprographic methods. Use of portable scanner is not permitted in the Reading Room. Researchers must apply to the librarian on duty for permission to photograph any material in the Research Collections Reading Room. Lights, copy stands, tripods and other such accessories are not permitted during open hours. If additional equipment is required, photographers must arrange a special appointment by calling (212) 870-1778. A fee will be charged for this appointment.

Recorded Sound: In order to make audio duplicates of the material from the Rodgers and Hanmerstein Archives of Recorded Sound, the material must no longer be available from commercial distributors, out-of-print dealers, or circulating library record collections and must be used for study purposes only. Written permission from the record company is required if any commercial use is intended. No copying of private, noncommercial material is allowed without the written permission of the proprietary rights holder.

Dance Division: Written permission from the donor, the union, the film company and/or the choreographer may be needed to view some films and videotapes in the Dance collection. The librarian will advise of restrictions. Restrictions have been placed also on some manuscripts and on some oral histories. For such restricted items, one day's notice must be given the library before viewing can be arranged. Call (212) 870-1657.

Copying of oral history recordings and manuscripts in the Dance collection is not permitted.

Permission to reproduce materials from the Billy Rose Theatre Collection for publication in books, magazines, documentaries or for other use including broadcasting, must be requested in writing. A fee may be charged. Users are responsible for obtaining reproduction and/or copyright clearances.

NEW YORK PUBLIC LIBRARY
SCHOMBURG CENTER FOR RESEARCH IN BLACK CULTURE

Facility Director: Howard Dodson, Director

Address: 515 Malcolm X Boulevard (formerly Lenox Avenue)   ♿
New York, NY 10037-1801

(Cross Street: Corner of 135th Street)

Phone: (212) 491-2200 (General Research and Reference Division)
(212) 491-2224 (Manuscripts, Archives and Rare Books Division)
(212) 491-2235 (Moving Image and Recorded Sound Division)
(212) 491-2057 (Photographs and Prints Division)

Fax: (212) 491-6760

E-mail: scgenref@nypl.org (General Research and Reference Division)
scmarbref@nypl.org (Manuscripts, Archives and Rare Books Division)
scphotoref@nypl.org (Photographs and Prints Division)

Website: www.nypl.org/research/sc/sc.html

Hours of Operation:

	General Research	Manuscripts, Archives.	Photographs & Prints
Tuesday	12:00 noon to 8:00pm	closed	12:00 noon to 5:00 pm
Wednesday:	12:00 noon to 8:00 pm	12:00 noon to 5:00 pm	12:00 noon to 5:00 pm
Thursday	12:00 noon to 8:00 pm	12:00 noon to 5:00 pm	12:00 noon to 5:00 pm
Friday:	12:00 noon to 6:00 pm	12:00 noon to 5:00 pm	12:00 noon to 5:00 pm
Saturday:	10:00 am to 6:00 pm	12:00 noon to 5:00 pm	10:00 am to 5:00 pm

An appointment is necessary for Moving Image and Recorded Sound Division.
The Center is closed Sunday, Monday and legal holidays. NOTE: Hours subject to change. Check before visiting.

Closest Public Transportation:

Subway: 2 or 3 to 135th Street
Bus: Bx33, M7 or M102 to Lenox Avenue and 135th Street

Directions:

Take the #2 or #3 train to the 135th Street station. Exit at the center of the platform to Lenox Avenue. The Library is on the corner.

Description of Resources:

The Schomburg Center specializes in Black history and has a rich collection of 5 million items documenting the experiences of peoples of African descent throughout the world. Its collection includes books, manuscripts, newspapers, photographs and videos that document the history of African-Americans, including:

1. Vital Records:

Afro-American vital records and 20th century abstracts: Richmond County/Staten Island 1915 and 1925, New York State census records, compiled by Richard Dickenson, et al. Staten Island, 1985. [Sc F 94-391]
American Negro Historical Society Collection, 1790–1905, includes Lebanon Cemetery, Philadelphia, PA burial vouchers, 1855–1901 and copies of death certificates, 1864–1884. [Sc Micro R-7104]
Assistant Commissioner for the State of Mississippi, Bureau of Refugees, Freedmen and Abandoned Lands, 1865–1869. Includes registers of indentures of colored orphans, August 1865–May 1866 and registers of marriages, 1863–1866. NOTE: Similar registers are available here for Alabama, Arkansas, Georgia, District of Columbia, North Carolina, South Carolina, Tennessee and Virginia.
Black birth book of Monmouth County, New Jersey, 1804–1848. Freehold, NJ, 1989. [Sc D 98-2926]
Blacks in the Marriage Records of the District of Columbia, Dec. 23, 1811–June 16, 1870, by Paul Sluby. Washington, 1988. [Sc F 90-47]
Black Marriage Records: Hart County, Georgia, edited by David T. Ray. Hartwell, GA, 1994. [Sc F 98-762]

Henry Davis Marriage Book, 1845–1873. Includes a list of 222 marriages performed by this minister of the African Methodist Episcopal Church in New York, New Jersey and Pennsylvania. [Manuscripts]

Newspaper Obituary clippings from the Baltimore Afro-American and the Washington Afro-American for the Year....1992–1994. Prince George's County, MD, 1992-1994. [Sc Ser - M N491]

St. Philips Episcopal Church Records, 1819–1969 (Harlem). Includes registers of marriages, 1865–1950, baptisms, 1819–1969, burials, 1875–1911 and interments, 1854–1933. [Sc Micro R-4368]

2. <u>U.S. Census</u>:

1790 to 1900 (including the fragmentary 1890 Census) - all states.

1910 - Twelve complete states (Alabama, Arkansas, Delaware, Georgia, Louisiana, Maryland, Mississippi, North Carolina, Ohio, South Carolina and Virginia), the District of Columbia and communities in 12 other states with significant Black populations.

1920 - Nine complete states (Alabama, Georgia, Louisiana, Maryland, Mississippi, North Carolina, South Carolina, Tennessee, Virginia) as well as the District of Columbia, the Panama Canal Zone and civilian, military and naval forces and most of the State of Arkansas.

The Library also has, *Free Black heads of households in the New York State federal census, 1790–1830,* by Alice Eichholz and James M. Rose. Detroit, [1981]. [Sc D 82-656]

See also U.S. census records available at the NATIONAL ARCHIVES, NORTHEAST REGION and NYPL IRMA AND PAUL MILSTEIN DIVISION OF UNITED STATES HISTORY, LOCAL HISTORY AND GENEALOGY.

3. <u>Genealogy Guides</u>: The following are available at the Information Desk in the Microforms Reading Room:

African American Genealogical Source book, edited by Paula K. Byers, Detroit, 1995. [Sc F 96-3]

African American Genealogical Research: How to Trace Your Family History, by Harry Bradshaw Matthews. [Baldwin, NY], 1992. [SC F 93-56]

African-American Genealogy: Exploring and Documenting the Black Family, by Tommie Morton Young. Clarksville, TN, [1980]. [Sc D 84-457]

Afro-American Genealogy Sourcebook, by Tommie Morton Young. New York, 1987. [Sc D 88-78]

Black Genealogy, by Charles L. Blockson with Ron Fry. Revised. Baltimore, 1991. [Sc D 95-908]

Black Genesis, by James Rose and Alice Eichholz. Detroit, 1978. [Sc D 87-929]

Family Pride: The Complete Guide to Tracing African-American Genealogy, by Donna Beasley. New York, 1997. [Sc D 97-572]

Generations Past: A Selected List of Sources for Afro-American Genealogical Research, compiled by Sandra M. Dawson. Washington, D.C., 1988. [Sc D 89-360]

Guide to Tracing Your African-American Civil War Ancestor, by Jeanette Braxton Secret. 3rd edition. Bowie, MD, 1997. [Sc D 98-858]

How and Where to Research Your Ethnic-American Cultural Heritage: Black Americans, by Robert D. Reed. Saratoga, CA, 1979. [Sc D 87-929]

4. <u>Military Records</u>: ("Sc Micro" in Microforms Reading Room)

List of Black servicemen compiled from the War Department collection of Revolutionary War records, compiled by Debra L. Newman. Washington, D.C., 1974. Special List #36, NARA. [Sc 973.34N]

Compiled Service Records of Volunteer Union Soldiers Who Served with United States Colored Troops, National Archives Microfilm. [Sc Micro R-3011; M594]; and index [Sc Micro R3016; M589]

A guide to local abolitionists and resource materials identifying African American soldiers of the Civil War from New York and other states, by Henry Bradshaw Matthews. [Oneonta, 1997.] [Sc F 97-357]

Black Confederates, compiled by Charles K. Barrow, et al. Gretna, LA, 2001. [Sc E 02-419]

New York's Black regiments during the Civil War, by William Seraile. New York, [2001]. [Sc E 01-571]

Returns from Regular Army Infantry Regiments, June 1821–December 1916. The 38th and 41st Infantry Regiments which later formed the 24th and 25th Regiments were Black regiments. [Sc Micro 3012]

Returns from Regular Army Cavalry Regiments, 1833–1916. 9th and 10th Cavalries were recruited from U.S. Colored Troops, volunteer units during the Civil War, and freed slaves in Southern States. [Sc Micro R3013]

The Negro in the Military Service of the United States, 1639–1886, U.S. Adjutant General's Office. Washington, DC, 1973. [Sc Micro R-2077] and National Archives Microfilm Pamphlet, M858. [Sc D 95-450]

5. <u>Cemetery Records</u> covering burials in the Washington, D.C. area, by P. E. Sluby and S.L. Wormley, include:

Register of Burials of the Joseph P. Birch Funeral Home, 4 vols. [Sc F 90-227]; *Records of the Columbian Harmony Cemetery...,1831–1931.* [Sc Ser-M R436]; *Rosemont Cemetery (formerly Moore's Cemetery)* [Sc F 93-

225]; *Records of Payne's Cemetery*, 4 vols., April 18, 1907–Feb. 14, 1952 [Sc Ser-M S58]; *Presbyterian Cemetery Records (Georgetown)...1856–1897* [Sc F 91-70]; *Woodlawn Cemetery...Brief History and Inscriptions* [Sc D 86-475]; and *Selected Small Cemeteries* (includes Union Baptist Cemetery) [Sc D88-475]. Washington, D.C., [1984-1996]

6. <u>Biographical Resources</u>: An extraordinary compilation of biographical resources can be found in the manuscript collection, *Black Biographical Dictionaries, 1790–1950,* which includes 297 biographical dictionaries (microfiche). See published cumulative index by Henry Louis Gates, Jr., Randell K. Burkett and Nancy Hall Burkett, 3 vols. Alexandria, 1991[Sc F 91-130] and Electronic Resources (below). In addition, the Center has:

African Biographical Index, compiled by Victor Herrero Mediavilla. 3 vols. Munich, 1999. Includes entries from 233 reference works published between 1807 and 1993; and includes c. 90,000 individuals. [Sc F 00775]
Black writers: a selection of sketches from Contemporary Authors. Detroit, 1999. [Sc F 00-119]
The Vanguard, "A tri-annual register of the active of African descent in New York and New Jersey," vols. 2–9, 1933–1941. [Sc Micro RS-624]
District of Columbia free Negro registers, 1821–1861, [by] Dorothy S. Provine. Bowie, 1996. [Sc F 99-227]
Free African-Americans of Maryland, 1832, by Jerry M. Hynson. Westminister, MD, 1998. [Sc D 00-777]
Notable Black American Scientists, edited by Kristine M. Krapp. Detroit, 1999. [Sc F99-241]
St. Thomas 1803, crossroads of the diaspora: the 1803 proceedings and register of the free Colored inhabitants in the town of Charlotte Amalie, on the island of St. Thomas in the Danish West Indies, edited and compiled by David W. Knight and Laurette de T. Prime. St. Thomas, [1999]. [Sc F 02-228]

7. <u>Resource Books and Archival Guides</u>: See *Handbooks, Manuals, Sourcebooks* (unpublished), compiled by Gilsa Stewart, Library Technical Assistant for materials available at the Schomburg Center. In addition, the Center has:

Records of the United States District Court for the District of Columbia Relating to Slaves, 1851–1863. These records, kept by the U.S. Circuit Court, District of Columbia, include emancipation papers, 1857–1863, manumission papers, 1851–1863, and case papers relating to fugitive slaves, 1851–1863. [Sc Micro R-2100]
A Guide to records of ante-bellum southern plantations from the Revolution to the Civil War, compiled by Martin Paul Schipper, Frederick, MD, 1985–1986. [Sc F 97-332, Series...]
Series A, selections from the South Carolina Library, University of South Carolina
Series B, selections from South Carolina Historical Society
Series C, selections from Holdings of the Library of Congress, Part 1- Virginia, Part 2- Alabama, Georgia and South Carolina.
Series E, selections from the University of Virginia Library, Part I, Virginia Plantations.
Series F, selections from the Manuscripts Department, Duke University Library, Part 3, North Carolina, Maryland and Virginia.
Series G, selections from the Barker Texas History Center, University of Texas at Austin, Part 1. Texas and Louisiana Collections.

8. <u>Freedman's Savings and Trust Company Records</u>, [1865–1874]. Registers of signatures of depositors in 26 branches. The bank, incorporated by Congress in 1865, had 37 branch offices in 17 states including one in New York. It failed in 1874 leaving thousands of Black family depositors in financial ruin. Registers include age, place of birth, occupation, parents' names and names of spouse, children, siblings and sometimes former owner. [Sc Micro R-2108]. NATIONAL ARCHIVES-NORTHEAST REGION has a surname index to these records [CD-ROM].

9. <u>Electronic Information Center</u>: The Center has free Internet access available for researchers. In addition, the following are available on 12 computers:

African American Biographical Database, 1790–1950. Includes *Black Biographical Dictionaries, 1790–1950* (see above), as well as newly uncovered sources, obituary files, slave narrative collections, Internet sites and more.
Ancestry.plus, Archives USA, Ethnic NewsWatch, and *Palmer's Index to the New York Times* are also available here. See NYPL - DIVISION OF UNITED STATES HISTORY, LOCAL HISTORY AND GENEALOGY for a description of these websites.
International Index to Black Periodicals includes 150 international scholarly and popular periodicals on Black studies from the U.S., Africa and the Caribbean.

10. <u>Other Manuscript, Archives and Rare Books Division Collections</u> include records of organizations including those of seven Ethiopian Hebrew Congregations. A sample of significant collections of interest to genealogists include:

African American Migration and Southern Folkways in New York City Oral History Project. [Manuscripts]
American Negro Theatre Scrapbook, 1945–1947, includes clippings on actors and actresses who appeared in the American Negro Theatre. [Sc MG 363]

Blacks in the Railroad Industry Collection, 1946–1954, includes membership rosters from the Brotherhood of Sleeping Car Porters. [Sc MG 50]

Black Women Oral History Project, 1976–1981. Includes 72 women across the U.S.A. [Sc MG 45]

California African-American Oral History Project, 1967–1979. 11 vols.

Papers of the NAACP, 1909–1950, a comprehensive collection including the NAACP Legal Department files, documentation of voter rights efforts, and efforts to combat discrimination in the Armed Forces.

11. Photographs and Prints Division includes over 300,000 images from mid-18th century graphics of major historical events to contemporary documentary and art photography. Circa 54,000 of these photographs are now on video disc. Among its collections are:

Austen Hansen Photograph Collection, from the 1930s to the late 1980s. Includes 530,484 items including an extensive wedding photography collection and photographs of school classes, businesses and funerals. Navy collection includes photographs of officers, sailors and natives on Manus Island, South Pacific, where Hansen served, 1944–1945. [Sc Photo, Hansen...]

Joe Nash Black Dance Collection, includes images of dancers. [*MGZR]

New York Jazz Museum Collection, was given to the Center when the Museum closed. It includes also Jewish jazz musicians. [Sc MG 346]

12. Moving Image and Recorded Sound Division (MIRS) directs and manages the Center's Oral History/Video Documentation Program which records life stories and viewpoints of persons representing a wide range of disciplines including physicians, scientists, labor leaders, dancers and community development leaders.

Finding Aids:

U.S. Census: The Center has the Soundex index for the 1880 Census for all states; and 1900 for 27 states. See Appendix A for a description of the National Archives Soundex system. Book indexes produced by Accelerated Indexing Systems, Inc. are available for 1790–1870 censuses for most, but not all states or all years. The Center plans to access the web for indexes to the Census in the future.

NOTE: The Center's microfilms can be viewed at the NEW YORK PUBLIC LIBRARY, MICROFORMS ROOM at 42nd Street by completing a call slip and submitting it at the Information Desk in the NYPL IRMA AND PAUL MILSTEIN DIVISION OF UNITED STATES HISTORY, LOCAL HISTORY AND GENEALOGY. Requests should be submitted at least one week in advance.

For other materials at Schomberg, check the CATNYP catalog. Over 80% of the holdings of Schomberg are already in this computerized catalog. The catalog is available online. The remaining holdings can be found in the *Dictionary Catalog of the Schomberg Collection of Negro Literature and History* located in the General Research Reading Room. Both the Manuscripts and Photographs Divisions have more detailed finding aids for many of their collections. Many of these are already online. Each of the photograph collections described above include name indexes.

Description of Facility:

The Schomburg Center is located in the heart of Harlem. The Center's Microforms Reading Room, General Research Reading Room and Photography Division, located on the Court level, are one floor below the entrance. The General Research Reading Room has 10 tables and seating for 72 researchers. There are 6 CATNYP terminals at the entrance to the room. The Microforms Room houses 11 microfilm reader/printers, 12 computers and 4 Internet workstations. There are 11 seats at 3 tables for researchers. A librarian is available to assist researchers. Encyclopedias, biographical dictionaries and catalogs of Black collections are on open shelves in the Reading Room. The Manuscripts Division, located on the second floor has 4 long tables that provide comfortable seating for 24 researchers. There are 2 microfilm readers, one photocopy machine and one computer with access to CATNYP in this room. Finding aids on open shelves in this room include the *National Union Catalog,* 1959–1993, and the *Index to Personal Names in the National Union Catalog of Manuscripts Collections,* 1959–1984. The Photographs and Prints Division has four video viewers and one computer with access to CATNYP. Finding aids in this Division must be requested from staff.

Fees/Copies:

Microfilm copies can be made using a Copico Card at $.20 per page. For copies of paper materials, staff make copies at $.25 per page (8 ½" x 11") or $.50 per page (11" x 17"). For other fees, see NYPL - GENERAL RESEARCH DIVISION.

Restrictions on Use:

Researchers must request each reel by call slip. Only 5 reels can be requested at one time. There may be a wait of 15 minutes before reels are delivered. Sign up is required for use of computers with Internet access. NOTE: See NYPL - GENERAL RESEARCH DIVISION, "Description of Facility" for photo ACCESS card to be required of all patrons.

NEW YORK PUBLIC LIBRARY
SCIENCE, INDUSTRY AND BUSINESS LIBRARY (SIBL)

Facility Director: Kristin McDonough, Director

Address: 188 Madison Avenue &
New York, NY 10016-4314

(Cross Street: Between East 34th & East 35th Streets)

Phone: (212) 592-7000
Fax: none
E-mail: sibleref@nypl.org
Website: www.nypl.org/research/sibl

Hours of Operation:

Tuesday to Thursday: 10:00 am to 8:00 pm
Friday and Saturday: 10:00 am to 6:00 pm

Closed Sunday, Monday and legal holidays.

Closest Public Transportation:

Subway: 6 to East 33rd Street/Lexington Avenue
B, D, F or Q to West 34th Street/6th Avenue

Bus: M2, M3, M4 and Q32 to East 34th/Madison (north)
M1 to East 34th/Park Avenue (north)
M1, M2, M3, M4, M5 and Q32 to 34th/5th Avenue (south)
M16, M34 to Madison/East 34th (east/west)

Directions:

Take the #6 (local) subway to 33rd Street and Park Avenue. Exit the station. Walk one block <u>north</u> to 34th Street and one block <u>west</u> to Madison Avenue.

Description of Resources:

The Science, Industry and Business Library (SIBL) of the New York Public Library opened in 1996 and is the nation's largest public information center devoted solely to science and business. This high-tech facility integrates the holdings of the former Economic and Public Affairs and Science and Technology Divisions of the New York Public Library. SIBL's Research Collection includes 1.5 million titles. Available resources include books, newspapers, periodicals, directories, and U.S. and foreign government publications. Of particular interest to genealogists are:

1. *Cole's Cross Reference Directory*, a reverse directory arranged by address and phone number, available for:

Manhattan, Bronx, Brooklyn, Queens and Nassau Counties, 1971to present.
Staten Island and Westchester-Putnam Counties, 1973 to present.
Suffolk County, 1970/1971 to present.

See NEW YORK PUBLIC LIBRARY, HUMANITIES AND SOCIAL SCIENCES LIBRARY, GENERAL RESEARCH DIVISION for earlier New York City and Westchester County cross reference directories.

2. <u>Telephone Directories</u>: SIBL has *Phonefiche* for U.S. and Puerto Rico cities for the two most current years. *Phonefiche Community Cross Reference Guide* [Microforms Desk], lists hundreds of local telephone directories available here.

For earlier *Phonefiche* and paper copies of telephone directories, see NEW YORK PUBLIC LIBRARY, HUMANITIES AND SOCIAL SCIENCES LIBRARY, GENERAL RESEARCH DIVISION.

Electronic resources at SIBL include *Reference USA* with 120 million residential and 12 million business listings. Business listings include name of owner, name/title of officers, type of business, and link to company website.

3. <u>Voter Registration Lists</u>, New York City, can be used to access Voter Registration records in the NEW YORK CITY DEPARTMENT OF RECORDS AND INFORMATION SERVICES, MUNICIPAL ARCHIVES.

List of Enrolled Voters, 1906–1975 (missing: 1915, all boroughs; 1919–1922, Manhattan) [*SYA+ 175] in bound volumes. Within each Assembly District and Election District, voters are listed alphabetically by first letter of surname.

*Registry of Voters (*bound volumes) are available for 1955 to 1969 [*SYA+]. Within each Assembly District and Election District, voters are listed by address. See NYPL - MILSTEIN DIVISION OF UNITED STATES. HISTORY, LOCAL HISTORY AND GENEALOGY for earlier years.

4. Patents: SIBL is a designated Patent and Trademark Depository Library and has a complete file of United States patents, as well as a significant collection of foreign patents. Full text and images of all U.S. patents from 1790 to date are available here. The Library has U.S. patents from 1790–1999 (microfilm); 1994–1999 (CD-ROM); and 1999 to date (DVD).

See also United States Patent and Trademark Office website at www.uspto.gov. Full text of patents, 1976 to the present and pending patent applications are searchable online. Full page images can be viewed for all patents, 1790 to present. Researchers can use keywords, including surname of inventor, to locate patents 1976 to present. As a result, names of earlier inventors or persons whose works are referenced in the text of a 1976 (or later) patent, can be found. For earlier patents, 1790–1975, an online search can only be made if patent number is known. Use *CASSIS: Classification and Search Support Information System,* available at SIBL in electronic form for 1969–1975 searches. See Finding Aids below, for searches of patents filed pre-1969.

Patents (abstracts or full text) filed in 44 countries and organizations including the following can be viewed at SIBL (earliest date shown): Australia (1904); Belgium (1884); Canada (1824); Denmark (1895); France (1811); Germany (1880); Japan (1905); Russia/USSR (1959); Sweden (1885); United Kingdom (1673). [Microforms]. NOTE: End dates vary for each country.

For later patents and related information, see *ESPACE* database index at SIBL [Microforms Room] covering European patent applications filed since 1978 when the European Patent Office was founded. See also the online websites of the European Patent Office (EPO), www.european-patent-office.org; and World Intellectual Property Organization (WIPO), www.wipo.org. EPO's website has links to member countries and many other patent offices around the world.

5. Real Estate Directories: SIBL has copies of *New York Boroughs* (except current year) from 1987 [*XLF-426]; and the current *Real Estate Directory of Manhattan,* 3 vols. [McGraw Reference Desk]. These provide property ownership information produced by First American Real Estate Solutions (formerly Real Estate Data, Inc., a.k.a. REDI). *New York Boroughs* (microfiche), arranged by block/lot, address and owner's name, is available for the outer boroughs (Brooklyn, Bronx, Queens and Staten Island). See NYPL MAP DIVISION for copies of current *New York Boroughs,* as well as Sanborn maps; and CITY REGISTER'S OFFICE, MANHATTAN for resources available in NYC offices and online.

6. Name Changes, 1812–1901, in New York State are included in the *General Index to the Laws of the State of New York, 1777–1901,* volume 2, pp. 1309–87 [XWZ]. These are arranged by groups of years, 1812–1857, 1858–1865, etc., and original name. New name, year name changed, chapter and page in Session Laws, are included. For name of court (after 1860) and exact date of court orders, request the published *New York State Statutes Sessions Laws* for the appropriate year, using the page number listed in the *General Index.* [XWZ]

NOTE: BROOKLYN PUBLIC LIBRARY, BUSINESS LIBRARY and the NEW YORK STATE LIBRARY in Albany have the *General Index,* as well as a *Supplement, 1902–1907,* pp. 469–567.

7. Ship Lists: *Lloyd's Register of Shipping (Merchant Ship Lists),* 1768, 1776, 1790, 1800, 1812, 1820, 1834 to present, includes British and foreign vessels, name of owner, builder (1860 to date), master (to 1947), as well as a description of the ship. [TRA+ (year)]. See www.mariners-l.freeserve.co.uk/ResLloydsRegister.htm for a description of these registers.

8. Biographical Resources: The Library has an extensive collection of published industry specific biographical directories for individuals employed in a wide variety of fields including energy, engineering, environment, fashion, nuclear science, petroleum and plastics, real estate, risk management, securities, venture capital, world oil and gas and more. A list of industry specific directories can be found on the website and in CATNYP. These include:

Who's Who in Finance and Industry, 1972 to present. [HF 3023.A2W5]. Latest copy at McGraw Information Desk.
D & B Reference Book of Corporate Managements: America's Corporate Leaders, 3 vols. [HD 2745.D85]

9. Electronic Resources: More than 130 databases and websites are available free at SIBL. One of the most useful to genealogists is *NEXIS*. *NEXIS* includes more than 2,300 sources, many of which are biographical dictionaries. But unlike other electronic biographies, a name search in *NEXIS* will also identify individuals whose mother's maiden name or wife's maiden name is the name sought. To find these biographies, go to PEOPLE database and select ALL BIO. Then, enter the surname sought. See also,

> *Business & Company Resource Center* includes names of executives and links to company websites which may include photographs and staff profiles.
> *Business Dateline* includes articles from more than 350 regional business journals, wire services and daily newspapers, 1989 to present.
> *Dow Jones Interactive* includes articles from 6,000 trade journals, magazines, news wires, and newspapers, including the Wall Street Journal. Search "Library" by key word such as surname.
> *D & B International Business Locator* includes 28 million companies in over 200 countries and can be searched by name of key executives.
> *Dun's Million Dollar Directory* includes over 1.6 million U.S. and Canadian businesses. Includes names of principal executives and some biographies.
> *Standard & Poor's Net Advantage* includes a register of executives providing birth place/year, and education.

Many of these databases (but not *NEXIS)* are also accessible at the NEW YORK PUBLIC LIBRARY, HUMANITIES AND SOCIAL SCIENCES LIBRARY.

Finding Aids:

CATNYP, the online catalog, includes all materials from 1972 to the present and serials, i.e. periodicals, cataloged prior to 1972. There is an ongoing effort to include all pre-1972 books in CATNYP. Researchers should check the NYPL *Dictionary Catalogs* for books not in CATNYP. A full set of the *Dictionary Catalogs* can be found in the lower level open-stack reference area behind the self-service photocopy center. See NYPL GENERAL RESEARCH DIVISION for a description of these catalogs. Use the LEO catalog to find books in the Circulating Library, street level. All books with call marks [*R-SIBL...] are on open shelves on the lower level. Books with call marks starting with "JB" or "JS" are kept in closed stacks and must be requested at the Delivery Desk. Call marks starting with "*Z" indicate the item is on microfilm or microfiche.

Patent Indexes available at SIBL, in addition to those online, include the *Official Gazette of the U.S. Patent and Trademark Office: Patents,* a weekly publication arranged by patent number, from 1872 to present; and an annual index of patents, arranged by inventor, assignee name and subject, and providing the registration date, and volume/page number where it can be found in the *Official Gazette.*

Description of Facility:

The Circulating Library is located on the street level. Non-circulating research and reference materials described above can be found on the lower level. The Solomon Reading Room on the lower level includes c. 200 study carrels wired for laptop use. In addition, there are 56 workstations in the Laptop Docking area, that allow researchers to connect laptops directly to the Internet and to many of the electronic resources available at SIBL. Users must have an Ethernet (Network Interface) card already installed in their computers to use this feature of the Library. The Library provides the RJ-45 Ethernet cable at docking stations. Instructions for connection (Help Sheet #9) are available.

The Rohatyn Electronic Information Center with 70 workstations, also on the lower level, connects users to the Internet and more than 130 internal and external databases. Twelve computers are dedicated to specific databases and the remainder can access all other Electronic Resources at SIBL. *NEXIS* is available on only one computer; and *Dow Jones Interactive* is available on two. One half-hour reservation can be made at the Electronic Information Center to use these special databases. For all other Electronic Resources, researchers should make one-hour reservations immediately upon entering the Library, using the touch-screen kiosks. Use those in the entrance hall, street level, for quickest access. These reservations fill up rapidly and can require a 2- to 3-hour wait. An additional 12 computers in the Circulating Library (street level) have access to Electronic Resources but are limited to ½ hour sessions. Users sign up for these computers at the "pink" sign. The Circulating Library also has 3 stand-up express computers for 15-minute Internet access. There are 30 computers terminals and printers on the lower level and 7 on the street level with exclusive access to CATNYP and LEO.

The Quade Microforms and Patents Reading Room on the lower level, at the far end of the Delivery Desk, has 19 microfilm/microfiche reader-printers, 2 microfilm readers and 3 microfiche readers. The Room also houses 4 computers dedicated to *CASSIS* (patent index).

The latest paper copy of *Cole's* directories can be found in the Microforms Room above the staff desk. Microfiche/microfilm are self-service and include the latest copy of Phonefiche for each locality and patents on microfilm. Earlier films must be ordered from the Delivery Desk.

NOTE: SIBL provides free orientation and training classes in the Electronic Training Center. Programs include, "Directories: Using Them to Find Companies and People," "Introduction to Patents," "Web Workshop for Beginners," "Searching the Library's Online Catalogs," and more. A schedule is available on SIBL's website. Reservations must be made on the same day at the Library. Use the touch-screen kiosks. There are c. 15 computers in each training room.

Fees/Copies:

For photocopy, photographic service or research fees, see NEW YORK PUBLIC LIBRARY, HUMANITIES AND SOCIAL SCIENCES LIBRARY, GENERAL RESEARCH DIVISION. There are 10 photocopy machines on the lower level in two glass enclosed areas.

Restrictions on Use:

Parcels, shopping bags, suitcases, large containers and wheeled conveyances are not permitted in the reading rooms. These must be deposited in the complementary checkroom to the left of the circulation desk on the street level.

Same day in-person reservations are required to use the Electronic Information Center and to attend classes or lectures. No more than two 1-hour reservations per day are permitted. Use of some databases is restricted to ½ hour per day. Only users with valid reservations may use the workstations. Names are checked when entering the Electronic Information Center.

NOTE: See NEW YORK PUBLIC LIBRARY - HUMANITIES AND SOCIAL SCIENCES LIBRARY, GENERAL RESEARCH DIVISION, "Description of Facility" for photo ACCESS card to be required of <u>all</u> patrons.

NEW YORK UNIVERSITY, ELMER HOLMES BOBST LIBRARY
TAMIMENT INSTITUTE LIBRARY AND ROBERT F. WAGNER LABOR ARCHIVES

Facility Director: Dr. Gail Malmgreen, Associate Head for Archival Collections

Address: 70 Washington Square South &
New York, NY 10012
(Cross Streets: LaGuardia Place and University Place)

Phone: (212) 998-2630
Fax: (212) 995-4070
E-mail: Gail.Malmgreen@nyu.edu
Website: www.nyu.edu/library/bobst/

Hours of Operation:

	School Semester:	Summer Schedule
Monday-Wednesday and Friday:	10:00 am to 5:45 pm	10:00 am to 5:45 pm
Thursday:	10:00 am to 9:00 pm	10:00 am to 5:45 pm
Most Saturdays:	11:00 am to 5:00 pm	closed

Closed Sunday and major legal holidays. The Library may be open on some holidays such as Election Day. During summer and semester breaks hours vary. Some collections are open by appointment only. Call for an appointment.

Closest Public Transportation:

Subway: N or R to 8th Street
A, B, C, D, E, F or Q to West 4th Street
6 to Astor Place or Bleecker Street

Bus: M5 or M6 to West 4th Street and Broadway (southbound) or West 4th Street and Avenue of the Americas (northbound)

Directions:

Take the N or R train to the 8th Street station. Exit the station and walk <u>south</u> on Broadway to West 4th Street. Turn <u>west</u> on West 4th Street and walk two blocks to Washington Square South (#70).

Description of Resources:

These collections cover labor history, socialism, communism, anarchism, utopian experiments, women's movements and other radical activities in the United States since 1865. Tamiment has a collection of 20,000 books, 500,000 pamphlets, leaflets, flyers and internal documents from labor and left organizations, and more than 300 manuscript collections. It has 5,000 non-current periodicals, roughly 800 current periodicals and 3,000 oral histories and other sound recordings. There are over 225,000 photographic images, posters, video and raw film footage.

The extensive archival holdings often include minutes, correspondence, reports, flyers and, in a few instances, membership lists and case histories. While organizational collections deal more with the leadership than with rank-and-file members, some individual members may be mentioned.

The following list is a sampling of the holdings of possible interest to genealogists:

1. <u>Socialist Collections</u>: There are over 35 collections, including organizations and personal papers of individuals including Harry Fleishman, Mendel Halushka, Morris Hillquit, Sergius Ingerman, Ben Josephson, Harry Laidler, Meyer London, Jacob Panken, Morris Paris, Abraham Shiplacoff, B. Charney Vladeck, Art Young and Sam Zagat.

2. <u>Communist Collections</u>: The 16 collections in this group include the personal papers of Israel and Sadie Amter, Alexander Bittleman, Sam Darcy, Edward Falkowski, David Gordon, Gil Green and Charlotte Stern.

3. <u>Other Radical Collections</u>: The more than 30 collections in this group include the personal papers of Max Bedacht, Alexander Berkman, Sam Dolgoff, Raya Dunayevskaya, Erwin Edelman, David Fender, Sol Feinstone, Albert Goldman, Emma Goldman, Bernard Goodman, Max Nomad, Annette Rubenstein, Morris U. Schappes, Max Shachtman, Myra Tanner Weiss and Isadore Wisotsky.

4. Labor Collections: There are over 50 labor collections, many of them relating specifically to New York City. These consist mostly of written records: minutes of meetings, newsletters, newspapers, memoranda, correspondence, organizing leaflets, issue-oriented files and personal accounts of union activists, including Elly Borochowitz, Victor Riesel, Fanny Simon and Max Zaritsky.

The holdings document activities of a wide range of New York working people including painters, printers, professors, postal workers, teachers, tunnel workers, department store clerks, librarians, clerical workers, transit workers, social service employees, city engineers, fire fighters, flight attendants, actors, burlesque and vaudeville artists, dancers, musicians and scenic artists.

Major categories of holdings include:

Central Bodies/Coalitions: Jewish Labor Committee, 1934–1980 (include case files on WWII refugees and orphans assisted by the JLC); NYC Central Labor Council, 1933–1982; New York Committee on Occupational Safety & Health, Campaign to Save OSHA, 1980–1981; New York State AFL-CIO Legislative Department, 1938–1983; Union Label & Service Trades Council of Greater NY, 1911–1980s.

Craft Employees: Bakery, Confectionary & Tobacco Workers Union Local 3; Building Trades Employers Association; Headwear Joint Board ACTWU, 1926–1980s; International Brotherhood of Electrical Workers, Local 3, 1902–1982; International Brotherhood of Teamsters Local 282, National Writers Union, NYC Chapter, 1980s; The Newspaper Guild of New York Local 3; Paperhangers Local 490, 1884–1952; Tunnelworkers Union, Local 174, 1939–1975; Typographical Union No. 6, Benefit Board ITU, 1907–1966.

Engineering Employees: Engineering and Professional Guild, Local 66 IFPTE, 1936–1979; Civil Service Technical Guild, Local 375 AFSCME, 1937–1984; Engineers Association of ARMA, Local 418 IUE, 1953–1983.

Entertainment Workers: Actors' Equity Association, 1913–1983; Actors' Fund, 1882–1980s; American Guild of Variety Artists, 1945–1980; American Federation of Musicians, Local 802, 1932–1978; Associated Actors & Artists of America, 1919–1982; Screen Actors Guild; Equity Library Theater, 1943–1964; The Labor Theater, 1979–1984; National Association of Broadcast Engineers and Technicians Local 15 (NABET); United Scenic Artists PAT Local 829.

Personal Papers: Including Albert Afterman (ILGWU); Julius Bernstein, Isaiah Minkoff (JLC); Carl Blum, Daniel French, Frank Schonfeld, Louis Weinstock, Sam Winn (Painters); Abram Flaxer (United Public Workers); Sidney Jonas Collection; Seymour Posner (NYS Assemblyman); Stanley Postek (Maritime Union); Jesse Simons (arbitrator).

Public Employees: District Council 37, American Federation of State, County and Municipal Employees (AFSCME), 1947–1983; New York Metro Area Postal Union, APWU, 1907–1981; New York Public Library Guild, Local 1930, District Council 37, AFSCME, 1962–1979; Professional Staff Congress, CUNY, Local 2334 AFT & AAUP, 1938–1980; Social Service Employees Union, Local 371, 1940–1981 and Local 372, 1966–1973; Transport Workers Union, 1933–1980s; Union of State Employees, 1937–1983; United Federation of Teachers, Local 2, AFT, 1935–1980.

Service/Communications: Communication Workers of America (CWA); Independent Union of Flight Attendants; Office and Professional Employees International Union (OPEIU); Taxi Drivers Rank and File Coalition.

Wholesale and Retail Employees: District 65, United Auto Workers (UAW), 1933–1970; Department Store Workers' Union, Local 1S RWDSU, 1939–1979.

5. Non-Print Collections: There are over 60 photographic collections and 100 documentary films on videotape of individuals and events in labor history and radical politics in NYC. There are separate graphic and cartoon collections, as well as songbooks, scores and recordings.

6. Oral History Collections: Each of the 44 collections has its own listing of the names of those interviewed. In some cases, abstracts are available. For example, there is a guide to the Oral History of the American Left which has over 750 interviews (see "Finding Aids"). The New York City Immigrant Labor History Collection, which has 285 interviews, and the Lower East Side Collection may also be of interest to Jewish genealogists. The collection New Yorkers at Work: Oral Histories of Life, Labor and Industry is a series of 150 interviews. The 3,000 interviews are on cassette tapes or transcribed. Some donor restrictions apply.

7. Abraham Lincoln Brigade Archives, formerly located at Brandeis University, includes information on American volunteers who fought in the Spanish Civil War, 1936-1939. The collection includes personal letters written by these soldiers, other manuscript materials, over 5,000 photographs and more than 500 audio tapes.

8. <u>Archives of Irish America</u>: Includes many collections such as the <u>County Societies Collection</u> with materials from 23 Irish county societies based in New York City; the papers of the <u>Ancient Order of Hibernians,</u> <u>Gaelic Athletic Association,</u> <u>Gaelic Society of New York</u> and more. See "Restrictions on Use."

9. <u>Vertical Files</u>: These contain pamphlets, leaflets, flyers, memoranda and clippings. The files are arranged by organization, author, subject and surname. The latter is the case for the biographical files included in this collection.

Finding Aids:

Entries for most of the Library's collection can be found in the New York University Bobst Library's computerized card catalog, BobCat, and via the Research Libraries Group's national bibliographic database (RLIN). BobCatPlus can be accessed on the Internet at www.nyu.edu/library/bobst/cat.htm. There are also several specialized archival card catalogs and vertical files which are well cross-referenced. In addition, finding aids with folder level control have been prepared for most of the archival collections. Descriptions of some of the archival collections can be found on the Internet. See *Finding Aids for Archival Collections in the New York University Libraries* (online).

The Library has a 4-page (free) bulletin, *Tamiment Institute Library & Robert F. Wagner Labor Archives, NYU Elmer Holmes Bobst Library, Information Bulletin #8*, which provides a brief overview of the scope of the entire collection. In addition, there are several published bibliographies including:

> Swanson, Dorothy. *Guide to the Manuscript Collection of the Tamiment Library.* [This guide is outdated but it describes the core of the collection.] 1977.

> *Socialist Collections in the Tamiment Library, a Guide to the Microfilm Edition.* New York, 1979.

> *Guide to Oral History of the American Left.* Tamiment, 1984.

> Wechsler, Robert. *New York Labor Heritage: A Selected Bibliography of New York City Labor History.* [This bibliography of secondary sources is arranged by industry, ethnic group and time period.] 1981.

> Malmgreen, Gail. *Labor and the Holocaust* (The Jewish Labor Committee). 1991.

Online finding aides include:

> *Archives of Irish America*

> *Guide to Yiddish Speaking Labor and Radical Movements,* by Jane H. Rothstein.

> *Sources in U.S. Women's Labor History,* by Kathleen M. Barry

Staff will provide advice to researchers in response to telephone inquiries. Patrons must come in to conduct actual research.

For Non-Print Collections (photographs, graphic materials and moving images), researchers should contact the Non-Print curator at (212) 998-2635.

Description of Facility:

The Library is located on the 10th floor of the Bobst Library between the elevator banks. The room can seat 40 people at tables. There is one staff member on duty at the reference desk. One microfiche and four microfilm readers are available. Some of the catalogs are to the left of the reference desk; the rest are behind the desk. Consult the staff.

Fees/Copies:

Some books and periodicals can be copied by the researcher after the librarian gives him/her a pass. Archival and fragile materials are only copied by the Library staff, after the researcher fills out a special form. Copies can be picked up or mailed. The cost is $.20 per page plus postage (if mailed).

Restrictions on Use:

The Tamiment Library and Wagner Labor Archives are open to the public without restriction. On inquiring at the entrance desk of Bobst Library, researchers will be given a one-day pass. Pass extensions are available at the Tamiment Library reading room. All photocopying is done at the discretion of the staff. Appropriate copyright restrictions apply.

<u>Archives of Irish America</u> are open by appointment only. Contact the founder/curator, Marion Casey, (718) 768-0151.

OLD YORK LIBRARY
CITY UNIVERSITY OF NEW YORK, GRADUATE CENTER

Facility Director: Madelyn Kent, Curator

Address: 365 Fifth Avenue   &
New York, NY 10016-4309

(Cross Streets: 34th and 35th Streets)

Phone: (212) 817-7241, or 7267
Fax: none
E-mail: info@oldyorklibrary.org
Website: www.oldyorklibrary.org

Hours of Operation:

Monday and Wednesday   9:30 am to 5:30 pm
Thursday   10:00 am to 2:00 pm

By appointment only. Closed Friday, Saturday, Sunday, and legal holidays.

Closest Public Transportation and **Directions:**

See NEW YORK PUBLIC LIBRARY - SCIENCE, INDUSTRY AND BUSINESS LIBRARY (SIBL). After exiting the subway station at 33rd Street and Park Avenue, walk one block <u>north</u> to 34th Street and two blocks <u>west</u> to Fifth Avenue. Or,

Take the B, D, F, N, Q, or R train to 34th Street/Herald Square station. Exit the train to 34th Street and 6th Avenue and walk one block <u>east</u> to 5th Avenue. The Library is on the northeast corner of 34th Street and 5th Avenue in the old B. Altman building. Enter through the Mina Rees Library to the right of the reception desk and go down one level to the Reading Room on the "C" Level. The Seymour B. Durst Reading Room is located opposite the elevators.

Description of Resources:

The Old York Library includes a unique collection of books, maps, images, newspapers and memorabilia encompassing four centuries of New York City history. The collection, founded in the 1960s by the late Seymour B. Durst, a real estate developer, chronicles the history, geography, architecture, culture and politics of New York City. In June, 2000, a significant portion of the Durst collection was gifted to the Graduate Center of the City of New York and the Seymour B. Durst Reading Room was established to house the collection and make it more accessible to the public. The collection includes over 9,000 books of which more than 3,000 are on open shelves in the Reading Room.

<u>Photograph Collection</u>: Includes 3,000 photographs and materials from the morgue of the now-defunct New York Herald Tribune.

<u>Postcard Collection</u>: Includes 20,000 postcards, many with personal reactions to landmark locations and events. The postcard collection is grouped by area and subject.

<u>Map Collection</u>: Includes such rare items as the 1814 *Commissioner's Grid Map* that outlined the City's path of development for the rest of the century.

<u>Book Collection</u>: Includes biographies of important NYC industrialists, labor leaders, bankers and merchants as well as diaries and other books of interest to genealogists. An extensive collection of early New York City histories can be found here such as:

The Annals of Newtown in Queens County, New York, by James Riker. New York 1852. See also NEW YORK PUBLIC
     LIBRARY, MANUSCRIPTS AND ARCHIVES, for additional materials in the James Riker Papers [W94a-231].
The Great Metropolis: A Mirror of New York, by Junius H. Browne. Hartford, NJ, 1869. Includes sketches of prominent
     places and persons in the City.
History of the City of Brooklyn, 2 vols., by Henry R. Stiles. Brooklyn, 1867 and 1869.
History of the City of New York, 1609–1909, by John William Leonard. New York, 1910. Includes brief biographies
     of men representative of the business interests of the City.
History of New York City, Embracing an Outline Sketch of Events from 1609 to 1830, and a Full Account of its
     Development from 1830–1884, 2 vols., by Benson J. Lossing. New York and Chicago, 1884. Includes portraits
     and biographies of prominent men active in NYC. (Deluxe edition)

History of the City of New York, by David T. Valentine. New York, 1853. Narrative history primarily of Dutch/English hostilities and prominent colonists of both countries.

History of Queens County, with Illustrations, Portraits, & Sketches of Prominent Families and Individuals, 1683–1882. New York, 1882.

Iconography of Manhattan Island (first edition), 6 vol., by I. N. Phelps Stokes. New York, 1915-1928. This visual description of the history of Manhattan covers the period 1498–1909.

Revised History of Harlem (City of New York), by James Riker. New York, 1904. Includes sketches of numerous families and the recovered history of land-titles.

Staten Island's Claim to Fame, "The Garden Spot of New York Harbor", by Vernon B. Hampton. Staten Island, 1925. Includes history and description; mostly famous persons.

Staten Island and Its People: A History 1609–1929, by Charles W. Leng and William T. Davis. 4 vols. New York, 1930. Includes information on old families and their homes.

The collection includes also such gems as:

An Account of the Malignant Fever Lately Prevalent in the City of New York, by James Hardie, A.M.. New York, 1799. Includes list of 2,086 burials (pp. 88–139) and a comparative review of the 1795 and 1798 fevers.

An Account of the Yellow Fever which Occurred in the City of New York in the Year 1822: In which is Prefixed a Brief Sketch of the Different Pestilential Diseases with which this City was Afflicted in the Years 1798, 1799, 1803 and 1805, by James Hardie, A.M. New York, 1822. Includes lists of persons who died of yellow fever (p.101–111).

America's Successful Men of Affairs: An Encyclopedia of Contemporary Biography, edited by Henry Hall. New York, 1895.

Encyclopedia of Biography of New York, by Charles Elliott Fitch. 3 vols. New York, 1916-1923.

Lives of the Clergy of New York and Brooklyn: Embracing Two Hundred Biographies of Eminent Living Men in All Denominations, by J. Alexander Patten. New York, 1874. Includes a history of each sect and congregation.

Manual of the Corporation of the City of New York, 1841–1868, and *Valentine's Manual,* 1916–1928. Unusual finds include, "Deaths 1864, 1865, 1866 and 1867 of Extreme Old Age" found in the 1868 volume, p.218.

Prominent Families of New York: being an account in biographical form of individuals and families distinguished as representatives of the social, professional and civic life of New York City, edited by Lyman Horace Weeks. New York, 1897.

Register in Alphabetical Order of the Early Settlers of Kings County, Long Island, New York from its First Settlement by Europeans in 1770, by Teunis G. Bergen. New York, 1881.

Report of the Mayor's Push-Cart Commission, Lawrence Veillier, Chairman. New York City, 1906. This small book includes maps of the City's "Jewish Quarter," lists of names/addresses of owners of 2 or more push-carts used by other men and the number of push-carts owned (p. 155–164).

The Witches of New York as Encountered, by Q. K. Philander Doesticks, P. S. [Notation: pseudonym of Mortimer Thomson]. New York, 1858.

Yearbook, New York Society of Architects, 1918–1919 and 1926. Includes lists names/addresses of architects practicing in New York City and New York State by community.

Finding Aids:

The Library has a computerized catalog available online. A search can be done by author, title, key word or subject. All books are now included. Photographs, newspapers, periodicals and most postcards are not included.

Description of Facility:

The Old York collection is housed in two locations at the Graduate Center. The Seymour B. Durst Reading Room, located on the C-Level (Room C196.09) lined with books from the collection, is a small beautifully designed room with two love seats, cocktail table, and two computers on which the catalog can be accessed. The postcard collection is currently in an off-site location. The remainder of the book collection and all maps and photographs are located one floor below on the "X" level. This room is also the office of the curator.

Fees/Copies:

Copies can be made at photocopy machines in the Graduate Center Library at $.25 per page.

Restrictions on Use:

This is not a lending library. Neither the Reading Room nor the room on the "X" level can be accessed without the curator. An appointment is necessary.

RESEARCH FOUNDATION FOR JEWISH IMMIGRATION
ARCHIVES

Facility Director: Dennis E. Rohrbaugh, Archivist

Address: 570 Seventh Avenue, Room 1803
New York, NY 10018

(Cross Street: Corner of 41st Street)

Phone: (212) 921-3871
Fax: (212) 575-1918
E-mail: none
Website: none

Hours of Operation:

Open to the public by appointment only. Call or write.

Closest Public Transportation:

Subway: 1, 2, 3, 7, 9, N, Q, R, S or W to Times Square/42nd Street

Bus: M10 (south) or M42 to 42nd Street and 7th Avenue
M6, M7 or M104 to 42nd Street and Broadway

Directions:

Take any of the above trains to the Times Square/42nd Street station. Exit the station and turn <u>south</u> on 7th Avenue to 41st Street. The building is on the southwest corner.

Description of Resources:

The collection consists of material on 25,000 individuals (on microfilm) gathered in preparation of a biographical dictionary on émigrés from <u>Germany</u>, <u>Austria</u> and German-speaking <u>Czechoslovakia</u>. It contains information on individuals — regardless of religion, profession or place of resettlement — who emigrated from these countries between 1933 and 1945.

There is information on the individual's personal and professional life and family both before and after emigration, including copies of published sources (e.g. *Who's Who,* newspapers, professional journals) and material from private sources (e.g. questionnaires compiled by the biographee, information from relatives). In addition, the Archives' Oral History Collection has 275 transcriptions of taped interviews with German-Jewish émigrés to the United States from the Nazi period on. A synopsis of each interview may be found in Volume 3, Part 1 of the series cited below. The interviews were conducted for the most part between 1970 and 1975.

See also LEO BAECK INSTITUTE, ARCHIVES - LIBRARY, which has a complete set of the microfilm and published materials. A third copy of these materials is available in Munich at the Institut fuer Zeitgeschichte. The originals have been deposited at the Zentrum fuer Antisemitismusforschung at the Technische Universitaet in Berlin.

Published materials of the Archives include:

1. *International Biographical Dictionary of Central European Emigres, 1933–1945,* edited by Herbert A. Strauss and Werner Roeder. Includes 8,700 biographies. 3 vols. Munich, 1980. Volume 1 covers nearly 4,000 individuals active in politics, commerce, industry and other areas of public life (German). Volume 2 records the lives of circa 4,700 persons of academic and cultural distinction (English). Volume 3 includes several indexes to volumes 1 and 2 including an index to: (a) names, pseudonyms, name changes; (b) countries of intermediate and final emigration; (c) occupation; (d) associations, institutions and parties; (e) members of parliament and of government; and (f) Nobel prize winners (German, English).

2. *Jewish Immigrants of the Nazi Period in the USA,* edited by Herbert A. Strauss.

   Vol. 1: *Archival Resources,* by Steven W. Siegel, 1979.

Vol. 2: *Classified and Annotated Bibliography of Books and Articles on the Immigration and Acculturation of Jews from Central Europe to the USA Since 1933,* by H. Friedlander, A. Gardner, K. Schwerin, H. Strauss and J. Wasserman, 1981.

Vol. 3: Part 1, *Guide to the Oral History Collection of the Research Foundation for Jewish Immigration, New York,* by Joan Lessing, 1982.

Vol. 3: Part 2, *Classified List of Articles Concerning Emigration in German Jewish Periodicals, January 30, 1933 to November 9, 1938,* by Daniel Schwarz and Daniel Niederland, 1982.

Vol. 4: Part 1, *Jewish Emigration from Germany, 1933–1944, A Documentary History: Programs and Policies until 1937,* by Norbert Kampe, 1992.

Vol. 4: Part 2, *Jewish Emigration from Germany, 1933–1944, A Documentary History: Restrictions on Emigration and Deportation to Eastern Europe,* by Norbert Kampe, 1992.

Vol. 5: *The Individual and Collective Experience of German-Jewish Immigrants, 1933–1984, An Oral History Record,* by Dennis Rohrbaugh, 1986.

Vol. 6: *Essays on the History, Persecution and Emigration of German Jews,* by Herbert A. Strauss, 1987.

Finding Aids:

1. Complete card index (microfilm) by surname of individuals in the collection.

2. Partial card index (microfilm) arranged by country of resettlement.

3. Partial card index (microfilm) arranged by profession.

4. Complete card index (microfilm) of émigrés to Israel (then Palestine), arranged by profession.

Description of Facility:

The Archives, located on the 18th floor of an office building, can serve 1-2 researchers at a time. One staff person is available by appointment to assist researchers. Biographical files, typed interview transcripts and a small collection of books and papers are on open shelves. Records can be viewed immediately. Mail requests are responded to within 2 weeks, on average. Requests for information may also be made by telephone.

Fees/Copies:

Small numbers of photocopies (c. 30 pages or less) can be made free-of-charge.

Restrictions on Use:

A small amount of personal biographical material has not been released to the public by the biographee. Some material may not be photocopied.

SURROGATE'S COURT - NEW YORK COUNTY (MANHATTAN)
RECORD ROOM

Facility Director: Jane Passenant, Chief Clerk, Surrogate's Court
                               Omar Colon, Record Room Supervisor

Address: 31 Chambers Street, Room 402
                               New York, NY 10007

                               (Cross Streets: Centre and Elk Streets)

Phone: (212) 374-8287
Fax: None
E-mail: None
Website: None

Hours of Operation:

Monday to Friday:

     Record Room 402:   9:00 am to 5:00 pm. (Files are pulled until 4:45 pm.)
     Liber Room 405:   9:00 am to 3:30 pm. (Closed for lunch, 1:00–2:00 pm.)

Closed Saturday, Sunday and legal holidays.

Closest Public Transportation and Directions:

See COUNTY CLERK'S OFFICE - STATE SUPREME COURT, NEW YORK COUNTY (MANHATTAN), DIVISION OF OLD RECORDS. The Surrogate's Court Record Room is on the 4th floor opposite the elevator bay. NOTE: There is a service entrance (steep incline) at the back of the building (Reade Street) which provides access to wheelchair users.

Description of Resources:

The County Surrogate's Court has wills and indexes, 1662 to the present; and all records of probate, letters of administration and estate taxes for New York County, 1830 to the present. Some estate files include a copy of the death certificate and testimony from individuals identifying family members, i.e. potential heirs. In addition, the Court has guardianship cases from 1808 and adoptions and commitments from 1924 to the present. NOTE: Family Court also has jurisdiction for adoptions since 1961.

Copies of probated wills are also found in Records of Will libers in the Liber Room (Room 405). Documents in will libers give the names and addresses of the witnesses and executor to a probated will, as well as the names of heirs mentioned in the will (but not necessarily all the heirs). These libers can be used as a quick way to see part of a probated case if the full file does not exist, i.e. pre-1830, or if the file is not in the building. Letters of Administration, in the room adjacent to the Liber Room, can also be used as a preliminary source for date of death and the name of the Executor pending retrieval of a full file. Delegations of power of attorney and other assignments can be found in the Records of Conveyances and Mortgages of Interests of Decedent Estates and Powers of Attorney, 1904 to the present. These records often include a description of relationship to the deceased which may not be included in the case file.

The Surrogate's Court records included records of residents of parts of the Bronx, 1874–1897, and all of the Bronx, 1898–1914.

NOTE: Inventories of estates, 1783–1844, are at the NYC MUNICIPAL ARCHIVES. See also NEW YORK STATE ARCHIVES for probated wills, 1787-1829 and recorded wills, 1787-1879 and QUEENS BOROUGH PUBLIC LIBRARY for microfilm copies of wills, 1662-1761, 1815-1829 and letters of administration, 1664-1683, 1743-1783.

Finding Aids:

There are Liber indexes for probate cases/wills, letters of administration, estate taxes and guardianships. Each type of record is indexed for groups of years in different libers. These include probate indexes, 1662–1949; letters of administration, 1743–1949 and guardianships, 1808–1963. Prior to 1743, letters of administration are recorded in the probate index libers. Separate liber indexes are available for Records of Conveyances and Mortgages...and Powers of Attorney.

All types of cases from 1950–1988 are maintained in card indexes. The cards are arranged alphabetically by last name of the deceased/guardianship of record and chronologically within two groupings, 1950–1963 and 1964–1988. Index cards, 1950–1963, include the will liber number in addition to the case number. Index cards, 1964–1988, include the date of death, last address and case number. From 1988 to the present, there is a computerized index which can be accessed in Room 402. Earlier records have not been entered in a consistent manner. Researchers cannot rely upon the computerized index.

Minutes to probate and administration records, 1924 to the present, are also available. This index includes will liber number and date of death.

Each probate, administration, guardianship and estate tax file is available upon request. Request forms must be filled out and submitted in the Record Room. See "Restrictions on Use."

NOTE: See also NEW YORK PUBLIC LIBRARY, IRMA AND PAUL MILSTEIN DIVISION OF UNITED STATES HISTORY, LOCAL HISTORY AND GENEALOGY and NEW YORK GENEALOGICAL AND BIOGRAPHICAL SOCIETY for published abstracts of wills, administrations and administration bonds filed in New York County.

Description of Facility:

The Record Room (Room 402) is opposite the elevators and can seat 8 researchers. There are two staff members available to pull files. The Record Room has 5 computers on which the 1988 to present index can be accessed.

The Liber Room (Room 405), open to the public, is located in the northwest corner of the 4th floor corridor. Floor to ceiling shelves line the walls of the room. All will libers, administration libers and Records of Conveyances and Mortgages...and Powers of Attorney libers are maintained here. The room can be dusty and there is no place to sit. You must pull the libers yourself and replace them yourself. It is suggested that researchers dress accordingly.

Index libers for probate records, 1662–1949, and administration, 1743–1949, are on open shelves under the long table opposite the entrance in the Liber Room. Liber indexes for guardianships, 1808–1963, are in the second room of the Liber Room along the wall to the right of the entrance (enter through Room 405). These guardianship liber indexes can be found on the top shelf of the sixth bookcase.

The card indexes, 1950–1988, can be found in four file cabinets now located on the window wall opposite the entrance to the Liber Room. Although unlabeled, the first two cabinets cover the 1950–1963 period and the third and fourth cover the 1964–1988 period. NOTE: For 1964–1988, surnames "A–F" are in the bottom two drawers of the third and fourth cabinets. The small index cards for surnames starting with "B" are in disarray. An open drawer on top of the cabinet holds some cards with surnames beginning with "G", and "T" to "V". The remaining drawers, "G–Z" are arranged alphabetically within these cabinets.

Adoption records are in Room 301. See "Restrictions on Use."

Fees/Copies:

Certified copies of wills and letters of administration are available at $5 per page. Two photocopy machines ($.15 per page) are available for public use. The clerks cannot make change.

Mail requests cost $70 for a search of records over 25 years old and $25 for records under 25 years, plus $5 per page for a copy of the record. The search fee is not charged if the file number is provided by the researcher.

Restrictions on Use:

Only 3 files per researcher per day will be pulled if the staff is busy. Cases prior to 1964 are stored off-site and require one week for retrieval. Special arrangements can be made for earlier retrieval. See the clerk. However, the will libers, administration libers and Records of Conveyances and Mortgages...and Powers of Attorney libers for any case may be examined on the spot.

Commitments and adoptions are sealed records. Commitments may only be examined after obtaining a court affidavit from the NY County Surrogate's Court and a court order to open the files. Adoption records can never be examined although a court affidavit and court order may be obtained for specific information, i.e. birth certificate or health information.

No papers may leave the Record Room at any time.

Visitors to 31 Chambers Street must present photo identification to the guards at the building entrance.

YESHIVA UNIVERSITY
ARCHIVES

Facility Director: Shulamith Z. Berger, Curator of Special Collections

Address: 2520 Amsterdam Avenue, Room 602   ♿
New York, NY

(Cross Streets: West 185th and West 186th Streets)

Mail Address: 500 West 185th Street
New York, NY 10033

Phone: (212) 960-5451
Fax: (212) 960-0066
E-mail: unilib@ymail.yu.edu
Website: www.yu.edu/libraries/arch/index.html

Hours of Operation:

Monday to Thursday: By appointment only.

Closed Friday, Saturday, Sunday, Jewish and legal holidays.

Closest Public Transportation:

Subway: 1 or 9 to 181st Street (and St. Nicholas Avenue)
A to 181st Street (and Ft. Washington Avenue)

Bus: M101 to 185th Street and Amsterdam Avenue (stops opposite the Library)
M3 to 186th Street and St. Nicholas Avenue
M4 to 186th Street and Ft. Washington Avenue

Directions:

Take the #1 or #9 train to the 181st Street station. Walk <u>north</u> on St. Nicholas Avenue to 185th Street. Turn <u>east</u> on 185th and walk two blocks to Amsterdam Avenue. Turn <u>north</u> on Amsterdam. The entrance is near the corner of 185th Street.

Or,

Take the A train to the 181st Street station. Use the exit to 184th Street and Overlook Terrace. Walk four blocks <u>east</u> on 184th Street to Amsterdam Avenue. Turn <u>north</u> on Amsterdam to 185th Street.

Description of Resources:

The Archives has more than 300 collections of mostly Orthodox Jewish institutions and individuals including material from 1605 to the present. Primarily organizational records, letters, memoirs, newspaper clippings, genealogies and photographs can be found here. The major collections of interest to genealogists are described below. Researchers should consult with the Archivist to determine whether other collections have documents related to their family histories or genealogy:

1.   <u>The Central Relief Committee Collection (1914–1959)</u>: Records, 1914–1918, include correspondence concerning requests to locate missing relatives, 1914–1916 [Boxes 10, 14]; correspondence requesting funds for transportation of relatives from Palestine to the U.S., 1916–1917 [Box 13]; lists of Palestine [Boxes 15–19] and Russian remittances, 1916 [Box 25]; and general correspondence with individuals. [Boxes 30–40]

Records, 1919–1929, include reports documenting the Jewish situation in Europe immediately after the end of WWI; eye witness accounts [Boxes 103–105]; list of orthodox congregations and shohatim (ritual slaughterers) in NYC [Box 111]; list of addresses of Rabbis and educational institutions in and Lithuania [Box 117]; list of 141 recipients of funds in Czechoslovakia (n.d.) [Box 114]; and letters of appeal for funds from individuals in Poland, Galicia, Estonia, Moravia and Slovakia, 1920–1922. [Box 115, 117]

Records, 1929–1947, include correspondence with yeshivot, institutions and individuals; lists of students (in Hebrew) from yeshivot in East European countries with biographical information such as age and hometown. These lists are most complete for Hungary and for Bobov institutions in Poland for 1930, some of which also include father's name. Lists of yeshivot and their students were also compiled in 1939 and 1940 for Latvia, Lithuania and Poland, and in 1941, for Hungary. Reports of yeshivot in Vilna being flooded with students seeking refuge; and lists of refugee students, their wives and children are included. [Box 224]

The papers of Rabbi Aaron Teitelbaum included in this collection contain correspondence with the U.S. State Department regarding emigration of 988 rabbinical students and faculty from 29 yeshivot in East Europe and Asia, 1940 and 1941; lists of students and visa applications of rabbinical students from yeshivot of Mir, Lublin, Radun, Kollel Kovno who proceeded to Japan; material on students and faculty from the Yeshiva Beth Joseph of Bialystok; and 100 affidavits, mostly from New York relatives and friends, for students living in Lithuania, Russia and Japan in 1941. [Boxes 254–255]

2. Mordechai Bernstein Collection, 1605–1965: Includes original documents of 58 Jewish communities in Germany and photocopies of documents of 38 Jewish communities. The earliest original document includes five records from the rabbinical court in Pappenheim, 1605–1619, on questions of heritage. Also included are a handful of marriage contracts, deeds of divorce and court records from such communities as Brakel, Castell, Darmstadt, Eppendorf, Luebeck, Petershagen, Muehlhausen, Warburg and Zinnwald. The documents include general meetings of the Jewish community of Esslingen on the Neckar (in Judeo-German), 1816–1825; a 1819–1843 volume of the burial society of Laupheim; excerpts of records of charitable endowments to the Jewish community of Laupheim, 1869–1872 (in German); a volume containing handwritten entries of circumcisions performed in an unidentified city, 1772–1796, and in Koenigsberg, 1852–1875; an account book of a burial society in Altenmuhr, 1845–1870, and a list of the Jewish residents of Fulda before 1933, with their location after 1945; documents regarding the Jewish cemetery and Jews living in Schiltz, 1935–1947; and a list of the Jewish residents of Stuttgart, 1940–1941.

Includes photocopies of the Memorbuecher from Koblenz, 1610–1850, and from Ehrenbreitstein, 1703–1883; photocopies of community records from Mikulow (Nikolsburg) in Moravia, 18th century; the records of a burial society in Prague, 1785–1870; and photographs of buildings, cemeteries and tombstones in over 50 Jewish communities in Germany, Czechoslovakia, Italy and Poland. This subseries contains a folder of transcriptions of the Hebrew text of tombstones in the Jewish cemetery of Sinsheim, 1891–1938.

Of note, this collection includes 115 inventories of Jewish records in Staatsarchivs in the following German communities:

Amberg	Frankfurt	Landshut	Regensburg
Amorbach	Friedberg	Ludwigsburg	Reugland
Ansbach	Fuerstenberg	Luebeck	Reutlingen
Assenheim	Goettingen	Marburg an der Lahn	Schweinfurt
Bamberg	Gunzenhausen	Memmingen	Sigmaringen
Birstein	Hamburg	Munich	Speyer
Braunschweig	Hameln	Neuburg	Stuttgart
Castel	Hannover	Neuenstein	Weikersheim
Coburg	Hesse	Neumarkt (Oberpfalz)	Wertheim
Darmstadt	Hildesheim	Neuwied	Wiesbaden
Donaueschingen	Huettenbach	Nuremberg	Wiesentheid
Duesseldorf	Jebenhausen	Oberehrenbreitstein	Wolfenbuettel
Esslingen	Karlsruhe	Pappenheim	Wuerzburg
Floss	Koblenz (Coblenz)		

3. National Council of Jewish Women, Service to the Foreign Born: Includes an estimated 350,000 records on individuals and families who came through the port of New York and whom the National Council helped to become citizens. The records include the New York Section, 1939–1968, and Brooklyn Section, 1942–1955. See "Restrictions on Use."

4. Vaad Hatzala Collection (1939–1963): Includes information on the rescue efforts of the Union of Orthodox Rabbis of the U.S. and Canada (Agudath Ha-Rabbonim). The files include correspondence, lists, visas and affidavits of support concerning rabbinical and student refugees, 1941–1948 [Boxes 4, 13–16, 19, 26–30, 38, 42–43]; searches for missing relatives, 1944–1948 [Boxes 17, 40, 44]; lists of non-quota immigrants, 1947, lists of sponsors, 1946, and lists of applicants for rabbinical positions, 1948 [Box 17]; lists of refugees in concentration camps [Bergen-Belsen - Box 18; Dachau - Box 30], in Displaced Persons Camps [Box 18], in Camp Vittel, France [Box 26], and elsewhere [Boxes 18, 22, 31, 38, 39]; identification papers (including photos) issued by the Vaad in Katowice, Poland [Box 18]; list of students of the Windsheim Yeshiva transported from Frankfurt, Germany to Lyons, France, 1948 [Box 31]; lists of Jews of various nationalities who arrived in Sweden, 1945 and n.d. [Boxes 34, 40]; list of

1,200 persons who left Theresienstadt for Switzerland, n.d. [Box 35]; lists of refugees to be transferred to Paris [Box 40]; and lists of Jews authorized to enter Tangier.

5. Louis Rittenberg Collection: Includes biographical data on famous American Jews. This data was accumulated for the preparation of the *Universal Jewish Encyclopedia* (1939–1944). These papers also include documentation of Jewish life in New York from the 1930s to 1960s, especially the rise of the Jewish community in Washington Heights.

6. Rescue Children, Inc. Collection (1946–1985): Includes files documenting the rescue of children who survived the Holocaust. RCI set up special centers in France, Belgium, Sweden and Germany. The organization supported 2,200 orphans between 1945 and 1948, and identified or located the families of more than two-thirds of the children. The bulk of the archival material is from information supplied by the children through interviews seeking biographical information and recollections of people in their home towns. See "Restrictions on Use."

7. Yeshiva University Records (1895–1970): Contains records of the University including biographical files on Presidents Bernard Revel, Samuel Belkin, Norman Lamm; on Deans Pinchos Churgin, Moses Isaacs, 1930–1970 and personal (family) files of Dr. Shelley R. Saphire, 1914–1960; applications for faculty positions at Yeshiva University and the High School, 1926–1952; faculty files, 1926–1946; files on foreign faculty, 1939–1941; Teacher's Time Book (Talmudical Academy) English Department, 1915–1921; and lists of faculty members and administrators, 1947, 1954–1955, 1957.

Records on students include grades, Talmudical Academy, 1917–1919, and Yeshiva College, 1936–1937; applications for admission, withdrawn or rejected applicants, 1926–1942; student (registration) cards 1924–1949; applications for stipends, dormitory applications or dormitory residents, 1929, 1943–1944, 1946–1947; lists of students, 1949–1950, 1957; and graduate school mailing list, 1946. This record group also includes alumni questionnaire replies, 1935–1936; a file on Talmudical Academy Alumni, 1942–1954; questionnaires, B. Revel Graduate School, 1930–1946; and records of donations with names/addresses of donors, by year, 1909–1934. Access to some files is restricted.

8. Institutional Synagogue Records (1917–1967): Includes annual membership meetings, 1928, 1929, 1938 and 1941, regarding election of Board members; Fanny Henning will, 1937; and a bound volume of the synagogue's bulletin, *The Institutional*, 1933–1940 (with gaps).

9. Shelley Ray Saphire Collection (1890–1970): Includes personal correspondence with his future wife and other family members; applications for teaching positions at the Talmudical Academy, the High School Department of Yeshiva University, 1944–1950.

10. Henry S. Morais Collection (1860–1935): Contains biographical sketches of eight persons mentioned in his book, *The Jews of Philadelphia:* Col. Mayer Asch, Victor Caro, Joseph Chumaceiru, Col. Max Friedman, Dr. Samuel J. Gittleson, Abraham Jacob, Rev. Lee Reich, and one signed "S.S.C." Also, invitations to weddings and correspondence, mostly incoming, covering his years as a journalist and Rabbi in Philadelphia and New York.

11. Jamie Lehmann Memorial Collection: Records of the Jewish Community of Cairo (1886–1961): Contains the records of three major institutions: The Sephardic Jewish community, the Ashkenazi community and the B'nai B'rith Lodges (Cairo Lodge and Maimonides Lodge). The collection contains account books, case files, certificates, correspondence, minutes and photographs. Most of the original documents were created between 1920 and 1960.

The records of the Jewish Community Council include proceedings of meetings, 1925–1934 [Box 1]; minutes of meetings of the B'nai B'rith Lodges, 1911–1928 [Box 11]; and proceedings of meetings of the Administrative Committee supervising the Cairo synagogue which include letters from synagogue personnel and ritual slaughterers [Box 8]. General correspondence, 1926–1957, includes a list of rabbis and employees of the Chancellerie, with their nationality (no date); correspondence regarding the Abraham Btesh school and its personnel; and correspondence on personal matters such as deeds of marriage and divorce, 1953. [Box 2]

Passport forms (in Arabic), are available for 1919, containing name, age, date and place of birth, father's citizenship, father's profession, date of arrival in Egypt and length of stay in Egypt, profession, address, previous country of residence, place of destination and reason for travel. Some contain photographs of individuals or families. [Box 2]

The records of the Chief Rabbinate include general correspondence, 1941–1959 [Box 3]. The correspondence deals with Palestinian Jewry regarding personal status and assistance to war prisoners. Correspondence with Alexandria, 1936–1946, include deeds of marriage and divorce and the status of foreign Jews. Out-going letters, 1947–1950, include letters about Jewish political detainees and complaints about attacks against Jews [Box 5]. A list of butchers in Alexandria, 1945, is in Box 4.

The Register of Deeds Regarding the Personal Status of Private Individuals, 1944–1946, includes birth, marriage and death certificates or affidavits (in Arabic). Each entry lists the name of the person involved in Arabic and French. The entries for Attestation of Personal Status, 1886, 1936–1937, 1947 (registration of requests for certificates) include the name of the person, date and a statement of purpose. The most frequent purposes attested to were birth, celibacy, betrothal, marriage, divorce, widowhood, death, notarization of judicial sentences and passport. [Box 5]

Accounting documents of the Chancellerie, 1946, include salaries of the staffs of the Rabbinate and the Arikha; a (Hebrew) list of ritual slaughterers in Cairo; and for 1949–1950, a ledger containing accounts of individuals, associations and schools in Cairo [Box 6]. Account books of contributions to the Ba'al Hanes Synagogue, 1890–1909 [Box 8]; and of the Synagogue Al Ostaz al Amshati in al Mahalla al Kubra (no date), are also available. Records of the Ashkenazi Community of Cairo, 1933–1955, list funds distributed to indigent families, 1947; and include accounting records for 1950. [Box 10]

Identification records (5 booklets) include entries for date, name, date and place of birth, profession, address, name of father, destination, spouse's name and place of birth and names of children, 1946–1947. Most entries also have a photograph. [Box 7]

The collection includes completed forms (in French) prepared by the Cairo Jewish Hospital on patients, 1959–1961; and forms (in Arabic and French) prepared by the Italian Hospital of Abbassieh, 1960–1961. [Box 9]

An unidentified register (may be assisted families) contains names of individuals living in Cairo neighborhoods. Each entry (in French) provides name, number of persons in family and address. An additional list, providing name, age and profession is scribbled on the back of a registration form of Yeshiva Ahaba Veahva in Cairo. [Box 9]

12. French Consistorial Collection (1809–1939): Includes also records of the Consistories of Rome, Italy, 1809–1810, and Treves and Koblenz, Germany, 1810–1812. The latter include tax exemption requests from individual Jews; lists of young men serving in the army; the decision of the mayor of Treves to expel Isaac Levy from that City, 1810; and letters by Simon Samuel, a British prisoner of war to the Central Consistory, 1812. [Box 1]

Extracts from the census of Parisian Jews, 1809, list all Jewish professionals and soldiers. Includes proceedings of the first meetings of the Consistory of Paris, 1809 and the records of the welfare committee containing certificates for foreign Jews, 1811–1813. [Box 1]

The records of the Administrative Commission for the Synagogues in Paris contain lists of synagogues' seat owners, 1834–1835, 1851 and 1853; and a contract hiring Cantor Israel Loevy, 1823 [Box 2]. Consistory of Paris, Central Administration records include lists of funeral processions in Paris, 1834–1839, 1884 and 1886, circumcisions, 1856, 1863, 1870–1871 and members of benevolent societies. [Box 3]

The "Ritual Bath" folder contains the certificates of many converts to Judaism, 1880–1885. The "Rabbinical Seminary" folder contains certificates of Lazard Wogue, 1817–1897, and Lazard Isidore, 1814–1888 attesting that converts underwent the ritual immersion in a mikve. Correspondence of the Central Consistory includes a letter from Rabbi Emmanuel Deutz, Chief Rabbi of the Central Consistory to Rabbi Abraham Andrade of Bordeaux concerning the marriage of a Jew from Bordeaux, 1936. The records include complaints against rabbis, cantors and ritual slaughterers. [Box 3 and 4]

The collection includes a list showing the Jewish population of the following communities: Auxerre, 1810, Dijon (n.d.), La Ferté s/ Jouarre, 1873, Fontainebleau, 1872, Nantes, 1848, Versailles (n.d.), La Orléans, c. 1810s, 1872, Reims, 1837, 1838, 1851, Tours (n.d.), and Le Havre, c. 1835. [Box 4]

Records of the Association Consistoriale Israélite de Paris include elections, 1908 and proceedings of meetings,1924 and 1939 [Box 4]. Records of the Departmental Consistories include a register of pupils at the Jewish vocational school in Marseilles, 1830; letters from Oran, Algiers regarding Moroccan refugees, 1859; Consistory of Strasbourg elections, 1835–1860 and Bordeaux elections, 1810–1812. [Box 5]

13. Chevra (Chebrah) Poel Zedek Anschei Illia Collection (1893–1961): Comprises the extant records of a defunct Lower East Side synagogue, the Forsyth Street shul (corner of Delancey Street), which was founded in the 1880s by immigrants from Illia, in the province of Vilna, Lithuania. Most of the collection consists of minutes and financial records, including lists of members' names and addresses, 1907–1944. A *Sefer HaZahav* [Golden Book] records the names and ages of members and their families in 1930; some applications for membership, 1929, 1937, 1943–1947 and cemetery records, 1926–1951.

14. <u>Benjamin and Pearl Koenigsberg Papers (1899–1977)</u>: Includes more than 100 affidavits and visa applications prepared by Benjamin Koenigsberg from 1938–1953 for European Jews with whom, in most cases, he had no personal relationship. These included families from Germany, Austria, Poland and Lithuania living in France and Portugal, as well as some still in Berlin (1939), Vienna (1940–1941), detained in British internment camps in the Isle of Man (1940) and some in Sydney, Australia (1941), Shanghai (1940) and Japan (1941) [Boxes 22–24]. The collection also includes personal family papers [Boxes 31–32]; correspondence of the Sienewar Chevra Anshe Sfard, 1908, 1929–1947 [Box 16]; and a list of congregations in NYC c. 1910. [Box 17]

15. <u>Peter Wiernik and Bertha Wiernik Collection, 1886–1950</u>: Includes records of the American Jewish Joint Distribution Committee, 1916–1946; personal papers of Peter Wiernik (1886–1936) and his sister, Bertha Wiernik (1914–1950); and maps showing the location of Jewish Schools in Poland, Lithuania and Latvia.

16. <u>Irving I. Herzberg Photograph Collection, 1962–1988</u>: Includes photographs of Hasidic life in Williamsburg and Crown Heights (Brooklyn, NY). The collection includes 2,500 negatives, 380 slides and 570 photographs.

Finding Aids:

Published inventories are available for some of these collections. Nevertheless, the records may be difficult to use because name indexes are not available in most cases. Some Yeshiva University Archives published inventories can be accessed on line at *Archives U.S.A.* (See YESHIVA UNIVERSITY LIBRARY, NEW YORK PUBLIC LIBRARY, IRMA AND PAUL MILSTEIN DIVISION OF UNITED STATES HISTORY, LOCAL HISTORY AND GENEALOGY or SCHOMBERG CENTER FOR RESEARCH IN BLACK CULTURE for free access to this website.)

1. <u>The Central Relief Committee</u>: The published inventories do not list names of individuals assisted but rather describe the type and subject of records included in each file. Only "Correspondence with individuals, 1914–17" is arranged alphabetically by surname. In order to find information on individuals in responses to questionnaires, researchers must know the name and location of the yeshiva, period of attendance and the person's function in the yeshiva.

2. <u>Mordechai Bernstein Collection</u>: Original documents, transcripts and some photographs in the collection are arranged alphabetically by city. A detailed list of the inventories of the Staatsarchivs and of microfilms of Jewish personal records is at the beginning of Box 17.

3. <u>National Council of Jewish Women, Service for the Foreign Born</u>: The records are arranged by code number. Researchers must have name, birth date and birth place for access. See "Restrictions on Use."

4. <u>Vaad Hatzala Collection</u>: A published inventory is available. Names of individuals assisted are not listed in the inventory. Most of the files of interest to genealogists are categorized under the series "Foreign Activities" [Boxes 22–44]. These are arranged primarily by country. Others are in the "Immigration and Rehabilitation" series [Boxes 15–21] and appear to be organized by correspondent. A description of the contents of each file is available which will allow researchers to narrow their search somewhat.

5. <u>Louis Rittenberg Collection</u>: A card catalog listing the contents of each box is available.

6. <u>Rescue Children, Inc. Collection</u>: A published inventory is available. Boxes 11–12 contain alphabetical index cards with the names of the children and biographical information prepared by the Stern College Rescue Children Inc. Project.

7. <u>Yeshiva University Records</u>: The preliminary published inventory has an index which allows relative ease in finding subject files. Some faculty members are listed under their own names. For others, see the "Faculty" listings. For records on students, see "Yeshiva College" or "Talmudical Academy" listings. For Alumni records, see "Alumni." NOTE: The published inventory includes the biographies of 10 former Administrators of Yeshiva University.

8. <u>Institutional Synagogue Records</u>: A published inventory is available. The Fanny Henning will is in folder 43.

9. <u>Shelley Ray Saphire Collection</u>: There is a published inventory for this collection. Personal correspondence is in folders 1–12. Applications for teaching positions at the Talmudical Academy are arranged by Department, e.g. Biology and Science, Business, Music, etc.

10. <u>Henry S. Morais Collection</u>: The published inventory to this collection has an alphabetical index to the correspondence in Morais' papers. Wedding invitations are not indexed but are arranged alphabetically by sender in folders 102 to 104. Biographical sketches are in folder 126.

11. Jamie Lehmann Memorial Collection, Records of the Jewish Community of Cairo: The published inventory provides a detailed description of the contents of each box and folder. General correspondence and correspondence with Alexandria are arranged alphabetically by name of the correspondent.

12. French Consistorial Collection: The published inventory provides a brief history of the Consistories and outlines the contents of each box. The arrangement of the records reflects the history of the Consistorial institution, i.e., the Napoleonic era, 1809–1822 [Box 1], the Central Consistory in Paris and provincial Jewish communities under its aegis, 1822–1905 [Boxes 2–4]; the records of the successor organization, the Association Consistoriale Israelite de Paris [Box 4]; and records of other departmental Consistories, including Bordeaux, Lyons, Marseilles, Metz, Nancy and Strasbourg. [Box 5]

13. Benjamin and Pearl Koenigsberg Papers (1899–1977): The published inventory lists alpha folders for affidavit and visa files. Some surnames are listed.

14. Irving I. Herzberg Photograph Collection, 1962–1988: Negatives are numbered, dated and identified briefly, i.e. "Gross Wedding." Some, but not all, photographs are identified.

15. Chevrah Poel Zedek Anschei Illia Collection and Peter Wiernik and Bertha Wiernik Collection, 1886–1950: Published inventories are available.

Description of Facility:

The Archives is located on the 6th floor in Room 602. An appointment is necessary. There are 2 staff persons who can assist researchers. In most cases, documents can be obtained immediately. The Archives has one microfilm reader.

Fees/Copies:

Copies can be made by Archives staff at $.25 per page. The published inventories can be purchased. They range in price from $5 to $12. The Inventories Order Form lists the cost of each.

Restrictions on Use:

Researchers may view only one box at a time. Specific restrictions are imposed by donors on some collections. Materials must be handled with care.

The National Council of Jewish Women, Service to the Foreign Born case files and the Rescue Children, Inc. files are restricted to the individual concerned or his/her immediate family.

Access to Yeshiva University Records should be requested from Yeshiva University's Senior Vice-President.

YESHIVA UNIVERSITY
MENDEL GOTTESMAN LIBRARY OF HEBRAICA-JUDAICA

Facility Director: Leah Adler, Head Librarian

Address: 2520 Amsterdam Avenue, 5th Floor   ♿
New York, NY

(Cross Streets: West 185th and 186th Streets)

Mail Address: 500 West 185th Street
New York, NY 10033

Phone: (212) 960-5382
Fax: (212) 960-0066
E-mail: unilib@ymail.yu.edu
Website: www.yu.edu/libraries/mgl/index.html

Hours of Operation:

School Year (September to mid-June)
Sunday to Thursday: 9:00 am to 1:00 am
Friday: 9:00 am to 12:30 pm

Closed Saturday, Jewish and legal holidays. NOTE: Summer hours vary. Call before coming.

Closest Public Transportation and Directions:

See YESHIVA UNIVERSITY - ARCHIVES.

Description of Resources:

The Gottesman Library is a major Judaica library with over 200,000 printed volumes in a variety of languages dating from the 15th century to the present. The Library's collection includes more than 800 current journal and newspaper subscriptions, 30,000 retrospective periodical volumes, 11,000 microform items which contain journals, dissertations, rare books, and manuscripts. Of special note are the Library's extensive collection of rabbinic materials including rabbinical responsa and rabbinic lexicons, family and community histories, biographies, genealogies, and a significant collection of yizkor books (see Appendix B). The Library's holdings also include the following (most on open shelves):

1. Vital Records:

    Czech Republic. Bohemia. *Matrikenverzeichnis der judischen Matriken Bohmens* [Register of Jewish vital statistics in Czech state archives pertaining to Bohemia], by F. Gundacker. Vienna, [1998]. [DS135 C96 B56 1998]
    Czech Republic. Moravia. *Matrikenverzeichnis der judischen Matriken Mahrens* [Register of Jewish vital statistics in Czech state archives pertaining to Moravia], by F. Gundacker. Vienna, 2000. [DS 135 C96 M62486 2000]
    England. London. *The Circumcision Register of Isaac and Abraham de Paiba (1715–1775): from the manuscript record preserved in the Archives of the Spanish and Portuguese Jews' Congregation of London,* transcribed and edited by R. D. Paiba. London, 1991. [BM295 S7 L6 v.4]
    France. Metz. *Tables du registre d'état civil de la communauté Juive de Metz, 1717–1792,* by Pierre Andre Meyer. Paris 1987. [Ref DS135 F85 M88 1987]
    Germany. Kassel. *Die Israelitische Gemeinde zu Kassel im 19. Jarhundert: Eheschliessungten, Geborene, Verstorbene, 1808–1886,* by Helmut Thiele. Kassel, 1986. [DS135 G4 K377445 1986]
    Lithuania. *Jewish Vital Records, Revision Lists and Other Jewish Holdings in the Lithuanian Archives,* compiled by Harold Rhode and Sallyann A. Sack. Teaneck, 1996. [CS856 J4 R53]
    Netherlands. Amsterdam. *Trouwen in mokum: Jewish marriage in Amsterdam, 1598–1811,* by Dave Verdooner and Harmen Snel. 's-Gravenhage, [1991]. Includes 15,238 Jewish couples. [Ref DS135 N5 A6884 1990z]

2. Names and their Origins:

    China. *The Nomenclature of Jews in China,* by Rudolf Lowenthal. Peiping, 1947. [CS3010 L68 1947]
    France. *Dictionnaire étymologique de noms de famille français d'origine étrangère et régionale,* by Laurent Herz. Paris, 1997. [Ref CS 2695.H47 1997]
    • *Les noms des Juifs de France au Moyen Age,* by Simon Seror. Paris, 1989. [Ref CS3010 S44 1989]

Greece. *Les noms des Juifs de Grèce: histoire, origine, signification des prénoms et des noms de famille de Juifs de Grèce,* by Asher Moissis. [1990]. [Ref CS3010 M6514 1990]

Israel. *Shemot ha-mishpachah be-Yisrael,* by Moshe Hanina Eshel. Haifa, [1967]. [Ref CS3010 E7]

Morocco. *Les noms des Juifs du Maroc: essai d'onomastique Judeo-Marocaine,* by Abraham I. Laredo. Madrid, 1978. [Ref CS3010 L37]

Spain. Majorca. *Origen genealogico de algunos apellidos existentes en Mallorca e historia de los Judios de Espana.* Valencia, 1965. [CS2749 M35 O75 1965]

3. Cemeteries:

Austria. Vienna. *Hunderttausend Steine: Grabstellen grosser Osterreicher judischer Konfession auf dem Wiener Zentralfriedhof: Tor I und Tor IV,* by Patricia Steines. Vienna, [1993]. [DS135 A93 A18 1993]

Czech Republic. Bohemia and Moravia. *Jewish Cemeteries in Bohemia and Moravia,* by Jan Herman. Prague, [1981]. [NB1880 C9 H47513]

Denmark. Copenhagen. *Jodiske gravstene 1886–1900 pa Mosaisk Vestre Begravelsesplads* [Jewish Tombstones, 1886–1900 in the Mosaisk Cemetery], by Elias Levin. Copenhagen, 1986. [DS135 D42 C68 1986]

England. London. *London's Jewish Cemeteries,* compiled and produced by Charles Tucker, Hannah and David Jacobs. London, 1989. [DS135 E55 L688 1989]

France. Alsace. *Le Cimetière Juif de Rosenwille,* by Robert Weyl. Strasbourg, 1988. [DS135 F85 A498 1988]

France. Jungholz. *Der Israelitische Friedhof in Jungholz,* by Dr. Moses Ginsburger. Gebweiler, 1904. [Uncl. G493 Isr]

France. Paris. *Cimetière de Montmartre: Division 3,* by Gilles Plaut. Paris, 1999. [DS135 F85 P375 1999]
  • *Cimetière du Père-Lachaise: Division Israélite,* by Gilles Plaut. Paris, 1999. [DS135 F85 P3755 1999]

Germany. Berlin. *Der Judische Friedhof Schonhauser Allee,* by Rosemarie Kohler and Ulrich Kratz-Whan. Berlin 1992. [DS135 G4 B4645 1992]
  • *Berliner Grabsteine,* by Heinz Knobloch. Berlin, [1988]. [DS135 G5 K57 1988]

Greece. Salonika. *Matsevot Saloniki: be-tseruf toldot hayehem shel gedole kehilah* [Precious Stones of the Jews of Salonica], by Isaac S. Emmanuel. 2 vols. Jerusalem, 1963–1968. [922.965 G793 T4 E54]

Netherlands. Hague. *De joodse begraafplaats aan de scheveningseweg in Den Haag: Geschiedenis en restauratieverslag,* by Francine Puttmann, et al. [Den Haag], 1992. [DS135 N5 H347 1992]

Netherlands. Muiderberg. *De Begraafboeken van Muiderberg, 1669–1811* [Burial books of Muiderberg, 1669–1811]. Meppel, [2000]. [DS135 N5 M85 2000]

Poland. Warsaw. *Cmentarze zydowskie w Warszawie* [Jewish Cemetery in Warsaw], by Leon Przysuskier. Radom, Poland,[1992]. [DS135 P62 W3288 1992]

United States. Connecticut. *Jewish cemeteries in five counties of Connecticut,* by Edward A. Cohen and Lewis Goldfarb. Bowie, MD., 1998. [F105 J5 C64 1998]

4. Holocaust Victims and Survivors:

Antisemetisch Verfolgte registriert in Bielefeld, 1933–1945: eine Dokumentation judischer einzelschiecksale, by Moniker Minninger, Joachim Meynert and Friedhelm Schaffer. Bielefeld, Germany, 1985. [DS135 G4 B523 1985]

Archives of the Holocaust: an international collection of selected documents, edited by Henry Friedlander and Sybil Milton. 22 vols. New York, 1989–. [D804.3 A7 1989]

Die Ausburgerung deutscher Staatsangehoriger, 1933–1945 nach den im Reichsanzeiger veroffenlichten Listen [Expatriation lists as published in the "Reichsanzeiger," 1933–1945], vol. 1, Chronological order, edited by Michael Hepp, Munich, 1985; vol. 2, Name Index; vol. 3, Index to Place of Birth/Last Known Residence. [CS614 A94 1985]

Catalogue of Camps and Prisons in Germany and German-occupied Territories, September 1,1939–May 8, 1945, compiled by the International Tracing Service. 1st issue. Arolsen, 1949–1950. [D805 G3 I46]

Kaddisj = Kadish: ter nagedachtenis van de joodse Rotterdamse burgers, 1940-1945. Gemeentarchief Rotterdam. Rotterdam, 2000. [DS135 N5 R675 2000]

Surviving Jews in Czestochowa. World Jewish Congress. New York, [1945]. [DS135 P62 C885 1945]

Totenbuch Theresienstadt. Judisches Komitee fur Theresienstadt. Vienna, 1971. [D805 C9 J84 1971]

5. Rabbinic Resources:

Dor rabanav ve-sofrav, by Benzion Eisenstadt. 6 vols. Warsaw, [1895–1903]. Rabbis of Europe and America. [922.964 E58D]

Dorot ha-aharonim, by Benzion Eisenstadt. 3 vols. Brooklyn, [1913–1915, 1936/37–1940/41]. [922.967 E36]

Hakhme Lita, by Naftali Ben-Menahem. Jerusalem, [1958 or 1959]. [DS135 R93 L555232 1958]

Meore Galitsyah: Encyclopedia of Galician Rabbis and Scholars, by Meir Wunder. 5 vols. Jerusalem, 1978–. [BM750 W83]

Otsar ha-rabbanim, by Nathan Zebi Friedmann. [Bnei Brak, 1975]. [BM 750 F73 1975]

Rabane Minsk va-hakhameha: sefer ha-zikaron, by Benzion Eisenstadt. Jerusalem, [1968 or 1969]. Includes epitaphs. [922.964 R969U 1968]

Sefer Anshe ha-shem be-Artsot ha-brit, by Benzion Eisenstadt. St. Louis, 1933. Biographies of Jews in U.S.A. [922.964 U58E]

Le-toledot Yisrael ve-hakhamav be-Polin, by Feivel Hirsch Wettstein. Krakow, [1908/09]. [DS135 P63 W42]

The Unbroken Chain, by Neil J. Rosenstein. New York, 1990. [BM750 R66 1990]

6.   Synagogues:

Algeria, Morocco, Tunisia. *Bate ha-keneset be-Afreika ha-tsefonit: Tunisyah, Algiryah, Maroko* [The Synagogues of North Africa...], by Jacob Pinkerfeld. Jerusalem, 1974. [NA6087 P56 1974]

Canada. Quebec. *A Checklist of Registers of Protestant and Jewish Congregations in Quebec,* by R. Neil Broadhurst. Calgary, Alberta, [1994]. [Ref CS88 Q4 B76 1994]

Greece. *Jewish Sites and Synagogues of Greece,* by Nicholas P. Stavroulakis and Timothy J. DeVinney. Athens, 1992. [BM319 S78 1992]

Hungary. *The Synagogues of Hungary: An Album,* by Imre Heller and Zsigmond Vajda. New York, 1968. [NA5512 H44 1968]

Italy. *Bate ha-Keneset be Italyah: mi-tekufat ha-renisans ad yamenu* [The Synagogues of Italy...], by Jacob Pinkerfeld. Jerusalem, 1954. [NA5614 P55 1954]

Spain. Toledo, Segovia and Cordoba. *Sinagogas de Toledo, Segovia y Cordoba,* by Francisco Cantera Burgos. Madrid, 1973. [NA5803 C36 1973]

Turkey. *The Old Synagogues of Turkey: a pictorial narrative,* by Don A. Halperin. Bristol, IN, 1986. [BM360 H35 1986]

7.   Guides to Archival Collections:

Catalogo descriptivo de los manuscritos hebreos de la Biblioteca Nacional [Catalog Description of the Hebrew Manuscripts in the National Library (Spain)], by Carlos del Valle Rodriguez. Madrid, 1986. [Z6621 S63 H4 1986]

A Handbook for Archival Research in the USSR, by Patricia Grimsted. [Washington, DC], 1989. [Ref CD 711 G68]

The German consulates in Palestine, 1842–1939 [RG 67], prepared by the Prime Minister's Office, State Archives. Jerusalem, 1976. [Ref CD1237.5 I85 1976]

Guide to Manuscripts and Documents in the British Isles Relating to the Middle East and North Africa, compiled by Noel Matthews and M. Doreen Wainwright. Oxford, 1980. [CD1048 N4 M37]

Guide to the Archives of Israel, edited by P. A. Alsberg. Jerusalem, 1973. [Ref CD2012 G84]

Guide to the Jewish Genealogical Records of Australia and New Zealand, compiled by Harvey A. Cohen and Beverly Davis. Melbourne, 1988. [Ref folio CS2007 J4 G84 1988]

Inventaris van de archieven van de Nederlands Israelitische gemeente te Rotterdam, 1737–1971, by A.M. van der Woel. Rotterdam, 1976. [DS138 N5 R6786 1976]

8.   Biographical Dictionaries:

Canada. *Canadian Jewish Women of Today: Who's Who of Canadian Jewish Women,* edited by Edmond Y. Lipsitz. Ontario, 1983–. [CT3270.J4 C3]
  • *Canadian Jewry: Prominent Jews of Canada,* edited by Zvi Cohen. Toronto, 1933. [922.964 C213C]
  • *Canadian Jewry Today: Who's Who in Canadian Jewry,* edited by Edmond Y. Lipsitz. Downsview, Ont., [1989]. [F1035 J5 C27 1989]

England. *Jewish Year Book.* [London], 1896/97–

Germany. Aschaffenburg. *Biographisches Handbuch der Juden in Stadt und Altkreis Aschaffenburg,* by Peter Korner. Aschaffenburg, 1993. [DS135.G4 A7825 1993]

Germany. Berlin. *Berliner Judische Arzte in der Weimarer Republik,* [Jewish Doctors in Berlin in the Weimar Republic], by Bernhard Meyer and Hans-Jurgen Mende. Berlin, 1996. [DS135 G5 A12545 1996]

Germany. Munster in Westfalen. *Judische Familien in Munster, 1918 bis 1945,* by Gisela Mollenhoff and Rita Schlautmann-Overmeyer. Munster, [1995]. [Ref DS135.G4 M93595 1995]

Israel. *Nashim be'Yisrael: lexicon* [Women of Israel: Lexicon], by Yael Roseman, et al. Tel Aviv, [1991]. [CT1919 P38 N38 1991]

- *Who's Who in Israel...*, 1945– (gaps). [DS125.3 A2 W62] and [DS126.6 A2 W5]
- *Yizkor...parashiyot hayehem u-motam shel ha-noflim* [Yizkor, in Memoriam: biographies and photographs of the fallen in the ranks of the Israel Defense Forces], by Reuven Avinoam. Vol 1: War of Liberation, 1955 and supplement, 1965; vol 2: War of Independence to 6 Day War, 1969; vol. 3: beginning with 6-day War, 1971. [Jerusalem]. [922.964 I85Y]

Switzerland. *Judisches Jahrbuch fur die Schweiz*, 1916–1922. [DS135 S9 J8]

9. <u>Newspapers and Periodicals</u>: NOTE: The years listed are the earliest and latest editions. Gaps exist.

Allgemeine Zeitung des Judentums (Berlin), 1837–1922
Bayerische Israelitische Gemeindezeitung (Munich), 1926–1928
Canadian Jewish Chronicle, 1948–1957
Chicago Jewish Forum, 1942–1968/9
Israelite (Bombay), 1926–1927
Jeschurun (Frankfurt), 1854–1870
Jewish Advocate (Boston), 1927–
Jewish Affairs (South Africa), 1946–
The Jewish Chronicle (London), 1904–1973

The Jewish Guardian (London), 1920–1924
Baltimore Jewish Times, 1984–1994
The Hebrew Standard (New York), 1893–1922
Jerusalem Post, 1952– (microfilm)
The Jewish Tribune (New York), 1920–1923
The Jewish Tribune and Hebrew Standard (New York), 1920–1930
The Jewish World (London), 1908–1934
Ha'Meilits (Odessa/St. Petersburg), 1861–1902
Palestine Post, 1933–1951
Ha'Tzefirah (Warsaw/Berlin), 1874–1904

The Library has many other newspapers in its collection. Check the YULIS catalog and with the librarian at the Information Desk. See also, the NYPL DOROT JEWISH DIVISION for additional Jewish newspapers and years.

10. <u>Manuscript Collection</u>:

The Library's Rare Book Room includes over 8,000 printed volumes and more than 1,000 manuscripts. About 400 Rabbinic manuscripts have been microfilmed (68 reels). In addition, the Library has on microfilm Hebrew manuscripts from the Jewish National and University Library in Jerusalem (900 reels); Hebrew manuscripts from the Vatican Library (189 reels) and Hebrew manuscripts from the Guenzberg collection in St. Petersburg (40 reels). The Jewish National and University Library microfilms include 8,756 Hebrew manuscripts filmed around the world. Manuscripts from the Library's own collection include:

<u>Letters of Rabbi Joseph Rozin, The "Rogachover Iluy" of Dvinsk</u> [MS 1142], a collection of 1,792 letters and 769 postcards sent to Rabbi Rozin from Israel, Europe and America between 1925–1936 with a variety of inquiries about Jewish law. The collection includes an alphabetical list of correspondents.

<u>Documents and lists from the Jewish Community of Frankfurt am Main</u>, [MS 281], collected by Judah Louis Lewin. Copied from the Memorbuch of the Klaus synagogue of the Jewish Community of Frankfurt.

<u>Documents from Odessa and Letters from Dayyanim in that City</u> [MS 1023] dealing with ritual slaughter, Jewish divorces and agunot. Primarily 1855–1866.

<u>*Rabane Risha u-matsevotehem...*</u> [The Rabbis of Rzeszow and their Tombstones from the year 1640 to the present], by Hayyim Duberish Friedberg (1876–1961). [MS 460]

<u>Record of Circumcisions kept by Samuel Conquy, Seder Milah</u> and a list of mahilim in Gibraltar, 1811. (Sephardic) [MS 1117, Folio 32–40]

<u>Isaac Lewin Collection</u> includes a rich variety of genealogical records of Jewish communities in Central and Eastern Europe especially in Posen, Silesia and other German-speaking areas including pinkasim (record books) of communities and societies, memorial books with lists of deaths, records of births and circumcisions, tax lists, property records, cemetery registers, synagogue seat records and other documents of communities such as:

Kempen (Kepno, Poland), 1771–1902
Militsch (Milicz, Poland), c.1830–c.1900
Fraustadt (Wschowa, Poland), 1835–1887)
Rawitsch (Rawicz, Poland), c.1838–c.1861
Nikolai (Mikolow, Poland), c.1849–1898
Myslowitz (Myslowice, Poland), 1810–1852

Schwerin, 1819–1869
Posen (Poznan, Poland), 1535–1538 (copies), 18th century, n.d.
Mecklenburg province, 1760–c. 1850
Breslau (Wroclaw, Poland); 1808–1844

See "Restrictions on Use."

11. Electronic Resources:

Includes access to the catalogs of Bar-Ilan Judaic Library, the Jewish National and University Library of the Hebrew University and the Jewish Theological Seminary Library (all available on the internet), as well as:

Bar-Ilan Judaic Library
Ethnic NewsWatch
FirstSearch Databases, includes 60 bibliographic, indexing and abstracting services and many text journals.
Index to Jewish Periodicals
Jerusalem Post, 1990–1998
RLG Archival Resources (see description NYPL IRMA AND PAUL MILSTEIN DIVISION OF UNITED STATES HISTORY, LOCAL HISTORY, AND GENEALOGY)
Takphone: Israeli Phonebook (Hebrew)

Finding Aids:

The Library's YULIS computerized catalog is available on line (www.yu.edu/libraries/yulis.htm) and can be searched in either Hebrew or English (Roman) script. YULIS includes the holdings of the Mendel Gottesman Library of Hebraica/Judaica, as well as Hedi Steinberg Library (Stern College for Women), Pollack Library - Landowne Bloom Collection, Yeshiva University Archives and the book collection of the Yeshiva University Museum.

For items not yet found in YULIS, search one of the Libraries' four card catalogs, starting with the New English Catalog, which is an integrated author/title/subject catalog. The New English Catalog has useful subject headings such as: Responsa (grouped by years, e.g. 1800 to 1900); Rabbis - biography; Jews - biography; Jews - [place name] - biography.

The Old English Catalog is a title/author catalog. A small but separate subject catalog is available but it is not comprehensive. The Old Hebrew (Dewey Decimal) and New Hebrew catalog are basically title catalogs only. Researchers looking for a specific book by title can use the Old English or Old and New Hebrew catalogs. Always search YULIS first.

For the Manuscripts Collection, check the published catalog, *Rabbinic Manuscripts: Mendel Gottesman Library, Yeshiva University* by Yosef Avivi, New York, 1998 [Z6621 M2547 H4 1998]. This volume includes a description of 400 Rabbinic manuscripts in the Rare Book Room (not the complete collection). The catalog is in both English and Hebrew. The Hebrew section is more detailed. There is a name index and a locality index in Hebrew (arranged by the name of the town used by its Jewish population). The Library also has a published catalog of 40 rare books in its collection that were printed pre-1500, *Sifre ha-defus ha-rishonim (inkunabulim): Bet ha-sefarim al-shem Mendel Gottesman, Yeshivah-Universitah,* by Gershon Cohen, New York, 1984. [Z240 C63]

For the remainder of the Rare Book Room Manuscript Collection, the Library has a card catalog located in the office of the Curator of Special Collections. The catalog is arranged by record group number. A separate card index arranged by surname, place and subject is available. See "Restrictions on Use."

The Library has a published guide and microfiche finding aid to the microfilmed Hebrew manuscripts from the Jewish National and University Library in Jerusalem. Check subject headings as "Divorce bills" (fiche 18) and "Marriage Contracts" (fiche 68–69) for manuscripts of interest to genealogists.

Description of Facility:

The Library is located on the fifth floor and on 5A. Most of the Library's books are on open shelves. A staff person is available to assist researchers. Seating is available for more than 150 persons. Six computers with access to the YULIS catalog and electronic resources are located on the 5th floor and 2 are located on 5A. The card catalogs are also on the 5th floor. The Library has two microfilm reader/printers and two microfiche readers.

Fees/Copies:

Two self-service photocopy machines are available in the Mendel Gottesman Library at $.15 per page or $.08 per page with a copy card. Three additional machines are located in the Photocopy Room on Level 2 of the Library Building. Microform reader-printers are located on the 5th and 2nd floors. Copies from microfilm are $.25.

Restrictions on Use:

Books in bad condition may not be copied. No mail research is conducted.

An appointment must be made to view the Rare Book Room Manuscript Collection card catalog.

YOUNG MEN'S & YOUNG WOMEN'S HEBREW ASSOCIATION (92nd STREET Y) ARCHIVES

Facility Director:	Steven W. Siegel, Library Director and Archivist
Address:	1395 Lexington Avenue New York, NY 10128
	(Cross Streets: East 91st and 92nd Streets)
Phone:	(212) 415-5542
Fax:	(212) 427-6119
E-mail:	library@92ndsty.org
Website:	www.92ndsty.org

Hours of Operation:

Sunday to Friday: By appointment only.
Closed Saturday, Jewish and legal holidays.

Closest Public Transportation:

Subway: 4, 5 (express) or 6 (local) to 86th Street

Bus: M101, M102 or M103 to Lexington Ave/ 92nd Street (southbound); 3rd Ave/91st Street (northbound)
       M86 to 86th Street and Lexington Avenue (crosstown)
       M96 to 96th Street and Lexington Avenue (crosstown)

Directions:

Take the #4, #5 (express) or #6 (local) train to the 86th Street station. Go up the staircase to the left as you exit the station. Walk <u>north</u> on Lexington Avenue to 92nd Street. The Archives is located on the 2nd floor in the Library.

Description of Resources:

The 92nd Street YM-YWHA is the oldest Jewish community center in North America in continuous existence. It was founded in 1874 as the Young Men's Hebrew Association. In addition to Jewish and secular genealogical reference materials and books on Jewish history and the Holocaust, the Archives at the 92nd Street Y holds records of the following organizations:

> Young Men's Hebrew Association (YMHA), 1874–1945, and its successor,
> Young Men's and Young Women's Hebrew Association (YM-YWHA), 1945 to date
> Young Women's Hebrew Association (YWHA), 1902–1945
> Clara de Hirsch Home for Working Girls, 1897–1962
> Surprise Lake Camp of the Educational Alliance and YMHA, 1902–1976
> Holy Society of the City of New York, 1849–1968

The records are arranged in record groups and sub-groups according to their organizational and departmental provenance, and in part by physical type (oral histories and memoirs; printed materials; audiovisual materials; art, artifacts and memorabilia). Of particular interest to genealogists are the following materials:

1. <u>YMHA Employment Department</u>

    Employers' ledgers, 1905–1928, and applicants' registers, 1911–1930, documenting the placement of thousands of young men with employers in New York City. Includes data about the applicants' backgrounds and job histories. (Arranged chronologically; no name index.)

    Applicant registration forms, 1930–1934, for approximately 1,200 men with last names Babbit to Bixgorin, Haar to Hymowitz, Rosanes to Ryvicker and Smith (Irving) to Sussman. Includes detailed personal histories and usually a photograph.

2. <u>YMHA Medical Department</u>

    Physical examination records, September 1904 to February 1905 for 198 men. Includes some family information. (Arranged chronologically; no name index.)

Medical record cards, 1930–1936, for approximately 3,800 men. Includes family and medical history. (Arranged alphabetically.)

3. YMHA and YM-YWHA Membership Department

Membership registers, 1882–1957. Includes name and address only. (Arranged chronologically; no name index.)
Published membership lists, 1886 and 1896–1916. Includes name and address only.
Membership record cards, 1900–1930, for approximately 24,000 men and boys. Includes name, address, other personal information and dates of membership. (Arranged alphabetically by category, i.e. older men, younger men, schoolboys.)
Membership record cards, 1930–1972, for tens of thousands of men and women. (Not completely arranged.)

4. YMHA Military and Veterans Activities

Personal information on, and photographs of, members in military service during World War II.

5. YMHA and YM-YWHA Residence Department (for young adults, 18 to 26)

Application cards, 1930–1958, for approximately 4,000 male residents, and 1930–1932, for approximately 500 men who applied for residence but did not move in.
Application cards, 1950–1958, for approximately 1,000 female residents (with last names Aaronson to Schwenkert).
Application forms, 1959–1968, for approximately 2,000 male and female residents.
Residents' registration cards, 1968–1990, for approximately 4,500 men and women.

NOTE: Contains personal and family information. Records since 1959 are restricted.

6. Young Women's Hebrew Association Residence

Residents' card files, 1920–1934, 1934–1942 and 1942–1950. Includes personal and family information. (Arranged alphabetically within each set of years.)

7. Clara de Hirsch Home for Working Girls

Record of applications, 1897–1900, and register of residents, 1897–1899. Include personal information. (Arranged chronologically with name indexes.)
Residence applications, 1954–1960. Include personal and family information. (Arranged by year of departure from the Home. No name index.)

8. Holy Society of the City of New York (one of the earliest non-synagogue Jewish benevolent societies to be incorporated in New York City. It was founded in 1846 and dissolved in 1968.)

Biographical data about members, c.1900–1930.
Burial permits, 1872–1927, for members interred in the Society's plot in Washington Cemetery, Brooklyn. (Arranged chronologically. No name index.)
Cemetery maps for the Society's plot.

Finding Aids:

The Archives has inventories and descriptions of each record group. Records are arranged alphabetically unless otherwise noted above.

Description of Facility:

Archival materials are consulted in the Library on the 2nd floor. Some of the materials described above are stored off-site. An advance appointment is necessary.

Fees/Copies:

The Library has one photocopy machine. The cost of a copy is $.10 per page.

Restrictions on Use:

The bulk of the records in the Archives may be used without restriction, although certain record series have restrictions to protect the privacy of individuals.

BRONX

Bronx Repositories

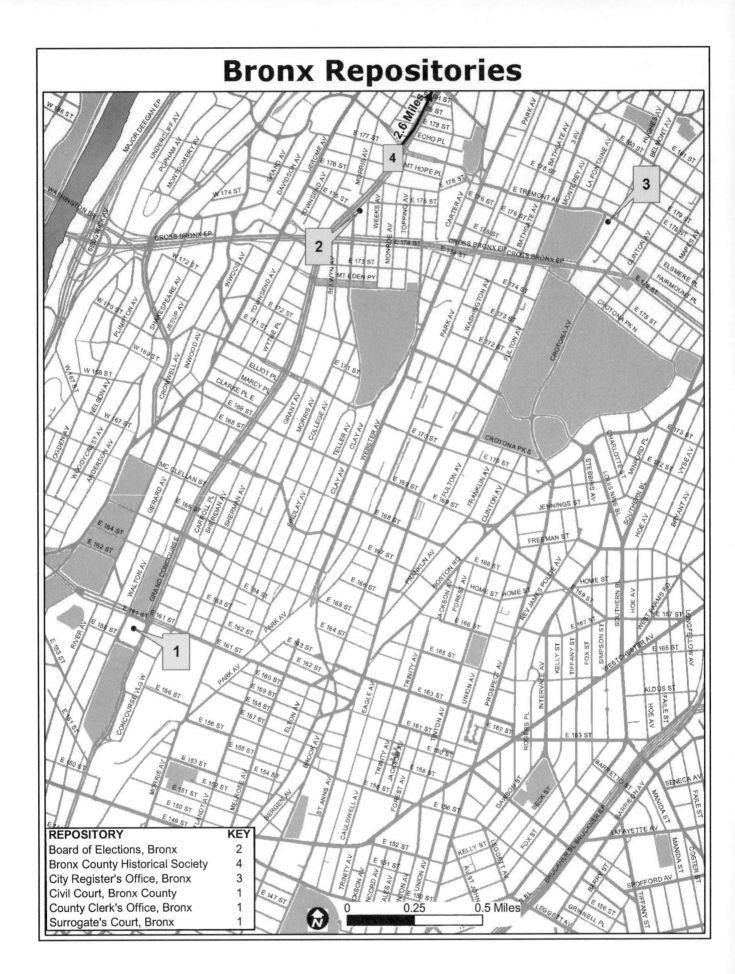

REPOSITORY	KEY
Board of Elections, Bronx	2
Bronx County Historical Society	4
City Register's Office, Bronx	3
Civil Court, Bronx County	1
County Clerk's Office, Bronx	1
Surrogate's Court, Bronx	1

BOARD OF ELECTIONS
BRONX BOROUGH OFFICE

Facility Director: Michael Benjamin, Deputy Chief Clerk
                          Victor B. Tosi, Deputy Chief Clerk

Address: 1780 Grand Concourse &
                          Bronx, NY 10457

                          (Cross Street: Eastburn Avenue)

Phone: (718) 299-9017
Fax: (718) 299-2140
E-mail: none
Website: www.vote.nyc.ny.us

Hours of Operation:

Monday to Friday: 9:00 am to 5:00 pm
Closed Saturday, Sunday and legal holidays.

Closest Public Transportation:

Subway: B or D to 174th-175th Street

Bus: Bx1 or Bx2 to 175th Street and Grand Concourse
           Bx36 to Tremont Avenue and the east side of the Grand Concourse

Directions:

Take the B or D train to the 174th-175th Street station. Exit toward the <u>north</u> end (3rd car from front) of the station. Exit to the <u>east</u> side of the Grand Concourse (to the right as one faces the token booth). The building is right behind the subway entrance. Take the elevator down to the "L4" level. (When exiting, take the elevator to the "GC" or Grand Concourse level.)

Description of Resources:

The Bronx office has voter registration records from 1897 to the present. Records, 1897–1956, are in bound ledgers arranged by year, Assembly/Election District (AD/ED) and then alphabetically by the first letter of the surname. Later records, 1957–1996 (microfilm), are arranged alphabetically.

Voter registrations that were still active in 1991 and registrations of voters who filed in 1991 or later were digitized and can be accessed through the Archival Voter Information Data (AVID) system.

See BOARD OF ELECTIONS, MANHATTAN BOROUGH OFFICE for a descriptions of these records and computer systems.

Finding Aids:

Current Bronx registrations and canceled registrations of Bronx voters who were still active when the computerized Election Administration System (EASY) index was created in 1986 are in the computerized database. This database can be accessed by name or by address.

In order to obtain information <u>pre-1957</u>, an address is necessary. The AD/ED is then located on maps available in this office. Canceled registrations ("buff cards"), 1957–1991, are arranged alphabetically and can be accessed by the staff in this office. A digitized copy of canceled registrations, 1991 to present, can be viewed through the AVID system accessible to staff only.

Description of Facility:

This NYC government office is on the Grand Concourse level of the building. There are 13 computers in the reception area that can access the EASY database. Staff conduct the search of records.

Fees/Copies:

Mail requests are accepted for a $3 fee (certified check or money order payable to the Board of Elections, City of New York). This covers a search for one name and one year. No refund is made if the record is not found. Transcripts are made by the clerk for pre-1957 records. Photocopies can be made from the AVID system for in-person researchers at $.25 per page or $3 certified. Provide the full name at registration, address where residing at the time of registration, and date of birth or age. For pre-1957 searches, use the address in a Presidential election year when the individual was more likely to have voted. Requests can be made by mail or fax.

There is no charge for viewing information in the EASY system.

Restrictions on Use:

Researchers visiting this office cannot view records directly. Staff will conduct the search of ledgers and microfilmed records and provide a copy for the $3 fee.

The AVID computerized database cannot be accessed by the public in this office. See BOARD OF ELECTIONS, QUEENS BOROUGH OFFICE and STATEN ISLAND BOROUGH OFFICE for direct access to the AVID system.

THE BRONX COUNTY HISTORICAL SOCIETY
RESEARCH LIBRARY AND ARCHIVES

Facility Director: Dr. Gary Hermalyn, Executive Director
                            Dr. Peter Derrick, Archivist

Address: 3309 Bainbridge Avenue
                            Bronx, NY 10467

                            (Cross Streets: East 208th and East 210th Streets)

Phone: (718) 881-8900
Fax: (718) 881-4827
E-mail: peterderrick@bronxhistoricalsociety.org
Website: www.bronxhistoricalsociety.org

Hours of Operation:

Monday to Friday: 9:00 am to 5:00 pm (by appointment only)

Closed Saturday, Sunday and legal holidays.

Closest Public Transportation:

Subway: D to 205th Street
         4 to Mosholu Parkway

Bus: Bx10, Bx16, Bx28, Bx30 or Bx34 to Bainbridge Avenue and East 208th or 210th Street
         Westchester #20 to Jerome Avenue and 210th Street

Directions:

Take the D train to the 205th Street station (last stop). Exit at the <u>south</u> end of the station. Go up the escalator (<u>not</u> the ramp). Turn right at the turnstile and go up the stairs to the street. Walk straight ahead (<u>north</u>) for 2 ½ blocks (same side of the street) until you see the 2-story brick building with a green awning marked "The Bronx County Historical Society." NOTE: The Archives is housed near the Research Library, at 3313 Bainbridge Avenue.

Description of Resources:

The Society, founded in 1955, collects all materials relating to the history of the Bronx. Its collection includes books, photographs, postcards, prints, paintings, maps, manuscripts, newspapers, pamphlets, as well as video and audio tapes about the Bronx. The following are some of the items of interest to genealogists:

1. <u>Photographs</u>: over 45,000 photographs and 5,000 slides showing a chronological progression of the Bronx from the 1860s to the present; and over 2,500 different post cards of Bronx scenes.

2. <u>Newspaper Clippings</u>: vertical files containing news clippings from local Bronx newspapers. Clippings are about Bronx neighborhoods as well as people from the Bronx.

3. <u>Bronx Newspapers</u>: The following local papers are available. One year is retained by the Library, and the remainder are in the Archives:

    Bronx Beat, 1982 to the present (selected issues)
    Bronx Chronicle, 1975–1976 (selected issues)
    Bronx Home News, 1907–1948
    Bronx News, 1975–1986, 1988
    Bronx Press Review, 1955 to the present (selected issues)
    City Island News (now *Island Current*), 1953 to the present
    Co-op City Times, 1970 to the present (selected issues)
    Fordham News Express, 1985 to the present (selected issues)
    Journal News, 1964–1976 (selected issues)
    Mosholu Parkway Press, 1976–1977 (selected issues)
    Parkchester News, 1973–1978 (selected issues)
    Parkchester Press Review, 1948–1949 (selected issues)

Parkway News, 1973–1975 (selected issues), 1976–1978
Riverdale Press, 1950–1981

The Library also has a complete set of *The Bronx County Historical Society Journal* from 1964 to 1998.

4. Map Collection: The Archives has over 100 maps and real estate atlases of the Bronx from 1868 to 1969 and some for Westchester and NYC. Early maps and even some later ones published through the 1940s show the names of landowners and boundaries of their property as well as block and lots that were to be laid out in later years. These atlases document the physical development of the Bronx down to the block/lot level.

   In addition to these maps, the Archives has the 19th Century Bronx Towns and Bronx Topographical Bureau Collection which includes records laying out the Bronx street system.

5. *Trow's New York City Directories* (includes Manhattan and part or all of the Bronx), 1850–1913, 1917 and 1918; and the 1907 Business Directory (microfilm).

6. Books: approximately 5,000 books about The Bronx and its people as well as information on other parts of New York City. Examples are:

   Brown, Martin B. *The Brown Book: A Biographical Record of Public Officials of the City of New York for 1898–1899.* New York, 1899. Contains biographical sketches and photos of city officials.
   Wells, James L., Louis F. Haffen and Josiah A. Briggs. *The Bronx and Its People: A History, 1609-1927.* 4 vols. New York, 1927.

7. Audio and Video Tapes: 1,000 audio and videotapes of the Society's lectures, forums and walking tours since 1985. In addition, films for the Bronx history shows aired on Channel 25, "Bronx Faces and Places," and tapes of the oral history radio program "Out of the Past" are available here.

8. Fire and Police Department Records: Fire Department journals, 1874–1913, and some later years; and Police Department blotters for various Bronx precincts, c. 1865–1950s, showing arrests each day.

9. New York State Census 1915 and 1925. The Society has the original paper copy of Bronx census volumes for these years. The first few pages are missing and some are in very poor condition. These volumes were donated to the Archives by the BRONX COUNTY CLERK'S OFFICE after they were microfilmed. See "Restrictions on Use."

10. Naturalization Certificate Receipt Books include the stubs for the certificates of naturalization provided to new citizens who filed their petitions in the State Supreme Court, Bronx County, 1918–1925. These stubs include the some information from the original certificate. See "Restrictions on Use."

11. Name Change Records, 1914–1922, filed in State Supreme Court, Bronx County. See "Restrictions on Use."

12. Business Incorporations, 1914–1924 (gaps). Paper copies in bound volumes are available here for select years. The Archives has volumes 1–27, 30, 32, 35 and 39. See "Restrictions on Use."

13. Morris High School Collection - including photographs and scrapbooks from 1897 to the 1930s.

14. Papers of Bronx Families, Businesses and Political Leaders - including Argenti, Ferris, Fleck, Tieck, and Schwartz families; political leaders Abrams, Lyons, Periconi, Badillo, Friedman, Bingham, Biaggi, Garcia and Massaro; business papers of Hoe, Lawrence, Lerner, Hallock, Davies, Gross and Keeler.

15. Bronx Old Timers Association, 1911-1986. Membership in this organization was limited to individuals who resided in the Bronx at least 50 years. The collection includes records and journals.

Finding Aids:

The Library has a computerized catalog accessible to staff. Materials under subject headings such as "Personalities," "Communities" and "Bronx Business" may be useful to genealogists. A list of archival collections and pending donations of materials can be found on the Library's website at www.bronxhistoricalsociety.org/index17.html.

A computerized index to the Photograph Collection is in process. Names of persons or businesses are included if they are identified on the back of the photograph. Buildings and street scenes are identified by cross streets. The card file for this collection is arranged by subject. A separate card file is available for slide and postcard collections.

The Newspaper Clipping vertical file is indexed in a card file.

The Library has a *Map Index: Guide for Atlases,* listing the various maps in its collection.

Description of Facility:

The Reading Room is open to the public. Four researchers can be accommodated at a time at one table. There is one microfilm reader/printer available to the public for viewing microfilm collections. The Archives building is nearby at 3313 Bainbridge Avenue.

Fees/Copies:

The staff will photocopy materials at $.25 per page. Copies from the microfilm reader/printer are $.35 per page. Fees for duplicating photographs range from $10 for a slide to $25 for photographs without negatives.

Annual membership dues start at $15 for students and senior citizens, $20 for an individual, and $25 for a family. Members receive a subscription to the semi-annual *The Bronx County Historical Society Journal, The Bronx Historian* newsletter and invitations to historical tours, lectures and educational programs.

There is a $20 per hour fee for research inquiries with a one-hour minimum and increments of 20 minutes at $10. For more involved research, the BHS requests that it be handled in 5 hour blocks (or $100) payable by check, Visa or MasterCard. A research request form can be found on the BHS website.

Publications of the Society for sale include:

Hermalyn, Gary, Laura Tosi and Narcisco Rodriguez. *The Bronx in Print: an annotated catalog of books dissertations, pamphlets, scripts and manuscripts about the Bronx.* 107 p. Bronx, 2000. ($25)

McNamara, John. *History in Asphalt: The Origin of Bronx Street and Place Names Encyclopedia.* Third edition. 556 p. Bronx, 1991. ($40)

Ultan, Lloyd. *The Bronx in the Frontier Era: from the beginning to 1696.* 236 p. Bronx, 1993. ($30)

Ultan, Lloyd. *The Beautiful Bronx, 1920-1950.* 192 p. New Rochelle, [1979]. ($25)

Ultan, Lloyd and Gary Hermalyn. *The Birth of the Bronx, 1609-1900.* 182 p. Bronx, 2000. ($30)

Ultan, Lloyd and Gary Hermalyn. *The Bronx in the Innocent Years, 1890–1925.* 192 p. Revised 1991. ($25)

Ultan, Lloyd and Gary Hermalyn. *The Bronx: it was only yesterday, 1935-1965.* 184 p. Bronx, [1992]. ($25)

Restrictions on Use:

Some of the material listed above, including newspapers more than one year old, are stored in another building and are not readily accessible. Call at least 2 days in advance to order them.

Paper copies of the NYS Census for the Bronx are in very poor condition. These census records are available on microfilm at the COUNTY CLERK'S OFFICE - STATE SUPREME COURT, BRONX COUNTY, the IRMA AND PAUL MILSTEIN DIVISION OF UNITED STATES HISTORY, LOCAL HISTORY AND GENEALOGY, the NEW YORK GENEALOGICAL AND BIOGRAPHICAL SOCIETY and the NEW YORK STATE DEPARTMENT OF EDUCATION, NEW YORK STATE LIBRARY.

There is no finding aid to the Naturalization Certificate Receipt Books, Name Change Records, or Business Incorporation Records located here. These records are arranged chronologically and are difficult to use without an index. See the COUNTY CLERK'S OFFICE - STATE SUPREME COURT, BRONX for naturalization petitions and declarations filed in the Bronx. Indexes are available for Name Change Records and Business Incorporations at the COUNTY CLERK'S OFFICE - STATE SUPREME COURT, BRONX COUNTY in theArchives and Records Management Room 7M. The COUNTY CLERK'S OFFICE has a copy of these records on microfilm.

Materials do not circulate.

CITY REGISTER'S OFFICE
BRONX

Facility Director: Dara Brown, Deputy City Register

Address: 1932 Arthur Avenue, Room 301
Bronx, NY 10457

(Cross Street: East Tremont Avenue)

Phone: (718) 579-6821 (Room 301, City Register's Office)
(718) 579-6830 (Room 201, Microfilm Unit)
(718) 579-6879 (Room 701, Real Estate Assessment Office)

Fax: none
E-mail: see website
Website: www.nyc.gov/html/dof/

Hours of Operation:

Monday to Friday: 9:00 am to 4:00 pm

Closed Saturday, Sunday and legal holidays.

Closest Public Transportation:

Subway: D to Tremont Avenue
4 to 161st Street/Yankee Stadium; transfer to the D to Tremont Avenue

and

Bus: Bx40 or Bx42 to Arthur and East Tremont Avenues
Bx15 or Bx55 to 3rd and East Tremont Avenues

Directions:

Take the D train to the Tremont Avenue station. Exit at the <u>north</u> end of the platform. Exit to the <u>east</u> side of the Grand Concourse (to the right when facing the token booth). Walk two short blocks <u>north</u> (passing Bush Street) to Burnside Avenue and the Grand Concourse. (Do not cross Burnside Avenue.) The Bx40/Bx42 bus stop is on the corner of Burnside Avenue on the <u>east</u> side of the Concourse. Take either bus to Arthur and East Tremont Avenues.

Description of Resources:

This Office has real property records (deeds, mortgages, maps) for Bronx County, 1674 to the present. Records are available on microfilm (all years) arranged chronologically, and in microfiche jackets arranged by block/lot number (1968–1991). A computerized index to Bronx property records, 1982 to the present may be available online by January 2003. Digitized records, 1966 to present, may be viewable online as early as 2004. See CITY REGISTER'S OFFICE - MANHATTAN for a description of records and computerized indexes.

NOTE: In 1874, New York City (and New York County) annexed the towns of Morrisania, West Farms and Kingsbridge; and in 1895, the town of Westchester and parts of the towns of Eastchester and Pelham. These were known as the Annexed District which became the borough of the Bronx in 1898 and Bronx County in 1914. See *Before the Five-Borough City: The Old Cities, Towns and Villages That Came Together to Form "Greater New York"* by Harry Macy Jr., published in *The NYG&B Newsletter,* Winter 1998. (Reprinted as Appendix H with the permission.

Finding Aids:

The Bronx City Register's Office has grantor/grantee, mortgagor/mortgagee and block/lot indexes but <u>not for all years</u>. Westchester County did not use block/lot designations for indexing purposes. Block/lot indexes therefore were not created until these areas were annexed to New York County. As a result, grantor/grantee and mortgagor/mortgagee indexes (microfilm and libers) are the only indexes available for western portions of the Bronx (formerly towns of Morrisania, West Farms and Kingsbridge) prior to 1874; and eastern portions of the Bronx (formerly towns of Westchester, parts of Eastchester and Pelham) prior to 1895. The relevant grantor/grantee indexes for these early years are *Index to Certified Copies of Westchester County Deeds*, 1674–1895 and *Alphabetical Index: District Annexed by*

Chapter 934 Laws of 1895, 1895–1917. NOTE: New York County (Manhattan) grantor/grantee and mortgagor/ mortgagee indexes, 1874–1891, also include western Bronx properties. See CITY REGISTER'S OFFICE, MANHATTAN.

To identify all records of a particular person or corporate body, use the grantor/grantee or mortgagor/mortgagee indexes available in ledgers or microfilm, 1674–1988.

A search can be made by computer, 1982 to the present. See CITY REGISTER'S OFFICE - MANHATTAN for a description of the computerized index and plans to add additional years. This computerized index may be online by January, 2003.

To locate records on a particular piece of property by address the tax block and lot numbers must first be determined. There are several ways to obtain these numbers:

1.   If the building still exists, use the computer index. See CITY REGISTER'S OFFICE, MANHATTAN for a description; or,

2.   Go to Room 701, the Real Property Assessment Office. The clerk at the desk in this office will assist researchers in identifying block and lot numbers. Or, researchers can check the NYC Department of Finance website (www.nyc.gov/finance) from this office or home. See CITY REGISTER'S OFFICE, MANHATTAN for directions. The Office will respond to phone inquiries. Call (718) 579-6879; or,

3.   Check *New York Boroughs* (on microfiche) produced by First American Real Estate Solutions, available at the NEW YORK PUBLIC LIBRARY, MAP DIVISION [*XLK-4]; or,

4.   Researchers can check the hanging maps in Room 201, located in a side room (last door to the left before the windows).

NOTE: For the years 1874–1917, records are recorded by (land) section number, as well as block and lot numbers. Index ledgers for this period are arranged by section number, and then block and lot. However, block ranges are shown on the spine of each volume (and on the box cover of each microfilm) making it easy to locate the correct index volume without knowing the section number. There is a chart pasted on the door behind the Microfilm counter listing block and lot numbers in each (land) section should this information be necessary. A map delineating sections is also posted on the wall to the right of the entrance to the Real Estate Assessor's Office, Room 701.

Once the block and lot numbers are known, go to the index arranged by block and lot numbers to get the liber and page numbers (or reel and page numbers) of the instruments filed. These are available on microfilm or in libers, 1874–1981, or computer, 1982 to the present. Liber and page number are necessary in order to find instruments recorded before 1968 (or reel and page number for instruments filed later). Reel and page numbers are not needed for instruments filed c.1968–1991 if the block/lot microfilm jacket is used. Starting in 1968, for the convenience of researchers, copies of microfilm frames were cut and placed in plastic jackets arranged by block and lot. These block/lot jackets look like microfiche. NOTE: Block/lot jackets may not include all recorded instruments.

For the period pre-1917, the Office has two sets of block/lot indexes covering part of the annexed areas. Volumes labeled, "Conveyances 1874–1890" and "Conveyances 1891–1917" cover blocks now in the western portion of the Bronx (Sections 9–13) annexed by New York County in 1874. Volumes labeled, "Conveyances 1895–1917" include blocks now in the eastern section of the Bronx (Sections 14–15) annexed by New York County in 1895. For earlier years, researchers must use the grantor/grantee or mortgagor/mortgagee indexes.

To complicate matters, there do not appear to be block/lot indexes for blocks 4336 to 5655 (a.k.a. Sections 16–18) prior to 1918 (formerly town of Eastchester and parts of Pelham and Westchester). Block/lot indexes do exist for Riverdale, a.k.a. Section 19, blocks 5700–5958, for the 1874–1917 period. During this period Riverdale was classified as "Section 13," blocks 3402–3428. See the Riverdale block/lot conversion chart hanging next to the door behind the Microfilm counter in Room 201. To search for ownership of a property pre-1918 in Sections 16–18 (blocks 4336–5655), researchers must use the grantor/grantee or mortgagor/mortgagee indexes or the indexes created by the Works Progress Administration (WPA) during the depression.

These WPA indexes are unlike those found in Manhattan or Brooklyn. They could be described as a "rough draft" compared to the WPA indexes found in the other boroughs. These indexes are arranged by block/lot and list, in separate volumes, all deeds and mortgages recorded for a particular lot. "Conveyance" (deed) and "Mortgage" volumes, for block numbers 3429–5655 (eastern Bronx annexation), circa 1895 to 1917, are in Room 301. WPA volumes covering the 1874–1895 period are in the basement. At the start of each block/lot, there is a sketch of the block with the lot location. These WPA indexes are not considered "official" records but are useful in searching the earlier years by block and lot number for Sections 16–18 (blocks 4336–5655).

To locate Bronx records, 1982 to the present, use the computers in Room 201 or 301. This index may be online as early as January 2003. See CITY REGISTER'S OFFICE, MANHATTAN for an explanation of how to use the computer to conduct a search by name or block/lot.

NOTE: There are about 580 Torrens properties in the Bronx. Torrens properties are now included in the computer system. The original ledger for these properties, arranged in order of the date of filing, previously located in the Deputy City Register's office, is missing. See CITY REGISTER'S OFFICE, MANHATTAN for a description of Torrens properties.

Description of Facility:

This is a New York City government office. Room 301 (3rd floor) has liber indexes grantor/grantee and mortgagor/mortgagee, and block/lot liber indexes pre-1930; WPA indexes ("Conveyances" and "Mortgages"), blocks, 3429–5655, and 4 public-access computers (1982 to the present). The Deputy City Register and cashier's office are also located here.

Room 201 (2nd floor) houses the Microfilm unit (microfilm of block/lot indexes, 1891–1981 and block/lot liber indexes, 1931–1981. Room 201 has 2 working computers in the last room off Room 201 (last door on the left). This room also houses the hanging maps. There are 10 microfiche and 15 microfilm readers of which 7 are reader/printers. Employees are very busy and cannot help researchers for more than a short time. Some Westchester grantor/grantee films are in the public access area and some are in the staff's microfilming room. Speak with the Microfilm supervisor if you wish to view these films.

Original record libers (deeds and mortgages) and additional WPA indexes, 1874–1895, are stored in an airless locked room in the basement. See the security guard in Room 201 if you wish to view these libers.

Fees/Copies:

See CITY REGISTER'S OFFICE, MANHATTAN. Certified copies of documents can be obtained in Room 301. There is a one week wait to for certified copies.

Restrictions on Use:

Grantor/grantee and mortgagor/mortgagee liber indexes pre-1918 in Room 301 are in disarray and some appear to be missing. Check with the Microfilm supervisor in Room 201 for the microfilmed copy.

NOTE: This Office may move in the next 2 years. Call before coming.

CIVIL COURT OF THE CITY OF NEW YORK
BRONX COUNTY

Facility Director: Andrew Hassell, Deputy Clerk of the County

Address: 851 Grand Concourse   ♿
Bronx, NY 10451

(Cross Streets: East 161st Street and Walton Avenue)

Phone: (718) 590-3601
Fax: none
E-mail: none
Website: see www.courts.state.ny.us

Hours of Operation:

Monday to Friday: 9:00 am to 5:00 pm

Closed Saturday, Sunday and legal holidays.

Closest Public Transportation:

Subway: B (rush hours only) or D to 161st Street/Yankee Stadium
4 to 161st Street/Yankee Stadium

Bus: Bx1 or Bx6 to Grand Concourse and East 161 Street
Bx13 to East 161 Street and River Avenue

Directions:

Take the D train to 161st Street Yankee Stadium station. Exit to Walton Avenue at the <u>north</u> end of the platform. You will emerge diagonally opposite the Court House. Cross East 161st Street and enter the Bronx Supreme Court building through the main entrance on East 161st Street. Take an "A" bank elevator to the Record Room on the ground level ("G"), also known as the basement level. Go to the door marked "Civil Court Record Room Windows 5-6-7." NOTE: Wheelchair accessible entrance on Grand Concourse.

Description of Resources:

The Civil Court has name change records filed in the Bronx from 1927 to the present.

See also COUNTY CLERK'S OFFICE - STATE SUPREME COURT, BRONX COUNTY for name changes recorded in State Supreme Court.

Finding Aids:

Records, 1927–1998, are indexed in ledgers in groups of years and arranged by the first letter of the original surname. The new name is listed in the ledger next to the old name but is not indexed. From May 1998 to the present, the index is computerized and can be searched by both old and new names. Request the ledger for the years desired from the clerk at Window 6. Fill out a yellow card to request a file.

Description of Facility:

Indexes are located behind the counter of "Civil Court Record Room Windows 5-6-7" on the ground level (also known as the basement). Indexes and case files are located in the same room and can be retrieved by staff upon request. There are two staff persons available to pull files. One desk is available in the public area for use by researchers.

Fees/Copies:

Photocopies can be made at $.15 per copy. See "Restrictions on Use." Certified copies of records cost $5 per page. Only cash or money orders are accepted.

Restrictions on Use:

The Office no longer has a photocopy machine. Copies can be made in Room 118 if photo identification is presented. Photo identification will be held at Window 6 until files are returned.

COUNTY CLERK'S OFFICE - STATE SUPREME COURT
BRONX COUNTY

Facility Director:	Hector L. Diaz, County Clerk Mark Nusenbaum, Records Management Officer
Address:	851 Grand Concourse, Room 118 ♿ * Bronx, NY 10451
	(Cross Streets: East 161st Street and Walton Avenue)
Phone:	(718) 590-4922, 7043 (Archives and Records Management, Room 7M) (718) 590-6091, 3629 (Miscellaneous Records, Room 118) (718) 590-3633, 3634 (Records and Filing, Room 118) (718) 590-7895 (Record Center, Room B124) (718) 590-3803 (Criminal Division, Room 123)
Fax:	(718) 590-8122 (Clerk's Office) (718) 590-4875 (Archives and Records Management)
E-mail:	contact@bronxcountyclerksoffice.com
Website:	www.bronxcountyclerksoffice.com

Hours of Operation:

Monday to Friday: 9:00 am to 5:00 pm

Closed Saturday, Sunday and legal holidays.

Closest Public Transportation and Directions:

See CIVIL COURT OF THE CITY OF NEW YORK, BRONX COUNTY. Take the elevator to the 8th floor. Walk down the "C" stairway to reach the Archives on the mezzanine level between the 7th and 8th floors. *NOTE: Wheelchair users should call in advance so that direct elevator access can be provided to Room 7M.

Description of Resources:

Bronx County was created in 1914. For earlier records see COUNTY CLERK'S OFFICE - NEW YORK COUNTY (MANHATTAN).

1. New York State Census, 1915 and 1925 (microfilm).

   NOTE: Original copies of the 1915 and 1925 Census formerly located here are now at the BRONX HISTORICAL SOCIETY. The 1915 and 1925 Census (on microfilm) are available also at the NEW YORK PUBLIC LIBRARY, IRMA AND PAUL MILSTEIN DIVISION OF UNITED STATES HISTORY, LOCAL HISTORY AND GENEALOGY, the NEW YORK GENEALOGICAL AND BIOGRAPHICAL SOCIETY and the NEW YORK STATE DEPARTMENT OF EDUCATION, NEW YORK STATE LIBRARY.

2. Naturalizations filed in State Supreme Court, Bronx County, 1914 to July 1932; Certificates, 1914–1926 and Declarations of Intention, 1914–1952. After July 1932, check the records of the U.S. District Courts now at the NATIONAL ARCHIVES - NORTHEAST REGION for naturalizations of Bronx residents.

3. Court Cases brought against an individual or corporation or actions filed by an individual or corporation, 1914 to the present. Civil cases more than 25 years old and criminal cases more than 20 years old are on microfiche. See "Restrictions on Use." This Office also has records and indexes for Bronx County Court, 1914–1926. NOTE: criminal case files, 1944–1950, were destroyed by fire in 1998.

4. Business Records

   Business Certificates (a.k.a. Businesses and Partnerships), 1914 to the present
   Certificates of Incorporation, 1914 to the present. (These include incorporations of synagogues and landsmanshaftn.) The Office also has records of Dissolution of Corporations, 1914 to the present.
   Limited Partnerships, 1920 to 1989

   NOTE: Business records (except Limited Partnerships) more than 5 years old are on microfilm. See also NYS DEPARTMENT OF STATE, DIVISION OF CORPORATIONS for limited partnerships, July 1, 1991 to present.

5. Military Records:

Military Discharge Records, 1917 to the present, for veterans who filed a copy of their DD 214 form (discharge papers) in this Office. See "Restrictions on Use."

1917 Militia Enrollment List, State of New York, Adjutant General's Office: Bronx (labeled "Military Enrollment List, Chapter 41 Laws 1909"). These typed soft-bound ledgers, arranged by first letter of the surname, include men age 18–45 liable for service. Lists name, address, age, date of birth, occupation, previous or existing military or naval service including date of enlistment, date of discharge and "in what grade."

6. Matrimonial Records: 1914 to the present for divorce, separations and annulments brought in State Supreme Court, Bronx County. See "Restrictions on Use."

7. Name Changes: filed by an individual or a business in Supreme Court, Bronx County, 1914 to the present.

8. Incompetency Records, Conservatorships and Guardianships: Incompetency Records involving persons who could not handle their own affairs or persons committed, 1914 to the present; and Conservatorships/Guardianships, 1977 to the present. See "Restrictions on Use." Cases closed 5 years are on microfilm filed together with other Court Cases. NOTE: Cases of incompetent persons remained open as long as the individual was alive and annual accountings were being filed.

9. Surrenders of Children: filed with the County Clerk, 1972 to the present. See "Restrictions on Use."

10. Registers of Professionals: The Office has ledgers for many professionals who were licensed to work in the Bronx. Data generally includes name, country and date of birth, address, date of license and license number:

Dentists, 1927–1949
Physicians, 1914–1924
Physiotherapists, 1927–1947
Registered nurses, 1934–1946
Trained attendants and practical nurses, 1921–1948

In addition, there are ledgers (unindexed) of affidavits filed by architects, 1918–1949; physicians and surgeons, 1917–1947; professional engineers and land surveyors, 1932–1949; veterinarians, 1914–1947, and nurses.

Finding Aids:

1. Census: Street address is needed to find information. Street maps of the Bronx detailing Assembly/Election Districts (AD/ED) are available for 1915 and 1925. Once the address is located on the map and the AD/ED numbers are identified, request the reel with that AD/ED from the clerk. Then search for the page with the address and family.

2. Naturalizations: The Office has microfilm and digitized copies of alphabetical card indexes for Naturalization petitions, 1914–1932, and for Declarations of Intention, 1914–1927 and 1927–1952. These indexes provide the name, Petition or Declaration number or liber and page number.

A separate microfilm copy of index cards arranged alphabetically and labeled "Certificates 1926 to present" includes names not necessarily in the indexes to petitions and should be checked also.

3. Court Cases (including Matrimonials and other civil cases) are indexed in libers, Index to Clerk's Minutes, 1914–1996, by year and arranged alphabetically by the first two letters of the surname and the first letter of the given name of the plaintiff. Liber indexes 1914 to 1960 are on microfilm. The County Clerk's Office also has index cards (microfilm) to court cases, arranged in groups of years, 1914–1975.

The Bronx County Clerk's Administration System, a computerized index, includes Civil Cases beginning in 1995. Older cases requiring some court action may be included in the computerized index.

Indexes to Criminal Cases, 1914–1989 (index cards) and 1983 to the present (computer) can be accessed by the clerks in Room 123. Index cards, 1914–1989, will be microfilmed and may be accessible to researchers in the future.

NOTE: An index to all pending Bronx County Supreme Court Civil Cases requiring judicial intervention ("RJI") is available on the NYS Unified Court System CaseTrac website. See COUNTY CLERK'S OFFICE, NEW YORK COUNTY for a description. Digitized copies of decisions are not yet available online for Bronx county. The online index to Criminal Cases can be searched only by case number. Unfortunately, cases are removed from both these online indexes two weeks after they close.

4. Business Records (except Limited Partnerships). Separate microfilms of card indexes are available for Business Certificates, Incorporations and Dissolution of Incorporation, 1914–1995. In addition, the Office has a cross reference alphabetical card index, Individuals Conducting Business, from 1938 to the present, an index by surname of owners of businesses and partnerships on file. For records after 1995, check the computer in the Miscellaneous Record Room.

There is a two-volume liber index to Limited Partnerships records, arranged by year and the first letter of the name of the business available at Law Department Window 13 on the first floor of Room 118.

NOTE: See NYS DEPARTMENT OF STATE, DIVISION OF CORPORATIONS for an online statewide index to corporations and limited partnerships active on or after December 5, 1977.

5. Military Records: Military Discharge index 1914–1995 (microfilm) and later years (index cards), are arranged alphabetically by surname of the veteran. Check with the clerk who will conduct the search. See "Restrictions on Use." The 1917 Military Enrollment lists are arranged by the first letter of the surname.

6. Name Changes for individuals and businesses are indexed together in two card files — one for new names and one for old names, 1914–1995. Both microfilmed card files are arranged alphabetically by surname. The Office also has liber indexes arranged by the first letter of the old name. The new name is listed with the old name but not indexed separately. The index to later records is also accessible by computers at the Docket counter (first floor Room 118) and the Records and Filing Room counter (mezzanine level, Room 118). However, there is no way to currently identify a name change record. These records are sometimes entered under the old name and sometimes under the new name. The computerized index does not show both names.

7. Incompetency Records and Conservatorships: A two-volume liber index, 1914–1995, covering both Incompetency Records and Conservatorships is arranged by year and alphabetically by the first letter of the surname. Conservatorships have case numbers beginning with 19000. Active cases in 1995 and all cases from 1996 to the present are included in the computerized index together with other civil cases. See "Restrictions on Use." The pre-1996 liber index is located in Room 118, Law Department. Request these libers at Window 6.

8. Surrenders of Children: See "Restrictions on Use."

9. Registers of Professionals are arranged by the first letter of the surname and then chronologically. Affidavit ledgers are not indexed.

Description of Facility:

The County Clerk's Office has undergone major cleanup and reorganization. Index volumes and records books are neatly arranged and easy to find. Many indexes are now on microfilm or computerized. Because of the volume of records in this office, a record location system has been created to assist researchers in locating materials. Basically, there are six primary locations in the building where records can be found:

1. Archives and Records Management (Room 7M, located on the mezzanine level between the 7th and 8th floors) is the repository for all inactive records including microfilm and paper copies of Naturalization records (Petitions and Declarations), Census Records, Assembly/Election District street maps (for Census searches), Civil Case files more than 15 years old, Matrimonial Records, 1914–1957, Military Records including Military Discharges (microfiche) and 1917 Militia Enrollment Lists, and Name Change Records (and ledgers) more than one year old. Closed Incompetency Records are included with Civil Case files. See "Restrictions on Use." The Archives also houses Supreme Court Criminal Case files, 1914–1943, 1960, 1964, and 1966–1982. Criminal case file index cards, 1914–1989 (microfilm) will be available here. Check with the clerks in Room 123, Supreme Court Criminal Court Division, for case file numbers of later records.

Take the "A" bank elevator (opposite Room 118) to the 8th floor and walk down one floor to the mezzanine level, located between the 7th and 8th floors. (Leave this office via the 7th floor elevator). The Archives has three desks and a stand-up table which can accommodate another 6 researchers. There is one photocopy machine, two microfilm/microfiche reader/printers, and a computer terminal where digitized Naturalization (Petitions and Declarations) indexes can be viewed.

2. The Miscellaneous Record Room (located on the mezzanine of Room 118M, opposite the staircase) houses current (filed last year) Name Changes and all Business Records. From Room 118 on the first floor, ascend the right staircase to the mezzanine. There are two staff persons available to assist researchers. This Room has one computer to access the Business Record index and a table for researchers

3. Records and Filing Room (located on the mezzanine level of Room 118M) houses current Supreme Court Civil Case files (cases opened in the last 5 years), all Matrimonial Records filed 1958 or later and Incompetency Records and Conservatorships (all active cases and cases opened in the last 5 years). Matrimonial Records more than 25 years old are on microfiche. Use the left staircase after entering room 118 to reach this area of the mezzanine. The area adjacent to the Record and Filing Room has seating available at 8 tables. However, researchers must compete for space in this area with attorneys taking depositions. Two computer terminals with access to the Bronx County Clerk's Administration System (computerized index) and 2 microfilm reader/printers are available at the counter. There are three photocopy machines located along the wall between the staircase and the Record and Filing Room.

4. The Records Center (basement, Room B-125) houses inactive records such as paper copies of Civil Cases (more than 5 years old but less than 15 years old). No Matrimonial records are located here. There is one photocopy machine in this room. NOTE: The location of the Records Center is often referred to as the "basement" level. However, it is the ground level ("G" in the elevator) if entering the building from the Walton Avenue entrance.

5. Liber Room (a small room, located on the mezzanine of Room 118 opposite the Miscellaneous Record Room) houses Civil Case liber indexes, 1961–1995. There is one seat available in the Liber room and a high table which can be used by 3-4 researchers.

6. Supreme Court Criminal Division, Clerk's Office, is located in Room 123 on the first floor. Only the clerks behind the windows in this room can access the computerized index for Criminal Cases, 1983 to the present, and original card indexes to criminal cases, 1914–1989. (See Archives and Records Management, Room 7M for microfilmed index cards, 1914–1989.) Criminal Cases filed, 1951–1959, 1961–1963, 1965, and 1983 to the present, can be accessed here. However, only cases 1994 to the present (and those in the Archives, Room 7M) are on-site. See "Restrictions on Use." NOTE: A new Supreme Court Criminal Court building is being constructed at 161st and Morris Avenue. The location of Criminal Case files and indexes may change. Check before coming.

NOTE: This Office plans to make records available on the internet in the future.

Fees/Copies:

Copies of Naturalizations are made by staff at $8 for a Petition and $4 for a Declaration. Researchers can hand copy these records at no charge. Certified copies are $10. For other Court Records, there are photocopy machines available at $.15 per page. Copies of microfilmed records can be made at $.25 per page. Copies of Court Records requested by mail are certified copies and cost $8 per document. A mail request for a Business Record is $5 (includes search fee and copy of the document). A search of Census Records and copy costs $10.00. For mail requests, payment is required by money order or certified check made out to the Bronx County Clerk.

Restrictions on Use:

Civil Court Cases of mentally ill persons (lunacy case) are sealed. The liber indexes include these cases but they cannot be accessed by computer without the case number.

Matrimonial records are closed except to a party of the action or his/her attorney.

Military Discharge Records and Surrenders of Children records and indexes are closed. Military Discharge records are open to the veteran or his representative. Incompetency Records of mentally ill persons are closed.

Criminal Case surname indexes are currently inaccessible to the public. However, index cards, 1914–1989, will be microfilmed and may be accessible to researchers in the future. Requests for searches can be made to the clerks behind the counter. For pre-1983 cases, the year of filing must be known. Case files 1944–1950 were destroyed in a fire in 1998. Cases filed, 1951–1959, 1961–1963, 1965, and 1983–1993 are stored off-site. Off-site files can be requested but will take at least one week for retrieval from approval of the requisition by the clerk.

NOTE: Adoptions records, 1914–1938, previously at the County Clerk's Office are now in the custody of the Surrogate's Court.

SURROGATE'S COURT - BRONX COUNTY
RECORD ROOM

Facility Director: Michael Prisco, Chief Clerk

Address: 851 Grand Concourse, Room 317 ♿
Bronx, NY 10451

(Cross Street: East 161st Street and Walton Avenue)

Phone: (718) 590-3616
Fax: (718) 537-5158
E-mail: none
Website: none

Hours of Operation:

Monday to Friday: 9:00 am to 5:00 pm
Closed Saturday, Sunday and legal holidays.

Closest Public Transportation and Directions:

See CIVIL COURT OF THE CITY OF NEW YORK, BRONX COUNTY. Take the elevator to the third floor.

Description of Resources:

Probate, administration, adoption and guardianship records are located here. The oldest records date back to 1914.

See SURROGATE'S COURT - NEW YORK COUNTY (MANHATTAN) for more detail on the content of these files and pre-1914 records of Bronx residents.

Finding Aids:

The office has a computerized index for probate, administration and guardianship records from 1914 to the present. NOTE: Some records were omitted from the computerized index. Check also the *General Index* libers on open shelves for *Wills* (probate), 1914–1989; *Administration*, 1927–1989; and *Guardianship*, 1949–1989. These are arranged by year and then alphabetically by the first letter of the surname.

A copy of the computerized index, 1914–1986, has been provided to the NEW YORK GENEALOGICAL AND BIOGRAPHICAL SOCIETY.

Description of Facility:

The Record Room is located on the third floor in Room 317. The room has tables which can seat 10-12 persons and two computers accessible to the public. There is one microfilm reader/printer behind the clerk's desk. One staff person is available to assist researchers.

Records, 1950 to the present, are available in the Record Room. Earlier paper records are stored in the basement and must be requested 3 days in advance. Researchers can call in advance for a computer search and record request.

Guardianship records, 1914–1979, and small estates, 1964–1988, are on microfiche and are available in the Record Room. However, since there is no microfiche reader available for public viewing, the clerk will print a full copy of the record upon request. A fee of $.25 per page is charged.

Fees/Copies:

There is a photocopy machine in the room at $.15 per page. Certified copies or copies by mail are $5 per page. Requests by mail which require a search (i.e. case number is not provided) cost $25 if the case is under 25 years old and $70 if the case is over 25 years, plus the $5 per page fee for copies. Cash or money orders are accepted — no personal checks.

Restrictions on Use:

Files on adoptions and certain guardianship records are confidential and are closed to the public.

General Index to Administration libers, 1914–1926 and *General Index to Guardianships*, 1914–1948 are not in the Record Room and are believed to be stored in the basement. These should be requested 3 days in advance.

BROOKLYN

(Kings County)

Brooklyn Repositories

Repository	Key
Board of Elections, Brooklyn	4
Brooklyn Historical Society	1
Brooklyn Public Library, Business Library	2
Brooklyn Public Library, Central Library	7
City Register's Office, Brooklyn	5
Civil Court, Brooklyn	6
County Clerk's Office, Kings County	3
Surrogate's Court, Kings County	3

(approx. 1.3 miles)

0   495   990 Feet

BOARD OF EDUCATION
SCHOOL RECORDS

Facility Director:	Cynthia Felix, Director
Address:	Office of Parent Outreach*
	Board of Education
	110 Livingston Street, Room 106
	Brooklyn, NY 11201
	Attention: School Records

Or, write directly to the local Elementary or High School:

Attention: Record Secretary
Re: Old Pupil Records

*NOTE: This Office is planning to move to 49 Chambers Street, New York, NY 10007 in 2003.

Phone:	(718) 935-5202
Fax:	(718) 935-3041
E-mail:	none
Website:	www.nycenet.edu/dist_sch/

Hours of Operation, Closest Public Transportation, Directions and Description of Facility:

Not applicable. Inquiries to determine location of records of schools that closed can be handled by mail or phone.

Description of Resources:

There are over 1,100 schools in the five boroughs that make up New York City. Every New York City school prepares and retains an Office Record Card on each of its students. This card includes a parent or guardian's name, address of student (sometimes changes of address), proof of age (possibly birth certificate number), birth date, birth place and schools attended.

Academic records are transferred from school to school with the child until graduation from high school. These records remain in the high school.

Records are maintained for 50 years. However, it is not uncommon for records to be kept much longer. The availability of records can be decreased by vandalism, fire, flood or loss during transfer from one school to another.

Finding Aids:

To find a record, identify the local school in the neighborhood where the child lived. If you know the school number or name and it still exists, write to that school first. To locate the address, telephone, fax number and name of principal of an existing school, check the Board of Education's website. Search "District & School Directory" or "School Search" by zip code, school name, school number, level, district or borough.

When a school closes permanently, its records are transferred to the school with which it merged, usually the nearest school. To determine which school this is, call or send a written request to the Office of Parent Outreach of the Board of Education (address above); or contact the applicable District Office. A map is available online which can assist researchers in identifying the appropriate Community School District. The Office of Parent Outreach has a loose-leaf binder, *School Records - All Boroughs, 2000–2001,* which lists every school that existed in NYC and if closed, the name and address of the school to which its records were transferred.

Written requests to a local school should include the student's name, when he/she attended, date of birth, parents' names and any other identifying information. State that your request is for genealogical research and specify the information you wish.

Restrictions on Use:

Requests should be made by a direct relative closest to the person in question. The principal of the school is the custodian of these records and has the right to deny the release of information. A record may be denied if the person making the request does not have a reasonable interest in it.

BOARD OF ELECTIONS
BROOKLYN BOROUGH OFFICE

Facility Director: Diane Haslett Rudiano, Chief Clerk

Address: 345 Adams Street, 4th floor
Brooklyn, NY 11201

(Cross Streets: Willoughby and Pearl Streets)

Phone: (718) 330-2271
Fax: (718) 522-6227
E-mail: nruiz@boe.nyc.ny.us
Website: www.vote.nyc.ny.us.

Hours of Operation:

Monday to Friday: 9:00 am to 5:00 pm
Closed Saturday, Sunday and legal holidays.

Closest Public Transportation:

Subway: 2, 3, 4 or 5 to Borough Hall
          M, N or R to Court Street/Borough Hall
          A, C or F to Jay Street/Borough Hall

Bus: B41, B45 or B51 to Joralemon and Court Streets
          B25, B26, B37, B38 or B52 to Fulton and Adams Streets
          B67 or B75 to Fulton and Jay Streets

Directions:

Take the Lexington Avenue #4 or #5 (express) train to Borough Hall station. After exiting the turnstile, go up the stairway to your left (under the Municipal Building). Cross the street and turn right. Adams Street will be straight ahead. Cross Adams to reach the building. NOTE: Wheelchair accessible entrance at rear of building (380 Pearl Street).

Description of Resources:

The Office has voter registration records from 1890 to the present. Prior to 1997, registration information included date of naturalization and court in which naturalized. Records 1890–1956 are in ledgers. See "Restrictions on Use." Records, 1957–1990, are on microfilm. Records active 1991 or later are digitized and maintained on computer in the Archival Voter Information Data (AVID) system.

Finding Aids:

This Office has the computerized system, Election Administration System (EASY Screens), implemented in Brooklyn in 1985/1986. All registrations active at the time of implementation or later are included in EASY. A search of EASY can be made from 1986 to the present by name or address using one of the public-access computers. In order to find date and court of naturalization, researchers will need to look at the actual registration record. For records of voters active in 1991 or later, request a search by name of AVID. Researchers can view digitized records on a staff-computer or request a printout from staff. NOTE: Public-access to AVID is anticipated as soon as funds are available for new computers. See BOARD OF ELECTIONS, MANHATTAN BOROUGH OFFICE.

In order to find records pre-1957 and canceled records, 1972–1986, the ward or Assembly/Election District must be provided. Address can be converted into ward or Assembly/Election District by staff using the maps available in this Office. Canceled records, 1957–1972, are arranged alphabetically by surname. See "Restrictions on Use."

Description of Facility:

This is a NYC government office. There are 10 public-access computers available to view EASY Screens to the area to the right of the reception desk. Staff conduct the search of pre-1987 records and records in the AVID system. Records, 1890–1956, are located in a warehouse off-site. Records from 1957–1990 (microfilm) are in the office.

Fees/Copies: See BOARD OF ELECTIONS, MANHATTAN BOROUGH OFFICE.

Restrictions on Use: Pre-1957 records (some in poor condition) are in the warehouse and may take 2-3 weeks to locate.

BROOKLYN HISTORICAL SOCIETY
THE DONALD F. AND MILDRED TOPP OTHMER LIBRARY

Facility Director: Jessie Kelly, President
        Richard Heaps, Vice-President, Operations

Address: 128 Pierrepont Street   ♯
    Brooklyn, NY 11201

    (Cross Street: Corner of Clinton Street)

Phone: (718) 222-4111
Fax: (718) 222-3794
E-mail: library@BrooklynHistory.org
Website: www.brooklynhistory.org

Hours of Operation:

Tuesday to Saturday: 10:00 am to 5:00 pm
Closed Sunday, Monday and legal holidays.

NOTE: The Library may close on Saturday if the next Monday is a legal holiday. Call in advance.

TEMPORARILY CLOSED DURING RENOVATION. REOPENING ANTICIPATED FALL 2003. During renovation, Society members may still have access to the digitized Image Collection at the Society's temporary office, 45 Main Street, Room 617, Brooklyn, NY 11201. An appointment is necessary.

Closest Public Transportation:

Subway: M, N or R to Court Street/Borough Hall
        2 or 3 to Clark Street or Borough Hall
        4 or 5 to Borough Hall

Bus: B25, B41 or B51 to Montague Street and Cadman Plaza West
    B38 or B52 to Tillary Street and Cadman Plaza West

Directions:

Take the M, N or R train to the Court Street/Borough Hall station. Exit to Clinton Street (back of the train if coming from Manhattan). Walk one block <u>north</u> to Pierrepont Street. The Society is on the corner. The Library's Reading Room, located on the second floor can be reached by walking up the grand staircase (one flight) or taking the accessible elevator located behind the stairs.

Description of Resources:

(The following was adapted from the "Guide to Genealogical Research in the Brooklyn Historical Society" prepared by Claire M. Lamers.)

The Brooklyn Historical Society, formerly known as the Long Island Historical Society, was founded in 1863 and has an extensive collection of research materials including 155,000 volumes, over 2,000 maps and atlases, 350 local and regional newspapers, 700 periodicals and serials and over 2000 feet of manuscripts and archival materials. The Library has genealogies, rare books, personal papers, oral histories and institutional records that document Brooklyn's many neighborhoods and ethnic groups. The following is a detailed description of the collections of interest to genealogists:

1. <u>Stiles-Toedteberg Family History Collection</u> contains over 14,000 family histories and charts, both published and unpublished. The collection includes the Society's <u>Family Bible Records</u> (both transcript and originals); and the <u>Collective Genealogy Collection</u>, which contains material on early families of Long Island, New York County and New England.

2. <u>Genealogical Reference Collection</u> consists of research guides, genealogical records surveys, catalogs of genealogy collections in other libraries, indexes to genealogical periodicals and histories of various ethnic groups who emigrated to the United States. This collection also includes bibliographies of ship passenger lists as well as published passenger lists, such as:

Filby, P. William, ed. *Passenger and Immigration Lists Index: A Guide to Published Arrival Records of about 500,000 Passengers Who Came to the United States and Canada in the Seventeenth, Eighteenth and Nineteenth Centuries.* Detroit, 1981–.

National Archives. *Index to Passenger Lists of Vessels Arriving at New York, 1820–1846.* (microfilm)

3. Vital Records Collection consists mainly of typescript material on births, marriages and deaths abstracted from church records (no synagogues), newspapers, cemetery records, court records and manuscripts. Most of the material (mainly 17th to 19th century) relates to Kings, Queens, Nassau and Suffolk Counties but material from New York County, New York State and other states is included. Of particular interest are:

Abstracts of Vital Records from Newspapers (see listing below).

Abstracts of Wills
Kings County, 1787–1842; indexes 1650–1850, 1850–1890.
Queens County, 1787–1850; indexes, Jamaica 1680–1781, 1787–1835.
New York County, 17th, 18th and part of 19th centuries; and indexes.

Hennenlotter Collection relates mostly to families in Flatbush, Flatlands and Gravesend and was compiled during the latter part of 19th and early 20th centuries. The index cards are arranged by surname and vital records pertaining to each individual are included.

Robbins Collection of Suffolk County wills and letters of administration, 1787–1880 (index cards).

4. Census Records. In addition to indexes to U.S. Census records of New York State, 1790–1850, and scattered volumes of other states, the Library has typescript copies of census records for various towns and counties in New York State. On microfilm, U.S. Census records are available for:

Kings, New York and surrounding counties, 1800–1880
Kings, Queens, Richmond and Suffolk counties, 1890 Union veterans
Kings County, 1900
New York State, 1910

5. Military Records include published histories and pension lists from the Colonial Wars to the late 19th century, with particular emphasis on regiments and people who served in the Civil War.

6. Local History Collection includes material on county, town and church histories of Kings, Queens, Nassau and Suffolk counties. The collection includes some material on other parts of New York City, New York State, the New England states and the southeast as well as material on Europe (particularly England and Holland).

Of particular interest to Jewish genealogists is the material on Brooklyn neighborhoods such as Williamsburg, Boro Park and Coney Island.

7. Manuscripts and Archives Collection includes histories, genealogies, official records and church records (no synagogue records) that contain genealogical information. Included here is the collection of abstracts of wills and letters of administration of New York Counties from the 17th to the mid-19th century compiled by William A. Eardeley. The Library has a card file index for this collection arranged by surname. Each card contains the name of the individual, date of the will or letters of administration, county seat and location of the material in Eardeley's files.

8. Newspaper Collection includes 350 local and regional newspapers, the majority of which are from Kings, Queens, Nassau and Suffolk Counties covering the 18th–20th centuries. See "Restrictions on Use." Other newspaper-related materials of interest to genealogists include:

The Brooklyn and Long Island Scrapbooks compiled from c. 1870 to 1970. These 160 volumes (on microfiche) include articles, obituaries, pictures, brochures and programs relating to the history, families and residents of Kings, Queens, Nassau and Suffolk counties. Most of the articles are from Brooklyn and Long Island newspapers, particularly the *Brooklyn Daily Eagle*.

Brooklyn Daily Eagle - abstracts of marriages and deaths, 1841–1880, 1907, 1909 (indexed); index to obituaries, 1891–1902; abstracts of vital statistics (excluding marriages and deaths), 1841–1846 (indexed).

Brooklyn newspapers - abstracts of marriages and deaths, 1791–1886 (indexed).

Long Island Democrat (Jamaica) - abstracts of births, marriages and deaths, 1835–1856 (indexed); scrapbook of clippings of vital records, 1861–1885 (indexed).

Long Island Star (Brooklyn) - card file index to vital records, 1807–1846.

Long Islander (Huntington) - index, 1839–1857; abstracts of marriages and deaths, 1839–1881; scrapbooks of clippings of vital records, 1847–1879 (indexed).

Newtown Register (Queens) - scrapbook of clippings of vital records, 1877–1882 (indexed).

New York Evening Post - abstracts of marriages and deaths, 1801–1890 (indexed).

The Christian Intelligencer of the Reformed Dutch Church (New York City) - abstracts of marriages and deaths, 1830–1871 (indexed).

In addition, the Library has the Genealogy Query Columns from the *Boston Evening Transcript,* 1896–1941, and the *Hartford Times,* 1957–1961 (microcards).

9. Periodicals and Serials Collections: The Library has over 700 periodical titles on a variety of subjects. Local history periodicals relate mainly to Kings, Queens, Nassau, Suffolk and New York counties. The Library also has periodicals from other state historical societies as well as national and foreign publications. This collection includes *The New York Genealogical and Biographical Society Record, National Genealogical Society Quarterly,* and the *New England Historic and Genealogical Register* as well as family newsletters.

10. Maps and Atlases Collection of 750 maps and atlases includes ward maps for use with census materials.

11. City Directories for Brooklyn, 1796, 1802/3, 1811/12, 1822–1826, 1829–1910, 1912/13 and 1933/4 and New York/Bronx, 1786–1933/4.

12. Image Collection includes 33,000 photographs, drawings and paintings of neighborhoods, streets, landmarks and the waterfront, as well as portraits of residents. The majority of photographs range from the 19th to 20th centuries. The entire collection has been digitized and is available on computer.

Finding Aids:

The Library's Image Collection and a small portion of its NYC book collection are now in electronic format. For all other materials, use the card catalogs.

The Library's Main Card Catalog is arranged by author, title and subject. Typical subject headings are "Genealogy," "Immigration" and "Passenger Lists." Geographic place names are interfiled alphabetically in the Main Card Catalog.

The Library also has a Genealogy Catalog by family name. This indexes published and manuscript materials.

There is a card file index for the Brooklyn and Long Island Scrapbooks. Entries are for persons, places and subjects. The index has two sections: one for Brooklyn clippings and the other for Long Island (including Queens) clippings.

The Society published a catalog of genealogies in its collection in 1935, *Catalogue of American Genealogies in the Library of the Long Island Historical Society.* This may be helpful to researchers who are unable to visit the Library, although it is not as up-to-date as the card catalog.

Of note, not all genealogical materials have been assigned call numbers (although all are included in the card catalog). These are arranged alphabetically by family name on the shelves.

The Library's Manuscript Catalog indexes its manuscript material. Entries are usually by the name of the individual or location. There is limited subject access. A catalog of the Brooklyn manuscripts was published by Brooklyn Rediscovery in 1980 as *A Guide to Brooklyn Manuscripts in the Long Island Historical Society.*

Another source which may help researchers utilize the Library's Long Island material is *Long Island Genealogical Source Material* (a Bibliography), Washington, DC: National Genealogical Society, 1962, by Herbert F. Seversmith and Kenn Stryker-Rodda.

The Library's Periodicals Catalog indexes all but the most current publications. Current publications are indexed in a file maintained by the Reference Librarian and in the Main Catalog.

The Maps and Atlases Catalog indexes these materials by subject (usually location), author and title. A selected list of atlases of Kings, Queens, Nassau and Suffolk counties is in the "Library Manual," a loose-leaf binder on the librarian's desk. Ward maps are kept with the census material.

Description of Facility:

The Library's Reading Room, located on the second floor, has a seating capacity of 35. This includes space for 24 researchers at 6 tables and 11 researchers at work-stations along the wall counters. Each of the tables has outlets for researchers using laptops. Two staff persons are available to assist researchers.

The Finding Aid Room, housing the 4 computer terminals, 2 microfilm/microfiche reader/printers and card catalogs, can be entered through the Reading Room (door to the right of the Reading Room entrance). To reach the Finding Aid Room, researchers pass through the Reference Room where reference books on NYC can be found on open shelves.

Fees/Copies:

Non-members must pay a fee of $2 per day (students $1 per day). Membership starts at $40 for individuals. Student and senior citizen membership is $20.

Copies of materials at $.30 per page are made by the staff. Copies can be made within 15 minutes. See "Restrictions on Use."

For a prepaid fee of $15 with mail requests, the Library will check two sources for a specific name and specific year. The fee includes 3 photocopies. Additional photocopies are $.30 per page. Up to 10 pages of a specific genealogy will be photocopied. The Library cannot guarantee a positive answer but makes every effort to secure the information. The fee is for the search. Mail requests take about 4 weeks. Enclose a self-addressed stamped envelope.

Restrictions on Use:

No more than three books may be requested at a time. Library staff retrieve all materials except those available on open shelves in the Reference Room.

Only one manuscript can be viewed at a time. In cases where a document is kept in the vault, special approval is needed to obtain it.

If material is too fragile, the staff will not photocopy it. No manuscripts or typescripts will be photocopied.

Due to age, condition and storage problems, the only newspapers that are available to the general public are the ones that have been microfilmed and issues of local papers for the current year. A list of "Newspapers on Microfilm" is available from the staff.

Researchers must use pencils only.

BROOKLYN PUBLIC LIBRARY
BUSINESS LIBRARY

Facility Director: Susan Phillis, Business Librarian

Address: 280 Cadman Plaza West   ♿
Brooklyn, NY 11201

(Cross Streets: Pierrepont and Clinton Streets)

Phone: (718) 623-7000, Ext. 3 (Reference desk); outside NYC: (800) 266-6696
Fax: (718) 222-5651, 5679
E-mail: busref@brooklynpubliclibrary.org
Website: www.biz.brooklynpubliclibrary.org

Hours of Operation:

Monday and Tuesday:	1:00 pm to 8:00 pm
Wednesday and Friday:	10:00 am to 6:00 pm
Thursday:	1:00 pm to 6:00 pm
Saturday:	10:00 pm to 5:00 pm

Closed Sunday and legal holidays.

Closest Public Transportation:

Subway: M, N or R to Court Street/Borough Hall
2 or 3 to Clark Street or Borough Hall
4 or 5 to Borough Hall

Bus: B25, B38, B41, B51 or B52 to Tillary and Cadman Plaza West

Directions:

Take the M, N or R train to the Court Street/Borough Hall station. Exit to Montague Street and Cadman Plaza West. Walk <u>north</u> two blocks to the entrance of the Library.

Description of Resources:

The Business Library, founded in 1943, has an extensive collection of materials including over 100,000 reference books and more than 30,000 circulating books covering business-related subjects. The following materials are of particular interest to genealogists:

1. <u>Newspapers and Periodicals</u>: The Library has 20 daily business newspapers, over 1,800 business and financial periodicals, and local newspapers such as the *Brooklyn Daily Eagle,* 1841–1963. Years vary for each periodical. The Library has Internet access to *Newspaper Source,* a full-text database of over 200 newspapers (1988 and later); the *New York Times* (latest 2 years); and CD-ROM, *Newspaper Abstracts,* covering the *New York Times, Wall Street Journal, Washington Post, Christian Science Monitor* and *Los Angeles Times,* 1985 to September 2000 and *Atlanta Constitution, Atlanta Journal, Boston Globe, Chicago Tribune* and *U.S.A. Today,* 1991 to September 2000.

2. <u>City Directories</u>: most of the available City Directories for Brooklyn and New York, 1786–1934:

    NYC Directories (Manhattan and parts of the Bronx) 1786–1933/4.
    Brooklyn, 1796, 1822–1826, 1829–1910, 1912/13, 1933/4.

3. <u>Biographical Directories</u>: an extensive collection of Who's Who of various countries and directories of specific professions. Examples of the latter include:

    Who's Who in Insurance, 1952–. [Orange label, Insurance]
    Who's Who in Finance and Industry, 1936–. [Orange label, Executives]
    Who's Who in American Law, 1977–. [Orange label, Lawyers]
    Who's Who in Canadian Business, 1980/81–. [Orange Label, Executives]
    Biography and Genealogy Master Index, 1980–1993. (See also "Electronic Resources" below.)

The Library also has *Social Register*, 1968– ; *D & B Business Locator* (CD-ROM), which includes names of 11 million corporations, many of which are names of people; *Dun & Bradstreet's Regional Business Directory: New York Metropolitan Area*, 1990–, and *Long Island*, 1996–. These directories, arranged alphabetically and geographically, include name, address, phone number, and names of owners/partners.

4. Telephone Directories: For the New York metropolitan area, the Library has the following directories on microfilm or microfiche:

	White Pages	Yellow Pages
Bronx	1929–1973/74, 1976/77–	same
Brooklyn, Queens, Staten Island	1924–1929	same
Brooklyn	1929–1973/74, 1976/77–	1944–1973/74, 1976/77–
Manhattan	1878–1973/74, 1976/77–	1828–1973/74, 1976/77–
Queens	1927–1973/74, 1976/77–	same
Staten Island	1927–1973, 1976/77–	same
Rockaways (Queens)	1928–1934, 1949–1973/74	
Nassau	1913–1973/74, 1977–	same
Suffolk	1928–1973/74, 1976/77–	1962/63–1973/74, 1976/77–
Rockland	1910–1973/74	same
Westchester	1906–1973/74, 1978–	
Westchester, Putnam, NY, Greenwich, CT	1915–1973/74	
Greenwich, CT	1961/62–1967/68, 1970/71–1973	

In addition, the Library has current Yellow Page directories for all New York State, as well as *Cole's Cross Reference Directory* (a.k.a. *Cole Directory*) for Brooklyn, from 1971 to present; Manhattan, 1980 to present and Queens, 1998 to present. These are reverse directories listing names by address and by phone number for listed numbers only.

5. Maps and Property Ownership: 21 volumes of the latest Sanborn maps for all land and properties in Brooklyn. In addition, the Library has the current First American Real Estate Solutions, *Real Estate Directory of Manhattan* (hard copy), and *Property Data* for Brooklyn (microfiche) which include real estate information including property ownership. See CITY REGISTER - MANHATTAN for a description of the content of these directories.

6. Passenger Ships: *Morton Allan Directory of European Passenger Steamship Arrivals for the years 1890 to 1930 at the Port of New York, and for the years 1904 to 1926 at the ports of New York, Philadelphia, Boston and Baltimore.* Baltimore, 1980. [R656-M88]

7. Name Change Records: 1812–1907, in New York State, are included in *General Index to the Laws of the State of New York, 1777–1901*, vol. 2, pp. 1309–1387; and Supplement, *1902–1907*, pp. 469–567. [345 N562 ST1 and ST2] These are arranged by groups of years, 1812–1857, 1858–1865, etc., and original name. New name, year name changed, chapter and page in Session Laws, are included. For name of court (after 1860) and exact date of court orders, check the published *New York State Statutes Sessions Laws* for the appropriate year (available at the NYPL, SCIENCE, INDUSTRY AND BUSINESS LIBRARY), using the page number listed in the *General Index*.

8. Electronic Resources ("e-resources"): The Library's computers have free Internet access to over 50 online databases available here and at the BROOKLYN PUBLIC LIBRARY, CENTRAL LIBRARY. The following resources are of interest to genealogists:

Biography and Genealogy Master Index, includes references to nearly 12 million biographical sketches.
Contemporary Authors (also known as *GLD Contemporary Authors)*, complete biographical references to more than 90,000 authors in the USA and around the world.
Ethnic NewsWatch, provides full-text access to c. 200 ethnic and minority newspapers, 1990–.
MEDLINEplus, includes under "Directories," the names, location and credentials of doctors/dentists in the USA.
New York Times (latest 2 years) through *UMI Proquest Direct*
Newspaper Source, provides full-text access to over 200 regional U.S.A. and international newspapers.
ReferenceUSA, a database of 12 million businesses and 90 million U.S. households. Customized reports and business profiles are available.

NOTE: Many of the Library's electronic resources can be accessed online from home for those patrons who have Brooklyn Public Library cards. Use the bar code numbers to access these databases.

Finding Aids:

The Business Library catalog is part of the Brooklyn Public Library's Online Public Access Catalog, *GeoWeb*. Use "Browse Searching" to search by author, title, subject or call number. See "Full Record" to determine if the title is available at the Business Library. Biographical Dictionaries can be found under "Biography-Indexes." Check "Who's Who" in "Title" for a complete listing of these volumes.

In addition, the Library has the following indexes:

The Business Index, from 1979 to 1990. This indexes such periodicals as *Barron's, Wall Street Journal* and the financial pages of the *New York Times*. (microfiche)

Business Periodicals Index, from 1958 to the present.

The New York Times Index, from 1851 to the present.

The National Newspaper Index, from 1979 to 1993, includes, the *Christian Science Monitor, Los Angeles Times, New York Times, Wall Street Journal* and *Washington Post.*

The Library has a free librarian-led walking tour of the Business Library (main floor) every Wednesday morning at 10:15 a.m. which last about a half hour.

Description of Facility:

The Business Library is on the first floor. It can accommodate up to 100 people. Most materials on the first floor are in self-service cabinets or on open shelves. There are librarians on duty who can provide assistance. The Library has 2 computers to access the online catalog in the Business Library (ground floor, left); and 12 computers with full Internet access in the Sylvia G. Mechanic Business Periodicals and Micro Materials Room. The Business Periodicals Room has 3 microfilm/microfiche reader/printers. There is one microfiche reader and 3 CD-ROM computers housing the *ABI/Inform Research, Business Dateline* and *Newspaper Abstracts*, in the Business Library room.

At least two-thirds of the collection is located in the basement (including the *Morton Allan Directory*). These materials can be retrieved by filling out a call slip. Service is very quick, i.e. less than 5 minutes.

Circulating books may be borrowed using a Brooklyn Public Library card. Books borrowed may be returned to any branch of the Brooklyn Public Library.

Most directories are located around the room and have color-coded labels, i.e. orange - Who's Who; yellow - products; red - state manuals; blue - foreign manuals; and green - services.

The Real Estate volumes and microfiche, and Dun & Bradstreet business reference materials can be obtained at the Reference Desk. Only staff have access to the *Dun's Business Locator*. Information from *Dun's Business Locator* is also provided by phone.

City Directories and telephone directories (microfilm) are in the self-service file cabinet to at the front of the Business Periodicals Room.

Cole's directories for Brooklyn, 1975/76, 1978 and 1988, are located on the counter above the Sanborn maps. These are located at the far end of the Business Library Room.

Fees/Copies:

The Library has 5 photocopy machines available. Copies can be made by the researcher at $.15 per page. Copies of microfilm/microfiche are $.10 per page. Up to 10 pages can be printed from the Internet at no charge.

Restrictions on Use:

Sanborn maps may not be photocopied. Researchers should bring identification (library card or driver's license) for use of materials located at the Reference Desk.

BROOKLYN PUBLIC LIBRARY
CENTRAL LIBRARY

Facility Director:	Judith Walsh, Division Chief, Brooklyn Collection
	Mark Levine, Division Chief, History/Biography/Religion Division
	Norman Eriksen, Division Chief, General Reference Center

Address: Grand Army Plaza   ♿
Brooklyn, NY 11238

(Cross Streets: Flatbush Avenue and Eastern Parkway)

Phone:	(718) 230-2100, Ext. 5 (Telephone Reference)
	(718) 230-2483 (Brooklyn Collection)
	(718) 280-2194 (History/Biography/Religion)
	(718) 230-2129 (Periodical and Micromaterials)
Fax:	(718) 857-2245 (Brooklyn Collection)
E-mail:	Use "e-resources" online, "Ask a BPL Librarian."
Website:	www.brooklynpubliclibrary.org

Hours of Operation:

	Central Library	Brooklyn Collection
Monday	9:00 am to 8:00 pm	closed
Tuesday and Thursday	9:00 am to 8:00 pm	2:00 pm to 7:30 pm
Wednesday	9:00 am to 8:00 pm	2:00 pm to 5:30 pm
Friday	9:00 am to 6:00 pm	10:00 am to 1:00 pm
Saturday:	9:00 am to 6:00 pm	1:00 pm to 5:30 pm
Sunday:	1:00 pm to 5:00 pm*	closed

*Closed on Sunday during the summer. Closed all legal holidays. NOTE: Winter and summer periods vary from year to year. Generally, winter hours begin the third week in September and end the first week in June. Check with the Library before a Sunday visit.

Researchers planning to use the Brooklyn Collection should call in advance for an appointment. While the browsing collection can be accessed on Sundays, the assistance of the Local History Librarian is not available.

Closest Public Transportation:

Subway: 2 or 3 to Eastern Parkway/Brooklyn Museum
              Q to 7th Avenue/Flatbush Avenue

Bus: B41, B69 or B71 to Prospect Park and Grand Army Plaza

Directions:

Take the #2 or #3 train to the Eastern Parkway/Brooklyn Museum station. Exit the station and turn left when reaching the street. Walk along the Park (on Eastern Parkway) to the end of the block. The main entrance to the Library is at the corner. NOTE: The "Youth Wing" entrance on Eastern Parkway is wheelchair accessible.

Description of Resources:

The Central Library of the Brooklyn Public Library opened on February 1, 1941 and includes 13 divisions of which three are described below:

A. Brooklyn Collection houses over 5,000 books, 50,000 photographs, 500 historic and contemporary maps and atlases, newspaper clippings (arranged under 7,000 subject headings), as well as other material about historic and present-day Brooklyn. Newspaper clippings include items on Brooklyn neighborhoods, schools, libraries, churches and synagogues. Clippings on people are limited to notable individuals or persons featured in newspaper articles.

1. Maps of current Brooklyn (coterminous with Kings County) as well as historic maps showing Brooklyn in colonial and Revolutionary times. Street maps of the City of Brooklyn are available from 1834.

2. Town records which were formerly part of the St. Francis College Collection are available here on microfilm. (These towns, later absorbed into the City of Brooklyn, became part of the City of New York in 1898 when the City

of Brooklyn became one of New York City's boroughs.) The original records are in the MUNICIPAL ARCHIVES. See NEW YORK CITY DEPARTMENT OF RECORDS AND INFORMATION SERVICES, MUNICIPAL ARCHIVES for additional information on the these records.

3. *Brooklyn Daily Eagle* index, July 1891–1902, original newspaper clipping files (morgue), 1904–1954, and photo collection belonging to the now-defunct *Brooklyn Daily Eagle* newspaper can be accessed here. The photo collection has been extensively "mined" for general scenes of Brooklyn (buildings, parks, etc.). Many of these photographs have been incorporated into the Brooklyn Collection. The Brooklyn Collection also includes copies of the *Brooklyn Eagle Almanac,* 1886–1929. These volumes include a section on "Necrology of Important Personages," listing people who died during the year by date of death. (See also "Periodical and Micromaterials Division" and "Restrictions on Use.")

4. Photograph Collections include the Daniel Berry Austin collection, c. 1900–1906, with photos of residential and public buildings, street scenes, and cemeteries in Brooklyn; the Ben Attas collection, 1960–1967, with photos of people in Prospect Park and photos of Sheepshead Bay; the Bob Arnold collection with views of cemeteries (mostly non-Jewish) and the Sephardic Jewish Center; the George Bradford Brainard collection, c. 1879–1887, with photos of people (by occupation), Brooklyn residences, schools, churches and parks; the Mal Gurian collection, c.1960–1970s, negatives of buildings under construction in Brooklyn and the *Brooklyn Daily Eagle* baseball photographs (portraits and action scenes) and miscellaneous negatives of street scenes and news events. There are additional views of Brooklyn subjects from the *Brooklyn Daily Eagle* and other sources, as well as the Irving Herzberg collection, which includes photos of Hasidic Jews in Brooklyn's Williamsburg section, 1962–1976, Jewish life on Ocean Parkway, 1960s–1970s, and photos of people at Coney Island, 1957–1977. Of note, more than 18,000 photographs from the *Brooklyn Daily Eagle* have been digitized for electronic viewing.

B. History/Biography/Religion Division has the following collections of interest to genealogists:

1. Yizkor Books: The History/Biography/Religion Division has a number of Yizkor books in its collection. Most are in Hebrew or Yiddish. (See Appendix B for Yizkor books available in other libraries in New York City.)

2. Biographies: The Division has a large number of biographies and collected biographies on open shelves. Check the library catalog for other biographies available in the stacks.

3. Maps and Atlases: The Library has U.S. Geographical Survey maps (topographical) covering all states and Defense Mapping Agency maps of the world. In addition, it has historical and contemporary maps of New York City and New York State, including Sanborn fire insurance maps for New York State, 1886–1915. See "Restrictions on Use." Maps of Brooklyn are in the Brooklyn Collection.

4. Civil War Collection: The Library has one of the most extensive collections about the Civil War in the U.S.A. including personal narratives of particular campaigns, memoirs and diaries of soldiers, muster rolls, and regimental histories.

5. History of Brooklyn: The Library houses a vast collection of books about Brooklyn, including:

Amusing the Million. Coney Island at the turn of the century, by John F. Kasson. New York, 1978.
  [+Ref 301.29 K]
Borough Park: centennial edition, 1898–1998, by Oscar Israelowitz. Brooklyn, [1998]. [+Ref 974.723 I]
Brooklyn! An illustrated history, by Ellen M. Snyder-Grenier. Philadelphia, 1996. [q974.723 S]
Brooklyn, People and Places, Past and Present, by Grace Glueck. New York, 1991. [f974.7239]
Brooklyn's Gold Coast: the Sheepshead Bay communities, by B. Merlis. Brooklyn, 1997. [+Ref q974.723 M]
Brownsville, the birth, development and passing of a Jewish community in New York, by Alter F. Landesman. New
  York, [1969]. [296.09747 L]
Encyclopedia of New York City, edited by Kenneth T. Jackson. New Haven, 1991. [q974.71 E]
Flatbush Odyssey: a journey through the heart of Brooklyn, by Allen Abel. Toronto, [1995]. [+Ref 974/723 A]
Gravesend, the Home of Coney Island, by Eric J. Ierardi. New York, [1975]. [Ref +974.723]
Gravesend, Brooklyn: Coney Island and Sheepshead Bay, by Eric J. Ierardi. Dover, NH, 1996. [778.94747 I]
Historic Flatbush: a brief review of pioneer days, published by the Green Point Savings Bank. Brooklyn, [1937].
  [+Ref 974.723 G798]
A History of New Lots, Brooklyn to 1887: including the villages of East New York, Cypress Hills and Brownsville,
  by Alter F. Landesman. Port Washington, NY, 1977. [974.723 L]
The Wealthy Men and Women of Brooklyn and Williamsburgh, by John Lomas. Brooklyn, 1847. [+917.472 L83]

C. Periodical and Micromaterials Room has the following materials of interest:

1. Newspapers: This Division has a unique collection of Brooklyn newspapers on microfilm. The following is a complete listing. (Gaps not shown):

Brooklyn Citizen, Jan. 1887 – Mar. 1947
Brooklyn Daily Eagle, Oct. 1841 – Jan. 1955
Brooklyn Daily Times (BDT), Jan. 1855 – Dec. 1936
BDT Home Edition, Jan. 1927 – Dec. 1933
BDT Long Island Edition, Jan. 1927 – Dec. 1933
BDT Noon Edition, Jan. 1927 – Dec. 1928
BDT Wall Street Edition, Jan. 1926 – Apr. 1937
Brooklyn Eagle, Nov. 1955; Oct. 1960 – June 1963
Brooklyn Heights Press, Nov. 1939 – Dec. 1959
Brooklyn Standard Union (a.k.a. *Standard Union*), Sept. 1863 – Jan. 1932
Brooklyn Sunday Review, Mar. 1873 – Dec. 1874
Brooklyn Sunday Star, Sept. 1927 – Mar. 1928
Brooklyn Sunday Sun, Nov. 1873 – Nov. 1876
Brooklyn Times Union, July 1932 – June 1937
Brooklyn Union, Mar. 1868 – Mar. 1869
Brooklyn Weekly Eagle, Mar. 1842 – Feb. 1845
Brooklyn Weekly News, May 1914 – Apr. 1915
Churchman, Mar. 1954 – Feb. 1955
Daily Long Island Democrat Greater Brooklyn, Apr. 1895 – Nov. 1895
Flatbush Kings & County, Feb. 1904 – Jan. 1906
Home Talk, June 1906– Dec. 1928
Home Talk Star, July 1928 – June 1931
Home Talk Star and Item, Jan. 1932 – Dec. 1938
Junior Eagle, Feb. 1907 – Dec. 1910
Kings County Inspector, Apr. 1892 – Aug. 1893
Kings County Rural & Brighton Gazette, Jan. 1880 – Dec. 1885
Long Islander, July 1839 – Dec. 1936
Standard Union Pictorial Edition, Jan. 1920 – Dec. 1922
Tablet, (formerly *Brooklyn Tablet*), Apr. 1908 – Mar. 1985
The Voice, Jan. 1885 – Dec. 1888
Weekly Chat, Feb. 1903 – Oct. 1929
Williamsburg Daily Times, Feb. 1848 – June 1854
Williamsburg Gazette, Nov. 1835 – Dec. 1850

The Library also has the *New York Times* from 1851 to the present, the *New York Times Index*, the *Personal Name Index to the New York Times Index*, 1851–1974 and 1975–1984. See also the Library's "E-Resources" for the *New York Times* (available online through *UMI Proquest Direct* for the last 2 years).

Published indexes available here include *Access,* 1992– (indexes the *Village Voice*), *Biography Index,* 1979–, *Business Periodicals Index,* 1958–, *The Education Index,* 1950–, *The (London) Times Index, 1939–, Los Angeles Times,* 1989–1995, *Index to Periodical Articles by and about Blacks* (a.k.a. *Index to Black Periodicals),* 1979–1986, *The Washington Post (*a.k.a. *The Official Washington Post Index),* 1985–1995, and *USA Today Index,* 1986–.

2. Brooklyn City Directories on microfilm are available for 1796, 1822–1826, 1829–1910, 1912/1913, 1933/1934.

Finding Aids:

The Library has an online catalog, *GeoWeb.* See "Finding Aids," BROOKLYN PUBLIC LIBRARY - BUSINESS LIBRARY for a description of *GeoWeb.*

1. Brooklyn Collection: Materials are indexed by subject, name of individual or organization in a card index accessible to the Local History Librarian only. Consult with the librarian to locate materials.

2. Town Records: The Local History Librarian has a folder listing the contents of each of the 52 microfilm reels that make up this collection. These are broad general headings only, e.g. "Roll 16 Gravesend Board of Health Minutes, Book 323, 1887–89."

3. *Brooklyn Daily Eagle:* Only July 1891 to 1902 are indexed in volumes. These indexes have headings such as "marriages," "obituaries" "murders and suicides," which list individual names. The Library received a grant to digitize the first 62 years (1841–1902), and has made the text fully searchable and available online. The morgue serves as the only "index" for the 1904–1954 period. Clippings are arranged by subject and name of individual or organization. See "Restrictions on Use."

4. Photographs: Most of the photograph collections include negative numbers, dates and identification of the subject. The *Brooklyn Eagle* collection generally identifies a photo by subject or name and the date the photo was used in the newspaper.

5. Yizkor Books: Check the *GeoWeb* catalog under "Jews in...," "yizker" or "yizkor" or by name of town.

6. Biographies and Brooklyn History: These are indexed in the *GeoWeb* catalog under subject, author and title of the book. Collected biographies can be located on open shelves under call numbers beginning with 920.

7. Civil War: Books on open shelves can be found in *GeoWeb*. There is a card catalog near the front of the History/Biography/Religion Room that catalogs rare books and other materials in the stacks. These are arranged by subjects such as "Biographies," "Personal Histories," "Campaigns" and "Regimental Histories."

8. Electronic Resources: See BROOKLYN PUBLIC LIBRARY, BUSINESS LIBRARY.

Internet access is available to some e-resources from home computers if the user has a valid Brooklyn Public Library card. All New York State residents are eligible to apply in-person. Bring 2 pieces of identification, one with the applicant's signature or photo and one showing the applicant's address in the last 2 months.

Description of Facility:

The main lobby of the Library has 9 computers with access to the *GeoWeb* catalog.

The History/Biography/Religion Division is located on the 2nd floor. Take the left escalator or stairs to reach it. This Division can seat c. 70 people. The Brooklyn Collection is in a separate room inside this Division and is not accessible to researchers. The librarian brings the material requested. The *Brooklyn Daily Eagle* clipping file is stored in the basement. See "Restrictions on Use." There are no microfilm readers available in this room but arrangements can be made to use the Town Records microfilms in the Periodical Room. See "Restrictions on Use." There are 4 computers that can access the *GeoWeb* catalog. One has access to e-resources and the Internet.

Identification is required to view some maps. Make an appointment with the map librarian (can be done by phone) to view historical maps.

The Periodical and Micromaterials Room, now part of the General Reference Center, is located on the 1st floor off the main lobby. Staff on duty can assist researchers. This room has 20 computers with Internet access; 9 additional computers with access to *GeoWeb* and e-resources (but not other Internet sites). Seventeen microfilm readers/printer, 4 microfiche readers and one microcard reader are available here. Seating at tables is available for an additional 64 people.

Fees/Copies:

The Library has 3 photocopy machines on the main floor, 3 in the micromaterials room and 2 outside the History/ Biography/Religion Division on the 2nd floor. Self-service copies can be made at $.15 per page. Copies from microfilm are also $.15 per page.

Restrictions on Use:

The librarian makes one trip weekly to the basement for materials stored there. Requests for *Brooklyn Daily Eagle* clippings should be made a week in advance. Copies of clippings can be requested by mail. A donation is recommended.

Researchers are requested to handle everything with care. Much of the Brooklyn Collection is already extremely fragile. Use only pencils, not ink, for note taking. Tracing of materials is not allowed.

When handling photographs, researchers are asked to wear the gloves provided.

Researchers must bring a library card or other identification showing name and address to use materials not on open shelves in this Library.

Use of the microfilm and microfiche readers may be limited to one hour per person if all machines are being used. A sign-in log is used during busy periods.

CITY REGISTER'S OFFICE
BROOKLYN

Facility Director: Lance Hermus, Deputy City Register

Address: Municipal Building
210 Joralemon Street, Room 2
Brooklyn, NY 11201

(Cross Streets: Court and Adams Streets)

Phone: (718) 802-3590 (City Register's Office)
(718) 802-3560 (Real Estate Assessment Office)

Fax: none

E-mail see website

Website: www.nyc.gov/html/dof/

Hours of Operation:

Monday to Friday: 9:00 am to 4:00 pm

Closed Saturday, Sunday and legal holidays.

Closest Public Transportation:

Subway: 2, 3, 4 or 5 to Borough Hall
M, N or R to Court Street/Borough Hall

Bus: B25, B26, B37, B38, B41, B45, B51 or B52 to Joralemon and Court Streets

Directions:

Take the #4 or #5 (express) train to the Borough Hall station. The exit is directly under the Municipal Building. Go to the City Register's Office in Room 2 (ground floor) or take the elevator to the 2nd floor. Room 203 is opposite the Marriage Bureau. NOTE: Entrance is wheelchair accessible.

Description of Resources:

This office has real property records (deeds, mortgages, filed maps) for Brooklyn (Kings County) from 1679 to the present. Records are available in paper copy (December 1949–December 1967), microfilm jackets arranged by block/lot number (July 1968 to November 1988), and microfilm arranged chronologically (all years). NOTE: An index to Brooklyn property records, 1982 to the present, may be online by January 2003; and digitized deed and mortgage records and indexes, 1966 to the present, by 2004. See CITY REGISTER'S OFFICE - MANHATTAN for a description of records and indexes; and CITY REGISTER'S OFFICE - BRONX for a description of microfilm jackets.

Finding Aids:

The Brooklyn office has indexes arranged by name (grantor/grantee and mortgagor/mortgagee) as well as block and lot number. Grantor/grantee indexes, arranged alphabetically by the first two letters of the surname and chronologically by date of recording, are difficult to use. NOTE: Lot numbers were assigned in Kings County beginning in 1900. Prior to that date, records are indexed by block and may be described by address, cross streets or distance from a corner.

To identify all records of a particular person or corporate body, use the grantor, grantee, mortgagor or mortgagee indexes. These are available on microfilm from 1679 to 1966. Ledgers are available from 1972–1988. A search can be made by computer, 1982 to present. NOTE: Grantor/grantee indexes, 1967–1971, could not be found.

To locate records on a particular piece of property by address, use one of the following:

1. If the building still exists, use one of the computers in Room 2 to determine the block and lot number. See CITY REGISTER'S OFFICE, MANHATTAN for a description of the computer index. Instructions for use of the computer are posted near the terminals. NOTE: Access to computerized indexes are available in this Office for Manhattan, Bronx and Queens in addition to Brooklyn. Or,

2. Go to Room 200, the Real Property Assessment Office. Clerks in this office will assist researchers in identifying block and lot numbers; or, researchers can check the NYC Department of Finance website (www.nyc.gov/finance)

from this office or home. See CITY REGISTER'S OFFICE, MANHATTAN for directions. The Office will respond to phone inquiries. Call (718) 802-3560. Or,

3. A 1988 copy of *Brooklyn Real Estate Register*, published by Real Estate Register, Inc., is accessible to the public at the counter of Room 200. Although the information on ownership and assessed valuation is out-of-date, locating tax block and lot number is very easy if this volume is used. NOTE: More current updates of this publication are available in *Real Estate Directory for Brooklyn,* published by First American Real Estate Solutions at the BROOKLYN BUSINESS LIBRARY, Reference Desk; and *New York Boroughs* (on microfiche) also produced by First American Real Estate Solutions [*XLK-4], at the NEW YORK PUBLIC LIBRARY, MAP DIVISION. These directories list properties by address and provide block and lot numbers, as well as other information such as name, address and telephone number of the current owner of each parcel.

4. "Land blocks" were used in Brooklyn prior to June 30, 1964 and "Tax blocks" after that date. Converting "Land block" number to "Tax Block" number is easy. These are listed in the red index books described below. To convert "Tax Block" number to "Land block," check the hanging charts at the front of the room (to the left of the entrance). To convert an address to a "Land block," see the *Block Book Index* on the atlas table in the middle of the room.

Once the block and lot numbers are known, consult the block and lot indexes in Room 2 (red books, 1895–1965; blue books, 1966–1968; grey books, 1968–1981; computer, 1982 to present) to obtain the liber and page numbers (or reel and page numbers after 1968) for deeds, mortgages and other instruments on file on a particular property. These list all conveyances by block and lot in chronological order. For recorded instruments, 1968–1988, researchers can skip this step and go directly to the block/lot jackets (described above). For a search of pre-1895 records, use the grantor/grantee indexes (microfilm).

Researchers can also use the Works Progress Administration (WPA) books which are available in this office (Room 2) to find liber and page numbers of earlier recorded instruments. These books where updated after the WPA project was completed (but not every transaction was added). See CITY REGISTER'S OFFICE, MANHATTAN for a description.

NOTE: More than 1,800 properties in Brooklyn (mostly Canarsie) are filed under the Torrens Land Title Registration System using Memorial Certificates rather than deeds. See CITY REGISTER'S OFFICE, MANHATTAN for a description of Torrens properties. Torrens properties are included in the computer index. The office also has a card index for these properties arranged three ways: grantor/grantee, block/lot numbers and certificate number. Each of these is further subdivided into "active" and "canceled."

To see a deed, mortgage or other conveyance, use the libers (hard copy) in Room 2 (December 1949 to December 1967) or go upstairs to Room 203 and get the block/lot microfilm jacket (1968 or later) or microfilm reel (all years) by filling out the appropriate form with the Land Block/Tax Block and lot number, liber (or reel) and page numbers and year. Be sure to indicate whether the instrument is a mortgage or deed.

Description of Facility:

This is a NYC government office. There are two staff persons on duty in Room 203 who can help researchers. Records can be obtained immediately.

Liber indexes to 1981 and records, December 1949–December 1967, are located on open shelves in Room 2 (ground floor). Indexes and records on microfilm or microfiche jackets are located on the second floor in Room 203. There are 14 computer terminals in Room 2. Room 203 has 17 microfiche and 22 microfilm readers of which 11 are reader/printers. One reader/printer can also make copies from microfiche.

The Real Property Assessment Office is located on the 2nd floor, Room 200 and has 3 computers which provide public access to the City Register's Office Internet website.

Fees/Copies:

See CITY REGISTER'S OFFICE - MANHATTAN. For a certified copy, apply at the main floor service desk. Copies will be ready in 5 business days.

Restrictions on Use:

There is a 15 minute limit on the use of computers if others are waiting.

CIVIL COURT OF THE CITY OF NEW YORK
BROOKLYN (KINGS COUNTY)

Facility Director: Stewart A. Feigel, Clerk of the County
                          Grace Cohen, Associate Court Clerk, Record Room

Address: 141 Livingston Street &
                          Brooklyn, NY 11201

                          (Cross Streets: Smith Street and Boerum Place)

Phone: (718) 643-8631 (Record Room)
Fax: none
E-mail: none
Website: see www.courts.state.ny.us

Hours of Operation:

Monday to Friday: 9:00 am to 5:00 pm. Closed Saturday, Sunday and legal holidays.

Closest Public Transportation:

Subway: A, C or F to Jay Street/Borough Hall
          M, N or R to Court Street/Borough Hall
          2, 3, 4 or 5 to Borough Hall

Bus: B41, B45, B61, B67 or B75 to Livingston and Smith Streets

Directions:

Take the A, C or F train to Jay Street/Borough Hall. From Manhattan, exit at the front of the station to Jay Street (Borough Hall exit). Walk south on Jay Street (becoming Smith Street) to Livingston. The building is on the corner.

Description of Resources:

Civil Court has name change records filed in Brooklyn from 1927 to the present. See also COUNTY CLERK'S OFFICE, STATE SUPREME COURT, KINGS COUNTY (BROOKLYN). Name changes also were recorded in State Supreme Court.

Finding Aids:

There are annual bound ledgers, 1927–1933 and 1938–1997, that list name changes. Ledgers 1927–1933 are arranged by the first letter of the old surname and then chronologically. Records are included in ledgers for this period. Ledgers 1938–1997, are arranged by the first letter of the old surname and include the new name in the index but no copy of the filing. Information in both sets of ledgers include the file number. Once the researcher identifies the file number, the original name change document can be requested. There is a computerized index to name changes filed 1998 to the present. A search can now be made by old or new name. NOTE: Indexes 1934–1937 could not be found. These were annual typed lists formerly housed in Room 301.

Description of Facility:

The Record Room (Room 7) located in the sub-basement, houses the name-change ledgers, 1927–1933 and 1938–1997. There is one public-access computer to the 1998+ index at the stand-up counter next to the door in Room 302. Instructions for use of the computer are posted on the wall next to the door. Records, 1927–1938, were in bundles. Records from 1939 to the present were in file folders. These are now being microfilmed.

Seating is available for 3 persons in the Record Room (Room 7). One microfilm reader/printer is available. Check in Room 303 for location.

Fees/Copies:

Copies can be made at $.15 per page in the Record Room. Staff will respond to mail requests, time permitting.

Restrictions on Use:

Indexes to name change records, 1934–1937, are missing. Records are available.

COUNTY CLERK'S OFFICE - STATE SUPREME COURT
KINGS COUNTY (BROOKLYN)

Facility Director: Wilbur A. Levin, County Clerk
Louis D. Fiorillo, Deputy County Clerk
James Blain, Administrator

Address: 360 Adams Street, Room 189   &
Brooklyn, NY 11201

(Cross Streets: Johnson, Court and Joralemon Streets)

Phone: (718) 643-5790 (Census and Incompetency records)
(718) 643-4149 (Naturalizations and all other records)

Fax: none
E-mail: none
Website: www.courts.state.ny.us/kingsclerk/default.htm

Hours of Operation:

<u>Monday to Friday</u>:
Room 189:   9:00 am to 5:00 pm
Record Room 079:   9:00 am to 3:00 pm
Room 122A: 9:00 am to 5:00 pm (closed 1–2 pm for lunch)

Closed Saturday, Sunday and legal holidays.

Closest Public Transportation:

Subway: 2, 3, 4 or 5 to Borough Hall
M, N or R to Court Street/Borough Hall
A, C or F to Jay Street/Borough Hall

Bus: B41, B45 or B51 to Joralemon and Court Streets
B25, B26, B37, B38 or B52 to Fulton and Adams Streets

Directions:

Take the #2 or # 3 (express) to the Borough Hall station. Exit the turnstiles and take the elevator behind the token clerk's booth to the street. The Supreme Court Building is the large, modern structure on your left as you exit the elevator. Enter the building through the <u>south</u> entrance.

Description of Resources:

1. <u>Naturalizations</u> including:

Petitions for Naturalization filed in State Supreme Court, Kings County, 1856–1924
Declarations of Intention, 1907–1924
Military Petitions ("Soldier Book"), 1918

After 1924, Brooklyn residents were naturalized in the U.S. District Court of either the Eastern or Southern Districts.

NOTE: Declarations, 1907–1924, and Petitions, 1907–1916 have been microfilmed. Filming of the remaining petition volumes to 1924 is underway. Declarations volume 85 and Petitons volume 31 are missing. The NATIONAL ARCHIVES, NORTHEAST REGION has dexigraph copies of Petitions, 1856–1907.

2. <u>Census Records</u> for Kings County (Brooklyn) available here include the original copies of New York State Census for 1855, 1865, 1875, 1892, 1905, 1915 and 1925; U.S. Census for 1850, 1860, 1870, 1880 and the 1880 "short form" for Kings County which can be used as an index to the 1880 census. Microfiche copies of the NYS Census records are also available here. See NEW YORK CITY DEPARTMENT OF RECORDS AND INFORMATION SERVICES, MUNICIPAL ARCHIVES, for a more detailed description of the 1880 census "short form."

NOTE: These Census records (except the 1880 Federal "short form") are available also at the NEW YORK PUBLIC LIBRARY, IRMA AND PAUL MILSTEIN DIVISION OF US HISTORY, LOCAL HISTORY AND GENEALOGY; NEW YORK GENEALOGICAL AND BIOGRAPHICAL SOCIETY; and the NEW YORK STATE DEPARTMENT OF EDUCATION, NEW YORK

STATE LIBRARY. The NYC MUNICIPAL ARCHIVES has microfilm copies of the NYS Census for Brooklyn (all years). It should be noted that county copies of U.S. censuses were generally the first copy made and could be more accurate than the federal copy available at other repositories.

3. Matrimonial Records from 15 December 1848 to the present for divorces, separations or annulments brought in State Supreme Court, Kings County (Brooklyn). See "Restrictions on Use."

4. Court Cases: brought against an individual or corporation or actions filed by an individual or corporation from June 1849 to the present.

5. Business Records including:

Certificates of Incorporation, 1845 to the present
Limited Partnerships, 1829 to June, 1991
Trade Names, "Doing business as...," (a.k.a. Assumed Name Certificates), 1895 to the present
Religious Corporations, 1785 to the present

See NYS DEPARTMENT OF STATE, DIVISION OF CORPORATIONS for limited partnerships, July 1, 1991 to present.

6. Incompetencies, Conservatorships and Guardianships:

Incompetency cases, 1918 to March 31, 1993
Conservatorships, 1952 to March 31, 1993
Guardianships, April 1, 1993 to the present

7. Military Records:

Military Discharge records, filed on a voluntary basis by veterans after the first World War to the present. See "Restrictions on Use."

1917 Militia Supplement List, State of New York, Adjutant General's Office, Brooklyn (labeled "1917 U.S. Military Census"). These typed soft-bound ledgers, arranged by the first letter of the surname, included men age 18–45 liable for service. Lists name, address, age, date of birth, occupation, previous or existing military or naval service including date of enlistment, date of discharge and "in what grade."

8. Name Changes: for individuals and organization from 1848 to the present.

9. Surrenders of Children and Adoptions: See "Restrictions on Use."

Finding Aids:

1. Naturalizations: Index libers, 1856–1924, are arranged by groups of years and then alphabetically by the first letter of the surname. The 1907–1924 index, including petitions and declarations, and a military index ("soldier book"), 1918, have been computerized and can be accessed on the Jewish Genealogical Society's website: www.jgsny.org. Users should read "Frequently Asked Questions" (FAQ) on this website.

NOTE: To locate information from certificate stubs of missing Petition volume 31, check the online finding aid in FAQ #22.

2. Census Records: A specific address is needed to locate data. With the address, the Assembly/Election District (AD/ED) can be located on the AD/ED maps. Census volumes are arranged by AD/ED and then address.

3. Matrimonial Records, Incompetency Records and other Court Cases: Each has index libers by groups of years and alphabetically by the first two letters of the surname. Index libers for Matrimonial and Court Cases are being microfilmed. Indexes to Matrimonial and Civil Cases from 1993 to the present are computerized and available online at http://www.courts.state.ny.us/kingsclerk/default.htm.

NOTE: A separate index to all pending Kings County (Brooklyn) Supreme Court Civil Cases requiring judicial intervention ("RJI" cases) is available on the NYS Unified Court System CaseTrac website. Digitized copies of decisions are added at the conclusion of the case. After a two week period, closed cases are removed from CaseTrac but decisions remain online. The State's website also includes an online index to Criminal Cases which can be searched only by case number. See COUNTY CLERK'S OFFICE, NEW YORK COUNTY.

4. Business Records: Indexes to records, 1785–1994, are in libers. The index to records 1992 to the present is computerized and available online. The online index to Business Records can be searched by business name, case number ("Id"), name of principals, street name ("Address") or date opened.

NOTE: The online index includes incorporations but provides only date filed and case number ("Id"). See NYS DEPARTMENT OF STATE, DIVISION OF CORPORATIONS for records on corporations and limited partnerships. A computerized index is available on DOS' website for corporations and limited partnerships active on or after December 5, 1977.

5. Military Records: There is a card index for Military Discharge records arranged in alphabetically. See "Restrictions on Use." 1917 Militia Enrollments lists are arranged by the first letter of the surname.

6. Name Changes: Liber indexes, 1848 to the present, are arranged by groups of years and alphabetically by the first letter of the new and old names. Indexes to Name Changes, 1994 to the present are also computerized. See the clerk at Window #11.

Description of Facility:

Naturalizations, Matrimonial Records, Business Records, Military Discharges, Name Changes, Surrenders of Children, Adoptions and other Court Cases are located in the basement. Take the elevator down to the "C" level, Room 079.

Naturalization indexes are located to the far left under the counter (on the clerk's side of the counter). Some volumes have been permanently removed to the "bindery" because of their poor condition. Microfiche copies are available for at least 3 volumes.

Court cases, 1990–1994, are stored in another part of the basement and are retrieved only at 9:30 am, 11:00 am and 2:30 pm.

Computer indexes and microfilm indexes to Matrimonial Records, Business Records, Name Changes and other Court Cases are located on the first floor (ground level) in Room 189.

Census records, 1917 Militia Enrollments, Conservatorships and Incompetency, and Guardianship index libers and records are located in Room 122A.

Room 079 can accommodate 16 people at the table. Rooms 122A and 189 have counter space for researchers but no seats.

Fees/Copies:

1. Naturalizations: For mail requests, the County Clerk's Office charges $10 for a search of the indexes and $10 for photocopies. There is no charge for in-person searches. Researchers who provide the volume/page numbers obtained from the Jewish Genealogical Society's online index (www.jgsny.org) pay only the $10 copy fee.

2. Census: The fee is $10 per address search conducted by staff. The staff will only conduct searches of the 1892–1925 Censuses. There is no refund if the name/address is not found. There is no charge for a search conducted by the researcher.

3. Other records: There are seven photocopy machines available in Room 079 and one in Room 105. Copies cost $.15 per page. Certified copies of records costs $8 per document (indexed records) and $10 for other records such as Business, Military Discharge and Adoptions. Exception: Military Discharge records are free to the individual who filed the record.

Restrictions on Use:

Matrimonial Records less than 100 years old may only be viewed by the parties or their attorneys. The indexes are open to the public.

Military Discharge Records may only be viewed by the concerned individual, a duly authorized agent or family member. Only staff can search the index.

Surrenders of Children and Adoption: There is no index to these cases files in the County Clerk's Office. They are filed by date and are closed to the public. These records may not be viewed without a court order.

SEPHARDIC COMMUNITY CENTER
SEPHARDIC ARCHIVES

Facility Director:	Martin Maskowitz, Executive Director
	Amir Levy, Sephardic Heritage Director
Address:	1901 Ocean Parkway
	Brooklyn, NY 11223
	(Cross Street: Corner of Avenue S)
Phone:	(718) 627-4300, ext. 223
Fax:	(718) 627-4993
E-mail:	none
Website:	none

Hours of Operation, Closest Public Transportation, Directions, Description of Facility, Fees/Copies:

See "Restrictions on Use." Materials currently inaccessible.

Description of Resources:

The Archives collects documents, memorabilia and artifacts from the Sephardic community with emphasis on, but not restricted to, the Syrian Jewish community of Brooklyn. The collection contains items relating to the history of this community in Syria as well as its years in the New York area. These include:

1. Magen David Congregation: Records of this first Syrian synagogue established in Brooklyn and its associated charities such as annual reports, 1921–1951, financial records, records of contributions, attendance record book, other school records, 1937–1953, and miscellaneous papers. Some records are in Hebrew and Spanish.

2. *Victory Bulletins* (1942–1945): A complete set of this newspaper published by the Girls Junior League, a community social organization. The newspaper included letters from and articles about soldiers, and photographs taken overseas and in Brooklyn about war-related activities. A reprinted volume, *Victory Bulletins, July 1942–September 1945: Wartime Newspapers of the Syrian Jewish Community in Brooklyn,* is available for sale.

3. Photographs and Slides: A small collection of photos, 1923–1946, including the Great Synagogue of Aleppo, Syria; group photos in front of the school in Aleppo and Damascus, 1923, 1928 and 1939; group photos of banquets of the Mapleton Lodge No. 452 at the Imperial Manor, 1930 and of the Magen David Community Center, 1946; and seven photos of the Sultan family, 1914–1983. There is also a slide collection, 1943–1983, including photos of Syrian Jews in service overseas during WWII and portraits of soldiers.

4. Legal Documents: Includes five ketubot in Hebrew, 1910–1920; one NYC marriage record, 1927; the passport of Selim Chammah, born in Aleppo, Syria, 1921; and the certificate of Naturalization of Raymond Zalta, 1926.

5. Oral Histories: There are c. 110 oral histories (in English), part of an on-going effort to record the story of how those who came from Syria transplanted themselves in New York. Sixty oral histories have been transcribed and are available in a book by Joseph Sutton, *Aleppo Chronicles,* 1987.

Finding Aids:

There is no central catalog. A published description of the holdings of the Archives is available in *Guide to Historical Resources in Kings County (Brooklyn) New York Repositories,* vol. I, 1987, by New York Historical Resources Center.

Restrictions on Use:

The Sephardic Community Center is planning a renovation project which may be completed by 2004. Plans for the Archives facility are not yet known. In the interim, archival materials are stored in Staten Island and are indefinitely inaccessible to researchers.

SURROGATE'S COURT - KINGS COUNTY (BROOKLYN) RECORD ROOM

Facility Director: Stephen Chepiga, Chief Clerk
        James Dillon, Supervisor, Record Room

Address: 2 Johnson Street (Supreme Court Building) ♿
        Room 109
        Brooklyn, NY 11201

        (Cross Streets: Adams Street and Cadman Plaza)

Phone: (718) 643-8016
Fax: none
E-mail: none
Website: none

Hours of Operation:

Monday to Friday: 9:00 am to 5:00 pm

NOTE: Records 1975 or earlier are retrieved only between 10:00 am and 3:00 pm
Closed Saturday, Sunday and legal holidays.

Closest Public Transportation and Directions:

See COUNTY CLERK'S OFFICE - STATE SUPREME COURT, KINGS COUNTY (BROOKLYN). Go to Room 109 at the <u>north</u> end of the ground floor. (Across the street from the Main Post Office.) NOTE: The main entrance and <u>south</u> end entrance are wheelchair accessible.

Description of Resources:

Surrogate's Court in Kings County has will libers from 1787, files of probate proceedings from 1866, administration proceedings from 1817, and guardianships from 1802. See SURROGATE'S COURT - NEW YORK COUNTY (MANHATTAN) for more detail on the content of these files.

Researchers may find published abstracts of early records very helpful. For example, the NEW YORK GENEALOGICAL AND BIOGRAPHICAL SOCIETY has *Abstracts of Wills of Kings County, Recorded at Brooklyn*, libers 1–6, 1787–1843 (typescript), by D. Van Buren; and, B-Ann Moorhouse and Joseph M. Silinonte's *Abstracts of Administration Proceedings Recorded in Kings County Surrogate's Court, 1817 to 1856* (to be published).

See also NEW YORK CITY DEPARTMENT OF RECORDS AND INFORMATION SERVICES, MUNICIPAL ARCHIVES, Town Records, Kings County, which include transcribed wills (3 vols.), 1658-1891, probated will proceedings, 1830-1866, 1881 and 1889, and more.

Finding Aids:

Computerized index for records filed 1990 to the present can be accessed through the computers in Room 109. Enter only the surname to obtain a list of all records with that surname. Older records will be added to this computerized index over time.

Index cards (1787–1992) located in this room are arranged alphabetically. Persons with aliases are often listed under both names (maiden name may be listed on the card). Each card includes name of individual, file number, year filed and notations "P" (Probate), "LA" (Letters of Administration), "G" (Guardianship) or "SDB" (Safety Deposit Box).

Index cards for cases filed between 1936/37 and 1951 also include date of death. Index cards for cases filed after 1951 include date of death and address of deceased. Index cards for guardianship files show date of birth.

If there is a probate liber number on the card, the will can be found in the indicated volume. A copy of the will may also be in the probate file.

NOTE: The Mormon Family History Library has microfilmed Kings County Surrogate's Court index cards, 1787–1971.

NEW YORK PUBLIC LIBRARY, IRMA AND PAUL MILSTEIN DIVISION OF UNITED STATES HISTORY, LOCAL HISTORY AND GENEALOGY and the NEW YORK GENEALOGICAL AND BIOGRAPHICAL SOCIETY have the following related finding aids:

Index of Wills Probated in Kings County, 1850–1890, by Gertrude A. Barber. 3 vols. (typescript), 1949.

Index to the Wills, Administrations and Guardianships of Kings County, New York, 1650–1850, compiled and edited by Milton Halsey Thomas and C. Shepard, 1926.

Description of Facility:

This is a government office. Seating for 16 researchers is available at four tables. Four computers are located on the counter. To order a file, fill out a request form found on the counter. Be sure to include the file number and the year of filing. There are two clerks available to pull files.

Drawers of card files are centrally located in the Record Room. Will libers through 1943 are located on open shelves under the card files. Case files, 1975 to the present, are located behind the counter in Room 109. Earlier files are maintained in the basement and must be accessed by the staff. Requests for these earlier files should be batched so that the clerks can retrieve them in one trip.

Fees/Copies:

Photocopies can be made in this room at $.15 per page. Two photocopy machines are available. For mail requests (even when the file number is provided by the researcher), the fee is $25 if the record is less than 25 years old, and $70 if it is more than 25 years, plus $5 per page for a certified copy.

Restrictions on Use:

Adoption records are closed and may be opened only by decision of the judge.

Records, c. 1866–1880, may be incomplete.

Researchers are limited to 3 files from the basement per day. Files will be retrieved from the basement only between 10:00 am and 3:00 pm.

QUEENS

Queens Repositories

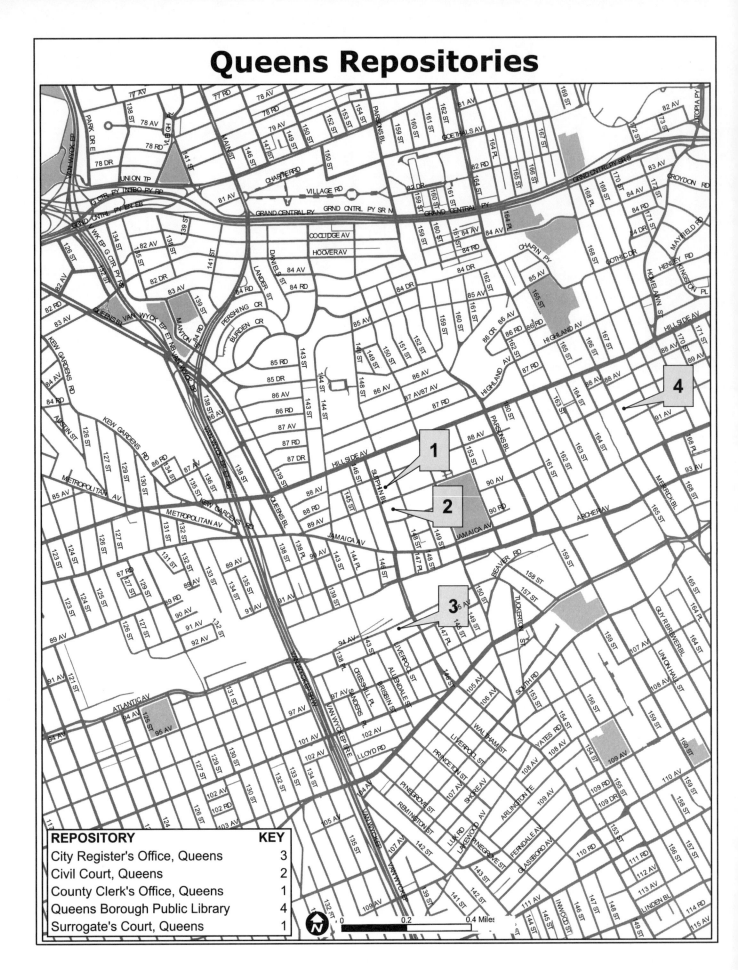

REPOSITORY	KEY
City Register's Office, Queens	3
Civil Court, Queens	2
County Clerk's Office, Queens	1
Queens Borough Public Library	4
Surrogate's Court, Queens	1

BOARD OF ELECTIONS
QUEENS BOROUGH OFFICE

Facility Director: Barbara A. Conacchio, Chief Clerk

Address: 42-16 West Street, 5th floor   NOTE: This Office will be moving in 2003/2004.*
Long Island City, NY 11101

(Cross Streets: Jackson Avenue and Queens Boulevard)

Phone Number: (718) 392-8989
Fax: (718) 392-8785
E-mail: none
Website: www.vote.nyc.ny.us

Hours of Operation:

Monday to Friday: 9:00 am to 5:00 pm. (No public access to computers between 12:30 pm and 1:30 pm.) Closed Saturday, Sunday and legal holidays.

Closest Public Transportation:

Subway: E, R, V to Queens Plaza
            7, N or W to Queensboro Plaza

Bus: M32, Q39, Q60, Q67, Q101, Q102 to Queens Boulevard and Jackson Avenue

Directions:

Take the E, V or R train to the Queens Plaza station. Exit to "Bridge Plaza South" or "Jackson Avenue." The building is southeast of the intersection of Queens Boulevard and Jackson Avenue. The entrance to this building complex, on West Street, is marked "QP's Market Place." (West Street looks more like a driveway than a street). Take the elevator to the 5th floor. NOTE: Wheelchair users should call ahead to use freight elevator. *New offices will be accessible.

Description of Resources:

The office has voter registration records from 1957 to the present. For records, 1898–1948, see NEW YORK CITY DEPARTMENT OF RECORDS AND INFORMATION SERVICES - MUNICIPAL ARCHIVES. Ledgers, 1949–1956, are missing.

Registration records pre-1995 can provide date of naturalization and court in which naturalized. Canceled registrations, 1957–2000, have been microfilmed and are arranged by year or groups of years, Assembly/Election District and then surname. Records of voters who were still active in 1992 and records of all new registrations filed 1992 or later have been digitized and can be viewed in the Archival Voter Information Data (AVID) system. See BOARD OF ELECTIONS, MANHATTAN BOROUGH OFFICE for a description of records and computerized systems.

Queens Board of Elections office has Assembly/Election District maps of Queens from 1919 to the present and published *Lists of Enrolled Voters*, 1916–1974.

Finding Aids:

The office has computerized the index to voter registrations from <u>1985 to the present</u>. A search can be made by name, surname or address using the AVID system. NOTE: AVID can access records from all boroughs. Borough offices implemented these systems over a range of years. Check each borough BOARD OF ELECTIONS for years covered.

For <u>1957–1985 records</u>, the voter's address and year of cancellation are needed in order to find a record. Staff check the Assembly/Election District (AD/ED) in the AVID system and then locate the block on the appropriate AD/ED map of the year requested. Staff search microfilm of that year to locate the canceled record.

Description of Facility:

This is a NYC government office. Microfilmed records of inactive voters are in a cabinet located on the 5th floor. AD/ED maps and *Lists of Enrolled Voters* are housed in a small room behind the reception desk. Although this office does not have dedicated public-access computers, researchers are accommodated at staff desks and can access the AVID system including digitized records.

Fees/Copies and Restrictions on Use: See BOARD OF ELECTIONS, MANHATTAN BOROUGH OFFICE.

CITY REGISTER'S OFFICE
QUEENS

Facility Director: Robert Schott, First Deputy City Register

Address: 144-06 94th Avenue, 1st floor ♿
Jamaica, NY 11435

(Cross Streets: Sutphin Boulevard and Liverpool Street)

Phone: (718) 298-7200 (City Register)
(718) 298-7099 (Real Property Assessment Bureau)
Fax: (718) 298-7153
E-mail: see website
Website: www.nyc.gov/html/dof/

Hours of Operation:

Monday to Friday: 9:00 am to 4:00 pm
Closed Saturday, Sunday and legal holidays.

Closest Public Transportation:

Subway: E, J or Z to Sutphin Boulevard/Archer Avenue

Railroad: Long Island Railroad (LIRR) to Jamaica

Bus: Q6, Q8, Q9, Q24, Q30, Q31, Q40, Q41, Q43, Q44, Q54, Q56 or Q60 to Sutphin Blvd/Jamaica Ave.

Directions:

Take the E, J or Z train to the Sutphin Boulevard station or take the Long Island Railroad to Jamaica. Exit the train and walk one block south (or turn right when exiting the LIRR) on Sutphin Boulevard. Cross 94th Avenue and turn west. The Department of Finance building is located is in the middle of the block.

Description of Resources:

All real property recorded instruments (deeds, mortgages, maps) for Queens County, recorded from 1683 to the present, are located here. Pre-1899 records for present-day Nassau County are included. Records are either on microfilm (all years), in block/lot microfilm jackets (1968–1987) or in ledgers (1839–1968). NOTE: A computerized index to Queens property records, 1982 to the present may be available online by January 2003. Digitized Queens records, 1966 to present, may be viewable online as early as 2004. See CITY REGISTER'S OFFICE - MANHATTAN for a description of records and computerized indexes; and CITY REGISTER'S OFFICE, BRONX for a description of the block/lot microfilm jackets.

Finding Aids:

Records in this office may be searched by name of property owner, or after 1914, by location. Records filed pre-1914 are indexed only in grantor/grantee indexes and mortgagor/mortgagee indexes arranged alphabetically. Block and lot numbers for each property were not used in Queens until 1914. A different numbering system known as "Land Blocks" was used from 1914 to June 1964. From July 1964 to the present, the Queens City Register's Office used "Tax Blocks." The computerized database, 1982 to present, provides Tax Block and lot numbers. Check with the staff at the UCC desk for a photocopy of the "City Register Public Access: Quick Reference Guide" pages explaining how to use the computers. To convert Tax Block number to Land Block number, check the small blue ledger, "Ridge Abstract - Conversion Book," located on the first long counter facing the public access computer area.

Tax Block and lot numbers can also be obtained:

1. From the Department of Finance, Real Property Assessment Bureau ("Assessment Office") on the second floor. This office will respond to telephone inquiries for block/lot number information. Call (718) 298-9285.

   Researchers with access to the Internet can also obtain block/lot numbers from the Department of Finance website. See CITY REGISTER'S OFFICE, MANHATTAN for a description. Or,

2. The QUEENS BOROUGH PUBLIC LIBRARY, Business, Science and Technology reference desk has a copy of *Property Data Microfiche* for Queens and NEW YORK PUBLIC LIBRARY, MAP DIVISION has *New York Boroughs* (on microfiche)

produced by First American Real Estate Solutions. Properties are listed alphabetically by name of owner as well as by street address. Each entry includes block/lot number.

From 1982 to the present, use the computer to locate records by either name of real property owner, block/lot number or address. See CITY REGISTER'S OFFICE, MANHATTAN for a description.

The 290 Torrens properties in Queens are included in the computerized index. These are properties previously recorded under the Torrens Land Title Registration System. See CITY CLERK'S OFFICE, MANHATTAN for a description.

Once the block/lot numbers are known, check with Library Services desk for the history of that block/lot from 1968 to 1987 (microfiche jacket with copies of actual records). See "Restrictions on Use." Or, check the large blue Tax Block ledgers, 1964–1981. These ledgers are arranged by tax block number and date of filing. Scan the lot number column for the one you are researching and note the name of the grantor/grantee, the type of record (deed, mortgage, etc) and the reel/page numbers. Reel/page numbers are necessary if you want to see the actual record.

For 1914–1964 records, check the small blue ledger, "Ridge Abstract - Conversion Book," to convert Tax Block number to Land Block number. There were no lot numbers assigned during this period. Check the large blue Land Block indexes (for deeds) or large orange indexes (for mortgages). These are arranged by Land Block number and then by date of recording. Note the liber/page numbers to locate the actual records. Scan the grantor or grantee columns for the name you seek to locate the property. (There are only a few pages for each block.) Small hand drawn sketch maps showing the property location are included with each entry, but unless distances from the corner are known to the researcher, these are difficult to use. Find the last owner (post-1964) in the Tax Block books if the owner during this period is not known.

Queens County did not use block/lot numbers pre-1914. For earlier records, check the 1683–1964 grantor (seller)/grantee (buyer) and mortgagor (borrower) indexes. Mortgagee indexes include primarily lending institutions. These indexes are arranged by the first two letters of the surname.

Description of Facility:

This is a NYC government office. Almost all Queens County real estate records are now located in the Main Room on the first floor. The Tax Block and Land Block ledgers are located under the long counters in the open area to the far left of the entrance. Microfilmed records (deeds and mortgages), grantor/grantee indexes (1683–1964) and mortgagor/ mortgagee indexes are on self-shelves near the back wall of the room.

Records were maintained in three series. The earliest records (1683–1965) were maintained in separate libers for Deeds and Mortgages. All are available on microfilm. Paper copies are also available in the Main Room for deeds libers (a.k.a. Conveyances), 1954–1965, (6691 to 7856) and in the basement, 1941–1954 (4483–6690).

From December 1965 to August 1968, Deeds and Mortgage records were kept together in grey Record Libers. These Record Libers (1–820) were microfilmed on 274 reels. Paper copies are also available in the Main Room. Paper copies of Deed and Record libers in the Main Room are located under the counters and along the back wall.

After 1968, records (Deeds and Mortgages) were maintained in Reel Libers (starting with Reel #275). These microfilms are located in self-service shelves. For the period 1968–1987, the City Register's Office also created microfilm jackets (look like microfiche) where records are arranged by tax block/lot numbers. Microfiche records are copies of the records in the Reel Libers. Microfiche are located in the Library Services area. See "Restrictions on Use."

Original paper grantor/grantee indexes for early years (1683–1915) are in the basement. For some letters of the alphabet, paper ledgers were retained through 1926. These ledgers are easier to use than microfilm. To reach this area, leave the City Register's Office and enter through the double doors of the Department of Finance passing the "Research Room." The entrance to the basement is in the "Self Service Area" through the door at the left marked, "Authorized Personnel Only." Use Stair D to reach the well-lit ledger room. Ask the clerk in the City Register's Office, Library Services Desk for permission to enter this area. One photocopy machine is located in the ledger room.

There are 15 public access computer terminals, 23 microfiche and 31 microfilm readers (including 2 microfiche reader/ printers and 12 microfilm/microfiche reader/printers) in the area behind the glass wall. The Office has 3 photocopy machines.

Fees/Copies: See CITY REGISTER'S OFFICE, MANHATTAN. NOTE: As a courtesy, the Library Services desk will make one free copy for researchers when there is a backlog of people waiting to use the microfilm/microfiche reader/printers.

Restrictions on Use: See CITY REGISTER'S OFFICE, MANHATTAN. Mail copies will be provided only if sufficient document location is supplied (document type, date, liber/reel and page numbers) and a check for the proper amount is enclosed. Mail copies take 3-4 weeks.

CIVIL COURT OF THE CITY OF NEW YORK
QUEENS COUNTY

Facility Director: Thomas J. Touhey, Clerk of the County
Joseph Traynor, Supervisor, Civil Term/Record Department

Address: Civil Court Building, Room 147   ♿
89-17 Sutphin Boulevard
Jamaica, NY 11435

(Cross Streets: 89th and 90th/Rufus King Avenues)

Phone: (718) 262-7138 (Record Room)
Fax: none
E-mail: none
Website: see www.courts.state.ny.us

Hours of Operation:

Monday to Friday: 9:00 am to 5:00 pm

Closed Saturday, Sunday and legal holidays.

Closest Public Transportation:

Subway: F to Sutphin Boulevard/Hillside Avenue
E, J or Z to Sutphin Boulevard/Archer Avenue

Bus: Q20A, Q20B, Q40, or Q43 to Sutphin Boulevard/89th Avenue

Directions:

Take the F train Sutphin Boulevard/Hillside Avenue station. From Manhattan, exit at the front of the station. Go up the stairs to the right, "To Court." Walk <u>two</u> blocks south on Sutphin Boulevard. The Civil Court building is on the left.

Description of Resources:

The Civil Court has name change records filed in Queens from 1927 to the present.

See also COUNTY CLERK'S OFFICE - STATE SUPREME COURT, QUEENS COUNTY. Name changes were recorded also in State Supreme Court.

Finding Aids:

The General Record Department has ledger books 1927–1997 arranged alphabetically by the first letter of the old surname. Ledgers 1927–1937 include the records for this period. Index ledgers 1938–1997 include the new name in the index but are alphabetized only by the first letter of the old name. There is a computerized index from 1998 to the present. Records can be accessed by either the old or new name in the computer.

Description of Facility:

All index ledgers for name change records and current files (less than 3 years old) are located on the main floor of the courthouse in Room 147. Go down the right corridor to reach the General Record Department windows. Ask to use the ledgers or to view a file at the last window. The ledgers are maintained at the entrance to this room. Public access computers are located at the first two window. Files more than 3 years old are stored in other parts of the building. See "Restrictions on Use." Researchers can use the bench opposite the windows to view files.

Fees/Copies:

Two photocopy machines are available at the end of the corridor. Copies cost $.15 per page.

Restrictions on Use:

Records more than 3 years old are retrieved once a week. No more than 3 files may be requested at one time.

COUNTY CLERK'S OFFICE - STATE SUPREME COURT
QUEENS COUNTY

Facility Director: Gloria D'Amico, County Clerk
                                    Sean Ford, Record Room Supervisor

Address: 88-11 Sutphin Boulevard, Room 105   ♿
                                    Jamaica, NY 11435

                                    (Cross Streets: 88th and 89th Avenues)

Phone: (718) 520-2877 (Record Room)
Fax: none
E-mail: none
Website: see www.courts.state.ny.us

Hours of Operation:

Monday to Friday: 9:00 am to 5:00 pm (County Clerk's Office, Rooms 100-106)
                                    9:00 am to 3:30 pm (Record Room, B-17)
                                    9:00 am to 12:00 noon (Vault)

Closed Saturday, Sunday and legal holidays.

Closest Public Transportation:

Subway: F to Sutphin Boulevard/Hillside Avenue
              E, J or Z to Sutphin Boulevard/Archer Avenue

Railroad: Long Island Railroad to Jamaica

Bus: Q20A, Q20B, Q40, Q43 or Q44 to 88th Avenue and Sutphin Boulevard

Directions:

From Manhattan, take the F train to the Sutphin Boulevard/Hillside Avenue station. Exit at the <u>front</u> of the station. Go up the stairs to the right, "To Court." Walk <u>one</u> block south on Sutphin Boulevard. The court building is on the left. Room 105 is down the hallway to the left of the entrance. NOTE: Wheelchair users can ride the mechanical chair lift located to the right of the main entrance.

Description of Resources:

1.   <u>Naturalizations</u>: Petitions filed in State Supreme Court, Queens County, 1794–1941; military petitions, 1918 (vol.1); and Declarations of Intention, 1890–1905, 1910–1926. After 1941, Queens residents could be naturalized in U.S. DISTRICT COURT. See "Restrictions on Use."

    NOTE: The NATIONAL ARCHIVES, NORTHEAST REGION has dexigraph copies of pre-September 1906 petitions filed in this Court. NEW YORK PUBLIC LIBRARY, MILSTEIN DIVISION OF UNITED STATES HISTORY, LOCAL HISTORY AND GENEALOGY has copies of pre-1906 petitions; index to petitions, 1906–1941; and Declarations, 1906–1926 (include volume indexes) microfilmed by the Mormon Family History Library. Declarations, 1824–1906, were also microfilmed by the Family History Library.

2.   <u>New York State Census</u>: for Queens County, 1892, 1915 and 1925 (originals). The 1892 Census for Queens includes present-day Nassau County. Two card indexes, one arranged by community, 1925, and the second arranged alphabetically by street name are available for 1915 and 1925. A surname index for Long Island City (volumes 1–5) is available for the 1892 census.

    NOTE: The NEW YORK GENEALOGICAL AND BIOGRAPHICAL SOCIETY has microfilm copies of the 1892, 1915 and 1925 censuses and indexes. NYPL, MILSTEIN DIVISION OF UNITED STATES HISTORY, LOCAL HISTORY AND GENEALOGY, QUEENS BOROUGH PUBLIC LIBRARY and the NEW YORK STATE DEPARTMENT OF EDUCATION , NEW YORK STATE LIBRARY in Albany have microfilm copies of the 1915 and 1925 censuses.

3.   <u>Matrimonial Records</u>: from 1847 to the present for divorces, separations and annulments brought in State Supreme Court, Queens County. See "Restrictions on Use." For earlier records, check Queens Court of Common Pleas (below).

This Office also has <u>Marriage Records</u> filed with the County Clerk, 1908–1910, 1913, 1915–1920; and indexes, 1908–1909, 1911–1917 and 1938. Records, 1908–1916, are hand-written in "summary" volumes. Records, 1917–1920, are typed transcripts of licenses. NOTE: It is possible that missing volumes will be found once renovation is completed.

4. <u>Military Records</u>: The Office has Military Discharge Records from 1917 to the present, for veterans who filed a copy of their DD 214 form (discharge papers) in this Office. See "Restrictions on Use."

5. <u>Court Cases</u>: cases brought against an individual or corporation or actions filed by an individual or corporation in State Supreme Court, Queens County, 1851 to the present. NOTE: Vol. 1 (1847–1850) is missing. Records, 1951–1987 are on microfiche. Filming of later records is continuing. *Docket of Judgements* ledgers include Judgements filed in other counties against Queens County residents, as well as those filed in Supreme Court of Queens. Judgements and orders issued, March 24, 2001 to date, are digitized and accessible from computers at the County Clerk's Office and online.

The Office also has records of the following Queens courts (gaps): Common Pleas, 1791–1847; Oyer and Terminer, 1812, 1859–1879, 1894–1897, Sessions and General Sessions, 1829–1897; County Court, 1813–1897.

6. <u>Business Records</u>:

Business Certificates (a.k.a. Trade Names, "Doing Business As..." and Assumed Business Names), 1900 to the present. (Records 1900–1996 are on microfiche; records 1993 to the present are digitized and can be viewed on computers in Room 106.)

Certificates of Incorporation, 1851 to the present. See "Restrictions on Use." Religious Incorporations, March 24, 2001 to the present are digitized and accessible from computers in this Office.

Limited Partnerships, 1943 to present. NOTE: From July 1991 to the present, these records are copies of those filed in NYS DEPARTMENT OF STATE.

7. <u>Incompetency, Conservatorship and Guardianship Records</u>:

Infants, Lunatics and Drunkards, 1860–1909, 1938–1946
Incompetency cases, 1880 to the present
Conservatorships/Guardianships, 1973 to the present

8. <u>Name Changes</u>:

Name Change records are available from 1847 to the present.

9. <u>Adoptions and Surrenders of Children</u>:

Adoptions (index only), 1928–1938 and Surrenders of Children, 1962 to the present, are available here. See "Restrictions on Use."

Finding Aids:

1. <u>Naturalizations</u>: There is an alphabetical card index to Petitions, 1794–1906, and two liber indexes covering this period (1794–1904, 1904–1906). For the period, 1906–1941, there is a separate card index for Petitions; and a liber index covering Petitions (c. 1906–1938) and Declarations (c. 1906–1924). Researchers wishing to view the card indexes should request access from the staff in Room 105. See also NYPL, MILSTEIN DIVISION OF UNITED STATES HISTORY, LOCAL HISTORY AND GENEALOGY which has the Family History Library microfilmed copy of the card index, 1906–1941. For pre-1907 petitions, researchers can check the WPA index to "Old Law" Naturalization Records for New York City, 1792–1906, which includes every court in NYC during this period. This Soundex index is available at the NATIONAL ARCHIVES, NORTHEAST REGION and at the NYPL, MILSTEIN DIVISION OF UNITED STATES HISTORY, LOCAL HISTORY AND GENEALOGY.

Military Petitions, 1918, are indexed in the front of that volume. NOTE: These petitions are <u>not</u> included in the card index.

For pre-1906 <u>Declarations of Intention</u>, only the index at the front of each volume is available. The indexes are arranged alphabetically by first letter of the surname. For c. 1906–1924 (Declaration volumes 1–50), the index is included in the same liber index as that for Petitions (see above). Separate liber indexes are available for Declarations, 1924–1950 (volumes 51–126), and 1950–1951 (volumes 127–131), arranged by first two letters of the surname and first letter of first name. Declaration records for most of this period are missing. See "Restrictions on Use."

2. <u>Census</u> records are searched by staff. For the 1892 Census, the name alone is sufficient. This office has a card index arranged by surname for most of the 1892 Census. Some communities are not included in this index. (NOTE: The 1892 Census did not include street addresses.) For the 1915 and 1925 Census, name/address are needed. This office has a master index for 1915 and 1925 arranged by community which shows the volume numbers corresponding to each community. A second card index arranged by volume number and street name lists the pages within each book that include that street name. These indexes were created by the County Clerk's Office. Census maps, 1925, are also available here.

See NEW YORK GENEALOGICAL AND BIOGRAPHICAL SOCIETY for microfilm copies of the 1892, 1915 and 1925 indexes.

3. <u>Matrimonial Records</u>, 1847–1929, can be located by looking in the *Common Rule* libers (microfiche) indexed in groups of years and then by first letter of the surname. For records, 1929–1946, use the alphabetical liber *Index to Matrimonial Actions* (microfiche). For later years through April 15, 1992, matrimonial records are in the same index libers as other cases. These libers (microfiche) include the names of the parties and the date of the action.

From 1992, <u>Matrimonial Actions</u> are included in the computerized index together with all other Court cases. Matrimonial cases are identified in the computer under "type" of case.

4. <u>Military Discharge Records</u>: The Record Room clerk has access to index cards (microfiche) filed by name. The clerk can advise if a record exists for a particular person. There are Military Discharge libers, 1941–1950, 1959–1967, arranged by year and then alphabetically. These libers can be viewed by researchers directly. The libers include name of veteran, date papers were filed and file number. Libers are useful for those who wish to look up many names. NOTE: Several of the liber indexes are missing. Earlier years could not be found.

5. <u>Court Cases</u> are indexed in *Common Rule* libers (microfiche) by year or groups of years and alphabetically by the first two letters of the surname from 1847 to 1992. The index to <u>Court Cases</u> is computerized, 1992 to the present.

NOTE: A separate index to all pending Queens County Supreme Court <u>Civil Cases</u> requiring judicial intervention ("RJI" cases) is available on the NYS Unified Court System CaseTrac website. Digitized copies of decisions are added at the conclusion of the case. After a two week period, closed cases are removed from CaseTrac but decisions remain online. The State's website also includes an online index to <u>Criminal Cases</u> which can be searched only by case number. See COUNTY CLERK'S OFFICE, NEW YORK COUNTY.

6. <u>Business Records</u>: The liber indexes to <u>Business Certificates</u>, 1900–1996 (microfiche) and <u>Limited Partnerships</u> are arranged by groups of years and alphabetically by the first letter of the name. Indexes to <u>Certificates of Incorporation</u> and <u>Limited Partnerships</u>, 1983–1991, are arranged in a similar manner but use the first <u>two</u> letters of the name. Separate libers are available for Religious Incorporations (Churches and Synagogues), 1924–1994 (microfiche), and Incorporation of Cemeteries, 1878–1912. There is a computerized index to <u>Business Records</u>, filed 1993 or later.

7. <u>Incompetency and Conservatorship</u> cases are indexed alphabetically by the first letter of the surname in libers to 1992. Later records are included in the computerized index. See "Restrictions on Use."

8. <u>Name Changes</u>: 1847–1929, can be located by looking in the *Common Rule* libers (microfiche) indexed in groups of years and then by first letter of the surname. Name Change records, 1929–1960 (microfiche), are indexed separately in the same manner by original surname. After 1960, these cases are indexed together with other court cases. Indexes 1992 to the present are computerized. Only original name can be searched. However, digitized copies of records filed March 24, 2001 or later can be accessed by computer to see the new name.

Description of Facility:

Make a left turn after passing the guards to reach Room 106. Computerized Indexes to <u>Court Cases</u>, <u>Matrimonial Actions</u>, <u>Name Changes</u> and <u>Business Records</u> can be accessed on computers in this room. Earlier cases are included in the index if there was any activity on the case after 1992.

The actual files for all <u>Court Cases</u>, <u>Matrimonial Records</u>, <u>Name Change</u>, <u>Business Records</u> and indexes (liber and microfiche), including the card indexes to the 1892, 1915 and 1925 <u>New York State Census</u> (but not indexes to <u>Naturalization</u> petitions), are in the basement Record Room (B-17). <u>Incompetency cases</u> and <u>Conservatorships</u> (liber index and records) are also in the basement. Some incompetency cases are closed to the public. See "Restrictions on Use." To reach the basement, go down the stairs on the left side of Room 106. The basement Record Room can seat 15-20 people. Request indexes from the clerk behind the counter. Once the file number is known, complete a requisition slip and provide to the clerk.

The card indexes to Petitions for <u>Naturalization</u> (1794–1906 and 1906–1941) are in locked file cabinets outside Room 105. Pre-1906 Petitions (tri-folds) are also in these locked cabinets. <u>Naturalization</u> and <u>Census</u> inquiries should be made to the two staff persons in Room 105 (enter this Administrative Office through Room 106). This is a working office. Space can be made for one researcher.

There is one microfilm reader/printer in Room 106 and three microfiche reader/printers (20 minute limit for use) in the basement Record Room (B-17). Room 106 has one computer dedicated to <u>Business</u> and incorporation filings; four computers dedicated to Civil Supreme <u>Court Case</u> filings; and six for <u>Judgments</u> and Property (block/lot searches). Judgments included are those awarded to Queens residents, Queens business owners, and persons who work in Queens by the Supreme Court in Queens as well as other (non-Queens) courts.

Fees/Copies:

There is no charge for in-person searches. Copies of records are $.15 per page if the researcher makes the copy. There are four photocopy machines located in the basement Record Room and three in Room 106. Mail requests cost $10 for search and copy of a <u>Census</u> record (one address) and $10 for a <u>Naturalization</u> record. For mail requests of other documents, the charge is $10 for the first two years searched and $5 for every 2-year search thereafter. Certified copies of <u>Business</u> records are $10; certified copies of all other records are $8.

Payment must be made by certified check, money order or cash. No credit cards, personal or corporate checks are accepted.

Restrictions on Use:

<u>Declarations</u>, pre-1889, 1906–1909 (vols. 1–4), 1927–1953 (vols. 66–131), could not be located and may be missing. Additional gaps may exist.

Researchers generally cannot search <u>Census records</u> themselves. In limited situations, when the office is not busy, these records may be searched in person.

<u>Matrimonial Records</u> are restricted to the parties or their attorneys. Matrimonial indexes, however, are open to researchers.

<u>Military Discharge</u> records are restricted to the concerned individuals. Liber indexes are open to the public. However, libers pre-1941 could not be located and there are gaps in later years.

<u>Business Records</u>, Certificates of Incorporation, 1851–1928; <u>Court Cases</u>, 1950 or earlier, and Judgement books (*Docket of Judgements)* are off-site. Records/libers can be delivered to the Court House within 3 days of request.

Records and indexes of <u>Surrenders of Children</u>, <u>Adoptions</u> and <u>Incompetency cases</u> involving persons in State hospitals are sealed. These records may not be opened without a court order.

QUEENS BOROUGH PUBLIC LIBRARY
LONG ISLAND DIVISION

Facility Director:	Judith Box, Curator
Address:	89-11 Merrick Boulevard ♿
	Jamaica, NY 11432
	(Cross Streets: 89th and 90th Avenues)
Phone:	(718) 990-0770
Fax:	(718) 658-8342
E-mail:	jbox@queenslibrary.org
Website:	www.queenslibrary.org/central/longisland/index.asp

Hours of Operation:

Monday	10:00 am to 9:00 pm
Tuesday to Thursday:	10:00 am to 7:00 pm
Friday:	10:00 am to 6:00 pm
Saturday:	10:00 am to 5:30 pm
Sunday:	12:00 am to 5:00 pm (except June, July and August)

Closed legal holidays and Sunday during the summer.

Closest Public Transportation:

Subway: F to 169th Street

Bus: Q1, Q2, Q3, Q, Q8, Q9, Q9A, Q36, Q41, Q17, Q75, Q76, Q77, N1, N2, N3, N6, N22, N22A, N24 or N26 to Jamaica Bus Terminal

Directions:

From Manhattan, take the F train to the 169th Street station. Exit at the back of the train to 168th Street. After exiting the turnstiles, go up the last stairway to the left. Walk one block west to Merrick Boulevard (166th Street) and turn left. Walk two blocks south on Merrick Boulevard to the Library. The Library is across the street from the Bus Terminal.

Description of Resources:

The Long Island Division of the Queens Borough Public Library, established in 1912, is a reference and research center devoted to the study of the four counties of Long Island — Queens, Kings (Brooklyn), Nassau and Suffolk. Materials include books, maps, photographs, manuscripts, census records and clipping files with emphasis on the history and genealogy of the area. Specific collections which may be of interest to genealogists include:

1. New York City - Vital Records: The Library has NYC Health Department indexes (microfilm) for:

   Births, Manhattan and Brooklyn, 1881–1897
   Births, all boroughs, 1898–1909
   Deaths, all boroughs, 1930–1948

2. Picture Collections: Includes over 100,000 pictures covering different localities in Queens and Long Island, from the early part of the 20th century to the present. In addition, the Division has over 46,000 images including more than 13,000 postcards, available on an in-house image database.

   The Long Island Division has a copy of the microfiche collection, *Photographic Views of New York City 1870's to 1970's*. See NEW YORK PUBLIC LIBRARY - IRMA AND PAUL MILSTEIN DIVISION OF U.S. HISTORY, LOCAL HISTORY AND GENEALOGY for a detailed description of this collection and finding aids.

3. Census: While the Long Island Division focuses on the four counties of Long Island, it has microfilm reels for some other New York State counties. The following New York metropolitan area census records are available:

   New York State and local census:
   Queens, 1915 and 1925
   NYC (Manhattan), 1819 and jury list [Reel AR-9]*

<u>Federal Census</u>:

Kings, Queens, Suffolk, 1800–1880, 1890 (Suffolk-Brookhaven Township only) and Veterans' schedules for the three counties. NOTE: Pre-1899, Queens County included present-day Nassau County.

Kings, Queens, Nassau, Suffolk, 1900, 1910, 1920, 1930

New York County, 1800, 1820 (part)

Richmond, 1800, 1810, 1890 (Veterans' schedules)

Rockland, 1800, 1820, 1830

Westchester, 1800, 1830, 1850

New York State (12 of 14 reels), U.S. Mortality Census, 1850–1880

New York State (entire State) Soundex, 1880, 1900

U.S. (entire) Index to the surviving 1890 schedules

New York State, U.S. Census Enumeration District Descriptions, 1900 and 1910

New Jersey, U.S. Census Enumeration District Descriptions, 1910

New York City, U.S. Census Enumeration District Descriptions, 1920

The Library has the following <u>published</u> indexes:

New York City 1870 Census Index, edited by Raeone C. Steuart. Bountiful, UT, 1997. [929.3747S]

New York 1890 Veterans Census Index, published by Heritage Quest. Bountiful, UT, 1999. [929.3747N]

New York City 1910 Census Index, published by Heritage Quest. 14 vols. North Salt Lake, UT, [2002]. Includes NYC, Nassau and Suffolk counties. [929.3747N]

See also *Ancestry.com* or *.plus* for an all-person index to the 1930 Federal Census for New York State, New Jersey, Connecticut and more, available at the CENTER FOR JEWISH HISTORY, NEW YORK PUBLIC LIBRARY (at all Research Libraries), and NEW YORK GENEALOGICAL AND BIOGRAPHICAL SOCIETY.

4.   <u>City Directories</u> (on microfilm, some in paper copies)

Brooklyn, 1796, 1802/3, 1811/12, 1822–1909/10, 1912, 1913, 1933/34

Brooklyn and Long Island (Business), 1878/79, 1899

New York City (generally includes Manhattan and parts of the Bronx), 1786–1924/25, 1933/34

Queens (Business and Residential), 1898–1902, 1904, 1906–1909/10, 1912, 1933

Flushing, 1887/88

Great Neck, 1937/38, 1946/47–1955

Hempstead/Freeport, 1897, 1901/2–1911/12

Long Island, 1864/65, 1872/73–1878/79, 1888/89

Long Island City, 1888/89

Montauk (Business), 1915–1917

Patchogue (Business and Residential), 1904

5.   <u>Telephone Directories</u> (on microfilm)

Brooklyn, 1929 to present

Brooklyn classified, 1928, 1944 to present

Brooklyn, Queens and Staten Island, 1924–1928/29

Manhattan, 1932/33–1973/74

Nassau, 1913 to present

Queens, 1927 to present

Queens classified, 1927/28–1930, 1957 to present

Suffolk, 1928 to present

Suffolk/Nassau/Queens supplement, 1908–1927

6.   <u>Newspapers and newspaper indexes</u>:

Herald Tribune picture morgue (file). NOTE: The clipping file formerly located here has been transferred to the University of Texas library in Austin, TX.

Brooklyn Daily Eagle, October 1841–January 1955; and indexes to deaths, 1841–1880; marriages, 1841–1880.

Christian Intelligencer, marriage index, 1830–1871

Newsday, 1973 to present (includes for various times Nassau, Nassau/Queens, Suffolk and NYC editions). In addition, the annual index to *Newsday,* 1977–1983, includes an alphabetical listing of obituaries.

New York Evening Post, death index, 1851–1890

New-York Weekly Post-Boy, 1743–1749, and *New-York Gazetteer/Weekly Post-Boy*, 1750–1773 [Reels NP]*

The Library has an extensive collection of Long Island newspapers on microfilm. A sample list of Queens newspapers follows (gaps exist):

Queens - Borough-wide
Long Island Democrat, 1835–1912
Long Island Freie Presse, 1891–1905
Long Island Daily Press, 1921–1967
Long Island Press, 1967–1977
Long Island Star Journal, 1938–1968
Queens Chronicle, 1984–
Queens Ledger, 1941–
Queens Review, 1935–1951
Queens Voice, 1965–1970

Astoria & Newtown
Astoria Gazette-Newtown Sentinel, 1852–1853
Astoria Herald & Newtown Gazette, 1863–1864

Bayside
Bayside Times, 1936–

Flushing
Broadway Flushing Times, 1936–1942
Flushing Daily Times, 1866–1925
Flushing Evening Journal, 1885–1930
Flushing Journal, 1842–1907; index 1841– 1865
Flushing Times, 1971–1975
Home Town News, 1954–1961
Long Island Herald, 1951–1974
Long Island Times, 1857–1896
North Shore News, 1940–1968

Forest Hills
Long Island Post, 1960–1970
Forest Hills Kew Gardens Post, 1926–1949
Queens Post, 1950–1960

Fresh Meadows
Fresh Meadows Times, 1993–

Glen Oaks
Glen Oaks News, 1952–1976

Glendale
Glendale Register, 1968–

Howard Beach
Forum of Howard Beach, 1978–1980

Jackson Heights
Jackson Heights News, 1918–1970

Jamaica
Community Chatter, 1970–1971
Community News, 1943–1948
Community Voice, 1973–1974
Daily Long Island Democrat, 1911–1912
Daily Long Island Farmer, 1912–1920
Jamaica Herald, 1927
Long Island Farmer, 1821–1911
New York Voice, 1971–
Queens Evening News, 1927–1939

Kew Gardens Hills
Kew Hills News, 1955–1976

Little Neck
Ledger, 1946–1989
Little Neck Ledger, 1989–

Long Island City
Daily Star, 1881–1933
Long Island Daily Star, 1933–1938
Long Island Graphic, 1952–1957

Maspeth (Northwest Queens)
Queens Ledger, 1941–

Newtown
Daily Register, 1935–1940
Long Island Register, 1940–1941
Newtown Register, 1873–1935; index 1880–1920

North Shore
North Shore Daily Journal, 1931–1938

Queens Village
Queens County Times, 1944–1975
Queens Illustrated News, 1973–1986
Times-Review, 1952–1958

Richmond Hill
Long Island News, 1884–1887, 1944–1945
Record, 1903–1948
Richmond Hill Courier, 1927–1928

Ridgewood
Long Island Daily Advocate, 1925–1966
Ridgewood Times, 1912–1989; index 1908–1915

Rockaway Beach
Rockaway Argus, 1914, 1934–1941
Rockaway Journal, 1906–
Rockaway News, 1905–1941
Rockaway Point News, 1961–1971
Rockaway Record, 1964–1981
Wave, 1896–

St. Albans
St. Albans Life, 1946–1952

South Jamaica
Inside Rochdale News, 1965–1978

South Queens
Forum of South Queens, 1981–1986
Forum of Queens, 1994–
Mirror/Mirror Tribune, 1985–1989
South Queens Star, 1968–1970

Whitestone
Whitestone Herald, 1871–1949

Woodhaven
Leader-Observer, 1912–

Woodside
Woodside Herald, 1975–

7. <u>Vertical Files</u>: On neighborhoods in Queens and communities on Long Island, including thousands of newspaper clippings.

8. <u>Property Records</u> (on microfilm)*

   Queens County Conveyances (Deeds), 1683–1806 [Reels QCV]
   Queens County Mortgages, 1754–1815 [Reel QMG]
   New York County (Manhattan) Conveyances (Deeds), 1654–1672 [Reels NCV]
   New York County Mortgages, 1665–1675 [Reel NCV], and 1754–1800 [Reel NMG]
   New York County, Foreclosures, 1849–1873, and index [Reel AAD-13]
   New York County, Assessment Rolls, 1699–1735 (gaps), 1790, 1792, 1799, 1802, 1807, 1810, 1820–1821
     [Reels AR]
   First American Real Estate Solutions, *Directory for Queens* (located at the Business, Science and Technology desk, main floor), current microfiche edition. The *Directory*, arranged by address and name of property owner, provides block and lot number, name of current owner and owner's mailing address, as well as other information about each property.

9. <u>Wills and Administration of Estates</u> (on microfilm)*

   New York County, Wills, 1698–1879, and indexes [Reels WL]
   New York County Surrogate's Court, Wills, 1662–1761, 1815–1829 [Reels SCW]
   New York County, Surrogate's Court, Letters of Administration, 1664–1683, 1743–1783, and Administration
     Bonds, 1753–1798 [Reels SAD]
   New York County, Supreme Court, record of Wills, 1821–1829, 1847–1927 [Reels SC]
   Albany, NY, Court of Appeals, Administration of Estates, 1666–1825 [Reels AIN]
   Albany, NY, Court of Appeals, Wills and indexes, 1629–1802; records, 1799–1839 [Reel UC-46]; and indexes,
     1830–1848 [Reels AW]
. Albany, NY, Court of Appeals, Administration Bonds, 1787–1791 [Reel AR-4]

10. <u>Town Records</u>: Records (on microfilm) include land transactions, wills and town meetings:

    Flushing, 1790–1892 [also Reels TFL & SD-9]*
    Hempstead, 1644–1874 [also Reels THS]*
    Newtown, 1653–1874 [also Reels TJM-4 & TNT; includes militia, 1861–1866]*
    Jamaica, 1656–1897 [Reels TFL & TJM]*
    Oyster Bay, 1684–1874 [Reels TOB]*
    Queens, 1788, 1828–1879 [Reels TFL-3 & TNT]*
    Westchester, 1665–1879 [Reels TJM-5 &TNT-8]*

    Brookhaven Town archives, Suffolk County, 1845–1924 (bulk 1880–1890), include fragmentary material from daily school registers, 1878–1921; registers of electors, election poll list and registration list, c. 1893–1924; tax assessment roll book and extracts of lists, 1872–1885.
    Flushing Village and Town archives, 1786–1881 (bulk 1817–1876), include roll book of public school, 1848–1853; minute book, Board of Education, District 5, 1841–1876; assessment roll (Town) 1817–1821 and (Village) 1857; Justice's Court docket book, c. 1877–1881; account book for census of Flushing inhabitants, 1786.
    New Amsterdam records include New York Colonial manuscripts, Dutch Council minutes, 1638–1649
      [Reels DM]*
    Ulster County records [Reels UL]* include lawyers papers; mortgages, 1792–1849; grand jurors, 1828–1850; court records, 1658–1766 and 1830–1857; wills and administration records, 1662–1822.

11. <u>Coroner's Office Inquests of Deaths</u> (on microfilm)*

    Coroner's Records, New York City (Manhattan), 1862–1864, 1868–1874 [Reel SCW-6], 1874–1918 [Reels CQ]

12. <u>Maps</u>: An extensive collection of maps including:

    Queens Assembly District, 1945–1948, 1957, 1965 and 1977
    Real Estate atlases of Queens, various years from 1890 to 1970
    Belcher Hyde and Sanborn Company maps for various years and neighborhoods (range of years shown): Brooklyn (1898–1913), Queens (1901–1991), Nassau (1909–1953) and Suffolk (1902–1959), showing every structure and address in these counties.
    U.S. Geological Survey maps for all of Long Island, topographical maps, 1900 to date

Long Island maps, including a map of Indian Villages c. 1600 and Hyde's Bicycle Map, c. 1897.
Long Island road and some railroad maps, 1903–1978

13. Genealogies/Family Histories: Approximately 3,500 genealogies and family histories including early Long Island settlers. In addition, the Library's Manuscript collection includes family papers and diaries of many individuals.

14. Passenger Records (on microfilm): Passenger lists of vessels arriving at New York harbor, 1820–1897. Arranged in order of arrival.

Surname index to passenger lists of vessels arriving at New York, 1820–1846. NOTE: See published indexes for the 1846 to June 15, 1897 period.

The Library has the following published indexes:
Migration from the Russian Empire: Lists of Passengers Arriving at the Port of New York, vols 1–6, 1875–1891 [929.347M]
Italians to America: Lists of Passengers Arriving at U.S. Ports, 1880–1899, 12 vols. [929.3089I]
Germans to America: Lists of Passengers Arriving at U.S. Ports, 1840–1845, 1850–1897, 69 vols. [929.3089G]

15. Blue Label Card File: Index cards with genealogical information about Long Island personalities abstracted from newspapers and records. The card file includes information from the 1700s and appears to run to the 1930s.

16. Revolutionary War Soldiers: U.S. Adjutant General's Office general index of Revolutionary War soldiers and sailors showing rank and regiment.

17. Civil War Veterans: The Manuscript collection includes:

Jamaica Post #368, Department of New York Grand Army of the Republic. Includes 59 applications for membership in the organization in the 1890s with age, birth place, occupation, regiment and length of service; membership rolls, 1889–1926; volume listing member deaths in alpha order. Includes unit in which served, length of service, rank, date of death and place of burial; and a list of deceased members compiled c. 1939.
George Huntsman Post #50 of the New York Grand Army of the Republic. Includes 1890s signature book of 75 members including village of residence; roll of members, 1888–1906, with addresses; a roll of deceased members prepared for a Memorial day service (c. 1909) and a Fragmentary Personnel Volume including name, age, birthplace, residence, occupation, residence, date of entry into military service, rank, company, regiment and date of discharge. These papers cover the 1870s through 1915.

18. William A. Eardeley Collection, c. 1920–1929, includes notes on Long Island families including birth, marriage and death dates; notebooks listing tombstone inscriptions from Brooklyn, Queens and Manhattan; listings of deaths from fevers in Manhattan between 1798 and 1822.

19. Exempt Firemen's Association of Queens and Flushing: Queens Collection includes notices of deaths of members, 1944–1947. Flushing Collection includes membership cards, c. 1916–1924.

20. Court Cases: (microfilm)*

The Library has various court records, 1674–1847, for Chancery Court, General Quarter Sessions, Court of Oyer and Terminer, Mayor's Court and the Court of Appeals, Albany, NY. [See Reels AIN, CC, CM and MC of the Queens College, Historical Documents Collection.]

21. Other Materials: Although the emphasis of this collection is on the counties of Long Island, the Library has an extensive collection of materials from other states in the Northeast. Example: The Connecticut State Library, Vital Records, c. 1750–1850 (on microfilm).

22. Cyber Center: In addition to the Internet-access computer in the Long Island Division, the Library has 48 computers on the main floor. Researchers can access the following reference databases of interest to genealogists at these computers:

AP Photo Archive: Associated Press Photo Archive containing 400,000 images, most 1995 to present. Historical images are being scanned in weekly.
Dialog@Carl: Includes c. 115 newspaper/news wire databases.
eLibrary Plus: Provides access to 800 journals, over 150 newspapers, more than 70 television and radio networks, 140,000 photographs and over 2,500 maps.
Ethnic NewsWatch, provides full-text search of c. 200 ethnic and minority newspapers, 1990–.
GaleNet: Includes Biography and Genealogy Master Index.

H.W. Wilson: Includes *Wilson's Biography Plus*, containing more than 46,000 in-depth profiles and hotlinks to related full-text articles. Provides combined coverage of *Current Biography Yearbooks,* 1940 to present; *World Authors; World Artists,* 1950–1990; *World Musicians* and more.

NOTE: An asterisk (*) indicates these items came from the Queens College Historical Documents Collection and can be found among the microfilms of that Collection.

Finding Aids:

The InfoLinQ catalog to the Queens Borough Public Library collection is online. The Long Island Division also has a card catalog which provides a separate index to community files, periodicals, manuscripts, genealogies and other books. All are indexed alphabetically.

The Long Island Division also has finding aids in binders arranged alphabetically by name for its Manuscript Collection. These are located inside the glass-enclosed area and must be requested from the librarian. A list of these c. 200 Collections is on the website.

The Queens College Historical Documents Collection is not cataloged. However, each microfilm box is labeled.

Description of Facility:

The Long Island Division is located on the second floor of the Library. Researchers must obtain a pass from the Information Desk, located at the front of the main floor. Take the elevator to the second floor. The Division seats 24 people. There are 3 microfilm/microfiche reader/printers available and one computer terminal with internet access. A librarian is available to assist researchers.

Microfilm and microfiche records are in open self-service cabinets providing easy access to researchers. However, the manuscript collection is located in the vault and must be requested from the librarian. See "Restrictions on Use."

The Library's Cyber Center is located on the main floor. Researchers must sign up at the Center for one-hour work sessions. The Business, Science and Technology Reference Desk is also located on the main floor.

Fees/Copies:

There is one photocopy machine in the Long Island Division. Copies cost $.15 per page and can be made by the researcher.

Restrictions on Use:

Materials located in the vault, e.g. original Town records, telephone directories (paper copies) and some biographies, cannot be retrieved on weekends.

Researchers must ask the librarian for the vertical files.

Librarians reserve the right to restrict the photocopying of material based on size, amount, and fragility of the item. Researchers are restricted to 50 copies per day.

Use of the Cyber Center is limited to one hour per day. Sign-in is required.

SURROGATE'S COURT - QUEENS COUNTY
RECORD ROOM

Facility Director: Alice Marie Rice, Chief Clerk
                            Joann Vennetter, Record Room and Microfilm Supervisor

Address: Supreme Court Building, Room 700   ♿
                88-11 Sutphin Boulevard
                Jamaica, NY 11435

                (Cross Streets: 88th and 89th Avenues)

Phone: (718) 520-5051
Fax: none
E-mail: none
Website: see www.courts.state.ny.us

Hours of Operation:

Monday to Friday: 9:00 am to 5:00 pm. Closed for lunch between 1:00 pm and 2:00 pm.
Closed Saturday, Sunday and legal holidays.

Closest Public Transportation and Directions:

See CIVIL COURT OF THE CITY OF NEW YORK - QUEENS COUNTY. Walk one block south from the subway station to the Supreme Court building. Take the elevator to the 7th floor.

Description of Resources:

The Record Room has probate, administration and guardianship records from 1787 to the present. Records, 1962–1985 are on microfiche. Filming of records is on-going.

NOTE: Through 1898, Queens County included what is now Nassau County.

Finding Aids:

The Record Room has alphabetical card indexes for records, 1787 to 1899 and 1900 to 1986. From January 1987 to the present the index is computerized. The card file index, c. 1940–1986, and computer index include name and last address of individual, date of death, type of proceeding filed and file number. Earlier index cards include name, file number and type of proceeding. NOTE: See also NEW YORK PUBLIC LIBRARY, IRMA AND PAUL MILSTEIN DIVISION OF UNITED STATES HISTORY, LOCAL HISTORY AND GENEALOGY and NEW YORK GENEALOGICAL AND BIOGRAPHICAL SOCIETY for published abstracts of wills filed in Queens County.

Description of Facility:

The Record Room is located on the 7th floor in Room 700. This room houses the card indexes. The dark green cabinet on the right wall has the 1787–1899 index cards. The cabinets inside the room hold the 1900–1986 cards. There are 4 computers and 3 microfiche reader/printers. Two 2 staff persons are available to retrieve records. A work table can seat 8 people. Will libers (real estate and personal), 1787 to 1998, are on shelves around the room.

Fees/Copies:

Two photocopy machines are available at \$.15 per page. Copies from microfiche reader/printers are free.

Mail requests cost \$70 for the search of a record by full name (not surname) over 25 years old and \$25 for records under 25 years, plus the cost of copying the record, i.e. \$5 per page for a certified copy. The search fee is not charged if the file number is provided by the researcher. NOTE: Indexes, 1787–1986, are available through any Mormon FAMILY HISTORY CENTER.

Restrictions on Use:

Files of mentally retarded persons, pre-1999 are sealed.

Researchers are required to submit appropriate identification (NYS Driver's License or Attorney's identification) together with the requisition slip when requesting a microfiche file. Requests of more than 10 files by an individual or firm in one day must be approved by the Record Room supervisor.

STATEN ISLAND

(Richmond County)

Staten Island Repositories

REPOSITORY	KEY
Board of Elections, Staten Island	5
Civil Court, Staten Island	1
County Clerk's Office, Staten Island	3
Staten Island Historical Society	6
Staten Island Institute of Arts and Sciences	2
Surrogate's Court, Staten Island	4

approx. 3 miles

0.5 0.25 0 0.5 Miles

BOARD OF ELECTIONS
STATEN ISLAND BOROUGH OFFICE

Facility Director: Barbara Kett, Chief Clerk

Address: 1 Edgewater Plaza, 4th floor &
Staten Island, NY 10305

(Cross Streets: Willow Avenue and Bay Street)

Phone: (718) 876-0079
Fax: (718) 876-0912
E-mail: bkett@boe.nyc.ny.us
Website: www.vote.nyc.ny.us

Hours of Operation:

Monday to Friday: 9:00 am to 5:00 pm. Researchers should arrive by 4:00 pm.

Closed Saturday, Sunday and legal holidays.

Closest Public Transportation:

Ferry: Staten Island Ferry from South Ferry Terminal (Manhattan) to St. George Ferry Terminal (S.I.), <u>and</u>

Bus: S51 from the St. George Ferry Terminal in Staten Island (Ramp B) to Willow Avenue and Bay Street, <u>or</u>

Staten Island Railway: SIR Train from St. George station to Clifton station

Directions:

Take the Staten Island Ferry from the South Ferry Terminal in Manhattan (near the South Ferry station of the #1 or #9 train; the Whitehall Street station of the N or R train; and the Bowling Green station of the #4 or #5 train). Exit the Ferry at the St. George Ferry Terminal in Staten Island. Proceed to Ramp B for the S51 bus to Willow Avenue and Bay Street. Walk one block toward the harbor to reach 1 Edgewater Plaza, a seven-story tan concrete building. Take the elevator to the 4th floor.

Description of Resources:

The Staten Island office has voter registration records from 1957 to the present. For records, 1898–1956, see NEW YORK CITY DEPARTMENT OF RECORDS AND INFORMATION SERVICES, MUNICIPAL ARCHIVES.

Finding Aids:

Active registrations are digitized and available in the Archival Voter Information Data (AVID) system. AVID combined and replaced the older Election Administration System (EASY Screens), a computerized database which was previously accessible to the public, and SCRIBE, the digitized copy of the voter application ("buff" card) and record previously accessible to staff only. The EASY system was implemented in Staten Island in 1987. SCRIBE was implemented in 1992. As a result, data on voters active in 1987 or who registered 1987 or later are in the AVID system. Digitized copies of records of voters still active in 1992 or who applied 1992 or later can also be seen in AVID. A search may be made by surname or address. The AVID system can access records from all boroughs. NOTE: Borough offices implemented these systems over a range of years, i.e. EASY (1985–1987), SCRIBE (1991–1993).

Canceled Staten Island records, 1957–1998, are on microfilm arranged by groups of years and then alphabetically. Original copies (active and canceled) "buff" cards, 1957 to 1995 and paper registrations, 1995 to the present are also available. Paper records and microfilm of Staten Island records are available in the Staten Island office only.

Description of Facility:

This is a NYC government office. There are 4 computer terminals with access to AVID and one microfilm reader.

Fees/Copies:

There is no charge for using the AVID system or viewing microfilm records in person. Photocopies of records are $.25 per page. The office will charge a $3 search fee for mail requests.

Restrictions on Use: None.

CIVIL COURT OF THE CITY OF NEW YORK
STATEN ISLAND (RICHMOND COUNTY

Facility Director:	Lorraine Stergious, Clerk of the County
Address:	927 Castleton Avenue ♿
	Staten Island, NY 10310
	(Cross Streets: Bement and Oakland Avenues)
Phone:	(718) 390-5417
Fax:	(718) 390-8108
E-mail:	none
Website:	www.courts.state.ny.us

Hours of Operation:

Monday to Friday: 9:00 am to 5:00 pm

Closed Saturday, Sunday and legal holidays.

Closest Public Transportation:

Ferry: Staten Island Ferry from South Ferry Terminal (Manhattan), <u>and</u>

Bus: S44 or S46 to Castleton and Bement Avenues

Directions:

Take the Staten Island Ferry from the South Ferry Terminal in Manhattan (near the South Ferry station of the #1 or #9 train; the Whitehall Street station of the N or R train; or the Bowling Green station of the #4 or #5 train). At the St. George Ferry Terminal in Staten Island, go to Bus Ramp C for the S46 (Castleton Avenue) bus or Bus Ramp D for the S44 (Henderson Avenue) bus to Castleton and Bement Avenues. Enter the court house and go down the stairs to the Record Room. NOTE: For direct wheelchair access to the record room, enter via Bement Avenue (around the corner). If the door is locked, ring the bell.

Description of Resources:

The Court has name change records for individuals who legally changed their names in Staten Island from 1927 to the present.

See also COUNTY CLERK'S OFFICE - STATE SUPREME COURT, RICHMOND COUNTY for name changes recorded in State Supreme Court.

Finding Aids:

Indexes to name change records, 1927–1998, are in ledgers in groups of years, alphabetized by the old name. Ledger, 1938–1962, is arranged also by new name for the early years. A computerized index is available from 1999 to the present. A search can be made by old or new name for this period.

Description of Facility:

The ledger indexes and records are stored in the basement of the Civil Court building. A public-access computer is available at the far end of the counter. The clerks on duty can assist researchers.

Fees/Copies:

A photocopy machine is located in the Record Room. Copies cost $.15 per page. Certified copies of records cost $5 per document. Only certified copies are provided in response to mail requests. Send a money order or certified check. Personal checks are not accepted. Include a self-addressed stamped envelope.

Restrictions on Use:

None. All records are located on-site.

COUNTY CLERK'S OFFICE - STATE SUPREME COURT
RICHMOND COUNTY (STATEN ISLAND)

Facility Director: Stephen J. Fiala, County Clerk
John Mansfield, Administrator
Felix Torres, Microfilm Supervisor
Maria Riccardi, Register Supervisor

Address: 130 Stuyvesant Place, 2nd Floor ♿
Staten Island, NY 10301

(Cross Streets: Schuyler and Hyatt Streets)

Phone: (718) 390-5389 (Law and Equity)
(718) 390-5386 (Real Property records)
(718) 390-5393 (Administrator's Office)
(718) 876-5893 (Microfilm unit)
Fax: (718) 390-8741
E-mail: none
Website: see www.courts.state.ny.us

Hours of Operation:

Monday to Friday: 9:00 am to 5:00 pm
Closed Saturday, Sunday and legal holidays.

Closest Public Transportation:

Ferry: Staten Island ferry from South Ferry Terminal (Manhattan) to St. George Ferry Terminal (Staten Island)

Directions:

Take the Staten Island Ferry from the South Ferry Terminal in Manhattan (near the South Ferry station of the #1 or #9 train; the Whitehall Street station of the N or R train; and the Bowling Green station of the #4 or #5 train). Exit the Ferry at the St. George Ferry Terminal in Staten Island. Cross Richmond Terrace and go up the steps* between the old Court House and Borough Hall emerging on Stuyvesant Place. 130 Stuyvesant Place is the green glass building across from the old Court House. *NOTE: The building is wheelchair accessible, however, the streets from the ferry go uphill. Do not use the ramp from Richmond Terrace. It does not lead to Stuyvesant Place.

Description of Resources:

The County Clerk's Office in Staten Island also performs the functions of the City Register's Office in recording real property instruments. The Office has deposited many of its old records with the NEW YORK CITY DEPARTMENT OF RECORDS AND INFORMATION SERVICES, MUNICIPAL ARCHIVES. Where this is the case, it is so noted. Some County records are also at the STATEN ISLAND HISTORICAL SOCIETY and the STATEN ISLAND INSTITUTE OF ARTS AND SCIENCES. The following records are at the County Clerk's Office:

1. Naturalizations (microfilm) include Petitions filed in County, Circuit and State Supreme Courts of Richmond County, 1869–1959 and Declarations of Intention, 1875–1961. Prior to 1907, most Petitions were filed in Richmond County Court. Petitions, 1907–1959, including Military Petitions, 1918–1924, were filed in State Supreme Court, Richmond County.

   NOTE: Petition volume 77 (with 14 Petitions, 1959/1960) and Declaration volume 1 (with 100 Declarations, 1907) are missing. The Office has 3 petitions filed in 1820, 1840 and 1864 respectively. These were filmed by the Mormon Family History Library together with the 1869–1906 Petitions and labeled "1820–1906."

   After 1960, Staten Island residents were naturalized in U.S. DISTRICT COURT of either the Southern or Eastern Districts. The NATIONAL ARCHIVES, NORTHEAST REGION has dexigraph copies of pre-September 1906 Naturalizations. See also NEW YORK CITY DEPARTMENT OF RECORDS AND INFORMATION SERVICES, MUNICIPAL ARCHIVES for Naturalization records from this office. The Mormon Family History Library has microfilmed Petitions, through 1924, and index to 1906.

2. <u>Census Records</u> (microfilm) for Richmond County include the U.S. Census, 1860 and 1870 (incomplete), and 1880; and the New York State Census, Richmond County, 1855 and 1865 (incomplete), 1875, 1915 and 1925.

   NOTE: See also NEW YORK PUBLIC LIBRARY, MILSTEIN DIVISION OF UNITED STATES HISTORY, LOCAL HISTORY AND GENEALOGY, and NEW YORK GENEALOGICAL AND BIOGRAPHICAL SOCIETY for these Census records; and STATEN ISLAND INSTITUTE OF ARTS AND SCIENCES for all but 1925. NYS Census records for Richmond County are available also at the NEW YORK STATE DEPARTMENT OF EDUCATION, NEW YORK STATE LIBRARY. Original copies of Census records formerly in this Office (in very poor condition) are now at the NEW YORK CITY DEPARTMENT OF RECORDS AND INFORMATION SERVICES, MUNICIPAL ARCHIVES.

3. <u>Court Cases</u> brought against an individual or actions filed by an individual, 1947 to the present. Cases filed 1947–1990 are on microfiche. The Office also has the records of the Court of Common Pleas, 1711–1833, on microfilm. For other Court records, 1706–1947, see NEW YORK CITY DEPARTMENT OF RECORDS AND INFORMATION SERVICES, MUNICIPAL ARCHIVES.

4. <u>Real Property Records</u> (deeds, mortgages, maps) recorded in Richmond County (Staten Island), 1683 to the present.

5. <u>Matrimonial Records</u>: Divorces, separations and annulments, 1934 to the present. See "Restrictions on Use."

   For earlier records, 1861–1933, see the NEW YORK CITY DEPARTMENT OF RECORDS AND INFORMATION SERVICES, MUNICIPAL ARCHIVES.

6. <u>Military Discharge Records</u> (microfilm) 1917 to the present, for veterans who filed a copy of a DD 214 form (discharge papers) in this Office.

7. <u>Business Records</u> including:

   Certificates of Incorporation, 1930 to the present
   Assumed Names (Trade Names, Doing Business As...) 1900 to present
   Limited Partnerships, 1930–June, 1991

   See NEW YORK CITY DEPARTMENT OF RECORDS AND INFORMATION SERVICES, MUNICIPAL ARCHIVES for Certificates of Incorporation, 1848–1929; and NYS DEPARTMENT OF STATE, DIVISION OF CORPORATIONS for limited partnerships, July 1, 1991 to present.

8. <u>Surrenders of Children</u>: Duplicate orders issued by the Surrogate's Court for Surrenders of Children are filed in the County Clerk's Office. See "Restrictions on Use."

9. <u>Name Changes</u> for individuals whose names were legally changed in State Supreme Court, Richmond County, 1930 to the present. This Office also has copies of final orders for Name Changes filed in Civil Court, Richmond County.

   For earlier records, 1840–1929, see NEW YORK CITY DEPARTMENT OF RECORDS AND INFORMATION SERVICES, MUNICIPAL ARCHIVES.

10. <u>Incompetency Records, Conservatorships and Guardianships</u>:

    Incompetency Records, 1930 to present
    Conservatorship Records, 1930–1993
    Guardianships, 1993 to present

    See NEW YORK CITY DEPARTMENT OF RECORDS AND INFORMATION SERVICES, MUNICIPAL ARCHIVES for earlier records, 1840–1929.

Finding Aids:

1. <u>Naturalizations</u>: The Office has the original card index, 1820–1906 (all but 3, 1869–1906), arranged alphabetically by surname. Liber indexes (2 volumes), arranged alphabetically by the first two letters of the surname and the first letter of the first name, are available for 1907–1931 and 1932–1960. These indexes are located in the Microfilm Unit office on the 2nd floor.

   Naturalization records (microfilm) are located behind the counter across from the Microfilm Unit office. However, requests to use these records are made in the Microfilm Unit office. Original record libers in the basement Record Room are not accessible to researchers.

   <u>Declarations of Intention</u>: one volume, 1875–1902 has no index. Three Declaration volumes for an overlapping period, 1884–1906, are indexed alphabetically by the first letter of the surname at the front of each volume. Declarations, 1907–1961, are indexed together with Petitions in the two libers described above.

2. <u>Census Records</u> were enumerated by Wards or AD/ED for NYS 20th century censuses. This Office has Ward maps for 1874, 1898, 1907 and 1917. Microfilm can be requested at the counter opposite the Microfilm Unit office. See also STATEN ISLAND INSTITUTE OF ARTS AND SCIENCES for additional Ward maps.

3. <u>Court Cases</u> and <u>Matrimonial Records</u>: For 1830–1832 and 1930–1992, liber indexes (<u>Index to Rule Book</u>) are available for <u>Court Cases</u>. Divorces and annulments (also known as Matrimonial cases) were indexed together with other court cases until 1974. There is no special case number designation to identify Matrimonial cases filed during this period. From 1974–1992, there are separate Matrimonial ledgers arranged in groups of years and alphabetically by the first letter of the surname. Separations were indexed separately, 1966–1974. From 1974–1992, they were indexed with other Matrimonial records. See "Restrictions on Use." These index ledgers, except 1830–1832, are located on the first floor Law and Equity Room 103. The 1830–1832 <u>Rule Book</u> index is in the basement. The index to <u>Court Cases</u>, 1993 to the present, is on a dedicated computer in the Law and Equity Room. The Office also has a computerized index to <u>Matrimonial Cases</u>, 1993 to the present, but it is not accessible to the public.

   NOTE: An index to all pending Richmond County (Staten Island) Supreme Court <u>Civil Cases</u> requiring judicial intervention ("RJI") is available on the NYS Unified Court System CaseTrac website. See COUNTY CLERK'S OFFICE, NEW YORK COUNTY for a description. Digitized copies of decisions are not yet available online for Richmond county. The online index to <u>Criminal Cases</u> can be searched only by case number. Unfortunately, cases are removed from both these online indexes two weeks after they close.

4. <u>Real Property Records</u>: Deeds recorded from May 1683 to October 1973 and from July 1986 to the present are indexed in libers by both grantor and grantee. These libers are arranged by groups of years and alphabetically by surname. The grantor/grantee indexes for deeds recorded between October 1981 and July 1986 are on microfiche. There is no grantor/grantee index for the period October 1973 to September 1981.

   Liber indexes for mortgagor/mortgagee from 1683 to September 1975 and from July 1986 to the present are arranged alphabetically by surname. Mortgagor/mortgagee indexes for mortgages recorded October 1981–July 1986 are on microfiche. There is no mortgagor/mortgagee index for the period September 1975 to September 1981.

   The above alphabetical indexes are the only indexes available for instruments filed pre-1923.

   Deeds and mortgages filed from <u>1923 to September 1981</u> are indexed also by Land Map Block and lot number. These numbers can be obtained by consulting a map in this office. (The index for this period is located in Section 4 opposite the counter on the 2nd floor.)

   Deeds and mortgages filed from <u>October 1, 1981 to October 16, 1986</u> are filed by Tax Block and lot numbers. These records are on microfiche. (Original binders are located in Section 3 but their use is not recommended.)

   Deeds and mortgages filed <u>after October 16, 1986</u> are indexed in computer printouts arranged by both Tax Block and lot numbers and grantor/grantee. NOTE: See the staff behind the counter in Room 201 for information recorded in the last month. (Printouts for 1986–1996 are located in Section 2; 1997 to present are located in Section 1.) Public access computers are available in the search area.

5. <u>Military Discharge Records</u>: Discharges pre-1945, are indexed alphabetically by first letter of the surname at the front of the record volume. There are separate liber indexes for records filed, 1945–1968 and 1969 to the present, available in the Microfilm Unit office. These are arranged also by first letter of the surname.

6. <u>Business Records</u>: The Office has index libers for Assumed Names from 1900–1991; and Certificates of Incorporations, 1881–1991, located in the first floor, Law and Equity Room 103. These indexes are arranged alphabetically by the first letter of the company's name. NOTE: Volume 1 of the Assumed Name index (1900–1930) is behind the counter. Limited Partnerships are indexed together with Assumed Names. A computerized index, 1992 to the present, is available on a dedicated computer in the Law and Equity Room.

   See also NYS DEPARTMENT OF STATE, DIVISION OF CORPORATIONS' statewide online index for corporations and limited partnerships active on or after December 5, 1977.

7. <u>Surrenders of Children</u>: See "Restrictions on Use."

8. <u>Name Changes</u>, <u>Incompetency Records</u> and <u>Conservatorship Records</u> filed in State Supreme Court can be found in the <u>Special Proceedings</u> ledger indexes, 1913–1927 (in the basement) and 1930–1992 (in Room 103). These indexes are arranged by groups of years and the first letter of the surname. <u>Name Changes</u> filed in Civil Court but recorded here can be found in the <u>Miscellaneous</u> ledger indexes, 1945 to present. The index for <u>Court Cases</u>, including <u>Name Changes,</u> 1993 to the present, is accessible on a dedicated computer in the Law and Equity Room.

Description of Facility:

The County Clerk's Office is on the first (ground) and second floors of 130 Stuyvesant Place. Law and Equity Room 103 on the first floor houses <u>Court Cases</u>, 1990 to the present, <u>Matrimonial Cases</u> (all), <u>Name Changes</u> filed in State Supreme Court and <u>Business Records</u>, (Assumed Names from September 1994 to present; and all other Business Records). <u>Court Cases</u>, 3–4 years old are located behind the counter. Records older than 4 years but filed after 1990 are stored in the basement and retrieved twice daily — at 11:00 am and 3:00 pm. <u>Court Cases</u>, 1947–1990, (microfiche) and <u>Business Records,</u> Assumed names, pre-September 1994 (microfilm) can be requested at the counter on the 2nd floor (Room 201).

Room 201 on the second floor houses all records on microfilm/microfiche and <u>Real Estate</u> records, 1683 to 1836 (microfilm) and 1836 to the present (paper copy). Microfilmed Real Estate records (pre-1836) are located in the Microfilm Unit office opposite the Microfilm counter. Index libers are on shelves marked "Section 1" to "Section 4" opposite the counters. Microfiche indexes, 1981 to 1986, can be requested at the Microfilm counter. For assistance with Real Estate records, check with the staff at the Register Department counter (far left of the entrance to the second floor). Deeds and mortgage record libers are on shelves or under the counters in Room 201 and extending the full length of the room to the left.

<u>Military Records</u> and liber indexes are located in the Microfilm Unit office.

There is seating for 4 researchers on the first floor and 3-4 researchers on the 2nd floor. Most work is done at standing counters. There are 3 microfiche/microfilm readers of which 2 are reader/printers on the 2nd floor.

Fees/Copies:

The office has 4 photocopy machines at $.25 per page. One is located on the first floor, one at each end of the 2nd floor and the remaining 2 are near the microfilm machines at the entrance to Room 201 on the 2nd floor. Microfilm and microfiche copies cost $.25 per page. There is no charge for copies of Naturalization or Census records unless a certified copy is requested. Certified copies cost $8 per document (regardless of the number of pages).

Restrictions on Use:

Many older records have been moved to the NEW YORK CITY DEPARTMENT OF RECORDS AND INFORMATION SERVICES, MUNICIPAL ARCHIVES. The Microfilm Unit office has an inventory list of the records in the MUNICIPAL ARCHIVES. The ARCHIVES does <u>not</u> have indexes to the records deposited with them. The only indexes available are those located in the Richmond County Clerk's Office.

Pre-1930 indexes for <u>Court Cases</u> (including <u>Matrimonials</u>) and indexes for <u>Special Proceedings</u> (including <u>Name Changes</u>, <u>Incompetency Records</u> and <u>Conservatorships</u>), pre-1913 and 1928–1929, cannot be located. The records (but not the indexes) for this period were transferred to the NEW YORK CITY DEPARTMENT OF RECORDS AND INFORMATION SERVICES, MUNICIPAL ARCHIVES.

<u>Matrimonial Records</u> are closed to the public for 100 years. These records may be viewed by the parties or their representatives. Available indexes are open to the public. <u>Surrenders of Children</u> records are also closed to the public and may not be examined without a court order. The actual case files and indexes are in the Surrogate's Court. These too are closed to the public.

The Office does not have sufficient staff to respond to mail inquiries.

STATEN ISLAND HISTORICAL SOCIETY
LIBRARY

Facility Director:	Elisabeth Sommer, Director, Research and Interpretation
	Carlotta DeFillo, Curatorial Assistant
Address:	P.S. 28
	276 Center Street
	Staten Island, NY
	(Cross Street: St. Patrick's Place)
Mail Address:	441 Clarke Avenue
	Staten Island, NY 10306
Phone:	(718) 351-1611, 1617 (Ext. 299)
Fax:	(718) 351-2352
E-mail:	sihs-esommer@si.rr.com
Website:	www.historicrichmondtown.org

Hours of Operation:

Tuesday: By appointment only.
The Library/Archives is closed Monday, Wednesday to Sunday and all legal holidays.

Closest Public Transportation:

Ferry: Staten Island Ferry from South Ferry Terminal (Manhattan), <u>and,</u>

Bus: S74 to St. Patrick's Place and Richmond Road

Directions:

See COUNTY CLERK'S OFFICE -STATE SUPREME COURT, RICHMOND COUNTY. Go up Bus Ramp B for the S74 bus to St. Patrick's Place/Richmond Road (Historic Richmond Town). Walk one block up the hill to the former school building (P.S. 28) which is now the Staten Island Historical Society Library. Use the stairs to the right. If the door is locked, ring the bell on the wall.

Description of Resources:

The Society's Library houses 1,200 cu. ft. of historic manuscripts and archival material and more than 15,000 books. The collection includes:

1. <u>Photographs</u>: More than 50,000 historic photographs of Staten Island scenes, buildings, portraits of Staten Island residents and personnel of the Volunteer Fire Departments.

2. <u>Staten Island Card Indexes</u>: covering thousands of people (94 drawers). These include vital records of Staten Island created as part of a Works Progress Administration (WPA) effort in the 1940s. The index cards include information about Staten Island families taken from wills, letters of administration, guardianships, deeds, mortgages, church records, tombstones, family bibles, newspaper articles, death notices and other published sources. Separate card indexes are available here for occupations, place names, road records and Black history on Staten Island.

   NOTE: The vital records index was microfilmed by the Mormon Family History Library in 1967 [Films #539053–#539071, *Index and genealogical data cards: births, deaths, marriages, baptisms, deeds, mortgages and other records from Staten Island and at the Historical Society...*]

3. <u>Biographical and Genealogical Correspondence Files</u>: The Library has files arranged by family name including correspondence on Staten Island families, genealogies, family records and news clippings. In addition, the Library has a collection of genealogies, some with dates from the late 1600s. NOTE: These are arranged alphabetically and were microfilmed by the Mormon Family History Library in 1967 [Films #509177–#509185, *Family Genealogies from the Staten Island Historical Society...*]. Genealogies received by the Staten Island Historical Society after 1967 are not included in these films.

4. <u>Manuscript Collection</u>: The Society has 115 processed manuscript collections including the papers of numerous Staten Island organizations, businesses and families, mostly non-Jewish. The exceptions are the Carl Isaacs papers

(1908–1978), which include the papers of Askel Isaacs, first vice president of B'nai Jeshurun Synagogue, and the papers of the Alter Mord family [MS-78]. The Society also has the Jewish Community Center's publication, *The Bulletin*, 1950–1965 [MS-52]; and records of Fire Departments, 1836–1964. [MS -53]

5 Staten Island Records, 1609–1967, (not indexed) include deeds, wills, marriage and death records, Surrogate Court decrees, patents and military records from various sources including the State Supreme Court (microfilm).

Richmond County public records (1741–1912) from the County Clerk's Office include coroner's reports and police records; fishing, hunting and oystering licenses; maps; and road records. "See Restrictions on Use."

The Society also has typescript abstracts of records including:

Letters of Administration of Richmond County, NY, 1787–1865, also Guardianship Papers, 1802–1865: Originals on file Surrogate's Office, St. George, Staten Island, NY, compiled by Frances S. Fast. 1941.

Index, Part I, Wills of Richmond County, NY, 1787–1863; and Index, Part 2, Letters of Administration and Guardianship, Richmond County, NY.

Wills of Richmond County, NY, 1787–1863: Originals on file Surrogate's Office, St. George, Staten Island, NY, compiled by Frances S. Fast. 1941.

Staten Island Patents taken from Certified Copies in the Possession of the Lancaster-Symes Foundation: Originals in State Building, Albany, NY, transcribed by Marion Bibb. 2 vols., 1937.

6. Staten Island Newspaper: The collection includes the WPA typescript, *Newspaper Items Relating to Staten Island, May 2, 1726 to December 20, 1890.* 4 vols. [Staten Island], 1935–1937. Articles abstracted were from newspapers in collections of New York Public Library and New-York Historical Society. Most were not Staten Island papers. The Society's vital records index includes items about people found in this typescript. NOTE: See also Mormon Family History Library, *Staten Island Newspaper Items, 1726–1890* [Film #509189].

In addition, the Society has the following Staten Island newspapers (microfilm) in its collection:

Daily Advance, 1917–1920   *Richmond County Democrat,* 1881–1892
Richmond County Advance, 1886–1918   *Staten Island Gazette and Sentinel,* 1859–1887

7. Hessian Revolutionary War Diaries (1776–1784): Microfilm copies of daybooks of Hessian regiments stationed on Staten Island. (Originals are in Marburg State Archive, Germany). The Society has typed transcripts of two daybooks: *Minnigerode Journal, 1776–1784* [973.342-M] and *Lossberg Journal, 1776–1783.* [973.342-L]

8. Maps: Printed, photocopied and manuscript maps of Staten Island from the 18th to 20th centuries.

9. Nursery School Records: Records and photographs from the Port Richmond Day Nursery (1906–1948), the Cradle Roll Nursery (1920–1938) and the West Brighton Day Nursery (1940).

10. Funeral Home Records: Records of the Connell Funeral Home (1907–1936).

11. Military Records: Register of all men from Staten Island who served in World War I.

12. Richmond County Public Records, 1741–1912. Include records from the County Clerk's Office such as coroner's reports and police records; fishing, hunting and oystering licenses; and road records. "See Restrictions on Use."

Finding Aids:

In addition to card file indexes, there are finding aids for many manuscript/archival collections in binders.

Description of Facility:

The Society is housed in the former P.S. 28 school building and is located on the grounds of Historic Richmond Town. The Library/Archives Room is on the first floor. Seating is available for 2 researchers.

Fees/Copies:

One microfilm reader (no printer) and one photocopy machine are available at $.25 per page. SIHS membership starts at $25 per year (individual) and $35 (family). Members receive the *Staten Island Historian,* free general admission to Historic Richmond Town, discounts on most programs and a 10% discount on Museum Store purchases.

Restrictions on Use:

In very few instances the Archivist may determine that records cannot be viewed for reasons of confidentiality or condition. Richmond County Public Records described above have not been cataloged and are currently inaccessible.

STATEN ISLAND INSTITUTE OF ARTS AND SCIENCES
HISTORY ARCHIVES AND LIBRARY

Facility Director: Patricia M. Salmon, Curator of History

Address: 75 Stuyvesant Place
Staten Island, NY 10301-1998

(Cross Streets: Wall Street and Hamilton Avenue)

NOTE: The Staten Island Institute of Arts and Sciences has begun a building campaign for the Museum and archives/library to move to larger quarters. Check address before visiting.

Phone:	(718) 727-1135, ext. 20
Fax:	(718) 273-5683
E-mail:	Salmonf@aol.com
Website:	www.siiasmuseum.org

Hours of Operation:

Tuesday, Wednesday, Thursday: 10:00 am to 4:00 pm for research purposes (by appointment only)
Closed Saturday, Sunday, and legal holidays.

Closest Public Transportation and Directions:

See COUNTY CLERK'S OFFICE - STATE SUPREME COURT, RICHMOND COUNTY. The archives and library are located at 51 Stuyvesant Place. Continue down Stuyvesant Place passing the SIIAS museum at #75 until reaching #51, next door. Enter through the door marked "District Health Center" (not "Borough Offices"). Take the elevator to the SIIAS offices in the basement. NOTE: Wheelchair users can use the ramp on the right side of the building to gain entry to the lobby.

Description of Resources:

The Institute was founded in 1881, houses an archives and library of more than 55,000 historical photographs, 3,000 maps and atlases, 15,000 books and many oral histories relating to Staten Island history. The following materials are of particular interest to genealogists:

1. Newspapers (on microfilm)

Richmond Argus, 1902–1904	*Staten Island* Advance, 1947–1994
Richmond County Free Press, 1834–1835	*Staten Island Gazette,* 1903–1904
Richmond County Gazette, 1860–1891	*Staten Island Independent,* 1894–1896, 1898–1900
Richmond County Mirror, 1837–1839	*Staten Island World,* 1902–1904
Richmond County Sentinel, 1876–1879, 1886–1889	*The Sepoy,* 1859–1860
	The Staaten Islander, 1856–1857
Richmond County Standard, 1882–1895, 1901	*The Staten Islander,* 1886–1927, 1934
Richmond Republican, 1827–1834	*Times-Transcript,* 1927–1941

   In addition, the Institute has a newspaper clipping file arranged by name and subject from 1910 to the present.

2. Architectural Survey Collection: Includes photographs and maps of Staten Island. This survey, conducted between 1975 and 1980 documents the architecture, building by building, of most of the north shore and parts of the south shore of Staten Island.

3. Biographies Collection: Letters, clippings, photographs and other biographical data on Staten Islanders compiled by William T. Davis and Charles Leng for their book, *Staten Island and its People.*

   In addition, the Institute has numerous collections of family papers, photographs and genealogies of Staten Island families. While mostly non-Jewish, the collection includes information on Isaac Abraham Almstaedt (Almstead).

4. Military Records Collection: Muster rolls of the Revolutionary War, 1776–1779; muster rolls of the Staten Island Militia, 1800–1814 and 1848; and Civil War enlistment records.

5. Photograph Collection: More than 55,000 photographs of people, Staten Island scenes, buildings, churches and cemeteries from the late 1800s to the present. Includes Cleaves, Crooke, Davis, Hoyer and Loeffler Collections.

6. <u>Richmond County Records</u>: Includes photocopies of the Supervisors* Book, 1766–1823; proceedings of the Board of Supervisors, 1877–1897; Justice of the Peace dockets, 1706–1896; and County Coroner papers, 1787 and 1879. Also included is an inventory of County and borough archives, 1940 and 1942.

   *Until 1898, the County was governed by a Board of Supervisors.

7. <u>Maps and Atlases</u>: Includes insurance atlases for Staten Island, 1874, 1878 and 1917–1935. Printed and photocopied maps are also available here.

8. <u>City Directories</u> (Business and Residential)

   Richmond County Directory, 1862
   Handbook of the Staten Island Railroad, 1870
   Webb's Consolidated Directory of the North and South Shore of Staten Island, 1882/83, 1884
   Standard Directory of Richmond County, 1893/94
   Standard Directory of Richmond Borough, 1897/98
   Industries of Staten Island Before Consolidation, 1898
   Trow's Business and Residential Directory of the Borough of Richmond, 1899, 1900
   Richmond Borough Directory, 1912
   Staten Island Advance Business and Telephone Directory, 1921/22, 1922/23
   Polk's Directory of Staten Island, 1933/34

9. <u>Census</u>: The Institute has the U.S. Census for Richmond County, 1800–1880, 1900–1920; and the NYS Census for Richmond County, 1835, 1855, 1865, 1875 and 1915. Ward maps are available for 1898, 1907 and 1917 (volumes 1 and 2).

   See COUNTY CLERK'S OFFICE - STATE SUPREME COURT, RICHMOND COUNTY (STATEN ISLAND) for the 1925 census as well as some of the above.

10. <u>Oral History Special Collection</u> collects and produces both video and audio taped testimonies central to the Institute's mission. Interviews are conducted with elderly residents of Staten Island from various occupations and communities.

Finding Aids:

The Institute has typewritten and computerized guides to its collections. Indexes are available for the following newspapers: *Richmond County Gazette, Richmond County Mirror, Richmond County Sentinel, Richmond Republican, The Sepoy* and *The Staaten Islander*. Indexes are available for some years for the *Richmond Standard* (1887–1894), *Staten Island Independent* (1898–1900), *The Staten Islander* (1934) and the *Staten Island World*.

Description of Facility:

The Archives/Library are not in the main building but are located next door, at 51 Stuyvesant Place, in the basement of the District Health Center. There is one staff person to assist researchers. Space is available for 2 researchers at one time. There is one microfilm reader/printer.

Fees/Copies:

There is a $7.50 research fee for non-members (students and senior citizens, $5; commercial users, $15). A photocopy machine is available at $.25 per page (up to 11"x 17") and $.30 for 11"x 17". Copies from the microfilm reader/printer arc $.50 per page. Research conducted by the Institute's Research Assistant cost $15 per hour (non-members) and $7.50 per hour (members). Add $5 postage and handling. Payment should be made after a bill is received. Individual membership is $35 or $25 for seniors (65+), students, artists and educators; family membership is $50.

Copies of photographs start from $40 for an 8"x 10" black and white print with existing negative. Color transparencies start at $150 for an existing transparency, 4"x 5". Color transparencies for publication purposes are provided for a 3-month rental period only. Color slides, 35mm, start at $15 for an existing slide. Add $5 for postage and handling. A complete list of charges is available at the Institute.

Pre-payment is required for all requests. Payments by check or money order must be drawn on a U.S. bank. Visa and Master Card are accepted. Requests are processed within 3-4 weeks. No date of delivery is guaranteed. For "rush service" (one week turn around), the cost of item(s) requested is doubled.

Restrictions on Use:

Researchers must explain intended use in writing when requesting permission to use Institute materials.

SURROGATE'S COURT - RICHMOND COUNTY (STATEN ISLAND) RECORD ROOM

Facility Director: Ronald M. Cerrachio, Chief Clerk

Address: County Court House &
18 Richmond Terrace, Room 201
Staten Island, NY 10301

(Cross Street: Schuyler Street. Opposite the Ferry Terminal.)

Phone: (718) 390-5400
Fax: (718) 390-8741
E-mail: none
Website: see www.courts.state.ny.us

Hours of Operation:

Monday to Friday: 10:00 am to 4:00 pm.
Record Room B-3 is closed between 1:00 pm and 2:00 pm.

Closed Saturday, Sunday and legal holidays.

Closest Public Transportation and Directions:

See COUNTY CLERK'S OFFICE - STATE SUPREME COURT, RICHMOND COUNTY (STATEN ISLAND). The County Court House is across from the Ferry Terminal in Staten Island and to the right of Borough Hall. To reach the Surrogate's Court Record Room, B-3, take the elevator to the Basement level. See COUNTY CLERK'S OFFICE for wheelchair accessibility.

Description of Resources:

The Surrogate's Court in Staten Island (Richmond County) has files 1787 to the present for probate and administration; and records of surrenders of children and adoptions from 1927. Guardianship files start in 1918. All closed guardianship files and probate files pre-1947 are on microfiche. See SURROGATE'S COURT - NEW YORK COUNTY (MANHATTAN) for a detailed description of these records.

Finding Aids:

The office has an index card file arranged alphabetically by surname, 1960 to the present. Earlier Probate and Administration records, 1787–1959, are indexed in two sets of libers by the first 2 letters of the surname. The index from 1992 to the present has been computerized. A public access computer is available in the Surrogate's Court office on the second floor, Room 201.

NOTE: See also STATEN ISLAND HISTORICAL SOCIETY, NEW YORK PUBLIC LIBRARY, IRMA AND PAUL MILSTEIN DIVISION OF UNITED STATES HISTORY, LOCAL HISTORY AND GENEALOGY and NEW YORK GENEALOGICAL AND BIOGRAPHICAL SOCIETY for published abstracts of wills, and letters of administrations filed in Richmond County (Staten Island).

Description of Facility:

The Record Room has seating available for 6 researchers. All records are on-site. There is one full-time and one part-time clerk who pull files.

Fees/Copies:

Two photocopy machines are available in the Record Room B-3 at $.15 per page. A microfiche reader/printer is available at $.25 per page. Certified copies are $5 per page.

Requests by mail which require a search (i.e. case number is not provided) cost $25 if the case is under 25 years old and $70 if the case is over 25 years, plus the $5 per page fee for copies. Uncertified copies can be mailed if the precise number of pages are identified.

Personal checks are not accepted.

Restrictions on Use:

Files on adoptions, surrenders of children and guardianship are closed to the public.

ALBANY

Albany Repositories

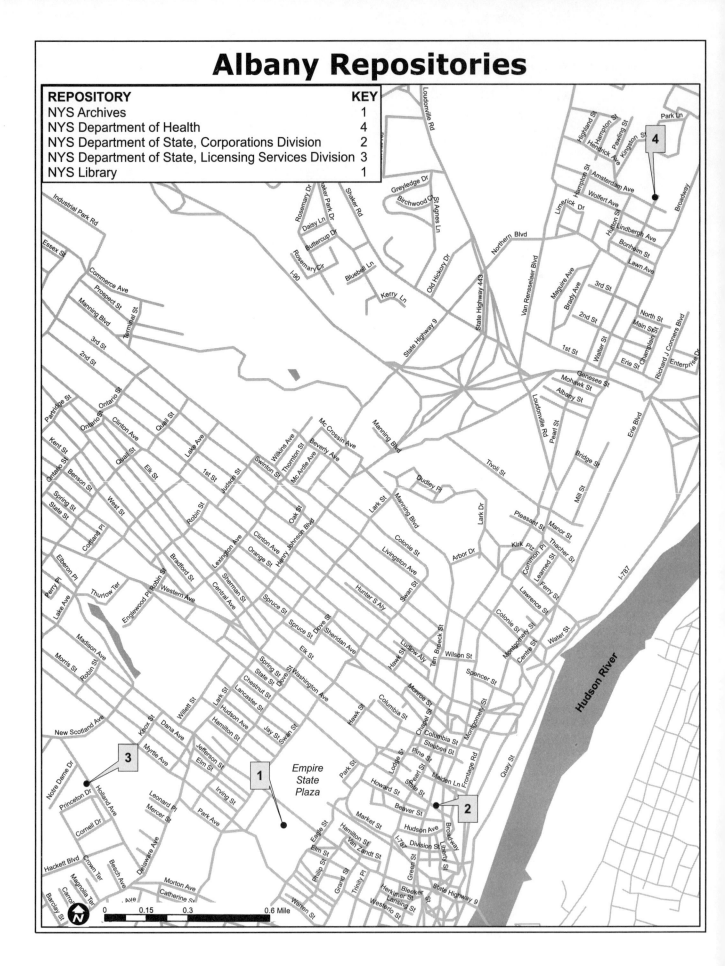

REPOSITORY	KEY
NYS Archives	1
NYS Department of Health	4
NYS Department of State, Corporations Division	2
NYS Department of State, Licensing Services Division	3
NYS Library	1

NEW YORK STATE DEPARTMENT OF EDUCATION
NEW YORK STATE ARCHIVES

Facility Director: Christine W. Ward, Acting State Archivist

Address: Cultural Education Center, 11th floor. ♿ [NOTE: Temporary location, 3rd floor to 2004.]
Empire State Plaza
Albany, NY 12230

(Cross Street: Madison Avenue)

Phone: (518) 474-8955
Fax: (518) 473-9985
E-mail: archref@mail.nysed.gov
Website: www.sara.nysed.gov

Hours of Operation:

Monday to Friday: 9:00 am to 5:00 pm.
Closed Saturday, Sunday and legal holidays. NOTE: A seat reservation must be made in advance. Call or email.

Closest Public Transportation:

Train: Amtrak to Albany (station in Rensselaer)
Bus: Greyhound or Trailways to Albany
CDTA buses: 3, 14, 15, 21X, 22, 23, 24, 30, 32, 33, 33X, 35X, 55X

Directions:

Take an Amtrak train to Albany. The station is across the Hudson River in Rensselaer. From the train station, take CDTA bus #14 or a taxi to the Empire State Plaza. The Cultural Education Center is at the south end of the Plaza, across Madison Avenue (Route 20). (The train ride takes 2 ½ hours from Manhattan. Ask for round trip excursion fare.) See the website at www.nysl.nysed.gov/locpar_ce.htm for driving and parking information.

Description of Resources:

The State Archives was created in 1971. At present, the Archives maintains approximately 74,000 cubic feet of Colonial and State government records including legislative and judicial records. The following records are of interest to genealogists. [Use of items noted with an "(R)" are restricted. Researchers who wish to view these records should contact the Archives in advance.]

1. Vital Records: Indexes to New York State vital records starting in 1880 (for deaths) and 1881 (for births and marriages) are available as follows:

    Births more than 75 years old
    Deaths and marriages more than 50 years old

    The indexes do not include births and deaths in Albany, Buffalo and Yonkers prior to 1914; or marriages in those cities prior to 1908. For New York City, only Queens and Richmond Counties, 1881–1897; eastern Bronx (part of Westchester County), 1881–1895; and towns in Kings County (Brooklyn), before the annexation to the City of Brooklyn in the 1880s and 1890s, are included in these indexes. See NEW YORK CITY DEPARTMENT OF RECORDS AND INFORMATION SERVICES, MUNICIPAL ARCHIVES for all other pre-1910 birth, pre-1950 death and pre-1952 marriage indexes; or NYPL, MILSTEIN DIVISION OF U.S. HISTORY, LOCAL HISTORY AND GENEALOGY for pre-1983 New York City birth and death indexes. For per-1914 births and deaths and pre-1908 marriages in Albany, Buffalo and Yonkers, contact the City Registrar's Offices in these cities.

    NOTE: New York State vital records indexes are accessible to the public also at the NATIONAL ARCHIVES AND RECORDS ADMINISTRATION, NORTHEAST REGION (NEW YORK CITY); at Onondaga County Public Library, 447 South Salina Street, Syracuse, NY; and at Rochester Public Library, 115 South Avenue, Rochester, NY.

2. Census Records: The Archives has the original copy (complete for all New York State Counties) of the 1915 and 1925 State censuses; and a card file index for Albany County, 1925 State census. See "Restrictions on Use." NOTE: NYS Census records for many counties are also available at NEW YORK GENEALOGICAL AND BIOGRAPHICAL SOCIETY and through any FAMILY HISTORY CENTER. Select counties are available at other NYC repositories.

3. Military Records include:

Revolutionary War accounts and claims, 1775–1809 [A0200]; certificates submitted by disabled Revolutionary War veterans claiming pensions, 1779–1789 [A0174] and index. [A0859]

Civil War records including abstracts of muster rolls, c. 1880–1890s (arranged by regiment, indexed by name) [13775]; bounty state registers (New York State and City), 1863–1868 (not indexed), and other records listing officers and enlisted men, 1861–1865 [A0389]

War of 1812, claim records [A0020]; and index [A1182]. (Published index also available at 973.52447 qA2.)

Spanish-American War, card file for NYS men who served with the U.S. Army, Navy and National Guard. [B0809]

New York National Guard units, muster rolls dating from 1878–1954 (not indexed). [13726]

World War I, summary service cards for U.S. Army, Navy and Marine personnel who served from New York; and scattered veterans' service data and photographs, 1917–1938. [A4012]

4. Court Records: All pre-1847 records of defunct higher-level state courts, including the Court of Chancery, 1684–1847; Supreme Court of Judicature (Albany, Geneva and Utica), 1797–1847; Court of Probates (and its predecessor, the Prerogative Court), 1664–1823; and Court for the Trial of Impeachments and Correction of Errors, 1777–1847 (except records deposited with the COUNTY CLERK'S OFFICE, NEW YORK COUNTY, DIVISION OF OLD RECORDS).

NOTE: Prior to 1788, the jurisdiction of the Court of Probates included all matters in New York, Kings, Orange, Rockland and Westchester counties and estates valued over fifty pounds elsewhere. After 1788, the Court's jurisdiction was limited to estates of New York residents who died out of State and to deceased non-residents who owned property in New York. Records include:

Recorded Wills, 1665–1787 [J0043]
Probated wills, 1661–1815 [J0038] (also available through any FAMILY HISTORY CENTER)
Administration papers, c. 1700–1823, and letters of administration, 1787–1823
Estate inventories and accounts, 1666–1822

After 1787, the Surrogate's Court in each county had jurisdiction over most estate matters (after 1823, all such matters). The Archives also has New York County records including probated wills, 1787–1829 [J1038], and recorded wills, 1787–1879 [J1043]. NOTE: These latter records were transferred from SURROGATE'S COURT, NEW YORK COUNTY, to the Queens College Historical Documents Collection in 1966; then transferred to QUEENS BOROUGH PUBLIC LIBRARY in the late 1980s and accessioned by the NYS Archives in 1992.

Jurisdiction of the Court of Chancery, New York's court of equity, 1683–1847, included business partnerships, land partitions and mortgage foreclosures, the appointment of guardians for minors, lunatics and drunkards, and, after 1787, divorces. A few naturalizations were also filed in the Court of Chancery (see below). The Archives has all the papers filed in this Court, except the records of the 1st Circuit (New York City and vicinity) which can be found in the COUNTY CLERK'S OFFICE - STATE SUPREME COURT - NEW YORK COUNTY (MANHATTAN), DIVISION OF OLD RECORDS. A name index for Chancery Decrees, 1800–1847, is available (on microfilm).

5. Naturalization Records: The Court of Chancery records described above also include a few naturalization papers (indexed), c. 1800–1847, for the 5th, 6th and 8th circuits. These circuits covered central and western New York State. In addition, a few naturalization papers for Albany, 1799–1812, Utica, 1822 and 1838–1839, filed in the Supreme Court of Judicature are available here.

6. Land Records include applications for land grants, 1642–1804 [A0272], land patents, 1664–1997 [12943], and Surveyor General maps, 1771–1913. [A0273]

7. Governor's Office records include:

Applications for executive clemency and pardon, c. 1860–1926 (R); and executive pardons (executive clemency records), 1799–1931 (indexed).
Application for restoration of citizenship rights, 1911–1918 (R)
Journal of pardons, proclamations and nomination for office, 1859–1916
Register of applications for appointment, 1859–1906 (not indexed)
Requisitions and mandates for extradition, 1857–1982

8. State Board of Charities records (arranged mostly by county) include:

Census of inmates in almshouses, 1875–1921 [A1978]
Census of non-institutionalized insane and idiots, 1871–1872 [A1979]
List of officers of incorporated charities, 1870

Register of children removed from poor houses, 1873–1874 [A1980]
Register of insane in county poor houses, 1871 [A1989]
Reports on institutionalized and non-institutionalized epileptics receiving poor relief, 1895 [A1991, A1992]
Register of tramps applying for relief to overseer of the poor, 1875–1876 [A1990]

9. Division for Youth: State Agricultural and Industrial School at Industry (Western House of Refuge) records include:

Records of admission, attendance and discharge, 1876–1960 (R) [A1970]
Case files of male inmates, 1849–1939 (R) [A1906]; and index, 1859–1867, 1891–1949 [A3063]
Case files of female inmates, 1876–1904, (indexed) [A1907] (R)

10. Department of Correctional Services holdings include the following:

Albion Correctional Facility, inmate admission ledgers (indexed) and case files, 1894–1981 (R)
Auburn Correctional Facility, inmate case files, 1914–1956 (R); register of male inmates received, 1817–1949 (incomplete); register of deaths, 1888–1937 (R); case files for inmates discharged by death, 1933–1959 (R); register of female inmates discharged, 1893–1919
Bedford Hills Correctional Facility, inmate case files, 1915–1930, 1955–1981 (R)
Clinton Correctional Facility (Dannemora Prison), inmate admission ledgers, 1846–1866, 1926–1948; medical and psychiatric reports of inmates, 1934–1967 (R)
Elmira Correctional Facility, inmate biographical ledger, 1879–1957; biographical register of returned men, 1913–1937 (R)
New York House of Refuge, Randall's Island, inmate case files (indexed), 1824–1935 (R) [A2064]; admission registers, 1859–1932 (R) [A2088]; parole register, 1892–1933 (R) [A2069]; register of deferred applications for parole, 1860–1891 (R) [A2068]
Ossining Correctional Facility (Sing Sing Prison), inmate admission registers, 1865–1971; case files of inmates sentenced to electrocution, 1939–1963 (R)

NOTE: See NYS Department of Corrections website (http://nysdocs.docs.state.ny.us) for "Inmate Population Information Search." This database includes all inmates from the early 1970s (except youth offenders).

11. Department of Education records include:

Inventory of church records, 1936–1942 [A4181]
Inventory of town, village and city records, 1936–1941 [A4180]

12. Department of Health records (most arranged alphabetically by surname) include:

Deceased and released typhoid carrier case files, 1920–1975 (R)
Polio confidential case report cards, 1921–1975 (R)
Raybrook State Tuberculosis Hospital, application book of patients, 1932–1942 (R)
Tuberculosis reporting cards, 1939–1975 (R)
Typhoid fever reporting cards, 1921–1954; and supplementary records, 1959–1971 (R)
Veteran's Home at Oxford, admission case files, 1897–1963 (arranged chronologically by year of discharge or death and then alphabetically by surname) (R)

13. Department of Social Services records include:

Indian census and annuity rolls, 1881–1950 (arranged by Tribe) (R)

14. Department of State records include documents from the Dutch Colonial period including land patents, 1630–1664, and deeds, 1652–1653. British Colonial records include marriage bonds filed by the Provincial Secretary, 1753–1784; appointment records, 1777–1994; executive pardons, commutations and restorations of citizenship rights, 1799–1994; incorporation certificates, 1811–1825; wills of out-of-State residents, 1823–1966 (indexed); and alien depositions of intent to become citizens, 1825–1913. These depositions were filed with the Secretary of State by aliens before they could acquire title to real property. The depositions contain the name of the individual and the county in which the deposition was made, and sometimes the country of origin.

15. Legislature: The following are records (on microfilm) from the sample survey of the Factory Investigating Commission. [A3000]. Most of the sample was taken in New York City factories. NOTE: These records are arranged by establishment. They are not indexed by name and as a result are not easily accessed.

Employee background cards, 1913–1914 (6,700 cards)
Establishment profile cards, 1912–1913 (3,800 cards)

Employment history cards, 1913–1914 (2,050 cards)
Individual annual earnings cards, 1912 (2,400 cards)
Personal financial history cards, 1913–1914 (2,050 cards)

16. <u>Department of Taxation and Finance</u>: Article 10 Estate Tax Files, 1885–1990 [19802] document taxation of estates included in life trusts (used by the very wealthy). The files are arranged alphabetically but have no index.

NOTE: In addition to NYS Vital Records indexes, the Archives has placed duplicate copies of microfilms at the NATIONAL ARCHIVES AND RECORDS ADMINISTRATION, NORTHEAST REGION (NEW YORK CITY). These include <u>Revolutionary War</u> [A0174] and <u>Civil War</u> records [A0389]; as well as records of the <u>Division for Youth</u> [A1907, A1970, A3063]; and <u>Department of Correctional Services</u>, New York House of Refuge, Randall's Island. [A2064, A2068-2069, A2088]

Finding Aids:

There are five types of finding aids available in the Archives. Researchers are encouraged to consult them before visiting the Archives.

1. The Archives has an online catalog, Excelsior (also known as WebCat). Excelsior is a comprehensive catalog combining the collections of the NEW YORK STATE LIBRARY (including Manuscript and Special Collections) and the NEW YORK STATE ARCHIVES. A search of the State Archives collections alone can be made by clicking on the "radio" button next to "Archives" and then on the "Login" button. Researchers can search by keyword, author, title, subject and series.

   NOTE: The complete *Historic Documents Inventory* (HDI) for each NYS county, prepared by Cornell University, 1976–1993, is now online and can be accessed also through WebCat. HDI includes more than 25,000 archives and manuscript collections housed in local repositories throughout New York State. NOTE: These HDI collections are <u>not</u> available in the NEW YORK STATE LIBRARY or ARCHIVES.

2. A published *Guide to Records in the New York State Archives,* 1993, contains brief histories of major State agencies and lists of archival record series that originated in each agency. Histories of agencies for which the Archives holds no records are also included. Additional *Guides* published by the NYS Archives include:

   "Duely & Constantly Kept": A History of the New York Supreme Court, 1691–1847 and An Inventory of Its Records (Albany, Utica, and Geneva Offices), 1797–1847. Albany, 1991. [COU, 402-4, DUECK, 91-8095]
   Guide to Records of the Department of Correctional Services in the New York State Archives. Albany, 1992. [ARC 952.4, GUIRD 95-8437]
   Guide to Records of the Governor's Office in the New York State Archives. Albany, 1995. [ARC 952.4, GUIRG, 97-7141]
   Guide to Records Relating to Native Americans. Albany, 1988. [ARC 952.4, GUIRR, 95-8434]
   Guide to Records Relating to the Revolutionary War in the New York State Archives. Albany, 1994. [ARC 952.4, GUIRR, 95-8438]
   The Greatest Reform School in the World: A Guide to the Records of the New York House of Refuge. Albany, 1989. [ARC 952.4, GRERS, 95-8436]
   The Lusk Committee: A Guide to the Records of the Joint Legislative Committee to Investigate Seditious Activities Held by the New York State Archives. Albany, 1992. [ARC 952.4, LUSCO 94-80078]
   A Spirit of Sacrifice: New York's Response to the Great War; A Guide to Records Relating to World War I Held in the New York State Archives. Albany, 1993. [ARC 952.4, SPISA 93-46964]
   The Union Preserved: A Guide to Civil War Records in the New York State Archives. New York, 1999. [016.9737, U58 99-103267]
   Working Lives: A Guide to the Records of the New York State Factory Investigating Commission in the New York State Archives. Albany, 1989. [ARC 952.4, WORLI 95-8433]

   In 2001, the Archives Partnership Trust also began publication of *New York Archives*, which highlights through scholarly articles, the results of research conducted at the State Archives and other New York repositories.

3. Descriptive inventories of the records of a few individual State government agencies are also available. These inventories contain more detailed information on the history and functions of an agency and narrative descriptions of the scope and content of information found in each record series. Copies of these inventories may be available at other libraries.

4. Detailed lists of the records in individual boxes, or the contents of specific volumes or individual microfilm reels within a particular record series, are available only in the Archives Research Room.

5. Specialized finding aids, which are usually detailed indexes or item descriptions of the contents of a single or several related series pertaining to a given topic are available. Some have been published but others, especially card indexes, are available only in the Research Room. Several of the these indexes are noted under "Description of Resources." Seven information leaflets are available from the Archives and can also be found online:

#1 *Genealogical Sources in the New York State Archives*
#2 *Vital Records*
#3 *Probate Records*
#4 *War Service Records & Searches*
#6 *Naturalization & Related Records*
#8 *Records Relating to African-Americans in the New York State Archives*
#9 *Records Relating to Criminal Trials, Appeals, and Pardons*

Description of Facility:

The Archives is located on the 11th floor of the Cultural Education Center in Albany's Empire State Plaza. Records may be viewed in the Research Room only. (NOTE: Temporary location on 3rd floor to 2004.) The Archives Research Room facilities are shared with the Manuscripts and Special Collections unit of the NEW YORK STATE LIBRARY. A reference archivist is on duty at all times to provide assistance to researchers. A seat reservation is necessary in order to use the Archives. Call or e-mail before coming.

There are 4 microfiche readers and 2 microform (film/fiche) reader/printers in the Research Room. Researchers may use their own computer or tape recording equipment on a space available basis. Arrangements should be made in advance to reserve space.

Fees/Copies:

A variety of photo duplication services are available. Photocopies made by staff are $.25 per page, self-service copies (from microfilm only) are $.10 per page; other charges apply for non-standard paper sizes. A fee schedule for photo duplication services is available from the Archives. Microfilm may be purchased at $25 per roll or borrowed through the New York State Interlibrary Loan network. (Contact your local library for information.)

Staff will respond to mail and telephone requests for information about holdings and copies. Searches can be made at a cost of $3 per record for Revolutionary War land grants to Continental officers and soldiers (not militia service); War of 1812 payroll cards and veterans' claims (post-1959); and Civil War abstracts of muster rolls. The fee is $1 for Spanish-American War summary service cards and WW1 summary service cards. Use the NYS War Service Records Search Request form available on the Archives website. Enclose a separate check or money order for each record requested. If no record is found, the check or money order will be returned.

Restrictions on Use:

Records in the official custody of the State Archives are made available to the public under provisions in the Freedom of Information Law (FOIL, Public Officers Law Article 6). Some records or portions thereof, are exempt from disclosure under FOIL. Examples of those legally restricted records in the State Archives are prison inmate files and mental hospital patient case files.

Because of their condition, some records including Census Records, are closed to researchers. Researchers are required to use microfilm copies when they are available. Researchers can view microfilm copies of the Census records in the NEW YORK STATE DEPARTMENT OF EDUCATION, NEW YORK STATE LIBRARY on the 7th floor of the Cultural Education Center in Albany or through any FAMILY HISTORY CENTER (LDS).

Coats, briefcases and other containers must be checked in lockers outside the Research Room. Only pencils may be used. Smoking, drinking and eating are prohibited.

Researchers must sign the annual registration form that includes an agreement to abide by the rules governing use of the Archives holdings. Researchers must sign in and out in the Research Room log book each day.

Only Archives staff may copy paper records. The Archives reserves the right to approve copying and to determine the method of photo duplication based upon the condition of the records. Some records are too fragile to be handled.

NOTE: The State Archives Reading Room on the 11th floor of the Cultural Education Center is being renovated. The Archives is expected to move back to the 11th floor in 2004. Patrons intending to visit the State Archives during the period of renovation should call or write ahead to determine the accessibility of records. There is no restriction on access to frequently used records available on microfilm or microfiche.

NEW YORK STATE DEPARTMENT OF EDUCATION
NEW YORK STATE LIBRARY

Facility Director: Mary Redmond, Interim Director
Janet M. Welch, State Librarian

Address: Cultural Education Center, 7th Floor   ♿
Empire State Plaza
Albany, NY 12230

(Cross Street: Madison Avenue)

Phone: (518) 474-5355 (Reference)
(518) 474-5161 (Genealogy and Local History)
(518) 474-6282 (Manuscripts and Special Collections)*

Fax: (518) 474-5786
E-mail: refserv@mail.nysed.gov
mscolls@mail.nysed.gov (seat reservation, Manuscripts and Special Collections)*

Website: www.nysl.nysed.gov

Hours of Operation:

Monday to Friday: 9:00 am to 5:00 pm*
Closed Saturday, Sunday and New York State legal holidays.

*NOTE: A seat reservation must be made in advance to use Manuscripts and Special Collections. Call or e-mail.

Closest Public Transportation and Directions:

See NEW YORK STATE DEPARTMENT OF EDUCATION, NEW YORK STATE ARCHIVES.

Description of Resources:

The New York State Library was established in 1818 to serve the government and the people of New York State. Today, its collection of more than 20 million items, includes the following of interest to genealogists:

1. Census Records (on microfilm)

    U.S. Census:

    Population schedules for New York State: 1790 (printed and manuscript), 1800–1930 (including surviving 1890 fragments and 1890 Union Veterans and Widows)

    Special schedules for New York State:
    Agriculture, 1850–1880
    Industry/Manufactures, 1820, 1850–1860, 1870 (Essex to Yates Counties), 1880
    Social Statistics, 1850, 1860, 1870 (Monroe to Yates Counties)
    Mortality schedules, 1850–1880
    Defective, Dependent and Delinquent Classes, 1880

    New York State Census for the following counties and years (records underlined are believed to be incomplete):

    Entire State (62 counties), 1915 and 1925

    Albany, 1855, 1865, 1875, 1892, 1905
    Allegany, 1855, 1865, 1875, 1892, 1905
    Broome, 1825, 1835, 1855, 1865, 1875, 1892, 1905
    Cattaraugus, 1825, 1835, 1845, 1855, 1865, 1875, 1892, 1905
    Cayuga, 1855, 1865, 1875, 1892, 1905 (Auburn only)
    Chautauqua, 1825, 1835, 1845, 1855, 1865, 1875, 1892, 1905
    Chemung, 1855, 1865, 1892, 1905
    Chenango, 1855, 1865, 1875, 1905
    Clinton, 1892, 1905
    Columbia, 1845 (City of Hudson only) , 1855, 1865, 1875, 1905
    Cortland, 1825, 1835, 1845, 1855, 1865, 1875, 1892, 1905

Delaware, 1855, 1865, 1875, 1892, 1905
Dutchess, 1865, 1875, 1892
Erie, 1855, 1865, <u>1875</u>, <u>1892</u>, <u>1905</u>
Essex, 1855, 1865, 1875, 1892, 1905
Franklin, 1875, 1905
Fulton, 1845, 1855, 1865, 1875, 1905
Genesee, 1875, 1892, 1905
Greene, 1855, 1865, 1875, 1892, 1905
Hamilton, <u>1892</u>, 1905
Herkimer, 1835, <u>1845</u>, 1855, 1865, 1875, 1892, 1905
Jefferson, <u>1865</u>, 1875, 1905
Kings, 1855, 1865, 1875, 1892, 1905
Lewis, 1825, 1835, 1855, 1865, 1875, 1892, 1905
Livingston, 1855, <u>1865</u>, 1875
Madison, 1855, 1865, 1875, 1892, 1905
Monroe 1855, 1865, 1875, 1892, 1905
Montgomery, 1855, 1865, <u>1875</u>, 1892, 1905
New York, <u>1855</u>
Niagara, <u>1855</u>, 1865, 1875, 1905
Onondaga, 1855, <u>1865</u>, 1875, 1892, 1905; and Syracuse street/ward index, 1850–1905.
Ontario, 1855, 1865, 1875, 1892
Orange, 1825, 1835, <u>1845</u>, 1855, 1865, 1875
Orleans, 1855, 1865, 1875, 1892, 1905
Oswego, 1855, 1865, 1875, 1892, 1905
Otsego, 1825, 1855, 1865, 1875, 1892, 1905
Rensselaer, 1855, 1865, 1875, <u>1905</u>
Richmond, 1855, 1865, 1875
Rockland, <u>1855</u>, 1865, 1875, 1892, 1905
St. Lawrence, <u>1845</u>, <u>1865</u>, 1905
Saratoga, 1855, 1865, 1875, 1892, 1905
Schenectady, 1835, 1845, 1855, 1865, 1875, 1892, 1905
Schoharie, 1825, 1835, 1855, 1865, 1875, 1892, 1905
Schuyler, 1855, 1865, 1875
Steuben, 1825, 1835, <u>1845</u>, 1855, 1865, 1875, 1892, 1905
Suffolk, 1865
Sullivan, 1855, 1875
Tioga, 1825, 1835, 1855, 1865, 1875, 1892, 1905
Tompkins, 1825, 1835, 1865, 1875, 1892, 1905
Ulster, 1855, <u>1865</u>, <u>1875</u>, 1905
Warren, <u>1855</u> (agricultural census only), 1865, 1875, 1892, 1905
Washington, 1825, 1835, 1855, 1865, 1875, 1892, 1905
Wayne, 1892, 1905
Westchester, 1905
Wyoming, <u>1875</u>
Yates, 1825, 1835, 1845, 1855, 1865, 1875, 1892

2. Vital Records:

New York City Health Department, birth and death indexes, 1907–1918. [R974.71 N532, 87-1534]
Guide to Public Vital Statistics Records in New York State, including New York City. [R016.312 H673]
New York Marriages Previous to 1784. [R974.7 N548 1968]
New York Marriage Bonds, 1753–1783, by Kenneth Scott. Abstracts the original marriage bonds salvaged from the 1911 State Capitol fire. [R974.7 S427n]

3. City and Telephone Directories: The Library has one of the most complete collections of City and Telephone Directories of New York State communities in books, microfilm and microfiche. It has all of the existing NYC Directories. A list of "City Directories and Selected Telephone Directories on Microfilm and Microfiche" in the Library's collection is available online at www.nysl.nysed.gov/genealogy/citydir.htm.

4. <u>Church and Cemetery Records</u>: NYS church (predominantly Protestant denominations) and cemetery records include published records, registers deposited in the State Library, and others compiled by New York State chapters of the Daughters of the American Revolution.

The collection also includes published records of many churches and cemeteries in the Northeast and English parish registers, primarily volumes published by county record societies.

5. <u>Wills</u>: The Library has an extensive collection of printed or microfilm copies of wills, administrative papers, abstracts, indexes and court calendars for NYS counties including:

Barber, Gertrude. *Abstracts of Wills of <u>Rockland</u> County, New York from May 6, 1845–December 24, 1870.* 4 vols. New York, 1950–1953. [R, 974.728, qAB239w]

Fernow, Berthold. *Calendar of Wills on file and recorded in the Offices of the Clerk of the Court of Appeals, of the County Clerk at <u>Albany</u>, and the Secretary of State, 1626–1836.* [Includes other <u>New York State</u> counties.] 1967. [R974.7, F36a]

Hix, Charlotte M. *<u>Staten Island</u> Wills and Letters of Administration, Richmond County, New York, 1670–1800: as found in the Surrogate's Court, New York County...* Bowie, MD, 1993. [R974.726, H626, 94-37612]

Kelly, Arthur C. M. *Index, Names of Principals: Abstracts of Wills on File in the Surrogate's Office, City of <u>New York</u>.* [Indexes names in *Abstracts of Wills, 1665–1800* published by the New-York Historical Society.] Rhinebeck, NY, 1981. [R929.37471, qK29, 86-30418]

Kelly, Arthur C.M. *<u>Dutchess</u> County, NY Probate records, 1787–1865, register of wills and letters testamentary and of administration in the Surrogate's Court, Poughkeepsie, NY.* 1997. [R974.733 qD975, 97-17430]

Sawyer, Ray C., editor. *Index of <u>New York State</u> Wills, 1662–1850, on file at the Office of the Surrogate for New York County in the Hall of Records, New York City.* 1932. [R974.71, qS27]

New-York Historical Society. *Abstracts of Wills 1665–1800, on file in the Surrogate's Office, County of <u>New York</u>.* 1892–1973. [R974.7, N552 v. 25–41]

Pelletreau, William Smith, ed. *Early Wills of <u>Westchester</u> County, New York, 1664–1784.* 1898. [R974.727, P38]

Pelletreau, William Smith, ed. *Early Long Island Wills of <u>Suffolk</u> County, 1691–1703. An unabridged copy of the manuscript volume known as "The Lester Will Book;" being the record of the Prerogative Court of the County of Suffolk, with genealogical and historical notes.* 1897. [R974.725 P38]

Scott, Kenneth. *Genealogical Data from Administration Papers from the <u>New York State</u> Court of Appeals in Albany.* 1972. [R929.374, S427, 74-5084]

6. <u>Daughters of the American Revolution (DAR) Records</u>: The Library is a depository for the following record series compiled by the New York State Chapters of the Daughters of the American Revolution: Bible records; Cemetery, Church and Town records; Family Histories; Genealogical Data - New Project (grandparents forms); Graves of Revolutionary Soldiers in New York; *Lineage Books*, 1890–1921; and DAR Patriot Index.

7. <u>Maps and Atlases</u> (Cartographic Collection): Geographic and historical printed maps of the Colony and State of New York from the mid-17th century to the present; manuscript maps, c. 1780–1870; and maps from the 19th and 20th centuries of towns, villages, land patents and, in some cases, individual farm lots.

The Library has over 1,000 atlases, including a nearly complete set of 19th century NYS and county atlases and Sanborn insurance atlases (on microfilm, not in color) for most of New York State. Atlases of the State begin in 1829 with the publication of David H. Burr's *Atlas of the State of New York.* County atlases, c. 1860–1880, often include names of persons.

8. <u>County Histories</u>: A majority of the county histories in the collection were published in the late 19th and early 20th centuries. These histories contain descriptions of the principal settlements within the county and genealogies or biographical sketches of early settlers and prominent citizens.

NOTE: *New York County and Regional Histories and Atlases,* a 116-reel microfilm set containing 481 items from the collection at the State Library, is available on interlibrary loan.

9. <u>Military Records</u>: Include lists (not always complete) of New Yorkers who served in the Colonial and State militia, War of 1812, Revolutionary War, Civil War and Spanish-American War. Most are printed compilations such as published indexes of federal pension files. The collection includes:

Civil War Unit Histories: Regimental Histories and Personal Narratives. The Library has the New England and Mid-Atlantic states portion of this microfiche collection. [MA/FF 973.741, C582, 93-13647]

A Bibliography of Military Name Lists from pre-1675 to 1900: a guide to genealogical sources, by Lois Horowitz. Metuchen, NJ, 1990. [R,929.373.H816, 90-14241]

The Union Preserved: A Guide to Civil War Records in the New York State Archives, compiled and edited by Daniel Lorello and Harold Holzer. New York, 1999. [R, 016.9737, U58, 99-10326]

Original records available in Manuscripts and Special Collections include letters, diaries and papers of individual soldiers, as well as Civil War muster rolls for the United States Army, 5th New York Artillery Regiment, Co. F, 1863–1865 [SC 16961]; the 3rd New York Cavalry Regiment, Co. G [SC 12256]; and the 15th Artillery Regiment, Co. M, 1864 [SC 14787]. The latter record group includes also payroll records and medical release certificates. Records of other Civil War regiments include:

- 34th New York Infantry Regiment, Co. D, 1861–1863 [SC 10000]. Descriptive books that contain information such as individual soldier's age, physical features, residence, occupation and date of enlistment.
- 43rd New York Infantry Regiment, 1861–1865 [SC 19552]. Record book listing soldiers absent from duty due to sickness or wounds; includes rank, company, nature of illness/wound, hospital admission date, date returned to duty, discharge from service or death.
- 121st New York Infantry Regiment, 1862–1865 [SC 17551]. Records related to enlistment, enrollment, discharges, transfers, promotions, desertions and casualties.

10. Passenger Records: The collection includes:

Index to Passenger Lists of Vessels Arriving at New York, 1820–1846 (103 rolls of microfilm). [MA-FM 929.37471 I38, 83-29199]

Filby, P. William with Mary K. Meyer, eds. *Passenger and Immigration Lists Index: A Guide to Published Arrival Records of about 500,000 Passengers Who Came to the United States and Canada in the Seventeenth, Eighteenth and Nineteenth Centuries.* 4 vols. and supps. Detroit, 1981–1985. [R929.373 qP287, 81-26439]

Filby, P. William, ed. *Passenger and Immigration Lists Bibliography, 1538–1900.* 2d ed. Detroit, 1988. [R,016.92933, q287, 82-20465]

Ptak, Diane S. *A Compilation of American and Canadian Passenger/Emigration Registers.* Albany, 1993.

11. Naturalization Records:

Neagles, James C. and Lila Lee Neagles. *Locating Your Immigrant Ancestor: A Guide to Naturalization Records.* rev. ed. Logan, UT, 1986. [R,929.1072073, N338, 90-48898]

Scott, Kenneth and Kenn Stryker-Rodda. *Denizations, Naturalizations and Oaths of Allegiance in Colonial New York.* Baltimore, 1975. [A,929.3747, S427, 76-285]

Scott, Kenneth. *Early New York Naturalizations: Abstracts of Naturalization Records from Federal, State, and Local Courts 1792–1840.* Baltimore, 1981. [R,929.3747, S427, 81-34067]

Scott, Kenneth and Rosanne Conway. *New York Alien Residents, 1825–1848.* Baltimore, 1978. [R,929.3747, S427, 81-34236]

12. Newspapers (all on microfilm)

The Library has the largest collection of NYS newspapers anywhere — over 4,000 titles, with c. 2,500 on film. The microfilm collection, amassed by the New York State Newspaper Project (NYSNP), significantly added to the State Library's newspaper collection. The NYSNP, started in 1987 to identify, describe and preserve all NYS newspapers since the first publication in 1725, has cataloged almost 21,000 titles. The collection includes:

Albany Evening Journal, 1830–1925
Binghamton Press, 1927–1960
Buffalo Courier, 1888–1926
Democrat and Chronicle (Rochester), 1884–
Elmira Star-Gazette, 1907–1963

The New York Age, 1905–1960
New York Herald, 1840–1919; *New York Herald-New York Tribune,* 1924–1926; *New York Herald Tribune,* 1926–1966
Post Standard (Syracuse), 1899–

The collection also includes such ethnic newspapers as:

Advocate (Irish), 1911–1988
L'Eco d'Italia (Italian Echo), 1890–1896
The Gaelic American, 1903–1951
Der Idisher zshurnal (The Jewish Journal), 1899–1906
Irish American Advocate, 1904–1911
Jewish Messenger, 1857–1902
The Jewish Recorder, 1893–1895

Nedlni New-Yorske Listy, 1891 (Czech)
New Yorker Volkszeitung, 1894–1932
Di Nyu-Yorker Yudishe Folkstsaytung, (New York Jewish people's newspaper), 1886–1889
Novoe russkoe slovo (New Russian word), 1967–
Il Progresso Italo-Americano, 1880–1950
Scottish American Journal, 1857–1861
Wochenblatt der deutschen Schnellpost, 1845-1849

The Library also has two major microfilm collections: *American Newspapers, 1860–1920* and *Early English Newspapers (1603–1818)*.

Check the New York State Newspaper Project web pages at www.nysl.nysed.gov/nysnp/nygcty.htm for a listing of the Library's New York State newspapers on microfilm arranged by county. NOTE: This website also includes a statewide inventory of local newspapers, by county and city, and identifies libraries throughout the State where these newspapers can be found. All newspapers on microfilm, except the *New York Times,* are available on interlibrary loan.

See also NEW YORK PUBLIC LIBRARY - GENERAL RESEARCH DIVISION, NEW-YORK HISTORICAL SOCIETY, BROOKLYN PUBLIC LIBRARY-CENTRAL LIBRARY, QUEENS BOROUGH PUBLIC LIBRARY - LONG ISLAND DIVISION, and the STATEN ISLAND INSTITUTE OF ARTS AND SCIENCES for additional newspaper collections.

13. Print Collection: Includes views of New York State and portraits of its citizens, past and present. The collection includes portrait volumes of the State Legislature, 1858–1879.

14. Genealogies: The collection includes about 12,500 family histories, national in scope, but with an emphasis on New York State families. In addition, the Manuscripts Collection includes family bibles, diaries, notebooks and correspondence.

Finding Aids:

The Library's computerized catalog is available onsite and online. See NEW YORK STATE ARCHIVES for a more detailed description. Also, there are several card files or indexes of local history and genealogy materials. Entries of interest to genealogists are: "Biography," "Deeds," "Family records," "Registers of birth," "Wills," etc. In addition, the Library has:

1. Surnames Card File (60 drawers) which identifies books, articles, pamphlets and manuscripts in the State Library alphabetically by surname.

2. Vital Records Card File (8 drawers) arranged by county: This card file indexes sources of county and other local birth, baptism and death records (not surnames or ethnic/religious groups). Cities, towns and communities are filed alphabetically within the county.

3. Census Records: The Library has published indexes, 1790–1870, to the U.S. censuses for all of New York State. In addition, it has the Soundex indexes for NYS, 1880, 1900, 1920; the 1910 street index for 37 U.S. cities; indexes to surviving 1890 population schedules and 1890 Union Veterans and Widows special schedules for New York; and indexes for New York State on CD-ROM for 1850, 1860, 1870, 1880 and 1910.

   No comprehensive indexes are available for New York State Census records. The NEW YORK STATE ARCHIVES has a card index for Albany County, 1925, arranged by surname. In addition, the ARCHIVES has Assembly/Election District maps for 1915 and 1925 censuses for the Bronx, Brooklyn and Manhattan.

4. City Directories and telephone books. In addition to the online list of directories on microfilm/microfiche (see above), the Library has a City Directories card file for those available in hard copy.

5. Church and Cemetery Records: These New York State records are accessed through the Vital Records Card File (see above). See also *Guide to Vital Statistics Records in New York State Churches (Exclusive of New York City).* 2 vols. 1942. Out-of-state records can be located through the online catalog. For church records, search by place, then by church name. To locate English parish registers, researchers should consult *A Guide to English Parish Registers in the New York State Library.* [RO16.942 N532]

6. Wills: For additional titles, check the catalog under the subject "Wills."

7. Daughters of the American Revolution Records are indexed in *Revised Master Index to the New York State Daughters of the American Revolution Genealogical Records Volumes,* 2 vols., 1998 [R929, qD23, 98-005610]. Bible records and Family Histories are listed in the Surnames Card File; and Cemetery, Church and Town Records are listed in the Vital Records Card File. Genealogical Data is indexed in the New Project Genealogical Data card index (17 drawers). Graves of Revolutionary War soldiers in New York are indexed in the Revolutionary War Soldiers Card Index (21 drawers). See also *Index to the Rolls of Honor (Ancestor Index) in the Lineage Books of the NSDAR.* [369.135 A]

8. Maps and Atlases are accessed by a card catalog with entries filed by geographic location. An annotated bibliography of selected New York State maps, 1793–1900 (www.nysl.nysed.gov/msscfa/mapsbibl.htm), can be found on the Library's website.

9. Print Collection. This collection is indexed by name and subject.

10. Military Records. Check the catalog for published materials. See also *Selected Civil War Collections held by the New York State Library*, a bibliography available on the NYSL website, arranged by name of soldier (for letters, diaries and other papers) and by State and regiment.

11. Electronic Publications

The New York State Library has created a variety of bibliographies and finding aids that are on its website. In addition to those mentioned above (City Directories, Maps, Military Records and Newspapers), these include:

Adoptees	*New York State Counties*
Cities, Towns and Villages in New York State	*New York State Wills*
Daughters of the American Revolution Collection	*Surnames - A Pathfinder*
Finding Places	*Tracing African-American Family History*
An Introduction to Genealogy at the State Library	*Tracing Your Immigrant Ancestors*
Loyalist Records	*Vital Records*

Description of Facility:

The 7th floor of the Cultural Education Center is the principal public service floor of the New York State Library. The general Reference Desk is at the left when entering from the elevators. The Local History and Genealogy Reference Center is to the left of the general Reference desk. Manuscripts and Special Collections are on the 11th* floor, where the Research Room (seats 24) is shared with the NEW YORK STATE ARCHIVES. [*NOTE: Temporary location, 3rd floor, to 2004.] A seat reservation is necessary for use of Manuscripts and Special Collections. Call or e-mail in advance.

While many of the materials of interest to genealogist are on open shelves on the 7th floor, the majority of the collection is in closed stacks. Materials, such as newspapers (microfilm), city directories and telephone books (paper editions) can be requested by submitting a call slip at the 7th floor Paging Desk. Materials are retrieved every half hour from 9:30 am to 4:00 pm. Materials in Manuscripts and Special Collections are retrieved twice daily, at 10:00 am and 2:00 pm.

"R" in the call number indicates that the item is in the Reference Collection on the 7th floor. The Genealogy/Local History Collection is part of the Reference Collection. Microforms formerly in Manuscripts and Special Collections have been transferred to the main collection and can now be accessed on the 7th floor. "A" or "N" in the call number indicates it is located on the 11th* [temporarily 3rd] floor in the Manuscripts and Special Collections area.

Most genealogies (call numbers beginning with 929.2) and New York State local histories (call number beginning with 974.7) are shelved in the Reference Collection on the 7th floor. Histories of all localities in any one county are grouped together on the shelves. Federal and State Census Records (population schedules) are located on the 7th floor.

The DAR Surnames Card File, Vital Records Card File, New Project Genealogical Data Card Index, Revolutionary War Soldiers Card Index and Index to the Rolls of Honor (Ancestor Index) in the *Lineage Books* of the NYSDAR can be found in the Local History and Genealogy Area.

The Library has 27 microfilm readers, 10 reader/printers, 7 microfiche readers, 5 microfiche reader/printers and one microcard reader located in the Local History and Genealogy area on the 7th floor. It shares microfilm and microfiche readers and reader/printers on the 11th* [temporarily 3rd] floor with the Archives.

Fees/Copies:

Photocopy machines, including overhead scanners, are located in the Local History and Genealogy area (7th floor). Copies on this floor can be made by researchers at $.10 a page. A bill changer (changes $1 and $5 into dimes) is also located in this area. Copying of materials in Manuscripts and Special Collections, 11th* floor [*Temporarily 3rd floor], must be done by staff. For information on charges for work done by New York State Library staff, call the Reference Desk or go to "Photoduplication Services" online at www.nysl.nysed.gov/photodup.htm.

Restrictions on Use:

See NEW YORK STATE DEPARTMENT OF EDUCATION, NEW YORK STATE ARCHIVES for photoduplication and other restrictions in using the Research Room on the 11th* [temporarily 3rd] floor.

Prior to publication of original materials, researchers should inquire about possible restrictions. Publication of any original materials from the Library's collections should credit the New York State Library as the source of the material.

NEW YORK STATE DEPARTMENT OF HEALTH
VITAL RECORDS SECTION

Facility Director: Peter M. Carucci, Director, Vital Records

Address: 800 North Pearl Street   ♿
Menands, NY   [NOTE: Moving to this address in 2003.]

(Cross Street: Amsterdam Avenue)

Mail Address: Genealogy Unit, Vital Records Section
PO Box 2602
Albany, NY 12220-2602

Phone: (518) 474-3077
Fax: none
E-mail   vr@health.state.ny.us
Website: www.health.state.ny.us/nysdoh/consumer/vr.htm

Hours of Operation:

Monday to Friday: 8:30 am to 4:30 pm

Closest Public Transportation:

Capital District Transportation Authority (CDTA): Bus #13 to "Channel 13"/North Pearl Street.

Directions:

Take the local CDTA #13 bus to "Channel 13" at North Pearl Street. Walk on North Pearl Street about 1000 feet (1/4 mile) to # 800. See "Restrictions on Use."

Description of Resources:

Birth, marriage and death records were filed with local vital record registrars or clerks (usually city, town or village). The original was sent to the NYS Department of Health, and a hand-transcribed copy or abstract retained locally. By the early 1970s, the procedure changed and an identical copy (not transcribed) was retained locally. The following are available at the State office:

1. Birth Records from 1881 and Death Records from 1880 for the entire State except records filed in Albany, Buffalo, Yonkers and New York City (and City of Brooklyn). For these cities, the Department has the following:

    Albany, Buffalo and Yonkers: Records from 1914 to the present.
    New York City: Only records for Queens and Richmond Counties, 1881–1897, the eastern portion of the Bronx (part of Westchester County), 1881–1895, and towns in Kings County before annexation to the City of Brooklyn, in the 1880s and 1890s.

    For pre-1914 birth and death records in Albany, Buffalo and Yonkers, contact the City Registrar's Office in these cities. For New York City birth records, 1910 to the present, and death records, 1949 to the present, see NEW YORK CITY DEPARTMENT OF HEALTH AND MENTAL HYGIENE, OFFICE OF VITAL RECORDS. For earlier New York City records, see NEW YORK CITY DEPARTMENT OF RECORDS AND INFORMATION SERVICES, MUNICIPAL ARCHIVES.

2. Marriage Records for the entire State from 1881 except for Albany, Buffalo, Yonkers and New York City (and City of Brooklyn). For these cities, the Department has the following:

    Albany, Buffalo, and Yonkers: Records from 1908 to the present.
    New York City: Only records for Queens and Richmond Counties, 1881–1897, the eastern portion of the Bronx (part of Westchester County), 1881–1895 and towns in Kings County before annexation to the City of Brooklyn.

    For marriage records in New York City, 1938 to the present and indexes 1952 to the present, see CITY CLERK'S OFFICE, MARRIAGE LICENSE BUREAU. For earlier New York City marriage records and indexes, see NYC DEPARTMENT OF RECORDS AND INFORMATION SERVICES, MUNICIPAL ARCHIVES. For pre-1908 records in Albany, Buffalo and Yonkers, contact the City Clerk's Office in these cities. See also County Clerk's Offices in upstate NY counties and Long Island for a duplicate set of marriage records, 1908–c.1935. NOTE: For NYC counties, only the QUEENS COUNTY CLERK'S OFFICE is known to have such records.

3. Divorces, 1963 to the present. Actual records (divorce decrees) are maintained at the county level in the 62 County Clerk's Offices around the State. Since January 1963, county courts are required to report marriage dissolutions to the State Department of Health. The NYS Department of Health can advise in which county the divorce took place and can issue a "dissolution" certificate to the parties or their legal representative. See "Restrictions on Use."

Finding Aids:

Statewide indexes for births, marriages and deaths (on microfiche) are arranged by year and then alphabetically by surname except birth indexes for 1882, marriage indexes, 1908–1914 and 1940 to the present, and death indexes, 1940 to the present, which are arranged by the NYS Health Department's Soundex system (see Appendix A). Marriage indexes include both bride's and groom's names and are indexed separately by name of bride and groom beginning in 1908. Indexes are open to the public for the same years that genealogical records can be ordered. See "Restrictions on Use."

Indexes show name, place, date and certificate number. Marriage indexes for 1908–1914 and from 1944 to the present include the first four letters of the last name of the spouse (although sometimes this information is not included). Death indexes from 1940 include the age of the deceased.

Researchers may not search the records directly. However, the indexes for the years released may be viewed at the NEW YORK STATE ARCHIVES in Albany, NATIONAL ARCHIVES AND RECORDS ADMINISTRATION, NORTHEAST REGION in New York City, the Onondaga County Public Library in Syracuse, and the Rochester Public Library.

Fees/Copies:

For a *certified* copy of a birth, marriage, death certificate or record of the dissolution of a divorce, or "No Record Certification," complete and mail the application form (available on the DOH's web site). There is an $15 fee for each copy of a birth, death and divorce certificate, and $5 for each marriage certificate. See "Restrictions on Use."

For a copy of a birth, marriage or death certificate, or "No Record Certification," *to be used for genealogical purposes only*, complete the "New York State Genealogy Request Form" and mail that application form (available in Appendix C-7). The fee is $11 (per one spelling of the name) for a copy of a birth, marriage or death certificate. This includes a three-year search if the certificate number is not provided. For additional years, the fee is as follows:

4 to 10 years, $21	31 to 40 years, $51	61 to 70 years, $81
11 to 20 years, $31	41 to 50 years, $61	71 to 80 years, $91
21 to 30 years, $41	51 to 60 years, $71	81 to 90 years, $101

A refund is made if the record is found in under the specified search period. If the record is not found, a "No Record Certification" will be sent (no refund). Payment may be made by money order or personal check (no cash or stamps).

The backlog of requests for copies of vital records "for genealogical purposes only" is 5-6 months. The waiting period can be shortened if the record number is provided with the request, i.e. Vital Records staff does not have to do the search. Genealogical requests dropped off at the Menands office are mailed within 2-3 weeks. Transcripts of copies (sometimes incomplete or abbreviated) of the birth, marriage and death certificates can also be obtained from local registrars or local vital record clerks (usually city, town or village) for the same fees, with the same restrictions, but usually in less time. Lists of the local registrars and clerks and their addresses are available at the same four locations as the indexes.

Restrictions on Use:

Copies of *certified* birth, marriage, death and divorce certificates can be provided only to the person to whom the record relates or to their legal representative. No divorce dissolution certificate is provided for genealogical purposes by the State Health Department. Genealogists are advised to contact the relevant County Clerk's Office for such certifications.

Not every record was filed with the State Department of Health before the 1920s. It is advisable to consult local city, village or town clerks if the State cannot locate an early birth, marriage or death record. To determine when a particular city, town or village began keeping vital records, see *Guide to Public Vital Statistics in New York State (including NYC)*, 3 vols., prepared by the Historical Records Survey of the Works Progress Administration. Albany, 1942.

The Health Commissioner's Administrative Rules and Regulations, Part 35.5, Vital Records (based on the Public Health Law, Section 4173, 4174) permits the release of records for genealogical purposes as follows: birth records on file at least 75 years and the person to whom the record relates is deceased; death records on file at least 50 years; and marriage records on file at least 50 years and the parties to the marriage named in the record are deceased. The time restrictions are waived if the applicant is a direct-line descendant (for example, child or grandchild, but not a brother, sister, niece, nephew, aunt, uncle or cousin). This ruling was adopted in March 1979. To obtain later records, provide copies of death certificates of the persons in the record required, along with the applicant's birth record showing direct relationship.

NEW YORK STATE DEPARTMENT OF STATE
DIVISIONS OF CORPORATIONS AND
DIVISION OF LICENSING SERVICES

Facility Director: Keith W. Stack, Deputy Secretary, Business and Licensing Services
Daniel E. Shapiro, Director, Division of Corporations

Address:

Division of Corporations	Division of Licensing Services
41 State Street &#	84 Holland Avenue &#
Albany, NY 12231-0001	Albany, NY 12208-3490
(Cross Streets: Broadway & James Street)	(Cross Street: Notre Dame & Princeton Drive)

Telephone: (518) 473-2492 (Corporations)
(518) 474-4429 (Licensing Services)

Fax: (518) 473-1654 (Corporations)
(518) 473-6648 (Licensing Services)

E-mail: corporations@dos.state.ny.us
licensing@dos.state.ny.us

Website: www.dos.state.ny.us

Hours of Operation:

Monday to Friday: 8:00 am to 4: 30 pm (office hours); 8:00 am to 4:45 pm (telephone inquiries)

Closest Public Transportation and Directions:

See NEW YORK STATE DEPARTMENT OF EDUCATION, NEW YORK STATE ARCHIVES. To reach the Division of Corporations from the railroad station, take a taxi or the #14 bus to State and Pearl Streets. Walk one block east to James Street.

To reach the Division of Licensing Services, take a taxi or the #14 bus to Swan Street and Washington Avenue. Cross Washington and transfer to the #13 bus. The #13 bus stops in front of 84 Holland Avenue. NOTE: Call or write this office before coming. Accessible entrance at the north end of the building — "C" wing entrance (Albany Medical Center).

Description of Resources:

The Office of the Secretary of State, known as the "Keeper of the Records," was established by state constitution in 1777. Its diverse functions today include recording pardons and commutations received from the Governor, filing certificates of incorporation other than those from banking, insurance and education; authorizing foreign corporations to do business in the state; administering oaths of office; appointing notaries public; registering charitable organizations; supervising the administration of cemetery corporations; and licencing and regulation many professions.

1. Division of Corporations (microfilm):

Corporations, 1811 to present
Limited liability companies and partnerships, October, 1994 to present
Limited partnerships, July, 1991 to present

For each type of business, the Division has current entity name, date organized, jurisdiction if other than NYS, county location, service of process address, registered agent, if any, and current status of the entity. Information for corporations may include the name and business address of the chief executive officer. The searchable online database includes all businesses in existence on or after December 5, 1977. For those that closed before December 31, 1984, the database includes a complete or partial history. Records of corporations that went out of existence prior to December 5, 1977 are available but must be searched manually. The names/addresses of incorporators are in the files but not computerized.

NOTE: For records of general partnerships and sole proprietorship filed as assumed names/trade name and "doing business as," see COUNTY CLERK'S OFFICE in the appropriate jurisdiction. Corporation filings are sent to the COUNTY CLERK'S OFFICE once completed. A microfilm copy is retained in Albany. For records of incorporations, 1811–1825, see NEW YORK STATE DEPARTMENT OF EDUCATION, NEW YORK STATE ARCHIVES.

2. <u>Division of Licensing Services</u> has records of more than 650,000 individuals licensed through this Division. Among those professions currently licensed by the department are:

Alarm Installers	Notaries Public
Apartment Information Vendors	Pet cemeteries and Pet Crematorium
Apartment Sharing Agents	Private Investigators
Appearance Enhancement (cosmetologists, etc.)	Real Estate Appraisers
Armored Car Carriers and Guards	Real Estate Branch Offices
Bail Enforcement Agents	Real Estate Brokers, Associate Brokers, Salespersons
Barbers	Security Guards
Central Dispatch Facilities	Watch, Guard and Patrol Agencies
Coin Processors	Telemarketer Businesses
Hearing Aid Dispensers and Businesses	

Only active records are retained (generally 6 years). Two-years of the licenses are maintained in the online database. The Division manually preserves the prior 4 years of the licensee's history. Earlier records are destroyed. NOTE: This may change in the future when computers are upgraded. The online database includes: registration number (ID number), name, profession, business name, business address and county. Frequently, only name, occupation and county are included. A copy of the complete record may be requested under the Freedom of Information Act. See "Restrictions on Use."

NOTE: For other licensed occupations such as physicians and attorneys, see NYS Physicians profile on NYS Department of Health website (www.nydoctorprofile.com/search_parameters.jsp); and the NYS Attorney Directory, on NYS Courts website (www.courts.state.ny.us).

See also NYS Department of Education, Office of the Professions, for online verification of licenses (www.op.nysed.gov/opsearches.htm) in 38 professions including: accountant, acupuncture, architect, athletic trainer, audiologist, chiropractor, dental assistance, dental hygienist, dentist, dietician/nutritionist, engineer, interior designer, land surveying, landscape architect, midwife, massage therapist, medical physics, occupational therapist, optometry, pharmacist, physician, podiatrist, practical nurse, psychologist, respiratory therapist, shorthand reporter, social worker, speech pathologist, and veterinarian.

3. <u>Miscellaneous Records Unit</u> (part of the Division of Corporations)

Records of <u>pardons</u> and <u>commutations</u> are retained for a period of 4 years and then transferred to the NEW YORK STATE ARCHIVES

Finding Aides:

1. <u>Corporations</u>: There is an online database for all corporations and business entities, including non-profit corporations such as landsmanshaftn, in existence on or after December 5, 1977. This database includes corporations and businesses entities that were active on December 5, 1977 but subsequently went out-of-business.

   The Division has an index card file, 1881–1990, by name of corporation which includes corporation and businesses entities that went out-of-business prior to December 5, 1977.

2. <u>Licenses</u>: A search of the online database can be made by registration number (ID number), name, or business name. Residential address is not included in the database and is protected by privacy law. See "Restrictions on Use."

3. <u>Miscellaneous Records Unit</u>: Index cards are available for pardon and commutation records.

Fees/Copies:

1. <u>Division of Corporations</u>: Callers to 1-900-TEL-CORP (835-2677) may request a search of the corporations database for up to 5 names. A fee of $4 is charged per call (charged to telephone bill). NOTE: This information is also available online, by mail or fax at no cost. Requests for more than 5 entities must be submitted by mail or in person at the Albany office together with a payment of $5 for each entity over 5.

   A drawdown (prepaid) account may be established to directly access the Division's computerized index of corporations and other business entity records at a fee or $.75 per transaction. A transaction allows access to the filing history of all business entities returned by the search. Special software is provided by the Department of State after the Drawdown Account Application is approved. A minimum deposit of $25 is required to establish an account.

For information not in the computer (names/addresses of incorporators or filers), a plain copy of the document can be requested for $5, and a certified copy for $10. Checks should be made payable to the "Department of State." There are additional fees for expedited processing. Faxed requests may be charged to a drawdown account or credit card (Visa or MasterCard). A Credit Card Authorization Form is available online. Copies are returned by first class mail, or Federal Express or similar service, not fax. To use Federal Express or similar service, provide your account number with the service provider or include a request to charge your credit card.

2. Division of Licensing Services and Miscellaneous Records: A fee of $15 is charged per record for a certified license history; and a fee of $5 plus $.50 per page for a copy of the license application. Requests must be made in writing by mail. Payment may be made by personal check, money order or credit card.

Description of Facility:

Division of Corporations card index to Corporation records is located on the 2nd floor of 41 State Street. Division of Licensing Services is on the first floor of 84 Holland Avenue.

Restriction on Use:

Corporations: The information maintained here does not include the names of officers or directors of a corporation. However, it can provide the name and address of the chief executive officer of a business corporation, the registered agent, if designated, and the principal business location of the corporation. The names and addresses of incorporator and filer may be obtained at no charge through examination of documents in person at this Albany office.

Licenses: Private investigators, watch guards, patrol agencies and armored car carriers are identified by business name only, not individual name, in the online database.

APPENDICES

APPENDIX A

SOUNDEX CODE SYSTEMS

		National Archives	HIAS	NYC Health Dept.	NYS Health Dept
1.	First letter of family name	Each code begins with the first letter of the surname.	Same as National Archives, except consonants that are similarly pronounced are <u>interfiled</u> in this system: C, K filed under C E, I filed under E J, Y filed under J S, Z filed under S V, W filed under V	Same as HIAS.	Same as National Archives.
2.	Code next 3 consonants (do not include first letter of the surname.)	<u>Code</u> <u>Key letter or equivalent</u> 1 B, F, P, V 2 C, G, J, K, Q, S, X, Z 3 D, T 4 L 5 M, N 6 R	<u>Code</u> <u>Key Letter or equivalent</u> 1 B, F, P, V, W Remainder same as National Archives.	Same as National Archives.	Same as National Archives.
3.	Exceptions	A, E, I, O, U, Y, H, W are not coded.	A, E, I, O, U, Y, H are not coded. W <u>is</u> coded (See rule #2.)	Same as National Archives.	Same as National Archives.
		When double consonants or two key letters or equivalent appear together, the two are coded as one letter. If two such consonants are separated by an H or W, the second consonant is ignored.	Same as National Archives. Also, if two such consonants are separated by an H, the second consonant is ignored. The W <u>is</u> coded. (See rule #2.) Three family names are arbitrarily assigned a coded number, regardless of spelling with -tz, -cz, -ts, -c, -z: Moskowitz M-213 Schwartz S-162 Horowitz H-613	Same as National Archives.	Same as National Archives.
		Names with prefixes such as *van, Von, de, le, Di, D', dela, or du*, may be coded both with or without the title or prefix.	Same as National Archives.	Same as National Archives.	Same as National Archives.
4.	Arrangement	Within each surname code, names are arranged alphabetically by the first name.	Same as National Archives.	Arranged by date of birth.	Same as National Archives.

The Soundex system used by the National Archives was patented by Robert C. Russell, April 2, 1918 (#1,261,167).

APPENDIX B
BIBLIOGRAPHY OF EASTERN EUROPEAN MEMORIAL (YIZKOR) BOOKS
WITH CALL NUMBERS FOR FIVE JUDAICA LIBRARIES IN NEW YORK

Memorial (or yizkor) books are among the most frequently consulted published sources on individual Eastern European Jewish communities. The narrative sections that comprise the bulk of a memorial book treat the history, culture and institutions of the town's Jewish community with particular emphasis on the period between the two world wars and the Holocaust. Many memorial books also include articles on prominent local rabbinical families and lists of Holocaust martyrs, which can be of particular value to the genealogist. Most are in Hebrew and/or Yiddish, though some also have sections in English or other languages. While some memorial books are written by individual authors, most represent the collective editorial efforts of organizations of former townspeople (also known as *landsmanshaftn*), which served as the publishers of the overwhelming majority of these works.

This edition of the Bibliography supersedes and expands upon the version included as Appendix A of *Genealogical Resources in the New York Metropolitan Area,* published by the Jewish Genealogical Society, Inc. in 1989, and updates the bibliography published by the JGS in 1992 and later supplements. The 1989 edition was based upon the work compiled by David Bass, *Bibliographical List of Memorial Books Published in the Years 1943-1972 (Yad Vashem Studies, 9, 1973)*; Zachary M. Baker's bibliography published in *Toledot: The Journal of Jewish Genealogy* (Fall 1979-Winter 1980 issue) and edited by Steven Siegel; and updates published in Baker's *From a Ruined Garden: The Memorial Books of Polish Jewry*, 1983 and 1985.

Most memorial books can be located in New York City, with its unequaled Judaica library resources. Five New York City Judaica collections have been surveyed for their holdings of memorial books. A sixth, the library of the Museum of Jewish Heritage, A Living Memorial to the Holocaust, has a collection of over 200 Yizkor books not included here. Yizkor books formerly part of the Bund collection, are now included in YIVO's collection. Call numbers at these libraries are listed after each citation:

YIVO: YIVO INSTITUTE FOR JEWISH RESEARCH LIBRARY (includes former Bund library)
NYPL: NEW YORK PUBLIC LIBRARY, JEWISH DIVISION
JTS: JEWISH THEOLOGICAL SEMINARY LIBRARY
YU: YESHIVA UNIVERSITY, MENDEL GOTTESMAN LIBRARY
HUC: HEBREW UNION COLLEGE-JEWISH INSTITUTE OF RELIGION, KLAU LIBRARY

This bibliography is arranged in three sections: General Reference Works, Countries and Regions, Localities. The last two sections are arranged alphabetically by place name.

In the Localities section, place names are given as originally compiled by Baker and Siegel. Alternate place names (current and former) are cross referenced where these were identified as the "subject" by one or more library. Country identified in parentheses is generally that of the locality today, as indicated by library "subject" designation. Use *Where Once We Walked* or other gazetteers to identify other alternate names or to verify current place name of a town. Country abbreviations include: (A) Austria, (B) Belarus, (Cr) Croatia, (Cz) Czech Republic, (Gr) Greece, (Hu) Hungary, (M) Moldova, (Mac) Macedonia, (P) Poland, (Ro) Romania, (R) Russia, (Sr) Serbia, (Slo) Slovakia, (U) Ukraine.

Book titles are given in transliteration (standard Romanization) of the Yiddish or Hebrew originals as used by most libraries today. English titles are supplied in brackets after the Hebrew or Yiddish titles. An asterisk (*) after an English title indicates that the translated title was supplied in the work itself. Most other titles were translated by Baker/Siegel.

The languages in which the book is written are noted at the end of each citation as follows: (H) Hebrew, (Y) Yiddish, (E) English, (Cz) Czech, (F) French, (G) German, (Gr) Greek, (Hu) Hungarian, (J) Judezmo, (P) Polish, (R) Russian, (Ro) Romanian, (S) Spanish, (Sc) Serbo-Croatian. NOTE: For translations of some of these books, check the Yizkor Book Project online at: www.jewishgen.org/yizkor.

The following cross-references are used:
a) A "see" reference sends the reader from a current or alternate spelling of a place name to the one citing the book.
b) A "see under" reference sends the reader from the name of a locality discussed in a special chapter of a book on another locality to the full citation for the latter book.
c) A "see also" reference sends the reader to other books that include chapters on a locality.

GENERAL REFERENCE WORKS

Arim ve-imahot be-Yisrael; matsevet kodesh li-kehilot Yisrael she-nehrevu bi-yede aritsim u-tmeim be-milhemet ha-olam ha-aharona [Towns and mother-cities in Israel; memorial of the Jewish communities which perished...]. Ed.: Y. L. Fishman (Maimon). Jerusalem, The Rav Kuk Institute (H)

vol. 1, Ostrog, Eisenstadt, Berlin, Vilna, Lwow, Munkacs. 1947. 371 p., ports.

vol. 2, Vienna-Hamburg-Wandsbek, Odessa, Budapest, Gomel, Nemirov, Krakow, 1948. 354 p., ports.

vol. 3, Warsaw. [By] D. Flinker. 1948. 308 p., ports.

vol. 4, Ungvar, Venice, Czernowitz, Nikolsburg. 1950. 313 p., ports.

vol. 5, Stanislawow. Eds.: D. Sadan, M. Gelerter. 1952. 429 p., ports., music.

vol. 6, Brody. [By] N. Gelber. 1956. 347 p., ports., map.

vol. 7, Bratislava (Pressburg). [By] Sh. Weingarten-Hakohen. 1960. 184 p., ports.

YIVO: BM 290 M3 1946   NYPL: *PXK Fishman
JTS: DS135 E8 M3 (vol. 1-7)   YU: 933.47 F537A
HUC: *HI 616 (vol.1-7)

Pinkas ha-kehilot; entsiklopediya shel ha-yishuvim ha-Yehudiyim le-min hivasdam ve-ad le-aher shoat Milhemet ha-olam ha-sheniyah [Pinkas hakehillot: encyclopedia of Jewish communities*]. Jerusalem, Yad Vashem Martyrs' and Heroes' Remembrance Authority, 1969-1998

YIVO: Ref DS135 E81   NYPL: *PXK 96-1252
JTS: Ref DS135 E83 P5   YU: Ref DS135 E83 P5
HUC: f DS135 E83 P5

Romania. vol. 1: Eds.: Theodore Lavi, Aviva Broshni. 1969. 224, 552 p., illus. (H)

YIVO: DS135 R78 1969 v.1   NYPL: *PXK 96-1252 v.1
HUC: fDS135.R7 P56 1969 (vol.1) YU: Ref DS135 E83 P5 v.1 pt.1

vol. 2: Eds.: Jan Ancel, Theodore Lavi. 1980. 5, 568 p., illus., maps (H)

YIVO: DS135 r78 1969 v.2   HUC: fDS135.R7 P56 1969 (vol.2)
YU: Ref DS135 E83 P5 v.1, pt.2.

Germany. vol. 1: *Bavaria.* Ed.: Baruch Zvi Ophir. 1972. 12, 683, 40 p., illus. (H,E)

YIVO: DS135 E81 G47 1972 v.1   NYPL: *PXK 96-1252 v.2 pt.1
HUC: fDS135.G33 P56 1972 (vol 1)   YU: Ref DS135 E83 P5 v.2, pt.1

vol. 2: *Württemberg, Hohenzollern, Baden.* Ed.: Joseph Walk. 1986. 12, 549 p., illus., maps, ports. (H)

YIVO: DS135 E81 G47 1986 v.2   NYPL: *PXK 96-1252 v.2 pt.2
HUC: fDS135.G33 P56 1972 (vol 2)   YU: Ref DS135 E83 P5 v.2, pt.2.

vol. 3: *Hesse, Hesse-Nassau, Frankfort.* Ed.: Henry Wassermann. 1992. 12, 725 p., illus., maps. (H)

YIVO: DS135 G37 G47 1972 v.3   YU: Ref DS135 E83 P5 v.2, pt.3.

Hungary. Ed.: Theodore Lavi. 1975. 8, 557 p., illus. (H)

YIVO: DS135 E81 H8 1976   NYPL: *PXK 96-1252 v.3
HUC: fDS135.H9 P55 1976   YU: Ref DS135 E83 P5 v.4

Poland. vol. 1: *The communities of Lodz and its region.* Eds.: Danuta Dabrowska, Abraham Wein. 1976. 15, 285, 15 p., illus. (H,E)

YIVO: DS135 E81 P65 1976 v.1   NYPL: *PXK 96-1252 v.4
HUC: fDS135.P6 P492 1976 (vol 1)   YU: Ref DS135 E83 P5 v. 3 pt 1

vol. 2: *Eastern Galicia.* Eds.: Danuta Dabrowska, Abraham Wein, Aharon Weiss. 1980. 31, 563 p., illus., maps (H,E)

YIVO: DS135 E81 P65 1976 v.1   NYPL: *PXK 96-1252 v.4 pt.2
HUC: fDS135.P6 P492 1976 (vol 2)   YU: Ref DS135 E83 P5 v. 3 pt.2

vol. 3: *Western Galicia and Silesia.* 1984. 23, 392 p., illus., maps (H)

YIVO: DS135 E81 P65 1976 v.3   NYPL: *PXK 96-1252 v.4 pt.3
HUC: fDS135.P6 P492 1976 (vol 3)   YU: Ref DS135 E83 P5 v. 3 pt 3

vol. 4: *Warsaw and its region.* 1989. 24, 482 p., illus., maps (H)

YIVO: DS135 E81 P65 1976 v.4   NYPL: *PXK 96-1252 v.4 pt.4
HUC: fDS135.P6 P492 1976 (vol.4)   YU: Ref DS135 E83 P5 v. 3 pt.4

vol. 5: *Volhynia and Polesie.* Ed.: Shmuel Spector. 1990. 9, 341 p., illus., maps (H)

YIVO: DS135 E81 P65 1976 v.5   NYPL: *PXK 96-1252 v.4 pt.5
HUC: fDS135.P6 P492 1976 (vol 5)   YU: Ref DS135 E83 P5 v. 3.pt 5

vol. 6: *Poznan and Pomerania Districts; Gdansk.* Ed.: A. Wein. 1999. 156 p., illus., maps, port. (H)

YIVO: DS135 E81 P65 1976 v.6   NYPL: *PXK 96-1252 v.4 pt 6
YU: Ref DS135 E83 P5 v. 3 pt 6

vol. 7: *Lublin and Kielce.* Ed.: A Wien. 1999. 628 p.

YIVO: DS135 E81 P65 1976 v7   NYPL: *PXK 96-1252 v.4 pt7

The Netherlands. Authors: Joseph Michman, Hartog Beem, Dan Michman. 1985. 10, 434 p., illus., maps, ports. (H)

YIVO: DS135 E81 N4 1985   NYPL: *PXK 96-1252 v.5
HUC: fDS135.N4 M5 1985   YU: Ref DS135 E83 P5 v. 5

Yugoslavia. Ed.: Zvi Loker. 1988. 382 p., illus., maps, ports. (H)

YIVO: DS135 E81 Y8 1988   NYPL: *PXK 96-1252 v.6
HUC: fDS135.Y8 P56 1988   YU: Ref DS135 E83 P5 v. 7

Latvia and Estonia. Ed.: Dov Levin. 1988. 11, 396 p., illus., maps, ports. (H)

YIVO: DS135E81 L38 1988   NYPL: *PXK 96-1252 v.7
HUC: fDS135.R93 L315 1988   YU: Ref DS135 E83 P5 v. 6

Lithuania. Eds.: Don Levin, Yosef Rozin. 1996. 17, 748 p., illus., maps, ports. (H). See trans below.

YIVO: DS135 E81 L58 1996   NYPL: *PXK 96-1252 v.8
HUC: fDS135.L5 P56 1996   YU: Ref DS135 E83 P5 v.8

Lithuania. The Litvaks: a short history of the Jews in Lithuania. Trans. from *Pinkas ha-kehilot* by A.Teller. Jerusalem, Yad Vashem, 2000. 282 p., illus., map. (E).
YIVO: DS135 E81 L5813 2000 NYPL: *PXW 00-6842
JTS: DS135 L5 L44513 2000 YU: DS135 R93 L5554313 2000
HUC: DS135 L5 L414513 2000

Libya-Tunisia. Ed.: Irit Abramski-Bligh. 1997. ix, 553, 12 p., illus., maps, ports. (H + E introduction)
YIVO: DS135 E81 L53 1997 NYPL: *PXK 96-1252 v.9
YU: Ref DS135 E83 P5 v.9

Greece (Yavan). Ed.: Berakhah Rivlin. 1998. 12, 453p, xviii maps, illus., facsims, ports. (H)
YIVO: DS135 E81 G7 1999 NYPL: *PXK 96-1252 v.10
YU: Ref DS135 E83 P5 v.10

COUNTRIES AND REGIONS

Bessarabia (M/U). *Al admat Besarabiyah; divre mehkar, zikhronot, reshimot, teudot... le-kviat ha-demut shel Yahadutah* [Upon the land of Bessarabia; studies, memoirs, articles, documents and essays depicting its image]. Ed: K. A. Bertini. Tel Aviv, United Assoc. of Former Residents of Bessarabia, [1958/1959-1962/1963] 3 vols.: 266, 213 p., illus., ports. (H)
YIVO:Bessarabia 1958 NYPL: *PXW(Bessarabia)
JTS: DS135 R93 B455 A4 HUC: Per

Bessarabia (M/U). *Bisarabyah ha-Yehudit be-ma'arakhoteha; ben shete milhamot ha-olam 1914-1940* [The Jews in Bessarabia; between the world wars 1914-1940*]. [By] David Vinitzky. Jerusalem, The Zionist Library, 1973. 2 vols.: 179 p., illus. (H)
YIVO: Bessarabia 1973 NYPL: *PXW(Bessarabia) 75-2345
JTS: DS135 R93 B455 V5 YU: DS135 R93 B48
HUC: HI 707.3

Bessarabia (M/U). *Pirke Besarabyah; measef la-avarah shel Yahadut Besarabyah* [Chapters from the history of Bessarabian Jewry]. Eds.: L. Kuperstein, Y. Korn. Tel Aviv, "Nativ," [1952]. 2 vols., ports. (H)
YIVO: Bessarabia 1952 NYPL: *PXW (Kuperstein..) v.1

Bessarabia (M/U). *Yahadut Bessarabyah* [The Jewry of Bessarabia]. Eds.: K.A. Bertini *et al.* Jerusalem, The Encyclopaedia of the Jewish Diaspora, [1971]. 950 columns, illus., maps, ports. (H)
YIVO: Bessarabia (Entsiklopedya, t.11) 1971
NYPL: *PX+ 96-485 v.11 JTS: Ref +DS135 E8 E55 v.11

Bulgaria. *Yahadut Bulgaryah* [Bulgaria*]. Eds.: A-. Romano *et al.* Jerusalem, The Encyclopaedia of the Jewish Diaspora, [1967]. 1018 columns, illus., maps, ports., facsims. (H)
YIVO: Bulgaria (Entsiklopdya, t.10) 1967
NYPL: *PX+ 96-485 v.10 YU: 933.503 E61 1953 v.10
JTS: Ref +DS135 E8 E55 v.10

Carpatho-Ruthenia (U) see Karpatalja

Crimea (U). *Yahadut Krim me-kadmutah ve-ad ha-Shoah* [The Jews of Crimea from their beginnings until the Holocaust]. Ed.: Yehezkel Keren. Jerusalem, Reuven Mass, 1981. 337 p., illus. (H)
NYPL: *PXW 00-3555 JTS: DS135 R93 C7 K4
YU: DS135 R93 K768 1981 HUC: DS135.R93 K768

Dabrowa Basin (Dombrowa Basin) (P/Cz) see Zaglebie

Galicia (P/U) *Gedenkbukh Galitsye* [Memorial book of Galicia]. Ed.: N. Zucker (Tsuker). Buenos Aires, Farlag "Zikhronot," [1964]. 334 p., ports., facsims. (Y)
YIVO: Galicia 1964 NYPL: *PXV(Galicia)
JTS: DS135 P62 G3 Z8 YU: DS135 P62 G34

Galicia (P/U). *Pinkes Galitsye* [Memorial book of Galicia]. Ed.: N. Zucker. Buenos Aires, Galitsyaner farband, 1945. xvi, 638 p., illus., ports. (Y)
YIVO: Galicia 1945 NYPL: *PXV(Galicia) 84-438
JTS: DS135 P62 E32 YU: DS135 G2 P5
HUC: HIW 445

Galicia (P/U). *Sefer Galitsye gedenk bukh* [Anales de Galitzia (Sefer Galitzia)*]. Ed.: Yosef Okrutni. Buenos Aires, Farlag "Galitsye" baym Tsentral Farband fun Galitsyaner Yidn in Buenos-Ayres, 1968. 408 p., illus., ports., facsims. (Y; introd.:S)
YIVO: Galicia 1968 NYPL: *PXV(Galicia) 89-11342
JTS: DS135 P62 G3 S4 YU: DS135 P62 G37 1968

Greece. *In memoriam; hommage aux victimes juives des Nazis en Grèce.,* Ed.: M. Molho. Vol. 2 by J. N. Salonique, N. Nicolaides, 1948-1953. 3 vols., illus, ports, facsims. (F); 2nd ed. revised vol. 2. Thessalonique, Communauté Israélite de Thessalonique, 1973. 469 p., illus, map. (F)
YIVO: /89383 (2nd ed.) JTS: DS135 G7 M59 (1st ed)
NYPL: *ZP 1357 No. 6 (1st ed.) and *PXM 80-3229 (2nd ed.)
YU: DS135 G7 M66 1948 (1st ed.) and DS135 G7 M66 1973 (2nd ed.)
HUC: HIW 486

Greece. *In memoriam; hommage aux victimes juives des Nazis en Grèce.,* Ed.: Michael Molho. Trans.: vols. 1 and 2 into Hebrew. Jerusalem, Yad Vashem, [1965]. 266, x p., map, ports. (H)
YU: DS135 G7 M6615 1965

Karpatalja (region) (U). *Karpatorus* [Karpatorus*]. Ed.: Y. Erez. Jerusalem, The Encyclopaedia of the Jewish Diaspora, 1959. 590 columns, ports., facsims. (H)
YIVO: Carpathos (Entsiklopedya, t.7) 1959
NYPL: *PX+ 96-485 v.7 JTS: Ref +DS135 E8 E55 v.7
YU: 933.503 E61 1959 v.7 HUC: HI 999

Karpatalja (region) (U). *Sefer Shefer harere kedem; golat Karpatoros-Marmarosh be-tifartah uve-hurbanah* [The beauty of the mountains of yore; the Karpatorus-

Marmarosh exile...]. [By] Sh. Rozman. Brooklyn, Zichron Kedoshim, vol. 1 [1991]. 528 p., illus., maps, ports. vol. 2 [1994]. 448 p., illus., map, ports., facsims. (H)

YIVO: Maramures 1991 (2 vols)

NYPL: *PXW (Transcarpathian) 91-899 v.1 & 2

JTS: DS135 R93 C26 R62 1991   YU: DS135 R93 Z277 1991

Karpatalja (region) (U). *Sefer zikhron kedoshim li-Yehude Karpatoros-Marmoresh* [Memorial book of the martyrs of Karpatorus-Marmarosh]. [By] Sh. Rozman. Rehovot, [1968]. 12, 32-543 p., illus., ports. (Y)

YIVO: Maramures 1968   NYPL: *PXW(Transcarpathian)

JTS: DS135 R93 C26 R6   YU: 933.5 C998K

Krymskaia Oblast (U) see Crimea

Latvia. *The Jews in Latvia.* Eds.: M. Bobe (Bobeh) *et al.* [Tel Aviv], Association of Latvian and Estonian Jews in Israel, [1971]. 384 p., illus, map, ports. (E)

YIVO: Latvia 1971   NYPL: *PXW 76-5880

JTS: DS135 R93 L25 J4   YU: 933.5 L36 5J

Latvia. *Yahadut Latviyah; sefer zikaron* [The Jews of Latvia; a memorial book]. Eds.: B. Eliav, M. Bobeh, A. Kremer. Tel Aviv, Former Residents of Latvia and Estonia in Israel, [1952 or 1953]. 458 p., ports., map (H)

YIVO: Latvia 1952   NYPL: *PXW (Lubotzky)

JTS: DS135 R93 L3 E4   YU: 933.547.5 L929

HUC: HIW 393

Latvia. *Yidn in Letland* [Latvian Jewry*]. Ed.: Mendel Bobe. Tel Aviv, Reshafim, 1972. 368 p., illus. (Y)

YIVO: Latvia 1972   JTS: DS135 R93 L25 B62

Lithuania. *Bleter fun Yidish Lite* [Lithuanian Jews; a memorial book*]. Ed.: Jacob Rabinovitch. Tel Aviv, Ha-Menora, 1974. 289 p., illus. (Y,H,E)

YIVO: Lithuania 1974   NYPL: *PXV(Lithuania) 75-5641

JTS: DS135 L5 R27   HUC: HIW 492

Lithuania. *Lite* [Lithuania], vol. 1. Eds.: M. Sudarski, U. Katsenelenbogn, Y. Kisn. [New York], Jewish-Lithuanian Cultural Society, [1951-1965]. 2070 columns, viii p., ports., maps, facsims. (Y); [Lithuania], vol. 2. Ed.: Ch. Leikowicz. Tel Aviv, I. L. Peretz, 1965. 894 columns, illus., ports., facsims. (Y)

YIVO: DS135 L5 L5   NYPL: *PXV+ 97-3520

JTS: +DS135 L5 L5 (vol. 1)   YU: 933.547.5 L776

Lithuania. *Lithuanian Jewish Communities.* [Eds.:] N. Schoenburg, S. Schoenburg. New York, Garland Pub., 1991. xi, 502 p., maps. Trans. from vol. 3 of *Yahadut Lita* (1967). (E)

YIVO: DS135 R93 L556 1991   JTS: DS135 L5 S32 1991

NYPL: *PXW (Lithuania) 91-405   YU: DS135 R93 L583 1991

HUC: DS135.L5 S38 1996 and DS135 R93 L556 1991

Lithuania. *Yahadut Lita* [Lithuanian Jewry*], vol. 1. Eds.: N. Goren, L. Garfinkel *et al.* Tel Aviv, Am-Hasefer,

[1959 or 1960]. 648 p., ports., maps, facsims., music (H); vol. 2, 1972 (H); vol. 3. Eds.: R. Hasman, D. Lipec *et al.* Tel Aviv, Igud yotse Lita be-Yisrael, 1967. 396 p., ports., maps (H); vol. 4: The Holocaust, 1941-1945. Ed.: Leib Garfunkel. Tel Aviv, 1984 (H)

YIVO: DS135 L5 Y3   NYPL: *PXV+ (Lithuania)

JTS: +DS135 R93 L5 Y3   YU: DS125 R93 L589 1959

Lithuania. *Yidishe shtet, shtetlekh un dorfishe yishuvim in Lite: biz 1918: historish-biografishe skitses* [Jewish cities, towns and villages in Lithuania*]. [By] Berl Kagan [Kohen]. New York, B. Kohen, 1991. ix, 791, v p. (Y)

YIVO: DS135 L5 K3 1991   NYPL: *PXV(Lithuania) 91-540

JTS: DS135 L5 K27 1991   YU: DS123 R93 L5548 1991

Maramures (region) (Ro). *Sefer Marmarosh; meah ve-shishim kehilot kedoshot be-yishuvan uve-hurbanan* [The Marmaros book; in memory of a hundred and sixty Jewish communities*]. Eds.: S. Y. Gros, Y. Yosef Kohen. Tel Aviv, Bet Marmarosh, [1983]. 151, 436, 58 p., illus., map, ports. (H,Y,E)

YIVO: Marmures 1983   NYPL: *PXR+ 84-457

JTS: +DS135 R72 M3 S4 1983   YU: DS135 R72 M377

Maramures (region) (Ro). *Sefer di sheyne fargangenheyt fun Marmarosh: di mishpohe in Marmorosh.* [Book of Marmarosh's beautiful history...], by Eliezer P. Soyfer. Brooklyn, Marmarosh Holocaust Memorial Fund of Cong. Beth Paksch, 1999. 515 p., illus., ports. (Y)

YIVO: Maramures 1999   NYPL: *PXR 99-2267

JTS: DS135 R72 M2 S8 1999   YU: DS135 R72 M375 1999

Maramures (region) (Ro) see also under Karpatalja

Poland. *Megilat Polin* [The scroll of Poland]. Ed.: Y. L. Levin. Part 5: Holocaust, vol. I. Jerusalem, Society of Religious Jews from Poland, [1961]. 351 p., illus., ports., facsims. (H,Y)

YIVO: Poland 1961   NYPL: *PXV+ 98-2232

Polesie (B/U). *Kuntres "Ve-ad dor va-dor emunato"...* [His faith extends from generation to generation; description of Jewish life that existed in Eastern European communities before the Holocaust*]. Jerusalem, The Memorial Committee for Kedoshe Polesie and Volin, [1987/88]. 118 p., illus., maps, ports. (H; introd.:E)

YIVO: Pripyat Marshes 1988   YU: BM 333 B44 VA 1988

Pripyat Marshes (B/U) see Polsie

Ruthenia (region) (U) see Karpatalja

Salaj (region) (Ro). *Sefer Yehude Salaz-Siladi: toldotehem, kehilotehem, mishpehotehem...* [Memorial-book of Salaj-Szilagy Jewry*]. Ed.: David Giladi. Tel Aviv, Council of Siladi Jews in Israel, 1989. 338, 414 p., illus., map, ports., facsims. (H,Hu,E)

YIVO: Salaj 1989   NYPL: *PXM+(Salaj) 90-3753

YU: 92-0515   YU: DS135 R72 S247 1989

Tokay Valley (region) (Hu) see Abaujszanto (under "Localities" below).

Transcarpathian Ruthenia (U) see Karpatalja

Transylvania (Ro). *Toldot ha-kehilot be-Transilvanyah; perakim mi-sivalot ha-Yehudim ve-nitsane ha-gevurah bi-tekufat ha-Shoah be-Hungaryah* [History of the communities of Transylvania]. [By] Y. Shvartz. Hadera, ha-Aguda Yad li-Kehilot Transylvania, [1975]. 293 p., illus. (H)

YIVO: Transylvania 1975   NYPL: *PXR 78-506
JTS: DS135 R72 T77 S32   YU: DS135 R72 T77
HUC: HIW 567

Transylvania (Ro) see also under Marosvarsarhely

Ukraine . *Shtet un shtetlekh in Ukraine un in andere teyln fun Rusland; forshungen in Yidisher geshikhte un Yidishn lebenshtayger* [Cities and towns in the history of the Jews in Russia and the Ukraine*]. By M. Osherowitch. New York, The M. Osherovitsh Jubillee [sic] Committee, 1948. 2 vols. (305, 306 p.) (Y)

YIVO: Ukraine 1948   NYPL: *PXW (Osherowitch)
JTS: DS135 R9 O8   HUC: HI 996.3

Ukraine. *Yidn in Ukraine* [Jews in the Ukraine*]. New York, Assoc. for Commemoration of the Ukrainian Jews, 1961-1967. 2 vols., illus., ports., maps, facsims. (Y)

YIVO: Ukraine 1961   NYPL: *PXW+ (Ukraine)
JTS: DS135 R93 U35 H4   YU: DS135 R93 U52 1961
HUC: HI 996.2

Zaglebie (P/Cz). *Pinkes Zaglembye; memorial book*. Ed.: I. Rapaport. Zaglembie Society and Pinkes Zaglembie Committee. Tel Aviv, HaMenorah, 1972. 612, 82 p., illus. (Y,E)

YIVO: Zaglebie Slasko-Dabrowskie 1972   HUC: HIW 481
NYPL: *PXV(Zaglebie) 75-5593
YU: DS135 P62 D244475 1972

Zakarpatskaya Oblast (U) see Karpatalja

LOCALITIES

Abauj-Torna Megye (Hu) see Sziksz.

Abaujzanto (Hu) *Wine and thorns in Tokay Valley: Jewish Life in Hungary: the history of Abaujzanto*, by Z. Stessel. Madison, NJ, Fairleigh Dickenson University Press, [1995]. 341 p., illus., maps. (E)

YIVO: /87587   NYPL: *PXT (Abaujzanto) 95-3509
JTS: DS135 H92 A22 S72 1995 YU: DS135 H92 A257 1995

Akkerman (U). *Akerman ve-ayarot ha-mahoz; sefer edut ve-zikaron* [Akkerman and the towns of its district; memorial book]. Chairman of the editorial board: Nisan Amitai [Stambul]. Tel Aviv, Society of Emigrants from Akerman and Vicinity, 1983. 511 p., illus., map (H)

YIVO: Bilhorod-Dnistrovskyy 1983
NYPL: *PXW (Bilhorod) 97-1095

Aleksandria (U). *Pinkas ha-kehila Aleksandriya (Wolyn); sefer yizkor* [Memorial book of the community of Aleksandria (Wolyn)]. Comp.: S. Yizreeli; ed.: N. Livneh. [Tel Aviv], Aleksandria Society, 1972. 314 p., illus. (H)

NYPL: *PXW(Aleksandriya) 79-2894
JTS: DS135 R93 A54 P5   YU: DS135 R93 A576

Aleksandrow (P). *Aleksander* [Aleksandrow - near Lodz]. Ed.: N. Blumental. Tel Aviv, Association of Former Residents of Aleksandrow in Israel, [1968]. 391 p., illus., maps, ports., facsims. (H,Y)

YIVO: Aleksandrow Lodzki 1968 JTS: DS135 P62 A53
NYPL:*PXV(Aleksandrow)   YU: 933.47 P762 S475B

Alt Lesle (P) see Wloclawek

Amdur (B) see Indura

Amshinov (Amszynow) (P) see under Zyrardow

Andrychow (P) see Wadowice

Annopol (P). *Rachov-Annopol; pirke edut ve-zikaron* [Rachov-Annopol; testimony and remembrance*]. Ed.: S. Nitzan. [Tel Aviv], Rachov/Annopol and Surrounding Region Society, 1978. 544, 80 p., illus. (H,Y,E)

YIVO: Rachiv & Annopil 1978 NYPL: *PXV(Rachow) 89-8502
JTS: DS135 P62 R25 N5   YU: DS135 P62 R323 1978

Antopol (B). *Antopol (Antepolye); sefer yizkor* [Antopol (Antepolie) yizkor book*]. Ed.: Benzion H. Ayalon. Tel Aviv, Antopol Societies in Israel and America, 1972. 11, 754, 170 p., illus. (H,Y,E)

YIVO: Antopol 1972   NYPL: *PXW+ (Antopol) 83-373
JTS: +DS135 R93 A6 A92   YU: DS135 R93 A67 1972f

Antopol (B). *Antopol (5400-5702); mi-toldoteha shel kehilah ahat be-Polesyah* [Antopol, 1648-1942; from the history of one Jewish community in Polesie]. Ed.: Y. Levin. Tel Aviv, 5727 [1966/67]. 164 p., illus., maps. (H)

NYPL: *PXW(Antopol) (Yosef...)   JTS: DS135 R93 A6 Y6

Apt (P) see Opatow

Ashmiany (B) see Oszmiana

Ataki (M). *Atik: a gedenk bukh nakh a Yidisher kehileh in Besarabye = Yad le-Ataki: sefer zikaron li-kehilah Yehudit be-Besarabiah* [Bessarabia = libro memorable de las comunidades judias de Ataky - Bessarabia*]. Eds: Z. Seker; and supplement, H. Zamir. Tel Aviv, Igud yotze Ataky be-Yisrael", 1993-1997. 2 vols, illus., ports., maps, facsims. (H, Y; table of contents in E)

YIVO: Otaci 1993; and 1997 (supp.) NYPL: *PXW (Ataki) 00-5321

Augustow (P). *Sefer yizkor li-kehilat Ogustov veha-sevivah* [Memorial book of the community of Augustow and vicinity]. Ed.: Y. Alexandroni. Tel Aviv, Association of Former Residents of Ogustov and Vicinity, [1966]. 549 p., illus., maps, ports. (H,Y)
YIVO: Augustow 1966   NYPL: *PXV(Augustow)
JTS: DS135 P62 A8   YU: 933.5 P762A

Auschwitz (P) see Oswiecim

Babi Yar (U). *Yisker-bukh fun di umgekumene Yidn in Babi-Yar* [The Babi Yar book of remembrance*]. Eds.: J. Vinokurov, S. Kipnis, N. Levin. Philadelphia, Publishing House of Peace, 1983. 82, 202 p., illus., ports. (Y,R,E)
YIVO: Kiev 1983   JTS: DS135 R93 K48 K65 1983

Bacau (Ro). *Kehilat Bacau; historyah Yehudit mefoeret* [The community of Bacau]. [By] Meir Eibeshits (Aibshits); [Ed.]: Y. Voldi-Vardi. Tel Aviv, Hasofrim, 1990. 240 p., illus., ports. (H)
YIVO: Bacau 1990   NYPL: *PXM(Bacau) 91-3072
YU: DS135 R72 B324 1990

Baia Mare (Ro) see Nagybanya

Baitsh (P) see Biecz

Baklerove (Bakalarzewo) (P) see under Suwalki

Baligrod (P) see under Lesko

Balin (U) see under Kamenets-Podolskiy

Balmazujvaros (Hu) see under Debrecen

Balti (M). *Sefer Baltsi Besarabyah: yad ve-zekher le-Yahadut Baltsi* [Balti Besarabia: a memorial of the Jewish community*]. Eds: Yosef Mazur (editor-in-chief), Mishah Fuks (editor). [Israel], Agudat yotse Baltsi, 1993. 665 p., illus., maps, ports., music, tables, facsims. (H)
YIVO: Balti 1993   NYPL: *PXW+ (Beltsy) 95-2708
YU: DS135 R93 B324 1992

Baltsi (M) see Balti

Banffy-Hunyad (Ro) see under Huedin

Baranovichi (Baranovichy) (B) see Baranowicze

Baranovka (U) see Novograd-Volynskiy

Baranow (P). *Sefer yizkor Baranov* [A memorial to the Jewish community of Baranow*]. Ed.: N. Blumental. Jerusalem, Yad Vashem, [1964]. 236, xvi, p., ports., tabs., facsims. (H,Y,E)
YIVO: Baranow Sandomierski 1964   NYPL: *PXV(Baranow)
YU: 933.5 P762 B225   HUC: HIW 466

Baranow Sandomierski (P) see Baranow

Baranowicze (B). *Baranovits; sefer zikaron* [Baranovits, memorial book]. Tel Aviv, Irgun yotse Baranovits be-

Yisrael, 1953. 668 columns, ports., map, facsims. (H,Y)
YIVO: Baranowchi 1953   NYPL: *PXW+ (Baranovichi)
JTS: DS135 B282 B2   YU: DS135 R93 B326 1953
HUC: HIW 601

Baranowicze (B). *Baranovitsh in umkum un vidershtand* [Baranowich in martyrdom and resistance*]. Ed.: Joseph Foxman. New York, Baranowicher Farband of America, 1964. vol. 1: 5, 107 p. (Y)
YIVO: Baranovichi 1964   NYPL: *PXW(Baranovichi)

Baranowicze (B). *Ha-Ma'avak le-hayim shel Yehude Bernovits: kovets zikhronot 'al ha-Sho'ah shel nitsole geto Baranovits ve-lohamav* [The life struggle of the Jews of Baranowicze: collection of memoirs of the Holocaust, by survivors and fighters of the Baranowicze ghetto]. Eds.: Yitshak Pozner, Hanah Binet. [Israel], Nehamah Tsukerman, 1992. iv, 240 p., illus., maps, ports. (H)
YIVO: Baranovichi 1992   NYPL: *PXW (Baranovichi) 93-1008
YU: DS135 R93 B3264 1992

Bardejov (Slo). *Be-ovdan moladeti: yad va-shem li-kehilah kedoshah Bardeyov, Tsekhoslovakyah: mi-yom hivasdah ve-ad hurbanah* [Bardejov remembered]. [By] Abraham L. Grussgott. Brooklyn, 1988. 189 p., illus., facsims., maps, ports. (H,Y,Cz)
YIVO: Bardejov 1988   NYPL: *PXT(Bardejov) 91-4000
YU: DS135 C96 B374 1988

Bardo (P) see Warta

Barylow (U) see under Radziechow

Baytsh (P) see Biecz

Beclean (Betlen) (Ro) see under Des

Bedzin (P). *Pinkas Bendin* [Pinkas Bendin; a memorial to the Jewish community of Bendin*]. Ed.: A. Sh. Stein [Shtain]. Tel Aviv, Association of Former Residents of Bedzin in Israel, 1959. 431 p., ports. (H,Y)
YIVO: Bedzin 1959   NYPL: *PXV+ (Bedzin)
JTS: +DS135 P62 B385   HUC: HIW 459.2
YU: 933.47 (438) B4135

Bedzin (P). *Ir ha-metim: hashmadat ha-Yehudim be-ezor Zaglembiyah.* Trans. by David Liver of the writings of A. S. Stein [Shtain]. Tel Aviv, N. Tverski, [1945/1946]. 215p, illus, facsims. (H)
NYPL: *ZP-1097 no 1 (microfilm)   JTS: DS135 P62 B38 L5
YU: DS 933.47 L784   HUC: DS135.P62 B38

Bedzin (P) see also under Piotrkow Trybunalski

Beklean (Ro) see under Des

Belchatow (P). *Belkhatov yisker-bukh* [Belchatow memorial book]. Buenos Aires, Association of Polish

Jews in Argentine, 1951. 511 p., illus., map, ports. (Y)

YIVO: Belchatow 1951   NYPL: *PXV(Belchatow)
JTS: DS135 P62 B45 Y4   YU: DS135 P62 B42 1951
HUC: LY

Belgorod-Dnestrovski (U) see Akkerman

Beligrod (P) see under Lesko

Belitsa (B) see Bielica

Beltsy (M) see Balti

Belz (P). *Belz; sefer zikaron* [Belz memorial book]. Ed.: Yosef Rubin. Tel Aviv, Irgun yotse Belz veha-sevivah, 1974. 559 p., illus., music. (H,Y)

YIVO: Belzec 1974   NYPL: *PXV(Belzec) 75-5700
JTS: DS135 P62 B458 S4   YU: DS135 P62 B415
HUC: HL

Belzec (P) see Belz

Bendery (M). *Kehilat Benderi; sefer zikaron* [Yizkor book of our birthplace Bendery*]. Ed.: M. Tamari. Tel Aviv, Bendery Societies in Israel and the USA, 1975. 446, 42 p., illus. (H,Y,E)

YIVO: Bender (Tighina) 1975   NYPL: *PXW(Bendery) 77-3793
JTS: DS135 R93 B364 K43   HUC: HIW 480

Bendin (P) see Bedzin

Beregszasz (U) see Berehovo

Berehovo (U) *Yahadut Berehovo-Beregsas bi-temunot* [Berehovo - Beregszasz Zsidosaga kepekben* = The Jews of Berehovo-Beregszasz in Pictures]. [Written and edited by] Yehoshua Halevi. Tel Aviv - Natanya, Irgun yotse Berehovo - Beregsas veha-sevivah, 1989. 274 p., illus., maps, ports., facsims. (H, Hu; photo captions in E)

YIVO: Berehove 1989   NYPL: *PXW(Berehove) 90-1306
YU: DS135 R93 B3734 1989

Beresteczko (U). *Hayeta ayarah:...sefer zikaron li-kehilot Berestechkah Beremelyah veha-sevivah* [There was a town...memorial book of Beresteczko...and vicinity]. Ed.: Mendel Singer. Haifa, Association of Former Residents of Beresteczko in Israel, [1960/1961]. 555 p., ports., map, facsims. (H,Y)

YIVO: Berestechko 1960   NYPL: *PXW(Berestechko)
JTS: DS135 R93 B38 S5

Bereza-Kartuska (B). *Kartuz-Berezeh; sefer zikaron ve-'edut li-kehilah she-hushmedah hy"d* [Kartuz-Breze, our town; memorial book*]. Ed.: C. Ben Israel, *et al.* Tel Aviv, Organization of Survivors of Kartuz-Breze, 1993. 292 p., illus., maps. (H, E [intro.], Y [poems only])

YIVO: Byaroza 1993   NYPS: *PXW (Biaroza) 96-1362
JTS: DS135 B38 B53 K37 1993   YU: DA135 R93 B495 1993

Bereza-Kartuska (B) see also under Pruzana

Berezhany (U) see Brzezany

Berezno (U). *Mayn Shtetele Berezne* [My town Berezne]. [By] G. Beijiel [Bigil]. Tel Aviv, Berezner Society in Israel, 1954. 182 p., illus., ports., map (H,Y)

YIVO: Berezna 1954   NYPL: *PXW(Berezna) 89-8336
YU: DS135 P62 B3853

Berezo (Slo) see under Postyen

Bershad (U). *Bershad: Be-tsel ayara* [Bershad*]. [By] Nahman Huberman. Jerusalem, The Encyclopaedia of the Jewish Diaspora, 1956. 247 p., port. (H)

YIVO: Bershad 1956   NYPL: *PXW(Bershad)
JTS: DS135 R93 B42 H8   YU: DS135 R93 B3874 1956
HUC: HI 956.3

Bershad (U). *Bershad.* New York, [o. fg.], 1946. [20]p., illus., map., ports. (Y)

YIVO: Bershad 1946   NYPL: *PXW (Bershad)

Berzhan (P) see Brzezany

Beszterce (Ro) see Bistrita

Betlen (Bethlen) (Ro) see under Des

Biala Podlaska (P). *Podliashe in Natsi-klem; notitsn fun hurbn* [Podlasie en las garras del nazismo*]. [By] M. J. Fajgnboim [Feigenbaum]. Buenos Aires, Committee of Friends, 1953. 241 p., illus. (Y)

YIVO: Biala Podlaska 1953
NYPL: *PXV(Biala Podlaska) 74-4931
JTS: DS135 P62 B5 F3

Biala Podlaska (P). *Sefer Byalah Podlaskah* [Book of Biala Podlaska]. Ed.: M. J. Feigenbaum. Tel Aviv, Kupat Gmilut Hesed of the Community of Biala Podlaska, 1961. 501 p., illus., maps, ports., facsims. (H,Y)

YIVO: Biala Podlaska 1961   NYPL: *PXV+ (Biala Podlaska)
JTS: DS135 P62 B5 F32   HUC: HIW 473

Biala Podlaska (P) see also under Parczew

Biala Rawska (P). *Sefer yizkor li-kedoshe Byalah Ravska* [Memorial book to the martyrs of Biala Rawska]. Eds.: E. Freudenreich, *et.al.* Tel Aviv, Biala Rawska Societies in Israel and the Diaspora, 1972. 255 p., illus. (H,Y)

YIVO: Biala Rawska 1972   NYPL: *PXV(Biala Rawska) 75-1503
YU: DS135 P62 B48 1972

Bialobrzegi (P). *Sefer zikaron li-kehilat Bialovzig* [Memorial book of the Byalovzig community*]. Ed.: David Avraham Mandelboim. Tel Aviv, Council of the Town of Bialobrzeg, 1991. 396 p., illus., maps, ports. (H)

YIVO: Bialobrzegi (Radom) 1991   NYPL: *PXV(Bialobrzegi) 91-969
JTS: DS135 P62 B516 1991   YU: DS135 P62 B4987 1991

Bialystok (P). *Byalistok; bilder album...* [Bialystok; photo album...*]. Ed.: David Sohn. New York, Bialy stoker Album Committee, 1951. 386 p., illus. (Y,E)

YIVO: Bialystok 1951 NYPL: *PXV+ (Sohn, D Byalistok)
JTS: +DS135 P62 B54 S6 YU: DS135 P62 B5349 1951
HUC: HI 996.3

Bialystok (P). *Der Byalistoker yisker-bukh* [Bialystoker memorial book*]. Ed.: I. Shmulevitsh. New York, Bialystoker Center, 1982. xi, 396, 205, x p., ports., illus. (Y,E)

YIVO: Bialystok 1982 NYPL: *PXV(Bialystock) 82-2354
JTS: +DS135 P62 B54 B5 YU: DS135 P62 B53455 1982

Bialystok (P). *Pinkes Byalistok; grunt-materyaln tsu der geshikhte fun di Yidn in Byalistok biz nokh der Ershter velt-milhome* [Pinkos Bialystok = The chronicle of Bialystok. Basic material for the history of the Jews in Bialystok till the period after the First World War*]. [By] A. Herschberg. Ed.: Yudl Mark. New York, Bialystok Jewish Historical Association, 1949-1950. 2 vols. (Y)

YIVO: Bialystok 1949 NYPL: *PXV Herschberg
JTS: DS135 P62 B54

Bialystok (P). *Sefer Byalistok: gevidmet dem heylikn ondenk fun undzere kedoyshim, tsum 20th yortog fun hurbn fun undzer heymshtot* [Sefer Bialystok: an everlasting memorial to the heroes and martyrs of annihilated Bialystok, published upon the 20th yahrzeit, 1943-1963*]. Eds: M. W. Bernshtayn (Bernstein) [et al.]. New York, Bialystoker Book Committee, April 1963-April 1964. 3 isssues (96 p.), illus., map, ports. (Y)

YIVO: Bialystok 1963-64

Biaroza (B) see Bereza-Kartuska

Bibrka (U) see Bobrka

Biecz (P). *Sefer zikaron li-kedoshe ayaratenu Baitsh* [Memorial book of the martyrs of Biecz]. Ed.: P. Wagshal (Vagshal). [Ramat Gan], Association of Former Residents of Biecz and Vicinity in Israel, [1959 or 1960]. 356p., illus., ports. (H,Y)

YIVO: Biecz 1959 NYPL: *PXV(Biecz)
JTS: DS135 P62 B5496 S4 YU: DS135 P62 B558 1959

Bielica (B). *Pinkas Belitsah* [Book of Belitzah-Bielica*]. Ed.: L. Losh. Tel Aviv, Former Residents of Bielica in Israel and the USA, [1968]. 511 p., ports., map, facsims. (H,Y,E)

YIVO: Belitsa 1968 NYPL: *PXV(Belitsa)
JTS: DS135 R93 B346 YU: DS135 R93 B346

Bielitz-Biala (P) see Bielsko-Biala

Bielsk-Podlaski (P). *Byelsk-Podlaski; sefer yizkor le-zikhram ha-kadosh shel Yehude Byelsk she-nispu ba-Shoah ha-natsit ba-shanim 1939-1944.* [Bielsk-Podliask; book in the holy memory of the Bielsk-Podliask Jews*].

Ed.: H. Rabin. [Tel Aviv], Bielsk Societies in Israel and the USA, 1975. 554, 44 p., illus. (H,Y,E)

YIVO: Bielsk Podliask1975 NYPL: *PXV(Bielsk) 80-3058
YU: DS135 P62 B56 1975

Bielsko-Biala (P). *Bielitz-Biala (Bielsko-Biala); pirkei avar* [chapters from the past]. [By] Elijahu Miron. Israel, 1973. 182 p., illus. (H,G)

NYPL: *PXV(Bielsko-Biala) 88-466

Biezun (P). *Sefer ha-zikaron li-kedoshe Byezshun* [Memorial book of the martyrs of Biezun]. Tel Aviv, Former Residents of Biezun in Israel, 1956. 186 p., ports. (H,Y)

YIVO: Biezun 1956 NYPL: *PXV(Biezun) 76-5564

Bikovsk (Bukowsko) (P) see under Sanok

Bilgoraj (P). *Bilgoray yisker-bukh* [Bilgoraj memorial book]. [By] Moshe Taitlboym [Teytleboym]. Jerusalem, 1955. 243 p., illus. (Y)

YIVO: Bilgoraj 1955 JTS: DS135 P2 B5737 1955
YU: DS135 P62 B5737 1955

Bilgoraj (P). *Hurbn Bilgorey* [Destruction of Bilgoraj]. Ed.: A. Kronenberg. Tel Aviv, [1955 or 1956]. x, 365 p., ports. (Y)

YIVO: Bilgoraj 1956

Bilhorod-Dnistrovskyy (U) see Akkerman

Bilki (U). See Bilky

Bilky (U). *Sefer zikaron li-kedoshe kehilat Bilkeh vehasevivah.* [The Bilker Memorial Book]. Ed.: Dr. M. Avital. New Rochelle, 1998. 2 vols., (1008 p.), illus., maps. (H)

YIVO: Bilky 1998 NYPL: *PXW (Bilky) 00-2215
JTS: DS135 U42 B45 S4 1998 YU: DS135 R93 B34757 1998

Bisk (P) see Busk

Bistrita (Ro). *Bistrits; 'ir ve-em be-Yisrael...* [Bistrits; mother city in Israel]. [By] Neta Aryeh Gafni (Vaynshtok). [Bene Berak], N.A. Gafni, [1990]. 157 p., illus., ports. (H)

YIVO: Bistrita-Nasaud 1990 YU: DS135 R72 B58 1990
NYPL: *PXM (Bistrita-Nasaud) 93-575

Bistrita-Nasaud (Ro) see Bistrita

Bitola (Bitolj) (Mac) see Monastir

Bitshutsh (U) see Buczacz

Bivolari (Ro). *Ayaratenu Bivolari* [Our town Bivolari]. Eds.: M. Abramovici *et al.* Haifa, Bivolari Immigrants Organization in Israel, 1981. 160, 37 p., illus. (H,Ro,E)

YIVO: Bivolari 1981 NYPL: *PXM(Bivolari) 87-4211
JTS: DS135 R72 B5 A95 YU: DS135 R72 B592

Bledow (Blendow) (P) see under Mogielnica

Bobrka (U). *Le-zekher kehilat Boberka u-venoteha* [Boiberke memorial book*]. Ed.: Sh. Kallay. [Jerusalem], Association of Former Residents of Bobrka and Vicinity, [1964]. 218, 38 p., ports., facsims. (H,Y,E)
YIVO: Bibrka 1964   NYPL: *PXW+ (Bobrka)
JTS: +DS135 R93 B588 K3   YU: DS135 R93 B58
HUC: HIW 488

Bobruisk (B). *Bobroisk; sefer-zikaron li-kehilat Bobroisk u-venoteha* [Memorial book of the community of Bobruisk and its surroundings]. Ed.: Y. Slutsky. Tel Aviv, Former Residents of Bobruisk in Israel and the USA, 1967. 2 vols. (871 p.), ports., map, facsims. (H,Y)
YIVO: Bobruysk 1967   NYPL: *PXW(Bobruisk)
JTS: +DS135 R93 B59   YU: DS135 R93 B59
HUC: HIW 489

Boiberik (U) see Bobrka

Bolechow (U). *Sefer ha-zikaron li-kedoshe Bolechov* [Memorial book of the martyrs of Bolechow]. Ed.: Y. and M. H. Eshel. [Haifa], Association of Former Residents of Bolechow in Israel, 1957. 352 p., ports. (H,Y)
YIVO: Bolekhiv 1957   NYPL: *PXW(Bolekhov)
JTS: DS135 P62 B65 E8   YU: 933.5 P762B

Bolekhiv (U) see Bolechow

Bolimow (P) see under Lowicz

Bonyhad (Hu). *Bonyhad: a destroyed community; the Jews of Bonyhad, Hungary.* By Leslie Blau; introd. by R. L. Braham. New York, Shengold Publishers, 1994. 164 p., illus., map, ports., facsims. (E)
YIVO: Bonyhad 1994   NYPL: *PXT 95-1549
JTS: DS135 H92 B65 B55 1994   YU: DS135 H92 B663 1994

Boremel (U) see under Beresteczko

Borsa (Ro). *Sefer zikhron Borshah, o: Ayarat-ahavim be-yarkete ha-Karpatim* [Memorial book of Borsha, or: The beloved village by the foot of the Carpat[h]ians*]. Written and edited by Gedaliahu Stein. Kiryat Motzkin, 1985. 655 p., illus., maps, ports. (H)
YIVO: Borsa 1985   NYPL: *PXM(Borsa) 89-10160
JTS: DS135 R72 B654 1985   YU: DS135 R72 B677 1985

Borsa (Ro). Kazot hayetah Borshah... [This was Borsa..]. Ed.: P. Heler. Bene Berak, [1998 or 1999]. 242 p., illus. (H)
YIVO: Borsa 1999   JTS: DS135.R72 B67 1998

Borshchiv (U) see Borszczow

Borszczow (U). *Sefer Borshtshiv* [The book of Borstchoff*]. Ed.: N. Blumental. Tel Aviv, Association of Former Residents of Borszczow in Israel, [1960]. 341

p., illus., map, ports., facsims. (H,Y)
YIVO: Borshchiv 1960   NYPL: *PXW(Borschchev)
JTS: DS135 R93 B6 B4   YU: DS135 R93 B6775 1960
HUC: HIW 420

Boryslav (U) see under Drohobycz

Bransk (P). *Braynsk; sefer ha-zikaron* [Brainsk; book of memories*]. [By] A. Trus and J. Cohen. [New York], Brainsker Relief Committee of New York, 1948. 440 p., ports., facsims. (Y)
YIVO: Bransk 1948   NYPL: *PXV(Bransk)
JTS: DS135 P62 B66

Bransk (P). *Ner le-Braynski tragedyah shel ayarah Yehudit yeduah be-mizah Eropah,* by Elchanan Mann. [S.1], E. Narkis, 2001. 239 p., illus., maps. (H)
YIVO: Bransk 2001

Braslau (Braslav) (B) see Braslaw

Braslaw (B). *Emesh Shoah; yad li-kehilot / gevidment di kehiles Braslaw...* [Darkness and desolation; in memory of the communities of Braslaw, Dubene, Jaisi, Jod, Kislowszczizna, Okmienic, Opsa, Plusy, Rimszan, Slobodka, Zamosz, Zaracz*]. Eds.: A. Machnes, R. Klinov. [Israel], Association of Braslaw and Surroundings in Israel and America; Ghetto Fighters' House and Hakibbutz Hameuchad Publishing House, 1986. 636 p., illus., maps, ports. (H,Y,E)
YIVO: Braslav 1986   NYPL: *PXW(Braslav) 89-8626

Bratislava (Pozsony) (Slo) see under General Reference Works, *Arim ve-imahot,* vol. 7

Braynsk (P) see Bransk

Brest Litovsk (Brest) (B) see Brzesc nad Bugiem

Breziny (P) see Brzeziny

Breziv (P) see Brzozow

Brezova nad Bradlom (Berezo) (Slo) see under Postyen

Briceni (M) see Brichany

Brichany (M). *Britshan; Britsani ha-Yehudit be-mahatsit ha-meah ha-aharonah* [Brichany; its Jewry in the first half of our century]. Eds.: Y. Amisur (Shtainhoiz) *et al.* Tel Aviv, Former Residents of Brichany, [1963]. 296 p., ports., map (H)
YIVO: Brichany 1963   NYPL: *PXW(Brichany)
JTS: DS135 R93 B77   YU: DS135 R93 B752 1963

Bricheva (M) see Brichevo

Brichevo (M). *Pinkas Britshivah* [Memorial book of Brichevo]. Ed.: K. A. Bertini. [Tel Aviv], Former Residents of Brichevo (Bessarabia) in Israel, 1970. 531 p., illus. (H,Y)

YIVO: Bricheva 1970 NYPL: *PXW(Bricheva)
JTS: DS135 R93 B75 P5

Briegel (P) see Brzesko

Brisk (B) see Brzesc nad Bugiem

Brisk Kuyavsk (Brzesc Kujawski) (P) see under Wloclawek

Brody (U) see under General Reference Works *Arim ve-imahot,* vol. 6

Broszniow (U) see under Rozniatow

Brzesc Kujawski (P) see under Wloclawek

Brzesc nad Bugiem (B). *Brisk de-Lita* [Brest Lit.(owsk) Volume*]. Ed.: E. Steinman. Jerusalem, Encyclopaedia of the Jewish Diaspora, 1954-1955. 2 vols., ports., map (H,Y)

YIVO: Brest (Entsiklopedya shel galuyot, t.2) 1954
NYPL: *PXV(Brest Litovsk)+ v.l; : *PX+ 96-485 v.2
JTS: Ref +DS135 E8 E55 v.2 HUC: HI 999

Brzesko (P). *Sefer yizkor shel kehilat Brigel-Barzesko veha-sevivah* [Memorial book of Briegel-Brzesko and vicinity]. Eds.: Hayim Teler, Liber Brenner (Yiddish). Ramat-Gan, [1980]. 267 p., illus. (H,Y)

YIVO: Brzesko 1980

Brzezany (U). *Bezezani, Narayuv veha-sevivah; toldot kehilot she-nehrevu* [Brzezany memorial book*]. Ed.: M. Katz. [Haifa, Brzezany-Narajow Societies in Israel and the USA, 1978.] 473, 28 p., illus., maps. (H,Y,E)

YIVO: Berezhany 1978 JTS: DS135 R93 B4 B4
NYPL: *PXW(Berezhany) 90-3756; *ZP-1749
YU: DS135 R93 B3843

Brzeziny (P). *Bzshezshin yisker-bukh* [Brzeziny memorial book*]. Eds.: A. Alperin, N. Sumer. New York, Brzeziner Book Committee, 1961. 288 p., map, ports. (Y)

YIVO: Brezeziny 1961 NYPL: *PXV+ (Brzeziny)
JTS: DS135 P62 B7 HUC: HIW 361

Brzeznica (P) see under Radomsko

Brzozow (P). *Sefer zikaron kehilat Breziv (Brzozow)* [A memorial to the Brzozow community*]. Ed.: Avraham Levite. [Israel], The Survivors of Brzozow, 1984. 348, [16], 195 p., illus., maps, ports. (H,Y,E)

YIVO: Brzozow (Rzeszow) 1984 NYPL:*PXV(Brzozow) 89-8504
HUC: f DS135 P62 B79 1984 YU: DS135 P62 B79 1984

Buchach (U) see Buczacz

Buczacz (U). *Sefer Butshatsh; matsevet zikaron li-kehilah kedosha* [Book of Buczacz; in memory of a

martyred community]. Ed.: I. Kohan (Cohen). Tel Aviv, Am Oved, [1955 or 1956]. 302 p., ports., facsims. (H)

YIVO: Buchach 1955 NYPL: *PXW(Buchach)
YU: DS135 R93 B8 1955 HUC: HIW 363

Budanow (Budaniv) (U) see Budzanow

Budapest (Hu) see under General Reference Works, *Arim ve-imahot,* vol. 1; see also Rakospalota.

Budzanow (U). *Sefer Budzanov* [Book of Budzanow*]. Ed.: J. Siegelman (Zigelman). Haifa, Former Residents of Budzanow in Israel and America, 1968. 319 p., ports., maps, facsims. (H,Y,E)

YIVO: Budaniv 1968 NYPL: *PXW(Budanow)
JTS: DS135 R93 B815 YU: 933.5 U35B

Bukaczowce (U) see under Rohatyn

Bukowsko (P) see under Sanok

Burshtyn (U) see Bursztyn

Bursztyn (U). *Sefer Burshtin* [Book of Bursztyn]. Ed.: S. Kants. Jerusalem, The Encyclopaedia of the Jewish Diaspora, [1960]. 426 columns, ports., facsims. (H,Y)

YIVO: Burshtyn 1960 NYPL: *PXW(Burshtyn)
JTS: DS135 R93 B83 K3

Busk (U). *Sefer Busk; le-zekher ha-kehilah she-harevah* [Busk; in memory of our community*]. Ed.: A. Shayari. [Israel], Busker Organization in Israel, [1965]. 343 p., illus., ports., facsims. (H,Y,E,P)

YIVO: Busk 1965 NYPL: *PXW(Busk) 94-680
JTS: DS135 R93 B87 S5

Byalovzig (P) see Bialobrzegi

Byaroza (B) see Bereza-Kartuska

Bychawa (P). *Bihvah: sefer zikaron* [Bychawa; a memorial to the Jewish community of Bychawa Lubelska*]. Ed.: Y. Adini. Bychawa Organization in Israel, [1969]. 636 p., ports., map, facsims. (H,Y)

YIVO: Bychawa 1969 NYPL: *PXV(Bychawa)
JTS: DS135 P62 B93 B5

Byten (B). *Pinkas Biten* [Memorial book of Byten]. Ed.: D. Abramowitz, M. W. Bernstein [Bernshtayn]. Buenos Aires, Former Residents of Byten in Argentina, 1954. 605 p., illus., map, facsims. (Y)

YIVO: Byten 1954 NYPL: *PXV(Byten)
JTS: DS135 R93 B98 A3 YU: DS135 R93 B9

Cakovec (Cr). *Megilat ha-Shoah shel kehilat kodesh Tsakavets* [Holocaust scroll of the holy community of Cakovec-Yugoslavia]. [By] Moshe Etz-Hayyim (Tibor Grunwald). Tel Aviv, 1977. 182, 12 p., illus., map. (H,Sc)

YIVO: Cakovec 1977 NYPL: *PXM(Cakovec) 89-9501
JTS: DS135 Y82 C3 E8 YU: DS135 Y82 C343

Calarasi (M) see Kalarash

Capresti (M) see Kapreshty

Cernauti (U) see under General Reference Works, *Arim ve-imahot,* vol. 4

Cetatea-Alba (U) see Akkerman

Charsznica (P) see under Miechow

Chelm (P). *Sefer ha-zikaron li-kehilat Helem; 40 shanah le-hurbanah* [Yizkor book in memory of Chelm*]. Ed.: Sh. Kanc and M. Grinberg. Tel Aviv, Chelm Society in Israel and U.S., [1980/1981]. 828 columns, illus. (H,Y)
YIVO: Chelm 1980   NYPL: *PXV(Chelm) 88-469
JTS: DS135 P62 C5   YU: DS135 P62 C48

Chelm (P). *Yisker-bukh Khelm* [Commemoration book Chelm*]. Ed.: M. Bakalczuk-Felin. Johannesburg, Former Residents of Chelm, 1954. 732 columns., ports., facsims. (Y)
YIVO: Chelm 1954   NYPL: *PXV + (Chelm)
JTS: DS135 P62 C5 B3   YU: K5 P762K

Chernovtsy (U) see under General Reference Works, *Arim ve-imahot,* vol. 4

Chervonoarmeisk (U) see Radziwillow

Chmielnik (P). *Pinkas Khmielnik* [Memorial book of Chmielnik].Ed.: E. Shedletski. Tel Aviv, Former Residents of Chmielnik in Israel, 1960. 1300 columns, maps, ports., facsims. (H,Y)
YIVO: Chmielnik 1960   NYPL: *PXV + (Chmielnik)
JTS: +DS135 P62 C52 P5   YU: DS135 P62 C52

Chodecz (P) see under Wloclawek

Cholojow (U) see under Radziechow

Chorostkow (U). *Sefer Horostkov* [Chorostkow book*]. Ed.: D. Shtokfish. Tel Aviv, Committee of Former Residents of Chorostkow in Israel, 1968. 418 p., ports., facsims. (H,Y)
YIVO: Khorostkiv 1968   NYPL: *PXW(Khorostkov)
JTS: DS135 R93 K42   YU: DS135 R93 K42

Chortkiv (U) see Czortkow

Chorzele (P). *Sefer zikaron li-kehilat Horzel* [Memorial book of the community of Chorzel]. Ed.: L. Losh. Tel Aviv, Association of Former Residents of Chorzele in Israel, 1967. 272 p., illus., map, ports., facsims. (H,Y)
YIVO: Chorzele 1967   NYPL: *PXV(Chorzele)
JTS: DS135 P62 C537   YU: 933.5 P762C L879

Chust (U) see Khust

Chrzanow (P). *Sefer Khzshanov; lebn un umkum fun a Yidish shtetl* [The book of Chrzanow]. [By] Mordechai

Bochner. Regensburg, [Obadia Field,1949]. xiii, 377 p., illus., ports. (Y)
YIVO: Chrzanow 1949 (use reprint below)
NYPL: *PXV (Chrzanow) 95-104; and *ZP-1062

Chrzanow (P). *Sefer Khzshanov = Chrzanow: the life and destruction of a Jewish shtetl.* [By] Mordechai Bochner; trans. by Jonathan Boyarin. Roslyn Harbor, NY, Solomon Gross, [1989]. xiii, 168, 320 p., illus., ports., map (Y,E)
YIVO: Chrzanow 1989   NYPL: *PXV (Chrzanow) 93-324
YU: DS135 C537 413 1989

Chrzanow (P) *Sefer Kheshanuv: le zikharam shel kedoshe ha-ir she-nispu ba-Sho'ah.* M. Bochner's book trans. from English to Hebrew. Tel Aviv, Irgun yotse Kheshanuv be-Yisrael, [1992]. 266 p., illus., ports. (H)
NYPL: *PXV (Chrzanow) 96-3560
JTS: DS135.P62 C538 B6416 1996

Ciechanow (P). *Yisker-bukh fun der Tshekhanover Yidisher kehile; sefer yizkor li-kehilat Ts'ehanov* [Memorial book of the community of Ciechanow]. Ed.: A. W. Yassni. Tel Aviv, Former Residents of Ciechanow in Israel and in the Diaspora, 1962. 535 p., ports. (H,Y)
YIVO: Ciechanow 1962   NYPL: *PXV(Ciechanow) 78-5220
YU: DS135 P62 C638 1962

Ciechanowiec (P). *Tsihanovits; mehoz Byalistok, sefer edut ve-zikaron* [Ciechanoviec-Bialystok district; memorial and records*]. Ed.: E. Leoni. [Tel Aviv], The Ciechanovitzer Immigrant Assoc. in Israel and the USA, [1964]. 936, 78 p., ports., facsims. (H,Y,E)
YIVO: Ciechanowiec 1964   NYPL: *PXV(Ciechanowiec)
JTS: DS135 P62 C54 L4   YU: DS135 P62 C647 1964

Ciechocinek (P) see under Wloclawek

Cieszanow (P). *Sefer zikaron di-kehilah kedosha Tsyeshinov* [Memorial book of the martyred community Cieszanow]. Ed.: D. Ravid. Tel Aviv, Former Residents of Cieszanow in Israel, [1969/1970]. 333 p., ports. (H,Y)
YIVO: Cieszanow 1969   NYPL: *PXV+ (Cieszanow)
JTS: +DS135 P62 C56

Cluj-Napoca (Ro) see Kolozsvar

Cmielow (P) see under Ostrowiec

Cracow (P) see Krakow

Csaktornya (Cr) see Cakovec

Csenger (Hu). *Sefer yizkor li-kedoshe Tshenger, Portsalmah veha-sevivah* [Memorial book of the martyrs of Csenger, Porcsalma and vicinity]. [By] Sh. Friedmann. Tel Aviv, 1966. 108, 60 p., ports., facsims. (H,Hu)
NYPL: *PXT(Csenger) 91-607

Czarny Dunajec (P) see under Nowy Targ

Czerbin (P) see under Ostroleka

Czernowitz (U) see under General Reference Works, *Arim ve-imahot,* vol. 4

Czestochowa (P). *Churban Czenstochow—The destruction of Czenstokov—Hurbn Tshenstokhov.* [By] Benjamin Orenstein. [Munich], Central Farwaltung fun der Czenstochower landsmanszaft in der Amerikaner Zone in Dajczland, 1948. 463 p., 52 p. of plates, illus., ports. (Y in Latin characters)
YIVO: Czestochowa 1948   NYPL: *ZP-774 No. 5
JTS: Restr DS135 P62 C92 O72   YU: 933.543.80
HUC: HIW 349

Czestochowa (P). *Czenstochov: our legacy* [Tshenstokhov: undzer yerushe*]. Edited and published by Harry Klein. Montreal, Harry Klein, 1993. xxiv, 360, 117 p., illus., map, ports., facsims. (E, Y)
YIVO: Czestochowa 1993   NYPL: *PXV (Czestochowa) 99-999
JTS: DS135 P62 C92 K5 1993   YU: DS135 P62 C8834 1993

Czestochowa (P). *Sefer Tsenstohov* [Memorial book of Czestochow]. Ed.: M. Schutzman. Jerusalem, The Encyclopaedia of the Jewish Diaspora, [1967-1968]. 2 vols., illus., fold. map, ports. (H,Y)
YIVO: Czestochowa 1967   NYPL: *PXV+ (Czestochowa)
JTS: Ref +DS135 E8 E55 v.8   HUC: HIW 539
YU: DS135 P62 C89

Czestochowa (P). *Tshenstokhover landsmanshaft in Montreal* [Czenstochover landsmanschaft of Montreal*]. Ed.: Benjamin Orenstein. Montreal, The Czenstochover Society in Montreal, 1966. 349 p., illus., ports. (Y)
YIVO: Czestochowa 1966   NYPL: *PXV(Czestochowa) 90-2743

Czestochowa (P). *Tshenstokhov; nayer tsugob-materyal tsum bukh "Tshenstokhover Yidn"* [Czenstochov; a new supplement to the book "Czenstochover Yidn"*]. Ed.: S. D. Singer. New York, United Relief Committee in New York, 1958. viii, 336, iv p., illus., maps, ports. (Y)
YIVO: Czestochowa 1958   NYPL: *PXV+ (Czestochowa)
JTS: +DS135 P62 C92 U5   HUC: HIW 458.2

Czestochowa (P). *Tshenstokhover Yidn* [The Jews of Czestochowa]. Ed.: R. Mahler. New York, United Czestochower Relief Committee and Ladies Auxiliary, 1947. 404, cxliv p., illus., ports., facsims. (Y)
YIVO: Czestochowa 1947   NYPL: *PXV+ (United Czestochover)
JTS: +DS135 P62 C9 U5   YU: 933.543.8 C9989 1947

Czortkow (U). *Sefer yizkor le-hantsahat kedoshe kehilat Tsortkov* [Memorial book of Czortkow*]. Ed.: Y. Austridan. Haifa, Former Residents of Czortkow in Israel, [1967]. 435, 36 p., ports., map, facsims. (H,Y,E)
YIVO: Chortkiv 1967   NYPL: *PXW(Chortkov)
JTS: DS135 R93 C5 S4   YU: 933.5 R969C A941

Czyzewo (P). *Sefer zikaron Tsizevah: Yizker Bukh nokh der horev gevorener Yidisher kehile Tshizsheve* [Memorial book Tshijewo*]. Ed.: Sh. Kanc. Tel Aviv, Former Residents of Czyzewo in Israel and the USA, 1961. 1206 columns, illus., ports., facsims. (H,Y)
YIVO: Czyzew 1961   NYPL: *PXV(Czyzew) 77-3791
YU: DS135 P62 C989 1961

Dabrowa Bialostocka (P). *Dubrowa: memorial to a shtetl.* By Michael A. Nevins. Spring Valley, NY: The Town House Press, [1982]. 38p., illus., maps, ports. (E); 2nd edition, [River Vale, NJ, M. Nevins, 2000], viii, 38 p., illus., maps, ports, facsims. (E)
YIVO: Dabrowa Bialostocka 1982 (1st ed.); 2000 (2nd ed.)
NYPL: PXV (Dabrowa) 99-2548 (1st ed.); 01-1076 (2nd ed)

Dabrowa Gornicza (P). *Sefer kehilat Yehude Dombrova Gornitseh ve-hurbanah* [Memorial book of Dombrawa Gornitza]. Eds.: M. Gelbart *et al.* Tel Aviv, Former Residents of Dombrowa Gornitza, 1971. 696 p., illus. (H,Y,E)
YIVO: Dabrowa Gornicza 1971 NYPL: *PXV+ (Dabrowa Gornicza)
JTS: +DS135 P62 D28 S4   YU: 933.47(438) D116G
HUC: HIW 373

Dabrowica (U). *Sefer Dombrovitsah* [Book of Dabrowica]. Ed.: L. Losh. Tel Aviv, Association of Former Residents of Dabrowica in Israel, 1964. 928 p., illus., ports., maps, facsims. (H,Y)
YIVO: Dubrovytsya 1964   NYPL: *PXW(Dombrovitza) 89-8304

Dabrowica (U) see also under Polesie (region)

Darabani (Ro) see under Dorohoi

Daugavpils (Lat). *Dvinsk; the rise and decline of a town.* [By] Yudel Flior; translated from the Yiddish by Bernard Sachs. Johannesburg, Dial Press, [1965]. 188 p. (E)
YIVO: Daugavpils 1965   NYPL: *PXW 72-331

Daugavpils (Lat). *Le-zekher kehilat Dvinsk* [In memory of the community of Dvinsk]. Haifa, Hativat benayim "Kiah," [1974]. 63 p., illus. (H)
NYPL: *PXW(Daugvpils) 77-3787   YU: DS135 R93 D3184

Daugeliszki (Li) see under Swieciany

Dauhinava (B) see Dolhinow

David Gorodok (B) see Dawidgrodek; see also under Polesie (region)

David Horodok (B) see Dawidgrodek; see also under Polesie (region)

Dawidgrodek (B). *David Horodoker memorial book - Memorial book of David-Horodok.* Partial trans. from the Yiddish and part of the Hebrew original [by] N. Helman. Oak Park, MI, B. Chase, [1981]. 129 p., map. (E)
YIVO: David-Gorodok 1981
NYPL: *PXW (David-Gorodek) 94-1957

Dawidgrodek (B). *Sefer zikaron David-Horodok* [Memorial book of Davidgrodek]. Eds.: Y. Eidan [Idan; Zeldin] *et al.* [Tel Aviv], Former Residents of Dawidgrodek in Israel, [1957]. 487 p., ports. (H,Y)

YIVO: David-Gorodok 1957   JTS: DS135 R93 D32 S4
NYPL: *PXW(David-Gorodek) 89-759
YU: 135 R93 D32 1957

Dawidgrodek (B) see also under Polesie (region)

Debica (P). *Sefer Dembits* [Book of Debica]. Ed.: D. Leibl. Tel Aviv, Association of Former Residents of Debica, 1960. 204 p., illus., maps, ports. (H,Y)

YIVO: Debica (Powiat) 1960   NYPL: *PXV(Debica) 88-465

Deblin (P). *Sefer Deblin-Modzits* [Demblin-Modrzyc book*]. Ed.: David Shtokfish. [Tel Aviv], Association of Former Residents of Demblin-Modrzyc, [1969]. 694 p., ports., music, facsims. (H,Y)

YIVO: Deblin 1969   NYPL: *PXV(Deblin)
JTS: DS135 P62 D38   YU: DS135 P62 D38 1969

Deblin (P). *Sefer Deblin-Modzjitz* [Demblin-Modrzyc book*]. Translation into English of writings of David Shtokfish. Tel Aviv, Demblin-Modrzyc in Israel & Abroad, 1994. 637 p., ports., facsims. (E)

NYPL: *PXV (Deblin) 96-3420

Debrecen (Hu). *Meah shana li-Yehude Debretsen; le-zekher kedoshe ha-kehilah ve-yishuve ha-sevivah* [Hundred years of Debrecen Jewry; in memory of the martyrs of Debrecen and vicinity]. [By] M. E. Gonda. [Haifa], Committee for Commemoration of the Debrecen Jewry, [1970]. 264, 409 p., ports., facsims. (H,Hu)

YIVO: Debrecen 1970   NYPL: *PXT 76-6740
JTS: DS135 H92 D4 G6   HUC: HIW 377

Dej (Ro) see Des

Delatycze (B) see under Lubcza

Dembits (P) see Debica

Demblin (P) see Deblin

Derechin (B) see Dereczyn

Derecske (Hu). *Sefer zikaron li-Yehude Deretskeh u-geliloteha* [Emlékkönyv Derecske és vidéke zsidósága* - Memorial book to the Jews of Derecske and its environs]. [By] Arje Moskovits. Tel Aviv, Society of Derecske Emigrants in Israel, 1984. 186, 185 p. [93] p. of plates, illus., facsims., ports. (H,Hu)

YIVO: Derecske 1984   NYPL: *PXT(Derecske) 89-9754
YU: DS135 H92 D475 1984

Derecske (Hu) see also under Debrecen

Dereczyn (B). *Sefer Deretsin* [The Dereczin Memorial Book: A Book of Remembrance Honoring the Communities of Dereczin, Halinka, Kolonia-Sinaiska].

Ed. Yekheskiel Raban. English translation by Jacob Solomon Berger. Mahwah, 2000. 401 p., map. (E)

YIVO: Derechin 2000   NYPL: *PXW (Derechin) 00-3691
JTS: DS135 R93 D47 S413 2000

Dereczyn (B). *Sefer Deretsin* [Deretchin memorial book*]. Ed.: Y. Raban. [Tel Aviv], Deretchiners Societies in Israel and USA, [1971 or 1972]. 494 p., illus. (H,Y)

YIVO: Derechin 1971   NYPL: *PXW(Derechin) 78-685
JTS: DS135 R93 D47 S4   YU: DS135 R93 D437 1971
HUC: HIW 525

Derewno (B) see under Rubiezewicze; Stolpce

Des (Ro). *Volt egyszer egy Des..., Bethlen, Magyarlapos, Retteg, Nagyilonda és kornyeke* [...and vicinity]. Ed.: Z. Singer. Tel Aviv, Former Residents of Des, [1970]. 2 vols. (683 p.), ports., facsims. (Hu, H, E)

YIVO: Dej 1970   NYPL: *PXM 75-6975
JTS: DS135 R72 D45 S5   YU: 933.5 H936D

Deutschkreutz (A). *Kehilat Tsehlim ve-hakhamehah: sefer zikaron li-kehilah kedoshah Tsehlim.* Eds.: S. Spitzer, M. Kinstlikher (Kunstlicher). Bnei Brak, Mekhon "Zikaron," [1999 or 2000]. 366 p., illus., ports., facsims. (H)

YIVO: Deutschkreutz 2000   JTS: DS 135.A92 D48 K44 1999
YU: DS135.A92 D4873 1999

Devenishki (B) see Dziewieniszki

Dibetsk (P) see under Dynov (*Hurbn Dynow*)

Dieveniskes (Li) see Dziewieniszki

Dinov (P) see Dynow

Dinovtsy (Dunivits) (U) see under Kamenets-Podolskiy

Disna (B) see Dzisna

Divenishok (Li) see Dziewieniszki

Dmytrow (U) see under Radziechow

Dnepropetrovsk (U) see Yekaterinoslav

Dobromil (U). *Sefer zikaron le-zekher kehilat Dobromil* [Memorial book Dobromil*]. Ed.: M. Gelbart. Tel Aviv, The Dobromiler Society in New York and the Dobromiler Organization in Israel, 1964. 389, 138 p., illus., map, ports., facsims. (H,Y,E)

YIVO: Dobromil 1964   NYPL: *PXW(Dobromil)
JTS: DS135 R93 D6 G4   YU: 933.5 R969 D634

Dobromil (U). *Dobromil: Life in a Galician Shtetl, 1890-1907.* By Saul Miller. New York: Lowentahl Press, 1980. 83, 50 p., port. (E, H)

NYPL: *PXW (Dobromil) 81-1493
JTS: DS135 R93 D6 M54   YU: DS135 R93 D63

Dobrin (P) see under Wloclawek

Dobrzyn (P). *Ayarati; sefer zikaron le-ayarot Dobzhyn-Golov* [My town; in memory of the communities Dobrzyn-Gollob*]. Ed.: M. Harpaz. [Holon], Association of Former Residents of Dobrzyn-Golub, 1969. 459, 29 p., ports., facsims. (H,Y,E)
YIVO: Golub-Dobrzyn 1969   NYPL: *PXV(Golub)
JTS: DS135 P62 G58

Dobrzyn (P). *Yisker bletlekh* [Our village*]. [By] S. Russak. Tel Aviv, [1971/1972]. 90, vi p., illus. (Y,E)
YIVO: Golub-Dobrzyn 1972
NYPL: *PXV(Golub-Dobrzyn) 75-1498

Dobrzyn nad Drweca (P) see Dobrzyn

Dobrzyn nad Wisla (P) see Wloclawek

Dokshitzy (B) see Dokszyce

Dokszyce (B). *Book in memory of Dokshits-Parafyanov...* Ed.: D. Stockfish; [excerpts] translated by Yariv Eldar. [Israel], Organization of Dokshits-Parafyanow Veterans in Israel and the Diaspora, [1990]. 116 p. (E)
YIVO: Dokshitzy & Parafyanovo 1990

Dokszyce (B). *Sefer yizkor Dokshits-Parafyanov* [Dokszyc-Parafianow book*]. Ed.: D. Shtokfish. [Tel Aviv], Assoc. of Former Residents of Dokszyce-Parafianow in Israel, [1970]. 350 p., illus., ports., facsims. (H,Y)
YIVO: Dokshitsy & Parafyanovo 1970   NYPL: *PXW(Dokshitsy)
JTS: DS135 R93 D648   YU: K5 R969D

Dolginovo (B) see Dolhinow

Dolhinow (B). *Esh tamid - yizkor le-Dolhinov; sefer zikaron li-kehilat Dolhinov veha-sevivah* [Eternal flame; in memory of Dolhinow]. Eds.: J. Chrust (Krust), M. Bar-Ratson. [Israel], Society of Dolhinow Emigrants in Israel, [1984 or 1985]. 718 p., illus., maps, ports. (H,Y,E)
NYPL: *PXW(Dolginovo) 87-2640

Dombrava Gornitsha (P) see Dabrowa Gornicza

Dombrovitsa (U) see Dabrowica

Dorohoi (Ro). *Dorot shel Yahadut ve-Tsiyonut Dorohoi: Savan, Mikhailan, Daraban, Hertsah, Radauts-Prut* [Generatii de Iudaism si Sionism Dorohoi, Saven, Mikhailen, Daraban, Hertsah, Radauts-Prut (Romania)* = Generations of Judaism and Zionism in Dorohoi...]. [Comp. and ed.:]David Shlomo (Shelomoh). Kiryat Bialik, Irgun yotse Dorohoi veha-sevivah be-Yisrael, 1992-1993. 4 vols., illus., maps, ports. (H, Ro)
YIVO: Dorohoi 1992 (vols. 2-4)
NYPL: *PXM (Dorohoi) 94-511 (vols.1-4)

Drahichyn (B) see Drohiczyn Poleski

Drodzyn (B) see under Stolin

Drohiczyn nad Bugiem (P). *Sefer Drohitshin* [Drohiczyn book]. Ed.: D. Shtokfish. [Tel Aviv], 1969. 576, 67 p., illus. (H,Y,E)
YIVO: Drohiczyn 1969   JTS: DS135 P62 D76
YU: DS135 P62 D767 1969

Drohiczyn Poleski (B). *Drohitshin; finf hundert yor Yidish lebn* [Memorial book Drohichyn*]. Ed.: D. B. Warshawsky (Varshavski). Chicago, Book-Committee Drohichyn, 1958. viii, 424 p., ports., map, facsims. (Y)
YIVO: Drahichyn 1958   NYPL: *PXW(Drogichin)
JTS: DS135 P62 D759

Drohobych (U) see Drohobycz

Drohobycz (U). *Sefer zikaron le-Drohobits, Borislav veha-sevivah* [Memorial to the Jews of Drohobycz, Boryslaw and surroundings*]. Ed.: N. M. Gelber. Tel Aviv, Assoc. of Former Residents of Drohobycz, Boryslaw and Surroundings, 1959. 224 p., ports. (H,Y)
YIVO: Drohobych & Boryslav 1959   YU: 933.5 R969D
NYPL: *PXW+ (Drogobych) 80-446

Droshkopol (U) see Druzkopol

Droye (Druia) (B) see Druja; see also under Glebokie

Druja (B). *Sefer Druyah u-kehilot Miyor, Droisk, ve-Leonpol* [The book of Druya and the communities of Miory, Druysk and Leonpol*]. Ed.: Mordekhai Neustadt (Naishtat). [Tel Aviv], Druja and Surrounding Region Society, [1973]. 255 p., illus. (H,Y)
YIVO: Druya 1973   NYPL: *PXW(Druia) 82-1573

Druja (Druya) (B) see also under Glebokie

Drujsk (B) see under Druja (*Sefer Druja*)

Druzkopol (U). *Ayaratenu Drushkopol* [Our town Droshkopol]. Eds.: Y. Shiloni *et al.* [Tel Aviv], Former Residents of Droshkopol in Israel, [1956 or 1957]. 91 p., illus., maps, ports. (H), mimeo.
YIVO: Druzhkopol 1957

Druzkopol (U). *Di geshikhte fun mayn shtetele Druzkopol* [The story of my "stetele Droshkopol"*]. [By] A. Boxer (Ben-Arjeh). Ed.: S. Eisenberg. Haifa, 1962. 108 p., ports (Y), mimeo

Dubasari (M) see Dubossary

Dubene (Dubinowo) (B) see under Braslaw

Dubetsko (Dubiecko) (P) see under Dynow (*Hurbn Dynow*)

Dubno (U). *Dubno; sefer zikaron* [Dubno; a memorial to the Jewish community of Dubno, Wolyn*]. Ed.: Y. Adini. Tel Aviv, Irgun yotse Dubna be-Yisrael, [1966]. 752

columns, illus., maps, ports, facsims. (H)

YIVO: Dubno 1966   NYPL: *PXW (Dubno)

JTS: DS135 R93 D8 A3   YU: 933.5 R969D

Dubossary (R). *Dubosari; sefer zikaron* [Dubossary memorial book]. Ed.: Y. Rubin.[Tel Aviv], Association of Former Residents of Dubossary in America, Argentina and Israel, [1965]. 377 p., ports., maps, music (H,Y)

YIVO: Dubasari 1965   NYPL: *PXW(Dubossary)

JTS: DS135 R93 D82   YU: 933.5 R969D R896

HUC: HIW 566.2

Dubrovitsa (Dubrovytsya) (U) see Dabrowica

Dubrowa (R) see Dabrowa (near Bialystok)

Dumbraveny (M). *Sefer Dombroven; ner-zikaron le-moshavah ha-haklait ha-Yehudit ha-rishonah be-Besarabyah* [Dombroven book; memorial to the first Jewish agricultural colony in Bessarabia]. Ed.: Haim Toren. Jerusalem, Dombroven Societies in Israel and The Diaspora, 1974. 252, 8 p., illus. (H,Y)

YIVO: Dumbraveni 1974   NYPL: *PXR(Dumbraveni) 75-5663

JTS: DS135 R72 D87 T68   HUC: LB-P

YU: DS135 $93 D853 1974

Dumbreven (M) see Dumbraveny

Dunajska Streda (Slo) see Dunaszerdahely

Dunaszerdahely (Slo). *Sefer ha-zikaron li-kehilat Dunaserdaheli* [A memorial to the Jewish community of Dunaszerdahely (Dunajska Streda)*]. [By] Abraham (Alfred) Engel. Tel Aviv, Committee of Dunaszerdahely Emigrants, 1975. 429, 157 p., illus, map. (H,Hu)

YIVO: Dunajska Streda 1975   NYPL: *PXT 76-5563

JTS: DS135 C96 D863 E55   YU: DS135 C96 D863 1975

HUC: HIW 558

Dunilovichi (Dunilowicze) (B) see under Glebokie

Dusetos (Li). *Ayarah hayetah be-Lita: Dusyat bi-re'i ha-zikhronot* [There was a shtetl in Lithuania: Dusiat reflected in reminiscences*]. Ed.: Sara Weiss-Slep (Vais-Slep). Tel Aviv, Society of Former Residents of Lita, 1989. 421 p., illus., maps, ports. (H)

YIVO: Dusetos 1989   NYPL: *PXW(Dusetos) 90-4663

JTS: DS135 L52 D8 A4 1989   YU: DS135 R93 D858 1989

HUC: DS135 L5 D885 1989

Dvart (P) see Warta

Dvinsk (Lat) see Daugavpils

Dyatlovo (B) see Zdzieciol

Dynow (P). *Hurbn Dynov, Sonik, Dibetsk* [The destruction of Dynow, Sanok, Dubiecko]. [By] David Moritz. New York, [1949/50]. 156 p., illus. (Y)

YIVO: Dynow 1949   NYPL: *PXV

JTS: DS135 P62 D88 M67   YU: DS135 P62 D927

Dynow (P). *Sefer Dynov; sefer zikaron li-kedoshe kehilat Dynov she-nispu ba-Shoah ha-Natsit* [The memorial book of Jewish Dinov*]. Eds.: Y. Kaseh, Moshe Rinat. [Israel], Dynow Society in Israel, 1979. 324 p., illus., map (H,Y)

YIVO: Dynow 1979   NYPL: *PXV(Dinow) 88-468

YU: DS135 P62 D927

Dzerzhinsk (B) see Koidanovo

Dzialoszyce (P). *Sefer yizkor shel kehilat Dzyaloshits veha-sevivah* [Yizkor book of the Jewish community in Dzialoszyce and surroundings*]. Tel Aviv, ha'Menorah, 1973. 423, 44 p., illus. (H,Y,E)

YIVO: Dzialoszyce 1973   NYPL: *PXV(Dzialoszyce) 75-1500

JTS: DS135 P62 D9 S4   YU: 933.5(438) D999

Dziewieniszki (B). *Sefer Divenishok; yad vashem le-ayara Yehudit* [Devenishki book; memorial book*]. Ed.: D. Shtokfish. [Tel Aviv], Divenishok Societies in Israel and the USA, 1977. 527 p., illus., maps. (H,Y)

YIVO: Dieveniskes 1977   NYPL: *PXW(Devenishki) 89-8360

JTS: DS135 P62 D53 S4   YU: DS135 R93 D59

Dzikow (P) see Tarnobrzeg

Dzisna (B). *Disnah; sefer zikaron li-kehilah* [Disna; memorial book of the community]. Eds.: A. Beilin *et al.* Tel Aviv, Former Residents of Disna in Israel and the USA, [1969]. 277 p., ports., facsims. (H,Y)

YIVO: Disna 1969   NYPL: *PXV(Disna)

JTS: DS135 R93 D533 B4   YU: 933.5 R969D

Edineti (Edinit/Edinita) (M) see Yedintsy

Eger (Hu). *Yehude Erlau* [The Jews of Eger]. Eds.: A. A. Ehrenfeld-Elkay (Aharonfeld-Alkai), T. Meir Klein-Z'ira. Jerusalem, Eger Commemorative Committee,1975. 64, 36, 100 p., illus. (H,Hu)

YIVO: Eger 1975   NYPL: *PXT 88-1941

JTS: DS135 H92 E353 E32   YU: DS135 H92 E353

HUC: HIW 493

Eisiskes (Li) see Ejszyszki

Ejszyszki (Li). *Aishishuk: its history and its destruction, documentaries, memoir and illustrations.* Compiled and edited by Peretz Alufi, Shaul Barkali; translated by Shoshanna Gavish. Jerusalem, 1989. 81 p., illus. (E)

YIVO: Esiskes 1949

Ejszyszki (Li). *Eshishok, koroteha ve-hurbanah* [Ejszyszki, its history and destruction]. Ed.: P. Alufi, Sh. Barkeli. Jerusalem, Committee of the Survivors of Ejszyszki in Israel, [1949 or 1950]. 136 p., ports. (H,Y)

YIVO: Eisiskes 1949   NYPL: *PXW (Eisiskes)

YU: DS135 R93 E363299 1949

Ejszyszki (Li). *There once was a world: a nine-hundred-year chronicle of the shtetl of Eishyshok.* By Y. Eliach. Boston, Little Brown, 1998. xiv, 818 p., illus., maps. (E)
YIVO: /92887   NYPL: *PXW (Eisiskes) 99-718
JTS: DS135 L52 E36 E4 1998   YU: DS135 R93 E36 1998

Ekaterinoslav (U) see Yekaterinoslav

Eremichi (B) see under Turzec

Erlau (Hu) see Eger

Falenica (P). *Sefer Falenits* [Falenica book*]. Ed.: D. Shtokfish. Tel Aviv, Former Residents of Falenica in Israel, 1967. 478 p., illus., ports., facsims. (H,Y)
YIVO: Falenica 1967   NYPL: *PXV (Falenica) 79-320
JTS: DS135 P62 F34 S8   YU: DS135 P62 F35

Falenica (P) see also under Otwock

Fehergyarmat (Hu). *Ayaratenu leshe-avar Feherdrmat* [Our former city Fehergyarmat]. [By] J. Blasz. Bnei Brak, [1965]. 44, 52 p., ports., music, facsims. (H,Hu)
YIVO: Fehergyarmat 1968   NYPL: *ZP-*PBM p.v. 1041 No. 2
JTS: DS135 H92 F4

Felsobanya (Hu) see under Nagybanya

Felshteen (U) see Felshtin

Felshtin (U). *Felshtin; zamlbukh tsum ondenk fun di Felshtiner kedoyshim* [Felshtin; collection in memory of the martyrs of Felshtin]. New York, First Felshtiner Progressive Ben. Assoc. 1937. 670 p., illus., maps. (Y,E)
YIVO: Gvardiyske (Felshtin) 1937   NYPL: *ZP-1111 No. 1
JTS: DS135 R93 F4

Filipow (P) see under Suwalki

Frampol (Lublin) (P). *Sefer Frampol* [Frampol book*]. Ed.: D. Shtokfish. Tel Aviv, [Book Committee], 1966. 414 p., illus., map, ports. (H,Y)
YIVO: Frampol 1966   NYPL: *PXV(Frampol)
JTS: DS135 P62 F7 S8

Frampol (Podolia) (U) see under Kamenets-Podolskiy

Gabin (P). *Gombin; dos lebn un umkum fun a Yidish shtetl in Poyln* [Gombin; the life and destruction of a Jewish town in Poland*]. Eds.: Jack Zicklin *et al.* New York, Gombin Society in America, 1969. 228, 162 p., illus., map. (Y,E)
YIVO: Gabin 1969   NYPL: *PXV(Gabin) 1969
JTS: DS135 P62 G2 G6   YU: Uncl G632 Gomb

Gargzdai (Li). *Sefer Gorzd, Lita; ayara be-hayeha u-be-hilyona* [Gorzd book; a memorial to the Jewish community of Gorzd]. Ed.: Y. Alperowitz. Tel Aviv, The Gorzd Society, 1980. 417, 79 p., illus. (H,Y,E)
YIVO: Gargzdai 1980   NYPL: *PXV(Gargzdai) 88-463
JTS: DS135 L52 G3 A4   YU: DS135 R93 G37 1980

Garwolin (P). *Garvolin yisker-bukh* [Garwolin memorial book]. Eds.: Z. Nokhgelt. Tel Aviv, New York, Garwolin Societies, 1972. 304 p., illus. (H,Y)
YIVO: Garwolin 1972   NYPL: *PXV + (Garwolin) 76-272
JTS: DS135 P62 G394 N3   YU: 933.47(438) G244N 1972

Ger (P) see Gora Kalwaria

Gherla (Ro) see Szamosujvar

Glebokie (B). *Hurbn Glubok, Sharkoystsene, Dunilovitsh, Postov, Droye, Kozan* [Destruction of Glebokie, Szarkowszczyzna, Dunilowicze, Postawy, Druja and Kaziany]. [By] M. and T. Rajak. Buenos Aires, Former Residents' Assoc. in Argentina, 1956. 426 p., ports. (Y)
YIVO: Glubokoye 1956   NYPL: *PXW(Glubokoye) 78-5719
JTS: DS135 R93 G55 R35

Glebokie (B). *Memorial book of Glebokie; a translation into English of Hurbn Glubok, by M. & Z. Rajak, which was originally published in 1956 in Yiddish by the Former Residents' Association in Argentina.* Canton, NY, Dr. Kendall Taylor (107 Main St., Canton, NY 13617), [1994?]. iv, 176 p., maps. (E)
YIVO: Glubokoye 1994

Glebokie (B) see also under Vilna (*Vilner zamlbukh...*)

Glina (U) see Gliniany

Gliniany (U). *Kehilat Galina, 1473-1943; toldoteha ve-hurbana* [The community of Glina 1473-1943; its history and destruction]. [By] Asher Korekh. Jerusalem, 1950. 138 p., illus. (H)
YIVO: Hlynyany (Kehilat Glina) 1950   NYPL: *PXV(Gliniany)
JTS: DS135 R93 G53 K6   YU: DS135 R93 G29 1950

Gliniany (U). *Hurbn Glinyane* [The tragic end of our Gliniany*]. New York, Emergency Relief Committee for Gliniany and Vicinity, 1946. [52] p. (Y,E)
YIVO: Hlynyany 1946   NYPL: *ZP-1100 no. 11
YU: 933.47 (438) \a.H

Gliniany (U). *Megiles Gline* [The book of Gline*]. Ed.: H. Halpern. New York, Former Residents of Gline, 1950. 307 p. (Y)
YIVO: Hlynyany (Megiles Gline) 1950   NYPL: *PXV (Halpern)
JTS: DS135 R93 G53 H3   YU: 933.47 H25M 1950

Glinojeck (P). *Mayn shtetele Glinovyetsk; un di vaytere vandlungen Plotsk-Vyezshbnik, zikhroynes* [My town Glinojeck...]. [By] Shlomo Moshkovitsh. Paris, 1976. 335 p., illus. (Y)
YIVO: Glinojeck 1976   NYPL: *PXV(Glinojeck) 87-536
JTS: DS135 P62 G52

Glubokoye (Glubok) (B) see Glebokie

Glusk (Glussk) (B) see under Bobruisk; Slutsk

Gniewaszow (P). *Sefer Gnivoshov* [Ginivashov Memorial book*]. Ed.: D. Shtokfish. [Tel Aviv], Association of Gnivoshov in Israel and the Diaspora, [1971]. 533, 19 p., ports. (H,Y,E)
YIVO: Gniewoszow 1971   NYPL: *PXV(Gniewoszow)
JTS: DS135 P62 G52 S75   YU: 933.5 P762G

Golshany (B) see under Holszany

Golub (P) see under Dobrzyn

Golynka (B) see under Dereczyn

Gombin (P) see Gabin

Gomel (B) see under General Reference Works, *Arim ve-imahot,* vol. 2

Goniadz (P). *Sefer yizkor Gonyondz* [Our hometown Goniondz*]. Tel Aviv, The Committee of Goniondz Association in the USA and in Israel, 1960. 808, xx columns, ports., maps (H,Y,E)
YIVO: Goniadz 1960   NYPL: *PXV(Goniadz)
JTS: DS135 P62 G6 S4   YU: 933.47(438) G638

Gora Kalwaria (P). *Megiles Ger.* Ed.: Gershon Sapoznikow. Buenos Aires, Ger Societies in Argentina, Israel and the USA, 1975. 512 p., illus. (Y)
YIVO: Gora Kalwaria 1975   JTS: DS135 P62 S36
NYPL: *PXV(Gora-Kalvaria) 89-8342
YU: DS135 P62 G65 1975

Gorki (B) see under Slutsk

Gorlice (P). *Sefer Gorlitsah; ha-kehilah be-vinyanah uve-hurbanah* [Gorlice book; the community at rise and fall*]. Ed.: M. Y. Baron. [Tel Aviv], Association of Former Residents of Gorlice and Vicinity in Israel, [1962]. 338 p., illus., map, ports., facsims. (H,Y)
YIVO: Gorlice 1962   NYPL: *PXV+ (Gorlice)
JTS: DS135 P62 G63 B3

Gorodenka (U) see Horodenka

Gorodets (B) see Horodec

Gorodishche (B) see Horodishche

Gorodnitsa (U) see under Novograd-Volynskiy

Gorodok (near Lviv) (U) see Grodek Jagiellonski

Gorokhov (U) see Horochow

Gorzd (Li) see Gargzdai

Gostynin (P). *Pinkes Gostinin; yisker-bukh* [Pinkas Gostynin; book of Gostynin*]. Ed.: Y. M. Biderman. New York, Gostynin Memorial Book Committees, 1960. 358, [81] p., illus., music, ports. (Y)
YIVO: Gostynin 1960   NYPL: *PXV(Gostynin)
JTS: DS135 P62 G66 B5   YU: DS135 P62 G66

Goworowo (P). *Goworovah; sefer zikaron* [Govorowo memorial book*]. Eds.: A. Burstin, D. Kossovsky. Tel Aviv, Irgune yotse Govorovah, 1966. 496, xvi p., ports., facsims. (H,Y,E)
YIVO: Goworowo 1966   NYPL: *PXV(Goworowo)
JTS: DS135 P62 G67

Grabowiec (P). *Sefer ha-zikaron li-kehilat Grabovits* [Memorial book Grabowitz*]. Ed.: S. Kanc. Tel Aviv, Grabowiec Society, 1975. 432, 26 p., illus. (H,Y,E)
YIVO: Grabowiec 1975   NYPL: *PXV(Grabowiec) 77-3821
JTS: DS135 P62 G693 S4   HUC: HIW 389

Grajewo (P). *Grayeve yisker-bukh* [Grayevo memorial book*]. Ed.: G. Gorin, et. al. New York, United Grayever Relief Committee, 1950. 311, [32], 51 p., illus. (Y,E)
YIVO: Grajewo 1950   NYPL: *PXV(Grajewo)
JTS: DS135 P62 G7   HUC: HIW 347

Greiding (U) see Grodek Jagiellonski

Gresk (Hresk) (B) see under Slutsk

Gritsa (P) see Grojec

Grodek (near Bialystok) (P). *Sefer zikaron li-kehilat Horodok 'a.y. Byalistok* [Horodok; in memory of the Jewish community*]. Ed.: M. Simyon (Shamen). Tel Aviv, Assoc. of Former Residents of Grodek in Israel and Argentina, 1963. 142 p., ports., facsims. (H,Y)
YIVO: Horodok 1963   NYPL: *PXV(Horodok) 89-8569
YU: DS135 P62 G8447 1963

Grodek Jagiellonski (U). *Sefer Grayding* [Book of Griding, Grodek Jagiellonski*]. Ed.: Yehuda Leibish Margel. Tel Aviv, Society of Grayding Emigrants, 1981. 120, 8 p., illus. (H,Y,E)

Grodno (B). *Grodnah* [Grodno*]. Ed.: Dov Rabin. Jerusalem, Grodno Society; The Encyclopaedia of the Jewish Diaspora, 1973. 744 columns, illus. (H,Y)
YIVO: Grodno 1973   NYPL: *PX+ 96-485 v.9
JTS: Ref +DS135 E8 E55 v.9   HUC: HI 999

Grodno (B). *Kovets Grodnah—zaml-heft Grodne* [Grodno collection]. Ed.: Yitshak Yelin. [Tel Aviv], Grodner Association of Israel, Dec. 1958. no. 1: 50 p., illus. (H,Y)
YIVO: Grodno 1958

Grojec (P). *Megilat Gritse* [Megilat Gritze*]. Ed.: Y. B. Alterman. Tel Aviv, Gritzer Association in Israel, 1955. 408 p., illus., ports. (H,Y)
YIVO: Grojec (Warsaw) 1955   NYPL: *PXV(Grojec)
YU: DS135 P62 G87 1955

Gross Magendorf (Nagymagyar) (Slo) see under Dunaszerdahely

Grosswardein (Ro) see Oradea

Grozovo (B) see under Slutsk

318

Gura Humora (Ro). *Gurah Humorah: 'ayarah bi-derom Bukovinah; koroteha shel kehilah Yehudit* [Gura Humora: a small town in southern Bukovina; the history of its Jewish community*]. Ed.: S. Yeshurun (Yurgrau). [Israel], The Society to Commemorate the Jewish Community of Gura Humora and Vicinity, [1992]. xvi, 338 p., illus., maps, ports, facsims. (H, G, Ro)
YIVO: Gura Homorului 1992   YU: DS125 R72 G874 1992
NYPL: *PXM (Gura Humorului) 97-521

Gura Humora (Ro). *Gura Humora: a small town in southern Bukovina: the history of a community.* Trans.: from Hebrew by Ike (Tulia) Katz. [Israel], Association of Former Residents of Gura Humora and Environs, [1997]. 225 p., illus., map. (E)
YIVO: Gura Humorului 1997   JTS: DS135 R72 G8713 1997

Gura Humorului (Ro) see Gura Humora

Gusiatyn (U) see Husiatyn

Gvardiyske (U) see Felshtin

Gwozdziec (U). *Sefer zikaron Gvozdzits veha-sevivah* [Memorial book for Gwozdziec and vicinity]. Ed.: Mendel Zilber. Ramat-Gan, 1974. 351p., illus.
YIVO: Hvizdets 1974 (photocopy)

Gyor (Hu). *Le-zekher kedoshe Gyor* [In memory of the martyrs of Gyor]. Ed.: Hana Spiegel. Haifa, [197-/8-]. 36 p., illus., maps (H)

Hajdunanas (Hu) see under Debrecen

Hajdusamson (Hu) see under Debrecen

Halinka (B) see under Dereczyn

Halmeu (Ro) see Halmi

Halmi (Ro). *Zikhron netsah la-kehilot ha-kedoshot Halmin-Turts veha-sevivah asher nehrevu ba-Shoah* [In memory of the communities of Halmin-Turcz and vicinity]. Ed.: Y. Shvarts (Schwartz). Tel Aviv, Halmin-Turcz and Vicinity Society, [1969]. 138 p., illus. (H)
YIVO: Halmeu & Turt 1969   NYPL: *PXM (Halmeu) 95-527
JTS: DS135 R72 H338

Haradzets (B) see Horodec

Harlau (Ro). *Der hoyv fun zikorn; mayn moldevish shtetl Harloy* [The duty of memory; my Moldavian town Harlau]. [By] C. Zaidman. Jerusalem, Yidishe kultur-gezelshaft, 1982. 398 p., illus., ports. (Y)
YIVO: Hirlau 1982   NYPL: *PWZ (Zaidman,C) 89-7503

Haydutsishok (Hoduciszki) (Li) see under Swieciany

Herta (Ro) see under Dorohoi

Hirlau (Ro) see Harlau

Hivniv (U) see Uhnow

Hlynyany (U) see Gliniany

Hlusk (Glusk) (B) see under Slutsk

Hoduciszki (Li) see under Swieciany

Holojow (Cholojow) (U) see under Radziechow

Holszany (B). *Lebn un umkum fun Olshan* [The life and destruction of Olshan]. Ed.: Shabtai Kaplan, et. al. Tel Aviv, Former Residents of Olshan in Israel, [1965]. 431, 136 p., ports., facsims. (H,Y)
YIVO: Golshany 1965   NYPL: *PXW(Ol'shany)
JTS: DS135 R93 O5 L4   YU: DS135 R93 O538 1965

Holynka (Hu) see under Dereczyn

Homel (Gomel) (B) see under General Reference Works, *Arim ve-imahot*, vol. 2

Horochow (U). *Sefer Horokhov* [Horchiv memorial book*]. Ed.: Y. Kariv. Tel Aviv, Horchiv Committee in Israel, [1966]. 375, 79 p., ports., maps, facsims. (H,Y,E)
YIVO: Horokhiv 1966   NYPL: *PXW(Gorokhov)
JTS: DS135 R93 G69 D3   YU: 933.5 R969G

Horodec (B). *Horodets; a geshikhte fun a shtetl, 1142-1942* [Horodec; history of a town, 1142-1942]. Ed.: A. Ben-Ezra. New York, Horodets Book Committee, [1949 or 1950]. 238 p., ports., map, facsims. (Y)
YIVO: Gorodets 1949   NYPL: *PXV+ (Ben-Ezra, A.)
JTS: +DS135 R93 G67 B4   YU: 933.547 G672B
HUC: HIW 351

Horodenka (U). *Sefer Horodenka* [The book of Horodenka]. Ed.: Sh. Meltzer. Tel Aviv, Former Residents of Horodenka and Vicinity in Israel and the USA, 1963. vii, 425 p., ports., map, facsims. (H,Y)
YIVO: Horodenka 1963   NYPL: *PXW(Gorodenka)
JTS: DS135 R93 G66 M44   YU: DS135 R93 G65
HUC: HIW 463

Horodishche (B).   *Der Horodishtser borg* [The Horodishche mountain]. Ed.: Benjamin Rubinshteyn (Rubinstein). New York, United Horodyszczer Relief Organizations, 1920. 44 p., ports. (Y)
NYPL: *ZP-*PBM p.v. 283 no. 4

Horodlo (P). *Di kehile fun Horodla; yisker-bukh...* [The community of Horodlo; memorial book...]. Ed.: Y. Ch. Zavidovits. Tel Aviv, Former Residents of Horodlo in Israel, [1962 or 1963]. 324 p., ports., facsims. (Y)
YIVO: Horodlo 1962   NYPL: *PXV(Horodlo)
JTS: DS135 P62 H659   YU: 933.5 P762H
HUC: HIW 363

Horodlo (P). *Kehilat Horodlah; sefer zikaron li-kedoshe Horodlah (Polin) veli-kedoshe ha-kefarim ha-semukhim* [The community of Horodlo; memorial book...]. Ed.: Y.

319

H. Zavidovits. Tel Aviv, Former Residents of Horodlo in Israel, [1959 or 1960]. 260 p., illus., ports., facsims. (H)

YIVO: Horodlo 1959   NYPL: *PXV(Horodlo) 84-370
JTS: DS135 P62 H658   YU: DS135 P62 H65

Horodno (B) see under Stolin

Horodok (P) see Grodek (near Bialystok)

Horokhiv (U) see Horochow

Horyngrod (U) see under Tuczyn

Hoshcha (U) see Hoszcza

Hoszcza (U). *Hoshtsh; sefer zikaron* [Hoshtch-Wolyn; in memory of the Jewish community*]. Eds.: B. H. Ayalon-Baranik, A. Yaron-Kritzmar. [Tel Aviv], Former Residents of Hoshtch in Israel, 1957. 269 p., ports. (H)

NYPL: *PXW (Goshcha) 93-1879

Hoszcza (U). *Sefer Hosht; yisker-bukh* [The book of Hosht—in memoriam*]. Ed.: R. Fink. New York and Tel Aviv, Society of Hosht, 1957. xvi, 294 p., illus., map, ports., facsims. (Y)

YIVO: Hoshcha 1957   NYPL: *PXW(Goshcha) (Fink R..)
JTS: DS135 R93 G65 F5

Hotin (U) see Khotin

Hresk (Gresk) (B) see under Slutsk

Hrodna (B) see Grodno

Hrubieszow (P). *Pinkas Hrubyeshov* [Memorial book of Hrubieshov]. Ed.: B. Kaplinski. Tel Aviv, Irgun yotse Hrubyeshov in Yisroel un in di fareynikte shtaten, [1962]. 812 col., xviii p., illus., maps, ports. (H,Y,E,P)

YIVO: Hrubieszow 1962   NYPL: *PXV+ (Hrubieszow)
YU: 933.47 (438) H873 K

Hrubieszow (P). *Shorashim shelanu: le-zekher kedoshe Hrubishov* [Our roots: in memory to the Jewish victims of the Holocaust 1939-1945*]. Tel Aviv, Organization of Former Jewish Inhabitants of Hrubieszow in Israel, 1990-1992. 2 vols., illus., ports. (H,Y,E,P)

YIVO: Hrubieszow 1990 (v.1), 1992 (v.2)
JTS: DS135 P62 H78 S56 1990   YU: DS135 P62 H78 1990

Huedin (Ro). *Zikhronotai me-Banfi-Hunyad; sefer zikaron li-Yehude Banfi-Hunyad* [Igy emlekszem Huedin/ Banffy-Hunyadra*=My memories of Banffy-Hunyadi]. [By] E. L. Klepner. Jerusalem, Sifre Ramot, [1990]. 38, 19, [12], 100 p., illus., maps, ports. (H,Hu)

YIVO: Huedin 1990   NYPL: *PXM(Huedin) 91-647
JTS: DS135 H92 H9 K55 1990   YU: DS135 R72 H845 1990

Husiatyn (U). *Husiatin; Podolyer gubernye...* [Husiatyn; Podolia-Ukraine*]. Ed.: B. Diamond. New York, [o. fg., 1968]. 146, 123 p., illus., ports. (Y,E)

YIVO: Husyatyn 1968   NYPL: *PXW(Gusyatin) 83-379
YU: DS135 R93 G854 1968

Husiatyn (U). *Kehilatayim: Husiatin ve-Kopitsintsah* [Two communities: Husiatyn and Kopyczynce*]. [By] Abraham Becker. Tel Aviv, Husiatyn Society, 1977. 286 p., illus., map. (H,Y)

YIVO: Husyatyn & Kopychyntsi 1977   JTS: DS135 R93 G88 B33
NYPL: *PXW(Gusyatin) 81-906   YU: DS135 R93 G852

Husiatyn (U). *Mi-bet aba; pirke zikhronot mi-yeme yaldut be-'ayarat moladeti Husyatin* [From my parents' home; memorial chapter...]. [By] A. Y. Avitov (Birnboim). Tel Aviv, [1964/1965], 155 p., illus., ports. (H)

YIVO: Husyatyn 1964   NYPL: *PWZ (Avituv)

Husiatyn (U). *Sefer zikaron Husiatyn veha-sevivah* [Memorial book of Husiatyn and the surrounding region]. Ed.: Abraham Becker. Tel Aviv, Husiatyn-Galicia Society, 1976. 499 p., illus. (H,Y)

Husyatyn (U) see Husiatyn

Hvizdets (U) see Gwozdziec

Iampol (U) see Yampol

Ianov (U) see under Trembowla

Ignatovka (Ignatowka) (U) see under Zofiowka

Iklad (Rom) see under Szamosujvar

Ileanda (Nagyilonda) (Ro) see under Des

Ilja (B). *Sefer Ilyah...*[alternate title: *Kehilat Ilyah: pirke hayim ve-hashmadah* [The community of Ilja; chapters of life and destruction]. Ed.: A. Kopelovits. [Tel Aviv], Association of Former Residents of Ilja in Israel, 1962. 466 p., illus., ports., facsims. (H,Y)

YIVO: Ilya 1962   NYPL: *PXW(Ilia) 88-464
JTS: DS135 R93 I49 K6

Ilya (B) see Ilja

Indura (B). *Amdur, mayn geboyrn-shtetl* [Amdur, my hometown]. [By] Iedidio Efron. Buenos Aires, 1973. 252, 33 p., illus. (Y,S)

YIVO: Indura 1973   NYPL: *PXW(Indura) 77-3818
JTS: DS135 R93 I54 E42   HUC: HL Efron
YU: DS135 R93 I54

Ipolysag (Slo) see Sahy

Istrik (Ustrzyki Dolne) (P) see under Lesko

Iue (B) see Iwie

Iustingrad (U) see Yustingrad

Ivano-Frankovsk (Stanislawow) (U) see under General Reference Works, *Arim ve-imahot*, vol. 5

Ivanovo (B) see Janow (near Pinsk)

Ivenets (B) see Iwieniec

Ivye (B) see Iwie

Iwacewicze (B) see under Byten

Iwie (B). *Sefer zikaron li-kehilat Ivyeh* [Ivie; in memory of the Jewish community*]. Ed.: M. Kaganovich [Kahanovich]. Tel Aviv, Association of Former Residents of Ivie in Israel and America, 1968. 738 p., illus., maps, music, ports. (H,Y)

YIVO: Ivye 1968   NYPL: *PXW(Iv'ye)
JTS: DS135 R93 I9   YU: DS135 R93 I927

Iwieniec (B). *Sefer Ivenits, Kamin veha-sevivah; sefer zikaron* [The memorial book of Iwieniec, Kamien, and the surrounding region]. [Tel Aviv, Defus Arzi, 1973]. 484 p., illus. (H,Y)

YIVO: Ivenets 1973   NYPL: *PXW(Ivenets) 74-2700
JTS: DS135 R93 I89 S4

Jablonka (P) see under Nowy Targ

Jadow (P). *Sefer Yadov* [The book of Jadow*]. Ed.: A. V. Yasni (Jasny). Jerusalem, Encyclopaedia of the Jewish Diaspora, 1966. 472, xxiii p., illus., map, ports. (H,Y,E)

YIVO: Jadow 1966   NYPL: *PXV(Jadow)
JTS: DS135 P62 J275   YU: DS135 P62 J275

Jaisi (Jejsa) (B) see under Braslaw

Janova (Li) see Jonava

Janow (near Pinsk) (B). *Yanov 'al-yad Pinsk; sefer zikaron* [Yanov near Pinsk; memorial volume*]. Ed.: M. Nadav (Katsikovits). Jerusalem, Assoc. of Former Residents of Janow near Pinsk in Israel, [1968 or 1969]. xvi, 420 p., illus., ports. (H,Y)

YIVO: Ivanovo 1968   NYPL: *PXW(Ivanovo)
JTS: DS135 R93 I88   YU: 933.5 R969Y

Janow (near Trembowla) (U) see under Budzanow; Trembowla

Jaroslaw (P). *Sefer Yaroslav* [Jaroslav book*]. Ed.: Yitzhak Alperowitz. Tel Aviv, Jaroslaw Society in Israel, 1978. 371, 28 p., illus, map. (H,Y,E)

YIVO: Jaroslaw 1978   NYPL: *PXV(Jaroslaw) 80-4339
JTS: DS135 P62 J29 S3   YU: DS135 P62 J297

Jaryczow Nowy (U). *Hurbn Yaritshov bay Lemberg; sefer zikaron li-kedoshe Yaritshov u-sevivoteha* [Destruction of Jaryczow; memorial book to the martyrs of Jaryczow and surroundings]. [By] Mordekhai Gerstl. New York, Boym, 1948. 78 p., ports. (Y)

YIVO: Novyy Yarychiv 1948   NYPL: *PXW(Novy Yarychev)
JTS: DS135 P62 J325 G4

Jaslo (P). *Toldot Yehude Yaslo; me-reshit hityashvutam be-tokh ha-ir ad yeme ha-hurban al yede ha-Natsim...* [History of the Jews of Jaslo...]. [By] M. N. Even-Hayim (Ibn-Chaim). Tel Aviv, Jaslo Society in Israel, 1953. 360 p., illus., map, ports. (H)

YIVO: Jaslo 1953   JTS: DS135 P62 J3 R3
HUC: HI 989.2   YU: DS135 P62 J333 1953

Jaworow (U). *"Yudenstadt Yavorov;" der umkum fun di Yavorover Idn* [Swastika over Jaworow*]. [By] S. Druck. New York, Independent Yavorover Association, 1950. 69, iv, 35 p., ports. (Y,E)

YIVO: Yavoriv 1950   NYPL: *PXW(Yavorov)
JTS: DS135 P62 J37 D7

Jaworow (U). *Matsevet zikaron li-kehilat Yavorov veha-sevivah* [Monument to the community of Jaworow and the surrounding region]. Ed.: M. Bar-Lev. Haifa, Jaworow Societies in Israel and the USA, [1978 or1979]. 252 p., illus., maps. (H,Y, E)

YIVO: Yavoriv 1978   NYPL: *PXW(Yavarov) 81-1019
JTS: DS135 P62 J37 B3   YU: DS135 B93 Y385

Jedrzejow (P). *Sefer ha-zikaron li-YehudeYendzeyov* [Memorial book of the Jews of Jedrzejow]. Ed.: Sh. D. Yerushalmi. Tel Aviv, Former Residents of Jedrzejow in Israel, [1965]. 490 p., illus., ports., facsims. (H,Y)

YIVO: Jedrzejow 1965   NYPL: *PXV(Jedrzejow)
JTS: DS135 P62 J43 Y4   YU: 933.47(438) Y47J

Jedwabne (P). *Sefer Yedvabneh; historiyah ve-zikaron* [Yedwabne; history and memorial book*]. Eds.: Julius L. Baker, Jacob L. Baker; assisted by M. Tzinovitz. Jerusalem-New York, Yedwabner Societies in Israel and the USA, 1980. 121, 110 p., illus. (E, H,Y)

YIVO: Jedwabne 1980   NYPL: *PXV(Jedwabne) 89-692
YU: DS135 P62 J4488 1980   HUC: DS135 P62 J448 1980

Jeleniewo (P) see Suwalki

Jeremicze (B) see under Turzec

Jezierna (U) *SeferYeziernah* [Memorial book of Jezierna*]. Ed.: Y. Siegelman. Haifa, Committee of Former Residents of Jezierna in Israel, 1971. 354 p., ports. (H,Y)

YIVO: Ozernyany 1971   NYPL: *PXW(Ozernyany)
JTS: DS135 R93 D958 S4   YU: DS135 R93 O958 1971

Jezierzany (U). *Sefer Ozyeran veha-seviva*h [Memorial book; Jezierzany and surroundings*]. Ed.: M. A. Tenenblatt. Jerusalem, The Encyclopaedia of the Jewish Diaspora, 1959. 498 columns, ports. (H,Y)

YIVO: Ozeryany 1959   NYPL: *PXW(Ozeryany)
JTS: DS135 R93 O97 T4   YU: DS135 R93 O97
HUC: HIW 459.2

Jeznas (Li). *Le-zikhram shel kedoshe kehilat Yeznah she-nispu bi-shenat 1941* [Memorial book of the martyrs of Jeznas who perished in 1941]. Ed.: Dov Aloni. [Tel Aviv], Former Residents of Jeznas in Israel, [1967]. 114 p., ports., maps, facsims. (H), mimeo.

YIVO: Jeznas 1967

Jod (Jody) (B) see under Braslaw

Jonava (Li). *Sefer Yanovah: le-hantsahat zikhram shel Yehude ha-'ayarah she-neherevah ba-Shoah* [Yizkor book in memory of the Jewish community of Yanova*]. Ed.: Shimeon Noi (Noy). Tel Aviv, Jonava Society in Israel, 1972. 35, 429 p., illus. (Y,E)

YIVO: Jonava 1972   NYPL: *PXW(Jonava) 75-1483
YU: DS135 R93 J65 1972

Jordanow (P) see under Nowy Targ

Jozefow (P). *Sefer zikaron li-kehilat Yozefof veli-kedosheha* [Memorial book to the community of Jozefow and its martyrs]. Ed.: Azriel Omer-Lemer. [Tel Aviv], Jozefow Societies in Israel and the USA, [1974 or 1975]. 462 p., illus. (H,Y)

YIVO: Jozefow 1974   NYPL: *PXV(Jozefow) 81-145
JTS: DS135 P62 J68 S4   YU: DS135 P62 J697

Jurbarkas (Li). *Sefer ha-zikaron li-kehilat Yurburg-Lita* [Memorial book for the community of Yurburg, Lithuania]. Ed.: Z. Poran. Jerusalem, Society of Yurburg Emigrants in Israel, 1991. 524 p., illus., ports. (H,Y; introd.:E)

YIVO: Jurbarkas 1991   NYPL: *PXW (Jurbarkas) 93-576
YU: DS135 R93 J8737 1991

Justingrad (U) see Yustingrad

Kadzidlo (P) see under Ostroleka

Kalarash (M). *Sefer Kalarash; le-hantsahat zikhram shel Yehude ha-'ayarah she-nehreva bi-yeme ha-Shoah* [Kalarash book in memory of the town's Jews, which was destroyed in the Holocaust]. Eds.: N. Tamir *et al.* Tel Aviv, [1966]. 533 p., map, ports., facsims. (H,Y)

YIVO: Calarasi 1966   NYPL: *PXW(Kalarash)
JTS: DS135 R93 K23   YU: 933.5 R969 Z78E
HUC: HIW 384

Kalisz (P). *The Kalish book.* Ed.: I. M. Lask. [Tel Aviv], Societies of Former Residents of Kalish and the Vicinity in Israel and the USA, 1968]. 327 p., illus., map. (E)

YIVO: Kalisz 1968   NYPL: *PXV(Kalisz) 73-1576
JTS: +DS135 P62 K291   YU: 933.5 P72 K14

Kalisz (P). *Kalish she-hayetah; ir ve-em be-Yisrael be-medinat "Polin-Gadol"* [The Kalisz that was...]. Haifa, Bet ha-sefer ha-reali ha-ivri and The Kalisz Society, [1979 or 1980]. 136 p., illus., ports., maps (H)

Kalisz (P). *Sefer Kalish* [The Kalish book *]. [Tel Aviv, The Israel-American Book Committee, 1964-1968.] 2 vols. (624, 598 p.), illus., map, ports., facsims. (H,Y)

YIVO: Kalisz 1964   NYPL: *PXV+ (Kalisz)
JTS: +DS135 P62 K29   YU: 933.5 P762 K14 1964

Kalisz (P). *Toldot Yehude Kalish* [History of the Jews of Kalisz]. [By] Yisrael David Bet-Halevi. Tel Aviv,

Author, [1960/61]. 448 p., illus., map, ports. (H)

YIVO: Kalisz 1960   NYPL: *PXV (Kalisz)(Bet Halevi)
JTS: DS135 P62 K29 B48 1961   YU: 933.543.8 B562TT
HUC: HI/909.3

Kalov (Hu) see Nagykallo

Kalusz (U). *Kalusz; hayeha ve-hurbanah shel ha-kehilah* [Kalusz; the life and destruction of the community]. Eds.: Shabtai Unger, Moshe Ettinger. Jerusalem, Kalusz Society, 1980. 576 p., illus. (H,Y,E)

YIVO: Kalusz 1980   NYPL: *PXW(Kalush) 82-1681
YU: DS135 R93 K244 1980

Kaluszyn (P). *Kehilat Kalushin* [The community of Kaluszyn]. Translated from Yiddish: Yitzhak Shoshani. Tel Aviv, I.L. Peretz and Society of Kaluszyn Emigrants in Israel, 1977. 77p., map. (H)

YIVO: Kaluszyn 1977   NYPL: *PXV (Kaluszyn) 96-1518

Kaluszyn (P). *Seyfer Kalushin; geheylikt der horev gevorener kehile* [Memorial book of Kaluszyn]. Eds.: A. Shamri, Sh. Soroka. Tel Aviv, Former Residents of Kaluszyn in Israel, America, Argentina, Germany and other lands, 1961. 545 p., illus., ports., facsims. (Y)

YIVO: Kaluszyn 1961   NYPL: *PXV+ (Kaluszyn)
JTS: Restr +DS135 P62 K3 S5   YU: DS135 P62 K36 1961

Kalwaria Zebrzydowska (Kalwaria) (P) see under Wadowice.

Kamenets-Litovsk (B) see Kamieniec Litewski

Kamenets-Podolskiy (U). *Kaminits-Podolsk u-sevivatah* [Kamenets-Podolsk and its surroundings]. Eds.: A. Rosen, *et. al.* Tel Aviv, Irgun yotse Kaminits-Podolsk u-sevivatah be-Yisrael, [1965]. 263 p., ports., facsims. (H)

YIVO: Kamyanets-Podilskyy 1965   JTS: DS135 R93 K25
YU: 933.5 R969K R813

Kamenets-Podolskiy (U). *Kamenetz-Podolsk; a memorial to a Jewish community annihilated by the Nazis.* Ed.: Leon S. Blatman. New York, Sponsors of the Kamenetz-Podolsk Memorial Book, 1966. 133 p., illus., ports. (E)

YIVO: Kamyanets-Podilskyy 1966   YU: Uncl. B644K
NYPL: *PXW (Kamenets-Podolski) 86-1459

Kamenets-Podolskiy (U). *Kaminits-Podolsk; excerpts from Kaminits-Podolsk u-sevivatah, a memorial book.* Translated by Bonnie S. Sohn. Washington, DC, [1990]. iii, 134 p. (E)

YIVO: Kamyanets-Podilskyy 1990

Kamenets-Podolskiy (U). *Kaminits-Podolsk and its environs: a memorial book of the Jewish communities in the cities of Kaminits-Podolsk, Balin, Dunivits, Zamekhov, Zhvanets, Minkovitz, Smotrich, Frampol, Kupin, and Kitaygorod annihilated by the Nazis in 1941.* Eds.: A. Rosen, H. Sarig and Y. Bernstein. Trans.: B.

Schooler Sohn. Bergenfield, 1999. xiii, 234 p. (E)
YIVO: Kamianets-Podilskyi 1999
NYPL: *PXW (Kamianets-Podilskyi) 00-2689
HUC: DS135 U42 K3613 1999   JTS: DS135 R93 K2513 1999

Kamianets (B) see Kamieniec Litewski

Kamien (B) see under Iwieniec

Kamien Koszyrski (U). *Sefer ha-zikaron li-kehilat Kamin Koshirski veha-sevivah.* [Kamin Koshirsky book; in memory of the Jewish community*]. Eds.: A. S. Stein *et al.* [Tel Aviv], Irgun yotse Kamin Koshirski veha-sevivah be-Yisrael, [1965]. 974 columns, illus., map, ports. (H,Y)
YIVO: Kamin Kashyrskyy 1965   NYPL: *PXW(Kamen-Kashirskiy)
JTS: +DS135 P62 K325   YU: 933.52 762K S819

Kamieniec Litewski (B). *Sefer yizkor li-kehilot Kamenits de-Lita, Zastavyah veha-kolonyot* [Kamenetz Litovsk, Zastavye, and colonies memorial book*]. Eds.: S. Eisenstadt (Aizenshtadt), M. Gelbart. Tel Aviv, Kamieniec and Zastavye Committees in Israel and the USA, 1970. 626, 185 p., illus., map (H,Y,E)
YIVO: Kamenets & Zastavye 1970
 NYPL: *PXW(Kamenets) 89-8630

Kamiensk (P) see under Radomsko

Kamin Kashyrskyy (U) see Kamien Koszyrski

Kammeny Brod (U) see under Novograd-Volynskiy

Kamyanets-Podilskyy (U) see Kamenets Podolskiy

Kapolnokmonoster (Ro) see under Nagybanya

Kapreshty (M). *Kapresht 'ayaratenu; Undzer shtetale Kapresht; sefer zikaron li-kehilah Yehudit be-Besarabyah* [Kapresht, our village; memorial book for the Jewish community of Kapresht, Bessarabia*]. Eds.: M. Rishpi (Fayarman), Av. B. Yanowitz. Haifa, Kapresht Society in Israel, 1980. 496 p., map, illus. (H,Y)
YIVO: Kapreshty 1980   NYPL: *PXW(Kapreshty) 89-8568
YU: DS135 R93 K2743 1980

Kapreshty (M). *Leket shel bikoret veha-'arakhah ha-sefer "Kapresht 'ayaratenu"= zamlung fun kritik un opshatsung in di shpurn fun bukh "Kapresht - undzer shtetl."* Eds: M. Rishpi, B. Yanowitz. Haifa, Irgun yotse Kapresht be-Yisrael, 1981. 109 p., illus., ports. (H, Y, Ro, E, S)
YIVO: Kapreshty 1981

Kapsukas (Li) see Marijampole

Kapulye (Kopyl) (B) see under Slutsk

Karcag (Hu). *Toldot kehilat Kartsag ve-kehilot mehoz Nad'kunsag* [History of the community of Karcag and the communities of the district of Nagykunsag]. [By] Moshe

Hershko. Jerusalem, Karcag Society, 1977. 219, 53 p., illus., ports., facsims. (H,Hu)
JTS: DS135 H92 K37 H47 1977

Karczew (P) see under Otwock

Kartuz-Bereze (B) see Bereza-Kartuska and also see under Pruzana; Biaroza

Kaszony (U) see Kosyno

Katowice (P). *Katovits: perihatah u-shekiatah shel ha-kehilah ha-Yehudit; sefer zikaron* [Katowice: the rise and decline of the Jewish community; memorial book]. Eds.: Yosef Khrust (Chrust), Yosef Frankel. Tel Aviv, The Society to Commemorate the Jews of Katowice, 1996. xx, 404 p., illus., map, ports. (H)
YIVO: Katowice 1996   NYPL: *PXV (Katowice) 97-378
YU: DS135 P62 K37555 1996

Kattawitz (P) see Katowice

Kaziany (B) see under Glebokie

Kazimierz (P). *Pinkas Kuzmir* [Kazimierz; memorial book*]. Ed.: D. Shtokfish. [Tel Aviv, Former Residents of Kazimierz in Israel and the Diaspora, 1970]. 655 p., illus., ports., facsims. (H,Y)
YIVO: Kazimierz 1970   NYPL: *PXV(Kazimierz)
JTS: DS135 P62 K38 P5   YU: K5 P762K
HUC: HIW 381

Kedainiai (Li). *Keydan; sefer zikaron* [Keidan memorial book*]. Ed.: Josef Chrust. Tel Aviv, Keidan Societies in Israel, South America, and the USA, 1977. 39, 313 p., illus. (H,Y,E)
YIVO: Kedainiai 1977   NYPL: *PXW(Kedainiai) 81-94
JTS: DS135 L5 K4 S4   YU: DS135 R93 L555

Kelme (Li). *Kelm - 'ets karut* [Kelm - an uprooted tree]. [By] Idah Markus-Karabelnik and Bat-Sheva Levitan-Karabelnik. [Tel Aviv], Authors, [1993]. 215 p., illus., ports. (H)
YIVO: Kelme 1993   NYPL: *PXW (Kelme) 93-2042
YU: DS135 R93 K34 1993

Kelts (P) see Kielce

Kesmark (Slo) see Kezmarok

Keydan (Li) see Kedainiai

Kezmarok (Slo). *Toldot Yehude Kezmarok veha-sevivah* [History of the Jews of Kezmarok and vicinity]. [By] Shemuel Dov Gevaryahu-Gotesman. Jerusalem, [1992]. 311 p., illus., facsims. (H)
YIVO: Kezmarok 1992   NYPL: *PXT (Kezmarok) 93-2041
JTS: DS135 S55 G48 1992   YU: DS135 C96 K494 1992

Kharshnitse (P) see Miechow

Khmelnitskii (U) see Proskurov

Khmelnytskyy (U) see Proskurov

Kholm (P) see Chelm

Khorostkiv (U) see Chorostkow

Khotin (U). *Sefer kehilat Hotin (Besarabyah)* [The book of the community of Khotin (Bessarabia)]. Ed.: Shlomo Shitnovitzer. Tel Aviv, Khotin (Bessarabia) Society in Israel, 1974. 333 p., illus. (Y, H)
YIVO: Khotyn 1974   NYPL: *PXW(Hotin) 75-3355
JTS: DS135 R93 K44 S4   YU: DS135 R72 H677

Khotyn (U) see Khotin

Khozhel (P) see Chorzele

Khust (U). *Kehilat Hust veha-sevivah: sefer zikaron.* [*Jewish community in Chust and its surrounding villages*]. Ed.: Tsevi Menshel. Rehovot, Irgun kehilat Hust veha-sevivah, 2000. 607 p., illus., maps, ports., facsims. (H)
YIVO: Khust 2000   NYPL: *PXW (Khust) 01-4488
YU: DS 135 R93 K484 2000

Kibart (Li) see Kybartai

Kielce (P). *'Al betenu she-harav—Fun der horever heym* [About our house which was devastated*]. Ed.: D. Shtokfish. Tel Aviv, Kielce Societies in Israel and the Diaspora, 1981. 246 p., illus., ports. (H,Y,P,E)
YIVO: Kielce 1981   YU: DS135 P62 K54 1981

Kielce (P). *Sefer Kelts; toldot kehilat Kelts...* [The history of the community of Kielce]. [By] P. Tsitron (Zitron). Tel Aviv, Former Residents of Kielce in Israel, [1956 or 1957]. 328 p., illus., ports. (H,Y)
YIVO: Kielce 1956   NYPL: *PXV(Kielce)
YU: DS135 P62 K545 1956

Kemelishki (B) see under Swieciany (Li)

Kiernozia (P) see under Lowicz

Kiev (U) see under Babi Yar

Kikol (P) see under Lipno

Kislowszczyzna (B) see under Braslaw

Kisvarda (Hu). *Sefer yizkor li-kehilat Klainwardain veha-sevivah* [Memorial book of Kleinwardein and vicinity]. [Eds.]: K. Joslez, E. Agon (Teichman). [Tel Aviv, s.n.], 1980. 190, 79 p., illus. (H,Hu,E)
YIVO: Kisvarda 1980   NYPL: *PXT 87-3579
JTS: DS135 H92 K5 J6   YU: DS135 H92 K574 1980
HUC: HIW 387 (Hung. ed.)

Kitai-Gorod (U) see under Kamenets-Podolskiy

Kitev (U) see Kuty

Klausenburg (Ro) see Kolozsvar

Kleck (B). *Pinkas Kletsk* [Pinkas Klezk; a memorial to the Jewish community of Klezk-Poland*]. Ed.: A. S. Stein. Tel Aviv, Former Residents of Klezk in Israel, 1959. 385 p., illus., map, ports., facsims. (H,Y)
YIVO: Kletsk 1959   NYPL: *PXV+ (Kleck)
JTS: DS135 R93 K65 S73   YU: 933.47 K64 SC2

Kleinwardein (Hu) see Kisvarda

Kletsk (Kletzk) (B) see Kleck

Klobuck (P) see Klobucko

Klobucko (P). *Sefer Klobutsk; mazkeret kavod la-kehilah ha-kedoshah she-hushmedah* [The book of Klobucko; in memory of a martyred community which was destroyed]. Tel Aviv, Former Residents of Klobucko in Israel, Germany and Australia, 1960. 439 p., ports., facsims. (Y; preface also H)
YIVO: Klobuck 1960   NYPL: *PXV(Klobuck) 89-8427
YU: DS135 P62 K58 1960

Knenitsh (Knihynicze) (U) see under Rohatyn

Kobrin (B) see Kobryn

Kobryn (B). *Kobrin; zamlbukh (an iberblik ibern Yidishn Kobrin)* [Kobryn; collection (an overview of Jewish Kobryn)]. Ed.: Melech Glotzer. Buenos Aires, Kobryn Book Committee, 1951. 310 p., illus., map. (Y)
YIVO: Kobrin 1951   NYPL: *PXW(Kobrin) 88-8508

Kobryn (B). *Sefer Kobrin; megilat hayim ve-hurban* [Book of Kobryn; the scroll of life and destruction]. Eds.: B. Shvarts (Schwartz), I. C. Biletzky. Tel Aviv, 1951. 347 p., ports. (H)
YIVO: Kobrin (Sefer Kobrin) 1951   NYPL: *PXW(Kobrin)
JTS: DS135 P62 K66   HUC: HIW 359

Kobryn (B). *Sefer Kobrin: The Book of Kobrin; the scroll of life and destruction.* Eds.: Bezalel Shwartz, Israel Chaim Biltzki (Biletzky); translated from the Hebrew by Nilli Avidan and Avner Perry; edited and printed by Joel Neuberg for HCNC. San Francisco, Holocaust Center of Northern California, 1992. iv, 447 p., illus., map, ports. (E)
YIVO: Kobrin 1992   NYPL: *PXW (Kobrin) 99-1858
YU: DS135 R93 K62713 1992

Kobylnik (B). *Sefer Kobilnik* [Memorial book of Kobilnik*]. Ed.: Y. Zigelman (Siegelman). Haifa, Committee of Former Residents of Kobilnik in Israel, 1967. 296 p., illus., map, ports. (H,Y)
YIVO: Kobylnik 1967   NYPL: *PXW(Kobyl'nik)
JTS: DS135 P62 K6614

Kock (P). *Sefer Kotsk* [Memorial book of Kotsk]. Ed.: E. Porat. [Tel Aviv], Former Residents of Kotsk in Israel..., [1961]. 424 p., ports., map, facsims. (H,Y)
YIVO: Kock 1961   NYPL: *PXV(Kock) 77-3769
JTS: DS135 P62 K662 P6   HUC: HIW 361.2
YU: DS135 P62 K6768 1971

Koden (P). *Koden, a shtetl no more*. By J. Schneider Oshrin. Hackettstown, Schneider Oshrin, 1995. (E)
NYPL: *XMH-3038 (3 microfiche)

Koidanovo (B). *Koydenov; zamlbukh tsum ondenk fun di Koydenover kdoyshim* [Koidanov; memorial volume of the martyrs of Koidanov]. Eds.: A. Reisin, A. Karlin. New York, United Koidanover Assn., 1955. 261, 207 p., illus., ports., facsims. (Y)
YIVO: Dzerzhinsk 1955   NYPL: *PBM p.v.1180, no. 1
JTS: DS135 R93 K652 R4   YU: DS135 R93 D97
HUC: HIW 419

Kolarovgrad (Bulgaria) see Shumla

Kolbuszowa (P). *Pinkas Kolbushov (Kolbasov)* [Kolbuszowa memorial book*]. Ed.: I. M. Biderman. New York, United Kolbushover, xii, 1971. 793, 88 p., illus., map, music, ports. (H,Y,E)
YIVO: Kolbuszowa 1971   NYPL: *PXV(Kolbuszowa)
JTS: DS135 P62 K663 B5   YU: DS135 P62 K649

Kolki (U). *Fun ash aroysgerufn* [Summoned from the ashes]. [By] Daniyel Kats (Kac). Warsaw, Czytelnik, Zydowski Instytut Historyczny w Polsce, 1983. 399 p., illus., map, ports. (Y)
YIVO: Kolky 1983

Kolno (P). *Sefer zikaron li-kehilat Kolnah* [Kolno memorial book*]. Eds.: A. Rembah, B. Halevi. [Tel Aviv], Kolner Organization, 1971. 680, 70 p., illus., ports., facsims. (H,Y,E)
YIVO: Kolno 1971   NYPL: *PXV(Kolno)
JTS: DS135 P62 K664 R4   YU: DS135 P62 K6645

Kolo (P). *Azoy zenen zey umgekumen - Kakh hem nispu* [This is how they perished*]. [By] A. M. Harap. [Israel], Memorial Book Committee and the Author, 1974. 169, 8 p., illus. (Y,H,E)
YIVO: Kolo 1974

Kolo (P). *Sefer Kolo* [Memorial book of Kolo]. Ed.: M. Halter. [Tel Aviv], Former Residents of Kolo in Israel and the USA, [1958]. 408 p., illus., ports. (H,Y)
YIVO: Kolo 1958   NYPL: *PXV(Kolo)
JTS: DS135 P62 K665 H34   YU: 933.5 P762K

Kolomyja (U). *Pinkes Kolomey* [Memorial book of Kolomey]. Ed.: Sh. Bickel. New York, [o. fg., 1957]. 448 p., illus., ports. (Y)
YIVO: Kolomyya 1957   NYPL: *PXW(Kolomea)
JTS: DS135 R93 K654 B5

Kolomyja (U). *Sefer zikaron li-kehilat Kolomeyah veha-sevivah* [Kolomeyer memorial book*]. Eds.: D. Noy (Noi), M. Schutzman. [Tel Aviv], Former Residents of Kolomey and Surroundings in Israel...[1972]. 395 p., illus., maps, ports., facsims. (H)
YIVO: Kolomyya 1972   NYPL: *PXW(Kolomea) 75-2279
JTS: DS135 R93 K654 S4   YU: DS135 R93 K655 1972

Kolonia (Kolonja) **Synajska**(B) see under Dereczyn

Kolozsborsa (Ro) see Borsa

Kolozsvar (Ro). *Sefer zikaron le-Yahadut Kluz-Kolozsvar* [Memorial volume of the Jews of Cluj-Kolozsvar*]. Ed.: M. Carmilly-Weinberger. New York, 1970. 155, 313 p., ports., facsims. (H,E,Hu)
YIVO: Cluj-Napoca 1970   JTS: DS135 R72 C59 C37
NYPL: *PXM (Carmilly-Weinberger)
YU: 933.47(498) C649C   HUC: DS135 R72 C59 1970

Kolozsvar (Ro). *Sefer zikaron le-Yahadut Kluz-Kolozvar* [Memorial volume of the Jews of Cluj-Kolozsvar*= A Kolozsvari zsidosag emlekkonyve*]. Ed.: Moshe Carmilly-Weinberger. 2nd ed. New York, Sepher-Hermon Press, Inc., for Alumni Association of Jewish High Schools in Kolzsvar, 1988. ix, 313, 155 p., illus., ports., facsims. (H,E,Hu) [Reprint of 1st ed., 1970]
NYPL: *PXM 01-1157   JTS: DS135 R72 C37 1988
HUC: DS135 R72 C59 1988

Kolozsvar (Ro). *Zikaron netsah la-kehilah ha-kedoshah Kolozhvar-Klauzenburg asher nehrevah ba-Shoah* [Everlasting memorial of the martyred community Kolozsvar-Klausenburg which perished in the Holocaust]. [Eds.]: Sh. Zimroni, Y. Shvarts (Schwartz). Tel Aviv, Former Residents of Kolozsvar in Israel, [1968]. 118 p., illus. (H,Hu), mimeo.
YIVO: Cluj-Napoca 1968   NYPL: *PXM (Cluj)
JTS: DS135 R72 C59

Koltyniany (Li) see under Swieciany

Komarno (U). *Bet Komarno;korot ha-'ir ve-toldoteha, me-hivsadah ve-'ad hurbanah: rabaneha, gedoleha ve-admoreha, isheha, hayehem ve-khilyonam* [The house of Komarno; history of the town and its history, from its founding until its destruction]. [By] Barukh Yashar (Shlikhter). Jerusalem, Author, [1965]. 204 p., illus., ports. (H)
YIVO: Komarne 1965   NYPL: *PXW (Komarno)
JTS: DS135 493 K66 Y3   YU: DS135 P62 K65

Konin (P). *Kehilat Konin be-ferihatah uve-hurbanah* [Memorial book Konin*]. Ed.: M. Gelbart. Tel Aviv, Assoc. of Konin Jews in Israel, 1968. 772, 24 p., illus., map, facsims. (H,Y,E)
YIVO: Konin 1968   NYPL: *PXV(Konin)
JTS: DS135 P62 K67 G4   YU: K5 P762K

Konyar (Hu) see under Debrecen

Kopin (U) see under Kamenets-Podolskiy

Koprzywnica (P). *Sefer Pokshivnitsah* [Memorial book of Koprzywnica]. Ed.: E. Erlich. [Tel Aviv], Former Residents of Koprzywnica in Israel, [1971]. 351 p., illus., ports., facsims. (H,Y)
YIVO: Koprzywnica 1971   NYPL: *PXV(Koprzywnica)
JTS: DS135 P62 K671 S4   YU: 933.47(438) K83E

Koprzywnica (P) *How I remember my home town, Pokshyvnitza.* By Samuel Kozinsky; translated from Yiddish to English by Esther Zweig. [New York, s.n., 1979]. 85 leaves. (E)
YIVO: Koprzywnica 1979   NYPL: *PXV (Koprzywnica) 97-2796

Kopychyntsi (Kopyczynce) (U) see under Husiatyn (*Kehilatiyim*)

Kopyl (B) see under Slutsk

Korczyna (P). *Kortshin (Kortshina); sefer zikaron...* [Korczyna memorial book*]. Eds.: I. England-Wasserstrom, M. Zucker. New York, Korczyna Memorial Book Committee, 1967. 495 p., illus., ports. (H,Y)
YIVO: Korczyna 1967   NYPL: *PXV(Korczyn)
JTS: DS135 P62 K672   YU: DS135 P62 K6735

Korolichi (B) see Korelicze

Korelicze (B). *Korelits-Korelitsh; hayeha ve-hurbanah shel kehilah Yehudit* [Korelitz; the life and destruction of a Jewish community]. Ed.: Michael Walzer-Fass. [Tel Aviv], Korelicze Societies in Israel and the USA, [1973]. 357 p., illus. (H,Y,E)
YIVO: Korelichi 1973   NYPL: *PXW(Korolichi) 76-2164
YU: DS135 R93 K59 1973   HUC: HIW 532

Korelicze (B) see also under Nowogrodek

Korets (U) see Korzec

Koriv (P) see Kurow

Korzec (U). *Korets (Vohlin); sefer zikaron li-kehilatenu she-'alah 'aleha ha-koret* [The Korets book (Volyn); in memory of our community that is no more*]. Ed.: E. Leoni.[Tel Aviv], Former Residents of Korets in Israel, [1959]. 791 p., illus., map, ports., facsims. (H,Y)
YIVO: Korets 1959   NYPL: *PXW(Korets) 75-5610
JTS: DS135 R93 K67 L4   HUC: HIW 457.2

Kosice (Slo). *Divre yeme kehilot Koshitseh* [The story of the Jewish community of Kosice*]. Hebrew version by Yehuda Schlanger; translated into English by Gabriela Williams. Yiddish title-page: *500 yor in Kashoy- Kosice: kurtse historishe faktn* [by] Shraga Peri; Hungarian title-page: *A kassai zsidosag tortenete es galleriaja* [by]

Gorog Artur. [Bne-Brak], 1991. vi, 340, [18], 92 p., illus., maps, ports. (H,Y,E,Hu)
YIVO: Kosice 1991   NYPL: *PXT (Kosice) 91-4630
JTS: DS135 S55 G67 1991   YU: DS135 C96 K6744 1991

Kosiv (U) see Kosow (East Galicia)

Kosow (East Galicia) (U). *Sefer Kosov-Galitsyah ha-mizrahit* [Memorial book of Kosow—Kosow Huculski*]. Eds.: G. Kressel, L. Olitzky. Tel Aviv, Former Residents of Kosow and Vicinity in Israel, 1964. 430 p., ports., map, facsims. (H,Y)
YIVO: Kosiv 1964   NYPL: *PXW(Kosov)
JTS: DS135 R93 K68 K7   YU: 933.5 R969K

Kosow (East Galicia) (U). *Megiles Kosov* [The scroll of Kosow]. [By] Yehoshua Gertner. Tel Aviv, Amkho, 1981. 156 p. (Y)
YIVO: Kosiv 1981   NYPL: *PXW(Kosow)

Kosow (Polesie) (U). *Pinkas kedoshe kehilat Kosov Polski* [Memorial book of Kosow Poleski]. Jerusalem, Relief Org. of Former Residents of Kosow Poleski in Israel, [1945]. 81 p., ports. (H)
YIVO: Kosiv 1945

Kosow Lacki (P). *Kosow Lacki.* General Ed.: Jacob Boas. San Francisco, Holocaust Center of Northern California, 1992. 75 p., illus., ports. (E,Y)
YIVO: Kosow Lacki 1992

Kostopil (U) see Kostopol

Kostopol (U). *Sefer Kostopol; hayeha u-motah shel kehilah* [Kostopol; the life and death of a community*]. Ed.: A. Lerner. Tel Aviv, Former Residents of Kostopol in Israel, [1967]. 386 p., illus., ports., maps. (H)
YIVO: Kostopil 1967   JTS: +DS135 P62 K675
NYPL: *PXW+ (Kostopol)

Kosyno (U). *The Jews of Kaszony, Subcarpathia.* By Joseph Eden (Einczig). New York, 1988. v, 131 p., illus., maps, ports. (E,H,Hu)
YIVO: Kosyny 1988   NYPL: *PXT 89-11421
JTS: DS135 R93 K678 EE

Kosyny (U) see Kosyno

Kotsk (P) see Kock

Kovel (U) see Kowel

Kowal (P) see under Wloclawek

Kowel (U). *Kovel; sefer edut ve-zikaron li-kehilatenu she-ala aleha ha-koret* [Kowel; testimony and memorial book of our destroyed community]. Ed.: E. Leoni-Zopperfin. Tel Aviv, Former Residents of Kowel in Israel, [1956 or 1957]. 539 p., illus., ports. (H,Y)
NYPL: *PXW(Kovel) 90-3569   YU: DS135 R93 K6845 1957

Kowel (U). *Pinkes Kovel* [Memorial book of Kowel]. Ed.: B. Baler. Buenos Aires, Former Residents of Kowel and Surroundings in Argentina, 1951. 511 p., illus., ports., facsims. (Y)

YIVO: Kovel 1951   YU: DS135 R93 K6846

Kozhan Gorodok (Kozangrodek, Kozanhorodok) (B) see under Luniniec

Koziany (B) see under Glebokie; Swieciany

Kozieniec (P). *The Book of Kozienice.* Ed.: B. Kaplinsky. Tel Aviv-New York, The Kozienice Organization, 1985. xxxvi, 677 p., illus. (E)

JTS: DS135 P62 K679 1985

Kozieniec (P). *Sefer Kozshenits* [Memorial book of the community of Kozieniec]. Ed.: B. Kaplinski. Tel Aviv, Former Residents of Kozieniec in Israel..., 1969. 516 p., illus., ports., maps, music, facsims. (H,Y)

YIVO: Kozienice 1969   NYPL: *PXV+ (Kozience)
JTS: +DS135 P62 K678   YU: 933.47(438) K88K 1969
HUC: HIW 383

Kozyany (Koziany) (B) see under Glebokie

Krakinovo (Li) see Krekenava

Krakow (P). *Dape hantsahah li-kehilat Krakov* [Memorial pages (dapeh hantzacha) dedicated to kehilat Cracow*]. Ed.: A. Kor. Tel Aviv, Municipal Secondary School No. 5, 1969. 91 p., illus., ports., map. (H)

YIVO: Krakow 1969

Krakow (P). *Memorial journal in honor of Jews from Cracow, perished 1939-1945.* Jamaica, NY, New Cracow Friendship Society, [1967]. vol. (unpaged), illus., maps, ports., facsims. (E)

YIVO: Krakow 1967   NYPL: *PXV (Cracow) 73-5132

Krakow (P). *Sefer Kroko, ir ve-em be-Yisrael* [Memorial book of Krakow, mother and town in Israel]. Eds.: Aryeh Bauminger, *et al.* Jerusalem, The Rav Kuk Inst. and Former Residents of Krakow in Israel, [1958 or 1959]. 429 p., ports., facsims. (H)

YIVO: Krakow 1958   NYPL: *PXV+ (Cracow) 84-306
JTS: DS135 P62 K6815   YU: 933.5 P762K
HUC: *HI 616

Krakow (P) see also under General Reference Works, *Arim ve-imahot,* vol. 2

Krakowiec (U) see under Jaworow (*Matsevet zikaron li-kehilat Jaworow...*)

Krasnik (P). *Sefer Krashnik.* [Krashnik Memorial Book*]. Ed.: D. Shtokfish. [Tel Aviv, Krasnik Societies in Israel and the Diaspora, 1973]. 673 p., illus. (H,Y)

YIVO: Krasnik 1973   NYPL: *PXV (Krasnik) 75-8552
JTS: DS135 P62 K693 S4   YU: DS135 P62 K69 1973

Krasnobrod (P). *Krasnobrod; sefer zikaron* [Krasnobrod; a memorial to the Jewish community*]. Ed.: M. Kroshnits (Kroshnitz). [Tel Aviv], Former Residents of Krasnobrod in Israel, 1956. 526 p., illus., ports., facsims. (H,Y)

YIVO: Krasnobrod 1956   NYPL: *PXV(Krasnobrod) 76-5703

Krasnopol (P) see under Suwalki

Krasnystaw (P). *Yisker tsum ondenk fun di kdoyshey Krasnistav* [Memorial book of the martyrs of Krasnystaw]. Ed.: A. Shtuntseyger. Munich, Publ. "Bafrayung"—Poalei Zion, 1948. 150 p., ports. (Y)

YIVO: Krasnystaw 1948   NYPL: *ZP-1100 no.13

Krekenava (Li). *Krakenowo; our town in Lithuania, the story of a world that has passed.* [Johannesburg], Krakenowo Sick Benefit and Benevolent Society, [1961]. 48 p., illus., facsims. (Y,E)

Kremenets (Kremenits) (U) see Krzemieniec

Kripa (Horyngrod) (U) see under Tuczyn

Krivichi (Krivitsh) (B) see Krzywicze

Kroscienko (P) see under Nowy Targ

Kroshnik (P) see Krasnik

Krosniewiec (P) see under Kutno

Krynki (P). *Krinik in hurbn: memoarn* [Krinki en ruines*]. [By] Alex Soyfer. Montevideo, Los Comites de Ayuda a los Residentes de Krinki de Montevideo y Buenos Aires, 1948. 269 p., illus., map, ports. (Y)

YIVO: Krynki 1949   NYPL: *ZP-1062 No. 2
JTS: DS135 P62 K7

Krynki (P). *Pinkas Krinki* [Memorial book of Krynki]. Ed.: D. Rabin. Tel Aviv, Former Residents of Krynki in Israel and in the Diaspora, 1970. 374 p., ports., map, facsims. (H,Y)

YIVO: Krynki 1970   NYPL: *PXV(Krynki)
JTS: DS135 P62 K7 P5   YU: 933.5 R969K

Krzemienica (B) see under Wolkowysk (*Volkovisker yisker-bukh*)

Krzemieniec (U). *Kremenits, Vizshgorodek un Potshayev; yisker-bukh* [Memorial book of Krzemieniec]. Ed.: F. Lerner. Buenos Aires, Former Residents of Kremenits and Vicinity in Argentina, 1965. 468 p., illus., ports., facsims. (Y)

YIVO:Kremenets 1965   YU: DS135 P62 K69 1965
NYPL: *PXV (Kremieniec) 92-1274

Krzemieniec (U). *Pinkas Kremenits; sefer zikaron* [Memorial book of Krzemieniec]. Ed.: A. S. Stein. Tel

Aviv, Former Residents of Krzemieniec in Israel, [1953 or 1954]. 453 p., illus., map, ports., facsims. (H,Y)

YIVO: Kremenets 1954   NYPL: *PXV(Krzemieniec)
JTS: DS135 R93 K7

Krzywicze (B). *Ner tamid; yizkor le-Krivits* [Kryvits yizkor book*]. Ed.: Matityahu Bar-Ratson. [Israel], Krivits Societies in Israel and the Diaspora, 1976. 724 p., illus. (H,Y)

YIVO: Krivichi 1976   NYPL: *PXW(Krivichi) 78-5704
JTS: DS135 R93 K746 N47   YU: DS135 R93 K746
HUC: HIW 527

Kshoynzh (Ksiaz Wielki) (P) see under Miechow

Ksiaz Wielki (P) see under Miechow

Kunow (P) see under Ostrowiec

Kurenets (B) Kurzeniec

Kurow (P). *Yisker-bukh Koriv; sefer yizkor, matsevet zikaron la-ayaratenu Koriv* [Yizkor book in memoriam of our hometown Kurow*]. Ed.: M. Grossman. Tel Aviv, Former Residents of Kurow in Israel, [1955]. 1152 columns, illus., ports., facsims. (Y)

YIVO: Kurow 1955   NYPL: *PXV+ (Kurow)
JTS: +DS135 P62 K8   YU: DS135 P62 K83
HUC: HIW 371

Kurzeniec (B). *Megilat Kurenits; 'ayara be-hayeha uve-motah* [The scroll of Kurzeniec; the town living and dead]. Ed.: A. Meirovitch. [Israel], Former Residents of Kurzeniec in Israel and in the USA, [1956]. 335 p., illus., ports. (H)

YIVO: Kurenets 1956   NYPL: *PXW (Kurenets) 93-1878
YU: 933.547 K96M   HUC: HIW 556

Kutno (P). *Sefer Kutnah veha-sevivah* [Kutno and surroundings book*]. Ed.: D. Shtokfish. [Tel Aviv, Irgun yotse Kutnah veha-sevivah be-Yisrael uve-huts la-arets, 1968]. 591 p., illus., ports., facsims. (H,Y)

YIVO: Kutno 1968   NYPL: *PXV+ (Kutno)
JTS: +DS135 P62 K86 S9   YU: 933.5 P762K 1968

Kuty (U). *Kitever yisker-bukh* [Kitever memorial book]. Ed.: E. Husen. New York, Kitever Sick and Benevolent Society, 1958. 240 p., ports. (Y)

YIVO: Kuty 1958   NYPL: *PXW(Kuty)
JTS: DS135 R93 K85 H8

Kuty (U). *Kitov 'iri: bene Kuti mesaprim et sipur ha-'ir* [Kitov my hometown: survivors of Kuty tell the story of their town*]. Ed: Hayim Tsins (Chaim Zins). Tel Aviv, Hotsa'at "Yair" 'a. sh. Avraham Shtern, 1993. 285 p., illus., map, facsims., ports. (H)

YIVO: Kuty 1993   NYPL: *PXW (Kuty) 93-248
JTS: DS135 U42 K8 K58 1993   YU: DS135 R93 K7975 1993

Kuzmir (P) see Kazimierz

Kybartai (Li). *Kibart (Lita).* By Yosef Rozin. Haifa, Executive Committee of the Society of Former Residents of Kibart in Israel, 1988. 2, 62 leaves, 20 [12] p., illus., map, ports., facsims. (H)

YIVO: Kybartai 1988

Lachowicze (B). *Lahovits; sefer zikaron* [Memorial book of Lachowicze]. Ed.: Israel Rubin Rivkai. Tel Aviv, Association of Former Residents of Lachowicze, [1948 or 1949]. 395 p., illus., maps, ports. (H,Y)

YIVO: Lyakhovichi 1948   NYPL: *PXW(Lyakhovice)
JTS: DS135 R93 L95 R5   YU: 933.5 R969L

Lachwa (B). *Rishonim la-mered; Lahva* [First ghetto to revolt, Lachwa*]. Eds.: H. A. Michaeli *et al.* Jerusalem, The Encyclopaedia of the Jewish Diaspora, [1957]. 500 columns, illus., maps, ports., facsims. (H,Y)

YIVO: Lakhva 1957   NYPL: *PXW(Lakhva)
YU: DS135 R93 L23

Lakhva (Lachwa) (B) see also under Polesie (region)

Lancut (P). *Lantsut; hayeha ve-hurbanah shel kehilah Yehudit* [Lancut; the life and destruction of a Jewish community*]. Eds.: M. Walzer-Fass, N. Kudish. Tel Aviv, Associations of Former Residents of Lancut in Israel and USA, [1963]. 465, lix p., ports., maps, illus., facsims. (H,Y,E)

YIVO: Lancut 1963   NYPL: *PXV(Lancut)
JTS: DS135 P62 L34   YU: 933.5 P7626 W242

Lanovitsy (Lanivtsi, Lanovits) (U) see Lanowce

Lanowce (U). *Lanovits; sefer zikaron li-kedoshe Lanovits she-nispu be-shoat ha-natsim* [Lanowce; memorial book of the martyrs of Lanowce who perished during the Holocaust]. Ed.: H. Rabin. [Tel Aviv, Association of Former Residents of Lanowce, 1970]. 440 p., illus., maps, ports. (H,Y)

YIVO: Lanivtsi 1970   NYPL: *PXW(Lanovtsy)
JTS: DS135 R93 L24   YU: 933.5 R969L

Lapichi (B) see under Bobruisk

Lask (P). *Lask; sefer zikaron* [Memorial book of Lask]. Ed.: Z. Tsurnamal. Tel Aviv, [Association of Former Residents of Lask in Israel], 1968. 737, 165 p., illus., ports., facsims. (H,Y,E)

YIVO: Lask 1968   NYPL: *PXV(Lask)
JTS: DS135 P62 L37   YU: 933.5 P762L

Lask (P) see also under Pabianice

Laskarzew (P). *Seyfer Laskazshev un Sobolev* [Laskarzew-Sobolew*]. Ed.: P. Gutmark. [France], La Société de Laskarzew-Sobolew en France, [197-/8-]. 708 p., illus., map, ports. (Y)

YIVO: Laskarzew-Sobolew 198?

Leczyca (P). *Sefer Lintshits* [Leczyca: in memory of the Jewish community*]. Ed.: Y.Y. Frenkel. [Tel Aviv], Former Residents of Leczyca in Israel, 1953. 224 p., illus., ports. (H)

YIVO: Leczyca 1953   NYPL: *ZP-721 no.8

JTS: DS135 P62 L42 S4

Lemberg (U) see Lwow

Lenin (B). *Kehilat Lenin; sefer zikaron* [The community of Lenin; memorial book]. Ed.: M. Tamari. Tel Aviv, Former Residents of Lenin in Israel and in the USA, [1957]. 407 p., illus., ports. (H,Y)

YIVO: Lenin 1957   NYPL: *PXW(Lenin)

JTS: DS135 R93 L4 T3   YU: 933.5 R969LHUC: HIW 487

Leonpol (B) see under Druja (*Sefer Druja*)

Lesko (P). *Sefer yizkor; mukdash li-Yehude ha-ayarot she-nispu ba-Shoah be-shanim 1939-44, Linsk, Istrik, Beligrod, Litovisk veha-sevivah* [Memorial book; dedicated to the Jews of Linsk, Istrik...and vicinity who perished in the Holocaust, 1939-44]. Eds.: N. Mark, Sh. Friedlander. [Tel Aviv], Book Committee of the "Livai" Organization, [1964/1965]. x, 516 p., illus., ports. (H,Y)

YIVO: Lesko 1964   NYPL: *PXV(Lesko)

JTS: DS135 P62 L47   YU: DS135 P62 L47

Lesko (P). *Sefer yizkor; mukdash li-Yehude ha-ayarot she-nispu ba-Shoah be-shanim 1939-44, Linsk, Istrik, Beligrod, Litovisk veha-sevivah.* Trans. from yizkor book Lesko and surrounding communities: chapters pertaining to town of Ustrzyki Dolne (Yiddish = Istrik). Trans. from Hebrew: S. Browd, Yiddish, L. Schwartzback. 32 p. Plainview, NY: R. H. Solomon, 1999. (E)

YIVO: Lesko 1999

Letychiv (U). *The road from Letichev: the history and culture of a forgotten Jewish community in Eastern Europe.* By: David A. Chapin. San Jose, CA, Writer's Showcase, 2000. 2 vols., illus., facsims, maps, ports. (E)

YIVO: Letychiv 2000   JTS: DS135.U42 L43 C43 2000

Levertev (P) see Lubartow

Lezajsk (P). *Lezansk; sefer zikaron li-kedoshe Lezansk she-nispu be-shoat ha-Natsim* [Memorial book of the martyrs of Lezajsk who perished in the Holocaust]. Ed.: H. Rabin. [Tel Aviv, Former Residents of Lezajsk in Israel, 1969]. 495 p., illus., map, ports., facsims. (H,Y)

YIVO: Lezajsk 1969   NYPL: *PXV(Lezajsk)

JTS: DS135 P62 L49   YU: DS135 P62 L49

Libovne (U) see Luboml

Lida (B). *Sefer Lida* [Book of Lida*]. Eds.: A. Manor *et al.* Tel Aviv, Former Residents of Lida in Israel and the

Relief Committee of the Lida Jews in USA, 1970. 438, xvii p., ports., illus., maps, facsims. (H,Y,E)

YIVO: Lida 1970   NYPL: *PXV+ (Lida)

JTS: +DS135 R93 L48   YU: DS135 R93 L48

Likeva (P) see Lukow

Linshits (P) see Leczyca

Linsk (P) see Lesko

Lipcani (M) see Lipkany

Lipkany (M). *Kehilat Lipkani; sefer zikaron* [The community of Lipkany; memorial book]. Tel Aviv, Former Residents of Lipkany in Israel, 1963. 407 p., illus., maps, ports. (H,Y)

YIVO: Lipcani 1963   NYPL: *PXW(Lipkany)

JTS: DS135 R93 L57 S5   YU: DS135 R93 L4934 1963

Lipkany (M). *Lipkan fun amol* [Lipcan of old*]. By A. Shuster. Montreal, Author, 1957. 217 p., illus., ports. (Y)

YIVO: Lipcani 1957   NYPL: *PXW(Lipkany) 89-7719

JTS: DS135 R93 L57

Lipniszki (B). *Sefer zikaron shel kehilat Lipnishok* [Memorial book of the community of Lipniszki]. Ed.: A. Levin. Tel Aviv, Former Residents of Lipniszki in Israel, 1968. 206 p., ports., map (H,Y)

YIVO: Lipnishki 1968   NYPL: *PXW(Lipnishki)

JTS: DS135 R93 L58   YU: DS135 R93 L494

Lipno (P). *Sefer Lipno: Skampah, Luvitsh, Kikol, veha-sevivah* [Sepher Lipno–The Lipno book: *Skepe, Lubicz, Kikol*]. Ed.: Shmuel Alon (Domb). Tel Aviv, Society of Former Residents of Lipno and Vicinity, 1988. viii, 327 p., illus., maps, ports. (H,Y,E)

YIVO: Lipno 1988   NYPL: *PXV(Lipno) 90-6229

YU: DS135 P62 L567 1988

Litevisk (Lutowiska) (P) see under Lesko

Liuboml (U) see Luboml

Lizhensk (P) see Lezajsk

Ljuban (B) see under Slutsk

Lodz (P). *Kehilat Lodz; toldot 'ir va-em be-Yisrael* [The community of Lodz; a Jewish mother-city]. [By] Aaron Ze'ev Aescoly (Escoli). Jerusalem, ha-Mahlakah le-inyane ha-no'ar shel ha-Histadrut ha-tsiyonit [Youth Section of the Zionist Organization], [1948]. 237 p. (H)

YIVO: Lodz 1948   NYPL: *ZP-1096, no.3

JTS: DS135 P62 L675 A4   YU: DS135 P62 L62

HUC: HI/ 905

Lodz (P). *Lodzer yisker-bukh* [Lodzer yiskor book*]. New York, United Emergency Relief Committee for the City of Lodz, 1943. 236, lxiv., 152 p., illus., ports. (Y)

YIVO: Lodz 1943   NYPL: *PXV (Lodz) 94-1288

JTS: DS135 P62 L675 U58

329

Lodz (P). *Yidish Lodzsh; a yiskor bokh.* [Yiddish Lodz, a yizker book*]. Melbourne, Lodzer Center, 1974. 243, 13 p., illus. (Y,E)

YIVO: Lodz 1974
NYPL: *PXV(Lodz) 78-2866
JTS: +DS135 P62 L675 Y5
YU: DS135 P62 L6875 1974

Lokachi (U) see Lokacze

Lokacze (U). *Sefer yizkor li-kehilat Lokats (Polin) - Gedenk bukh far di shtetl Lokatsh* [Lokatch (Poland) memorial book*]. Comp.: Eliezer Verba; ed.: Shimon Matlofsky. Jerusalem, Shimon Matlofsky, 1993. 98 p., [32] p. of plates, illus., map, ports. (H,Y; E introd.)

YIVO: Lokachi 1993
NYPL: *PXW (Lokachi) 93-563
JTS: DS135 R93 L6554 1993
YU: DS135 R93 L6537 1993

Lomazy (P). *Sefer Lomaz: 'ayarah be-hayehah uve-khilyonah.* Ed.: Yitshak Alperovits. Tel Aviv, Irgune Lomaz be-Yisrael uve-Artsot ha-Berit, 1994. 166, 70 p., illus., ports., map. (H, Y, E)

YIVO: Lomazy 1994
NYPL: *PXV (Lomazy) 95-2709
YU: DS135 P62 L69366 1994

Lomza (P). *Lomzshe; ir oyfkum un untergang* [The rise and fall of Lomza]. Ed.: H. Sobotka. New York, American Committee for the Book of Lomza, 1957. 371 p., illus., map, ports., facsims. (Y)

YIVO: Lomza 1957
NYPL: *PXV+ (Lomza) 79-1103
JTS: DS135 P62 L678 L6 1957

Lomza (P). *Lomze: momentn un zikhroynes.* New York, United Lomzer Relief Committee, 1946. 63, 27 p., illus. (Y,E)

NYPL: *PXV (Lomza) 93-569

Lomza (P). *Sefer zikaron li-kehilat Lomzah* [Lomza -In memory of the Jewish community*]. Ed.: Y. T. Lewinski. [Tel Aviv], Former Residents of Lomza in Israel, 1952. x, 337 p., illus., maps, ports., facsims. (H)

YIVO: Lomza 1952
NYPL: *PXV+ (Lomza) 77-169
JTS: +DS135 P62 L678 L4
YU: 933.4 P762 L846L 1952
HUC: HI 997.2

Lopatyn (Lopatin) (U) see under Radziechow

Losice (P). *Loshits; le-zekher an umgebrakhter kehile* [Losice; in memory of a Jewish community, exterminated by Nazi murderers*]. Ed.: M. Shinar. Tel Aviv, Former Residents of Losice in Israel and the Diaspora, 1963. 459 p., illus., ports., facsims. (H,Y)

YIVO: Losice 1963
NYPL: *PXV(Losice) 76-5778
JTS: DS135 P62 L679 L6
YU: DS135 P62 L694 1963

Lowicz (P). *Lovitsh; a shtot in Mazovye un umgegnt* [Lowicz; a town in Mazovia, memorial book*]. Ed.: G. Shaiak (Shayak-Tsharnezon). [Tel Aviv], Former Residents of Lowicz in Melbourne and Sydney, Australia, 1966. 395, xxii p., illus., ports., facsims. (H,Y,E)

YIVO: Lowicz 1966
NYPL: *PXV+ (Lowicz) 94-169
JTS: +DS135 P62 L68 S5
YU: DS135 P62 L7 1966

Lozisht (Ignatowka) (U) see under Zofiowka

Lubartow (P). *Hurbn Levertov* [The destruction of Lubartow]. Ed.: B. Tshubinski. Paris, Association of Lubartow, 1947. 118 p., illus., ports., facsims. (Y)

YIVO: Lubartow 1947
NYPL: *PXV+ (Lubartow)
JTS: +DS135 P62 L82 C45

Lubcza (B). *Lubats u-Delatits; sefer zikaron* [Lubtch - Delatich; in memory of the Jewish community*]. Ed.: K. Hilel. [Haifa], Former Residents of Lubtsh-Delatitsh in Israel, 1971. 480 p., illus., ports., map, facsims. (H,Y)

YIVO: Lyubcha & Delyatichi 1971
NYPL: *PXW(Lyubcha)
JTS: DS135 R93 L99 L8

Lubenichi (B) see under Bobruisk

Lubicz (P) see under Lipno

Lublin (P). *Dos bukh fun Lublin* [The memorial book of Lublin]. [Eds.]: M. Litvin, M. Lerman. Paris, [Former Residents of Lublin in Paris], 1952. 685 p., illus., ports., facsims. (Y)

YIVO: Lublin 1952
NYPL: *PXV+ (Lublin)
YU: DS135 P62 L767 1952

Lublin (P). *Lublin* [Lublin volume*]. Eds.: N. Blumental, M. Korzen. Jerusalem, The Encyclopaedia of the Jewish Diaspora, [1957]. 815 columns, ports., map. (H,Y)

YIVO: Lublin (Entsiklopedya) 1957
NYPL: *PX+ 96-485 v.5
JTS: Ref +DS135 E8 E55 v.5

Luboml (U) *Luboml: The memorial book of a vanished shtetl;* [English trans. of the Yizkor book of Luboml. N. Sobel, Ed.] Hoboken, NJ: KTAV Publishing House; copyright Libovner-Voliner Benevolent Society, [1997]. xx, 427 pl, illus., map, facsims., ports. (E)

YIVO: Luboml 1997
NYPL: *PXW (Lyuboml) 98-2516
YU: DS135 R93 L59313 1997

Luboml (U). *Sefer yizkor li-kehilat Luboml* [Yizkor book of Luboml*]. Ed.: Berl Kagan. [Tel Aviv, 1974]. 393 p., illus. (H,Y)

YIVO: Liuboml 1974
NYPL: *PXW(Lyuboml) 79-2913
JTS: DS135 R93 L995 S4
YU: DS135 R93 L593 1974

Lubraniec (P) see under Wloclawek

Luck (U). *Sefer Lutsk* [Memorial book of Lutsk]. Ed.: N. Sharon. Tel Aviv, Former Residents of Lutsk in Israel, 1961. 608 p., illus., maps, ports., facsims. (H,Y)

YIVO: Lutsk 1961
NYPL: *PXW+ (Lutsk)
JTS: DS135 R93 L83
YU: 933.547.7 L974 I67

Ludmir (U) see Wlodzimierz

Ludwipol (U). *Sefer zikaron li-kehilat Ludvipol* [Ludvipol-Wolyn; in memory of the Jewish community*]. Ed.: N. Ayalon. Tel Aviv, Ludvipol Relief Society of Israel, [1965]. 335 p., illus., ports., map. (H,Y)

YIVO: Sosnove 1965   NYPL: *PXW+ (Sosnovoye)
JTS: +DS135 R93 S68 A9   YU: 933.5 R969L

Lukow (P). *Sefer Lukov; geheylikt der horev- gevorener kehile* [The book of Lukow; dedicated to a destroyed community]. Ed.: B. Heller. Tel Aviv, Former Residents of Lukow in Israel, [1968]. 652 p., illus., ports. (H,Y)

YIVO: Lukow 1968   NYPL: *PXV(Lukow)
JTS: DS135 P62 L85 H4   YU: DS135 P62 L8 1968

Lukow (P). *Lukover kdoyshim un heldi: yizker-oysgabe.* Comp.: M. Tirman. Lodz, Komitet fun Lukover Yidn, 1947. 48 p., illus., ports. (Y)

YIVO: Lukow 1947

Luninets (B) see Luniniec

Luniniec (B). *Yizkor: kehilot Luninyets/Kozanhorodok* [Memorial book of the communities of Luniniec/ Kozanhorodok]. Eds.: Y. Zeevi (Wilk) *et al.* Tel Aviv, Assoc. of Former Residents of Luniniec/Kozhanhoro-dok in Israel, [1952]. 268 p., illus., map, ports. (H,Y)

YIVO: Luninets & Kozhan Gorodok 1952
NYPL: *PXW(Luninets) 76-5565   YU: DS135 R93 L8549 1952

Luniniec (B) see also under Polesie (region)

Lutowiska (P) see under Lesko

Lutsk (U) see Luck

Lviv (U) see Lwow; see also General Reference Works, *Arim ve-imahot,* vol. 1

Lwow (U). *Levov* [Lwow volume*], part I. Ed.: N. M. Gelber. Jerusalem, The Encyclopaedia of the Jewish Diaspora, [1956]. 766 columns, ports., facsims. (H)

YIVO: Lviv (Entsiklopedya) 1956   NYPL: *PX+ 96-485 v.4
JTS: Ref +DS135 E8 E55 v.4

Lwow (U) see also General Reference Works, *Arim ve-imahot,* vol. 1

Lyakhovichi (B) see Lachowicze

Lyngmiany (B) see under Stolin

Lynki (B) see under Stolin

Lyntupy (B) see under Swieciany (Li)

Lyskow (B) see under Wolkowysk (*Volkovisker yisker-bukh*)

Lyszkowice (P) see under Lowicz

Lyuban (B) see under Slutsk

Lyuboml (U) see Luboml

Mad (Hu). *ha-Kehilah ha-Yehudit shel Mad, Hungaryah* [The Jewish community of Maad, Hungary*]. Ed.: Arieh Lewy. Jerusalem, Mad Commemorative Committee, [1974]. 154, 31 p., illus. (H,E,Hu)

YIVO: Mad 1974   NYPL: *PXT 76-5639
JTS: DS135 H92 M28 L485   YU: DS135 H92 M424 1974
HUC: HIW 474

Magyarlapos (Ro) see under Des

Makow-Mazowiecki (P). *Sefer zikaron li-kehilat Makow-Mazovyetsk* [Memorial book of the community of Makow-Mazowiecki]. Ed.: Y. Brot. Tel Aviv, Former Residents of Makow-Mazowiecki in Israel and the USA, [1969]. 505 p., illus., map, ports., facsims. (H,Y)

YIVO: Makow Mazowiecki 1969   YU: DS135 P62 M34 1969
NYPL: *PXV(Makow-Mazowiecki)   JTS: DS135 P62 M28 S4

Makow Podhalanski (P) see under Nowy Targ

Malecz (B) see under Pruzana

Marghita (Margareten) (Ro) see Margita; see also under Saplacu

Margita (Ro). *Sefer yizkor li-kehilat Margaretin veha-sevivah* [Memorial book of the community of Margareten and surrounding region]. Ed.: A. Kleinmann. Jerusalem, Hayim Frank, 1979. 275 p., illus. (H,Hu)

YIVO: Marghita 1979   NYPL: *PXM(Marghita) 89-682
YU: DS135 R72 M3738 1979

Marijampole (Li). *Mariyampole Lita* [Marijampole, Lithuania]. Ed.: A. Tory (Tori-Golub). Tel Aviv, Vaad Sefer Mariyampol, 1986. 245, 74 p., illus., map, ports. (H, E)

YIVO: Marijampole 1986   YU: DS135 R93 M33 1986
NYPL: *PXW(Marijampole) 90-2442   JTS: +DS135 L5 M3 M3

Markuleshty (M). *Markuleshti; yad le-moshavah Yehudit be-Bessarabyah* [Markuleshty; memorial to a Jewish colony in Bessarabia]. Eds.: L. Kuperstein, M. Kotik. Tel Aviv, Markuleshty Society in Israel, [1977.] 272 p., illus. (H,Y)

YIVO: Markulesti 1977   JTS: DS135 R93 M335
NYPL: *PXW(Markuleshty) 79-1033   YU: DS135 R93 M335

Markulesti (M) see Markuleshty

Markuszow (P). *Hurbn un gevure fun shtetl Markushov* [The destruction and heroism of the town of Markuszow]. Ed.: D. Shtokfish. Tel Aviv, Former Residents of Markuszow in Israel, 1955. 436 p., illus., ports. (Y)

YIVO: Markuszow 1955   NYPL: *PXV(Markuszow)

Marosvasarhely (Ro). *Perakim be-toldot ha-Yehudim be-Transilvanyah ba-'et ha-hadashah.* Vol. 1, *Korot Yehude Marosvasarhely veha-sevivah* [History of the

Jews in Marosvasarhely]. [By] Yitzhak Peri (Friedmann). 2 vols. Tel Aviv, Ghetto Fighters House, Ha-Kibbutz ha-Meuhad, [1977]. (H)

YIVO: Transylvania (Tirgu Mures) 1977

NYPL: *PXM 88-9992 vol. 1 & 2

JTS: DS135 R72 T5 P4   YU: DS135 R72 T576

Mattersburg (A). *Zihkronot mi-kehilat Mattersdorf: das Leben und der Untergang einer juedischen Gemeinde.* [By] Samuel Hirsch. Bnei Brak, Institute for the Memory of Hungarian Jewry, [2000]. 150 p., illus., ports. (H)

YIVO: Mattersburg 2000   JTS: DS135.A92 M2 H5 2000

Medenice (P) see under Drohobycz

Melits (P) see Mielec

Melnitza (U) see Mielnica

Melnytsya (U) see Mielnica

Meretsh (Li) see Merkine

Merkine (Li). *Meretsh; 'ayara Yehudit be-Lita* [Merkine*]. Ed.: U.Shefer. Tel Aviv, [Society of Meretsh Immigrants in Israel], 1988. 195 p., illus., map, ports. (H)

YIVO: Merkine 1988   NYPL: *PXW (Merkine) 90-1196

YU: DS135 R93 M474 1988

Mervits (Muravitsa) (U) see under Mlynow

Meytshet (B) see Molczadz

Mezhirechye (Mezhyrichia) (U) see Miedzyrzec-Wolyn

Mezritsh (P) see Miedzyrzec

Miava (Myjava) (Slo) see under Postyen

Michalovce (Slo) see Nagymihaly

Michow (P). *Mikhov (Lubelski); sefer zikaron li-kedoshe Mikhov she-nispu be-Shoat ha-Natsim be-shanim 1939-1942* [Memorial book to the martyrs of Michow who perished in the Holocaust]. Ed.: C. Rabin. [Israel], Former Residents of Michow, [1987]. 343 p., illus., map, ports. (H,Y)

YIVO: Michow 1987   NYPL: *PXV(Mikhov) 90-3755

Miechow (P). *Sefer yizkor Maikhov, Kharshnitsah, u-Kshoinz* [Miechov memorial book, Charshnitza and Kshoynge*]. Eds.: N. Blumental, *et al.* Tel Aviv, Former Residents of Miechov, Charshnitza and Kshoynzh, 1971. 314 p., illus., ports. (H,Y,E)

YIVO: Miechow 1971   NYPL: *PXV(Miechow) 82-2352

YU: DS135 P62 M4877

Miechow Lubelski (P) see Miechow

Miedzyrzec (P). *Mezritsh; zamlbukh* [The Mezritsh volume]. Ed.: Y. Horn. Buenos Aires, Assoc. of Former Residents of Mezritsh in Argentina, 1952. 635 p., illus., ports., facsims. (Y)

YIVO: Miedzyrzec Podlaski 1952   NYPL:*PXV(Miedzyrecz) 90-2739

Miedzyrzec (P). *Sefer Mezritsh; le-zekher kedoshe irenu* [Mezritsh book, in memory of the martyrs of our city]. Eds.: B. Heller, Y. Ronkin. Israel, Mezritsh Societies in Israel and the Diaspora, 1978. 821 p., illus. (H,Y)

YIVO: Miedzyrzec Podlaski 1978   HUC: DS135 P62 M497

NYPL: *PXV(Miedzyrecz) 85-2013

Miedzyrzec (P). *Di Yidn-shtot Mezritsh; fun ir breyshes biz erev der velt-milhome* [Historia de Mezritch (Mezritch Podlasie); su población Judía*]. [By] M. Edelbaum. Buenos Aires, Sociedad de Residentes de Mezritch en la Argentina, [1957]. 424 p., port., facsims. (Y)

YIVO: Miedzyrzec Podlaski 1957   NYPL: *PXV(Miedzyrzecz)

JTS: DS135 P62 M38 E3   HUC: DS135 P62 M38 1957

YU: DS135 P62 M488 1957

Miedzyrzec Podlaski (P) see Miedzyrzec

Miedzyrzec-Wolyn (U). *Meziritsh gadol be-vinyanah uve-hurbanah* [Mezhiritch-Wolyn; in memory of the Jewish community*]. Ed.: B. H. Ayalon-Baranik. [Tel Aviv], Former Residents of Mezhirith in Israel, 1955. 442 columns, illus., ports., facsims. (H,Y)

YIVO: Yemilchyne (Mezhyricka) 1955   JTS: +DS135 R93 M4 A85

Miedzyrzec-Wolyn (U). *Pinkas ha-kehilah Mezhirits* [Memorial book of Mezhirits]. Ed.: Natan Livneh. Tel Aviv, Committee of Former Residents of Mezhirits in Israel, [1973]. 71 p., illus. (H,Y)

NYPL: *PXW(Mezhirech'ye) 75-3249

JTS: +DS135 R93 M4 P45

Mielec (P). *Melitser Yidn* [Mielec Jews]. [By] Shlomoh Klagsbrun. Tel Aviv, Nay-Lebn, [1979]. 288 p., illus. (Y)

YIVO: Mielec 1979   NYPL: *PXV(Mielec) 82-1666

JTS: DS135 P62 M45 K54

Mielec (P). *Sefer zikaron li-kehilat Mielets; sipur hashmadat ha-kehilah ha-Yehudit* [Remembering Mielec; the destruction of the Jewish community*]. [New York], Mielec Yiskor-Book Committee, 1979. 84, 122 p., illus., ports. (H,Y,E)

YIVO: Mielec 1979

Mielnica (U). *Melnitsah, pelakh Vohlin-Ukrainah: sefer hantsahah, 'edut ve-zikaron li-kehilat Melnitsah* [Melnitza: in memory of the Jewish Community*]. Ed.: J. Lior. Tel Aviv, Melnitza Survivors in Israel and the Diaspora, 1994. 276, 78 p., illus., maps, ports., facsims. (H,Y,E)

YIVO: Melnytsya 1994   NYPL: *PXW (Melnitsa) 95-61

JTS: DS135 U42 M45 M45 1994

Mielnica (U) see also under Kowel (*Pinkes Kowel*)

Mihaileni (Ro) see under Dorohoi

Mikepercs (Hu) see under Debrecen

Mikolajow (U) see under Radziechow

Mikulince (U). *Mikulintsah; sefer yizkor* [Mikulince yizkor book*]. Ed.: Hayim Preshel. [Israel], Organization of Mikulincean Survivors in Israel and in the USA, [1985]. 356, 266 p., illus., ports. (H,E,Y)
YIVO: Mykulyntsi 1985   NYPL: *PXW (Mykulyntsi) 90-6228
YU: DS135 R93 M956 1985

Mikulov (Nikolsburg) (Cz) see under General Reference Works, *Arim ve-imahot,* vol. 4

Milosna Nowa (P) see under Rembertow

Minkovtsy (U) see under Kamenets-Podolskiy

Minsk (B). *Albom Minsk* [The Minsk album; selected pictures collected by David Cohen from the two volumes of the book "The Jewish Mother-City Minsk"*]. Eds.: Shelomo Even-Shoshan, Nehemiya Maccabee. [Israel], Association of Olim from Minsk and its Surroundings in Israel, ha-Kibuts ha-meuchad, [1988]. 71 p., illus., maps, ports. (H,E)
YIVO: Minsk 1988   NYPL: *PXW (Minsk) 96-1164
HUC: DS135 R93 M556 1988

Minsk (B). *Minsk ir va-em* [Minsk; Jewish mother city: a memorial anthology*]. Ed.: S. Even-Shushan. [Tel Aviv], Association of Olim from Minsk and its Surroundings in Israel; Ghetto Fighters' House; Kiryat Sefer, [1975-1985]. 2 vols., illus., ports. (H)
YIVO: Minsk 1975   NYPL: *PXW(Minsk) 83-311
JTS: DS135 R93 M59 M55   YU: DS135 R93 M555

Minsk-Mazowiecki (P). *Sefer Minsk-Mazovyetski* [Minsk-Mazowiecki memorial book*]. Ed.: Efrayim Shedletski. Jerusalem, Minsk-Mazowiecki Societies in Israel and Abroad, 1977. 633, vi p., illus. (H,Y,E)
YIVO: Minsk Mazowiecki 1977
NYPL: *PXV(Minsk-Mazowiecki) 87-6485
JTS: DS135 P62 M5 S5   YU: DS135 P62 M537

Miory (B) see under Druja (*Sefer Druja*)

Mir (B). *Sefer Mir* [Memorial book of Mir]. Ed.: N. Blumental. Jerusalem, The Encyclopaedia of the Jewish Diaspora, [1962]. 768, 62 columns, map, ports. (H,Y,E)
YIVO: Mir 1962   NYPL: *PXW(Mir)
YU: DS135 R93 M5965 1962

Miskolc (Hu). *Kedoshe Miskolc veha-sevivah; ha-kehilot me-Hidasnemeti ad Mezokovesd ume-Ozd ad Szerencs* [The martyrs of Miskolc and vicinity; the communities from Hidasnemeti to Mezokovesd and from Ozd to Szerencs]. [By] Slomo Paszternak. Bnei Brak, 1970. 14, 38, 277 p., illus., ports. (Hu,E,H)

Mizoch (U) see Mizocz

Mizocz (U). *Mizots; sefer zikaron* [Memorial book of Mizocz]. Ed.: A. Ben-Oni. Tel Aviv, Former Residents of Mizocz in Israel, [1960 or 1961]. 293, [26] p., ports., illus., facsims. (H)
YIVO: Mizoch 1960   NYPL: *PXW(Mizoch)
JTS: DS135 R93 M62   YU: DS135 R93 M5995 1960

Mlawa (P). *Mlavah ha-Yehudit; koroteha, hitpathutah, kilayonah—Di Yidishe Mlave; geshikhte, oyfshtayg, umkum* [Jewish Mlawa; its history, development, destruction*]. Ed.: J. Alter, D. Shtokfish. [Israel], Mlawa Societies in Israel and in the Diaspora, [1984]. 2 vols. (536, 584 p.), illus., maps, ports. (H,Y,E)
YIVO: Mlawa 1984   NYPL: *PXV(Mlawa) 87-6488
YU: DS135 P62 M598 1984

Mlawa (P). *Pinkes Mlave* [Memorial book of Mlawa]. [Ed.: Y. Shatski]. New York, World Assoc. of Former Residents of Mlawa, [1950]. 483, 63 p., illus., ports. (Y)
YIVO: Mlawa 1950   NYPL: *PXV(Mlawa)
JTS: DS135 P62 M6 P5

Mlinov (Mlyniv, Mlynuv) (U) see Mlynow

Mlynow (U). *Sefer Mlynov-Mervits* [Mlynov-Muravica memorial book*]. Ed.: Y. Siegelman (Zigelman). Haifa, Former Residents of Mlynov-Muravica in Israel, 1970. 511 p., illus., ports. (Y,H)
YIVO: Muravitsa & Mlyniv 1970   NYPL: *PXW(Mlinov)
JTS: DS135 R93 M637   YU: 933.5 R969M

Modrzyc (P) see Deblin

Mogielnica (P) *Sefer yizkor Mogelnitsah-Bledov* [Memorial book of Mogielnica-Bledow]. Ed.: Yisrael Zonder. Tel Aviv, Mogielnica and Bledow Society, 1972. 808 p., illus., map, ports. (H,Y)
YIVO: Mogielnica & Blendow 1972   JTS: +DS135 P62 M65 S4

Molchad (B) see Molczadz

Molczadz (B). *Sefer-zikaron li-kehilat Maitshet* [Memorial book of the community of Meytshet]. Ed.: Benzion H. Ayalon. Tel Aviv, Meytshet Societies in Israel and Abroad, 1973. 460, 12 p., illus. (H,Y)
YIVO: Molchad 1973   JTS: DS135 R93 M647 S4
NYPL: *PXW(Molchad) 75-866   YU: DS135 R93 M647

Monasterzyska (U). *Sefer Monastrishts* [Monasterzyska; a memorial book*]. Ed.: Meir Segal. Tel Aviv, Monasterzyska Association, 1974. 126 p., illus. (H,Y,E)
YIVO: Monastryryska 1974

Monastir (Mac). *Ir u-shemah Monastir* [A city called Monastir]. [By] Uri Oren. Tel Aviv, Naor, [1972]. 167 p., illus. (H)
NYPL: *PXM 89-7664   JTS: DS135 Y82 B5 O74

Monastir (Mac). *A town called Monastir.* [By] Uri Oren; translated from the Hebrew by Mark Segal. Tel Aviv,

Dror Publications, 1971. 240 p., illus., ports. (E)

YIVO: Bitola (Monastir) 1971   JTS: DS135 Y82 B5 O4713
YU: 933.5 Y94M

Mosty (B) see under Piaski

Mosty-Wielkie (U). *Sefer zikaron Mosti-Vielkeh--Most Rabati,* [Mosty-Wielkie memorial book*]. Eds.: Moshe Shtarkman, Abraham Ackner, A.L. Binot. [Tel Aviv], Mosty Wielkie Societies in Israel and the USA, 1975-1977. 2 vols., illus. (H,Y,E)

YIVO: Velyki Mosty 1975   JTS: DS135 R93 V375 M67
NYPL: *PXW(Velikiye-Mosty) 82-2367   YU: DS135 R93 V375

Motele (B) see Motol

Motol (B). *Hurban Motlah* [The destruction of Motele]. [By] A. L. Polik. Jerusalem, Council of Motele Immigrants, [1955 or 1956]. 87 p. (H)

Mszczonow (P) see under Zyrardow

Mukacevo (Munkacs) (U) see under General Reference Works, *Arim ve-imahot,* vol. 1

Muravitsa (Muravica) (U) see under Mlynow

Myjava (Slo) see under Postyen

Mykulyntsi (U) see Mikulince

Mysleniec (Myslenice) (P) see under Wadowice

Myszyniec (P) see under Ostroleka

Nadarzyn (P) see under Pruszkow

Nadvornaya (Nadvirna) (U) see Nadworna

Nadworna (U). *Nadvurnah; sefer edut ve-zikaron* [Nadworna, Stanislav district; memorial and records*]. Ed.: Israel Carmi (Oto Kramer). [Tel Aviv], Nadworna Societies in Israel and the USA, 1975. 281, 67 p., illus. (H,Y,E)

YIVO: Nadvirna 1975   NYPL: *PXW(Nadvornaya) 88-498
YU: DS135 R93 N326

Nadzin (Nadarzyn) (P) see under Pruszkow

Nagybanya (Ro). *Sefer zikaron li-kedoshe Nadi-Banyah veha-sevivah* [Nagybanya and the surrounding region]. Ed.: Naftali Stern. Bnei Brak, [1976]. 245, 176 p., illus. (H,Hu)

YIVO: Baia Mare (Nagybanya) 1976

Nagybanya (Ro). *Emlek Konyv Nagybanya, Nagysomkut, Felsobanya, Kapolnok Monostor es Kornyeke Zsidosaganak tragediajarol.* Alternate title: *Gal-'ed le-Yahadut Nagi-Banyah, Nagi-Shumkut, Felsho Banyah, Kapolnok Monoshtor veha-sevivah* [A monument to the Jews of Nagybanya...and vicinity*]. Ed.: Ichak Joszef Kohen. Tel Aviv, Organization of Former Inhabitants of Baia-Mare (Nagybanya) in Israel,

1996. 415, 176 p., illus., maps, ports. (H, Hu, E [pp.255-261 only])

YIVO: Baia Mare 1996   NYPL: PXM+ 97-2496
YU: DS135 R72 B3544 1996

Nagyilonda (Ro) see under Des

Nagykallo (Hu). *Ha-Tsadik mi-Kalov u-kehilato; tsiyun le-nefesh hayah uli-kehilah nikhehedet...* [The tsadik of Kalov and his community...]. [By] T. (Laszlo) Szilágyi-Windt; trans. from Hungarian and ed.: Y. Edelshtein. [Tel Aviv, 1970]. 208 p., facsims., illus., music, ports. (H)

YIVO: Nagykallo 1970   NYPL: *PQV (Szilagyi-Windt)
JTS: BM755 T23 S916

Nagykunsag (H) see under Karcag

Nagymagyar (Slo) see under Dunaszerdahely

Nagymihaly (Slo). *Sefer Mikhalovtsah veha-sevivah* [Book of Michalovce*]. Ed.: M. Ben-Zeev (M. Farkash). [Tel Aviv], Committee of Former Residents of Michalovce in Israel, 1969. 240, 64, 103 p., illus., ports., facsims. (H,E,Hu)

YIVO: Michalovce 1969   NYPL: *PXT(Michalovce)
JTS: DS135 C96 M537   YU: 933.5(437) M999B

Nagyshumkut (Ro) see under Nagybanya

Nagyszollos (U). *Sefer zikaron li-kehilat Selish veha-sevivah* [A memorial to the Jewish community of Sevlus (Nagyszollos) District*]. Ed.: Sh. ha-Kohen Weingarten. [Israel], Selish Society, [1976]. 326 p., illus. (H)

YIVO: Vinogradiv 1976   NYPL: *PXW(Vinogradov) 87-6493
YU: DS135 R93 V587 1976

Nagyszollos (U). *Sefer zikaron...* [Memorial book*]-*Musaf* [Addenda]. Eds.: J. H. Klein, J. M. Hollander. Israel, The Committee of Olei Nagyszollos and Vicinity in Israel, 1981. 94 p., ports. (H,E)

Nagytapolcsany (Slo) see Topolcany

Nagyvarad (Ro) see Oradea

Naliboki (B). *Unzer shtetle Nalibok: ir lebn un unkum* [Our town Nalibok, its existence and destruction*]. Tel Aviv, Former Residents of Nalibok, 1967. 230 p., illus., ports., map (H,Y)

YIVO: Naliboki 1967

Naliboki (B) see also under Stolpce

Narajow (U) see under Brzezany

Navahrudak (Navaredok) (B) see Nowogrodek

Naymark (P) see Nowy Targ

Nemirov (U) see under General Reference Works, *Arim ve-imahot,* vol. 2

Nestilye (U) see Uscilug

Nesvizh (B) see Nieswiez

Neumarkt (P) see Nowy Targ

Nevel (B) see under Vitebsk (*Sefer Vitebsk*)

Nieswiez (B). *Sefer Nisviz*. Ed.: David Shtokfish. [Israel], Nieswiez Societies in Israel and the Diaspora, 1976. 531 p., illus. (H,Y)
YIVO: Nesvizh 1976   NYPL: *PXW+(Nesvizh) 86-2667
YU: DS135 R93 N457 1976

Nieszawa (P) see under Wloclawek

Nikolsburg (Cz) see under General Reference Works, *Arim ve-imahot,* vol. 4

Noua Sulita (U) see Novoselitsa

Novohrad-Volynskyi (U) see Novograd-Volynskiy

Novograd-Volynskiy (U). *Zvhil (Novogrodvolinsk).* Eds.: A. Uri, M. Bone. [Tel Aviv], Association of Former Residents of Zvhil and surrounding area, [1961 or 1962]. 2 pts. in 1, illus., maps, ports. (H,Y,E)
YIVO: Novograd Volynskiy 1961
NYPL: *PXW (Novagrad Volynsky)
JTS: DS135 R93 N63 Z8   YU: 933.5 R969N

Novogrudok (B) see Nowogrodek

Novo Minsk (P) see Minsk Mazowiecki

Novoselitsa (U). *Novoselitsah.* Ed.: Shalom Dorner. Tel Aviv, Irgun Yotse Novoselitsah be-Yisrael, 1983. 578 p., illus., ports., maps. (H,Y)
YIVO: Novoselitsa 1983

Novoselitsa (U). *Zikhron Novoselitsah (Bessarabia); goralot ba-Shoah* [In memory of Novoselitsa (Bessarabia); its fate during the Holocaust]. [By] Dov Rains. [Israel]. Irgun Yotse Novoselitsa be-Yisrael, 1993. 143 p. (H)
YIVO: Novoselitsa 1993

Novoselytsia (U) see Novoselitsa

Novyi Vitkov (Witkow Nowy) (U) see under Radziechow

Novyi Yarichev (U) see Jaryczow Nowy

Novvy Sverzhen (B) see under Stolpce

Novyy Vitkov (Witkow Nowy) (U) see under Radziechow

Novyy Yarychiv (U) see Jaryczow Nowy

Nowe Miasto (P) see under Plonsk

Nowogrod (P) see under Lomza (*Lomzhe; ir oyfkum un untergang*)

Nowogrodek (B). *Pinkes Navaredok* [Navaredok memorial book*]. Eds.: E. Yerushalmi *et al.* [Tel Aviv, Alexander Harkavy Navaredker Relief Committee in the USA, 1963]. 419 p., illus., ports., maps. (H,Y)
YIVO: Novogrudok 1963   NYPL: *PXW(Novogrudok)
JTS: DS135 R93 N69 P5   YU: DS135 R93 N68

Nowo-Swieciany (Li) see under Swieciany

Nowy Dwor (near Warszawa) (P). *Pinkas Nowi Dvor* [Memorial book of Nowy-Dwor]. Eds.: A. Shamri, D. First. Tel Aviv, Former Residents of Nowy-Dwor in Israel, USA, Argentina..., [1965]. 556, 19p., ports., map, facsims. (H,Y,E)
YIVO: Nowy Dwor Mazowiecki 1965   NYPL: *PXV(Nowy Dwor)
JTS: DS135 P62 N643 S5   YU: DS135 P62 N6

Nowy Dwor (P). *Andenk bukh fun Nowi Dvor* [Memorial book of Nowy Dwor]. Los Angeles, Nowy Dwor Relief Committee, [1948]. 60 p., illus., ports. (Y)
YIVO: Nowy Dwor 1948

Nowy Dwor (P) see also under Szczuczyn (*Sefer zikaron li-kehilot Szczuczyn, Wasiliszki...*)

Nowy Dwor Mazowiecki (P) see Nowy Dwor

Nowy Sacz (P). *Le-zekher kehilat Tsants* [In memory of the community of Tsants]. Ed.: Y. Tefuhah. Jerusalem, Bet ha-sefer ha-tikhon ha-dati la-banot Oylinah di Rotshild, [1967 or 1968]. 174 p., illus., facsims., ports. (H)
JTS: DS135 P62 N648 L49 1968

Nowy Sacz (P). *Sefer Sants* [Book on the Jewish community of Nowy Sacz*]. Ed.: R. Mahler. New York, [Former Residents of Sants in New York], 1970. 886 p., illus., ports., facsims. (H,Y)
YIVO: Nowy Sacz 1970   NYPL: *PXV(Nowy Sacz)
JTS: DS135 P62 N648 M3   YU: 933.5 P762S

Nowy Targ (P). *Sefer Novi Targ veha-sevivah* [Remembrance book Nowy Targ and vicinity*]. Ed.: M. Walzer-Fass. [Israel], Townspeople Assoc. of Nowy Targ and Vicinity, 1979. 432, 100 p., illus. (H,Y,E)
YIVO: Novy Targ 1979   NYPL: *PXV(Nowy-Targ) 89-8486
YU: DS135 P62 N657 1957

Nowy Zagorz (P) see under Sanok

Odessa (U) see under General Reference Works, *Arim ve-imahot,* vol. 2

Oleksandriia (U) see Aleksandria

Okmieniec (B) see under Braslaw

Okuniew (P) see under Rembertow

Olizarka (U) see under Rafalowka

Olkeniki (Li). *ha-Ayara bi-lehavot; sefer zikaron li-kehilat Olkenik pelekh Vilnah* [Olkeniki in flames; a memorial book*]. Ed.: Sh. Farber. Tel Aviv, Association of Former Residents of Olkeniki and Surroundings, [1962]. 287 p., illus., ports. (H,Y)

YIVO: Valkininkas 1962   JTS: DS135 L5 F28 1962

Olkeniki (Li). *ha-'Ayarah she-haytah...Olknik: 'ayarah bi-medinat Lita.* [Haifa], Hanhalat...Irgun yotse Olknik, [1969]. 70 p., illus., maps, facsims. (H)

YIVO: Valkininkas 1969

Olkusz (P). *Olkush = (Elkish): sefer zikaron li-kehilah she-hukhehadah ba-Shoah* [Olkusz; memorial book to a community that was exterminated during the Holocaust]. Ed.: Zvi Yasheev. Tel Aviv, Olkusz Society in Israel, 1972. 280 p., map, illus. (H,Y)

YIVO: Olkusz 1972   NYPL: *PXV(Olkusz) 90-2302
YU: DS135 P62 O436 1972

Olshan (B) see Holszany

Olyka (U). *Pinkas ha-kehilah Olyka; sefer yizkor* [Memorial book of the community of Olyka]. Ed.: Natan Livneh. Tel Aviv, Olyka Society in Israel, 1972. 397 p., illus. (H,Y)

YIVO: Olyka 1972   NYPL: *PXW(Olyka) 75-3326
JTS: DS135 R93 O536 L55   YU: DS135 R93 O536

Opatow (P). *Apt (Opatov); sefer zikaron le-ir ve-em be-Yisrael* [Apt; a town which does not exist any more*]. Ed.: Z. Yasheev. Tel Aviv, The Apt Organization in Israel, USA, Canada and Brazil, [1966]. 441, 20 p., illus., maps, ports. (H,Y,E)

YIVO: Opatow 1966   NYPL: *PXV+ (Opatow)
JTS: +DS135 P62 O63 Y3   YU: 933.47 (438) O61Y

Opatow (P). *Yizkor: Yehude Apta: reshimat Yehude 'ir ha-mehoz Opatow me-ha-shnim 1940-41* [The list of the Jewish people of the district city Opatow in the years 1940-1941*]. [Israel], Irgun Yotse Apta be-Yisrael. 79 p. (H)

Opatow (P) see also under Ostrowiec (*Ostrovtse; geheylikt dem ondenk...*)

Opoczno (P). *Sefer Opotshnah; yad vashem li-kehilah she-harvah* [The book of Opoczno]. Ed.: Y. Alfasi. Tel Aviv, Assoc. of Emigrants from Opoczno and Vicinity, [1989]. 394, 21 p., illus., ports., diagrams (H,Y,E)

YIVO: Opoczno 1989   NYPL: *PXV(Opoczno) 90-2296
YU: DS135 P62 O647 1989

Opole (P). *Sefer Opole-Lubelski* [Memorial book of Opole-Lubelski*]. Ed.: D. Shtokfish. [Israel], Opole Societies in Israel and Diaspora, [1977]. 467 p., illus. (H,Y)

YIVO: Opole Lubelskie 1977

Opole Lubelskie (P) see Opole

Opsa (B) see under Braslaw

Orchei (M) see Orgeyev

Oradea (Ro). *A Tegnap városa; a nagyváradi zsidóság emlékkönyve* [Ir ve-etmol; sefer zikaron li-Yehude Grosswardein* = A city and yesterday; memorial book to the Jews of Grosswardein]. Eds.: Schön Dezső et al. Tel Aviv, 1981. 446 p., illus., maps, ports. (Hu)

NYPL: *PXR+ 86-3819   JTS: +DS135 R72 O7 T4
YU: DS135 R72 O677 1981

Oradea (Ro). *Tegnap varosa. Hebrew. Sefer zikaron le-Yahadut Grossvardain-Oradeah-Nagvarad veha-sevivah, mi-shnat yisudah ve-ad-hurbanah* [Memorial book to the Jews of Grosswardein-Oradea-Nagyvarad and vicinity...]. Ed.: Tsevi Grosman. Tel Aviv, Grosswardein Society in Israel, 1984. 451, 67 p., illus., maps, ports. (H)

YIVO: Oradea 1984   NYPL: *PXR+ 88-562
JTS: +DS135 R72 O716 G7 1984   YU: DS135 R72 O67714 1984

Orgeev (M) see Orgeyev

Orgeyev (M). *Orhiyov be-vinyanah uve-hurbanah* [Orheyev alive and destroyed]. Eds.: Y. Spivak et al. [Tel Aviv, Committee of Former Residents of Orheyev, 1959.] 216 p., illus., ports. (H,Y)

YIVO: Orchei 1959   NYPL: *PXM(Orgeyev)
JTS: +DS135 R93 O7 S6   YU: DS135 R72 O7

Orlovo (Orlowa) (B) see under Zoludek

Oshmyany (Oshmena) (B) see Oszmiana

Oshpitsin (P) see Oswiecim

Osiek (P) see under Staszow

Osipovichi (B) see under Bobruisk

Ostra (U) see Ostrog

Ostrog (U). *Le-zekher kehilat Ostra'ah; hantsahat kehilat Ostra'ah* [In memory of the Jewish community of Ostrog]. Ramat-Hasharon, Bet-sefer "Oranim," 1969. 55 p., illus. (H)

YIVO: Ostroh 1969

Ostrog (U). *Osta'ah.* [By] Yehuda Leyb Levin. Jerusalem, Yad Yahadut Polin, [1965 or 1966]. 111 p., map, ports., illus. (H)

NYPL: *PXW(Ostrog)   JTS: DS135 R93 O88 L4

Ostrog (U). *Pinkas Ostra'ah; sefer zikaron...* [Ostrog-Wolyn; in memory of the Jewish community*]. Ed.: H. Ayalon-Baranik. Tel Aviv, Association of Former Residents of Ostrog, 1960. 640 columns, ports., maps, facsims. (H,Y)

YIVO: Ostroh 1960   NYPL: *PXW(Ostrog)
JTS: DS135 R93 O88 A9   YU: DS135 R93 O74

Ostrog (U). *Sefer Ostra'ah (Vohlin); matsevet zikaron li-kehilah kedoshah* [Ostrog book; a memorial to the Ostrog holy community*]. Ed.: Yitzhak Alperowitz; Chief Coordinator: Chaim Finkel. Tel Aviv, The Ostrog Society in Israel, 1987. 402, 34 p., illus., ports., map (H,Y,E,P)

YIVO: Ostroh 1987 NYPL: *PXW(Ostrog) 89-10742
JTS: DS135 R93 O88 S4 HUC: DS135 493 O75 1987
YU: DS135 R93 O75 1987

Ostrog (U). *Ven dos lebn hot geblit* [When life was blooming]. [By] M. Grines. Buenos Aires, 1954. 17, 471 p., illus., ports. (Y)

YIVO: Ostroh 1954 NYPL: *PXW
HUC: HIW 454

Ostrog (U) see also under General Reference Works, *Arim ve-imahot*, vol. 1

Ostroh (U) see Ostrog

Ostroleka (P). *Sefer kehilat Ostrolenkah* [Book of kehilat Ostrolenka*]. Ed.: Y. Ivri. Tel Aviv, Association of Former Residents of Ostrolenka in Israel, 1963. 579 p., illus., map, ports. (H,Y)

YIVO: Ostrolenka 1963 YU: DS135 P62 O748 1963
NYPL: *PXV+ (Ostroleka) 89-8554 JTS: +DS135 P62 O7 S4

Ostrowiec (P). *Ostrovtse; geheylikt dem ondenk...fun Ostrovtse, Apt...* [Ostrovtse; dedicated to the memory of Ostrovtse, Apt...]. Buenos Aires, Former Residents of Ostrovtse...in Argentina, 1949. 217 p., ports. (Y)

YIVO: Ostrowiec Swietokryzski 1949 JTS: DS135 P62 O8
NYPL: *PXV(Ostrowiec) 84-351 YU: 933.5 P7628

Ostrowiec (P). *Sefer Ostrovtsah: le-zikaron ule-edut* [Ostrowiec; a monument on the ruins of an annihilated Jewish community*]. Eds.: G. Silberberg, M. S. Geshuri. [Tel Aviv], Society of Ostrovtser Jews in Israel, [1971]. 560, [106], 134 p., illus., maps, ports. (Y,H,E)

NYPL: *PXV(Ostrowiec) JTS: DS135 P62 O8 S4

Ostrow-Lubelski (P). *Sefer-yizkor Ostrov-Lubelski – Yisker-bukh Ostruv-Lubelski* [Memorial-book Ostrow-Lubelski*]. Ed.: David Shtokfish. [Israel], Association of Former Residents of Ostrow-Lubelski in Israel, [1987]. 422 p., illus., ports. (H,Y,E)

NYPL: *PXV(Ostrow-Lubelski) 90-3606
YU: DS135 P62 O767 1987

Ostrow-Mazowiecka (P). *Ostrov Mazovyetsk.* [By] Yehuda Leyb Levin. Jerusalem, [Yad Yahadut Polin, 1965 or 1966]. 164 p., ports., illus. (H)

NYPL: *PXV(Ostrow) JTS: DS135 P62 O78 L4

Ostrow-Mazowiecka (P). *Sefer ha-zikaron li-kehilat Ostrov-Mazovyetsk* [Memorial book of the community of Ostrov-Mazovyetsk]. Ed.: A. Margalit. Tel Aviv, Association of Former Residents of Ostrow-Mazovyetsk, [1960]. 653 p., illus., maps, ports. (H,Y)

YIVO: Ostrow-Mazowiecka 1960 NYPL: *PXV(Ostrow)
JTS: DS135 P62 O78 G6 YU: DS135 P62 O79 1960

Ostryna (B) see under Szczuczyn (*Sefer zikaron li-kehilot Szczuczyn, Wasiliszki...*)

Oswiecim (P). *Sefer Oshpitsin* [Oswiecim-Auschwitz memorial book*]. Eds.: H. Wolnerman, A. Burstin, M. S. Geshuri. Jerusalem, Oshpitsin Society in Israel, 1977. 622, [3] p., illus., maps, ports. (H,Y)

YIVO: Oswiecim 1977

Oszmiana (B). *Sefer zikaron li-kehilat Oshminah* [Oshmana memorial book*]. Ed.: M. Gelbart. Tel Aviv, Oshmaner Organization in Israel, 1969. 659, 109 p., illus., maps, ports. (H,Y,E)

YIVO: Oshmyany 1969 NYPL: *PXW(Oshmyany)
JTS: DS135 R93 O67 YU: 933.5 L776O

Otaci (Otik) (M) see Ataki

Otvotsk (P) see Otwock

Otwock (P). *Hurbn Otvotsk, Falenits, Kartshev* [The destruction of Otvotsk, Falenits, Kartshev.] [By] B. Orenstein. [Bamberg], Former Residents of Otvotsk, Falenits and Kartshev in the American Zone in Germany, 1948. 71 p., ports. (Y)

YIVO: Otwock, Karczew, Falenica 1948 HUC: HIW 373
JTS: DS135 P62 O86 O72 NYPL: *ZP-739 No.11

Otwock (P). *Yisker-bukh tsu fareybiken dem ondenk fun di horev-gevorene Yidishe kehiles Otvotsk, Kartshev* [Memorial book of Otvotsk and Kartshev*]. Ed.: Sh. Kanc [Kants]. Tel Aviv, Former Residents of Otvotsk in Israel, 1968. 1088 columns, illus., map, ports. (H,Y)

YIVO: Otwock & Karczew 1968 NYPL: *PXV(Otwock)
JTS: DS135 P62 O86 Y5 YU: DS135 P62 O8

Ozarow (P). *Memoires d'une ville juive eteinte Ozarow.* [By] Hillel Adler. [Charenton-le Pont, France], Hillel Adler, [1994]. 247 p., illus., ports., map. (F)

YIVO: Ozarow 1994 NYPL: *PXV (Ozarow) 97-2617

Ozarow (P). *Memories of Ozarow: a little Jewish town that was.* [By] Hillel Adler; translated from the French by William Fraiberg. Montreal, Ozarow Press, 1997. xxviii, 214 p., illus., map, ports. (E)

YIVO: Ozarow 1997

Ozarow (P) see under Ostrowiec

Ozernyany (U) see Jezierna

Ozeryany (Ozieran) U) see Jezierzany

Ozorkow (P). *Ozorkov.* [By] Y. L. Levin. Jerusalem, Yad Yahadut Polin, [1966]. 128 p., illus. (H)

YIVO: Ozorkow 1966 NYPL: *PXV(Ozorkow)
JTS: DS135 P62 O9

Pabianice (P). *Sefer Pabyanets* [Memorial book of Pabianice]. Ed.: A. V. Yasni (Jasny). Tel Aviv, Former

Residents of Pabianice in Israel, 1956. 419 p., illus., map, ports., facsims. (H,Y)

YIVO: Pabianice 1956   NYPL: *PXV(Pabianice) 90-2271

Paks (Hu). *Mazkeret Paksh* [Paks memorial book]. Ed.: D. Sofer. Jerusalem, [h.mo.l, 1962-]. 3 vols., ports., facsims. (H)

YIVO: Paks 1962 (vols. 2-3)   NYPL: *PXT(Paks) 83-468
JTS: DS135 H92 P3   YU: DS135 H92 P3 1962

Papa (Hu). *Sefer zikaron Papa; le-zekher kedoshe ha-kehilah ve-yishuve ha-sevivah* [Memorial book of Papa..], [By] Jehuda-Gyula Lang. [Tel Aviv], Papa Memorial Committee, [between 1972-1974]. 28, 188 p., illus., ports. (H,Hu)

YIVO: Papa 1972   NYPL: *PXT(Papa) 84-505

Parafianowo (B) see under Dokszyce

Parczew (P). *Partsev - sefer zikaron li-kedoshe Partsev veha-sevivah* [Parczew - memorial book of the martyrs of Parczew and vicinity]. Eds.: Sh. Zunnshin *et al.* [Israel], Association of Former Residents of Parczew in Israel, [1977]. 328 p.,illus., ports. (H,Y)

YU: DS135 P62 P373 1977

Parichi (B) see under Bobruisk

Parysow (P). *Sefer Porisov* [Parysow; a memorial to the Jewish community of Parysow, Poland*]. Ed.: Y. Granatstein. [Tel Aviv], Former Residents of Parysow in Israel, 1971. 625 p., illus., ports. (H,Y)

YIVO: Parysow 1971   NYPL: *PXV(Parysow)
JTS: DS135 P62 P376 S4   YU: K5 P762P

Perehinsko (U) see under Rozniatow

Peski (B) see Piaski

Petrikov (P) see Piotrkow Trybunalski

Piaski (B). *Pyesk u-Most; sefer yizkor* [Piesk and Most, a memorial book*]. [Tel Aviv], Piesk and Most Societies in Israel and the Diaspora, [1975]. 588, [70], 52 p., illus. (H,Y,E)

YIVO: Peski & Mosty 1975   NYPL: *PXW(Peski) 77-3794
JTS: DS135 R93 P4 S4   YU: DS135 R93 P9 1975

Piatnica (P) see under Lomza (*Lomzhe, ir oyfkum un untergang*)

Pidhaitsi (Pidhaytsi) (U) see Podhajce

Pidvolochysk (U) see Podwoloczyska

Piesk (B) see Piaski

Piestany (Slo) see Postyen

Pilev (P) see Pulawy

Pinczow (P). *Sefer zikaron li-kehilat Pintsev; in Pintshev togt shoyn nisht* [A book of memory of the Jewish community of Pinczow, Poland*]. Ed.: M. Shinar (Shner). Tel Aviv, Former Residents of Pinczow in Israel and the Diaspora, 1970. 480 p., illus., map, ports. (H,Y)

YIVO: Pinczow 1970   NYPL: *PXV(Pinczow)
JTS: DS135 P62 P495   YU: 933.5 P762P

Pinsk (B). *Pinsk sefer edut ve-zikaron li-kehilat Pinsk-Karlin* [Pinsk*]. Ed.: Z. Rabinovits, N. Tamir (Mirski). Tel Aviv, Former Residents of Pinsk-Karlin in Israel, 1966-1977. 3 vols., illus., map, ports., facsims. (H,Y)

YIVO: Pinsk 1973 (v.1, pt 1) 1977 (v.1,.pt.2), 1966 (v.2)
NYPL: *PXW (Pinsk) 76-279
JTS: +DS135 R93 P5 P5   YU: DS135 R93 P54

Pinsk (B). *Toyznt yor Pinsk; geshikhte fun der shtot, der Yidisher yishuv, institutsyes, sotsyale bavegungen, perzenlekhkeytn, gezelshaftlekhe tuer, Pinsk iber der velt* [A thousand years of Pinsk; history of the city, its Jewish community, institutions, social movements, personalities, community leaders, Pinsk around the world]. Ed.: B. Hoffman. New York, Pinsker Branch 210, Workmen's Circle, 1941. xv, 500 p., illus., maps, ports. (Y)

YIVO: Pinsk 1941   NYPL: *PXV+ (Hoffman..)
JTS: +DS135 R93 P5 H6

Piotrkow Trybunalski (P). *Pyotrkow Trybunalski un ungegent* [Piotrkow Trybunalski and vicinity*]. Eds.: Y. Maltz, N. Lau-Lavie (Lavi). [Tel Aviv, h.mo.l, 1965]. 1192 columns, illus., maps, ports., facsims. (H,Y)

YIVO: Piotrkow Trybunalski 1965 NYPL: *PXV+ (Piotrkow)
YU: DS135 P62 P558 1965   JTS: +DS135 P62 P5

Piotrkow Trybunalski (P). *A tale of one city: Piotrkow Trybunalski*. Ed.: Ben Giladi. New York, Shengold Publishers with The Piotrkow Trybunalski Relief Association, [1991]. 408 p., illus., maps, ports. (E)

YIVO: Piotrkow Trybunalski 1991   JTS: DS135 P62 P5 T36 1991
NYPL: *PXV (Piotrkow-Trybunalski) 92-3507
YU: DS135 P62 P56 1991

Pitshayev (U) see Poczajow; see also under Krzemieniec

Plantsh (Polaniec) (P) see under Staszow

Plawno (P) see under Radomsko

Plintsk (P) see Plonsk

Plock (P). *Plotsk: bletlekh geshikhte fun Idishn lebn in der alter heym* [Plock; páginas de historia de la vida judía de Allende el Mar*]. Ed.: Yosef Horn. Buenos Aires, Sociedad de Residentes de Plock en la Argentina, 1945. 255 p., illus., ports. (Y)

YIVO: Plock 1945   NYPL: *PXV
JTS: DS135 P62 P57 S6   YU: DS135 P62 P57

Plock (P). *Plotsk; toldot kehilah 'atikat-yomin be-Polin* [Plotzk; a history of an ancient Jewish community in Poland*]. Ed.: E. Eisenberg (Aizenberg). Tel Aviv, ha-

Menorah, [1967]. 684, 96 p., illus., ports., maps. (H,Y,E)

YIVO: Plock 1967 NYPL: *PXV+ (Plock)
JTS: DS135 P62 P566 YU: DS135 P62 P566
HUC: HIW 383

Plock (P). *Yidn in Plotsk* [Jews in Plotzk*]. [By] S. Greenspan (Grinshpan). New York, [1960]. 325 p., illus., ports. (Y)

YIVO: Plock 1960 NYPL: *PXV (Plock)
JTS: DS135 P62 P56 G74 YU: 933.5 P762 P729E

Plonsk (P). *Sefer Plonsk veha-sevivah* [Memorial book of Plonsk and vicinity]. Ed.: Sh. Zemach (Tsemah).[Tel Aviv], Former Residents of Plonsk in Israel, [1963]. 775 p., ports., illus., map, facsims. (H,Y)

YIVO: Plonsk 1963 NYPL: *PXV (Plonsk) 76-5726
YU: DS135 P62 P57674 1963

Plotsk (P) see Plock

Plusy (B) see under Braslaw

Pochaiv (Pochayiv) (U) see Poczajow; see also under Krzemieniec.

Poczajow (U). *Pitshayever yisker bukh* [Memorial book dedicated to the Jews of Pitchayev-Wohlyn executed by the Germans*]. Ed.: H. Gelernt. Philadelphia, The Pitchayever Wohliner Aid Society, 1960. 311 p., illus., ports. (Y)

YIVO: Pochayiv 1960 NYPL: *PXW (Pochaiv) 89-758
JTS: DS135 R93 P58 G4 YU: DS135 R93 P58 1960

Poczajow (U) see also under Krzemieniec

Podbrodzie (Li) see under Swieciany

Podgaytsy (U) see Podhajce

Podhajce (U). *Sefer Podhaitsah.* Ed.: M. S. Geshuri. Tel Aviv, Irgun yotse Podhaitsah veha-sevivah be-Yisrael, [1972]. 295, 17 p., illus. (H,Y,E)

YIVO: Pidhaytsi 1972 NYPL: *PXW(Podgaytsy) 74-2705
HUC: HIW 506 YU: DS135 R93 P59 1972

Podwoloczyska (U). *Sefer Podvolotsiskah veha-sevivah* [The book of Podwoloczyska and environment; Podvolocisk book*]. Ed.: Avraham Ahuvyah. Haifa, Podwoloczyska Community in Israel, 1988. 207 p., illus., ports., map. (H; introd.: E)

YIVO: Pidvolochysk 1988 NYPL: *PXW (Pidvolochysk) 95-582
YU: DS135 R93 P492 1988

Pogost (Pohost) (B) see under Slutsk

Pogost Zagorodskiy (B) see Pohost Zahorodzki

Pohost Zahorodzki (B). *'Edut ve-zikaron li-kehilat Pohost Zahorodzki veha-sevivah.* Tel Aviv, [1978/79]. [Cited in Pinkas ha-kehilot - Poland, vol. 2, p.275.]

Pokshivnitsa (P) see Koprzywnica

Polaniec (P) see under Staszow

Poligon (Li) see under Swieciany

Polonnoye (U) see under Novograd-Volynskiy

Porcsalma (Hu) see under Csenger

Porisov (P) see Parysow

Porozow (B) see under Wolkowysk (*Volkovisker yisker-bukh*)

Postawy (B). *Mayn shtetl Postov* [My town Postov]. [By] Israel Reichel. Tel Aviv, published by the Author, 1977. 215 p. (Y)

YIVO: Postavy 1977

Postavy (Postov) (B) see Postawy; see under Glebokie

Postyen (Slo). *Sefer zikaron li-kehilot Pishtani, Verbovah (Verbo), Miyavah u-Brezovah u sevivatan* [Memorial for the Jewish communities Piestany, Vrbove (Verbo), Myjava, Brezova and vicinities*]. [By] Sh. Grunwald. Jerusalem, 1969. 111 leaves, illus., ports. (G)

NYPL: *PXT(Piestany) 92-117 YU: 933.5 C998P
JTS: DS135 C96 P52 G78

Pozsony (Slo) see General Reference Works, *Arim ve-imahot,* vol. 7

Praga (P). *Sefer Pragah; mukdash le-zekher kedoshe irenu* [Praga book; dedicated to the memory of the martyrs of our town]. Ed.: G. Weisman (Vaisman). [Tel Aviv], Praga Society in Israel, [1974]. 563 p., illus. (H,Y)

YIVO: Praga (Warsaw) 1974 NYPL: *PXV(Praga) 77-3783
JTS: DS135 P62 P66 S4 YU: DS135 P62 W338 1974

Premisle (P) see Przemysl

Pressburg (Pozsony) (Slo) see under General Reference Works, *Arim ve-imahot,* vol. 7

Proshnits (P) see Przasnysz

Proskurov (U). *Hurbn Proskurov; tsum ondenken fun di heylige neshomes vos zaynen umgekumen in der shreklikher shhite, vos iz ongefirt gevoren durkh di Haydamakes* [The destruction of Proskurov; in memory of the sacred souls who perished during the terrible slaughter of the Haidamaks]. New York, Levant Press [1923 or 1924]. 111 p., illus. (Y,H)

YIVO: Khmelnytskyy (Proskurov) 1923
NYPL: *PXW(Proskurov) JTS: DS135 R93 P76 H87

Pruszkow (P). *Sefer Pruskow, Nadzin veha-sevivah* [Memorial book of Pruszkow, Nadzin and vicinity]. Ed.: D. Brodski. [Tel Aviv], Former Residents of Pruszkow in Israel, [1966]. 334 p., illus, maps, ports., facsims. (H,Y)

YIVO: Pruszkow 1966 NYPL: *PXV(Pruszkow)
JTS: DS135 P62 P7

Pruzana (B). *Pinkas fun finf-fartilikte kehiles Pruzshene, Bereze, Maltsh, Shershev*, Selts [Chronicle of destroyed communities of the towns of Pruzana, Bereza, Malch, Scherschev and Seltz...]. Ed.: M. W. Bernstein. Buenos Aires, Former Residents of Pruzana... in Argentina, [1958]. 13, 972 p., illus., ports. (Y)

YIVO: Pruzhany & Bereza 1958   NYPL: *PXW (Bernstein, M.)
JTS: DS135 R93 W43 B4   YU: DS135 R93 P78535

Pruzana (B). *Pinkas Pruzani veha-sevivah; [tol]dot ve-zikaron li-kehilot she-hushmedu ba-Shoah* [Pinkas Pruz'any and its vicinity (Bereze, Malch, Shershev, Seltz and Lineve); chronicle of six communities perished in the Holocaust*]. Ed.: Joseph Friedlaender. Tel Aviv, Irgun yotse Pruzani veha-sevivah be-Yisrael uve-Artzot ha-Brit, 1983. 542, 169 p., illus., maps, ports. (H,E)

YIVO: Pruzhany 1983   NYPL: *PXW(Pruzhany) 85-1938
JTS: DS135 P93 P785   YU: DS135 R93 P785

Pruzhany (B) see Pruzana

Pryborzhavske (U) see Zadna

Przasnysz (P). *Sefer zikaron kehilat Proshnits* [Memorial book to the community of Proshnitz*]. Ed.: Shlomo Bachrach. [Tel Aviv], Proshnitz Society in Israel, [1974]. 273 p., illus. (H,Y,E)

YIVO: Prasznysz 1974   NYPL: *PXV(Przasnysz) 75-762
JTS: DS135 P62 P73 S4 YU: DS135 P62 P7375 1974

Przeclaw (P) see under Radomysl Wielki

Przedborz (P). *Pshedboz—33 shanim le-hurbanah* [Przedborz memorial book*]. Ed.: S. Kanc (Kants). Tel Aviv, Przedborz Societies in Israel and America, 1977. 548, 84 p., illus., map, port. (H,Y,E)

YIVO: Przedborz 1977   NYPL: *PXV(Przedborz) 89-8445
JTS: DS135 P62 P737 P7 YU: DS135 P62 P73765 1977

Przedborz (P) see also under Radomsko

Przedecz (P). *Sefer yizkor li-kedoshe ir Pashyatsh korbanot ha-Shoah* [Memorial book to the Holocaust victims of the city of Pshaytsh]. Eds.: Mosheh Bilavski *et al.* Tel Aviv, Przedecz Societies in Israel and the Diaspora, 1974. 400 p., illus., map. (H,Y)

YIVO: Przedecz 1974   NYPL: *PXV(Przedecz) 87-532
JTS: DS135 P62 P7377 S4 YU: DS135 P62 P7377

Przemysl (P). *Sefer Pshemishel* [Przemysl memorial book*]. Ed.: A. Mentser. [Tel Aviv], Former Residents of Przemysl in Israel, [1964]. xvi, 522 p., illus., maps. ports., facsims. (H,Y)

YIVO: Przemysl 1964   NYPL: *PXV(Przemysl)
JTS: DS135 P62 P75 M4 YU: DS135 P62 P758 1964

Przerosl (P) see under Suwalki

Przytyk (P). *Sefer Pshitik.* Ed.: David Shtokfish. Tel Aviv, [Przytyk Societies in Israel, France and the USA],

1973. 7, 461 p., illus. (H,Y; introd. in E)

YIVO: Przytyk 1973   NYPL: *PXV(Przytyk) 75-5589
JTS: DS135 P62 P787 S4 YU: DS135 P62 P787

Pshaytsh (P) see Przedecz

Pshedbozh (P) see Przedborz

Pshemishl (P) see Przemysl

Pshetslav (Przeclaw) (P) see under Radomysl Wielki

Pshitik (P) see Przytyk

Pulawy (P). *Yisker-bukh Pulav* [In memoriam—the city of Pulawy*]. Ed.: M. W. Bernstein. New York, Pulawer Yiskor Book Committee, 1964. 494 p., ports., maps, facsims. (Y)

YIVO: Pulawy 1964   NYPL: *PXV(Pulawy)
JTS: DS135 P62 P84 B4 YU: DS135 P62 P849 1964

Pultusk (P). *Pultusk; sefer zikaron* [Pultusk memorial book]. Ed.: Yitzhak Ivri. Tel Aviv, Pultusk Society in Israel, 1971. 15, 683 p., illus. (H,Y)

YIVO: Pultusk 1971   NYPL: *PXV(Pultusk)
JTS: DS135 P62 P86 I85

Punsk (P) see under Suwalki

Raab (Hu) see Gyor

Rabka (P) see under Nowy Targ

Rachev (U) see under Novograd-Volynskiy

Rachow (Rachov) (P) see under Annopol

Raciaz (P). *Galed li-kehilat Ratsyonz* [Memorial book of the community of Racionz*]. Ed.: E. Tsoref. Tel Aviv, Former Residents of Raciaz, [1964 or 1965]. 446, 47 p., illus., ports., facsims. (H,Y,E)

YIVO: Raciaz 1964   NYPL: *PXV(Raciaz)
JTS: DS135 P62 R27 Z6

Raczki (P) see under Suwalki

Radashkovichy (B) see Radoszkowice

Radauti (Ro). *Radauti: kehilah Yehudit be-tsemihatah uve-sheki'atah* [Radauti: a Jewish community in bloom and in decline]. [By] Yisrael Margalit (Pustilnik). Tel Aviv, Irgun yotse Radauti (Bukovina), 1990. 297 p. (H)

Radauti-Prut (Ro) see under Dorohoi

Radekhov (Radekhiv) (U) see Radziechow

Radevits (Ro) see Radauti

Radikhov (U) see Radziechow

Radom (P). *Dos Yidishe Radom in hurves; ondenkbukh* [The havoc of Jewish Radom*]. Stuttgart, The Committee of Radom Jews in Stuttgart, 1948. 277 p., iv, [8] leaves of plates, illus. (Y)

YIVO: Radom 1948　　　　JTS: DS135 P62 R32
YU: 933.47(438)

Radom (P). *Radom* [Radom; a memorial to the Jewish community of Radom, Poland*]. Ed.: A. Sh. Stein. [Tel Aviv, Former Residents of Radom in Israel and in the Diaspora, 1961]. 346 p., ports., facsims. (H)

YIVO: Radom 1961　　　　NYPL: *PXV+ (Radom)
YU: DS135 P62 R319 1961

Radom (P). *Sefer Radom* [The book of Radom; the story of a Jewish community in Poland destroyed by the Nazis*]. Ed.: Y. Perlov; [English section]: Alfred Lipson. Tel Aviv, Former Residents of Radom in Israel and the USA, 1961 (Hebrew); and New York, 1963 (English). 451, lxxviii, 120 p., illus., ports. (Y,E)

YIVO: Radom (Sefer Radom) 1961　　NYPL: *PXV+ (Radom)
JTS: +DS135 P62 R32 P4　　　　YU: DS135 P62 R32 1961

Radomsko (P). *Sefer yizkor li-kehilat Radomsk veha-sevivah* [Memorial book of the community of Radomsk and vicinity]. Ed.: L. Losh. [Tel Aviv], Former Residents of Radomsk..., [1967]. 603 p., illus., ports., maps, facsims. (H,Y)

YIVO: Radomsko 1967　　　NYPL: *PXV+ (Radomsko)
JTS: +DS135 P62 R34 L6　　　YU: 933.5 P762R 1967

Radomysl Wielki (P). *Radomysl rabati veha-sevivah; sefer yizkor* [Radomysl Wielki and neighbourhood; memorial book*]. Eds.: H. Harshoshanim *et al.* Tel Aviv, Former Residents of Radomysl and Surroundings in Israel, [1971]. 1067 columns, illus., ports., map, facsims. (H,Y,E)

YIVO: Radomysl Wielki 1971　NYPL: *PXV+ (Radomysl)
JTS: DS135 P62 R3267　　　　YU: 933.5 P762R 1971

Radoszkowice (B). *Radoshkovits; sefer zikaron* [Radoshkowitz; a memorial to the Jewish community*]. Eds.: M. Robinson *et al.* Tel Aviv, Former Residents of Radoshkowitz in Israel, 1953. 222 p., illus., ports. (H)

YIVO: Radoshkovichi 1953　　NYPL: *PXW(Radoshkovichi)
JTS: DS135 R93 R3　　　　　YU: DS135 R93 R3
HUC: HIW 351

Radyvyliv (U) see Radziwillow

Radzanow (P) see under Szransk

Radziechow (U). *Sefer zikaron li-kehilot Radihov, Lopatin, Vitkov Novi, Holoyov, Toporov, Stanislavtshik, Stremiltsh, Shtrovits, veha-kefarim Ovin, Barilov, Volitseh-Vigodah, Skrilov, Zavitsh, Mikolayov, Demitrov, Sinkow, ve-od* [Memorial book of Radihov, Lopatin, Novyi Vitkov, Cholojow, Toporov, Stanislavchik, Stremilch, Shchurovichi, and the villages Ubin, Barylow, Wolica-Wygoda, Skrilow, Zawidcze, Mikolajow,

Dmytrow, Sienkow, etc.]. Ed.: G. Kressel. Tel Aviv, Society of Radikhov, Lopatyn and Vicinity, 1976. 656 p., illus., ports. (H,Y)

YIVO: Radekhiv 1976　　NYPL: *PXW(Radekhov) 89-10906
YU: DS135 R93 R2958 1976

Radzin (P). *Radzin 1939-1943.* Ed.: Y. Rosenkrantz. Tel Aviv, Committee of Former Residents of Radzin and Pudel in Israel. 17 p. (H), mimeo.

Radzin (P). *Sefer Radzin* [The book of Radzin]. Ed.: Y. Siegelman. Tel Aviv, Council of Former Residents of Radzin (Podolski) in Israel, 1957. 358 p., illus. (H,Y)

YIVO: Radzyn Podlaski 1957　JTS: DS135 P62 R33 S55
NYPL: *PXV (Radzim-Podlaski) 93-57

Radzin Podlaski (P) see Radzin

Radziwillow (U). *Radzivillov; sefer zikaron* [A memorial to the Jewish community of Radziwillow, Wolyn*]. Ed.: Y. Adini. Tel Aviv, The Radziwillow Organization in Israel, [1966]. 438 p., illus., ports., maps, facsims. (H,Y)

YIVO: Radyvyliv 1966　　NYPL: *PXW (Chervonoarmeisk)
JTS: DS135 R93 R32　　　　YU: 933.5 R969 R133 A235

Radzymin (U). *Sefer zikaron li-kehilat Radzimin* [Le livre du souvenir de la communauté Juive de Radzymin*]. Ed.: Gershon Hel. Tel Aviv, The Encyclopaedia of the Jewish Diaspora, 1975. 389, 72 p., illus. (H,Y,F)

YIVO: Radzymin 1975　　NYPL: *PXV+ (Radzymin) 77-3792
JTS: +DS135 P62 R342 S4　YU: DS135 P62 R3287
HUC: HIW 3805

Rafalowka (U). *Ner tamid: le-zekher ha-'ayarot Rafalovkah ha-yeshenah, Rafalovkah he-hadashah, Olizarkah, Zolutsk veha-sevivah* [Memorial book for the towns of Old Rafalowka, New Rafalowka, Olizarka, Zolutsk and vicinity]. Eds.: Pinhas and Malkah Hagin. Tel Aviv, Irgun yotse Rafalovkah ha-yeshanah, Rafalovkah he-hadashah, Olizarkah, Zolutzk veha-sevivah, 1996. 530 p., illus., maps, ports. (H, Y)

NYPL *PXW (Rafalovka) 99-438　YU: DS135 R93 R33356 1996

Rakishok (Li) see Rokiskis

Rakospalota (Hu). *Toldot kehilat Rakoshpalota* [History of the Rakoshpalota community]. [By] Rachel Aharoni. Tel Aviv, 1978. 204, 52 p., illus. (H,Hu)

YIVO: Budepest 1978　　　NYPL: *PXT 85-2618

Rakow (P). *Sefer zikaron li-kehilat Rakov* [Memorial book of the community of Rakow]. Ed.: Ch. Abramson. Tel Aviv, Former Residents of Rakow in Israel and the USA, 1959. 184, [15] p., ports., facsims. (H,Y)

YIVO: Rakov 1959　　　　YU: DS135 B38 R34 1959

Ratno (U). *Ratnah; sipurah shel kehilah Yehudit she-hushmedah* [Ratne; the story of a Jewish community that

341

was destroyed]. Ed.: N. Tamir. Tel Aviv, Ratno Society in Israel, 1983. 331 p., illus., map, ports. (H)

Ratno (U). *Yisker-bukh Ratne; dos lebn un umkum fun a Yidish shtetl in Volin* [Memorial book of Ratno; the life and destruction of a Jewish town in Wolyn]. Eds.: Y. Botoshansky, Y. Yanosovitsh. Buenos Aires, Former Residents of Ratno in Argentina and the USA, 1954. 806 p., illus., ports., map (Y)

Rawa Ruska (U). *Sefer zikaron li-kehilat Ravah Ruskah veha-sevivah* [Rawa Ruska memorial book*]. Eds.: A. M. Ringel, J. H. Rubin. Tel Aviv, Rawa Ruska Society and vicinity in Israel. [1973]. 468 p., illus. (H,Y,E)

Rawicz (P). *Le-korot kehilat Ravitsh* [Annals of the community of Rawitsch (Rawicz)*]. By Arthur Posner (Pozner), Jerusalem, Hotsaat Erez, [1962]. 84, xvi p., illus., map, ports. (H, E summary)

Raysha (P) see Rzeszow

Rayvits (P) see Rejowiec

Rejowiec (P). *"Shtil vi in Rayvits..."; oyfn hurbn fun mayn heym* ["As silent as in Rayvits..."; on the destruction of my home]. [By] Shmuel Drelikhman. Bergen-Belsen, [1947]. 46 p., illus., ports. (Y)

Rembertow (P). *Sefer zikaron li-kehilot Rembertov, Okunyew, Milosnah* [Yizkor book in memory of Rembertov, Okuniev, Milosna*]. Ed.: Shimon Kanc (Kants). Tel Aviv, Rembertow, Okuniew and Milosna Societies in Israel, the USA, France, Mexico City, Canada, Chile and Brazil, 1974. 465 p., illus. (H,Y)

Reteag (Retteg) (Ro) see under Des

Rietavas (Li). *Sefer Ritovah; galed le-zekher ayaratenu* [Memorial book: the Ritavas community; a tribute to the memory of our town*]. Ed.: Alter Levite.[Israel], Ritova Societies in Israel and the Diaspora, [1975]. 223, xxvii p., illus. (H,Y,E)

Rietavas (Li). *Hoveret Ritovah: tosefet l'sefer ha-zikaron.* [Tel Aviv], Ritova Societies in Israel and the Diaspora, [1977]. 24 p., illus. (H, Y)

Rietavas (Li). *A yizker book to Riteve: a Jewish shtetl in Lithuania.* Ed.: Alter Levite. Revised edition by Dr. Dina Porat and Roni Stauber. Capetown, Kaplan Kushlick Foundation, 2000. 206 p. (E)

Rimszan (Rymszany) (B) see under Braslaw

Riskeva (Ro) see Ruscova

Rivne (U) see Rowne

Rogatin (U) see Rohatyn

Rohatyn (U). *Kehilat Rohatin veha-sevivah*[Rohatyn; the history of a Jewish community*]. Ed.: M. Amihai. [Tel Aviv], Former Residents of Rohatyn in Israel, [1962]. 362, 62 p., illus., ports., facsims. (H,Y,E)

Rokiskis (Li). *Yisker-bukh fun Rakishok un umgegnt* [Yizkor book of Rakishok and environs*]. Ed.: M. Bakalczuk-Felin. Johannesburg, Rakishker Landsmanshaft of Johannesburg, 1952. 626, vi p., illus., ports., facsim. (Y, E=preface)

Rokitno (U). *Rokitnah (Vohlin) veha-sevivah; sefer edut ve-zikaron* [Rokitno-Wolyn and surroundings; memorial book and testimony]. Ed.: E. Leoni. Tel Aviv, Former Residents of Rokitno in Israel, 1967. 459 p., illus., ports., maps (H,Y)

Rokytne (U) see Rokitno

Romanova (B) see under Slutsk

Rotin (U) see Rohatyn

Rovno (U) see Rowne

Rowne (U). *A zikorn far Rovne* [In memory of Rowne]. Eds.: Y. Margulyets, Z. Finkelshteyn, Y. Shvartsapel. [Germany], Rowne Landsmanshaft in Germany, [1947]. 43 p., ports. (Y), mimeo.

Rowne (U). *Rovneh; sefer zikaron* [Rowno; a memorial to the Jewish community of Rowno, Wolyn*]. Ed.: A. Avitihi. [Tel Aviv], "Yalkut Wolyn"—Former Residents of Rowno in Israel, 1956. 591 p., illus., ports., maps, facsims. (H)

YIVO: Rivne 1956   NYPL: *PXV(Rovno)
JTS: DS135 R93 R6 A9   YU: DS135 R93 R6

Rozan (P). *Sefer zikaron li-kehilat Rozan (al ha-Narew)* [Rozhan memorial book*]. Ed.: Benyamin Halevi. [Tel Aviv], Rozhan Societies in Israel and the USA, [1977]. 518, 96 p., illus. (H,Y,E)

YIVO: Rozan 1977   NYPL: *PXV(Rozan) 82-1627
JTS: DS135 P62 R6 S4   YU: DS135 P62 R63

Rozana (P). *Rozinoi; sefer zikaron li-kehilat Rozinoi veha-sevivah* [Rozana; a memorial to the Jewish community*]. Ed.: M. Sokolovski. Israel, Former Residents of Rozinoi in Israel, [1957]. 232 p., illus., ports. (H,Y)

YIVO: Ruzhany 1957   NYPL: *PXW(Ruzhany)
JTS: DS135 R93 R65 S4   HUC: HIW 389
YU: DS135 R93 R8

Rozanka (B) see under Szczuczyn (*Sefer zikaron li-kehilot Szczuczyn, Wasiliszki...*)

Rozhan (P) see Rozan

Rozhinoy (P) see Rozana

Rozhishche (U) see Rozyszcze

Rozhnyativ (U) see Rozniatow

Rozniatow (U). *Sefer zikaron li-kehilat Rozniatov, Prahinsko, Broshnyov, Swaryczow veha-sevivah* [Yizkor-book in memory of Rozniatow, Perehinsko, Broszniow, Swaryczow and environs*]. Ed.: Shimon Kanc. Tel Aviv, Rozniatow, Perehinsko, Broszniow and Environs Societies in Israel, 1974. 537, 58 p., illus., map. (H,Y,E)

YIVO: Rozhnyativ 1974   YU: DS135 R93 R689 1974

Rozprza (P) see under Piotrkow Trybunalski

Rozwadow (P). *Sefer yizkor Rozvadov veha-sevivah* [Rozwadow memorial book*]. Ed.: N. Blumental. Jerusalem, Former Residents of Rozwadow in Israel...America...Belgium, [1968]. 349, xix p., illus., ports. (H,Y,E)

YIVO: Rozwadow 1968   NYPL: *PXV+ (Rozwadow)
JTS: +DS135 P62 R65 S4   YU: DS135 P62 R65

Rozyszcze (U). *Rozishts 'ayarati* [Rozyszcze my old home*]. Ed.: Gershon Zik. Tel Aviv, Rozyszcze Societies in Israel, the USA, Canada, Brazil, and Argentina, 1976. 482, 76 p., illus. (H,Y,E)

YIVO: Rozhishche 1976

Rubeshov (P) see Hrubieszow

Rubezhevichi (B) see Rubiezewicze

Rubiel (B) see under Polesie (region)

Rubiezewicze (B). *Sefer Rubizevits, Derevnah veha-sevivah* [Rubiezewicze and surroundings book*]. Ed.: D. Shtokfish. Tel Aviv, 1968. 423 p., illus., maps. (Y,H)

YIVO: Rubezhevichi & Derevna 1968   JTS: DS135 R93 R77
NYPL: *PXW(Rubezhevichi)

Rubiezewicze (B) see also under Stolpce

Rudki (U). *Rudki; sefer yizkor li-Yehude Rudki veha-sevivah* [Rudki memorial book; of the Jews of Rudki and vicinity*]. Ed.: Josef Chrust (Y. Krust). [Israel], Rudki Society, [1977]. 374 p., illus. (H,Y,E)

YIVO: Rudky 1977   NYPL: *PXW(Rudki) 84-303

Rudky (U) see Rudki

Ruscova (Ro). *Sefer le-zikhron kedoshe Ruskovah ve-Zoblas, Mehoz Marmarosh* [Memorial book of the martyrs of Ruskova and Soblas, Marmarosh District]. Ed.: Y. Z. Moskovits. Tel Aviv, Former Residents of Ruskova and Soblas in Israel and in the Diaspora, [1969]. 128 p., illus., ports., facsims. (H,Y)

YIVO: Ruscova 1969   NYPL: *PXM(Ruscova) 77-1765
JTS: DS135 R72 R85 S4   YU: DS135 R72 R877

Ruzhany (B) see Rozana

Ryki (P). *Yisker-bukh tsum fareybikn dem ondenk fun der horev-gevorener Yidisher kehile Riki* [Ryki; a memorial to the community of Ryki, Poland*]. Ed.: Shimon Kanc. Tel Aviv, Ryki Societies in Israel, Canada, Los Angeles, France, and Brazil, 1973. 611 p., illus. (H,Y)

YIVO: Ryki 1973   NYPL: *PXV(Ryki) 76-2058
JTS: DS135 P62 R93 Y59   HUC: HIW 379

Rypin (P). *Hantsahat kehilat Rypin-Polin* [Dedicated to the Jewish community of Rypin, Poland]. [By a group of students.] Bene Berak, Bet ha-sefer "Komemiyut," [1966]. 64 p., illus., map, ports. (H)

YIVO: Rypin 1966   NYPL: *PXV (Rypin)
JTS: DS135 P62 R82 H3

Rypin (P). *Sefer Ripin* [Ripin; a memorial to the Jewish community of Ripin–Poland*]. Ed.: Sh. Kanc. Tel Aviv, Former Residents of Ripin in Israel and in the Diaspora, 1962. 942 columns, 51 p., ports., facsims. (H,Y,E)

YIVO: Rypin 1962   NYPL: *PXV+ (Rypin)
JTS: DS135 P62 R82 S4   YU: DS135 P62 R867 1962

Rytwiany (P) see under Staszow

Rzeszow (P). *Kehilat Resha; sefer zikaron* [Rzeszow Jews; memorial book*]. Ed.: M. Yaari-Wold. Tel Aviv, Former Residents of Rzeszow in Israel and the USA, 1967. 620, 142 p., illus., ports., maps, facsims. (H,Y,E)

YIVO: Rzeszow 1967   NYPL: *PXV+ (Rzeszow)
JTS: +DS135 P62 R95   YU: DS135 P62 R95

Sahy (Slo). *Orokmecses; Sahy-Ipoolysag [Ipolysag] es kornyeke* [Eternal light; in memory of the Jews of

Ipolysag and vicinity=*Ner tamid; le-zekher Yahadut Ipolysag veha-sevivah**]. Eds.: S. Asher, Gy Gartenzaum. [Kfar Vradim, A.I. Gidron, 1994.] 212, 194 p., illus., map, ports., facsims. (H, Hu)

YIVO: Sahy 1994   NYPL: *PXT 00-7106
YU: NC (In Process)

Saloniki (Gr). *Saloniki; ir va-em be-Yisrael* [Salonique, ville-mère en Israël*]. Jerusalem, Centre de recherches sur le Judaisme de Salonique, Union des Juifs de Grèce, [1967]. 358, xviii p., illus., ports., maps, facsims. (H,F)

YIVO: Thessaloniki 1967   NYPL: *PXM+ (Saloniki, 1967)
JTS: +DS135 G72 S2   HUC: HIW 475
YU: 933.5 G793 T267T 1967

Saloniki (Gr). *Zikhron Saloniki; gedulatah ve-hurbanah shel Yerushalayim de-Balkan* [Zikhron Saloniki; grandeza i destruyicion de Yeruchalayim del Balkan*]. Ed: D. A. Rekanati. Tel Aviv, Committee for the Publication of the Saloniki Book, [1971/72-1985/86]. 2 vols., illus., facsims., ports. (H,J)

YIVO: Thessaloniki 1971   NYPL: *PXM 76-2119
JTS: +DS135 G72 S2 Z5   YU: DS135 G72 T59
HUC: HIW 475

Sambir (U) see Sambor

Sambor (U). *Sefer Sambor-Stari Sambor; pirke edut ve-zikaron li-kehilot Sambor-Stari Sambor me-reshitan ve-ad hurbanan* [The book of Sambor and Stari Sambor; a memorial to the Jewish communities of Sambor and Stari Sambor, the story of the two Jewish communities from their beginnings to their end*]. Ed.: A. Manor. Tel Aviv, Sambor/Stari Sambor Society and vicinity in Israel, 1980. 323, xlvi p., illus. (H,Y,E)

YIVO: Sambir & Staryy Sambir 1980   JTS: DS135 P62 S15 M3
NYPL: *PXV(Sambor) 82-2353   YU: DS135 R93 S147

Samorin (Somorja, Sammerein) (Slo) see under Dunaszerdahely

Sandomierz (P). ʻEt ezkerah: sefer kehilat Tsoizmir (Sandomyez) [Whenever I remember: Memorial book of the Jewish Community in Tzoizmir (Sandomierz)*]. Ed.: Eva Feldenkreiz-Grinbal. Tel Aviv, Association of Tzoyzmir Jews in Israel; Moreshet Publishing, 1993. 586 p., illus., maps, ports, facsims. (H,Y,E)

YIVO: Sandomierz 1993   NYPL: *PXV (Sandomierz) 94-874
JTS: DS135 P62 S154 F4   YU: DS135 P62 S1484 1993

Sanok (P). *Sefer zikaron li-kehilat Sanok veha-sevivah* [Memorial book of Sanok and vicinity]. Ed.: E. Sharvit. [Tel Aviv], Irgun yotse Sanok veha-sevivah be-Yisrael, [1969]. 12, 686 p., illus., music, ports., facsims. (H,Y)

YIVO: Sanok 1969   NYPL: *PXV(Sanok)
JTS: DS135 P62 S16   YU: 933.5 P762 S228

Sanok (P) see also under Dynow (*Hurbn Dynov*)

Sants (P) see Nowy Sacz

Sarkeystsene (Sharkovshchina) (B) see under Glebokie

Sarnaki (P). *Sefer yizkor li-kehilat Sarnaki* [Memorial book of the community of Sarnaki]. Ed.: D. Sobel (Shuval). Haifa, Former Residents of Sarnaki in Israel, 1968. 415 p., illus., map, ports. (H,Y)

YIVO: Sarnaki 1968   NYPL: *PXV(Sarnaki)
JTS: DS135 P62 S2 S4   YU: 933.47(438) S246S

Sarny (U). *Sefer yizkor li-kehilat Sarni* [Memorial book of the community of Sarny]. Ed.: Y. Kariv. Jerusalem, Yad Vashem, [1961]. 508 p., illus., maps, ports., facsims. (H,Y)

YIVO: Sarny 1961   NYPL: *PXW(Sarny)
JTS: DS135 R93 S3   YU: DS135 R93 S3
HUC: HIW 393

Sarny (U) see also under Polesie (region)

Sasiv (U) see Sasow

Sasow (U). *Mayn shtetl Sasov* [My town Sasow]. [By] Mosheh Rafael. [Israel, 1979]. 128p. port. (Y)

YIVO: Sasiv 1979   NYPL: *PXW (Sasov) 94-170

Satmar (Ro) see Satu Mare

Satoraljauhely (Satorujhely) (Hu) see under Zemplen Megye

Satu Mare (Ro). *Zekhor et Satmar: sefer ha-zikaron shel Yehude Satmar* [Remember Satmar; the memorial book of the Jews of Satmar]. Ed.: Naftali Stern. Bnei Brak, [1984]. 160, 240 p., illus., maps, ports. (H,Hu)

NYPL: *PXT+ 89-10893   YU: DS135 R27 5389 1984

Saveni (Ro) see under Dorohoi

Schodnica (U) see under Drohobycz

Schuchin (B) see Szczuczyn

Schutt Szerdahely (Slo) see Dunaszerdahely

Secureni (U) see Sekiryani

Sedziszow (P) see under Wodzislaw

Sejny (P) see under Suwalki

Sekiryani (U). *Sekuryan (Bessarabyah) be-vinyanah uve-hurbanah* [Sekiryani, Bessarabia—alive and destroyed]. Ed.: Z. Igeret. [Tel Aviv, Committee of Former Residents of Sekiryani, 1953 or 1954]. 260 p., illus., ports. (H)

YIVO: Sokyryany 1953   NYPL: *PXW(Sekiryany)

Sekiryany (U) see Sekiryani

Selib (Wsielub) (B) see under Nowogrodek

Selish (U) see Nagyszollos

Selts (Sielec) (B) see under Pruzana

Semezhevo (B) see under Slutsk

Semyatichi (P) see Siemiatycze

Sendishev (Sedziszow) (P) see under Wodzislaw

Sepolno (P) see Sompolno

Serock (P). *Sefer Serotsk* [The book of Serock]. Ed.: M. Gelbart. Tel Aviv, Former Residents of Serock in Israel, 1971. 736 p., illus., ports. (H,Y)

YIVO: Serock 1971   NYPL: *PXV(Serock) 75-3340
JTS: DS135 P62 S4 S4   YU: 933.47(438) S486G

Sevlus (U) see Nagyszollos

Sharkovshchina (Sharkoystsene) (B)   see under Glebokie

Shchedrin (B) see under Bobruisk

Shchuchyn (B) see Szczuczyn

Shchurovichi (U) see under Radziechow

Shebreshin (P) see Szczebrzeszyn

Shedlets (P) see Siedlce

Shelib (Wsielub) (B) see under Nowogrodek

Shemezovo (B) see under Slutsk

Sherpts (P) see Sierpc

Shidlovtse (P) see Szydlowiec

Shimsk (U) see Szumsk

Shkud (Li) see Skuodas

Shpola (U). *Shpolah; masekhet haye Yehudim be-'ayarah* [Shpola; a picture of Jewish life in the town]. [By] David Cohen. [Haifa], Assoc. of Former Residents of Shpola (Ukraine) in Israel, [1965]. 307 p., illus., ports. (H)

YIVO: Shpola 1965   NYPL: *PXW(Shpola)
JTS: DS135 R93 S47   YU: 933.47 S559C

Shransk (P) see Szransk

Shtruvits (Szczurowice) (U) see under Radziechow

Shumen (Bulgaria) see Shumla

Shumla (Bulgaria). *Yehude Bulgaryah—kehilat Shumlah* [The Jews in Bulgaria—The community in Shumla*]. [By] B. Arditi. Tel Aviv, Community Council, [1968]. 179 p., illus., ports. (H)

JTS: DS135 B83 S53   NYPL: *PXM (Arditi, B...)
YU: nc 75-950846

Shumskoye (U) see Szumsk

Shvenchionis (Li) see Swieciany

Siauliai (Li). *Pinkas Shavli: yoman mi-geto Litai, 1941-1944.* By Eliezer Yerushalmi. Jerusalem, Mosad Byalik

Yad va-shem, [1958]. 420 p., illus. (H)

NYPL: *PXV (Siauliai)   JTS: DS135 L52 S5 J47

Siedlce (P). *Oyf di hurves fun mayn heym (Hurbn Shedlets)* [On the ruins of my home; the destruction of Siedlce]. [By] M. Fainzilber. Tel Aviv, Committee of Townspeople, 1952. 260 p., illus., map, ports. (Y)

YIVO: Siedlce 1952   NYPL: *PXV (Siedlce) 01-1156

Siedlce (P). *Sefer yizkor li-kehilat Shedlits* [Memorial book of the community of Siedlce]. Ed.: A. W. Yasni (Jasny). Buenos Aires, Former Residents of Siedlce in Israel and Argentina, 1956. xvi, 813 p., map, ports., facsims. (H,Y)

YIVO: Siedlce 1956   NYPL: *PXV(Siedlce)
YU: 933.543.8 B928

Siedliszcze (P). *Sefer zikaron li-kehilat Shedlishts'eh veha-sevivah* [Memorial book of the community of Siedliszcze and vicinity]. Ed.: B. Haruvi. Tel Aviv, Former Residents of Siedliszcze in Israel, 1970. 360 p., ports., facsims. (H,Y)

YIVO: Siedliszcze 1970   NYPL: *PXV(Siedliszcze) 75-1502
JTS: DS135 P62 S544 S4   YU: DS135 P62 S552275 1970

Sielec (B) see under Pruzana

Siemiatycze (P). *Kehilat Semyatits* [The community of Semiatich*]. Ed.: E. Tash (Tur-Shalom). [Tel Aviv, Assoc. of Former Residents of Semiatich in Israel and the USA, 1965.] 449, xiii p., illus., ports., map, facsims. (H,Y,E)

YIVO: Siemiatycze 1965   NYPL: *PXV(Siemiatycze)
JTS: DS135 P62 S555 T3

Sienkow (U) see under Radziechow

Sierpc (P). *Kehilat Sherpts; sefer zikaron* [The community of Sierpc; memorial book]. Ed.: E. Talmi (Wloka). Tel Aviv, Former Residents of Sierpc in Israel and Abroad, 1959. 11, 603 p., illus., ports., map, facsims. (H,Y)

YIVO: Sierpc 1959   NYPL: *PXV+ (Sierpc)
JTS: DS135 P62 S557 T3   YU: DS135 P62 S9565 1959

Sierpc (P). *Hurbn Sierpc 1939-1945; zikhroynes fun di ibergeblibene landslayt vos gefinen zikh in der Amerikaner Zone in Daytshland* [The destruction of Sierpc 1939-1945; memories of the remnants of the community of Sierpc in the American Zone in Germany]. Eds.: A. Meirantz, H. Nemlich. Munich, Committee of the Former Residents of Sierpc in the American Zone in Germany, 1947. 55 p., ports. (Y)

YIVO (BUND): 94526

Sierpc (P). *Zaml-bukh fun Sherptser sheyres ha-hurbn, 1939-1945* [Collection of Sierpc Holocaust survivors, 1939-1945]. [Germany], Sherpcer Jewish Committee (U.S. Zone, Germany), 1948. 93 p., illus., ports. (Y)

YIVO: Sierpc 1948

Siniawka (B) see under Kleck

Sislevitsh (B) see Swislocz

Skala (U). *Sefer Skalah.* Ed.: Max Mermelstein (Weidenfeld/Videnfeld). New York, Skala Benevolent Society, 1978. 98, 261 p., illus., maps, ports. (H,Y,E)
YIVO: Skala Podilska 1978 JTS: DS135 R93 S5 S4
NYPL: *PXW (Skala-Podolskaya) 78-4402
YU: DS135 R93 S536 1978

Skala-Podilska (U) see Skala

Skalat (U). *Death of a shtetl.* By A. Weissbrod; English trans. arranged by L. Milch and J. Kofler, English text and additional testimonies of witnesses edited by L. Milch. [New York, 1995]. vi, 128 p., illus., maps, ports. "Published (in Yiddish) by the Central Historical Commission of the Central Committee of Liberated Jews in the American Zone of Germany, Munich, 1948." (E)
YIVO: Skalat 1995   NYPL: *PXW (Skalat) 97-2085
JTS: DS135 R93 S5373 W5392 (1995)

Skalat (U). *Es shtarbt a shtetl; megiles Skalat* [Skalat destroyed*]. [By] Abraham Weissbrod (Vaysbrod). Ed.: Y. Kaplan. Munich, Central Historical Commission of the Central Committee of Liberated Jews in the U.S. Zone of Germany, 1948. 184 p., illus., maps, ports. (Y)
YIVO: Skalat 1948   NYPL: *ZP-515
JTS: DS135 R93 S537 W4   YU: 933.47 W342

Skalat (U). *Skalat; kovets zikaron li-kehilah she-harvah ba-Shoah* [Skalat; memorial volume of the community which perished in the Holocaust]. Ed.: H. Bronstein (Bronshtain). [Petah-Tikvah, The Yaacov Krol School and former Residents of Skalat in Israel, 1971. 160 p., illus., ports., facsims. (H)
YIVO: Skalat 1971   NYPL: *PXW (Skalat)
JTS: DS135 R93 S537 S55   YU: DS135 R93 S537

Skarzysko-Kamienna (P). *Skarzisko-Kamiennah sefer zikaron* [The "yischor" book in memoriam of the Jewish community of Skarzysko and its surroundings*]. [Tel Aviv, Skarzysko Society, 1973]. 260 p., illus. (H,Y)
YIVO: Skarzysko Kamienna 1973
NYPL: *PXV+ (Skarzysko) 78-5229

Skarzysko-Kamienna (P). *Zahhor: yad li-kehilat kedoshe Skarzisko Kamiyennah.* Ed.: Yerahmiel Shi'ar. Tel Aviv, Irgun Yotse Skarzysko Kamienna; Moreshet, 1997. 205 p., illus., map, ports. (H)
YIVO: Skarzysko-Kamienna 1997 JTS: DS135 P62 656 Z35 1997
NYPL: *PXV (Skarzysko-Kammienna) 98-246

Skepe (P) see under Lipno

Skierniewice (P). *Sefer Skernivits* [The book of Skierniewice]. Ed.: Y. Perlov. Tel Aviv, Former Resi-

dents of Skierniewice in Israel, 1955. 722 p., illus., maps, ports., facsims. (Y)
YIVO: Skierniewice 1955   NYPL:*PXV (Skierniewice) 75-5640
JTS: DS135 P62 S57 P4   YU: DS135 P62 S57 1955

Sknilow (U) see under Radziechow

Skole (U). *Le-zekher kedoshe Skolah veha-sevivah* [In memorium [sic] to the Jewish community of Skole and neighbouring villages who perished in the Holocaust*]. [Israel], Jewish Committee of Skole in Israel, 1986. 180 p., illus. (H)
NYPL: *PXW+ (Skole) 90-1720

Skole (U) see also under Galicia (*Gedenkbukh Galicia*)

Skuodas (Li). *Kehilat Shekod; kovets zikaron* [Memorial book of Skuodas]. Tel Aviv, Former Residents of Skuodas, [1957 or 1958]. 68 p., illus., ports., facsims. (H,Y)
YIVO: Skuodas 1957   NYPL: *PXV(Skuodas) 84-448
HUC: HIW 564.8

Slobodka (B) see under Braslaw

Slonim (B). *Pinkas Slonim* [Memorial book of Slonim]. Ed.: K. Lichtenstein. Tel Aviv, Former Residents of Slonim in Israel, [1961-1979]. 4 vols., illus., ports. (H,Y,E)
YIVO: Slomin 1961   NYPL: *PXW+ (Slonim)
JTS: DS135 P62 S54 L5   YU: 933.5 R969SP

Slupia (P) see under Ostrowiec

Slutsk (B). *Pinkas Slutsk u-venoteha: Ortseyah, Horke, Hlusk, Hrozovah, Hresk, Vizna, Vrahotin, Timkovits, Luban, Starobin, Staridorogi, Pahust, Kapoli, Rumnovah, Shmezevah* [Slutsk and vicinity memorial book*]. Eds.: N. Hinits, Sh. Nachmani (Nahmani). New York, Yizkor-Book Committee, [1962]. 540 p., illus., ports., maps, facsims. (H,Y,E)
YIVO: Slutsk 1962   NYPL: *PXW (Slutsk)
JTS: DS135 R93 S56 P55   YU: DS135 R93 S57
HUC: HIW 468

Sluzewo (P) see under Wloclawek

Smorgon (B) see Smorgonie

Smorgonie (B). *Smorgon mehoz Vilno; sefer edut ve-zikaron* [Smorgonie, District Vilna; memorial book and testimony]. Ed.: A. Gordon, *et al.* [Tel Aviv], Assoc. of Former Residents of Smorgonie in Israel, 1965. 584 p., illus., map, ports., facsims. (H,Y)
YIVO: Smorgon 1965   NYPL: *PXW (Smorgon)
JTS: DS135 R93 S58   YU: 933.5 L7765

Smotrich (U) see under Kamenets-Podolskiy

Sobibor (P), see under Wlodawa

Soblas (Ro) see under Ruscova

Sobolew (P) see under Laskarzew

Sobota (P) see under Lowicz

Sochaczew (P). *Pinkas Sokhatshev* [Memorial book of Sochaczew]. Eds.: A. Sh. Stein (Shtayn), G. Weissman (Vaysman). Jerusalem, Former Residents of Sochaczew in Israel, [1962]. xii, 843 p., illus., map, ports. (H,Y)
YIVO: Sochaczew 1962   NYPL: *PXV (Sochaczew)
JTS: DS135 P62 S64 F8 1962   YU: DS135 P62 S6

Sofiyivka (Sofyovka) (U) see Zofiowka

Sokal (U). *Sefer Sokal, Tartakov, Varenz, Stoyanov veha-sevivah* [Memorial book of Sokal, Tartakov...and surroundings]. Ed.: A. Chomet (Homet). [Tel Aviv], Former Residents of Sokal and Surroundings, 1968. 576 p., illus., map, ports., facsims. (H,Y)
YIVO: Sokal 1968   NYPL: *PXW(Sokal)
JTS: DS135 R93 S59 S4

Sokolivka (U) see Yustingrad

Sokolka (P). *Sefer Sokolkah* [Memorial book of Sokolka]. Ed.: E. Mishkinski. Jerusalem, The Encyclopaedia of the Jewish Diaspora, [1968]. 768 columns, illus., map, ports., facsims. (H,Y)
YIVO: Sokolka 1968   NYPL: *PXV+ (Sokolka)
JTS: +DS135 P62 S63   YU: DS135 P62 S63

Sokolovka (U) see Yustingrad

Sokolow (P). *In shotn fun Treblinke (Hurbn Sokolov-Podliaski)* [In the shadow of Treblinka*]. [By] S. Polakiewicz (Polyakevitsh). Tel Aviv, Sokolow-Podlaski Society in Israel, [1957]. 167 p. (Y)
YIVO: Sokolow Podlaski 1957   NYPL: *PXV (Polakiewicz, 1957)
JTS: DS135 P62 S65 P6   YU: DS135 P62 S634 1957

Sokolow (P). *Mayn horev shtetl Sokolo; shilderungen, bilder un portretn fun a shtot umgekumene Yidn* [My destroyed town of Sokolow]. [By] Perets Grantstein (Granatshteyn). Buenos Aires, Union Central Israelita Polaca en la Argentina, 1946. 188 p., illus. (Y)
YIVO: Sokolow Podlaski 1946   NYPL: *PXV(Sokolow)
JTS: DS135 P62 S65 G7

Sokolow (P). *Sefer ha-zikaron; Sokolov-Podliask* [Memorial book Sokolow-Podlask]. Ed.: M. Gelbart. Tel Aviv, Former Residents of Sokolow-Podlask in Israel and the USA, [1962]. 758 p., illus., map, ports. (Y,H)
YIVO: Sokolow Podlaski 1962   YU: 933.5 P762S G314
NYPL: *PXV(Sokolow-Podlaski) 75-5625

Sokolow (P). *Yoyvl-bukh gevidmet dem ondenken fun di kdoyshim un martirer fun Sokolov* [Jubilee book dedicated to the memory of the hallowed martyrs of Sokolow*]. Ed.: A. S. Lirick. New York, Sokolower

Young Friends Progressive Aid Society, 1946. 180, 30 p., illus., ports. (Y,E)
YIVO: Sokolow Podlaski 1946

Sokoly (P). *Sefer zikaron li-kedoshe Sokoli* [Memorial book of the martyrs of Sokoly]. Ed.: M. Grosman. [Tel Aviv, 1962]. 625 p., illus., ports. (Y)
YIVO: Sokoly 1962   NYPL: *PXV(Sokoly) 75-3422
JTS: DS135 P62 S64 G76

Sokoly (P). *Sokoli—ba-ma'avak le-hayim* [Sokoly—in a struggle for survival]. Trans. of *Sefer zikaron li-kedoshe Sokoli*. Trans. and ed.: Shmuel Klisher. Tel Aviv, Sokoly Society in Israel, 1975. 438 p., illus. (H)
NYPL: *PXV(Sokoly) 84-375

Sokyryany (Sokyriany) (U) see Sekiryani

Sombor (Sr) see Zombor

Somcuta Mare (Ro) see under Nagybanya

Somorja (Slo) see under Dunaszerdahely

Sompolno (P). *Dape ed shel sarid ha-'ayarah Sompolno* [Pages of witness of the remnants of the town Sompolno]. [By] Y. Kominkovski. Tel Aviv, Alef, 1981. 103 p., illus., ports. (H)
NYPL: *PXK 00-1223   JTS: DS135 P62 S67
YU: DS135 P62 S64 1984

Sonik (P) see Sanok

Sopockinie (B). *Kol adam ve-zikhrono: ayarah, perihatah ve-hurbanah, hayeha, demuyoteha ve-tipusehah: Sopotkin nikra otah...* By Y. Yehezkieli. [Tel Aviv, 1964]. 100 p., illus., port. (H)
NYPL: *PXW (Sopotskin)   JTS: PJ 5054 Y417 K6

Sopockinie (B). *Korot 'ayarah ahat; megilat ha-sigsug veha-hurban shel kehilat Sopotkin* [Sopotkin; in memory of the Jewish community*]. [By] Alexander Manor (Menchinsky). [Tel Aviv], Sopotkin Society in Israel, 1960. 124 p., illus., ports. (H)
YIVO: Sopotskin 1960

Sopotskin (B) see Sopockinie

Sosnovoye (Sosnove) (U) see Ludwipol

Sosnowiec (P). *Sefer Sosnovits veha-sevivah be-Zaglembyah* [Book of Sosnowiec and the surrounding region in Zaglebie]. Ed.: M. S. Geshuri (Brukner). Tel Aviv, Irgun yotse Sosnovits veha-sevivah be-Yisrael, [1973-1974]. 2 vols., illus. (H,Y)
YIVO: Sosnowiec 1974   NYPL: *PXV(Sosnowiec) 85-2020
JTS: DS135 P62 S69 S4   YU: DS135 P62 S657

Stanislawczyk (Stanislavchik) (U) see under Radziechow

Stanislawow (U). *Al horvotayikh Stanislavuv; divre edut le-khilyon kehilat Stanislavov u-sevivatah mipi adei-*

re'iah ve-al-pi teudot [On the ruins of Stanislawow; concerning the annihilation of the community of Stanislawow and vicinity...]. [By] Emmy Weitz (Veyts). Tel Aviv, Vaad yotse Stanislovov be-Erts Yisrael, [1947]. 112 p., illus. (H)

YIVO: Ivano-Frankivsk (Stanislav) 1947   NYPL: *ZP-1106 no.1
JTS: DS135 R93 S79 W45

Stanislawow (U) see also under General Reference Works, *Arim ve-imahot,* vol. 5

Starachowice (P) see under Wierzbnik

Starobin (B) see under Slutsk

Staryi Sambir (Staryy Sambir) (U) see under Sambor

Starye Dorogi (Staryja Darohi) (B) see under Slutsk

Staszow (P). *Sefer Stashov* [The Staszow book*]. Ed.: E. Ehrlich. [Tel Aviv], Former Residents of Staszow in Israel, [1962]. 690 p., illus., map, ports., facsims. (H,Y,E)

YIVO: Staszow 1962   NYPL: *PXV(Staszow)
JTS: DS135 P62 S72 E4   HUC: HIW 362
YU: DS135 P62 S738 1962

Stavische (U). *Stavishtsh.* Ed.: A. Weissman (Vaisman). New York, The Stavisht Society, [1961]. 251 p., illus., ports. (H,Y)

YIVO: Stavyshche 1961   NYPL: *PXW(Stawiszcze) 90-3675
YU: DS135 R93 S66 1961

Stavyshche (U) see Stavische

Stawiski (P). *Stavisk; sefer yizkor* [Stawiski memorial book]. Ed.: Y. Rubin. [Tel Aviv], Stavisk Society in Israel, 1973. 379, v p., illus. (H,Y,E)

YIVO: Stawiski 1973   NYPL: *PXV(Stawiski) 76-2105
JTS: DS135 P62 S737 R8   YU: DS135 P62 S7397 1973

Stawiszcze (U) see Stavische

Stefanesti (Ro). *Mi-Shtefaneshti le-Erets-Yisrael: sipurah shel ayarah* [Din Stefanesti spre Eretz-Israel: saga unui orasel*]. [By] Idel Evron-Nachberg. Haifa: Author, 1989. 181 p., illus., map, ports. (H)

NYPL: *PXM(Stefanesti) 90-3757   YU: DS135 R72 S746 1989

Stepan (U). *Ayaratenu Stepan* [The Stepan Story; excerpts*]. Ed.: Y. Ganuz (Ganusovitch). [Tel Aviv], Irgun yotse Stepan veha-sevivah be-Yisrael, 1977. 4, 364 p., illus., maps, ports. (H,E)

YIVO: Stepan 1977   NYPL: *PXW(Stepan) 89-8310
JTS: DS135 P62 S7385 G3   YU: DS135 R93 S663

Steybts (B) see Stolpce

Stiyanev (Stojanow) (U) see under Sokal

Stoczek-Wegrowski (P). *Pinkes Stok (bay Vengrov); matsevet netsah* [Memorial book of Stok, near Wegrow].

Ed.: Y. Zudicker (Tsudiker). Buenos Aires, Stok Society in Israel, 1974. 654 p., illus. (H,Y)

YIVO: Stoczek 1974   NYPL: *PXV(Stok) 79-1032
JTS: DS135 P62 S74 P55

Stojaciszki (Li) see Swieciany

Stojanow (U) see under Sokal

Stok (P) see Stoczek-Wegrowski

Stolbtsy (B) see Stolpce

Stolin (B). *Albom Stolin* [Stolin album]. Ed.: P. Doron. [Jerusalem, 1960]. 88 p., illus., ports. (H,Y)

YIVO: Stolin 1960

Stolin (B). *Stolin: sefer zikaron li-kehilat Stolin veha-sevivah* [Stolin; a memorial to the Jewish communities of Stolin and vicinity*]. Eds.: A. Avatihi, J. Ben-Zaccai (Zakai). Tel Aviv, Former Residents of Stolin and Vicinity in Israel, 1952. 263 p., illus., map, ports. (H)

YIVO: Stolin 1952   NYPL: *PXW(Stolin)
YU: DS135 R93 S6877 1952   HUC: HIW 382

Stolin (B) see also under Polesie (region)

Stolpce (B). *Sefer zikaron; Stoibts-Sverna veha-ayarot ha-semukhot...* [Memorial volume of Steibtz-Swerznie and the neighbouring villages...*]. Ed.: N. Hinits. [Tel Aviv], Former Residents of Steibtz in Israel, 1964. 537, xxiii p., illus., ports., map, facsims. (H,Y,E)

YIVO: Stolbtsy & Sverzen 1964 NYPL: *PXW(Stolbtsy)
JTS: DS135 R93 S86 H5   YU: DS135 R93 S68

Stoubtsy (B) see Stolpce

Stoyanov (U) see under Sokal

Stropkov (Slo). *Sefer zikron Stropkov: di historye fun der shtot Stropkov: fun zint di kehile hot zikh gegrindet biz dem yor 1914, ven di ershte velt milhome hot oysgebrokhen in unzer dor* [Stropkov memorial book: the history of the town of Stropkov since the founding of the community until the year 1914, the outbreak of WW1*]. By Abraham Abish haKohen Vaynshtayn [Weinstein]. Brooklyn, NY, A. Vaynshtayn, [1967 or 1968]. 61p. (Y)

NYPL: *PXT (Stropkov) 90-2269   JTS: DS135.C96 S7 W4

Stropkov (Slo). *Stropkov memorial book: the history of the town of Stropkov since the founding of the community until the year 1914, the outbreak of WWI.* Translation of *Sefer zikron Stropkov.* By Avraham Abish Weinstein. Brooklyn, NY, A.A. Weinstein,1968. 82 columns. (E)

NYPL: *PXT+ 86-3677

Stropkov (Slo). *Between Galicia and Hungary: the Jews of Stropkov.* By Melody Amsel. Bergenfield, [2002]. 204, 86 p., 40 p. of plates. (H, E).

YIVO: Stropkov 2002   NYPL: *PXT 02-2335

Stramtura (Ro). *Agadot Strimtereh; sipurah shel kehilah Yehudit me-reshitah ve-ad ahritah* [Tales of Strimtera; the story of a Jewish community from beginning to end]. [By] Sh. Avni. Tel Aviv, Reshafim, [1985/86]. 270 p., illus., port. (H)

NYPL: *PXM (Strimtura) 90-2903   JTS: DS135 R93 C26 A9
YU: DS135 R7 S77 1985

Stremiltsh (Strzemilcze; Stremilch) (U) see under Radziechow

Strimtera (Ro) see Stramtura

Strusov (Strusow) (U) see under Trembowla

Stryj (U). *Sefer Stri* [Yizkor book of the Jewish community of Stryj*]. Eds.: N. Kudish *et al.* [Tel Aviv], Former Residents of Stryj in Israel, [1962]. 260, 68 p., map, ports., facsims. (H,Y,E)

YIVO: Stryy 1962   NYPL: *PXW(Stryj)
JTS: DS135 R93 S87   YU: DS135 R93 S83
HUC: HIW 394

Strzegowo (P). *Stshegove yisker-bukh* [Memorial book of Strzegowo]. Ed.: Florence Youkelson. New York, United Strzegower Relief Committee, 1951. 135 p., xi p., ports., facsims. (H,Y,E)

YIVO: Strzegowo-Osada 1951   NYPL: *PXV(Strzegowo)
JTS: DS135 P62 S75 U5   YU: DS135 P62 S747 1951

Strzegowo (P). *Stshegove yizker-bukh: the life and death of a Polish shtetl.* Eds: F. Bisberg-Youkelson, R. Youkelson. Trans. by G. Bluestein. Lincoln, University of Nebraska Press, 2000. xv, 125 p., map. (E)

YIVO: Strzegowo-Osada 2000   JTS: DS135.P62 S746713 2000
YU: DS135 P62 S74713 2000

Stregowo (P). *Pictures related to the life and death of a Polish shtetl.* [By] Aaron M. Bisberg. [Lincoln, 2000]. xv, [16 p.]. (E)

YIVO: Strzegowo-Osada 2000

Strzemilcze (U) see under Radziechow

Strzyzow (P). *Sefer Strizov veha-sevivah* [Memorial book of Strzyzow and vicinity]. Eds.: Y. Berglas, Sh. Yahalomi (Diamant). [Tel Aviv], Former Residents of Strzyzow in Israel and Diaspora, [1969]. 480 p., illus., map, ports., facsims. (H,Y)

YIVO: Strzyzow1969   NYPL: *PXV+ (Strzyzow)
JTS: DS135 P62 S77   YU: 933.5 P762S

Strzyzow (P). *The book of Strzyzow and vicinity.* Eds.: Itzhok Berglass, Shlomo Yahalomi-Diamond; trans.: Harry Langsam. Los Angeles, Harry Langsam, [1990]. viii, 560 p., illus., ports., facsims. (E)

YIVO: Strzyzow 1990   NYPL: *PXV (Strzyzow) 96-2383
JTS: DS135 P62 S7713 1990 YU: DS135 P62 S7513 1990

Sulita (U) see Novoselitsa

Stutshin (B) see Szczuczyn

Sucha Beskidzka (Sucha) (P) see under Wadowice

Suchocin (P) see under Plonsk

Suchowola (P). *Hurbn Sukhovolye; le-zikorn fun a Yidish shtetl tsvishn Byalystok un Grodne* [The Holocaust in Suchowola; in memory of a Jewish shtetl between Bialystok and Grodno]. Ed.: S. Lazar, Sh. Zabludovski. [Mexico, Suchowola Landslayt in Mexico, 1947]. 72 p., illus., ports. (Y)

YIVO: Suchowola 1947   YU: DS135 P62 S757

Suchowola (P). *Sefer Suhovolah* [Memorial book of Suchowola]. Eds.: H. Pribulsky Steinberg *et al.* Jerusalem, The Encyclopaedia of the Jewish Diaspora, [1957]. 616 columns, illus., ports., map, facsims. (H,Y)

YIVO: Suchowola 1957   NYPL: *PXV(Suchowola)
YU: DS135 P62 S8

Suplacu (Ro). *Olami: sefer zikaron li-kehilat Seplak u-gelil Margaretin: le-korot mishpehot Vainberger, Feldman...* By A. T. Ayalon (Weinberger). Bnai Brak, Zikaron - Mif`al le-hantsahat Yahadut Hungaryeah, 1998. 10, 510 p., illus, ports, maps. (H)

NYPL: *PXM (Suplacu) 98-2219   JTS: DS135 R72 S87 1998
YU: DS135 R72 S87 1998

Suplacu de Barcau (Ro) see Suplacu

Suprasl (P). *Hayim u-mavet be-tsel ha-ya'ar: sipurah shel Suprasl ha-Yehudit, 'ayarah be-mizrah Polin* [Life and death in shadow of the forest: the story of Suprasl, a shtetl in Eastern Poland*]. [By] Yaakov Pat (Patt). [Israel, 1991]. 182, 60 p., illus., maps, ports. (H,Y,E)

YIVO: Suprasl 1991   NYPL: *PXV(Suprasl) 92-256
JTS: DS126.33 P379 1991   YU: DS135 P62 S8356 1991

Suwalki (P). *Sefer kehilat Suvalk u-venotehah* [Jewish community book Suwalk and vicinity: Baklerove, Filipove, Krasnopole, Punsk, Ratzk, Vizhan, Yelineve*]. Eds.: Yehuda Elroi, Yosef Chrust (Krust). Tel Aviv, The Yair-Abraham Stern Publishing House, 1989. 446, 86 p., illus., maps, ports. (H,E)

YIVO: Suwalki 1989   NYPL: *PXV(Suwalki) 90-5658
HUC: DS135 P62 S8581 1989   YU: DS135 P62 S856 1989

Suwalki (P). *Yisker-bukh Suvalk un di arumike shtetlekh: Baklerove, Vizshan, Yelineve, Sayni, Punsk, Psherasle, Filipove, Krasnefalye, Ratsk* [Yizkor book: Suwalki and vicinity]. Ed.: B. Kahan [Kagan]. New York, The Suvalk and Vicinity Relief Committee, [1961]. 825 columns, illus., ports., facsims. (Y)

YIVO: Suwalki 1961   NYPL: *PXV(Suwalki) 84-229
JTS: DS135 P62 S8 K3   YU: DS135 P62 S858

Svencionys (Li) see Swieciany

Sverzen (B) see under Stolpce

349

Svir (B) see Swir

Svisloch (B) see Swislocz

Swaryczow (U) see under Rozniatow

Swieciany (Li). *Sefer zikaron le-esrim ve-shalosh kehilot she-nehrevu be-ezor Shventsion* [Svintzian Region; memorial book of twenty-three Jewish communities*]. Ed.: Sh. Kanc. Tel Aviv, Former Residents of the Svintzian District in Israel, [1965]. 1954 columns, illus., ports., map, music, facsims. (H,Y)

YIVO: Svencioys 1965   NYPL: *PXW+ (Shvenchionis)
JTS: +DS135 L5 S85 K3   YU: DS135 R93 S89 1965

Swierzen (B) see under Stolpce

Swir (B). *Ayaratenu Svir* [Our townlet Swir*]. Ed.: H. Svironi (Drutz). Tel Aviv, Former Residents of Swir in Israel, 1959. 240 p., illus., ports., map (H,Y)

YIVO: Svir 1959   NYPL: *PXW (Swir) 76-2191
JTS: DS135 R93 S94 S9

Swir (B). *Hayoh haytah 'ayarat Svir; ben shete milhemot ha-olam* [There once was a town Swir; between the two world wars]. [By] H. Vayner (Vainer). [Kfar Saba], Swir Society in Israel, [1975]. 227 p., illus. (H,Y)

YIVO: Svir 1975   NYPL: *PXV (Svir) 77-3730
JTS: DS135 R93 S944 V35   YU: DS135 R93 S92

Swislocz (B). *Kehilat Swislots pelekh Grodno* [The community of Swisocz, Grodno District]. Ed.: H. Rubin. [Tel Aviv,] Former Residents of Swislocz in Israel, [1960 or 1961]. 159 p., illus., ports. (H,Y)

YIVO: Svisloch 1960   NYPL: *PXW (Svisloch) 88-467
YU: DS135 R93 S93 1960

Swislocz (B). *Sefer Swislocz* [Swislocz book], [vol.] 2. Ed.: Y. Lifshits. Netanya, Former Residents of Swislocz in Israel, 1984. 289 p., illus., facsims., maps, ports. (H)

Swislocz (B) see also under Wolkowysk (*Volkovisker yisker-bukh*)

Szamosujvar (Ro). *Sefer zikaron shel kedoshe ayarotenu Samoshuivar-Iklod veha-sevivah...* [Memorial book of the martyrs of our town Szamosujvar-Iklad and surroundings]. Eds.: M. Bar-On, *et al.* [Tel Aviv, Former Residents of Szamosujvar-Iklad and Surroundings in Israel, 1971]. 190, 90 p., illus., ports., facsims. (H,Hu)

YIVO: Gherla 1971   NYPL: *PXM (Sefer Zikaron...)
JTS: DS135 R72 G46 S4   YU: DS135 R72 G457

Szarkowszczyzna (B) see under Glebokie

Szatmarnemeti (Ro) see Satu Mare

Szczawnica (P) see under Nowy Targ

Szczebrzeszyn (P). *Sefer zikaron li-kehilat Shebreshin* [Book of memory to the Jewish community of Shebre-

shin*]. Ed.: Dov Shuval. Haifa, Association of Former Inhabitants of Shebreshin in Israel and the Diaspora, 1984. 518, xiv p., illus., maps, ports. (Y,H,E)

YIVO: Szczebrzeszyn 1984   YU: DS135 P62 S877 1984
NYPL: *PXV (Szczebrzeszyn) 89-8558

Szczekociny (P). *Pinkas Shatskutsin* [A memorial book to the Jewish community of Szczekociny*]. Ed.: Y. Shvaytser (Schweizer). Tel Aviv, Former Residents of Szczekociny in Israel, 1959. 276 p., illus., ports. (H,Y)

YIVO: Szczekociny 1959

Szczuczyn (District Bialystok) (B). *Hurban kehilat Shtsutsin* [The destruction of the community of Szczuczyn]. Tel Aviv, Former Residents of Szczuczyn in Israel, 1954. 151 p., illus., ports. (Y)

YIVO: Shchuchin 1954   NYPL: *PXW (Shchuchin) 77-3675

Szczuczyn (B). *Sefer zikaron li-kehilot Shtsutsin, Vasilishki, Ostrin, Novidbor, Rozanke.* [Memorial book of the communities Szczuczyn...]. Ed.: L. Losh. Tel Aviv, Former Residents of Szczuczyn, Wasiliszki..., 1966. 456 p., illus., ports., map, facsims. (H,Y)

YIVO: Ostryna 1966   NYPL: *PXW (Shchuchin)
YU: DS135 R93 S43 1966

Szczurowice (U) see under Radziechow

Szekesfehervar (Hu). *Zahor: Sefer zikaron li-kehilot Sekeshfehervar veha-sevivah* [Remember: The Jews of Szekesfehervar and its environs*]. Eds.: E. Even, B. Ravid. Jerusalem, 1997. 247, 131 p., illus. (H,E,Hu)

YIVO: Szekesfehervar 1997   NYPL:*PXT (Szekesfehervar) 98-951
JTS: DS135 H92 S89 Z35

Szereszow (B) see under Pruzana

Szikszo (Hu). *Nitsotsot—mi-kehilat Siksa u-mehoz Abaui-Torna she-nidmu...* ["Orok fenyck" = Sparks; from the community of Szikszo and the region of Abauj Turna]. [By] I. Fleishman. Bnei Brak, [1971 or1972]. 374, 96 p., illus. (H,Hu)

YIVO: Abauj-Torna Megye 1972   NYPL: *PXT 86-2010
JTS: DS135 H92 S93 F5   YU: DS135 H92 A236 1972

Szkudy (Li) see Skuodas

Szransk (P). *Kehilat Shrensk veha-sevivah; sefer zikaron* [The Jewish community of Szrensk and the vicinity; a memorial volume*]. Ed.: Y. Rimon (Granat). Jerusalem, [Former Residents of Szrensk], 1960. 17, 518, 70 p., illus., ports., maps, facsims. (H,Y,E)

YIVO: Szrensk 1960   NYPL: *PXV(Szrensk) 82-1598
YU: DS135 P62 S94 1960

Szrensk (P) see Szransk

Szumsk (U). *Shumsk: sefer zikaron li'kedoshe Shumsk she-nispu be sho'at ha-natsim bi-shenat 1942.* [Shumsk: memorial book to the martyrs of Shumsk who died during the Nazi Holocaust]. Eds.: Hayim Rabin, Refael Sapir, Pesah Lerner. [Tel Aviv, Former Residents of Szumsk in Israel, 1968]. 477 p., illus., facsims, map, ports. (H,Y)

YIVO: Shumsk 1968   NYPL: *PXW(Shumskoye)
JTS: DS135 R93 S495   YU: 933.5 R9695

Szurdok (Ro) see Stramtura

Szydlow (P) see under Staszow

Szydlowiec (P). *Shidlovtser yisker-bukh* [Yizkor book Szydlowiec*]. Ed.: Berl Kagan (Kohen). New York, Shidlovtser Landsmanshaft in New York, 1974. vii, 912, 22 p., illus., maps, ports. (Y,E)

YIVO: Szydlowiec 1974   NYPL: *PXV(Szydlowiec) 76-5553
JTS: DS135 P62 S957 K34   YU: DS135 P62 S9572 1974

Szydlowiec (P). *Memorial book Szydlowiec.* Ed.: Berl Kagan; trans. from Yiddish: Max Rosenfeld. New York, Shidlowtzer Benevolent Association in New York, 1989. 349 p., [43] p. of plates, illus., map, ports. (E)

YIVO: Szydlowiec 1989   NYPL: *PXV(Szydlowce) 90-795
JTS: DS135 P62 S8 S4 1989   YU: DS135 P62 S957 2513 1989
HUC: DS135 P62 S957 2513 1989

Tacovo (U) see Tiacevo

Targowica (U). *Sefer Trovits* [Memorial book of Targovica*]. Ed.: Y. Zigelman. Haifa, Former Residents of Targovica in Israel, 1967. 452 p., illus., ports., map, facsims. (H,Y)

YIVO: Torhovytsya 1967   NYPL: *PXW (Torgovitsa)
JTS: DS135 R93 T64   YU: 933.5 R969T

Targu-Lapus (Magyarlapos) (Ro) see under Des

Targu-Mures (Ro) see Marosvasarhely

Tarnobrzeg (P). *Kehilat Tarnobzeg-Dzikov (Galitsyah ha-ma'aravit)* [The community of Tarnobrzeg-Dzikow (Western Galicia)]. Ed.: Y. Y. Fleisher (Flaisher). Tel Aviv, Tarnobrzeg-Dzikow Society in Israel, 1973. 379 p., illus. (H,Y)

YIVO: Tarnobrzeg & Dzikow 1973   JTS: +DS135 P62 T37 K44
NYPL: *PXV+ (Tarnobrzeg) 77-3795

Tarnogrod (P). *Yisker-bukh: nokh der horev-gevorener Yidisher kehile Tarnogrod.* [Sefer Tarnogrod Memorial book Tarnogrod*]. Ed.: Sh. Kanc (Kants). Tel Aviv, Organization of Former Residents of Tarnogrod in Israel, 1966. 592 p.,illus., maps, ports. (H,Y)

YIVO: Tarnogrod, 1966

Tarnopol (U). *Tarnopol* [Tarnopol volume*]. Ed.: Ph. Korngruen (Korngrin). Jerusalem, The Encyclopaedia of the Jewish Diaspora, [1955.] 439 columns, illus., ports., facsims. (H,Y,E)

YIVO: Ternopil (Entsiklopedya...) 1955   NYPL: *PX+ 96-485 v.3
JTS: Ref +DS135 E8 E55 v.3

Tarnow (P). *Tarne; kiem un-hurban fun a Yidisher shtot* [The life and decline of a Jewish city]. Ed.: A. Khomet (Humet). Tel Aviv, Association of Former Residents of Tarnow, 1954-1968. 2 vols. (xx, 928, 433 p.), illus., ports., facsims., map (H,Y)

YIVO: Tarnow 1954   NYPL: *PXV(Tarnow)
JTS: DS135 P62 T34   YU: 933.5 P762T V.2

Tartakow (Tartakov) (U) see under Sokal

Tasnad (Ro). *Tashnad; te'ur histori le-zekher kehilat Tashnad (Transilvanyah) veha-sevivah vi-yeshivat Maharam Brisk, me-reshitan ve-ad le-ahar yeme ha-Shoah* [Tasnad; description, in memory of the community of Tasnad (Transylvania) and the surrounding region, and the Brisk Yeshiva, from their beginnings until after the Holocaust]. [By] Avraham Fuks (Fuchs). Jerusalem, 1973. 276 p., illus. (H)

YIVO: Tasnad 1973   NYPL: *PXR 75-2347
JTS: DS135 R72 T373 F8   YU: DS135 R72 T378

Tecso (U) see Tiacevo

Teglas (Hu) see under Debrecen

Telc (Ro). *Telts: toldot kehilah Yehudit be-mordot ha-Karpatim: yesodah, hayeha ve-hurbanah.* By Yehezkel Harpanes. Jerusalem, Feldhaim, [1989 or 1990]. 2 v. [705 p.], illus., ports. (H)

YIVO: /83208   NYPL: *PXT (Telc) 90-1185
YU: DS135 R72 T442 1989   JTS: DS135 C96 T34 H3 1990

Telechany (B). *Telekhan* [Telekhan memorial book*]. Ed.: Sh. Sekuler. Los Angeles, Telekhan Memorial Book Committee, 1963. 189, 15 p., illus., ports., map (H,Y,E)

YIVO: Telekhany 1963   NYPL: *PXW(Telekhany)
YU: DS135 R93 T45

Telciu (Ro) see Telc

Telenesti-Targ (M). *Ha-ayara ha-ketana she-be-Bessarabyah; le-zekher Teleneshti - ayaratenu* [A small town in Bessarabia; in memory of our town Telenesti]. Ed.: R. Fels. Kefar Habad, Bet ha-sefer li-defus "Yad ha-Hamisha," 1981. 127, [25] p., illus., map, ports. (H,Y)

Telenesti (M). *Pinkas Teleneshti: sefer-zikaron li-Yehude Teleneshti-Besarabyah* [Ondenkbuk far di Yidn fun Teleneshti*]. Eds.: Aryeh Horshi and Alter Hartsuvski Tel Aviv, Irgun yotse Teleneshti be-Yisrael, 1982. 345 p., illus., maps, ports. (H,Y)

YIVO: Telenesti 1982

Telsiai (Li). *Sefer Telz (Lita); matsevet zikaron li-kehilah kedoshah* [Telsiai book*]. Ed.: Yitzhak Alperovits. Tel Aviv, Telz Society in Israel, 1984. 505 p., illus., map, ports. (H,Y)

YIVO: Telsiai 1984   NYPL: *PXV (Telsiai) 88-518
JTS: +DS135 L52 T4 A4   YU: DS135 R93 T454 1984

Telz (Li) see Telsiai

Teplik (U). *Teplik, mayn shtetele; kapitlen fun fuftsik yor lebn* [My town Teplik; chapters from fifty years of life]. [By] Valentin Chernovetzky. Buenos Aires, El Magazine Argentino, 1946-1950. 3 vols., illus. (Y)
YIVO: Teplyk 1946 (v.1); Teplyk 1950 (v. 2)   NYPL: 16841
JTS: DS135 R93 T46 C45

Terebovlya (U) see Trembowla

Ternivka (U) see Ternovka

Ternopil (U) see Tarnopol

Ternovka (U). *Ayaratenu Ternovkah; pirke zikaron u-matsevah* [Our town Ternovka; chapters of remembrance and a monument]. [By] G. Bar-Zvi (Tsevi). Jerusalem, Ternovka Society, [1970]. 103 p., illus. (H)
YIVO: Ternivka 1970   NYPL: *XMH - 1061
JTS: DS135 R93 T47   YU: DS135 R93 T47

Tetsh (U) see Tiacevo

Thessaloniki (Gr) see Saloniki

Tiacevo (U). *Tapuah: kovets peratim mitoledot kehilat Tetsh* [Apple: collection of names and details from the history of the Jewish community of Tetsh]. [Collected and edited by] Yitshak Gershuni. Be'er Sheva, Igad yotse Tetsh veha-sevivah...be-Yisreal, [1987-1994]. 496 p., illus., maps, ports. (H)
YIVO: Tyachiv 1987   JTS: DS135 R93 T538 (1987)

Tighina (M) see Bendery

Tiktin (P) see Tykocin

Timkovichi (B) see under Slutsk

Tirgu Lapus (Ro) see Des

Tirgu-Mures (Ro) see Marosvasarhely

Tishevits (P) see Tyszowce

Tlumach (U) see Tlumacz

Tlumacz (U). *Tlumats=Tolmitsh=Tlumacz; sefer edut ve-zikaron* [Memorial book of Tlumacz*]. Eds.: S. Blond *et al.* Tel Aviv, Tlumacz Society in Israel, [1976]. 533, 188, clxxxvii p., illus. (H,Y,E)
YIVO: Tlumach 1976   NYPL:*PXW(Tlumach)77-3790
JTS: DS135 R93 T55 B55   YU: DS135 R93 T577

Tluste (U). *Sefer Tlustah* [Memorial book of Tluste]. Ed.: G. Lindenberg. [Tel Aviv,] Association of Former Residents of Tluste and Vicinity in Israel and USA, 1965. 289 p., illus., ports., map, facsims. (H,Y)
YIVO: Tovste 1965   NYPL: *PXW(Tolstoye)
JTS: DS135 R93 T6   YU: DS135 R93 T687 1965

Tluszcz (P). *Sefer zikaron li-kehilat Tlushtsh* [Memorial book of the community of Tluszcz]. Ed.: M. Gelbart. Tel Aviv, Association of Former Residents of Tluszcz in Israel, 1971. 340 p., illus. (H,Y)
YIVO: Tluszcz 1971   NYPL: *PXV(Tluszcz)
JTS: DS135 P62 T55   YU: DS135 P62 S477 1971

Tolmitsh (U) see Tlumacz

Tolstoye (U) see Tluste

Tomaszow-Lubelski (P). *Sefer zikaron shel Tomashov-Lub.* [Memorial book of Tomaszow-Lubelski]. Ed.: M. Gordon. [Jerusalem, 1972]. 28, 549 p., illus. (H)
YIVO: Tomaszow Lubelski 1972   JTS: DS135 P62 T654
NYPL: *PXV(Tomaszow) 76-5720 YU: DS135 P62 T641 1972

Tomaszow-Lubelski (P). *Tomashover (Lubelski) yisker-bukh* [Memorial book of Tomaszow Lubelski]. Brooklyn, Tomashover Relief Committee, 1965. 912 p., illus., ports., facsims. (Y)
YIVO: Tomaszow Lubelski 1965   YU: DS135 P62 T65
NYPL: *PXV(Tomaszow Lubelski) JTS: DS135 P62 T6 T64

Tomaszow Mazowiecki (P). *Sefer zikaron li-kehilat Tomashov Mazowietsk* [Tomashow-Mazowieck; a memorial to the Jewish community of Tomashow-Mazovieck*]. Ed.: M. Wajsberg. [Tel Aviv], Tomashow Organization in Israel, 1969. 648 p., illus., ports., map, facsims. (H,Y,E,F)
YIVO: Tomaszow Mazowiecki 1969   JTS: +DS135 P62 T67
NYPL: *PXV+ (Tomaszow Mazowiecki)   YU: 933.5 P762T 1969

Tomaszow Mazowiecki (P). *Bet ha-'almin ha-Yehudi be-Tomashov-Mazovyetskl: sikum peulot hantsahah* 756 [Jewish cemetery]. Ed.: Benjamin Yaari-Wald. [Israel], Irgun yots'e Tomaszov Mazowyetski be-Yisrael, 1996. 127 p., xlix p., illus. (H, E, P)
NYPL: *PXV (Tomaszow-Mazowiecki) 98-64
YU: DS135 P62 T645 1996

Topolcany (Slo). *Korot mekorot li-kehilah Yehudit-Topoltsani* [The story and source of the Jewish community of Topoltchany*]. [By] Y. R. Buchler. [Lahavot Haviva], Topolcany Book Committee in Israel, 1976. 74, 174, [44] p., illus. (H,E,G)
YIVO: Topolcany 1976   NYPL: *PXT(Topolcany) 83-380
JTS: DS135 C96 T6 B8   YU: DS135 C96 T663 1976

Topolcany (Slo). *Topolcany: the story of a perished ancient community.* [By] Yehoshua Robert Buchler. Lahavot Haviva, 1989. [30] p. (E)

Toporow (Toporov) (U) see under Radziechow

Torczyn (U). *Le-zikhron 'olam fun di umgekumene kdoyshim fun dem Idishen yishuv in Tortshin... "Yisker" bukh fun Torczyn* [Torchin, our lost but not forgotten town*]. Brooklyn, Torchiner-Woliner Young Men's Assoc., 1948. 1 vol., illus., ports., maps (E,Y)

YIVO: Torchyn 1948

Torhovytsya (Torgovitsa) (U) see Targowica

Torna (Galicia) (P) see Tarnow

Torna (Turna nad Bodvou) (Slo) see Turna

Torun (Karpatalja) (P). *Ayarah she-hayetah: Torun sheba-Karpatim* [A town that once was: Torun in the Carpathians]. [By] Yosef Ha-Gelili (Fikl). Tel Aviv, Moreshet, 1956. 179 p., illus., ports. (H)

YIVO: Torun 1956

Tovste (U) see Tluste

Trakai (Li) see Troki

Trembowla (U). *Sefer yizkor li-kehilot Trembovlah, Strusov ve-Yanow veha-sevivah* [Memorial book for the Jewish communities of Trembowla, Strusow, Janow and vicinity*]. Bnai Brak, Trembowla Society and vicinity, [1981]. 379, li p., illus., maps (H,E)

YIVO: Terebovlya 1981   NYPL: *PXW(Terebovlia) 87-6491
YU: DS135 R93 T467   HUC: DS135 R93 T467

Trisk (U) see Turzysk

Trokhenbrod (U) see Zofiowka

Troki (Li). *Troki.* Tel Aviv, [1954]. 79 p., map (H)

YIVO: Trakai 1954

Trovits (U) see Targowica

Trzebinia (P). *Kehilat Tshebin* [The community of Trzebinia*]. Eds.: P. Goldwasser *et al.* Haifa, Committee of Trzebinians in Israel, 1969. 21, 435, 35 p., ports., map, facsims. (H,E)

Tshebin (P) see Trzebinia

Tshekhanov (P) see Ciechanow

Tshekhanovets (P) see Ciechanowiec

Tshenstokhov (P) see Czestochowa

Tsheshanov (P) see Cieszanow

Tshizheva (P) see Czyzewo

Tshmelev (Cmielow) (P) see under Ostrowiec

Tsoyzmir (P) see Sandomierz

Tuchyn (U) see Tuczyn

Tuczyn (U). *Sefer zikaron li-kehilat Tutshin-Kripeh* [Tutchin-Krippe, Wolyn; in memory of the Jewish community*]. Ed.: B. H. Ayalon. Tel Aviv, Tutchin and Krippe Relief Society of Israel, 1967. 384 p., illus., ports., map, facsims. (H,Y)

YIVO: Tuchyn 1967   NYPL: *PXW (Tuchin)
JTS: +DS135 R93 T75 A9   YU: Folio 933.5 R969T 1967

Tuczyn (U). *Yehude Tutsin u-Kripeh mul rotshehem: 'esrim ve-arba' 'eduyot* [Jews of Tuchin and Kripa in front of their murderers*]. Comp.: A. Sadeh; ed.: L. Deror. Tel Aviv, Council of Emigrants from Tuczyn-Kripa; Moreshet, 1990. 160 p., illus., maps, ports. (H)

YIVO: Tuchyn 1990   NYPL: *PXW (Tuchyn) 98-918
JTS: DS135 U42 T8 Y4

Turbin (P) see Turobin

Turcz (Ro) see Halmi

Turek (P). *Sefer zikaron li-kehilat Turek veli-kedosh-eha* [Turek: a memorial to the Jewish community of Turek, Poland*]. Tel Aviv, The Turek Society in Israel, 1982. 450, xviii p., illus. (H,Y,E)

YIVO: Turek 1982   NYPL: *PXV (Turek) 93-574

Turets (B) see Turzec

Turiysk (U) see Turzysk

Turka (U). *Turkah: sefer zikaron* [*Sefer zikaron li-kehilat Turka al nehar Stryj veha-sevivah* = Memorial book of the community of Turka on the Stryj River and vicinity]. Ed.: Y. Zigelman. (Siegelman), Haifa, Former Residents of Turka (Stryj) in Israel, 1966. 472 p., illus., ports., map, facsims. (H,Y)

YIVO: Turka 1966   NYPL: *PXW (Turka)
JTS: DS135 R93 T8   YU: 933.5 R969T S571

Turna (Slo). *Torna - Turna n/Bodvou; zsidósága* [The Jews of Torna]. Ed.: H. Gasner-Gutmann. [Israel, 197-/8-]. 321-384 p., illus., ports. (Hu)

Turna (Slo). *K. K. Turna veha-sevivah.*]. Eds.: Y. Gutmann, H. Gasner-Gutmann, *et al.* [Israel, h. mo. l., 1995] 76 p., illus. (H)

NYPL: *PXT (Turna) 97-1093   JTS: DS135 S552 T686
YU: DS135 C96 T755 1990Z

Turna nad Bodvou (Slo) see Turna

Turobin (P). *Sefer Turbin; pinkas-zikaron* [The Turobin book; in memory of the Jewish community*]. Ed.: M. S. Geshuri. Tel Aviv, Former Residents of Turobin in Israel, 1967. 397 p., illus., ports., map, facsims. (H,Y)

YIVO: Turobin 1967   NYPL: *PXV (Turobin)
JTS: DS135 P62 T86

Turt (Ro) see under Halmi

Turzec (B). *Kehilot Turzets ve-Yeremits; sefer zikaron* [Book of remembrance—Tooretz-Yeremitz*]. Eds.: M. Walzer-Fass (Valtser-Fas), M. Kaplan. Israel, Turzec and Jeremicze Societies in Israel and America, 1978. 421, 114 p., illus., ports. (H,Y,E)

YIVO: Turets & Yeremichi 1978   NYPL: *PXW (Turets) 89-8382
JTS: DS135 R93 T88 K4   YU: DS135 R93 T784

Turzysk (U). *Pinkas ha-kehilah Trisk; sefer yizkor* [Memorial book of Trisk]. Ed.: Natan Livneh. Tel Aviv, Trisk Society in Israel, 1975. 376 p., illus. (H,Y)

YIVO: Turiysk 1975   NYPL: *PXW (Turiysk) 78-463
JTS: DS135 R93 T785 P55

Tyachevo (Tyachiv) (U) see Tiacevo

Tykocin (P). *Pinkes Tiktin* [Anshe Tiktin historical book; Pincus Tiktin, Tiktiner historical book*]. Ed.: Moshe Toltshin; comp.: Alter Hoffman. Chicago, Anshe Tiktin, [1949]. 100, [28], 59 p., illus. (Y,E)

YIVO: Tykocin 1949

Tykocin (P). *Sefer Tiktin* [Memorial book of Tiktin]. Eds.: M. Bar-Yuda, *et al.* Tel Aviv, Former Residents of Tiktin in Israel, [1959]. 606 p., illus., ports., facsims. (H)

YIVO: Tykocin 1959   NYPL: *PXV (Tykocin)
JTS: DS135 P62 T92

Tysmienica (U). *Tismenits: matseyve oyf di hurves fun a farnikhteter Yidisher kehileh* [Tysmienica; a memorialbook*]. Ed.: Shlomo Blond. Tel Aviv, Ha-Menorah, 1974. 262 p., illus. (H,Y)

YIVO: Tysmenitsya 1974   NYPL: *PXW(Tysmonitsa) 78-491
JTS: DS135 R93 T933 B55

Tysmenitsya (Tysmenytsia) (U) see Tysmienica

Tyszowce (P). *Pinkes Tishivits* [Tiszowic book*]. Ed.: Y. Ziper. Tel Aviv, Association of Former Residents of Tiszowic in Israel, 1970. 324 p., illus., map, ports., facsims. (H,Y)

YIVO: Tyszowce 1970   NYPL: *PXV (Tyszowce)
JTS: DS135 P62 T98

Ubinie (U) see under Radziechow

Ugnev (Uhniv) (U) see Uhnow

Uhnow (U). *Sefer zikaron li-kehilat Hivniv (Uhnow) veha-sevivah* [Hivniv (Uhnow) memorial book*]. Ed. N. Ortner. Tel Aviv, Irgun yotse Uhnow veha-sevivah in Israel, 1981. 298, 83 p., illus. (H. E)

YIVO: Ugnev 1981   NYPL: *PXW (Ugnev) 84-304
YU: DS135 R93 U286

Ujhely (Satorujhely) (Hu) see under Zemplen Megye

Ujpest (Hu). *Az ujpesti zsidóság története= Sefer zikhronot shel k(ehila) k(edosha) Uipesht* [Memorial book of the community of Ujpest]. [By]

Laszlo Szilagyi-Windt; Hebrew translation: M. Miron. Tel Aviv, 1975. 325, 27 p., illus., ports. (H,Hu)

YIVO: Ujpest (Budapest) 1975   NYPL: *PXT 89-7534
JTS: DS135 H92 U52 S9

Ungvar (U). *Shoat Yehude Rusyah ha-Karpatit- Uzhorod* [The Holocaust in Carpatho-Ruthenia-Uzhorod]. [By] Dov Dinur. Jerusalem, Section for Holocaust Research, Institute of Contemporary Jewry, Hebrew University of Jerusalem; World Union of Carpatho-Ruthenian Jews; and Hebrew Schools, [1983]. 6, 123, 15 p., facsims. (H)

NYPL: *PXW (Uzhgorod) 90-3718   JTS: DS135 R93 C26 D53
YU: DS135 R93 U953 1983

Ungvar (U). *Ungvar.* By Yehuda Spiegel. Tel Aviv, Y. Shpigel (Spiegel), [1993]. 279, 48 p., illus. (H).

NYPL: *PXW (Uzhgorod) 94-875   JTS: DS135 U42 U937

Ungvar (U) see also General Reference Works, *Arim ve-imahot,* vol. 4

Urechye (Urecca) (B) see under Slutsk

Uscilug (U). *Kehilat Ustilah be-vinyanah uve-hurbanah* [The growth and destruction of the community of Uscilug]. Ed.: A. Avinadav. [Israel], Association of Former Residents of Uscilug, [1961]. 334 p., illus., ports. (H,Y)

YIVO: Ustilug 1961   ·   NYPL: *PXW(Ustilug) 89-8566
YU: DS135 R93 U884 1961

Ustila (U) see Uscilug

Ustrzyki Dolne (P) see under Lesko

Ustyluh (U) see Uscilug

Utena (Li). *Yisker-bukh Utian un umgegent* [Memorial book of Utyan and vicinity]. Tel Aviv, [Nay Lebn], 1979. 296 p., illus., ports. (Y)

YIVO: Utena 1979

Utyan (Utian) (Li) see Utena

Uzhhorod (Uzhgorod) (U) see Ungvar; see also under General Reference Works, *Arim ve-imahot,* vol. 4;

Uzlovoye (Cholojow) (U) see under Radziechow

Valkininkas (Li) see Olkeniki

Valozhyn (B) see Wolozyn

Vamospercs (Hu) see under Debrecen

Varenz (U) see under Sokal

Vas (Hu). *Sefer zikaron mehoz Vas* [Memorial book of the region of Vas]. Ed.: Avraham Lowinger. [Jaffa], Vas Commemorative Committee, 1974. 214 p., illus. (H, Hu)

YIVO: Vas Megye 1974   NYPL: *PXT 77-3365

Vas Megye (Hu) see Vas

Vashilkov (P) see Wasilkow

Vashniev (Wasniow) (P) see under Ostrowiec

Vasilishok (P) see Wasiliszki

Vaukavysk (B) see Wolkowysk

Vayslits (P) see Wislica

Velky Mager (Nagymagyar) (Slo) see under Dunaszerdahely

Velyki Mosty (U) see Mosty-Wielkie

Vengrov (P) see Wegrow

Venice (Italy) see under General Reference Works, *Arim ve-imahot,* vol. 4

Verbo (Slo) see under Postyen

Verkhutina (B) see under Slutsk

Verzhbnik (P) see Wierzbnik

Vidz (Vidzy) (B) see Widze

Vileyka (Vileikas) (B) see Wilejka

Vilna (Li). *Bleter vegn Vilne; zamlbukh* [Pages about Vilna; a compilation]. Eds.: L. Ran, L. Koriski. Lodz, Association of Jews from Vilna in Poland, 1947. 77, xvii p., illus., ports., music, facsims. (Y)
YIVO: Vilnius 1947   NYPL: *ZP-1105 No. 11
JTS: DS135 R93 V5 R35

Vilna (Li). *Vilner zamlbukh - measef Vilnah* [Vilna collection*]. Ed.: Yisrael Rodnitski. Tel Aviv, World Federation of Jews from Vilna and Vicinity in Israel, [1974]. 140 p., illus., facsims. (Y,H)
YIVO: Vilnius 1974   NYPL: *PXV (Vilma) 99-2457

Vilna (Li). *Yerusholayim de-Lita* [Jerusalem of Lithuania, illustrated and documented*]. Collected and arranged by Leyzer Ran. New York, Vilna Album Committee, 1974. 3 vols., illus. (H,Y,E,R)
YIVO: Vilnius 1974   NYPL: *PXW+ (Vilna) 76-2170
JTS: DS135 R93 V5 Y47   YU: DS135 R93 V584

Vilna (Li). *Vilne: a zamelbukh gevidmet der shtot Vilne.* Ed.: Ephim H. Jeshurin. New York, Vilner Branch 367 Arbayter Ring, 1935. x, 3-1012 p., illus. (Y)
YIVO: Vilnius 1935   NYPL: *ZP-1108 No. 5
JTS: DS135.R93 V5 J4   YU: 933.547 J58V

Vilnius (Li) see Vilna; see also under Lithuania and under General Reference Works, *Arim ve-imahot,* vol. 1

Vinogradov (Vinogradiv) U) see Nagyszollos

Vilshany (U) see Holszany

Vishneva (B) see Wiszniew

Vishnevets (U) see Wisniowiec Nowy

Vishnevo (B) see Wiszniew

Vishogrod (P) see Wyszogrod

Viskit (Wiskitki) (P) see under Zyrardow

Visooroszi (Ro) see Ruscova

Visotsk (U) see Wysock

Vitebsk (B). *Vitebsk* [Memorial book of Vitebsk]. Ed.: B. Karu. Tel Aviv, Former Residents of Vitebsk and surroundings in Israel, [1957]. 508 columns, illus., ports., facsims. (H)
YIVO: Vitebsk 1957   NYPL: *PXW(Vitebsk) 89-8567
YU: 933.547 V838K

Vitebsk (B). *Vitebsk amol; geshikhte, zikhroynes, hurbn* [Vitebsk in the past; history, memoirs, destruction]. Eds.: G. Aronson, J. Lestschinsky, A. Kihn. New York, 1956. 644 p., illus., ports. (Y)
YIVO: Vitebsk 1956   NYPL: *PXW(Vitebsk)
JTS: DS135 R93 V6   YU: DS135 R93 V6

Vitkov (Novyy) (Witkow Nowy) (U) see under Radziechow

Vizna (B) see under Slutsk

Vladimir-Volynskiy (Vladimirets) (U) see Wlodzimierz

Vloyn (P) see Wielun

Voislavitsa (P) see Wojslawice

Volchin (B) see under Wysokie Litewskie

Volkovysk (B) see Wolkowysk

Volodymyrets (U) see Wlodzimierzec

Volodymyr-Volynsky (U) see Wlodzimierz

Volozhin (B) see Wolozyn

Voltshin (B) see under Wysokie-Litewskie

Voronovo (B) see Werenow

Voydislav (P) see Wodzislaw

Vrbove (Verbo) (Slo) see under Postyen

Vurka (P) see Warka

Vynohradiv (U) see Nagyszollos

Vyshgorodok (U) see under Krzemieniec

Vysokoye (B) see Wysokie-Litewskie

Vysotsk (U) see Wysock

Wadowice (P). *Sefer zikaron li-kehilot Vadovitseh, Andrikhov, Kalvaryah, Mishlenits, Suka* [Memorial book of the communities Wadowice...] Ed.: D. Jakubowicz (Yaakobovits). [Tel Aviv], Former Residents of

Wadowice..., [1967]. 454 p., illus., maps, ports., facsims. (H,Y)

YIVO: Wadowice 1967   NYPL: *PXV(Wadowice)
JTS: DS135 P62 W353   YU: DS135 P62 W2237 1967

Warez (Li) see under Sokal

Warka (P). *Vurkah; sefer zikaron* [Vurka memorial book]. [Israel], Vurka Society in Israel, 1976. 407 p., illus., ports. (H,Y)

YIVO: Warka 1976   NYPL: *PXV(Warka) 89-8627

Warsaw (P). *Dos amolike Yidishe Varshe, biz der shvel fun dritn hurbn,1414-1939* [Jewish Warsaw that was: a Yiddish literary anthology*]. [Montreal], Farband of Warsaw Jews in Montreal, 1966. 848, 56 p., facsims., illus., ports. (Y)

YIVO: Warsaw 1966   NYPL: *PXV(Warsaw)
JTS: PJ5125 A5

Warsaw (P). *Pinkes Varshe* [Book of Warsaw]. Eds.: P. Kats *et al.* Buenos Aires, Former Residents of Warsaw and Surroundings in Argentina, 1955. v. [1351 columns, lvi p.], ports., music, map (Y)

YIVO: Warsaw 1955   NYPL: *PXV+(Warsaw) 90-2974
JTS: +DS135 P62 W3 P5   YU: 933.5 (438) W295P

Warsaw (P). *Varshah* [Warsaw volume*]. Ed.: Y. Gruenbaum. Jerusalem, Encyclopaedia of the Jewish Diaspora, [1953-1973]. 3 vols., illus., ports., maps. (H,Y)

YIVO: Warsaw 1 (Entsiklopedya) 1953, 2 -1959, 3-1973
NYPL: *PX+ 96-485 v.1,6,12   JTS: Ref +DS135 E8 E55 v.1, 6, 12

Warsaw (P) see Rembertow and Ryki; see also under General Reference Works, *Arim ve-imahot,* vol. 3.

Warszawa (P) see Warsaw

Warta (P). *Sefer Devart.* Ed.: Eliezer Estrin. Tel Aviv, Devart Society in Israel, [1974]. 567 p., illus. (H,Y)

YIVO: Bardo 1974   NYPL: *PXV(Bardo) 79-205
JTS: DS135 P62 W325 S4   YU: DS135 P62 B346

Wasiliszki (P). *Tahat shilton ha-germani ba-shanim 1941-1945* [Under German rule in the years 1941-1945]. Tel Aviv, Former Residents of Wasiliszki in Israel, [1986/87]. 1 vol., illus. (H)

Wasiliszki (P) see also under Szczuczyn (*Sefer zikaron li-kehilot Szczuczyn, Wasiliszki*)

Wasilkow (P). *Pinkes Vashilkover yisker-bukh; a spets-yele oysgabe vegn lebn mord un toyt fun a Yidishn yishev* [The Wasilkower memorial book; memories of our town Wasilkow which has been annihilated by the Nazis*]. Author and ed: L. Mendelewicz; trans. by M. Langsam, B. Gothajner. Melbourne, [Wasilkower Committee], 1990. 339, 152 p., illus., maps, ports., facsims. (Y,E)

YIVO: Wasilkow 1990   NYPL: *PXV (Wasilkow) 93-562
JTS: DS135 P62 W327 M46   YU: DS135 P62 W42955 1990

Wasniow (P) see under Ostrowiec

Wegrow (P). *Kehilat Vegrov; sefer zikaron* [Community of Wegrow; memorial book]. Ed.: M. Tamari. Tel Aviv, Former Residents of Wegrow in Israel and Argentina, [1960/1961]. 418 p., illus., map, ports., facsims. (H,Y)

YIVO: Wegrow 1961   NYPL: *PXV(Wegrow)
YU: DS135 P62 W5375 1969

Werenow (B). *Voronovah: sefer zikaron li-kedoshe Voronovah she-nispu be-Shoat ha-Natsim...1941-1944* [Voronova; memorial book to the martyrs of Voronova who died during the Nazi Holocaust]. Ed.: H. Rabin. [Tel Aviv], Voronova Society in Israel, [1970 or 1971]. 440 p., illus., map. (H,Y)

YIVO: Voronovo 1971   NYPL: *PXW(Voronovo)
JTS: DS135 R93 V73 R3

Widze (B). *Fertsik yor nokhn umkum fun di Vidzer Yidn z"l* [Forty years after the annihilation of the Jews of Widze]. [By] Y. Parmunt. Kefar Giladi, Society of Widze Jews in the Land of Israel, [1982/83]. 8 leaves. (Y)

Widze (B). *Sefer Vidz: 'ayarah behayeha uve-khilayonah* [Widze memorial book*]. Edited by Gershon Winer, Yizhak Alperovitz. Tel Aviv, Widze Association in Israel, 1998 [date in English t.p.: 1997]. 540, 17 p., illus., map, ports. (H,Y,E)

YIVO: Vidzy 1998   NYPL: *PXW (Vidzy) 98-695
YU: DS135 R93 V38587 1998

Widze (B) see also under Swieciany

Wieliczka (P). *Kehilat Vilitskah: sefer zikaron* [The Jewish community of Wieliczka; a memorial book*]. Ed.: S. Meiri. [Israel], The Wieliczka Association in Israel, [1980]. 160, 93 p., illus., ports. (H,Y,E,P)

YIVO: Wieliczka 1980   NYPL: *ZP-1260
JTS: DS135 P62 W365 K44   YU: DS135 P62 W624 1980

Wielun (P). *Sefer zikaron li-kehilat Veyelun* [Wielun memorial book*]. Tel Aviv, Irgun yotsey Veyelun, 1971. 534, 24 p., illus., ports. (H,Y,E)

YIVO: Wielun 1971   NYPL: *PXV+ (Wielun)
JTS: +DS135 P62 W37 S4   YU: DS135 P62 W638
HUC: HIW 382

Wieruszow (P). *Virushov; sefer yizkor* [Wieruszow; memorial book]. Ed.: Y. Zelkovits, *et. al.* [Tel Aviv, Former Residents of Wieruszow Book Committee], 1970. 907 p., illus., map, ports., facsims. (H,Y)

YIVO: Wieruszow nad Prosna 1970   NYPL: *PXV(Wieruszow)
JTS: DS135 P62 W64   YU: 933.5 P762W

Wieruszow nad Prosna (P) see Wieruszow

Wierzbnik (P). *Sefer Virzbnik-Starakhowits* [Wierzbnik-Starachowitz; a memorial book*]. Ed.: Mark Schutzman. Tel Aviv, Wierzbnik-Starachowitz Societies in Israel and the Diaspora, 1973. xxix, 399, [118], 83 p., illus., maps, ports. (H,Y,E)

YIVO: Wierzbnik & Starachowice 1973   JTS: DS135 P62 W376 S4

NYPL: *PXV(Wierzbnik) 76-5651   YU: DS135 P62 W6537 1973

Wilejka (B). *Sefer zikaron kehilat Vilaikah ha-mehozit, pelekh Vilnah* [Memorial book of the community of Vileika*]. Eds.: K. Farber, J. Se'evi (Ze'evi). [Israel], Wilejka Society, 1972. 326 p., illus., map. (H,Y,E)

YIVO: Vileyka 1972   NYPL: *PXW(Vileyka) 89-8261

JTS: DS135 R93 V4 S4   YU: DS135 R93 V387

Wilno (Li) see Vilna

Wiskitki (P) see under Zyrardow

Wislica (P). *Sefer Vayslits; Sefer edut ve-zikaron.* [Book of Wislica]. [Tel Aviv]. Ed.: Y. Eisenberg. Association of Former Residents of Wislica, 1971. 299 p., illus., map, ports. (H,Y,P)

YIVO: Wislica 1971   NYPL: *PXV(Wislica)

JTS: DS135 P62 W38 S4

Wislowiec (P) see Wojslawice

Wisniowiec Nowy (U). *Visnivits: sefer zikaron li-kedoshe Visnivits she-nispu be-shoat ha-Natsim* [Wisniowiec; memorial book of the martyrs of Wisniowiec who perished in the Nazi Holocaust]. Ed.: H. Rabin. [Tel Aviv, Former Residents of Wisniowiec, [1970]. 540 p., illus., map, ports. (H,Y)

YIVO: Vishnevets 1970   NYPL: *PXW(Vishnevets)

JTS: DS135 R93 V59   YU: 933.5 U35V

Wiszniew (B). *Vishnivah, ke-fi she-hayetah ve-enenah od; sefer zikaron* [Wiszniew; as it was and is no more; memorial book]. Ed.: H. Abramson. [Tel Aviv], Wiszniew Society in Israel, [1972]. 216 p., illus. (H,Y)

YIVO: Vishnevo 1972   NYPL: *PXV(Vishnevo) 75-1443

JTS: DS135 R93 V598 V5   YU: DS135 R93 V598

Witkow Nowy (U) see under Radziechow

Wizajny (P) see under Suwalki

Wloclawek (P). *Velotslavek veha-sevivah; sefer zikaron* [Wloclawek and vicinity; memorial book*]. Eds.: K. F. Tchorsh (Thursh), M. Korzen. [Tel Aviv], Assoc. of Former Residents of Wloclawek in Israel and the USA, 1967. 16 p., 1032 cols., illus., maps, ports, facsims. (H,Y)

YIVO: Wloclawek 1967   NYPL: *PXV+ (Wloclawek)

JTS: +DS135 P62 W4   YU: DS135 P62 W76

Wlodawa (P). *Wlodawa; ner zikaron* [In memory of Wlodawa]. Ed.: D. Rovner. Haifa, 1968. 211 p., ports., facsims. (H,Y,E,P), mimeo.

Wlodawa (P). *Sefer zikaron Vlodavah veha-sevivah Sobibor* [Yizkor book in memory of Vlodava and region Sobibor*]. Ed.: Shimon Kanc [Kants]. Tel Aviv,

Wlodawa and Vicinity Society in Israel..., 1974. 1290, 128 columns, illus. (H,Y,E)

YIVO: Wlodawa & Sobiber 1974   JTS: +DS135 P62 W43 S4

NYPL: *PXV(Wlodawa) 75-8553

Wlodzimierz (U). *Pinkas Ludmir; sefer zikaron li-kehilat Ludmir* [Wladimir Wolynsk; in memory of the Jewish community*]. Tel Aviv, Former Residents of Wladimir in Israel, 1962. 624 columns, illus., ports., facsims. (H,Y)

YIVO: Volodymyr-Volynsky 1962   YU: DS135 R93 V6354 1963

NYPL: *PXW(Vladimir-Volynskii) 89-8558

JTS: DS135 V42 V638 P54 1962

Wlodzimierzec (U). *Sefer Vladimerets* [The book of Vladimerets]. Ed.: A. Meirovits. [Tel Aviv], Former Residents of Vladimerets in Israel, [1963]. 515 p., illus., ports., map (H,Y,E)

YIVO: Volodymyrets 1963   NYPL: *PXW(Vladimirets) 79-198

YU: DS135 R93 V6354 1963

Wlodzimierzec (U) see also under Polesie (region)

Wodzislaw (P). *Sefer Vaidislav-Sendzishov.* Ed.: M. Shutsman. Tel Aviv, Community Council of Wodzislaw-Sedziszow Emigrants in Israel, [1978 or 1979]. 437 p., illus., maps. ports. (H,Y)

YIVO: Wodzislaw & Sedziszow 1978

Wojslawice (P). *Yizker-bukh tsum fareybikn dem ondenk fun derhorev-gevorener Yidisher kehile Voyslavits* [Yizkor book in memory of Voislavize*]. Ed.: Sh. Kanc. Tel Aviv, Former Residents of Voislavize in Israel, 1970. 515 p., illus., map, ports., facsims. (H,Y)

YIVO: Wislowiec 1970   NYPL: *PXV(Wislowiec)

JTS: DS135 P62 W65 Y5

Wolborz (P) see under Piotrkow Trybunalski

Wolbrom (P). *Volbrom irenu* [Our town Wolbrom]. Ed.: M. Geshuri (Bruckner). Tel Aviv, Association of Former Residents of Wolbrom in Israel, [1962]. 909 p., ports., map (H,Y)

YIVO: Wolbrom 1962   NYPL: *PXV(Wolbrom)

JTS: DS135 P62 W73 G4

Wolczyn (B) see under Wysokie-Litewskie

Wolica-Wygoda (U) see under Radziechow

Wolkowysk (B). *Hurbn Volkovisk be-milhemet ha-olam ha-sheniyah 1939-1945* [The destruction of Wolkowysk during WW2 1939-1945]. Tel Aviv, Va'ad irgun yotse Wolkowysk b'Eretz Yisrael, 1946. 96 p., illus., ports. (H)

YIVO: Volkovysk 1946   NYPL: *PXW(Volkovysk)

JTS: DS135 R93 V64 H8

Wolkowysk (B) *Le-zekher kehilat Volkovisk* [In Memory of the community of Volkovisk]. Haifa, "Aliyah," [1969]. 50 p., illus. (H)

NYPL: *PXW (Volkovysk) 96-1535

357

Wolkowysk (B). *Volkovisker yisker-bukh* [Wolkovisker yizkor book*]. Ed.: Moses Einhorn (Aynhorn). New York, 1949. 2 vols. (990 p.), illus., ports. (Y,E)
YIVO: Volkovysk 1949 NYPL: *PXW(Volkovysk)
JTS: DS135 R93 V64 YU: 933.5 R969V
HUC: HIW 353

Wolkowysk (B). *Volkovisk: sipurah shel kehilah Yehudit-Tsiyonit, hushmedah ba-Shoah 1941-1943* [Wolkovisk; the story of a Jewish community*]. Ed.: K. Lashovits. Tel Aviv, 1988. 159 p., illus., map, ports. (H)
YIVO: Volkovysk 1988 NYPL: *PXW(Volkovysk) 89-8542
YU: DS135 R93 V667 1988

Wolkowysk (B) *The Volkovysk memorial book: a trilogy comprised of Wolkovisker Yizkor book, edited by Dr. Moses Einhorn; Hurbn Volkovysk, published by the Committee of Volkovisk Emigres..; Volkovisk, published by Katriel Lashowitz...* Trans. by J. S. Berger. Mahwah, NJ, 2002. [4], xv, 480, 82, vi. 176 p., map. (E)
YIVO: Volkovysk 2002 NYPL: *PXW (Volkovysk) 02-2201
JTS: DS135.B38 V64 B47 2002

Wolma (B) see under Rubiezewicze

Wolomin (P). *Sefer zikaron kehilat Volomin* [Volomin; a memorial to the Jewish community of Volomin (Poland)*]. Ed.: Shimon Kanc (Kants}. Tel Aviv, Wolomin Society in Israel, 1971. 600 p., illus. (H,Y)
YIVO: Wolomin 1971 NYPL: *PXV(Wolomin)
JTS: DS135 P62 W67 S4 YU: 933.5 P762V

Wolozyn (B). *Volozin; sifrah shel ha-ir ve-shel yeshivat "Ets hayim"* [Wolozin; the book of the city and of the Etz Hayyim Yeshiva*]. Ed.: E. Leoni. Tel Aviv, Former Residents of Wolozin in Israel and the USA, 1970. 679, 35, 47 p., illus., ports., map, facsims. (H,Y,E)
YIVO: Volozhin 1970 NYPL: *PXW(Volozhin)
JTS: DS135 R93 V67 YU: DS135 R93 V67

Wolczyn (B) see under Wysokie-Litewskie

Wolpa (B) see under Wolkowysk (*Volkovisker yisker-bukh*)

Wsielub (B) see under Nowogrodek

Wysock (near Rowne) (U). *Ayaratenu Visotsk; sefer zikaron* [Our town Visotsk; memorial book]. [Rehovot], Association of Former Residents of Visotsk in Israel, [1963]. 231 p., illus., ports., maps (H,Y)
YIVO: Vysotsk 1963 NYPL: *PXW(Vysotsk)
JTS: DS135 R93 V56 A9 YU: DS135 R93 V69 1963

Wysock (U) see also under Polesie (region)

Wysokie-Litewskie (B).*Yizkor! gevidmet dem heyligen ondenk fun di kdoyshim fun Visoka-Litovsk un Voltshin* [Entertainment and ball given by the United Wisoko-

Litowsker and Woltchiner Relief...*]. Eds.: S. Levine, M. Gevirtz. New York, United Wisoko-Litowsker and Woltchiner Relief, 1948. [16] p., illus., ports. (Y)
YIVO: Vysokye & Volchin 1948

Wysokie-Mazowieckie (P). *Visokie-Mazowyetsk yizker bukh* [Visoka-Mazovietsk*]. Ed.: Y. Rubin. Tel Aviv, Wysokie-Mazowieckie Society in Israel, 1975. 280 p., illus. (H,Y,E)
YIVO: Wysokie Mazowieckie 1975 JTS: DS135 P62 W888 V57
NYPL: *PXV(Wysokie-Mazowieckie) 80-600

Wyszkow (P). *Sefer Vishkov* [Wishkow book*]. Ed.: D. Shtokfish. [Tel Aviv], Association of Former Residents of Wishkow in Israel and Abroad, [1964]. 351 p., illus., ports., facsims. (H,Y)
YIVO: Wyszkow 1964 NYPL: *PXV+ (Wyszkow)
JTS: +DS135 P62 W9 YU: 933.5 P792 W995S 1964

Wyszogrod (P). *Vishogrod; sefer zikaron* [Vishogrod; dedicated to the memory...*]. Ed.: H. Rabin. [Tel Aviv], Former Residents of Vishogrod in Israel, [1971]. 316, 48 p., illus., ports., facsims. (H,Y,E)
YIVO: Wyszogrod 1971 NYPL: *PXV+ (Wyszogrod)
JTS: +DS135 P62 W958 YU: 933.5 P672V 1970

Wyszgrodek (U) see under Krzemieniec

Yagistov (P) see Augustow

Yampil (U) see Yampol

Yampol (U). *Ayara be-lehavot; pinkas Yampala, (pelekh Vohlin)* [Town in flames; book of Yampola, district Wolyn]. Ed.: L. Gelman. Jerusalem, Commemoration Committee for the Town with Yad Vashem and the World Jewish Congress, [1963]. 154 p. (H,Y)
YIVO: Yampil 1963 NYPL: *PXW (Iampol) 89-8324

Yanova (Li) see Jonava

Yanovichi (B) see under Vitebsk (*Vitebsk amol*)

Yartshev (U) see Jaryczow Nowy

Yavoriv (U) see Jaworow

Yedintsy (M). *Yad le-Yedinits; sefer zikaron li-Yehude Yedinits-Bessarabyah* [Yad l'Yedinitz; memorial book for the Jewish community of Yedintzi, Bessarabia*]. Eds.: M. Reicher (Raikher), Y. Magen-Shits. Tel Aviv, Yedinitz Society in Israel, 1973. 4 p., 1022 columns., illus. (H,Y)
YIVO: Edinita 1973 NYPL: *PXM (Edinita) 75-1514
JTS: +DS135 R93 Y42 Y3

Yedwabne (P) see Jedwabne

Yekaterinoslav (U). *Sefer Yekaterinoslav-Dnepropetrovsk.* Eds.: Zvi Harkavi, Yaakov Goldburt.

Jerusalem, Yekaterinoslav-Dnepropetrovsk Society in Israel, [1972]. 167 p., illus. (H)

YIVO: Dnipropetrovsk 1972   NYPL: *ZP-1068
YU: DS135 R93 D597

Yemilchyne (Mezhyricka) (U) see Miedzyrzec-Wolyn

Yendrikhov (Andrychow) (P) see under Wadowice

Yendzheva (P) see Jedrzejow

Yeremichi (B) see under Turzec

Yurburg (Li) see Jurbarkas

Yustingrad (U). *Sokolievka / Justingrad; a century of struggle and suffering in a Ukrainian shtetl, as recounted by survivors to its scattered descendants.* Eds.: Leo Miller, Diana F. Miller. New York, Loewenthal Press, 1983. 202 p., facsims., illus., maps, ports. (E,H,Y) Incl. facsim. and tr. of 1972 Mashabei Sadeh booklet.

YIVO: Sokolivka & Yustingrad 1983   JTS: DS135 R93 Y87 S66
NYPL: *PXW (Sokolievka) 85-2337   HUC: DS35.R93 S66 1983

Yustingrad (U). *Yustingrad-Sokolivkah; ayarah she-nehrevah* [Yustingrad-Sokolivka; a town that was destroyed]. Ed.: B. Bernstein. Kibbutz Mashabe Sadeh, [1971 or 1972]. 63, [17] p., ports., map, illus. (H)

YIVO: Yustingrad 1971   NYPL: *PXW (Yustingrad) 75-2343
JTS: DS135 R93 Y87 Y86   YU: DS135 R93 Y87

Zablotow (U). *Ir u-metim; Zablotov ha-meleah veha-harevah* [A city and the dead; Zablotow alive and destroyed]. Ed.: M. Henisch, G. Kressel. Tel Aviv, Former Residents of Zablotow in Israel and the USA, [1949]. 218 p., illus., ports. (H,Y)

YIVO: Zabolotiv 1949   NYPL: *PXW+ (Zablotov) 88-502

Zabludow (P). *Zabludov: dapim mi-tokh "Yisker-bukh"* [Zabludow: pages from yizkor book*]. Eds.: N. Shmueli-Schmusch *et al.* [Israel], Former Residents of Zabludow in Israel, 1987. 170 p., illus., map (H)

YIVO: Zabludow 1987   NYPL: *ZP-1529 No.2

Zabludow (P). *Zabludove yisker-bukh* [Zabludowo; in memoriam*]. Eds.: Sh. Tsesler *et al.* Buenos Aires, Zabludowo Book Committee, 1961. 507 p., illus., ports., map, facsims. (Y)

YIVO: Zabludow 1961   NYPL: *ZP-1529 No. 1
YU: DS135 P62 Z3 1961

Zadna (U). *Sefer yizkor li-kedoshe kehilot Zadnye veha-sevivah* [Memorial book to the martyrs of Zadnye and vicinity]. Comp.: Shraga Faitil Yosovits. [Israel, between 1983-1993.]4, 2, 145 p., illus, ports, map, facsims. (H,Y)

NYPL: *PXW (Zadneye) 93-2583   YU: DS135 R93 Z246 1984

Zadneye (U) see Zadna

Zagaipol (U) see Yustingrad

Zaklikow (P). *Hayiti sham* [I was there:"Shemot anshe

Zelikor she-hayu mahanot 'avodah ve-rikuz," *], p 281-282. By Y. Laks. [Tel Aviv, h.mo. L., 1993]. 289 p., illus., ports. (H)

YIVO: /86814   NYPL: *PXV (Zaklikow) 94-1111
JTS: DS135 P62724 L35

Zakopane (P) see under Nowy Targ

Zaloshits (P) see Dzialoszyce

Zaluche (U) see under Rafalovka and see Zoludzk

Zambrow (P). *Sefer Zambrov: zichron li-kehilat ha-kodesh...* [The book of Zambrov*]. Ed.: Y. T. Lewinski. Tel Aviv, Zambrover Societies in USA, Argentina and Israel, 1963. 627, 69 p., ill., map, ports., facsims. (H,Y,E)

YIVO: Zambrow 1963   NYPL: *PXV(Zambrow)
JTS: DS135 P2 Z27   YU: 933.5 P762Z

Zamekhov (U) see under Kamenets-Podolskiy

Zamosc (P). *Pinkes Zamoshtsh; yizker-bukh...* [Pinkas Zamosc; in memoriam*]. Ed.: M. W. Bernstein. Buenos Aires, Committee of the Zamosc Memorial Book, [1957]. 1265 p., illus., ports., facsims. (Y)

YIVO: Zamosc 1957   NYPL: *PXV(Zamosc)

Zamosc (P). *Zamoshts bi-geonah uve-shiverah* [The rise and fall of Zamosc]. Ed.: M. Tamari. Tel Aviv, Former Residents of Zamosc in Israel, [1952 or 1953]. 327 p., illus., ports., facsims. (H,P)

YIVO: Zamosc 1952   NYPL: *PXV(Zamosc) 83-381
JTS: DS135 P62 Z3   YU: 933.5 P762Z T153

Zamosze (B) see under Braslaw

Zarachye (Zaracze, Zarache) (B) see under Braslaw

Zareby Koscielne (P). *Le-zikhron olam; di Zaromber Yiden vos zaynen umgekumen al kidush-hashem* [For eternal remembrance; the Jews of Zaromb...]. Eds.: Zelig Dorfman, *et al.* Brooklyn, United Zaromber Relief, 1947. 68 p., ports., map, facsims. (Y)

YIVO: Zareby Koscielne 1947

Zarki (P). *Kehilat Zarki; ayarah be-hayehah uve-khilyonah* [The community of Zarki; life and destruction of a town]. Ed.: Y. Lador. [Israel], Former Residents of Zarki in Israel, [1959]. 324 p., illus., ports. (H,Y)

YIVO: Zarki 1959   NYPL: *PXV(Zarki)
JTS: DS135 P62 Z35 L3   YU: DS135 P62 Z36 1959

Zaromb (P) see Zareby Koscielne

Zarszyn (P) see under Sanok

Zastavye (B) see under Kamieniec Litewski

Zassow (P) see under Radomysl Wielki

Zastawie (B) see under Kamieniec Litewski

Zawidcze (U) see under Radziechow

Zawiercie (P). *Sefer zikaron: andenk-bukh k.k. Zaviertshe veha-sevivah* [Memorial book of the martyrs of Zawiercie and vicinity]. Ed.: Sh. Spivak. Tel Aviv, Former Residents of Zawiercie and Vicinity, [1957 or 1958]. 570 p., map, ports. (H,Y)
YIVO: Zawiercie 1957   NYPL: *PXV(Zawierce)
YU: DS135 P62 Z37 1957

Zbaraz (U). *Sefer Zbaraz* [Zbaraz: the Zbaraz memorial book*]. Ed.: Moshe Sommerstein. Tel Aviv, Former Residents of Zbaraz, 1983. 178, 45 p., illus., ports. (H,Y,E)
YIVO: Zbarazh 1983   NYPL: *PXW (Zbarazh) 97-1092

Zbarazh (U) see Zbaraz

Zboriv (U) see Zborow

Zborow (U). *Sefer zikaron li-kehilat Zborov* [Memorial book of the community of Zborow]. Ed.: Eliyahu (Adik) Zilberman. Haifa, Zborow Society in Israel, 1975. 477 p., illus., ports. (H,Y)
YIVO: Zboriv 1975   NYPL: *PXW(Zborov) 89-8498
JTS: DS135 U43 Z8

Zdunska Wola (P). *Zdunskah Vola* [The Zdunska-Wola book*]. Ed.: E. Erlich. Tel Aviv, Zdunska-Wola Associations in Israel and in the Diaspora, 1968. 714, 58 p., illus., maps, ports., facsims. (H,Y,E)
YIVO: Zdunska Wola 1968   NYPL: *PXV+ (Zdunska Wola)
JTS: DS135 P62 Z38

Zdzieciol (P). *Pinkes Zshetl...* [Pinkas Zetel; a memorial to the Jewish community of Zetel*]. Ed.: B. Kaplinski. Tel Aviv, Zetel Association in Israel, [1957]. 482 p., illus., maps, ports., facsims. (H,Y)
YIVO: Dyatlovo 1957   NYPL: *PXW(Dyatlovo)
JTS: +DS135 R93 D95 K36   YU: 933.5 R969 D994 K17

Zelechow (P). *Yisker-bukh fun der Zshelekhover Yidisher kehile* [Memorial book of the community of Zelechow]. Ed.: A. W. Yasni. [Chicago], Former Residents of Zelechow in Chicago, 1953. 398, xxiv p., illus., ports., facsims. (Y)
YIVO: Zelechow 1953   NYPL: *PXV(Zelechow) 89-8570
JTS: +DS135 P62 Z39 J3   YU: 933.47(438) Z49J

Zelem (A) see Deutschkreutz

Zelow (P). *Sefer zikaron li-kehilat Zelov* [Memorial book of the community of Zelow]. Ed.: Avraham Kalushiner. [Israel], Zelow Society in Israel, [1976]. 447 p., illus. (H,Y)
YIVO: Zelow 1976   NYPL: *PXV(Zelow) 80-605
JTS: DS135 P62 Z4 K3   YU: DS135 P62 Z4 1976

Zelva (B) see Zelwa

Zelwa (B). *Sefer zikaron Zelvah.* [Zelva memorial book]. Ed.: Yerachmiel Moorstein (Morshtain). [Israel], Irgun

yotse Zelvah be-Yisrael, 1984. 4, 193, xiii p., illus. (H, Summary E)
NYPL: *PXW (Zelva) 93-1007   YU: DS135 R93 Z35 1984

Zelwa (B). *Sefer zikaron Zelvah* [Zelva memorial book*]. Ed.: Yerachmiel Moorstain; English trans.: J. S. Berger. Mahwah, NJ, Berger, 1992. vii, 141 p. (E)
YIVO: Zelva 1992   NYPL: *PXW(Zelva) 92-762
JTS: DS135 R93 Z43 S4   YU: DS135 R93 Z3513 1992

Zemplen (Hu) see Zemplen Megye

Zemplen Megye (Hu). Vanished communities in Hungary; the history and tragic fate of the Jews in Ujhely and Zemplen County. By Meir Sas [Szasz]; trans. from Hebrew by Carl Alpert. Toronto, Memorial Book Committee, 1986. 214, 170. 140 p., illus., ports., maps, facsims. (H,Hu,E)
YIVO: Zemplen Megye & Satoraljauhely 1986
NYPL: *PXT 89-4569   YU: DS135 H92 Z47 1986

Zetel (B) see Zdzieciol

Zgierz (P). *Sefer Zgyerz, mazkeret netsah li-kehilah Yehudit be-Polin* [Memorial book Zgierz*], vol. 1: Ed.: D. Shtokfish; vol. 2: Eds: Sh. Kanc, Z. Fisher. [Tel Aviv, Zgierz Society in Israel, 1975-1986]. 2 vols., illus. (H,Y)
YIVO: Zgierz 1975 (v.1); Zgierz 1986 (v.2)
NYPL: *PXV(Zgierz) 76-389   YU: DS135 P62 Z5 1975

Zhelekhov (P) see Zelechow

Zheludok (B) see Zoludek

Zhetl (B) see Zdzieciol

Zholkva (U) see Zolkiew

Zholudsk (U) see Zoludzk

Zhovkhva (U) see Zolkiew

Zhvanets (Zbanits) (U) see under Kamenets-Podolskiy

Zinkiv (U) see Zinkov

Zinkov (U). *Pinkas Zinkov: gedenkbukh* [Zinkover memorial book*]. Ed. S. Eisenstadt (Aizenshtadt) [Tel Aviv], Va'ad Zinkov, [1966]. 239, 16 p., illus., map, ports. (H,Y,E)
YIVO: Zinkiv 1966   NYPL: *PXW(Zinkov)
JTS: DS135 R93 Z5   YU: 933.5 R969 Z78E

Zlochiv (U) see Zloczow

Zloczew (Lodz) (P). *Sefer Zlotsev* [Book of Zloczew]. [Tel Aviv, Committee of the Association of Former Residents of Zloczew in Israel, 1971]. 432 p., illus., ports., facsims. (H,Y)
YIVO: Zloczew 1971   NYPL: *PXV(Zloczew)
JTS: +DS135 P62 Z557 S4   YU: DS135 P62 Z557

Zloczow (U). *Der Untergang fun Zloczów* [The destruction of Zloczów]. [By] Szlojme Mayer. Munich, Farlag

"Ibergang," 1947]. 45 p., illus., ports. (Y in Latin alpha.)
YIVO: Zolochiv 1947

Zloczow (U). *Sefer kehilat Zlotsov* [The city of Zloczow*]. Ed.: B. Karu (Krupnik). Tel Aviv, Zloczow Society, 1967. 540, 208 cols., illus., maps, ports. (H,E)
YIVO: Zolochiv 1967   NYPL: *PXW(Zolochev)
JTS: +DS135 R93 Z48   YU: 933.5 R969 Z86K

Zofiowka (U). *ha-Ilan ve-shorashav; sefer korot Tal: Zofyovkah-Ignatovkah* [The tree and the roots (Sofyovka and Ignatovka)*]. Eds.: Y. Vainer *et al.* Givataim, Agudat Beit-Tal, 1988. 572, xxxv p., illus., maps, ports. (H,Y,E)
YIVO: Sofiyivka & Ignatovka 1988   YU: DS135 R93 S5855 1988
NYPL: *PXW(Sofyovka) 89-8491

Zolkiew (U). *Sefer Zolkiv (kiryah nisegavah)* [Memorial book of Zolkiew]. Eds.: N. M. Gelber, Y. Ben-Shem. Jerusalem, The Encyclopaedia of the Jewish Diaspora, 1969. 844 columns, ports., illus., map, facsims. (H)
YIVO: Zhovkhva 1969   NYPL: *PXV(Zholkva)
JTS: +DS135 R93 Z48

Zolochev (U) see Zloczow

Zoludek (B). *Sefer Zoludok ve-Orlovah; galed le-zikaron* [The book of Zoludek and Orlowa; a living memorial*]. Ed.: A. Meirovitz. [Tel Aviv], FormerResidents of Zoludek in Israel and the USA, [1967]. 329 p., illus., ports., map (H,Y,E)
YIVO: Zheludok & Orlovo 1967   NYPL: *PXW(Zheludok)
JTS: DS135 R93 Z47   YU: 933.5 R969Z

Zoludzk (U). *Ner tamid le-zekher kehilat Zelutsk* [Memorial book of the community of Zoludzk]. Ed.: A. Avinadav. [Tel Aviv], Irgun yotse Zoludzk in Israel, 1970. 185, 3 p., illus., ports., map (H,Y)
YIVO: Zholudsk 1970   NYPL: *PXW(Zhelutsk) 85-1927

Zoludzk (U) see also under Rafalowka

Zombor (Sr). *Kehilat Sombor be-hurbanah; dape zikaron li-kedoshe ha-kehilah* [The Sombor community in its destruction; pages of commemoration to the martyrs of the community]. [By] E. H. Shpitser (Spitzer). Jerusalem, 1970. 29 p., illus., ports. (H)
NYPL: *PXM(Sombor) 92-920

Zuromin (P). *Zoromin-Polin: sipurah shel kehilah she-nikhtah.* [*Zuromin memorial book: the Holocaust remembered.] Teaneck, Puffin Foundation, 2002. 1 vol. (various pagings), illus. (H, prologue E)
YIVO: Zuromin 2002

Zvihil (Zwiahel) (U) see Novograd-Volynskiy

Zwolen (P). *Zvoliner yisker-bukh* [Zwolen memorial book]. Ed.: Berl Kagan. New York, Zwolen Society in New York, 1982. vii, 564, 112 p., illus., ports. (Y,E)
YIVO: Zwolen 1982   NYPL: *PXV(Zwolen) 87-4199
JTS: DS135 P62 Z97 Z95

Zychlin (P). *Sefer Zihlin* [The memorial book of Zychlin*]. Ed.: Ami Shamir. Tel Aviv, Zychlin Society of Israel and America, 1974. 350 p., illus. (H,Y,E,)
YIVO: Zychlin 1974   NYPL: *PXV(Zychlin) 76-2190
JTS: DS135 P62 Z878 S4   YU: DS135 P62 Z878 1974

Zyrardow (P). *Pinkes Zshirardov, Amshinov un Viskit* [Memorial book of Zyrardow, Amshinov and Viskit]. Ed.: M. W. Bernstein. Buenos Aires, Association of Former Residents in the USA, Israel, France and Argentina, 1961. 699 p., illus., ports., facsims. (Y)
YIVO: Zyrardow 1961   NYPL: *PXV(Zyrardow)
JTS: DS135 P62 Z98 B4   YU: DS135 P2 Z9 1961

APPENDIX C-1

THE CITY OF NEW YORK
OFFICE OF THE CITY CLERK
MARRIAGE LICENSE BUREAU

MAIL REQUEST FOR MARRIAGE RECORDS
(From 1930 to present)*

NOTE: Marriage records less than fifty (50) years old will be released **only:**
   (a) to parties to the marriage;
   (b) to persons presenting written authorization from one of the parties to the marriage; or
   (c) to attorneys in cases where such records are required as evidence *(When making a request, attorneys, on their official stationery, must indicate the party or parties that they represent, the nature of any pending action, and make an affirmative statement that such records are required as evidence in such proceedings.)*

(PRINT CLEARLY IN BLACK INK)

Date of marriage ceremony:	Month:	Day:	Year:	Borough where the license was issued:
If uncertain, specify other years you want searched:				License number:
Groom (male) Full legal name:				Birth date:
Bride (female) Full maiden name:				Birth date:
If woman was previously married, give **last name** of former husband(s):				
Reason search & copy are needed:		Number of copies requested:		
Name of person requesting search:		Your relationship to bride or groom:		
Your address:	Street	City	State	Zip Code
Name and address to which marriage record will be mailed: Name	Street	City	State	Zip Code

I solemnly swear, under penalty of perjury, that the foregoing information is true and correct (*check the correct box*) and

(__)   **I am a party to the marriage. (BRIDE OR GROOM ONLY)**

(__)   **The written authorization from a party to the marriage is a genuine request from such party and such party has authorized me to request and receive such records. (THIRD PARTY WITH WRITTEN AUTHORIZATION ONLY)**

(__)   **I am an attorney in good standing and such records are required as evidence in a legal proceeding. (ATTORNEYS ONLY)**

(__)   **I am the spouse or prospective spouse of the above-named (__) groom (__) bride. (SPOUSE OR PROSPECTIVE SPOUSE ONLY)**

(__)   **I am the _____ (relation) of the above-named (__) groom (__) bride and the marriage record will be used for a proper purpose. (RELATIVE OF BRIDE OR GROOM ONLY)**

X _____   **Date:** _____
      Signature   (DO NOT PRINT)

*Records from 1866 to 1929 can be obtained from the Municipal Archives, 31 Chambers Street, Rm. 103, New York, NY 10007

FORM CC2002B 5/01/02

THE CITY OF NEW YORK
DEPARTMENT OF HEALTH AND MENTAL HYGIENE
OFFICE OF VITAL RECORDS
125 Worth Street, CN 4, Room 133
New York, N.Y. 10013-4090

SEE IDENTIFICATION REQUIREMENTS *
ON REVERSE

APPLICATION FOR A BIRTH RECORD
(Print All Items Clearly)

1. LAST NAME ON BIRTH RECORD	2. FIRST NAME	3. ❑ FEMALE ❑ MALE

4. DATE OF BIRTH Month ⬚ Day ⬚ Year ⬚⬚⬚	5. PLACE OF BIRTH (NAME OF HOSPITAL, OR IF AT HOME, NO. AND STREET)	6. BOROUGH OF BIRTH

7. MOTHER'S **MAIDEN** NAME (NAME BEFORE MARRIAGE) FIRST LAST	8. CERTIFICATE NUMBER (IF KNOWN)

9. FATHER'S NAME FIRST LAST	*(FOR OFFICE USE ONLY)*

10. NO. OF COPIES	11. YOUR RELATIONSHIP TO PERSON NAMED ON BIRTH RECORD IF SELF, STATE "SELF"	

| 12. FOR WHAT PURPOSE ARE YOU GOING TO USE THIS BIRTH RECORD | |

NOTE: Copy of a birth record can be issued only to persons to whom the record of birth relates, if of age, or a parent or other lawful representative. IF THIS REQUEST IS NOT FOR YOUR OWN BIRTH RECORD OR THAT OF YOUR CHILD, NOTARIZED AUTHORIZATION FROM THE PARENT OR THE PERSON NAMED ON THE CERTIFICATE MUST BE PRESENTED WITH THIS APPLICATION.

Section 3.19, New York City Health Code provides, in part: ". . .no person shall make a false, untrue or misleading statement or forge the signature of another on a certificate, application, registration, report or other document required to be prepared pursuant to this Code."

Section 558 (e) of the New York City Charter provides that any violation of the Health Code shall be treated and punished as a misdemeanor.

SIGN / PRINT YOUR NAME AND RECORD YOUR ADDRESS BELOW

SIGNATURE	PRINT NAME
STREET ADDRESS	APT. NO.
CITY	STATE	ZIP CODE

DAYTIME TELEPHONE NUMBER ⬚⬚⬚ ⬚⬚⬚ — ⬚⬚⬚⬚
Area Code   Telephone Number

NOTE: PLEASE ATTACH A STAMPED, SELF-ADDRESSED ENVELOPE

FEES

SEARCH FOR TWO CONSECUTIVE YEARS AND ONE COPY, OR A CERTIFIED "NOT FOUND STATEMENT"	$15.00
EACH ADDITIONAL COPY REQUESTED	$15.00
EACH EXTRA YEAR SEARCHED (WITH THIS APPLICATION)	$ 3.00

1. Make check or money order payable to: N.Y.C. Department of Health and Mental Hygiene. **CASH NOT ACCEPTED BY MAIL.**
2. If from a foreign country, send an international money order or check drawn on a U.S. Bank.

* Reverse side not shown

THE CITY OF NEW YORK
DEPARTMENT OF HEALTH AND MENTAL HYGIENE
OFFICE OF VITAL RECORDS
125 Worth Street, CN 4, Room 133
New York, N.Y. 10013-4090

SEE IDENTIFICATION REQUIREMENTS ON REVERSE *
VEA REQUISITOS DE IDENTIFICACIÓN AL DORSO

APPLICATION FOR A COPY OF A DEATH RECORD
(Print All Items Clearly)

1. LAST NAME AT TIME OF DEATH	2. FIRST NAME	3. ❏ FEMALE ❏ MALE
4. DATE OF DEATH Month ☐ Day ☐ Year ☐	5. PLACE OF DEATH	6. BOROUGH / 7. AGE
8. NO. OF COPIES / 9. SPOUSE'S NAME	10. OCCUPATION OF DECEASED	
11. FATHER'S NAME	12. SOCIAL SECURITY NUMBER	
13. MOTHER'S **MAIDEN** NAME (Name Before Marriage)	14. BURIAL PERMIT NUMBER (IF KNOWN)	
15. FOR WHAT PURPOSE ARE YOU GOING TO USE THIS CERTIFICATE	16. YOUR RELATIONSHIP TO DECEDENT	

NOTE: Section 205.07 of the Health Code provides, in part:" . . . The confidential medical report of death shall not be subject to subpoena or to inspection." Therefore, copies of the medical report of death cannot be issued.

SIGN/PRINT YOUR NAME AND RECORD YOUR ADDRESS BELOW

SIGNATURE	PRINT NAME	
ADDRESS		APT. NO.
CITY	STATE	ZIP CODE
DAYTIME TELEPHONE NUMBER ☐☐☐ ☐☐☐ — ☐☐☐☐ Area Code Telephone Number		

INFORMATION: APPLICATION SHOULD BE MADE IN PERSON AT 125 WORTH STREET OR BY MAIL TO THE ABOVE ADDRESS

NOTE: PLEASE ATTACH A STAMPED, SELF-ADDRESSED ENVELOPE

FEES	(FOR OFFICE USE ONLY)
SEARCH FOR TWO CONSECUTIVE YEARS AND ONE COPY .... $15.00 EACH ADDITIONAL COPY REQUESTED .... $15.00 EACH EXTRA YEAR SEARCHED (WITH THIS APPLICATION) .... $ 3.00 IF RECORD IS NOT ON FILE, A CERTIFIED "NOT FOUND STATEMENT" WILL BE ISSUED. 1. Make check or money order payable to: N.Y.C. Department of Health and Mental Hygiene. **CASH NOT ACCEPTED BY MAIL.** 2. If from a foreign country, send an international money order or check drawn on a U.S. Bank. 3. Stamps or foreign currency will not be accepted.	

VR 66 (REV. 8/02)

* Reverse side not shown

NEW YORK CITY
DEPARTMENT OF RECORDS AND INFORMATION SERVICES
MUNICIPAL ARCHIVES
31 Chambers Street
New York, N.Y. 10007
(212) 788-8580
www.nyc.gov/html/doris

BIRTH

APPLICATION FOR A SEARCH AND/OR CERTIFIED COPY OF A BIRTH RECORD:

FEES:

$10.00   Search of birth records in one year and one City/Borough for one name
and issuance of one certified copy or "not found" statement.

$ 2.00   Per additional year to be searched in one City/Borough for the same name.

$ 2.00   Per additional City/Borough to be searched in one year for same name.

$ 5.00   Per additional copy of record.

$ 5.00   Issuance of certified copy, when certificate number is provided.

• Enclose stamped, self-addressed envelope.

• Make check or money order payable to: NYC Department of Records.

• To expedite processing, please send each request separately.

PLEASE PRINT OR TYPE

Last name on birth record	First name	Female/Male

Date of birth

Month   Day   Year

Place of birth – if at home, house number and street	City/Borough

Father's name, if known	Mother's name, if known	

Your relationship to person named above	Certificate no., if known

Purpose for which this record will be used

Your Name, please print	Signature

Address

City	State	Zip Code

MA-22(1-99)

NEW YORK CITY
DEPARTMENT OF RECORDS AND INFORMATION SERVICES
MUNICIPAL ARCHIVES
31 Chambers Street
New York, N.Y. 10007
(212) 788-8580
www.nyc.gov/html/doris

DEATH

APPLICATION FOR A SEARCH AND/OR CERTIFIED COPY OF A DEATH RECORD:

FEES:

$10.00   Search of death records in one year and one City/Borough for one name
         and issuance of one certified copy or "not found" statement.

$ 2.00   Per additional year to be searched in one City/Borough for the same name.

$ 2.00   Per additional City/Borough to be searched in one year for same name.

$ 5.00   Per additional copy of record.

$ 5.00   Issuance of certified copy, when certificate number is provided.

• Enclose stamped, self-addressed envelope.

• Make check or money order payable to: NYC Department of Records.

• To expedite processing, please send each request separately.

PLEASE PRINT OR TYPE

Last name on death record	First name	Middle name

Date of death			Cemetery, if known	
Month	Day	Year		
Place of death			City/Borough	Age
Father's name, if known			Mother's name, if known	
Your relationship to person named above			Certificate no., if known	
Purpose for which this record will be used			Number of copies requested	

Your Name, please print	Signature

Address		
City	State	Zip Code

MA-23(1-99)

366

NEW YORK CITY
DEPARTMENT OF RECORDS AND INFORMATION SERVICES
MUNICIPAL ARCHIVES
31 Chambers Street
New York, N.Y. 10007
(212) 788-8580
www.nyc.gov/html/doris

MARRIAGE

APPLICATION FOR A SEARCH AND/OR CERTIFIED COPY OF A MARRIAGE RECORD:

FEES:

$10.00   Search of marriage records in one year and one City/Borough for one Groom and/or Bride and issuance of one certified copy or "not found" statement.

$ 2.00   Per additional year to be searched in one City/Borough for the same name(s).

$ 2.00   Per additional City/Borough to be searched in one year for same name(s).

$ 5.00   Per additional copy of record.

$ 5.00   Issuance of certified copy, when certificate number is provided.

• Enclose stamped, self-addressed envelope.

• Make check or money order payable to: NYC Department of Records.

• To expedite processing, please send each request separately.

PLEASE PRINT OR TYPE

Last name of Groom	First name of Groom
Last name of Bride (Maiden name)	First name of Bride

Date of Marriage

Month   Day   Year(s)

Place of marriage	City/Borough
Your relationship to people named above	Certificate no., if known
Purpose for which this record will be used	Number of copies requested
Your Name, please print	Signature

Address

City	State	Zip Code

MA-24(1-99)

NEW YORK STATE DEPARTMENT OF HEALTH
Vital Records Section, Genealogy Unit
P.O. Box 2602
Albany, New York 12220-2602

General Information and Application
For Genealogical Services

VITAL RECORDS COPIES CANNOT BE PROVIDED FOR COMMERCIAL PURPOSES.

1. FEE - $11.00 includes search and uncertified copy or notification of no record.
2. Original records of births and marriages for the entire state begin with 1881, deaths begin with 1880, EXCEPT for records filed in Albany, Buffalo and Yonkers prior to 1914. Applications for these cities should be made directly to the local office.
3. The New York State Department of Health does not have New York City records except for births occurring in Queens and Richmond counties for the years 1881 through 1897.
4. Please read the Administrative Rule Summary on the reverse side of this sheet which specifies years available for genealogical research.

To insure a complete search, provide as much information as possible. Please complete for type of record requested, birth, death OR marriage.

Birth

Name at Birth _____

Date of Birth _____

Place of Birth _____

Father's Name _____

Mother's Maiden Name _____

Birth

Name at Birth _____

Date of Birth _____

Place of Birth _____

Father's Name _____

Mother's Maiden Name _____

Marriage

Name of Bride _____

Name of Groom _____

Date of Marriage _____

Place of Marriage and/or License _____

Marriage

Name of Bride _____

Name of Groom _____

Date of Marriage _____

Place of Marriage and/or License _____

Death

Name at Death _____

Date of Death _____ Age at Death _____

Place of Death _____

Names of Parents _____

Name of Spouse _____

Death

Name at Death _____

Date of Death _____ Age at Death _____

Place of Death _____

Names of Parents _____

Name of Spouse _____

For what purpose is information required?_____

What is your relationship to person whose record is requested?_____

In what capacity are you acting?_____

SIGNATURE OF APPLICANT_____ DATE_____

ADDRESS _____

Send record to: (please print)

Name _____

Address _____

City _____ State_____ Zip Code _____

If requesting birth and marriage records, please sign the following statement:
To the best of my knowledge, the person(s) named in the application are deceased.

SIGNATURE OF APPLICANT

DOH-1562 (9/98)

(over)

City Directories pre-1861 are generally on microfiche and can be requested in Room 100 (Microforms Room) or Room 121 (Genealogy Division). Post-1861 City Directories on microfilm (classmark *R-ZAN-G67) can be found in self-service cabinets in Room 100. Those with other classmarks are in the stacks and can be requested either in Room 100 or 121. Gaps of less than 10 years are not shown. Check with the staff at the Information Desk in Room 100 for additional City Directories.

Aberdeen, SD	1903-1931, 1940-1960	Ardsley, NY See Tarrytown/North		Beckley, WV	1921-1934, 1944-1960
Abilene, TX	1909-1960	Tarrytown	1914-1919	Bedford, IN	1912-1927, 1942-1960
Acushnet, MA See Dartmouth/Acushnet/...		Arkansas City, KS	1925-1932		
		Arlington, MA	1902-1935	Bedford/Maple Heights	
Adams, MA	1887-1932	Arlington, NJ See Harrison/Kearny...		OH	1939-1960
Adams, PA	1904-1932			Bellefontaine, OH	1941-1959
Adams/Franklin/ Lincoln Co., WA	1910-1918	Ashbury Park, NJ	1885-1955	Belleville, IL	1860, 1891-1959
Adrian, MI	1903-1960	Asheville, NC	1902-1960		
Akron, OH	1859-1860, 1889-1935	Ashland, KY	1908-1960	Belleville, NJ	1909, 1921-1960
		Ashland, OH	1917-1959		
Alaska/Yukon Terr.	1902-1918	Ashland, WI	1888-1922	Bellingham, WA	1902-1960
Albany, GA	1946-1960	Ashtabula, OH	1908-1960	Bellows Falls/	
Albany, NY	1813-1969, 1988	Astoria, OR	1902-1960	Springfield, VT	1902-1959
		Atchinson, KS	1860-1880, 1891-1959	Belmont, MA	1907-1955
Albany County, NY	1983			Beloit, WI	1858, 1904-1933
Albany/Rensselaer, NY	1902-1904, 1935-1937	Athens, TN	1941-1960		
		Athol, MA	1902-1934	Bend, OR	1936-1960
Albany/Rensselaer/ Menands, NY	1937-1940	Athol/Orange, MA	1936-1960	Bennington, VT	1908-1960
		Atlanta, GA	1859-1960	Benton/Franklin/	
Albany/Troy, NY	1904-1905	Atlantic City, NJ	1902-1958	Klickitat Co., WA	1911-1918
Albany/Troy/ Schenectady, NY	1910, 1923	Attleboro, MA	1883-1960	Benton Harbor, MI	1902-1960
		Auburn, NY	1857-1959	Berks/Lehigh Cos., PA	1908-1918
Albert Lea/Freeborn County, MN	1902-1929	Augusta, GA	1841-1960	Berlin, CT	1914-1930
		Augusta, ME	1867-1960	Berlin, NH	1903, 1920-1956
Albuquerque, NM	1904-1960	Aurora, IL	1902-1960		
Alexandria, VA	1882-1959	Austin, TX	1857, 1881-1960	Bessemer, AL	1913-1960
Alexandria, LA	1912-1935			Bethel, CT	
Alexandria/ Pineville, LA	1938-1960	Austin, MN	1909-1912, 1922-1959	See Danbury/Bethel, CT	
				Bethlehem, PA	1927-1960
Alhambra, CA	1910-1956	Ayer/Groton/Harvard/ Littleton, MA	1907-1929	Beverly, MA	1882-1960
Allentown, PA	1885-1960			Biddeford, ME	1856-1857, 1882-1956
Alpena, MI	1883-1960	Baker City, OR	1908-1950		
Alton, IL	1858, 1889-1935	Bakersfield, CA	1906-1960	Biddeford/Saco, ME	1936-1956
		Baltimore, MD	1752-1959	Big Spring, TX	1928-1935
Altoona, PA	1882-1960	Bangor, ME	1834-1960	Billings, MT	1901-1960
Amarillo, TX	1903-1960	Bar Harbor, ME	1928-1935	Biloxi, MS	1913-1958
Americus, GA	1916-1923	Barnstable/Falmouth/ Bourne, MA	1903-1908, 1926-1929	Binghamton, NY	1857-1860, 1883-1960
Amesbury, MA See Newburyport/..					
		Barre, VT	1902-1935	Birmingham, AL	1888-1960
Amherst, MA	1903, 1913-1935	Barre/Montpelier, VT	1937-1960	Bisbee, AZ	1914, 1927
		See also Montpelier/Barre, VT		Bismarck, ND	1914-1933
Amsterdam, NY	1883-1959	Barrington/Warren/ Bristol, RI	1942-1955	Bloomfield, NJ See Montclair/Bloomfield...	
Anaconda, MT	1902-1960				
Anderson, IN	1902-1903, 1914-1959	See also Bristol/Warren/...		Bloomington, IL	1889-1960
		Bartlesville, OK	1938-1959	Bloomington, IN	1913-1935
Anderson, SC	1905-1960	Bartow, FL	1955-1960	Bluefield, WV	1915-1960
Andover, MA	1885-1901	Batavia, NY	1904-1906, 1923-1960	Boise, ID	1901-1960
Andover/N. Andover, MA	1937-1953			Boone, IA	1904-1932
		Bath, ME	1867-1955	Boston, MA	1789-1960
Androscoggin Co., ME	1894-1901	Baton Rouge, LA	1905-1960	Boulder, CO	1903, 1913-1932
Androscoggin, ME	1902-1925	Battle Creek, MI	1884-1960		
Ann Arbor, MI	1886-1960	Bay City, MI	1883-1960	Bourne, MA See Barnstable/Falmouth...	
Annapolis, MD	1910, 1924-1929	Beacon, NY	1915-1925, 1955-1960		
				Bowling Green, KY	1905-1935
Anniston, AL	1908-1960	Beardstown, IL	1911, 1926-1929	Bozeman, MT	1902-1959
Ansonia, CT	1881-1960			Braddock, PA	1902-1926
Appleton, WI	1884-1934	Beatrice, NE	1904-1907, 1925-1935	Bradentown, FL	1921-1950
Arcadia, FL	1915-1926			Bradenton/Palmetto, FL	1951-1960
Ardmore, OK	1907-1960	Beaumont, TX	1903-1960	Bradford, PA	1885-1915
		Beaver Valley, PA	1910-1928	Brainerd, MN	1903-1907, 1937-1959

Braintree, MA 1916-1935
Branford, CT 1895-1960
Brattleboro, VT 1901-1960
Bremerton, WA 1909-1914,
1929-1960
Bridgeport, CT 1855-1858,
1862-1960
Bridgeton, NJ 1921-1959
Brighton, MA 1850
Bristol, CT 1882-1960
Bristol, VA &TN 1903-1960
Bristol/Warren/
Barrington, RI 1906-1927
See also Barrington/Warren/...
Brockton, MA 1874-1958
Brookfield, MA
See Spencer/Warren/...
Brookline, MA 1868-1944
Brownwood, TX 1909-1931
Brunswick, GA 1914-1960
Brunswick, ME 1910-1960
Bryan, OH 1923-1934
Bucyrus, OH 1909-1959
Buffalo, NY 1828-1960
Bureau Co., IL 1858-1859
Burlingame, CA
See San Mateo/Burlingame, CA
Burlington, IA 1856-1859,
1890-1960
Burlington, NC 1920-1958
Burlington, NJ 1926-1929
Burlington Co., NJ 1881-1911
Burlington, VT 1861-1960
Butler, PA 1903-1960
Butte, MT 1884-1960
Cairo, IL 1904,
1915-1925
Caldwell, NJ
See Montclair/Bloomfield...
Cambridge, MA 1847-1954
Camden, NJ 1860-1943
Camden, SC 1816-1824
Canadaigua, NY 1904-1912,
1930-1932
Canastota, NY See Oneida/...
Canton, NY See Massena/...
Canton, OH 1888-1934
Canyon/Gem/Payette/
Washington, ID 1913-1931
Cape Girardeau, MO 1912-1913,
1928-1960
Carbondale, PA 1903-1959
Carlsbad, NM 1954-1960
Carlisle, PA 1924-1960
See also Chambersburg/...
Carnegie, PA 1902-1935
Carthage, MO 1937-1953
See also Joplin/Carthage...
Carthage, NY 1927-1930,
1943-1958
Carthage/West Carthage, NY 1904,
1923-1933
Casco Bay, ME 1902-1935
Casper, WY 1917-1960
Cateret, NJ
See Perth Amboy/Cateret...
Cedar Grove, NJ
See Montclair/Bloomfield...
Cedar Rapids, IA 1903-1960
Central Nyack, NY 1924-1925

Centralia/Chehalis, WA 1939-1959
Chambersburg/
Carlisle, PA 1882-1888
Champaign/Urbana, IL 1923-1935
Chanute, KS 1903-1931
Charles City, IA 1911-1921
Charleston, SC 1785-1901
Charleston, WV 1902-1935
Charlestown, MA 1831-1874
Charlotte, NC 1889-1935
Charlottesville, VA 1904-1934
Chattanooga, TN 1861-1960
Cheboygan, MI 1910-1916
Chehalis, WA
See Centralia/Chehalis, WA
Chelan/Douglas/
Grant/Okanogan, WA 1910-1921
Chelsea, MA 1847-1946
Chester, PA 1859-1860,
1902-1929
Chester Co., PA 1884-1901
Cheyenne, WV 1905-1934
Chicago, IL 1839-1929
Chico, CA 1902-1960
Chillicothe, OH 1855-1859,
1888-1934
Chippewa Falls, WI 1907-1929
Chouteau Co., MT 1902-1912
Cicero, IL 1913-1927
Cincinnati, OH 1819-1960
Circleville, OH 1859
Claremont/
Newport, NH 1905-1934
Clarksburg, WV 1902-1935
Clarksville, TN 1859-1860,
1911-1929
Clearfield, PA 1915-1934
Clearwater, FL 1920-1931
Cleburne, TX 1907-1928
Cleveland, OH 1837-1935
Clifton, NJ See Passaic/Clifton...
Clinton, IA 1903-1904,
1921-1935
Clinton, IN 1912-1930
Clinton, MA 1856,
1882-1935
Clinton/Lancaster, MA 1937-1959
Coeur D'Alene, ID 1910-1932
Coffeyville, KS 1925-1935
Coldwater, MI 1902-1935
Colorado Springs, CO 1902-1960
Columbia, SC 1859-1860,
1903-1935
Columbus, GA 1859-1860
1886-1960
Columbus, IN 1915-1935
Columbus, MS 1912-1931
Columbus, OH 1843-1935
Concord, MA 1905-1934
Concord, NH 1830-1860
1902-1935
Connecticut 1849-1859
Conn. River Valley 1902-1935
Connersville, IN 1911-1913,
1931/32
Connesville, PA 1923-1934
Connesville/Uniontown,
PA 1917-1921
Coos County, OR 1907-1924
Corning, NY 1893-1959

Corning/Painted Post,
NY 1897-1905
Corsicana, TX 1901-1931
Cortland, NY 1902-1960
Cortland/Homer/
Marathon/
McGrawville, NY 1896-1900
Cos Cob, CT 1904-1911
Coshocton, OH 1910-1911,
1930-1934
Council Bluffs, IA 1889-1959
Covington, KY 1861-1881,
1902-1960
Cowlitz County/Kelso,
WA 1926-1933
Cranford, NJ See Westfield/...
Cranston, RI 1913-1927
Crawfordsville, IN 1914-1926
Creston, IA 1910-1927
Cumberland, MD 1884-1935
Cumberland Co., NJ 1875-1912
Cumberland, RI 1902-1935
Dallas, TX 1875-1960
Dalles, OR 1905-1906,
1925-1931
Danbury, CT 1882-1960
Danbury/Bethel, CT 1936
Danville, IL 1922-1935
Danville, VA 1882-1921
Darien, CT 1918-1935
Darien/New Canaan, CT 1936-1959
Dartmouth/Acushnet/
Westport, MA 1905-1932
Davenport, IA 1855-1935
Dayton, OH 1850-1935
Daytona Beach, FL 1902-1935
Decatur, IL 1889-1903,
1922-1932
Dedham/Westwood, MA 1902-1931
Delaware, OH 1859, 1905-
1906, 1930
Denison, TX 1887-1934
Denver, CO 1859-1960
Derby, CT 1883-1896
Derby/Shelton, CT 1883/84
Des Moines, IA 1866-1935
Detroit, MI 1857-1935
Dickinson, ND 1910-1919
Dighton, MA
See Somerset/Dighton...
Dillon, MT 1906-1917
Dixon, IL 1908-1928
Dobbs Ferry, NY
See Tarrytown/North
Tarrytown ... 1914-1919
Dorchester, MA 1850
Douglas, AZ 1915-1929
Douglas, WA
See Chelan/Douglas/Grant/...
Dover, NH 1830-1935
Dover, MA
See Needham/Wellesley...
DuBois, PA 1830-1859
1902-1933
Dubuque, IA 1858-1881,
1902-1935
Dunkirk, NY 1944-1959
Dunkirk-Fredonia, NY 1887-1942
Durham, NC 1887-1900,
1936-1960

370

Dutchess Co., NY	1883-1896	
East, The	1846	
East Boston, MA	1848-1850	
East Liverpool, OH	1902-1934	
East Newark, NJ		
See Harrison/Kearny...		
East Orange, NJ	1889-1894	
East Port Chester, NY	1912-1926	
East Providence, RI	1902-1935	
East St. Louis, IL	1905-1906,	
	1924-1930	
East Williston, NY	1938	
Easton, PA	1883-1935	
Eau Claire, WI	1884-1935	
Edwardsville, IL	1925-1934	
El Dorado, AR	1927-1935	
El Dorado, KS	1927-1935	
El Paso, TX	1902-1935	
Elgin, IL	1903-1935	
Elizabeth, NJ	1865-1959	
Elkhart, IN	1910-1960	
Elkins, WV	1921-1934	
Ellensburg, WA	1904-1932	
Elmira, NY	1857-1960	
Elwood, IN	1906-1933	
Emporia, KS	1902-1960	
Enfield, CT	1906-1927	
Enfield/Suffield, CT	1906	
See also Thompsonville/...		
Englewood, NJ	1930-1931	
Englewood/		
Hackensack, NJ	1900-1908	
Enid, OK	1902-1935	
Erie, PA	1853-1960	
Erie County, NY	1924-1931	
Erie County, PA	1859-1860	
Escanaba, MI	1902-1935	
Essex County, MA	1883-1896	
Essex County, NJ	1859-1860,	
	1889	
Essex Fells, NJ		
See Montclair/Bloomfield...		
Eugene, OR	1902-1935	
Eureka, CA	1902-1960	
Evanston, IL	1882-1935	
Evansville, IN	1858-1934	
Everett, MA	1902-1934	
Everett, WA	1902-1935	
Exeter/Newmarket,		
NH	1911-1929	
Fairfield Co., CT	1885-1888	
Fairfield /Southport, CT	1895	
Fairmont, WV	1913-1935	
Fall River, MA	1853-1935	
Falmouth, ME	1902-1912	
Falmouth, MA		
See Barnstable/Falmouth...		
Fargo, ND	1902-1934	
Fayetteville, NC	1902-1912	
Fergus Falls, MN	1902-1912	
Findlay, OH	1904-1935	
Fitchburg, MA	1847-1860,	
	1882-1935	
Flint, MI	1885-1935	
Fond du Lac, WI	1857-1858,	
	1884-1926	
Fort Myers, FL	1902-1960	
Fort Dodge, IA	1902-1935	
Fort Pierce, FL	1916-1931	
Fort Scott, KS	1888-1909	

Fort Smith, AZ	1907-1911,	
	1930	
Fort Wayne, IN	1858-1879,	
	1902-1960	
Fort Worth, TX	1877-1959	
Framingham, MA	1906-1935	
Franklin, PA		
See Oil City/Franklin...		
Franklin Co., PA		
See Benton/Franklin...		
Franklin Co., WA		
See Adams/Franklin/Lincoln		
Frankfurt, KY	1910-1932	
Freaborn Co., MN		
See Albertlea/Freaborn Co.		
Frederick, MD	1859-1860,	
	1902-1960	
Fredonia, NY		
See Dunkirk-Fredonia, NY		
Freeport, IL	1894-1899	
Freeport, NY	1914-1931	
Fremont, NE	1902-1935	
Fresno, CA	1887-1901	
Fulton, NY	1903-1960	
Gadsden, AL	1912-1931	
Gainesville, FL	1915-1928,	
	1942-1960	
Galena, IL	1854-1860,	
	1900	
Galveston, TX	1856-1935	
Gardner, MA	1882-1935	
Gary, IN	1902-1935	
Gem, ID See Canyon/Gem...		
Geneva, NY	1857-1858,	
	1901-1960	
Georgia, Regional	1850	
Glen Falls, NY	1882-1959	
Glen Ridge, NJ		
See Montclair/Bloomfield...		
Gloucester, MA	1860,	
	1869-1909,	
	1910-1960	
Gloucester, NJ See Salem/...		
Gloversville, NY	1882-1935	
Gloversville/		
Johnstown, NY	1888-1960	
Goodhue Col, MN		
See Red Wing/Goodhue...		
Grand Forks, ND	1882-1959	
Grand Junction, CO	1902-1935	
Grand Rapids, MI	1859-1935	
Grant, WA		
See Chelan/Douglas/Grant/...		
Great Falls, NH	1848	
Great Falls, MT	1903-1935	
Green Bay, WI	1898-1935	
Greene County, AL	1855-1856	
Greenfield, MA	1902-1935	
Greensboro, NC	1902-1935	
Greenville, SC	1905-1935	
Greeenwich, CT	1898-1960	
Greenwich, CT/		
Portchester, NY	1902-1909	
Greenwich, NY & area 1894/95		
Greenpoint, NY	1854	
Groton, MA		
See Ayer/Groton/Harvard...		
Hackensack, NJ	1906-1931	
Hamilton, OH	1858-1859,	
	1888-1901	

Hammond, IN	1911-1935	
Hanover/		
McSherystown, PA	1923-1935	
Harrisburg, PA	1861-1935	
Harrison, NJ	1882-1901	
Harrison/Kearny/		
East Newark/		
Arlington, NJ	1907-1929	
Harrison/Kearny, NJ	1907-1958	
Harrison, NY	1898-1911	
Hartford, CT	1799-1960	
Harvard, MA		
See Ayer/Groton/Harvard...		
Hastings, NE	1891-1935	
Hastings, NY		
See Tarrytown/North Tarrytown		
Hattiesburg, MS	1906-1935	
Haverhill, MA	1853-1958	
Hazelton, PA	1923-1935	
Helena, MT	1889-1935	
Hempstead, NY	1915-1916,	
	1930-1936	
Henry County, IA	1859-1860	
Herkimer Co., NY See Otsego/..		
Hibbing, MN	1909-1924	
High Point, NC	1902-1935	
Holyoke, MA	1882-1960	
Homer, NY		
See Cortland/Homer...	1896-1900	
Homestead, PA	1902-1932	
Honolulu, HI	1882-1960	
Hoosick Falls, NY	1889-1934	
Hoosick Falls/		
Hoosick Town, NY	1908-1916,	
	1926-1931	
Hopkinsville, KY	1924-1935	
Hornell, NY	1908-1915	
Hornesville, NY	1893-1900	
Hot Springs, AR	1903-1960	
Houlton, ME	1895-1900	
Houston, TX	1882-1935	
Hudson, NY	1851-1935	
See also New York State 1842/3		
Huntington, IN	1906-1932	
Huntington, WV	1902-1935	
Huron, SD	1907-1934	
Hutchison, KS	1904-1935	
Hyde Park, IL	1883-1901	
Idaho Falls, ID	1911-1933	
Illinois	1847-1860	
Imperial Valley, CA	1910-1960	
Indiana	1858-1861	
Indianapolis, IN	1855-1960	
Iowa State	1846-1857,	
	1901-1923	
Iowa City, IA	1857,	
	1901-1959	
Ironwood, MI	1893-1901	
Irvington, NY		
See Tarrytown/North		
Tarrytown ...	1914-1919	
Ithaca, NY	1883-1935	
Jackson, MI	1882-1935	
Jackson, MS	1860	
Jacksonville, FL	1882-1960	
Jamestown, NY	1905-1934	
Janesville, WI	1858-1860	
Jefferson County, IN	1859	
Jersey City, NJ	1852-1926	
Jersey Coast, NJ	1886-1888	

Johnson City, TN	1908-1935	
Johnston, RI	1890-1898	
See also North Providence/...		
Johnstown, PA	1884-1901	
Joliet, IL	1872-1935	
Joplin/Carthage, MO	1902-1907	
Joplin, MO	1909-1935	
Kalamazoo, MI	1889-1935	
Kalispell, MT	1903-1934	
Kane County, IL	1859-1860	
Kankakee, IL	1904-1935	
Kansas City, KS	1904-1934	
Kansas City, MO	1849-1935	
Kearny, NJ		
See Harriaon/Kearny...		
Keene, NH	1827-1830, 1861-1935	
Kennebec County, ME	1903-1924	
Kenosha, WI	1858, 1903-1935	
Kentucky	1859-1860	
Keokuk, IA	1854	
Key West, FL	1887-1888	
Kingston, NY	1857-1935	
Kinston, NC	1908-1928	
Kittanning, PA	1904-1935	
Klickitat Co., PA		
See Benton/Franklin...		
Knoxville, TN	1861-1935	
Kokomo, IN	1912-1959	
La Crosse, WI	1884-1934	
La Jolla, CA	1945-1952	
La Salle/Peru, IL	1891-1899, 1905-1935	
Lackawanna, NY	1914	
Laconia, NH	1895-1935	
Lafayette, IN	1858-1960	
Lake, IL	1885-1889	
Lake Charles, LA	1911-1934	
Lake View, IL	1882-1901	
Lakeland, FL	1915-1960	
Lakewood, NJ	1909	
Lambertville, NJ	1889-1900	
Lancaster, MA		
See Clinton/Lancaster, MA		
Lancaster, PA	1843-1857, 1882-1935	
Lancaster Co., PA	1859-1860	
Lansing, MI	1882-1935	
Laporte, IN	1904-1932	
Laramie, WY	1902-1935	
Lawrence, KS	1902-1928	
Lawrence, MA	1848, 1883-1936	
Lawrenceburgh, IN	1859-1860	
Lawton, OK	1903-1933	
Leadville, CO	1882-1911	
Leavenworth, KS	1860-1881, 1902-1934	
Lebanon, PA	1889-1934	
Lehigh Co., PA		
See Berks/Lehigh Cos., PA		
Leominster, MA	1882-1960	
Lewis County, WA	1925-1934	
Lewis, Pacific Co, WA	1904-1923	
Lewiston/Auburn, ME	1883-1896	
Lewistown, MT	1902-1935	
Lexington, KY	1806, 1818, 1864-1881, 1898-1935	

Lexington, MA	1902-1934	
Lima, OH	1903-1934	
Lincoln, NE	1882-1935	
Lincoln Co., WA		
See Adams/ Franklin/Lincoln		
Little Falls, NY	1882-1928	
Little Rock, AR	1871-1935	
Littleton, MA		
See Ayer/Groton/Harvard...		
Livingston, MT	1904-1935	
Livingston, NY	1894	
Lockport, NY	1882-1935	
Logan, UT	1904-1935	
Logansport, IN	1859-1860, 1902-1960	
Long Beach, CA	1907-1960	
Long Island, NY	1864-1872	
Los Angeles, CA	1872-1960	
Louisville, KY	1832-1935	
Lowell, MA	1832-1960	
Lowville, NY	1890-1892	
Lubbock, TX	1910-1935	
Ludington, MI	1883, 1893-1900	
Luneburgh, MA	1834	
Lynchburg, VA	1882-1935	
Lynn, MA	1832-1880, 1902-1960	
Macon, GA	1897-1960	
Madera, CA See Merced-Madera...		
Madison, IN	1859-1860	
Madison, WI	1855-1935	
Maine State	1849-1856, 1893-1900	
Malden, MA	1869-1960	
Malone, NY	1897-1933	
Mamaroneck, NY	1898-1903	
Manchester, CT	1888-1935	
Manchester, NH	1844-1935	
Mankato, MN	1892-1935	
Mansfield, OH	1858-1859, 1882-1935	
Marathon, NY		
See Cortland/Homer..	1896-1900	
Marietta, OH	1860-1861, 1902-1936	
Marinette/ Menominee, WI/MI	1903-1934	
Marion, IN	1901-1960	
Marion, OH	1913-1934	
Marlboro, MA	1883-1900	
Marquette, MI	1882-1901	
Marshalltown, IA	1891-1934	
Marysville, CA	1853-1858, 1922-1935	
Mason City, IA	1900-1935	
Massachusetts	1850-1859	
Massena/Potsdam, NY	1919-1933	
Massena/Potsdam/ Canton, NY	1930	
Massillon, OH	1902-1932	
Mattoon, IL	1902-1911, 1927	
Maysville, KY	1913-1934	
McGrawville, NY		
See Cortland/Homer	1896-1900	
McAlester, OK	1907-1930	
McKeesport, PA	1893-1935	
Meadville, PA	1902-1915, 1925-1932	

Mechnicville/Ballson Spa, NY	1915-1930	
Medford, MA	1849, 1885-1930	
Melrose, MA	1902-1935	
Memphis, TN	1849-1960	
Menominee, MI	1887-1901	
See also Marinette/Menominee...		
Merced-Madera, CA	1938-1960	
Meriden, CT	1872-1960	
Meridian, MS	1888-1935	
Merrill, WI	1908-1930	
Methuen, MA	1904-1932	
Miami, FL	1904-1960	
Miami, OK	1927-1931	
Michigan, Regional	1856-1860	
Michigan City, IN	1902-1960	
Michigan State	1902-1929	
Middleboro, MA	1889-1930	
Middlesboro, KY	1912-1913, 1926-1935	
Middlesex Co., MA	1882-1890	
Middletown, CT	1868-1960	
Middletown, NY	1857-1858, 1905-1935	
Middletown/Goshen, NY	1897-1901	
Middletown/Port Jervis, NY	1890-1892	
See also Port Jervis/...		
Middletown, OH	1910-1935	
Miles City, MT	1914-1931	
Miles City/Glendive, MT	1909-1912	
Milford, CT	1909-1960	
Milford, MA	1856-1859, 1869-1950	
Millburn, NJ See Summit/...		
Millville, NJ	1921-1929, 1937-1938	
Milton, MA	1902-1934	
Milwaukee, WI	1847-1935	
Mineral Point, WI	1859	
Mineral Wells, TX	1907-1928	
Minneapolis, MN	1861-1960	
See also The West, St. Anthony, MN,	1837 and 1859/60	
Mineola, NY	1938	
Minot, ND	1922-1934	
Mishawaka, IN	1925-1935	
Mississippi Valley	1844	
Missoula, MT	1901-1934	
Missouri, Regional	1860	
Mitchell, SD	1902-1931	
Moberly, MO	1905-1911, 1932	
Mobile, AL	1837-1960	
Modesto, CA	1910-1960	
Mohawk Valley, NY	1928-1930	
Moline, IL	1855-1859, 1891-1935	
Moline/Rock Island, IL	1882-1902	
See also Rock Island/Moline...		
Monmouth Co., NJ	1896-1899	
Monmouth, IL	1903-1923	
Monongahela, PA	1859, 1902-1929	
Monroe, LA	1912-1934	
Monrovia, CA	1911-1935	
Montana	1861-1882	
Montclair, NJ	1893-1900	

Montclair/Bloomfield/Caldwell/
  Essex Fells/Glen Ridge/Verona
  Cedar Grove, NJ   1908-1939
Monterey, CA
  See Salinas/Monterey...
Montgomery, AL   1880-1960
Montgomery Co., OH   1912-1929
Montpelier, VT   1904-1915
Montpelier/Barre, VT   1918-1921
  See also Barre/Montelier...
Morgantown, WV   1914-1935
Morris Co., NJ   1883-1909
Morrisania, NY   1853
Morristown, NJ   1887-1935
Mt. Vernon, NY   1882-1937
  See also Westchester   1878-1888
Mt. Vernon, IL   1906-1915,
    1929-1930
Mt. Vernon, OH   1858-1859,
    1903-1933
Muncie, IN   1889-1960
Moundsville, WV   1924-1935
Muscatine, IA   1856-1860,
    1889-1934
Muskogee, OK   1902-1960
Muskegon, MI   1883-1935
Mystic, CT   1912-1932
Mystic/Stonington/
  Noank, CT   1929-1930
Nanticoke, PA   1903-1924
Nantucket, MA   1909-1927
Napa, CA   1902-1960
Narragansett, RI
  See South Kingstown/...
Nashua, NH   1841-1935
Nashville, TN   1853-1935
Natchez, MS   1922-1935
Natick, MA   1905-1931
Naugatuck, CT
  See Waterbury/Naugatuck, CT
Needham/Wellesley/
  Dover, MA   1905-1935
Nevada City, CA   1856
Nevada Territory   1861-1882
New Albany, IN   1856-1860,
    1888-1960
New Albany/
  Jeffersonville, IN   1947-1960
New Bedford, MA   1836-1934
New Bern, NC   1904-1926
New Britain, CT   1882-1960
New Brunswick, NJ   1855,
    1886-1933
New Canaan, CT
  See Darien/New Canaan...
New Castle, IN   1911-1934
New Castle, PA   1889-1931
New England   1849-1860
New Hampshire   1849,
    1902-1921
New Haven, CT   1840-1935
New Ipswich, NH   1858
New Jersey, Region   1850-1851
New Jersey State   1870-1871
New Kensington, PA   1911-1928
New London, CT   1855-1960
New Milford, CT   1878-1897,
    1902-1927
New Orleans, LA   1805-1960

New Philadelphia/Canal
  Dover, OH   1903-1908,
    1921
New Rochelle, NY   1882-1934
  See also Westchester   1878-1888
New York State   1842-1859
New York Counties   1896
  includes Cortland/
  Onandago/Oswego
Newark, NJ   1835-1935
Newark, OH   1902-1960
Newburgh, NY   1856-1935
Newburyport, MA   1849-1936
Newburyport/
  Amesbury, MA   1937-1959
Newport, NH
  See Claremont/Newport, NH
Newport, RI   1856-1858,
    1882-1935
Newport News, VA   1902-1935
Newton, MA   1868-1960
Newton, NJ   1902-1905,
    1926-1934
Niagara Co., NY   1908-1935
Niagara Falls, NY   1886-1935
Noank, CT
  See Mystic/Stonongton/Noank...
Norfolk, NE   1911-1935
Norfolk, VA   1801-1901,
    1924-1935
Norristown, PA   1860-1861,
    1882-1935
North Adams, MA   1883-1935
North Andover, MA   1905-1935
  See also Andover...
North Essex, MA   1907-1917
North Hollywood/
  Studio City, CA   1941-1946
North Hudson Co., NJ   1902-1923
North Providence/
  Johnston, RI   1910-1926
North Tarrytown, NY   1885-1886,
  See alsoTarrytown/North
  Tarrytown...   1914-1919
North Yakima/Yakima
  Co., WA   1903-1916
Northampton, MA   1882-1901
Northampton/Easthampton,
  MA   1902-1935
Norwalk, CT   1882-1960
Norwich, CT   1846-1960
Norwich/Oxford/   1908-1909,
  Sherburne, NY   1930-1934
Norwich, PA   1846-1860
Norwood, MA   1903-1933
Norwood, OH   1909-1935
Nutley, NJ
  See Belleville/Nutley, NJ
Nyack, NY   1885-1886,
    1902-1932
Oak Park, NJ   1921-1929
Oakland, CA   1861-1935
Ocala, FL   1908-1930
Ocean City, NY   1937-1938
Ogden, UT   1890-1935
Ogdensburg, NY   1857,
    1882-1934
Ohio, Regional   1853-1861
Oil City/Franklin, PA   1902-1927
Oklahoma City, OK   1902-1935

Oklahoma State   1911-1912
Olean, NY   1898-1934
Olympia, WA   1902-1934
Omaha, NE   1861-1935
Onandago Co., NY
  See New York Counties 1896
Oneida, NY   1884-1941
Oneida/Canastota, NY   1898
Oneida Co., NY   1910-1917
Orange, MA   1902-1934
  See also Athol/Orange
Orange, NJ   1882-1934
Orange Co., CA   1903,
    1924-1951
Orange Co., NJ   1904
Orlando, FL   1915-1960
Orleans Co., NY   1910-1911,
    1921-1926
Oshkosh, WI   1857-1934
Ossining, NY   1912-1931
Oswego, NY   1852-1935
  See also New York Counties
Otsego/Herkimer Co.,
  NY   1917
Ottawa, IL   1904-1935
Ottawa, KS   1903-1933
Ottumwa, IA   1902-1935
Outagamie Co., WI   1908-1910
Owatonna/Steele Co.,
  MN   1903-1929
Owensboro, KY   1889-1935
Owosso, MI   1905-1932
Oxford, NY
  See Norwich/Oxford/...
Oxford Co., ME   1915-1928
Pacific Grove, CA
  See Salinas/Monterey...
Paducah, KY   1906-1936
Painted Post, NY
  See Corning/Painted Post, NY
Palatka, FL   1915-1928
Palestine, TX   1911-1914,
    1935
Palmer, MA   1892-1901
Palmetto, FL
  See Bradenton/Palmetto, FL
Palo Alto, CA   1914-1935
Pampa, TX   1929-1935
Paris, IL   1904-1906,
    1926-1930
Paris, TX   1908-1929
Parkersburg, WV   1905-1932
Parsons, KS   1902-1931
Pasadena, CA   1902-1960
Passaic, NJ   1882-1937
Passaic/Clifton, NJ   1937-1956
Paterson, NJ   1855-1935
Pawtucket, RI   1857-1935
Pawtuxet Valley, RI   1892-1896,
    1908-1927
Payette, ID
  See Canyon/Gem/Payette/...
Peekskill, NY   1875,
    1903-1935
  See also Westchester   1878-1888
Pekin City, IL   1887-1934
Pendleton, OR   1925-1935
Penn Yan, NY   1913,
    1927-1930
Pennsylvania   1844-1860

Pensacola, FL	1885-1934	
Peoria, IL	1844-1935	
Pepperell/Townsend, MA	1905-1926	
Perth Amboy, NJ	1912-1935	
Perth Amboy/Cateret/Port Reading/Seawaren/ Woodbridge, NJ	1900-1910, 1929-1938	
Peru, IL See La Salle/Peru, IL		
Peru, IN	1905-1920	
Peterborough, NH	1830	
Petersburg, VA	1859, 1882-1935	
Petoskey, MI	1902-1935	
Peyette, ID See Canyon		
Philadelphia, PA	1785-1935	
Phoenix, AZ	1903-1960	
Piermont, NY	1924-1925	
Pine Bluff, AR	1908-1913, 1927-1931	
Pineville, LA See Alexandria/Pineville, LA		
Piqua, OH	1907-1934	
Pittsburg, KS	1902-1933	
Pittsburgh, PA	1760-1935	
Pittsfield, MA	1859-1860, 1882-1935	
Pittston, PA	1905-1928	
Pittston/West Pittston, PA	1887-1898	
Plainfield, NJ	1883-1935	
Plymouth, MA	1846-1860, 1887-1935	
Plymouth, PA	1887-1891	
Pocatello, ID	1902-1935	
Pomona, CA	1909-1934	
Port Chester, NY	1898-1926	
Port Chester/Rye, NY	1910-1932	
See also Westchester	1878-1888	
Port Jervis/Middletown, NY	1891	
See also Middletown/...		
Port Reading, NJ See Perth Amboy/Cateret...		
Port Washington, NY	1951	
Portland, ME	1823-1935	
Portland, OR	1863-1935	
Portsmouth, NH	1821-1934	
Portsmouth, OH	1858-1859, 1902-1935	
Postsdam, NY See Massena...		
Pottsville, PA	1887-1934	
Poughkeepsie, NY	1843-1935	
Prescott, AZ	1916-1929	
Princeton, IN	1907-1935	
Princeton, NJ	1909-1937	
Providence, RI	1824-1935	
Provo, UT	1902-1935	
Pueblo, CO	1899-1935	
Punxsutawney, PA	1910-1924	
Putnam, CT	1907-1933	
Quincy, IL	1855-1860, 1884-1927	
Quincy, MA	1868-1955	
Racine, WI	1850-1859, 1882-1935	
Rahway, NJ	1904-1934	
Raleigh, NC	1886-1935	
Randolph County, IL	1859	

Randolph/Holbrook/ Avon, MA	1908-1927	
Range Towns, MN	1903-1908	
Rapid City, SD	1918-1935	
Reading, PA	1806-1935	
Red Wing/Goodhue Co., MN	1907-1925	
Redlands, CA	1902-1950	
Redondo Beach, CA	1915-1931	
Redwood City, CA	1911-1933	
Rehoboth, MA See Somerset/Dighton...		
Reidville, NC	1929-1935	
Reno, NV	1913-1935	
Rensselaer, NY See Albany/Rensselaer		
Revere, MA	1911-1933	
Rhinelander, WI	1921-1930	
Rhode Island	1849	
Rice County, MN	1903-1926	
Richmond, CA	1937-1960	
Richmond, IN	1857-1861, 1883-1935	
Richmond, VA	1819-1960	
Richmond Hill, NY	1922-1923	
Ridgewood, NJ	1926-1935	
Riverside, CA	1905-1951	
Riverside, CT See Sound Beach/Riverside, CT		
Roanoke, VA	1888-1935	
Rochester, MN	1909-1935	
Rochester, NY	1827-1935	
Rock County, WI	1857-1858	
Rock Island, IL	1855-1859, 1901-1935	
Rock Island/Moline, IL	1936-1960	
Rockford, IL	1857-1860, 1902-1960	
Rockland, MA	1888-1898	
Rockland, ME	1882-1892	
Rockville, CT	1882-1958	
Rocky Neck, CT	1898-1899	
Rome, NY	1857-1860, 1883-1934	
Roswell, NM	1902-1935	
Roxbury, MA	1847-1860	
Rutherford, NJ	1909-1931	
Rutland, VT	1884-1935	
Rye, NY	1898-1899, 1902-1926	
Saco, ME	1849	
See also Biddeford/Saco, ME		
Sacramento, CA	1851-1935	
Saginaw, ME	1883-1934	
St. Albans, VT	1886-1900	
St. Anthony, MN	1859-1860	
St. Augustine, FL	1911-1960	
St. Cloud, MN	1894-1900	
St. Johnsbury, VT	1904-1935	
St. Joseph, MO	1902-1935	
St. Louis, MO	1821-1935	
St. Louis Co., MO	1909-1934	
St. Paul, MN	1856-1935	
St. Petersburg, FL	1914-1960	
Saginaw, MI	1883-1934	
Salem, MA	1837-1960	
Salem, NJ	1897-1904, 1923-1931	
Salem/Gloucester/ Woodbury, NJ	1897-1902, 1937/38	

Salem, OH	1902-1903, 1923-1934	
Salem, OR	18891893	
Salina, KS	1904-1935	
Salinas/Monterey/Pacific Grove, CA	1926-1930	
Salisbury/Spencer, NC	1907-1914, 1928-1929	
Salt Lake City, UT	1861-1960	
San Angelo, TX	1908-1934	
San Antonio, TX	1861-1935	
San Bernardino, CA	1904-1949	
San Diego, CA	1897-1935	
San Fernando Valley, CA	1921-1951	
San Francisco, CA	1850-1960	
San Jose, CA	1901-1960	
San Mateo/Burlingame, CA	1907-1909, 1929	
San Pedro, CA	1906-1959	
Sandusky, OH	1855-1935	
Sanford, FL	1909-1926	
Sanford/Springvale, ME	1913-1925	
Santa Ana, CA	1910-1911, 1921-1923	
Santa Barbara, CA	1886-1888, 1904-1960	
Santa Cruz, CA	1902-1935	
Santa Fe, NM	1928-1935	
Santa Monica, CA	1911-1933	
Santa Rosa, CA	1903-1935	
Sarasota, FL	1926-1930	
Saratoga Springs, NY	1882-1935	
Sault St. Marie, MI	1888-1901	
Savannah, GA	1848-1934	
Schenectady, NY	1841-1935	
See also Albany/Troy...		
Scranton, PA	1861-1960	
Seattle, WA	1872-1935	
Seawaren, NJ See Perth Amboy/Cateret...		
Selma, AL	1904-1959	
Shamokin, PA	1884-1893	
Shawnee, OK	1902-1935	
Shelbyville, IN	1860-1861	
Shelton, CT See Derby/Shelton, CT		
Sherburne, NY See Norwich/...		
Shreveport, LA	1902-1960	
Sidney, OH	1902, 1929-1931	
Sioux City, IA	1882-1959	
Sioux Falls, SD	1889-1935	
Skagit Co., WA	1902-1930	
Somers, CT See Thompsonville/Enfield/...		
Somerset/Dighton/Swansea/ Seekonk/Rehoboth, MA	1904-1931	
Somerville, NJ	1917-1931	
Somerville, MA	1851, 1869-1933	
Sound Beach/ Riverside, CT	1825-1926	
South, The	1854	
South Bend, IN	1882-1935	
South Berkshire, MA	1907-1960	
South Boston, MA	1852	
South Kingstown/ Narragansett, RI	1910-1925	

South Nyack, NY	1885-1886, 1924-1925	
South Pasadena, CA	1920-1953	
Southbridge, MA	1854, 1907-1931	
Southern Berkshire Co., MA	1910-1921	
Southington, CT	1882-1960	
Sparkil, NY	1924-1925	
Spencer/Warren/Brookfield, MA	1902-1906, 1928-1929	
Spokane, WA	1889-1935	
Springfield, NJ See Summit/...		
Springfield, IL	1855-1935	
Springfield, MA	1845-1935	
Springfield, MO	1890-1950	
Springfield, OH	1852-1860, 1894-1935	
Springfield, VT See Bellows Falls/Springfield		
Springvale, ME See Sanford/Springvale...		
Stafford, CT	1906	
Stamford, CT	1881-1960	
Statesville, NC	1909-1917, 1932-1933	
Staunton, IL	1921-1929	
Staunton, VA	1888-1934	
Steubenville, OH	1856-1857, 1899-1934	
Stevens Point, WI	1903-1904, 1917-1927	
Stillwater, MN	1890-1931	
Stockton, CA	1852-1856, 1888-1960	
Stonington, CT	1881	
See also Mystic/Stonington...		
Stoughton, MA	1902-1907, 1918-1931	
Streator, IL	1904-1912, 1925-1935	
Suffield, CT See Enfield/Suffield, CT See also Thompsonville/...		
Summit, NJ	1905-1934	
Summit County, NJ	1898-1901	
Summit/Millburn/ Springfield, NJ	1928-1934	
Superior, WI	1889-1935	
Swansea, MA See Somerset/Dighton...		
Syracuse, NY	1851-1935	
Tacoma, WA	1889-1935	
Tallahassee, FL	1904-1934	
Tampa, FL	1899-1935	
Tarrytown, NY	1885-1886, 1902-1919	
Tarrytown/North Tarrytown/ Irvington/Dobbs Ferry/Ardsley/ Hastings, NY	1914-1919	
Taunton, MA	1850-1881, 1902-1935	
Tennessee	1860	
Terre Haute, IN	1858-1860, 1887-1935	
Texarkana, AR	1902-1935	

Thompsonville/Enfield/ Somers/Suffield, CT	1907-1909	
Toledo, OH	1858-1935	
Topeka, KS	1868-1880, 1902-1935	
Torrington, CT	1902-1960	
See also Winsted/...		
Townsend, MA See Pepperell/Townsend...		
Traverse City, MI	1902-1935	
Trenton, NJ	1844-1932	
Trinidad, CO	1910-1935	
Troy, NY	1829-1935	
See also Albany/Troy...		
Tucson, AZ	1899-1935	
Tulsa, OK	1909-1935	
Tuolumne Coutny, CA	1856	
Tuscaloosa, AL	1913-1932	
Union County, NJ	1898-1901	
Uniontown, PA See Connesville/Uniontown...		
Upper Nyack, NY	1885-1886, 1924-1925	
Urbana, IL See Champaign/Urbana, IL		
Urbana, OH	1904-1918	
Utica, NY	1817-1935	
Valley Stream, NY	1923-1924	
Vancouver, WA	1907-1934	
Ventura, CA	1902-1935	
Vermont	1849-1860	
Verona, NJ See Montclair/Bloomfield...		
Vicksburg, MS	1860, 1902-1935	
Vincennes, IN	1888-1901	
Vineland, NJ	1921-1938	
Virginia	1852	
Waco, TX	1882-1935	
Wakefield, MA	1882-1934	
Walla Walla, WA	1902-1935	
Wallingford, CT	1882-1960	
Waltham, MA	1882-1935	
Warren, RI See Bristol/Warren/... See also Barrington/Warren/...		
Warren, MA See Spencer/Warren/...		
Washington, DC	1822-1960	
Washington, PA	1903-1935	
Waterbury, CT	1876, 1882-1935	
Waterbury/Naugatuck, CT	1887-1898, 1941	
Watertown, NY	1840-1855, 1882-1935	
Watertown, WI	1885-1935	
Waterville, ME	1885-1892	
Watts Compton, CA	1913-1928	
Waukegan, IL	1901-1960	
Waukesha, WI	1858	
Wausau, WI	1908-1933	
Waverly, NY	1903-1931	
Wellesley, MA See Needham/Wellesley...		

West, The	1837	
West Bay City, MI	1902-1904	
West Carthage, PA See Carthage/West Carthage...		
West Chester, PA	1857, 1902-1935	
West Hempstead, NY	1935-1936	
West Palm Beach, FL	1902-1935	
West Pittston, PA See Pittston/..		
Westbrook, ME	1902-1935	
Westchester Co., NY	1861-1888	
Westerly, RI	1882-1935	
Western Reserve	1852	
Westfield/Cranford, NJ	1929-1939	
Westfield, MA	1902-1935	
Westport, CT	1902-1960	
Westport, MA See Dartmouth/Acushnet/...		
Westwood, MA See Dedham/Westwood, MA		
Weymouth, MA	1888-1933	
Wheeling, WV	1839-1851	
See The West	1837	
See also Virginia	1852	
White Mountains, NH	1914-1934	
White Plains, NY	1902-1934	
Whitewater, WI	1858	
Whitman, MA	1904-1932	
Whitman County, WA	1904-1909	
Whittier, CA	1920-1937	
Wichita, KS	1886-1892, 1902-1935	
Wichita Falls, TX	1909-1935	
Wildwood, NJ	1928-1938	
Wilkes-Barre, PA	1882-1935	
Williamsburgh, NY	1847-1854	
Williamsport, PA	1866-1883, 1902-1935	
Willimantic, CT	1884-1960	
Wilmington, DE	1814, 1845-1959	
Wilmington, NC	1889-1934	
Wilson, NC	1902-1935	
Winona, MN	1908-1934	
Winsted/Torrington, CT	1882	
Winston-Salem, NC	1889-1935	
Wisconsin	1857-1859	
Woburn, MA	1868-1901	
Woodbridge, NJ See Perth Amboy/Cateret...		
Woodbury, NJ See Salem/...		
Woodbury County, IA	1884-1899	
Woonsocket, RI	1890-1935	
Worcester, MA	1828-1935	
Wythe County, VA	1857	
Yonkers, NY	1859-1860, 1885-1931	
See also Westchester	1878-1888	
York, PA	1902-1935	
Youngstown, OH	1882-1935	
Yukon Territory, Alaska See Alaska/Yukon	1902-1918	
Zanesville, OH	1851-1865, 1883-1935	

The above was based upon "Updated City Directory List As of March, 2000," prepared by Alice Dowd, Chief, Microforms Division and revised December 2002.

APPENDIX E

NEW YORK PUBLIC LIBRARY - SELECT FOREIGN TELEPHONE DIRECTORIES

This list includes Foreign Telephone Directories formerly at the Annex and those on microform available in the Microfilm Room (Room 100). The list is not complete. Check also SCHOMBURG, the JEWISH DIVISION, SLAVIC AND BALTIC DIVISION and the Bill Blass Public Catalog Room, Room 315. The most current directories are at the SCIENCE, INDUSTRY AND BUSINESS LIBRARY. NOTE: All holdings are paper except as noted below. Microfilm or Phonefiche indicated by (*).

COUNTRY	CITY	HOLDINGS
ARGENTINA	Buenos Aires	1918, 1920*, 1921-1933, 1938, 1942, 1946-1952, 1955, 1957/58
AUSTRALIA	Australia	1988*- (Phonefiche)
	Adelaide	1931-1937
	Brisbane	1932-1938, 1947-1949, 1952-1954, 1956, 1957, 1959, 1960
	Melbourne	1931-1939, 1946-1961
	Perth	1936, 1939, 1947
	Sidney	1931, 1935, 1937-1939, 1946-1961
AUSTRIA	Vienna	1928*-1930*, 1932*-1934*, 1936*-1938*, 1948-1961
BELGIUM	Brussels	1947-1962
BOLIVIA		Scattered years 1991-1993
BRAZIL	Rio de Janeiro	1918, 1920, 1931, 1935, 1939, 1942-1943, 1947-1949, 1951-1961
	Sao Paulo	1930, 1933-1934, 1939, 1943, 1945, 1947
CANADA	Calgary	1918-1921, 1923-1938, 1945, 1947, 1951, 1953-1956, 1960-1962
	Edmonton	1919-1921, 1923-1938, 1940, 1947-1955, 1961-1962
	Montreal	1911, 1913, 1915-1939, 1943-1962
	Ottawa	1919, 1927, 1929, 1938, 1940-1959
	Quebec	1913-1915, 1917, 1921, 1923-1937, 1943, 1948-1959, 1961
	Toronto	1912-1921, 1923-1930, 1932-1933, 1935-1962
	Winnipeg	1912, 1917-1938, 1940, 1943-1962

Note: The Canada collection includes also Phonefiche for 61 metropolitan area directories in the provinces of Ontario and Quebec, 1988-.

COUNTRY	CITY	HOLDINGS
CHILE	Santiago	1924, 1927, 1932-1937, 1939, 1946-1948, 1952, 1954, 1959, 1961-1962
CHINA	China	1988
	Hong Kong	1938, 1947-1950, 1954-1962
	Shanghai	1928, 1930, 1932-1939
COLOMBIA	Bogota	1961-1962
COSTA RICA	San Jose	1960-1961, 1996*
CUBA	Havana	1920, 1923-1933, 1935-1938, 1940, 1945, 1947-1949, 1951-1957, 1959
CYPRUS	Nicosia	1960
CZECHOSLOVAKIA	Prague	1932*-1938*, 1940*, 1947*, 1950, 1952, 1954
	Bohemia	1934-1935, 1935-1936, 1936-1937, 1937-1938
	Moravia/Silesia	1932, 1933, 1936
	Slovakia/Russian Lower Carpathia	1934-1935
DENMARK	Copenhagen	1911, 1917-1919, 1928*-1938*, 1940*-1947*, 1949-1963
EGYPT	Cairo	1935-1936, 1937*, 1957
	Port Said	1932-1935
FINLAND	Helsingfors	1948, 1952-1954, 1956
	Helsinki	1957-1959, 1961-1962
FRANCE	Paris	1914, 1923-1924, 1926-1931, 1932*-1938*, 1946*, 1947-1961
GERMANY	Berlin	1882, 1913, 1926*-1928*-1930*-1935*, 1937*-1938*, 1941, 1952-1963
	Dusseldorf	1931, 1932*-1935*, 1936, 1937*, 1959-1960
	Frankfurt	1927*, 1930*-1937*
	Hamburg	1927*, 1930*-1931*-1933*, 1934, 1935*
	Leipzig	1932*-1934*, 1936*
	Munich	1932*-1936*, 1937
	Stuttgart	1936
GREAT BRITAIN	Great Britain	1988*- (Phonefiche)
	London	1927-1978 (also Northern Ireland, Scotland, South Wales)
HUNGARY	Budapest	1913, 1928-1933, 1934*, 1936*, 1937, 1938*, 1940*, 1947-1950, 1954

COUNTRY	CITY	HOLDINGS
INDIA	Bombay	1923, 1934-1939, 1946, 1948-1949, 1951, 1953-1956, 1960-1961
	Calcutta	1934-1939, 1941, 1952-1953, 1956, 1960-1961
INDONESIA	Bandung	1959
IRAQ	Baghdad	1948
IRELAND	Dublin	1929-1938, 1945-1948, 1952-1961
ITALY	Lazia	1953-1960
	Milano	1931*-1934*, 1948-1962
	Rome	1932, 1945-1951, 1959-1960
JAMAICA	Jamaica	1961-1962
KENYA	Kenya	1961-1962
LATVIA	Daugavpils	1932*-1937*
	Liepaja	1932/33*
	Jelgava	1934/34*
	Riga	1936/37*, 1992*
LITHUANIA	Kaunas	1937*
	Various places	1932-1937*
MALAYA		1961-1962
MEXICO	Mexico City	1921-1922, 1928-1936, 1942-1961
NETHERLANDS	Netherlands	1931*-1936*
	Amsterdam	1929-1939, 1947-1961
	Hague	1947-1948, 1950, 1953-1960
	Rotterdam	1953-1961
NETHERLANDS WEST INDIES	Aruba	1960
	Curacao	1960
NEW GUINEA		1960
NEW ZEALAND	Wellington	1946, 1948, 1950, 1952-1954, 1956, 1961
NORTHERN RHODESIA		1961-1962
NORWAY	Oslo	1928, 1937, 1946, 1949
NYASALAND		1961-1962
PAKISTAN	Karachi	1951, 1955, 1957
PANAMA	Panama y Colon	1960-1961
PARAGUAY		1958
PERU	Lima	1921, 1932-1938, 1946-1949, 1953, 1961-1962
PHILIPPINES	Cebu	1933, 1935-1938, 1960
	Luzon	1933, 1935-1938
	Manila	1929-1950
POLAND	Warsaw	1931*-1940*, 1955-1959, 1964/65, 1977/78
	All Districts except Warsaw	1936*-1937*
PORTUGAL	Lisbon	1933, 1935-1937, 1947-1949, 1951-1962
RUSSIA	St. Petersburg (Leningrad)	1939
SOUTH AFRICA	Johannesburg	1928
SOUTHERN RHODESIA		1961-1962
SPAIN	Barcelona	1926*-1946*, 1947-1962
	Madrid	1928*-1935*, 1947-1960
SWEDEN	Stockholm	1923, 1928*-1937*, 1941-1945, 1946*, 1947--1961
SWITZERLAND	Switzerland	1990*- (Phonefiche)
UGANDA		1961-1962
URUGUAY		1920, 1932-1933, 1947-1948, 1958
VENEZUELA	Caracas	1953-1954, 1955
YUGOSLAVIA	Belgrade	1934, 1955

APPENDIX F

NEW YORK PUBLIC LIBRARY

SELECTED U.S. AND FOREIGN NEWSPAPERS

This is a selected list of NYPL General Research Division holdings. Most can be accessed through the Microforms Room. Check with the Information Desk in the Bill Blass Catalog Room for other cities and additional papers. The years listed do not necessarily represent a complete run of the paper for that period. Gaps exist.

STATE/COUNTRY	CITY	NEWSPAPER	HOLDINGS
U.S. NEWSPAPERS:			
Alabama	Birmingham	*Birmingham News*	1966-
Alaska	Anchorage	*Anchorage DailyTimes*	1962-
Alaska	Juneau	*Juneau Alaska Empire*	1964-1968
Alaska	Juneau	*Southeast Alaska Empire*	1968-1980
Alaska	Juneau	*Juneau Empire*	1980-
Alaska	Fairbanks	*Tundra Times*	1962-1978
Arizona	Phoenix	*Arizona Republic*	1968-
Arkansas	Little Rock	*Arkansas Gazette*	1819-1821, 1866, 1968-
California	Los Angeles	*Los Angeles Times*	1954-
California	Sacramento	*Sacramento Bee*	1987-
California	San Diego	*San Diego Union*	1987-
California	San Francisco	*San Francisco Chronicle*	1865-
Colorado	Denver	*Denver Post*	1969-
Colorado	Denver	*Rocky Mountain News*	1958-1968
Connecticut	Hartford	*American Mercury*	1784-1829
Connecticut	Hartford	*Hartford Courant*	1764-1994
Connecticut	New Haven	*Connecticut Journal*	1767-1820
Connecticut	Norwich	*Norwich Courier*	1796-1831
D.C.	Washington	*Evening Star*	1852-1981
D.C.	Washington	*Washington Post*	1914-
Florida	Miami	*Miami Herald*	1957-
Georgia	Atlanta	*Atlanta Constitution*	1945-
Hawaii	Honolulu	*Honolulu Star Bulletin*	1959-
Illinois	Chicago	*Chicago Tribune*	1947-
Indiana	Indianapolis	*Indianapolis Star*	1967-
Iowa	Des Moines	*Des Moines Register*	1968-
Kansas	Witchita	*Witchita Eagle Beacon*	1969-
Kentucky	Louisville	*Courier-Journal*	1967-
Louisiana	New Orleans	*Times-Picayune*	1837-
Maine	Portland	*Eastern Argus*	1803-1829
Maine	Portland	*Portland Gazette*	1789-1814
Maine	Portland	*Portland Press Herald*	1969-
Maryland	Baltimore	*Federal Gazette*	1796-1801
Maryland	Baltimore	*Sun*	1837-
Maryland	Silver Spring	*National Observer*	1962-1977
Massachusetts	Boston	*Christian Science Monitor*	1908-
Massachusetts	Boston	*Boston Gazette*	1719-1820
Massachusetts	Boston	*Boston Globe*	1972-
Massachusetts	Boston	*Boston Daily Globe*	1872-1878
Massachusetts	Boston	*Boston Herald*	1894-1967
Massachusetts	Boston	*Boston Herald Traveler*	1967-1972
Massachusetts	New Bedford	*New Bedford Mercury*	1807-1837
Massachusetts	Pittsfield	*Pittsfield Sun*	1800-1849
Michigan	Detroit	*Detroit News*	1945-
Minnesota	Minneapolis	*Minneapolis Star and Tribune*	1967-
Mississippi	Jackson	*Clarion Ledger*	1967-
Missouri	Kansas City	*Kansas City Star*	1987-
Missouri	Kansas City	*Kansas City Times*	1987-
Missouri	St. Louis	*St. Louis Post Dispatch*	1939-
Montana	Great Falls	*Great Falls Tribune*	1969-
Nebraska	Omaha	*Omaha World Herald*	1969-
New Hampshire	Amherst	*Farmers' Cabinet*	1802-1867
New Hampshire	Keene	*New Hampshire Sentinel*	1799-1833
New Hampshire	Manchester	*Manchester Union Leader*	1971-
New Jersey	Bridgeton	*Washington Whig*	1815-1820
New Jersey	Elizabethtown	*New Jersey Journal*	1786-1798

STATE/COUNTRY	CITY	NEWSPAPER	HOLDINGS
New Jersey	Mount Pleasant	*Jersey Chronicle*	1795-1796
New Jersey	Newark	*Centinel of Freedom*	1796-1820
New Jersey	Newark	*Star Ledger*	1972-
New Jersey	Newark	*Evening News*	1968-1972
New Mexico	Albuquerque	*Albuquerque Journal*	1969-
New York	Albany	*Albany Times Union*	1968-
New York	Albany	*Albany Argus*	1813-1820
New York	Balston Spa	*Balston Spa Gazette*	1821-1825
New York	Cooperstown	*Otsego Herald*	1795-1821
New York	Hudson	*Northern Whig*	1809-1820
New York	Ithaca	*American Journal*	1817-1820
New York	Kingston	*Ulster Plebeian*	1815-1829
New York	Mount Pleasant	*Westchester Herald*	1818-1820
New York	Nassau-Suffolk	*Newsday*	1959-
New York	Ogdensburgh	*St. Lawrence Gazette*	1817-1818
New York	Poughkeepsie	*Independence*	1832-1834
New York	Rochester	*Democrat and Chronicle*	1969-
New York	Rochester	*Rochester Telegraph*	1818-1820
New York	Sag Harbor	*Sag Harbor Gazette*	1804-1811
New York	Salem	*Northern Post*	1804-1806
New York	Saratoga Springs	*Saratoga Sentinel*	1819-1822
New York	Sing Sing	*Hudson River Chronicle*	1837-1850
New York	Utica	*Patrol*	1815-1816
North Carolina	Charlotte	*Charlotte Observer*	1966-
North Dakota	Fargo	*Forum*	1971-
Ohio	Cincinnati	*Cincinnati Enquirer*	1968-
Ohio	Cleveland	*Plain Dealer*	1965-
Oklahoma	Oklahoma City	*Daily Oklahoman*	1969-
Oregon	Portland	*Oregonian*	1958-
Pennsylvania	Philadelphia	*Philadelphia Inquirer*	1860-
Pennsylvania	Pittsburgh	*Pittsburgh Press*	1967-1992
Pennsylvania	Reading	*Readinger Adler*	1801-1854
Puerto Rico	San Juan	*El Mundo* (Spanish)	1962-1982
Puerto Rico	San Juan	*El Imparcial*	1962-1973
Rhode Island	Newport	*Newport Mercury*	1758-1836
Rhode Island	Providence	*Providence Journal*	1969-
South Carolina	Charleston	*City Gazette*	1787-1805
South Carolina	Charleston	*News & Courier*	1968-
South Dakota	Sioux Falls	*Argus Leader*	1971-
Tennessee	Nashville	*Tennessean*	1968-
Texas	Dallas	*Dallas Morning News*	1958-
Texas	Houston	*Houston Post*	1969-1995
Utah	Salt Lake City	*Deseret News*	1949-
Vermont	Bennington	*Vermont Gazette*	1783-1832
Vermont	Burlington	*Burlington Free Press*	1971-
Virginia	Richmond	*Times-Dispatch*	1966-
Virginia	Richmond	*Richmond Enquirer*	1804-1828
Washington	Seattle	*Seattle Times*	1966-
West Virginia	Charleston	*Charleston Gazette*	1969-
Wisconsin	Milwaukee	*Milwaukee Journal*	1966-1973

FOREIGN NEWSPAPERS:

Albania	Tirana	*Bashkimi*	1956-1976
Argentina	Buenos Aires	*La Prensa*	1857-1917, 1941-1950, 1957-1995
Argentina	Buenos Aires	*Herald*	1941-1973
Australia	Sydney	*Sydney Morning Herald*	1940-1994
Australia	Canberra	*Australian*	1944-1976
Austria	Vienna	*Arbeiter Zeitung*	1907-1910, 1912-1925
Belarus	Minsk	*Belaruski Chas*	1993-
Belgium	Brussels	*Le Soir*	1949-
Brazil	Sao Paulo	*O Estado De Sao Paulo*	1875-1939, 1968-
Canada	Vancouver	*The Sun*	1966-
Canada	Montreal	*Montreal Star*	1940-1979
Canada	Toronto	*Globe and Mail*	1966-
Ceylon	Colombo	*Ceylon Daily News*	1966-1972
Chile	Santiago	*El Mercurio*	1915-1917, 1944-1947, 1969-1972
Columbia	Bogota	*El Tiempo*	1968-1993
Costa Rica	San Jose	*La Prensa Libre*	1969-1988
Cuba	Havana	*Granma* (formerly *Revolucion*)	1959-1997

COUNTRY	CITY	NEWSPAPER	HOLDINGS
Czechoslovakia	Prague	*Lidova Demodracie*	1945-1994
Denmark	Copenhagen	*Berlingske Tidende*	1935-1941, 1949-1997
Dominican Republic	Santo Domingo	*El Caribe*	1969-1973
Ecuador	Quito	*El Comercio*	1940-1947
Egypt	Cairo	*Egyptian Gazette*	1968-1994
England	Leeds	*Yorkshire Eve Post*	1971-
England	London	*The Observer*	1923-
England	London	*The Observer* (Sunday Supplement)	1964-
England	London	*Sunday Times*	1822-
England	London	*Times*	1785-
England	London	*Daily Worker*	1930-1966
England	London	*Morning Star*	1974-1981
England	Manchester	*The (Manchester) Guardian*	1821-
Ethiopia	Addis Ababa	*Ethiopian Herald*	1957-1999
Finland	Helsinki	*Helsingin Sanomat*	1959-
France	Paris	*Le Figaro*	1880-
France	Paris	*Le Monde*	1944-
France	Paris	*Le Temps*	1923-1942
France	Paris	*International Herald Tribune*	1887-
France	Paris	*Le Combat*	1944-1974
France	Paris	*L'Humanité*	1906-1998
France	Paris	*Le Peuple*	1921-1924, 1946-1968, 1990-1998
Germany	Berlin	*Der Angriff*	1938-1945
Germany	East Berlin	*Neues Deutschland*	1969-
Germany	West Berlin	*Der Tagesspiegel*	1949- 1999
Germany	Frankfurt	*Frankfurter Allgemeine Zeitung*	1967-1999
Germany	Hamburg	*Die Welt*	1969-
Germany	Stuttgart	*Die Neue Zeit*	1883-1923
Greece	Athens	*Io Vema*	1969-
Guatemala	Guatemala City	*Diario de Centro America*	1947-1972, 1980-
India	Calcutta	*Amrita Bazar Patrika*	1962-1996
India	Calcutta	*Statesman*	1914-
India	Bombay	*Times of India*	1919-1997
Indonesia	Djakarta	*Indonesian Observer*	1965-1992
Iran	Tehran	*Teheran Journal*	1971-1979
Iraq	Baghdad	*Baghdad Observer*	1964-1974
Ireland	Dublin	*Irish Times*	1859-
Ireland	Belfast	*Belfast Telegraph*	1970-
Italy	Turin	*La Stampa*	1867-1993
Italy	Milan	*Corriere Della Sera*	1914-
Japan	Tokyo	*Japan Times*	1897-1997
Kenya	Nairobi	*Daily Nation*	1969-1973, 1994-1997
Korea	Seoul	*Korea Times*	1964-
Mexico	Mexico City	*El Universal*	1951-1986
Netherlands	Rotterdam	*NRC Handelsblad*	1938-1973
New Zealand	Auckland	*New Zealand Herald*	1966-1992
Norway	Oslo	*Aftenposten*	1915-1941, 1949-1969, 1989-
Panama	Panama City	*The Panama Tribune*	1928-1971
Panama	Panama City	*Estrella de Panama*	1858-1909, 1971-1972
Peru	Lima	*El Comercio*	1969-1973
Philippines	Manila	*Bulletin Today*	1973-1986
Portugal	Lisbon	*O Seculo*	1910-1979, 1986-
Rhodesia	Salisbury	*Rhodesia Herald*	1969-1979
Scotland	Edinburgh	*Scotsman*	1959-
Singapore	Singapore	*Straits Times*	1956-
South Africa	Cape Town	*Cape Times*	1913-
Spain	Madrid	*El Pais*	1983-
Spain	Madrid	*ABC Madrid*	1915-1939
Sweden	Stockholm	*Svenska Dagblandet*	1969-
Switzerland	Geneva	*Journal de Geneve*	1899-1947, 1975, 1991-
Switzerland	Zurich	*Neue Zuercher Zeitung*	1914-1986
Thailand	Bangkok	*Bangkok Post*	1953-1988
U.S.S.R.	Moscow	*Moscow News*	1930-
Vatican	Vatican City	*L'Osservatore Romano*	1849-1997
Venezuela	Caracas	*El Nacional*	1968-1998
Vietnam, North	Hanoi	*Vietnam Courier*	1964-
Vietnam, South	Saigon	*Saigon Post*	1964-1975

APPENDIX G
CEMETERIES IN THE NEW YORK METROPOLITAN AREA

Acacia. 83-84 Liberty Avenue, Ozone Park, NY 718-845-9240 County: Queens

201 East Broadway, New York, NY 10002 212-477-2221

Records available at Manhattan central office for Acacia/Machpelah/Mokom Sholom. Records can be retrieved by date of burial.

Arlington Jewish. *See North Arlington Jewish Cemetery.*

Baron Hirsch. 1126 Richmond Avenue, Staten Island, NY 10314 718-698-0162 County: Richmond

Records are on microfiche and arranged alphabetically by last name of the deceased. Records after 1901 are cross-indexed by date of burial.

Bayside. 80-35 Pitkin Avenue, Ozone Park, NY 11417 718-843-4840 County: Queens

Bay View-New York Bay Cemetery. 321 Garfield Avenue, Jersey City, NJ 07305 201-433-2400 County: Hudson

This is a non-Jewish cemetery that has a few Jewish burial society plots in the New York Bay section. New York Bay Cemetery merged with Bay View Cemetery.

Beth Abraham. 617 Cranberry Road, East Brunswick, NJ 732-257-7460 County: Middlesex

P.O. Box 6905, East Brunswick, NJ 08816

Beth David (Elmont). 300 Elmont Road, Elmont, NY 11003 516-328-1300 County: Nassau

Some records have been computerized. Basic indexing is by deceased's last name. Plot maps exist for landsmanschaftn/burial society areas.

Beth David (Kenilworth, NJ). Located off the Garden State Parkway, exit # 138. 908-245-7100 County: Union

Administered by Sanford B. Epstein, Inc., 731 Boulevard, Kenilworth, NJ 07033

Beth El (New Union Field. 80-12 Cypress Hills Street, Ridgewood, NY 718-366-3558 County: Queens

Records available from Salem Field Cemetery Office

Beth El (Westwood). Forest Avenue, Paramus, NJ 201-261-7878 County: Bergen

P.O. Box 329, Westwood, NJ 07675

This is one section of the same cemetery as Cedar Park.

Beth Israel (Cedar Knolls). Ridgedale Ave, Hanover Township, NJ 973-543-9740 County: Morris

Contact: Alise Ford, 73 Hampshire Dr., Cedar Knolls, NJ, 07945

Beth Israel Memorial Park. U.S. Highway 1, Woodbridge, NJ 732-634-2100 County: Middlesex

P.O. Box 706, Woodbridge, NJ 07095

Beth Moses. Founded 1949. Wellwood Avenue, Pinelawn, NY 631-249-2290 County: Suffolk

P.O. Box 340, Farmingdale, NY 11735

See also: Wellwood. Records are arranged alphabetically by deceased's last name.

Beth Olom. Founded 1856. 2 Cypress Hills Street, Brooklyn, NY 718-277-6255 County: Kings

P.O. Box 211263, Woodhaven, NY 11421

The cemetery is jointly owned by three Manhattan congregations:

1. Shearith Israel (Spanish Portuguese), 8 West 70 St, NY, NY 10023 212 873-0300
2. B'nai Jeshrun, 270 West 89 St, NY, NY 10024 212 787-7600
3. Shaaray Tefila, 250 East 79 St, NY, NY 10021 212 535-8008

Records are available at the Cemetery Office and at each congregation.

Bnai Abraham Memorial Park. 2600 Route 22 East, Union, NJ 07083 908-688-3054 County: Union

Owned by Temple Bnai Abraham, Livingston, NJ

Bnai Israel (Newark). *See McClellan Street Cemeteries below.* County: Essex

Bnai Jacob. Passaic Avenue, Lodi, NJ (near Home Place) 201-939-8170 County: Bergen

Contact: Sabetay Behar, 200 Murray Hill Parkway, East Rutherford, NJ 07073

Breslau Cemetery Association.

Newark Street & Monroe Street, Lindenhurst, NY 11757 631-884-2323 County: Suffolk

See Lindenhurst Hebrew Congregation. This is a non-denominational cemetery founded in the 1880's. Lindenhurst Hebrew Congregation is the Jewish section.

Cedar Park. Forest Avenue, Paramus, NJ 201-262-1100 County: Bergen

P.O. Box 329, Westwood, NJ 07675

One section of the same cemetery is Beth El (Westwood).

Chevra Kadisha (Sag Harbor). Route 114, Sag Harbor, NY 631-725-1080 County: Suffolk

Contact: Gertrude Katz, Ferry Road, Sag Harbor, NY 11963

Congregation Bnai Israel-Ahavas Joseph. Midland Ave, Saddle Brook, NJ 973-278-5366 County: Bergen

Contact Mrs. Ida Ezorsky 35 E 40th St, Paterson, NJ 07544.

Congregation Shearith Israel.   212-873-0300   County: New York (Manhattan)

    Chatham Square (55 St. James Place, opposite Chatham Square), 1682-1828

    11th Street (76 W. 11th Street, between 6th & 7th Avenues), 1805-1829

    21st Street (between 6th & 7th Avenues), 1829-1851

    Mail address: 8 West 70th Street, New York, NY 10023

    The congregation's original cemeteries are all in Manhattan. Their newer cemetery is Beth Olam in Brooklyn. The records for the Manhattan cemeteries are all at the congregation office.

Congregation Sons of Jacob. Route 202 (off of Route 9W), Haverstraw, NY

    Mail address: 37 Clove Ave, Haverstraw, 10927   845-429-4644   County: Rockland

Cypress Hills. 833 Jamaica Ave, Brooklyn, NY 11208   718-277-2900   County: Kings

    This is a non-sectarian cemetery that has several Jewish burial society plots.

Dover Mt. Sinai. Chrystal Street, Randolph, NJ   973-539-4440   County: Morris

    Mail address: Marcia Waxler, Dover Mt. Sinai Cemetery, c/o Adath Shalom Synagogue, 841 Mountain Way, Morris Plains, NJ 07950. *The synagogue is not affiliated with the cemetery. It simply serves as a place for receipt of mail and messages.*

East Ridgelawn. Founded 1905. 255 Main Avenue, Clifton, NJ 07014   973-777-1920   County: Passaic

    See Menorah. This is a non-denominational cemetery. Menorah is the Jewish section. Some records are cross referenced by burial society plot.

Elmweir. *This is the old name for Mt. Zion*   County: Queens

Floral Park /Washington. Founded c. 1930.

    104 Deans Rhode Hall Road, Monmouth Junction, NJ 08852   732-297-2336   County: Middlesex

    Records are arranged alphabetically by deceased's last name and by burial society.

Grove Street & South Orange Avenue. Includes the Grove Street, Talmud Torah and Union Field Cemeteries.

    Grove St. & So. Orange Ave., Newark, NJ   908-245-7100   County: Essex

    Sanford B. Epstein, Inc., 731 Boulevard, Kenilworth, NJ 07033

    NOTE: Grove Street Cemetery is located on Grove Street between South Orange Ave & Central Avenues. Talmud Torah is on South Orange Avenue opposite #616 South Orange Ave. Union Field is on the opposite site of South Orange Avenue between Grove & 19th Street.

Highland View Cemetery Association. *See Mt. Judah*

Hungarian Union Field.

    8299 Cypress Avenue & Cypress Hills Street, Glendale, NY 11385   718-366-3434   County: Queens

    The parent organization, Mutual Benevolent Society, was founded in 1865 by 44 Hungarian immigrants on New York's Lower East Side. The cemetery was opened in the late 1800's.

Huntington Jewish Center. Old Country Road, Huntington, NY 11743   631-427-9486   County: Suffolk

    Contact person is Murry Nierenberg.

Independent Jewish. Route 114, Sag Harbor, NY   631-287-0383   County: Suffolk

    Contact: Kerri Howland Cruse, 525 E 14 St, Apt MA, New York, NY 10009

Independent Lodzer Young Mens. McBride Avenue, West Paterson, NJ   973-546-1099   County: Passaic

    Contact: Isidore Steinfeld, 257 7th Street, Apt O5, Clifton, NJ 07011

Jewish Federation of North Jersey Cemetery Association.

    P.O. Box 436, Totowa, NJ 07511   973-492-2969   County: Passaic

    Owns and manages twelve small one congregation / one landsmanshaft cemeteries in north Jersey. Cemeteries are as follows:

        Americus Lodge, Midland Avenue, Saddle Brook, NJ
        A.M. White Lodge, Riverview Drive, Totowa, NJ
        Bnai Sholom Organization, Dewey Avenue, Saddle Brook, NJ
        Independent United Jersey Verein, McBride Avenue, West Paterson, NJ
        Nathan & Miriam Barnert Organization, McBride Avenue, West Paterson, NJ
        Passaic County Club, McBride Avenue, West Paterson, NJ
        Stein-Joelson Lodge, Riverview Drive, Totowa, NJ
        Temple Emanuel of North Jersey, Dewey Avenue, Saddle Brook, NJ
        Workmen's Circle Branch #121, Dewey Avenue, Saddle Brook, NJ
        Workmen's Circle Branch #970, Dewey Avenue, Saddle Brook, NJ
        Workmen's Circle Branch #13, Chobot Lane, Elmwood Park, NJ
        Yanover Lodge, Dewey Avenue, Saddle Brook, NJ

    NOTE: Knoble Construction manages the above cemeteries for the Jewish Federation. In addition, it maintains the Congregation Bnai Yeshurun/Yavne Academy, Midland Ave, Saddle Brook, NJ

        Ozorkower Ben. Society, Dewey Ave, Saddle Brook, NJ

Kensico. 273 Lakeview Avenue, P.O. Box 7, Valhalla, NY 10595   914-949-0347   County: Westchester

    See Sharon Gardens. This is a non-denominational cemetery. Sharon Gardens is the Jewish section.

King David Memorial Park. 101 Mill Street, Putnam Valley, NY 10579   914-528-3516   County: Putnam

King Solomon Memorial Park. Dwas Line Avenue & Allwood Road, Clifton, NJ   973-473-5646   County: Passaic

    P.O. Box 1041, Clifton, NJ 07014

    Originally opened as West Ridgelawn Cemetery

Kings Park Jewish Center Cemetery. P.O. Box 301, Kings Park, NY 11754   631-269-1133   County: Suffolk

    Cemetery is located on border of Kings Park and Commack in residential development called Country Woods on east side of Indian Head Road. Contact person is Gary Spiegel at 516-724-6321.

Knollwood Park. Founded 1947.

    57-80 Cooper Avenue at Cypress Avenue, Ridgewood, NY 11385   718-386-6700   County: Queens

Linden Hill. Founded c. 1850. 52-22 Metropolitan Avenue, Ridgewood, NY 11385   718-821-2279   County: Queens

    Founded by Congregation Ahavat Chesed/Central Synagogue

Lindenhurst Hebrew Congregation. Newark Street & Monroe Street, Lindenhurst, NY; 516-226-2022   County: Suffolk

    P.O. Box 100, Lindenhurst, NY 11757

    This congregation owns the property for Jewish burials within the non-denominational Breslau Cemetery.

Machpelah. Founded 1800's. 82-30 Cypress Hills Street, Ridgewood, NY   718-366-5959   County: Queens

    201 East Broadway, New York, NY 10002   212-477-2221

    Records available at Manhattan central office for Acacia/Machpelah/Mokom Sholom. Records can be retrieved by date of burial. Records are poorly organized but can be retrieved by date of burial. Harry Houdini is buried here.

Maimonides – Brooklyn. 895 Jamaica Avenue, Brooklyn, NY   718-347-0095   County: Kings

    P.O. Box 125, Elmont, NY 11003

    Records are available at Maimonides-Elmont Cemetery Office

Maimonides - Elmont. 90 Elmont Road, Elmont, NY   718-347-0095   County: Nassau

    P.O. Box 125, Elmont, NY 11003

    The Maimonides Elmont office holds the records for both Maimonides Elmont and Maimonides Brooklyn. Some records exist for burial society plots. See also: Maimonides-Brooklyn

McClellan Street Cemeteries. Located Off Route #1 in Newark, NJ   908-245-7100   County: Essex

    Sanford B. Epstein, Inc., 731 Boulevard, Kenilworth, NJ 07033

    Includes many burial societies including Bnai Israel Cemetery and Gomel Chesed. These society plots cluster around McClellen Street and Mt. Olive Avenue in Newark..

Menorah. 600 Passaic Avenue, Clifton, NJ 07014   973-777-1920   County: Passaic

    Jewish section of East Ridgelawn Cemetery.

Mokom Sholom. 80-07 Pitkin Avenue, Ozone Park, NY   718-845-6030   County: Queens

    201 East Broadway, New York, NY 10002   212-477-2221

    Records available at Manhattan central office for Acacia/Machpelah/Mokom Sholom. The office has poorly organized records and poor plot maps. You must have the date of death to retrieve records. Recent burials are computerized.

Montefiore. Founded 1908. 121-83 Springfield Blvd., St. Albans, NY   718-528-1700   County: Queens

    P.O. Box 120098, St. Albans, NY 11412

    Owned by Springfield Long Island Cemetery Society. Records are available by burial date or alphabetically by last name of the deceased. See also: New Montefiore

Mt. Ararat. Route 109 and Southern State Parkway, No. Lindenhurst, NY   631-957-2277   County: Suffolk

    P.O. Box 355, Farmingdale, NY 11735

Mt. Carmel Queens. 83-45 Cypress Hills Street at Cooper Avenue, Glendale, NY 11385; 718-366-5900   County: Queens

    See also: New Mt. Carmel

Mt. Eden. 20 Commerce Street, Hawthorne, NY 10532   914-769-0603   County: Westchester

    Records are arranged alphabetically by last name of deceased, chronologically by date of burial, and by burial society.

Mt. Golda. 500 Old Country Road, Huntington Station, NY 11746   631-427-2577   County: Suffolk

Mt. Hebron. Founded late 1800's. 130-04 Horace Harding Expressway., Flushing, NY   718-939-9405   County: Queens

    P.O. Box 228, Flushing, NY 11352

    Records are most easily retrieved alphabetically by deceased's last name.

Mt. Hope (Hastings-On-Hudson).

    50 Jackson Ave, Saw Mill River Road, Hastings-On-Hudson, NY   914-478-1855   County: Westchester

    P.O. Box 248, Hastings-On-Hudson, NY 10706

Mt. Hope (Brooklyn). 927 Jamaica Avenue, Brooklyn, NY   718-347-0095   County: Kings

    P.O. Box 125, Elmont, NY 11003

    Records are available from Maimonides-Elmont

Mt. Judah. Cypress Avenue, Ridgewood, NY   718-821-1060   County: Queens

    P.O. Box 860177, Ridgewood, NY 11385

    See also: Highland View Cemetery Association

Mt. Lebanon/New Mt Lebanon – NJ. Gill Lane, Iselin, NJ   732-283-1010   County: Middlesex
P.O. Box 135, Iselin, NJ 08830

Mt. Lebanon, New Mt. Lebanon and Mt. Lebanon Part 2 are all part of the same cemetery. They are bounded by the Garden State Parkway, U.S. Highway Route 1, Mt. Hope Avenue and Forest Lawn Memorial Gardens Cemetery.

Mt. Lebanon – NY. Founded 1915. 78-00 Myrtle Avenue, Glendale, NY 11385   718-821-0200   County: Queens

Mt. Moriah. Founded c. 1910. 685 Fairview Avenue, Fairview, NJ 07022   201-943-6163   County: Bergen

Mt. Moriah also owns Fairview Cemetery, 500 Fairview Ave., Fairview, NJ 201-943-6161. Fairview is a non-denominational cemetery that has no Jewish section, but may have Jewish burials. Their records are computerized.

Mt. Nebo. 195 Totowa Road, Totowa, NJ 07512   973-942-5361   County: Passaic

Mt. Neboh. Founded 1853. 82-07 Cypress Hills Street, Glendale, NY 11385   718-366-4141   County: Queens

Mt. Pleasant. 80 Commerce Street, Hawthorne, NY   914-769-0397   County: Westchester
P.O. 286, Hawthorne, NY 10532

Mt. Richmond. Founded 1909. 420 Clark Avenue, Staten Island, NY 10306   718-667-0915   County: Richmond
224 West 35th Street, New York, NY 10001   212-239-1662

Records can be found at both the cemetery office and at the Hebrew Free Burial Association. Most records are on microfilm and are arranged chronologically by burial date. The last couple of years have been computerized.

Mt. Sinai Cemetery. *See Dover Mt. Sinai Cemetery*   County: Morris

Mt. Zion. 59-63 54 Avenue, Maspeth, NY   718-335-2500   County: Queens
P.O. Box 355, Maspeth, NY 11378

Opened as Elmweir Cemetery. Their records are well organized by last name of the deceased, chronologically by date of burial, and by burial society. They have good maps of each of the burial society plots. Records for grave sites that are under active care have been computerized.

New Montefiore. Wellwood Avenue, West Babylon, NY   631-249-7000   County: Suffolk
P.O. Box 130, Farmingdale, NY 11735
See also: Montefiore

New Mt. Carmel. Founded 1902.
Cooper Avenue at Cypress Hills Street, Glendale, NY 11385   718-366-5900   County: Queens
Records are available from the old Mt. Carmel Office. First burial was in 1906.

New Mt. Lebanon. *See Mt. Lebanon/New Mt. Lebanon - NJ*   County: Middlesex

New Mt. Zion. 742 Rutherford Avenue, Lyndhurst, NJ   201-438-1612   County: Bergen
P.O. Box 53, Rutherford, NJ 07070
Alphabetically by last name of the deceased and chronologically by date of burial.

New York Bay Cemetery. *See Bay View -New York Bay Cemetery.*

North Arlington Jewish Cemetery. Bellville Turnpike, North Arlington, NJ   908-245-7100   County: Bergen
Sanford B. Epstein, Inc., 731 Boulevard, Kenilworth, NJ 07033

At the extreme southern end of Bergen County. Across the street from the cemetery is Kearny, Hudson County. Records are not clearly organized.

Ocean View Cemetery (non-sectarian). 33-15 Amboy Road   718-351-1870   County: Richmond
Staten Island NY 10306

A portion of this cemetery is owned by the Hebrew Free Burial Society/Mt. Richmond and the records are at Hebrew Free Burial Society/Mt. Richmond.

Passaic Junction Cemeteries (Part). Dewey Avenue, Saddle Brook, NJ   201-794-7474   County: Bergen
Contact: Darius Chludzinski, 21-00 Morlot Avenue, Fair Lawn, NJ 07410

Not a real cemetery, but an area with the following society plots:

Adas Israel Center
Congregation Ahavath Sholom
Congregation Ahavath Torah (purchased Nathan & Miriam Barnert Org. plot on Dewey Ave.)
Independent Worker's Association Br. #5
Passaic Hebrew Independent Benevolent Association
Paterson Worker's Alliance, Farband
Paterson Zion Camps #6
Temple Beth El (aka Hackensack Hebrew Institute)
Tifereth Israel
United Brotherhood Congregation
Young Israel Passaic & Clifton (aka Bikur Cholim)

NOTE: See Jewish Federation of North Jersey Cemetery Association for other cemetery plots on Dewey Ave.

Patchogue Congregation Cemetery. Buckley Road, Holtsville, NY   631-289-0375   County: Suffolk
P.O. Box 293, Patchogue, NY 11772

Records can be requested from Harriet Gordon c/o the P.O. Box address. The cemetery was founded by Patchogue Hebrew Congregation now Temple Beth-el of Patchogue around 1893. Contact person is Dr. Girshoff.

Riverside (Saddle Brook). Founded c. 1907.

    12 Market Street, P.O. Box 930, Saddlebrook, NJ 07662   201-843-7600   County: Bergen

    Was founded as Saddle Brook Cemetery. Records are available chronologically by date of burial, and by burial society.

Saddle Brook. Founded c. 1907. *Name changed to Riverside Cemetery.*   County: Bergen

Salem Fields (Temple Emanu-El). Founded 1852.

    775 Jamaica Avenue, Brooklyn, NY 11208   718-277-3898   County: Kings

    First cemetery was in Brooklyn. The congregation gave that up and opened here in 1852. See also: Beth El (New Union Field).

Sharon Gardens (Jewish division of Kensico Cem.).

    273 Lakeview Avenue, P.O. Box 7, Valhalla, NY 10595   914-949-0347   County: Westchester

    Records are available from the Kensico Cemetery Office

Silk City Benevolent Association McBride Avenue, Paterson, NJ   201-797-3469   County: Passaic

    Contact: Sol Schiffman, 1 Fernwood Drive, Fairlawn, NJ 07410. *Records are in his home.*

Silver Lake. Founded 1890's. 926 Victory Blvd., Staten Island, NY 10301   County: Richmond

    Silver Lake is a 'full cemetery' and is closed to new burials. The office burned down but records are available through the Hebrew Free Burial Association and from the cemetery office at Mt. Richmond Cemetery. See also: Hebrew Free Burial Association.

Talmud Torah Cemetery (Newark). *See Grove Street. This is one of three cemeteries in the Grove Street/South Orange Avenue area.*

Temple Israel of the City of New York.

    388 Saw Mill River Road, Hastings-on-Hudson, NY 10706   914-478-1343   County: Westchester

    The temple is located at 112 East 75 Street, New York, NY 10021 (212) 249-5000.

Union Field (Ridgewood, NY). Founded 1854.

    82-11 Cypress Avenue, Ridgewood, NY 11385   718-366-3748   County: Queens

    Records are cross-indexed chronologically by date of burial, and by burial society

Union Field (Newark, NJ). *See Grove Street. This is one of three cemeteries in the Grove Street/South Orange Avenue area.*

United Hebrew Founded 1908. 122 Arthur Kill Road, Staten Island, NY   718-351-0230   County: Richmond

    P.O. Box 6, Staten Island, NY 10306-0006

    Some records arranged by burial society. Indexes also available by last name of deceased and chronologically by burial date. Maps are also maintained for landsmanschaftn/burial society plots.

United Orthodox Synagogue of Plainfield. New Market Avenue, South Plainfield, NJ 908-245-7100   County: Middlesex

    Administered by Sanford B. Epstein, Inc., 731 Boulevard, Kenilworth, NJ 07033

United Synagogue. 4003 Middle County Road, Calverton, NY   212-533-7800   County: Suffolk

    155 Fifth Avenue, New York, NY 10010

Washington (Brooklyn). Founded 1867.

    5400 Bay Parkway at MacDonald Avenue, Brooklyn, NY 11230   718-377-8690   County: Kings

    Records can be retrieved alphabetically by deceased's last name, chronologically by date of burial, and by burial society. They have excellent maps of each burial society plot area.

Washington (NJ). 104 Deans Hall Road, Monmouth Junction, NJ 08852   732-297-2336   County: Middlesex

    See also Floral Park..

Water Street Shul. McBride Avenue, Paterson, NJ   201-794-2807   County: Passaic

    Contact: Marcey Morgenstern, 16-20 Collitt Dr., Fairlawn, NJ 04410.

Wellwood. Wellwood Avenue, Pinelawn, NY   631-249-2300   County: Suffolk

    P.O. Box 340, Farmingdale, NY 11735

    See also: Beth Moses.

Westchester Hills (Free Synagogue). Founded 1921.

    400 Saw Mill River Road, Hastings-On-Hudson, NY 10706   914-478-1767 County: Westchester

    Records are available from the cemetery office and from the congregation office at: Stephen Wise Free Synagogue, 30 West 68th Street, New York, NY 10023 (212) 877-4050

NEW YORK AREA JEWISH CEMETERIES

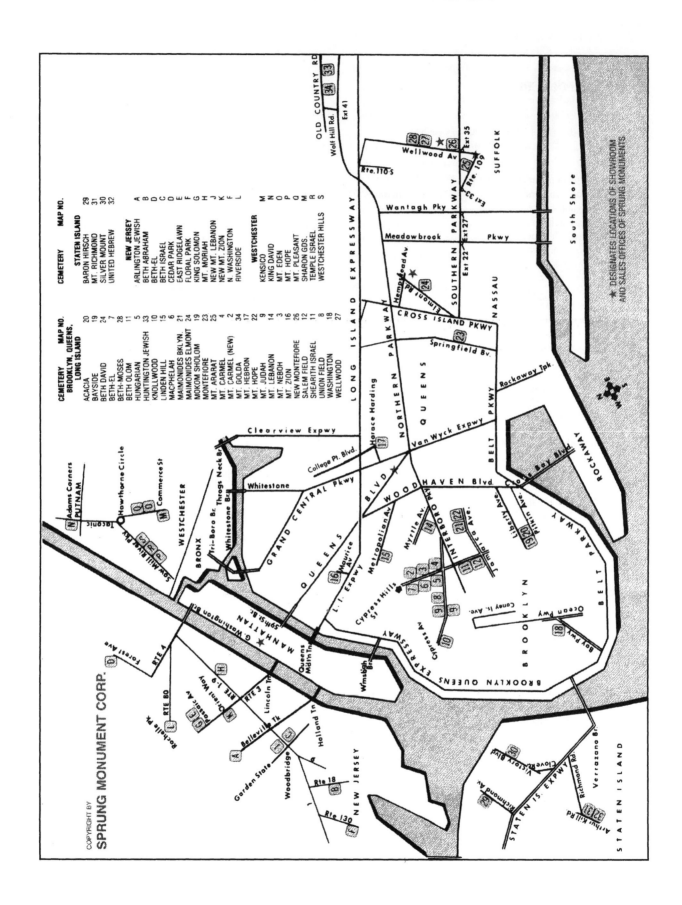

COPYRIGHT BY

SPRUNG MONUMENT CORP.

CEMETERY BROOKLYN, QUEENS, LONG ISLAND	MAP NO.
ACACIA	20
BAYSIDE	19
BETH DAVID	24
BETH-EL	7
BETH-MOSES	28
BETH OLOM	11
HUNGARIAN	5
HUNTINGTON JEWISH	33
KNOLLWOOD	10
LINDEN HILL	15
MACPHELAH	6
MAIMONIDES BKLYN.	21
MAIMONIDES ELMONT	24
MOKOM SHOLOM	19
MONTEFIORE	23
MT. ARARAT	25
MT. CARMEL	4
MT. CARMEL (NEW)	2
MT. GOLDA	34
MT. HEBRON	17
MT. HOPE	22
MT. JUDAH	9
MT. LEBANON	14
MT. NEBOH	3
MT. ZION	16
NEW MONTEFIORE	26
SALEM FIELD	12
SHEARITH ISRAEL	11
UNION FIELD	8
WASHINGTON	18
WELLWOOD	27

CEMETERY	MAP NO.
STATEN ISLAND	
BARON HIRSCH	29
MT. RICHMOND	31
SILVER MOUNT	30
UNITED HEBREW	32
NEW JERSEY	
ARLINGTON JEWISH	A
BETH ABRAHAM	B
BETH-EL	C
BETH ISRAEL	D
CEDAR PARK	D
EAST RIDGELAWN	E
FLORAL PARK	F
KING SOLOMON	G
MT. MORIAH	H
NEW MT. LEBANON	J
NEW MT. ZION	K
N. WASHINGTON	F
RIVERSIDE	L
WESTCHESTER	
KENSICO	M
KING DAVID	N
MT. EDEN	O
MT. HOPE	P
MT. PLEASANT	Q
SHARON GDS.	M
TEMPLE ISRAEL	R
WESTCHESTER HILLS	S

★ DESIGNATES LOCATIONS OF SHOWROOM AND SALES OFFICES OF SPRUNG MONUMENTS

APPENDIX H

BEFORE THE FIVE-BOROUGH CITY:
The Old Cities, Towns and Villages That Came Together to Form "Greater New York"

by Harry Macy, Jr., F.A.S.G., F.G.B.S.

Copyright © 1998, 2002, The New York Genealogical and Biographical Society

January 1, 1998, marked the 100th anniversary of the creation of the five-borough New York City. This article focuses on the world which that city *replaced*, for the consolidation of 1898 (and others which preceded it) wiped off the map many jurisdictions which genealogists are going to encounter in their research. Most modern maps do not show these old cities, towns, or villages, so it is often difficult for genealogists to understand the place names they encounter in census, land, vital, and other records before 1898.

After the English seized the City of New Amsterdam in 1664 and renamed it New York, they extended its boundaries to include all of Manhattan Island. In 1683, when the Province of New York was first divided into counties, the City of New York also became New York County.

At first the actual city was limited to the island's southern tip, the rest of Manhattan consisting of scattered farms and rural villages. Slowly the urbanized area spread northward. In 1874, to accommodate this growth, New York City and County annexed from Westchester County what is now the western Bronx. Meanwhile, the village of Brooklyn had become a city and was expanding to eventually cover all of Kings County.

In 1894 a vote was taken in New York, Westchester, Kings, Queens, and Richmond counties on a proposal to combine New York City with Brooklyn, the eastern Bronx, part of Queens County, and all of Richmond County, to form the second largest city in the world (after London). There was a large majority for the proposal, but only because of the vote in New York County. Only 50.1% of Kings County voters were in favor, and some towns, such as Flushing in Queens County, were solidly opposed.

Nevertheless, the overall majority ruled, and consolidation went ahead. In 1895 New York City annexed the eastern Bronx. On January 1, 1898, the City of Brooklyn, Long Island City, and the towns and villages of western Queens and all of Richmond were replaced by the Boroughs of Brooklyn (Kings County), Queens (Queens County), and Richmond (Richmond County). With the Boroughs of Manhattan and The Bronx (New York County) they formed a new City of New York, briefly called "Greater New York."

Since 1898 there have been two important changes. In 1914, The Bronx became a separate county of the same name. In 1975, the Borough of Richmond was renamed the Borough of Staten Island, though remaining Richmond County.

Sources dated after January 1, 1898, may carry either the borough or county name, or both. In general, records generated by a city agency (such as the Department of Health) use the borough names, while those created by agencies of the state

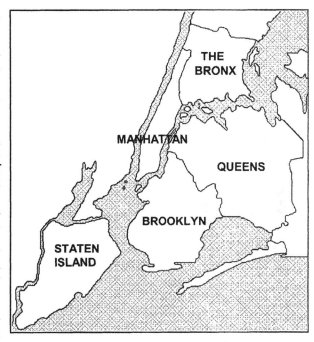

Map. 1. The Five Boroughs of New York City.

(such as the Surrogate's Court) use the county names, but this usage may not be consistent. Genealogists should be familiar with both sets of names.

Prior to 1898, the City of Brooklyn maintained records very similar to those of its sister city of New York, including vital records as early as 1848. When Long Island City was created in 1870 it also began to keep vital records. The towns of Kings, Queens, Richmond, and Westchester (later Bronx) counties kept records similar to those maintained by towns in the rest of the state, including vital records in 1847-49 and beginning again in 1881. Within the towns, incorporated villages sometimes kept their own vital records after 1880-81 (Morrisania kept some at least as early as 1872). For the surviving vital records of the old cities, towns, and villages see *Genealogical Resources in New York*, NEW YORK CITY DEPARTMENT OF RECORDS AND INFORMATION SERVICES, MUNICIPAL ARCHIVES.

To understand the maps that follow, keep in mind that in New York State, counties are made up of towns and cities. Towns in turn consist of villages, which may be incorporated (and thus have some records of their own), or unincorporated (in which case their affairs are covered by the town records).

387

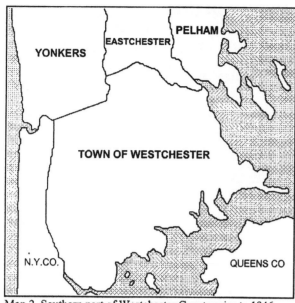

Map 2. Southern part of Westchester County prior to 1846, showing the town boundaries. The manor of Morrisania was made a town in 1788 but annexed to Westchester in 1791.

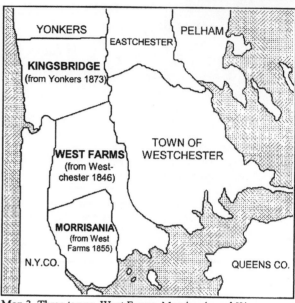

Map 3. Three towns, West Farms, Morrisania and Kingsbridge, were created between 1846 and 1873. In 1864 the entire town of Morrisania was also incorporated as a village.

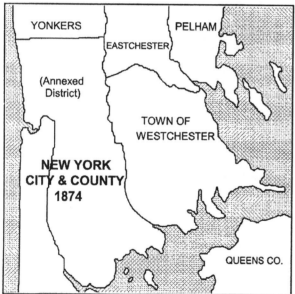

Map 4. In 1874 New York City and County annexed from Westchester County the area south of the City of Yonkers and west of the Bronx River. The former towns of Morrisania, West Farms, and Kingsbridge became Wards 23 and 24 of the City, and were known as the "Annexed District." (NOTE: Although New York City continued to be divided into wards until the 1930s, the wards lost their political function as a result of reforms in the 1890s.)

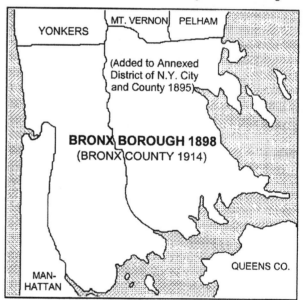

Map 5. In 1895 the Annexed District and Ward 24 were extended eastward to include all of the town of Westchester and parts of Pelham and Eastchester. These towns included some incorporated villages, of which South Mount Vernon and Wakefield had vital records which survive. At the consolidation of 1898, the Annexed District became the Borough of the Bronx, but remained part of New York County until Bronx County was created in 1914.

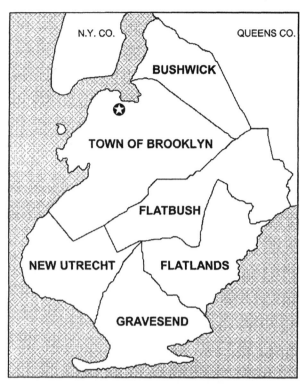

Map 6. Kings County towns before 1834. The star indicates the Village of Brooklyn, incorporated in 1816.

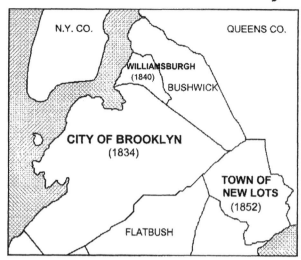

Map 7. In 1834 the Village and Town of Brooklyn were combined to form the City of Brooklyn. In 1827 the village of Williamsburgh was incorporated within the town of Bushwick; in 1840 it became a separate town, and in 1851 a city. In 1852 the eastern part of Flatbush became the Town of New Lots. In 1854 Williamsburgh and Bushwick were annexed to Brooklyn as the Eastern District of that city, usually abbreviated "E.D." (the original city was then briefly called the Western District).

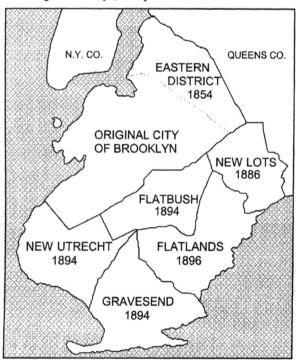

Map 8. Brooklyn annexed all the remaining towns 1886-96.

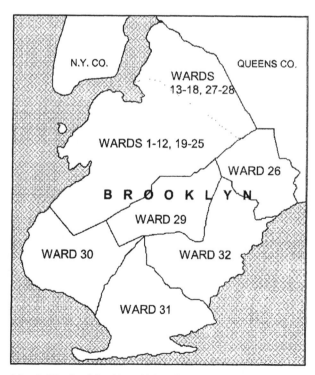

Map 9. Wards of the City 1896, and Borough 1898–.

389

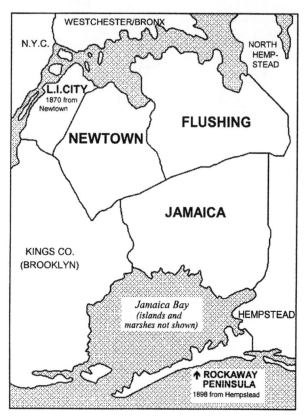

Queens

Map 10. Before 1870, Queens County consisted of the towns of Newtown, Flushing, Jamaica, North Hempstead, Hempstead, and Oyster Bay (not shown). The Rockaway Peninsula was part of the town of Hempstead.

In 1870 the western part of Newtown closest to New York City, including the village of Astoria, was incorporated as a separate city, called Long Island City.

On January 1, 1898, Long Island City, Newtown, Flushing, Jamaica, and the Rockaway Peninsula of Hempstead became the Borough of Queens, and were replaced by five wards: Long Island City became Ward 1, Newtown Ward 2, Flushing Ward 3, Jamaica Ward 4, and Rockaway Ward 5.

There had been a number of incorporated villages in the former towns. Several of these briefly kept their own vital records which survive, namely: in the town of Flushing, the villages of Flushing, College Point, and Whitestone; in the town of Jamaica, the villages of Jamaica and Richmond Hill; and in the Rockaway Peninsula of Hempstead, the villages of Far Rockaway and Rockaway Beach.

The creation of the borough left the larger eastern portion of Queens County (Hempstead, North Hempstead and Oyster Bay) outside of the city. This political complication was resolved on January 1, 1899 when the three eastern towns became the new county of Nassau. After that date Queens County consisted only of the Borough of Queens, but it retained all of the pre-1899 county records.

Staten Island (Richmond)

Map 11. Richmond County was originally divided into four towns, Castleton, Northfield, Southfield, and Westfield. In 1860 a fifth town, Middletown, was created from parts of Castleton and Southfield.

Castleton was the closest town to New York City (by ferry), and the first to lose its rural character. Its north shore was incorporated in 1866 as the village of New Brighton, and in 1872 the village boundaries were extended to include the entire town, so that Castleton and New Brighton covered the same area.

There were smaller incorporated villages in the other towns, of which the following have surviving vital records in addition to those of the towns: Port Richmond in Northfield, Edgewater in both Middletown and Southfield, and Tottenville in Westfield.

On January 1, 1898 the Borough of Richmond was created, and the former towns became wards: Castleton/ New Brighton was Ward 1, Middletown Ward 2, Northfield Ward 3, Southfield Ward 4, and Westfield Ward 5.

In 1975 the Borough of Richmond was renamed the Borough of Staten Island. The county continues to be known as Richmond.

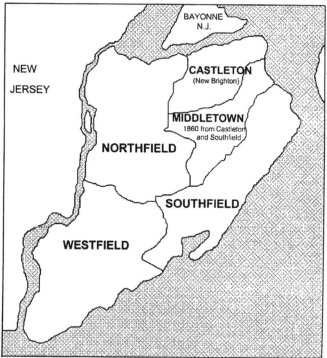

SUBJECT INDEX

This index covers subjects listed primarily under "Description of Resources." In rare cases (i.e., when citing a published resource not covered under "Description of Resources"), "Finding Aids" are also indexed. Entries in CAPITAL LETTERS are repositories included in this book. Underlining is used to denote either a primary source of the records or a more significant collection than found on other pages cited. Where two pages are connected by a hyphen, the subject continues to the second page. In all other cases, a hyphen is used as a space saver to connect 3 or more pages mentioning the subject.

NAME INDEX

Includes authors, editors, names in collections and names in titles of collections.

PLACE INDEX

Includes place names listed primarily under "Description of Resources." Does not include places mentioned in Appendices.

409

412

ESTELLE M. GUZIK, compiler and editor of *Genealogical Resources in New York,* served as President of the Jewish Genealogical Society, Inc., from 1996 to 2001 and Vice-President from 1985-1990. Estelle has been a member of the JGS almost from its inception in 1977. She served as editor of the JGS' *Resources for Jewish Genealogy in the New York Area* in 1985, *Genealogical Resources in the New York Metropolitan Area*, published in 1989, and is a frequent contributor to *Dorot,* the JGS newsletter and other genealogical publications. The 1989 edition of *Genealogical Resources in the New York Metropolitan Area* was selected by the New York Public Library, Research Libraries, as the best reference book of that year. During her term as president, the JGS completed a project cataloging over 10,000 landsmanshaftn, synagogues, family circles, labor unions and other Jewish organizations with cemetery plots in New York-New Jersey cemeteries. She coordinated the creation of an award-winning database — the work of over 100 volunteers of the Jewish Genealogical Society, Inc., the German Genealogy Group and the Italian Genealogy Group — that computerized the index to over 253,000 naturalization records filed in the Kings County Clerk's Office, 1907-1924. The result of these efforts can be found on the JGS' website (www.jgsny.org). Estelle has a B.A. in political science from Brooklyn College and a master's degree in urban planning from Hunter College. She served as director of compliance for the U.S. Department of Housing and Urban Development, and was formerly staff director to the Federal Regional Council in New York.

Estelle began to research her own family history in 1970 when she realized she did not know the names of aunts, uncles and cousins killed in the Holocaust. Her parents, David and Helen Guzik (z'l), were supportive from the start and were her best resource. This book is dedicated to their memory.

The **JEWISH GENEALOGICAL SOCIETY, Inc. (JGS)** was founded in 1977 to address the growing interest of American Jews in researching their family roots. Today, the Society has over 1,000 members.

Based in New York City, the JGS offers monthly programs given by experts on diverse topics for both beginning and advanced researchers. The JGS publishes a quarterly newsletter, *Dorot*; sponsors an annual Beginners' Workshop; arranges visits to local cemeteries and repositories; and maintains a website with useful information for genealogists.

In 2000, the Jewish Genealogical Society moved to a new home at the Center for Jewish History, an outstanding resource for Jewish scholarship that houses the American Jewish Historical Society, American Sephardi Federation, Leo Baeck Institute, Yeshiva University Museum and the YIVO Institute for Jewish Research. The collections of these organizations are among those described in this book.

The JGS is an activist organization. In addition to contributing funds enabling libraries and archives to purchase genealogical materials, the JGS was instrumental in the transfer of historic records to the New York City Municipal Archives and the National Archives-Northeast Region. JGS members are actively involved in volunteer projects including indexing and computerizing important historical records of interest to genealogists.

The JGS is open to people of all backgrounds. Membership includes a subscription to *Dorot.* For information, write to the Jewish Genealogical Society, Inc., P.O. Box 286398, New York, NY 10128. Telephone: 212-294-8326. Website: www.jgsny.org E-mail: info@jgsny.org

NOTES

NOTES

NOTES

NOTES

NOTES